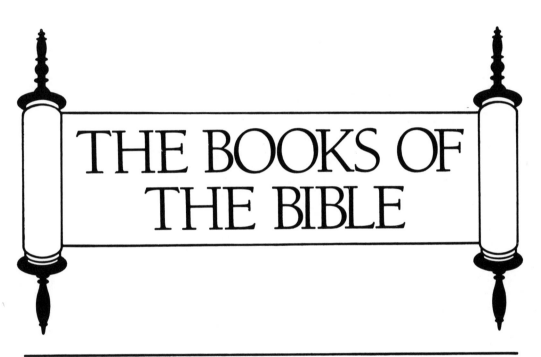

THE BOOKS OF THE BIBLE

The Old Testament / The Hebrew Bible

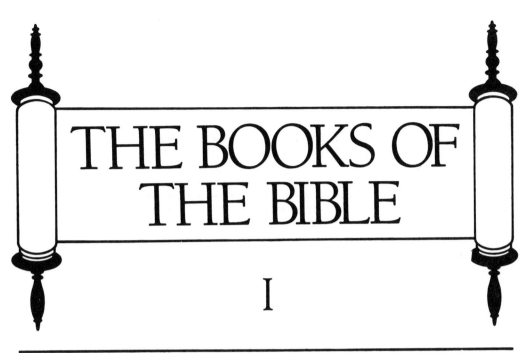

THE BOOKS OF THE BIBLE

I

The Old Testament / The Hebrew Bible

Bernhard W. Anderson, Editor

CHARLES SCRIBNER'S SONS

NEW YORK

Charles Scribner's Sons
Macmillan Publishing Company
866 Third Avenue, New York, NY 10022

Collier Macmillan Canada, Inc.

Library of Congress Catalog Card Number: 89:10074

PRINTED IN THE UNITED STATES OF AMERICA

printing number

2   3   4   5   6   7   8   9   10

The Books of the Bible/Bernhard W. Anderson, editor.
   p. cm.
   Bibliography: v. 1, p.
   Includes indexes.
   Contents: v. 1. The Old Testament/The Hebrew Bible—v. 2. The
Apocrypha and the New Testament.
   ISBN 0-684-18487-7 (set: alk. paper)—ISBN
0-684-19098-2 (v. 1: alk. paper)—ISBN 0-684-19099-0
(v. 2: alk. paper)
   1. Bible—Criticism, interpretation, etc.   I.   Anderson,
Bernhard W.
BS540.B62   1989
220.6'1—dc20   89-10074
                                            CIP

The paper in this book meets the guidelines
for permanence and durability
of the Committee on Production Guidelines
for Book Longevity of the Council on Library Resources.

Editorial Staff

Managing Editors
Daniel J. Calto and John Fitzpatrick

EDITORIAL

Associate Editors
Lesley Ann Beneke   Ilene Cohen   Michael Scott Cooper   Eric Haralson
Karen Ready   Irina Rybacek   Joan Zseleczky

Proofreaders
Emily Garlin   Carol Holmes

Editorial Assistant
Brigitte M. Goldstein

Indexer
AEIOU, INC.

PRODUCTION

Director
Matthew M. Kardovich

Book Designers
A Good Thing, Inc.   Mike McIver
(text)   (case)

Production Assistant
Frederick A. Aiese

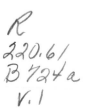

Contents

PREFACE, *xi*

THE OLD TESTAMENT CANON, *xiv*

CHRONOLOGY, *xvi*

LIST OF ABBREVIATIONS, *xix*

THE BIBLE AS SACRED LITERATURE

Bernhard W. Anderson, 1

INTRODUCTION TO THE OLD TESTAMENT

Walter Harrelson, 11

GENESIS

Walter Brueggemann, 21

EXODUS

Nahum M. Sarna, 47

LEVITICUS

Jacob Milgrom, 63

NUMBERS

Katherine Doob Sakenfeld, 71

DEUTERONOMY

James A. Sanders, 89

JOSHUA

Marvin L. Chaney, 103

CONTENTS

JUDGES

Philip J. King, 113

RUTH

Katheryn Pfisterer Darr, 123

I AND II SAMUEL

Bruce C. Birch, 127

I AND II KINGS

Burke O. Long, 141

I AND II CHRONICLES, EZRA, NEHEMIAH

David Noel Freedman and Bruce E. Willoughby, 155

ESTHER, ADDITIONS TO ESTHER

Katheryn Pfisterer Darr, 173

JOB

David J. A. Clines, 181

PSALMS

Patrick D. Miller, Jr., 203

PROVERBS

James L. Crenshaw, 223

ECCLESIASTES

Phyllis Trible, 231

THE SONG OF SOLOMON

Roland E. Murphy, 241

ISAIAH

Ronald E. Clements, 247

JEREMIAH

Robert Wilson, 281

CONTENTS

LAMENTATIONS

Claus Westermann, 303

EZEKIEL

Peter R. Ackroyd, 319

DANIEL, ADDITIONS TO DANIEL

W. Sibley Towner, 333

HOSEA

Carole R. Fontaine, 349

JOEL

Theodore Hiebert, 359

AMOS

Simon B. Parker, 367

OBADIAH, NAHUM

Elizabeth Achtemeier, 375

JONAH

Katheryn Pfisterer Darr, 381

MICAH

James Luther Mays, 385

HABAKKUK

J. J. M. Roberts, 391

ZEPHANIAH

Robert A. Bennett, 397

HAGGAI, ZECHARIAH, MALACHI

Ben C. Ollenburger, 405

LIST OF CONTRIBUTORS, 415

INDEX, 419

Preface

The Books of the Bible is a two-volume reference work that contains discussions of
the various writings found in the Old Testament (or Hebrew Bible) and the New
Testament. The first volume treats the thirty-nine books of the Old Testament,
following the familiar order of English Bibles rather than that of the Hebrew Bible;
and the second discusses the primary apocryphal—or, in Catholic usage,
deuterocanonical—writings and the twenty-seven books of the New Testament.
(Some of the shorter Apocrypha, such as the additions to Esther and Daniel, are
treated at the appropriate points in the Old Testament volume.) In addition to essays
on each book of the Bible, there are introductory essays on the Old Testament, the
Apocrypha, and the New Testament, as well as an initial essay on "The Bible as
Sacred Literature."

Those who seek an entry into the Bible will find that two types of reference
works are readily available. On the one hand is the commentary (for instance the
Jerome Biblical Commentary), which typically offers a chapter-by-chapter explanation of the text; on the other hand, the biblical encyclopedia or dictionary, such as
Harper's Bible Dictionary, is usually an alphabetical compendium of explanations or
definitions. The present work helps to fill the gap that lies between the commentary
and the dictionary. It is neither a collection of definitions nor a set of small
commentaries but rather a series of interpretive essays, arranged according to the
order of the biblical canon, that deal descriptively with the content, purpose, and
theological perspective of each book of the Bible, from Genesis to Revelation.
Readers are given the necessary information to begin their study and to enhance
their appreciation of literature that has had a major impact upon human culture.
Each essay is accompanied by a selected bibliography for the purpose of supporting or
elaborating the views expressed and guiding the reader into further study.

In these essays, the primary emphasis falls upon the Bible as literature, that is,
"scripture," or what is written. When pertinent, consideration is given to the
prehistory of the final texts, showing how previous traditions have been utilized or
how editors have incorporated traditional materials. The main purpose, however, is
to understand a biblical book in its final literary form. Contributors may indicate
now and then how a biblical book has been read confessionally by religious
communities, but the primary concern is to view a book as a literary work in its own
right.

The essays are addressed to that eager, inquiring type of person known as the
"general reader": students in high schools and seminaries, church school teachers or
college instructors, ministers and rabbis, literary browsers, seekers who desire a
larger understanding. At the same time, specialists will find that these essays may
excite their interest and sharpen their own thinking. Contributors have endeavored

to bring the reader to the creative frontier of biblical scholarship without burdening the discussion with technical matters or with views that are faddish and lack widespread scholarly support. Readers will discover that biblical scholarship is not pedantic and boring; it can reveal new horizons of interpretation that will provide an invitation to read and to reread the books of the Bible.

This work appears at a time of changing emphases in biblical scholarship. Indeed, in the larger perspective of the history of interpretation a major upheaval has occurred since the mid twentieth century. The once-dominant historical approach to the Bible, championed preeminently by the American archaeologist W. F. Albright in his monumental *From the Stone Age to Christianity* (1940), has given way to other methods of study, particularly those that deal with the Bible as literature: the study of literary genre (form criticism), style (rhetorical criticism), structure (structuralism), editing (history of redaction), and the canonical process that led to the composition and arrangement of the books in their final form (canonical criticism). In addition, the sociological approach has been receiving increasing attention, in both the Old and New Testament fields. No single approach to biblical interpretation governs the essays in these volumes. Contributors have been free to use the methods that, in their opinion, best suit the material and are most helpful to the reader. The result is that these essays, when taken together, give the reader a sense of being in a time of ferment in biblical interpretation.

The contributors all belong to the scholarly ranks of the United States and Great Britain, with the exception of the German scholar Claus Westermann, whose essay on the Book of Lamentations shows how the method of form criticism helps us to understand the text. My participation in the Society of Biblical Literature, of which I am a past president, enabled me to turn to a number of my colleagues in this Society. The selection of contributors was made on the basis of special competence in a particular area of biblical studies and with the intention of including young scholars, established teachers, emeriti professors, as well as representatives of minority groups. The considerable number of women included in the list bears witness to women's increasing participation in biblical studies. Furthermore, the list includes Roman Catholic, Protestant, and Jewish scholars who share the common task of biblical criticism and interpretation. That these scholars do not follow a single line, but vary in their opinions and differ in their approaches, is not a weakness but a strength. Each essay is a separate piece of work that can be read and appreciated apart from the others. But taken as a totality they all testify to the vigor with which scholars pursue the never-ending task of biblical interpretation and attest to that strange power of scripture to become, in some sense, "word of God" to people of every age.

Confident that readers will find that these essays illuminate the sacred pages of Scripture, I venture, on their behalf, to thank the various contributors for their cooperation. To some of these colleagues in particular I am grateful for counsel, especially to George Nickelsburg who, besides writing his own introductory essay, gave advice in the area of the Apocrypha. I am grateful too to Roland M. Frye, a professor of English literature who has a profound interest in the Bible, for his gracious encouragement and counsel at the beginning of this project. Finally, I wish to thank Charles Scribner, Jr., who personally invited me to become the editor of this reference work. Unexpected difficulties arose along the way but, after all has been written and done, I am pleased that these volumes will join the splendid line of Scribner reference works.

BERNHARD W. ANDERSON

The Old Testament Canon

JEWISH (The Hebrew Bible, *Tanakh*)	ROMAN CATHOLIC	PROTESTANT

Law (*Torah*)
1. Genesis (*Bereshit*)
2. Exodus (*Shemot*)
3. Leviticus (*Vayiqra'*)
4. Numbers (*Bemidbar*)
5. Deuteronomy (*Devarim*)

Prophets (*Nevi'im*)
6. Joshua (*Yehoshua'*)
7. Judges (*Shoftim*)
8. 1 Samuel (*Shemu'el 1*)
9. 2 Samuel (*Shem'uel 2*)
10. 1 Kings (*Melakhim 1*)
11. 2 Kings (*Melakhim 2*)
12. Isaiah (*Yesha'yah*)
13. Jeremiah (*Yirmeyah*)
14. Ezekiel (*Yehezqe'el*)
15. The Twelve (*Tere Asar*)
    Hosea (*Hoshea'*)
    Joel (*Yo'el*)
    Amos (*'Amos*)
    Obadiah (*'Ovadyahu*)
    Jonah (*Yonah*)
    Micah (*Mikhah*)
    Nahum (*Nahum*)
    Habakkuk (*Havaqquq*)
    Zephaniah (*Tsefaneyah*)
    Haggai (*Haggai*)
    Zechariah (*Zekareyah*)
    Malachi (*Mal'akhi*)

Writings (*Ketuvim*)
16. Psalms (*Tehillim*)
17. Proverbs (*Mishlei*)
18. Job (*Yyyov*)

1. Genesis
2. Exodus
3. Leviticus
4. Numbers
5. Deuteronomy
6. Joshua
7. Judges
8. Ruth
9. 1 Samuel (1 Kings)
10. 2 Samuel (2 Kings)
11. 1 Kings (3 Kings)
12. 2 Kings (4 Kings)
13. 1 Chronicles (1 Paralipomenon)
14. 2 Chronicles (2 Paralipomenon)
15. Ezra (1 Esdras)
16. Nehemiah (2 Esdras)
17. Tobit*
18. Judith*
19. Esther (with additions*)
20. Job
21. Psalms
22. Proverbs
23. Ecclesiastes
24. Song of Solomon (Song of Songs)
25. Wisdom of Solomon*
26. Ecclesiasticus (Wisdom of Jesus, Son of Sirach)*
27. Isaiah
28. Jeremiah
29. Lamentations
30. Baruch*
31. Ezekiel

1. Genesis
2. Exodus
3. Leviticus
4. Numbers
5. Deuteronomy
6. Joshua
7. Judges
8. Ruth
9. 1 Samuel
10. 2 Samuel
11. 1 Kings
12. 2 Kings
13. 1 Chronicles
14. 2 Chronicles
15. Ezra
16. Nehemiah
17. Esther
18. Job
19. Psalms
20. Proverbs
21. Ecclesiastes
22. Song of Solomon
23. Isaiah
24. Jeremiah
25. Lamentations
26. Ezekiel
27. Daniel
28. Hosea
29. Joel
30. Amos
31. Obadiah
32. Jonah
33. Micah
34. Nahum
35. Habakkuk

The Old Testament Canon

JEWISH (The Hebrew Bible, *Tanakh*)	ROMAN CATHOLIC	PROTESTANT
19. Song of Songs (*Shir ha-Shirim*)	32. Daniel (with additions*)	36. Zephaniah
20. Ruth (*Rut*)	33. Hosea	37. Haggai
21. Lamentations (*Eikhah*)	34. Joel	38. Zechariah
22. Ecclesiastes (*Qohelet*)	35. Amos	39. Malachi
23. Esther (*Ester*)	36. Obadiah	
24. Daniel (*Dani'el*)	37. Jonah	
25. Ezra (*'Ezra'*)	38. Micah	
26. Nehemiah (*Nehemeyah*)	39. Nahum	
27. 1 Chronicles (*Divrei ha-Yamim 1*)	40. Habakkuk	
28. 2 Chronicles (*Divrei ha-Yamim 2*)	41. Zephaniah	
	42. Haggai	
	43. Zechariah	
	44. Malachi	
	45. 1 Maccabees*	
	46. 2 Maccabees*	

- Roman Catholic practice is to treat the books marked with an asterisk (*) as deuterocanonical and to include them in the Old Testament in roughly the order of the Septuagint (which more or less corresponds to the historical setting of the books). Because the Septuagint knows the Hebrew books of Ezra and Nehemiah as "1 Esdras" and "2 Esdras," the Greek books of those titles (excluded from the Catholic canon) are sometimes called 3 and 4 Esdras.

- Eastern Orthodox tradition likewise accepts the deuterocanonical books listed above and also includes the following books in the same category: 1 Esdras, Psalm 151, and the Prayer of Manasseh. (Third and Fourth Maccabees are included as an appendix to Orthodox Bibles.)

- Protestant Bibles exclude all these books from the Old Testament canon and append them (plus 2 Esdras) in a separate unit called the Apocrypha.

Chronology

ca. 3000–2700 B.C.E.	The art of writing develops among the peoples of the Near East.
	Gilgamesh, the oldest known epic, is written down in cuneiform in Mesopotamia.
	Hieroglyphic writing emerges in Egypt.
2700–2500	The Egyptian pharaohs Khufu and Khafre build the great pyramids and the great sphinx of Giza.
2060–1950	The first city-states are founded in Canaan.
	Art and literature flourish in Mesopotamia during the IIIrd Sumerian Dynasty of Ur.
1990–1700	Egypt becomes the strongest power in the Near East under the XIIth Dynasty, and her empire reaches its greatest geographic extent.
	The Babylonian empire supersedes the Sumerian.
	Hammurabi issues the first law code (1750).
	Canaan comes under Egyptian control.
	The Hyksos begin their incursions into Egyptian territory.
	Abraham migrates from Ur to Haran and from there to Canaan.
1700–1600	Canaan comes under Hyksos control.
	Jacob and his family migrate to Egypt.
	The Hyksos assume power in Egypt as the XVth and XVIth dynasties.
1600–1400	The indigenous rulers in Egypt overthrow the Hyksos and Egypt becomes again a major power under the XVIIIth Dynasty.
	Queen Hatshepsut (1503–1482) expands Egyptian rule into Africa.
	Pharaoh Thutmose III gains control over Canaan and Phoenicia after his victory at Megiddo (1480).
	The city of Babylon is destroyed by invading Hittites (1531).
1400–1300	Amenhotep IV takes the name Akhenaton and introduces the monotheistic worship of Aton, the sun disk.
1300–1200	**Moses** leads the Exodus of the Israelites out of Egypt into the Sinai desert (*ca.* 1280).
	Joshua leads the Israelites into the Promised Land in a series of conquests between 1250 and 1200.
	Assyria becomes the dominant power in the Near East.
1200–1000	The Philistines build a series of city-states in the coastal area of Canaan.
	The Israelites consolidate their settlements in Canaan under the leadership of the **Judges.**
	Israelites and Philistines clash at Megiddo (*ca.* 1125).
	The Philistines capture the sacred ark during the battle at Shiloh (*ca.* 1050), and the city is burnt.
	The continuous pressure exerted on the Israelites by Philistines and Ammonites leads to the creation of a monarchy.
	The prophet and judge **Samuel** anoints **Saul** king.
	Pharaoh Rameses III repels the invading Sea Peoples, but he cannot halt the weakening of Egypt's power.

CHRONOLOGY

The Hittite empire succumbs to virulent attacks from the Sea Peoples.

1000–900   **David** establishes his rule over Judah and the northern tribes (*ca.* 1000), taking the name of Israel for the kingdom. Jerusalem becomes his capital.

His son **Solomon** succeeds to the throne (*ca.* 961).

His reign marks Israel's most glorious period.

Solomon builds the first Temple at Jerusalem.

At the end of **Solomon**'s reign (*ca.* 922), the kingdom is divided among feuding factions—Israel (Ephraim) in the north and Judah in the south (ruled by the Davidic dynasty in Jerusalem).

The alphabet, first used by Phoenician traders, comes into general use.

By the end of the century, Assyria recovers from a period of decline to become an aggressive conquering force.

900–750   Tense relations prevail between Judah and Israel (Ephraim).

Internal strife marks the history of Israel.

Elijah prophesies against the House of **Omri** of the kingdom of Israel (*ca.* 850).

King **Ahab** of Israel joins the Syro-Aramaean alliance formed to curb Assyrian aggression.

Amos prophesies against the oppression of the poor by the wealthy in the reign of **Jeroboam II** of Israel.

Hosea denounces Baal worship among the Israelites.

Assyria's power increases steadily, while Egypt's geopolitical importance wanes.

The Assyrian king Tiglath-pileser III institutes a ruthless policy of torture, executions, and deportation to subjugate the conquered nations.

750–600   **Isaiah** prophesies in Judah at various times, mostly during the reign of **Hezekiah** (727–698).

Micah denounces injustice and idolatry in Samaria, capital of the kingdom of Israel.

The kingdom of Israel is destroyed by invading Assyrian armies, and the population is dispersed among the peoples of the empire (722/721).

Judah having been spared, King **Josiah** institutes a series of "Deuteronomic" reforms (621), which revive traditional worship.

The Assyrian armies sweep southward into Egypt and sack Thebes, the Egyptian capital (663).

The sudden rise of Babylonia under Nabopolassar (626–605) ends Assyrian hegemony.

Assyria falls after defeats at Haran (609) and Carchemish (605).

600–538   **Jeremiah** prophesies in the kingdom of Judah (*ca.* 626–587), warning of impending doom.

The kingdom of Judah comes under Babylonian domination. The first wave of deportations takes place in 597.

After the destruction of Jerusalem and the Temple in 587, the bulk of the population is deported to Babylonia.

Ezekiel becomes the prophetic voice of the Babylonian Exile (*ca.* 593–573).

538–400   Babylonian dominance ends in 538, superseded by a new, non-Semitic power, the Persians.

The exiles begin to return, following the Edict of Cyrus, king of Persia (538).

Urged on by **Zechariah,** the people set out to rebuild the Temple (520–515).

Ezra returns from exile (*ca.* 458) and reads the Law of Moses in public.

Nehemiah is appointed governor of Judah by the king of Persia (444); he rebuilds the wall of Jerusalem and restores the Temple cult.

The Pentateuch is canonized.

The Persian empire flourishes under a long line of strong rulers, beginning with Xerxes I (485–465), the biblical **Ahasuerus** of the Book of **Esther.**

400–100   The Persian empire succumbs to the armies of Alexander the Great of Macedon (334–330).

Judah comes under Greek control in 332.

After the battle at Gaza between Alexander's successors (312), Judah falls to the Ptolemaic empire.

Ptolemaic Alexandria becomes a center of Jewish learning. The famous library is established around 280.

The Septuagint, a Greek translation of the Bible, is produced by Jewish scholars in Alexandria (3d century).

The Seleucids gain control of Judah in 183 and impose Greek customs and religious practices on the population.

Judas Maccabeus leads a successful revolt against Antiochus IV Epiphanes' attempt to erect a shrine to Zeus at the Temple of Jerusalem (168).

Several books of the **Apocrypha** are written during this period, and the Book of **Daniel** achieves its final form (167–164).

List of Abbreviations

BIBLICAL BOOKS

Genesis (Gen)
Exodus (Exod)
Leviticus (Lev)
Numbers (Num)
Deuteronomy (Deut)
Joshua (Josh)
Judges (Judg)
Ruth
1 Samuel (1 Sam)
2 Samuel (2 Sam)
1 Kings (1 Kgs)
2 Kings (2 Kgs)
1 Chronicles (1 Chron)
2 Chronicles (2 Chron)
Ezra
Nehemiah (Neh)
Esther (Esth)
Additions to Esther (Add Esth)
Job
Psalms (Ps, Pss)
Proverbs (Prov)
Ecclesiastes (Eccl)
Song of Solomon (Song)
Isaiah (Isa)
Jeremiah (Jer)
Lamentations (Lam)
Ezekiel (Ezek)

Daniel (Dan)
Additions to Daniel (Add Dan)
Hosea (Hos)
Joel
Amos
Obadiah (Obad)
Jonah
Micah (Mic)
Nahum (Nah)
Habakkuk (Hab)
Zephaniah (Zeph)
Haggai (Hag)
Zechariah (Zech)
Malachi (Mal)
1 Esdras (1 Esdr)
2 Esdras (2 Esdr)
Tobit (Tob)
Judith (Jdt)
Wisdom of Solomon (Wis)
Sirach (Sir)
Baruch (Bar)
Letter of Jeremiah (Let Jer)
Prayer of Manasseh (Pr Man)
1 Maccabees (1 Macc)
2 Maccabees (2 Macc)
Matthew (Matt)
Mark

Luke
John
Acts
Romans (Rom)
1 Corinthians (1 Cor)
2 Corinthians (2 Cor)
Galatians (Gal)
Ephesians (Eph)
Philippians (Phil)
Colossians (Col)
1 Thessalonians (1 Thess)
2 Thessalonians (2 Thess)
1 Timothy (1 Tim)
2 Timothy (2 Tim)
Titus
Philemon (Phlm)
Hebrews (Heb)
James (Jas)
1 Peter (1 Pet)
2 Peter (2 Pet)
3 Peter (3 Pet)
1 John
2 John
3 John
Jude
Revelation (Rev)

TRANSLATIONS

Ancient Near Eastern Texts (ANET; nonbiblical)
Authorized Version (AV; informally known as the King James Version, KJV)
Jerusalem Bible (JB)
Jewish Publication Society (JPS)
New American Bible (NAB)
New English Bible (NEB)
New International Version (NIV)

New Jerusalem Bible (NJB)
New Jewish Version (NJV; published as *Tanakh* by the JPS)
Revised Standard Version (RSV)
Revised Version (RV)
Today's English Version (TEV; also known as the Good News Bible)

The Bible
as Sacred Literature

THE TITLE OF this work, *The Books of the Bible*, takes one back ultimately to the ancient city of Byblos, a thriving Phoenician port on the Mediterranean Sea in the second millennium B.C.E. For our English word "Bible" is based on the ancient Greek word *biblia* ("documents" or "books"), which in the singular (*biblos*) referred to the papyrus imported from that city for the making of scrolls. In one sense the Bible is a collection of books, a library. In the Jewish community the Bible consists of those writings found in the Hebrew Bible, generally known as the Old Testament; in the Christian community the Bible is a two-volume work, consisting of the books of the Old Testament and the New Testament.

THE BIBLE AND THE COMMUNITY
OF FAITH

Often these books are referred to as Scripture, which means something that is written, a literary work. As literature the Bible may be classified with other classics that make an enduring claim upon generations of readers and may be studied with the methods that are applicable to other great literary compositions. For synagogue and church, however, the Bible is Holy Scripture and as such is authoritative in some sense for theological understanding and for daily life.

When introducing the essays dealing with the books of the Bible, then, the proper place to begin is with the recognition that these books belong to and reflect the life and thought of a community of faith. In the Old Testament (Hebrew Bible) this community is known as Israel, an ancient personal name from the premonarchic period that means "may God contend" or perhaps "may God rule." Eventually the name was given a national meaning by being applied to the kingdom of David (*ca.* 1000 B.C.E.) and, after the split of the empire (*ca.* 922), to the northern kingdom (otherwise known as Ephraim), just as today the name designates a state of the Middle East. In the Old Testament, however, the term is not reducible to nationhood. Before becoming a state, Israel was a people, the "people of Yahweh" (Judg 5:11, 13), and hence the name was appropriately carried by Jacob, one of the ancestors of the people (Gen 32:28). In this larger sense, as a people drawn together by faith in God—as *The People Called* (Hanson 1986)—the early Christian church could trace its origins to God's call of Abraham and could even be regarded as "the Israel of God" (Gal 6:16). In the view of the Apostle Paul, the Christian community has been incorporated into Israel as a branch grafted onto a vine; therefore the two communities, Jewish and Christian, coexist in the elective purpose of God (Rom 9–11), both sharing the same scriptural tradition.

In the New Testament, whenever the word "scripture(s)" (*graphe, graphai*) appears, the reference is almost without exception to the Hebrew Bible, which is divided into three parts: Torah (Teaching, often translated "Law"), Prophets, and Writings (see "Introduction to the Old Testament"). Eventually the Christian community produced its own canonical writings and placed them under the rubric "the New Covenant" [Testament] (*cf.* Jer 31:31–33). Consequently, the Christian Bible is a bipartite canon consisting of the Old Testament and the New Testament. Here the adjective "new" does not mean that the Old Testament became antiquated or obsolete with the coming of Jesus Christ; this view, first advocated by Marcion in the second century, is regarded as heresy by orthodox Christianity. Rather, the adjective signifies that the new age, anticipated by prophets like Jeremiah, was beginning to dawn. To be "in Christ," that is, in the new community of which he is the head, is to be part of a "new creation" that is taking place in the world (2 Cor 5:16–19).

In discussions of the canon of biblical books, some scholars place the emphasis upon the "canonical process," that is, the long history of the transmission and shaping of the religious tradition (Sanders 1987). Others stress the result of that process: the final form of biblical books and the meaning these books have when placed side by side in a canonical whole (Childs 1979, 1985). But whether one thinks of canon as a dynamic process or as a finished collection of books, the community of faith determined through usage of the received traditions—not by vote in an "official council"—what material gave a valid and reliable expression of religious faith. What we find in the biblical canon is a selection from a vast body of literature that was actually produced, some of which has survived, and much of which has vanished.

Various factors entered into the community's selection of the biblical "books" as valuable and authoritative, such as usage in worship or religious education, the need to have a basis for survival in times of catastrophe or persecution, intuition about the divine revelation contained. A major factor in the formation of the canon was growing controversy between the Jewish and Christian communities, which resulted in the Jewish rejection of a number of works found in the Greek translation of the Hebrew Bible (Septuagint) that was used in the early Christian community. These extra books, often called the Apocrypha, are regarded as outside the Bible proper by Protestants and are considered deuterocanonical by Catholics (see "Introduction to the Apocrypha").

Neither Judaism nor Christianity is a "religion of the Book" in the same sense as Islam, whose holy scripture is the Koran. The community of faith known as Israel existed in advance of the composition of the Torah, Prophets, and Writings; and the Christian church flourished before there were any Christian writings or any accepted canon. The books of the Bible give expression to the religious faith of the community, Israel, and the church respectively, which is not static and bookish, but living and personal.

STORY AND HISTORY

The literature of the Bible is characterized by great diversity in literary genre, style of expression, and theological outlook. Various attempts have been made to comprehend the Bible under a unifying theological doctrine or theme, but in vain; scripture resists all attempts at systematization and harmonization. Yet in the midst of its great diversity one thing stands out clearly: Israel's faith characteristically is narrative in character. This is especially evident when one turns to the Torah (Genesis through Deuteronomy), the basic and most authoritative part of the Hebrew Bible in Jewish tradition. The Hebrew term *torah* is inadequately rendered as "Law"; the Jewish translation, *Tanakh*, properly renders the term as "Teaching." The Torah includes laws (especially in Exodus and Leviticus), but fundamentally it is teaching in the form of a history or story, which begins with the creation and extends to the eve of the occupation of the Promised Land. The theme of the Torah story is "God's promise on the way to fulfillment" (Harrelson: "Introduction to the Old Testament," below).

For centuries people believed that the Bible presented a reliable account of ancient history, including such events as the expulsion from the garden of Eden, the great flood, the migration of Abraham from Ur of Babylonia, and Joseph's administration of Egypt. However, it has become increasingly apparent, especially since the Enlightenment, that the biblical account has the ambiguity of the German term *Geschichte*, which may be rendered as either "history" or "story." At points the account reflects crucial historical experiences, such as the Exodus from Egypt, the Babylonian conquest of Jerusalem and the exile of the people, the crucifixion of Jesus and the persecution of his followers by leaders of the Roman empire. To the degree that these events are historical, they are open to critical historical inquiry and may be corroborated or challenged by the study of ancient history and by archaeology. But the biblical account goes beyond history in the strict sense of the word into the realm of storytelling and poetry. The biblical narrative is a mixture of what we would distinguish as history and story. It is a history-like story or a story-like history (Barr 1976); and it is often impossible to distinguish sharply between these two dimensions.

From the very first the Israelite community recognized the primacy of story—a story that centers in the deliverance from Egyptian oppression and the experience at Mount Sinai. All Jewish tradition reaches back ultimately to these two "root experiences"—the "saving experience" and the "commanding experience" (Fackenheim 1970). The Christian community inherited and transformed this "narrative mode" of confessing faith (Niebuhr 1941). The gospel or "good news" it proclaimed was essentially an exposition of "the great story plot of all time and space," which opens with the creation and moves through the Old Testament, reaching a climax in the life, death, and resurrection of Jesus of Nazareth (Wilder 1964).

One way to interpret the Bible, particularly the Old Testament, is to arrange the literature in its approximate historical sequence, following the pilgrimage of Israel from the time of the Exodus, or even from the preceding period of the ancestors of Israel (Gen 12–50), through the rise and fall of the monarchy and to the period of the Second Temple, when Christianity emerged from the heart of Judaism (Anderson 1986). Critical study of biblical literature, sometimes with the aid of archaeology, has made this historical approach preferable to a book-by-book treatment. An approach of this kind, however, has to take into account that the literature of the Bible was not written with our historical interests in view and certainly not as a source for ancient history. This is

confessional literature, written to confess faith in the holy God, who chooses to be involved in the life of a small people in acts of judgment and mercy and, through the history of that people, to be recognized as Creator and Redeemer by all peoples. Contrary to modern views of history, God is the chief actor in the unfolding drama of human life and particularly in the career of Israel, "the people of God." In the view of the early Christian community, God's involvement in the world through Jesus of Nazareth, confessed to be the Messiah (Heb. *mashiach*) or Christ (Gk. *christos*), is the climactic outcome of the biblical story.

Some interpreters have construed the overall biblical story as a "history of salvation" (*Heilsgeschichte*) or history of God's redemptive activity. So regarded, the unity manifest within the diversity of scripture is the dramatic movement of God's purpose from creation to consummation. At the denouement or climax of this unfolding drama occurred decisive events that give meaning to the whole. For the Jewish community, the crucial events are Exodus and Sinai, and the continuing tradition based on those "root experiences" commemorated even yet in the Passover Seder (Herberg 1976). "The Bible is not a book to be read but a drama in which to participate," writes Rabbi Abraham Joshua Heschel (1976, p. 254). For the Christian community, the decisive event that gives unity to the whole is the Christ event—the life, death, and resurrection of Jesus Christ, which is celebrated especially at Easter and is remembered in every service of the Eucharist (Anderson 1988, pp. 89–93).

This dramatic view of redemptive history is rooted in scripture itself, for instance, in Luke-Acts and the epistles of Paul. In the second century the view was advocated by the great theologian Irenaeus, and in the modern period it has been championed by a line of theologians extending from Johannes Cocceius in the seventeenth century to Gerhard von Rad (1962, 1965) and Oscar Cullman (1967) in the twentieth.

FROM TRADITION TO SCRIPTURE

For the community of faith, the literature of the Bible is sacred not only because it is the dramatic narrative of "God who acts" (Wright 1952) but also because it mediates "the word of God." To invoke a Christian formulation, the Bible sets forth "the word of God in human words." This calls attention to another aspect of the Bible as literature: its sacred *words* that were once spoken and transmitted orally and eventually were written down as "scripture."

In recent times a great deal of attention has been given to investigating how the literature of the Bible was composed over a period of time, that is, diachronically. Behind many of the books of the Bible, it was observed, lies a history of composition or process of literary transmission that extends from a period of oral discourse to the eventual rendering of the tradition in written or scriptural form. Thus there was tradition before there was scripture (Anderson 1981).

Several methods have been used in the diachronic study of the biblical tradition. Source critics have attempted to analyze and arrange the putative sources used in the composition of a literary work (Habel 1971). For instance, it was discovered that in the Pentateuch (Torah), several sources have been blended together: an old epic tradition in two versions (J for Yahwist, E for Elohist) found, for instance, in the ancestral history (Gen 12–50); a Deuteronomic tradition (D) found preeminently in the book of Deuteronomy; and a Priestly tradition (P) found, for example, in the book of Leviticus. Similarly, New Testament scholars discovered that Matthew and Luke drew upon Mark as a source, as well as a putative document known as Q (for *Quelle*, or "source").

Again, form critics, working in both Testaments, attempted to go behind literary sources into the period of oral tradition, and to isolate the various genres that related to particular "situations in life" (*Sitze im Leben*) in the community (Tucker 1971). In the Old Testament have been found literary genres such as legends, oracles of judgment, laments, hymns, disputations, wisdom sayings; and in the New Testament literary forms such as parables, miracle tales, pronouncement stories, epistles.

Finally, redaction critics have studied the way editors used these literary units like building blocks to construct larger literary structures, and also the various phases that the tradition went through on its way to receiving final scriptural form (Perrin 1969).

These methods have helped the reader to realize

that scripture cannot be read simply on a "flat surface," as we read the page of a book, for it has a "dimension of depth" (von Rad). The sixty-six chapters of the present book of Isaiah, for instance, reflect a long history of the reinterpretation of Isaiah's message, from the time of the eighth-century prophet himself to the apocalyptic rendition of his message in the time of the restoration of the Jewish community in the fifth century B.C.E. or even later.

All of these methods, which may be gathered together under the umbrella of "historical criticism," attempt in their respective ways to understand the words of Scripture in their historical setting. The assumption is that historicocritical study can illuminate the concrete human situation—political, cultural, social—in which the biblical message was expressed, and to which it was directed. A relatively new horizon in this kind of study is the sociological approach, which seeks to understand the social location presupposed in biblical texts (Gottwald 1985; Wilson 1984). For instance, prophets who stood within the political establishment spoke with a different accent than did those who were peripheral to the political structure (Wilson 1980), and the writings of the New Testament are illumined by a study of the social status of early urban Christians (Meeks 1983).

An increasing number of scholars advocate a shift from the diachronic study of scripture to a synchronic approach, which views a literary work as a finished product without regard to historical antecedents or to the social setting in which it was composed. Whereas historical criticism attempts to trace the process by which a biblical book came to be, the newer literary criticism concentrates on the completed work and considers such matters as its structure, dynamic, place in the canon, and impact upon the reader (see "Job").

In this connection may be mentioned rhetorical or stylistic criticism (Muilenburg 1969). Although related to form criticism, from which it sprang, this type of study goes beyond it, in the sense that it is not so concerned about "situation in life" (*Sitz im Leben*) but concentrates rather on stylistic and structural features of a text. Using this approach, a "close reading" yields new appreciation, both aesthetic and theological, of familiar texts like the creation story or the story of paradise lost (Trible 1978). Some literary critics interpret the text by treating the stylistic features that are evident on the surface of the text (Alter 1981; Fishbane 1979). Others, who advocate the method of structuralism, delineate the deep structure that lies beneath the text and that surfaces in it (Patte 1976; Polzin 1977). Many literary studies, whether rhetorical or structuralist, are carried out without regard to the history of Israel or to the theological significance of the text.

Both of these general approaches, the diachronic and the synchronic, coexist rather amicably, sometimes influencing and correcting each other. Those who stress the diachronic dimension will consider primarily the *process* of transmission in which the heritage of the community was appropriated and reinterpreted as the community faced new situations during its ongoing historical pilgrimage. According to this view the word of God is not frozen in a text but is a living word that becomes the "word of God" as the past tradition is contemporized in a new historical situation (Sanders 1987). Those who stress the synchronic dimension, if they face the theological question at all, may advocate a poetic appreciation of the words of scripture as "holy words" (Jer 23:9) that function as windows into the world of divine transcendence or, in other terms, as vehicles of the word of God.

THE RELATION BETWEEN THE TESTAMENTS

In the Jewish community the relation between the Hebrew Bible and the New Testament is not an issue, for the Talmud (that is, the authoritative body of Jewish law, comprising the Mishnah and the Gemara) is regarded as the continuation and supplement of the "Old Testament" (Tsevat 1986). For the Christian community, on the other hand, this is a major question precisely because this community claims the Old Testament as its scripture too. As we have seen, early Christians not only used the storytelling mode to confess their faith, thereby proving themselves to be the heirs of Israel's prophets, poets, and narrators, but they also affirmed that Scripture tells *one* story about the people of God, Israel, which reaches its climax in the life, death, and resurrection of Jesus Christ (Luke 24:13–35).

Some Christian interpreters have seized the Old Testament with such possessive passion that they have read into it the content of the Christian gospel, thereby absorbing the Old Testament into the New. The Old Testament, however, has an integrity of its own, as attested by the fact that the Christian Bible contains not one Testament, but two.

The essays in these volumes disclose many areas of agreement between the two Testaments. Creation theology, as set forth classically in the opening chapters of Genesis (Gen 1–11), some of the psalms (Pss 8, 19, 33, 104, 145), prophetic poetry (Isa 40–55), and Wisdom literature (Prov 8; Job), is presupposed in the New Testament. It is to the Old Testament that one must turn to find the texts that deal with the original creation, the order of the cosmos, and ecological issues (Anderson 1984).

Furthermore, the New Testament ethic of love presupposes and builds upon the Old Testament message that God, the Holy One of Israel, places the plumb line of judgment against the structures of society, humbles the mighty and lifts up the poor and helpless (see the Magnificat, Luke 1:46–55), and calls for repentance, or change in way of life, in view of the coming of God's kingdom. Marcion's attempt to say that the God of Jesus Christ is not the same God as the Creator and Judge of the Old Testament has no scriptural basis.

In other ways the Old Testament supplements the New. Wisdom literature, represented by the books of Proverbs, Job, and Ecclesiastes and in the Apocrypha by Sirach and the Wisdom of Solomon, provides rich resources for understanding the good life and the wisdom that governs God's creation. During the third century the book of Sirach came to be known in the Christian church as Ecclesiasticus, meaning "the church book," owing to the special favor that it enjoyed among the deuterocanonical writings.

In some respects there are strong elements of discontinuity between the Testaments. The sacrificial system of the temple, as set forth in the book of Leviticus, was irrelevant to the church, whose primary affinity was with the synagogue, not the temple. Christians could appropriate the priestly legislation of the book of Leviticus only by interpreting it typologically in relation to the once-for-all atonement made by Jesus Christ (Letter to the Hebrews).

Moreover, the Old Testament includes heroes of faith who dared to wrestle with and even challenge God. Beginning with Abraham, who on the eve of the holocaust of Sodom and Gomorrah boldly questioned God's ways (Gen 18:23–33), the Old Testament includes a long line of individuals who expostulated with God, preeminently Job. A great number of poems in the book of Psalms are laments in which people in distress cry out "My God, why?" or "O Lord, how long?" with a faith that seeks understanding (Pss 13, 22, etc.; Brueggemann 1984). In contrast to the New Testament, which often seems to encourage an otherworldly hope, the literature of the Old Testament on the whole is infused with a love for this earth with its marvelous beauty, an enjoyment of the senses and bodily passions including sexual expression (Song of Solomon), and a passion for understanding the ways of God here and now.

The early Christians' rereading of the Old Testament resulted in some shifts of emphasis. This is evident in the way the sacred Torah story is understood. To take an example: The early church was much influenced by the story of the ancestors of Israel, especially the promises of grace made to Abraham—that his descendants would become a numerous people, that they would be given the land of Canaan as an "everlasting possession," and that they would mediate blessings to other nations of the earth (Gen 12:1–3, 17:1–21). Paul, however, fastened on only the first and last of these promises. The second, concerning the land of Israel, he reinterpreted to mean "inherit the world" (Rom 4:13).

Even more important, in appropriating Israel's scriptures the Christian church shifted the canonical center to the Prophets. In Judaism the center is the sacred Torah, the so-called five books of Moses; the other two parts of the canon, the Prophets and the Writings, form concentric circles around this center. In the Christian view, however, central attention focuses on the Prophets, in which is announced the divine purpose that in the fullness of time became manifest in Jesus Christ.

Even when turning from the Torah to the Prophets, however, early Christians read the Prophets with different eyes. Certain aspects of the messianic hope were pushed into the background or reinterpreted, as in the case of Isaiah's prophecies of the king who was to come (Isa 9:2–7, 11:1–9, 32:1–8). These portrayals do not exactly fit Jesus, who, though he claimed to be of Davidic lineage, was not a king of the Davidic type. The prophets of Israel sometimes looked forward to the coming of the Messiah, or the Christ, who would rule as God's representative on earth; but when the Christ came, he was not exactly the one who was expected. Instead, he proved to be more like the Servant, rejected but glorified through suffering, as depicted by the prophet of the Exile often called the Second Isaiah (Isa 52:13–53:12).

In attempting to understand the relation between the Old Testament and the New, due attention must be given to both continuity and discontinuity, to agreement and disagreement. From the Christian perspective the old anticipates the new, the new fulfills the old. When the new is come, the old is not rendered obsolete but is transfigured with new meaning.

THE BIBLE IN MODERN EXPERIENCE

The Bible, regarded as a story or history in which God acts and speaks, is inevitably read from the standpoint of our own time and situation in life. The biblical story touches people where they are living—it sometimes clashes with, and sometimes illuminates, "my story" or "our story." Any discussion of scriptural interpretation would be incomplete without consideration of some of the ways in which people in the community of faith have responded, and are responding, to the Bible as sacred scripture.

During the twentieth century many people have sensed the tension, if not the conflict, between the Bible and the modern scientific worldview. "Conservative" interpreters have valiantly attempted to overcome the problem by maintaining that the Bible—for instance, the story of creation and paradise lost (Gen 1–3)—harmonizes with modern science. In the final analysis, however, honesty compels the careful biblical student to admit that the Bible is composed in nonscientific language and reflects a prescientific worldview. A much discussed "liberal" proposal for resolving this problem was to "demythologize" the Bible, that is, to translate it from its prescientific cosmology or "three-storied view of the universe" (heaven, earth, underearth or hell) into the terms of human existence, that is, the personal relationship between God and the existing person (Bultmann 1941). This proposal has merit insofar as it testifies that faith does not involve a "sacrifice of the intellect." But, by reducing the biblical message to existentialist terms, this view fails to deal adequately with the communal, historical, and cosmic dimensions of scripture. It is more prudent to abandon the rationalism inherent in both "conservative" and "liberal" views and recognize the poetic or, better, mythopoeic character of biblical language (Anderson 1984).

Other responses to the biblical story have come from liberation theologians who reread scripture from the standpoint of the experience or "story" of a particular group of people. Representatives of the black community have shown how the Bible speaks with liberating power to their situation. Indeed, black experience is held to be a key for interpreting scripture (Cone 1986). Latin American theologians, struggling against the entrenched economic and political power of the establishment, have found in the Exodus story a paradigm of God's liberation from oppression (Segundo 1976; Croatto 1981; Gutierrez 1973). In South Korea, Minjung theologians have turned to the stories of the Bible (*e.g.*, the Exodus story or the stories of the responses of the crowd to Jesus) to find the assurance of divine power for releasing the "common people" (*minjung*) from the experience of oppression by rulers (Kane 1987). These are a few illustrations of how people in various parts of the world identify with the biblical story—or certain aspects of it—in their own experience.

One major group, which represents at least half of the membership of the community of faith, is only beginning to be heard from: women. From the standpoint of women's experience, feminist theologians have been developing a theology of liberation— liberation from all those structures of power, social practices, and ways of thinking that have kept women in subjugation for centuries (Schüssler-Fiorenza 1984). For women, unlike other liberation theologians, the Bible, at least as it has been interpreted in the church, is something to be liberated from, because in it patriarchal tradition is dominant, the major metaphors for God are male (king, warrior, shepherd, father), and even language about God assumes the masculine gender (he, his, him). Feminist approaches

to scripture cover a wide gamut, from total rejection of the Bible as hopelessly androcentric to the view that, when properly interpreted, it is a witness to human liberation (Achtemeier 1988; Osiek 1985; Sakenfeld 1988).

All of these liberation theologies share a common assumption: there is no "objective" or neutral ground from which to approach scripture. The historicocritical study of scripture is naive if it attempts to go back to "what scripture originally meant," thus excluding the interest or point of view of the modern reader. "Reader response" is part of the interpretive process, for the meaning of the text is influenced in some degree by personal and social experience. However, the crucial question, which is yet to be faced fully, is whether the authority is vested in scripture primarily, though in dialogue with modern experience, or whether a particular experience is the "canon" by which scripture is judged or reinterpreted. It is one thing to identify with the biblical story and find correlations with modern experience; it is another to say that the biblical story is identical with "our story." Some theologians ask for "an openness on the part of the reader and the community to biblical texts which do not confirm personal history and social experience but which call into question the interpretations given to them" (Stroup 1988, pp. 29–32).

Some of the great interpreters of the past, at least until the modern period, when the Newtonian view of the universe exerted imperial sway, spoke of God's accommodation to the limitations of human language. *Synkatabasis* in the Greek, or *accommodatio* in the Latin, refers to God's condescension to meet human beings at the human level, just as a parent gets down on the floor and speaks baby talk to a child (Battles 1977). Modern difficulty with scripture would be considerably reduced if readers were to consider that "the word of God" is couched in human words, words that were formulated in a particular cultural situation but that carry figurative and metaphorical overtones. "The capacity and the practice of perceiving the poetic word," writes a Catholic theologian, "is a presupposition of hearing the word of God" (Rahner 1966, p. 363). The recovery of this poetic capacity, which other ages have had in greater measure, would provide a healthy corrective to preoccupation with the plain, literal meaning of scripture that has afflicted conservative and liberal interpreters in their respective ways. Such recovery would enable the reader to take seriously the "root metaphors" and "archetypal myths" found in the biblical text (Rothschild 1971). A professor of English literature who has displayed a profound interest in the literature of the Bible sees signs that we may have moved "out of an era in which the literal equation was supreme, and once again are in a world in which the metaphor and approximation are recognized as invaluable" (R. M. Frye 1980, pp. 66f.). If so, appreciation of the poetics of scripture may put the reader in touch once again with that dimension of transcendence which, in theological terms, is symbolized as the word of God.

Bibliography

Achtemeier, Elizabeth. "The Impossible Possibility: Evaluating the Feminist Approach to Bible and Theology." *Interpretation* 42 (1988): 45–57.

Alter, Robert. *The Art of Biblical Narrative.* New York, 1981.

Anderson, Bernhard W. "Tradition and Scripture in the Community of Faith." *Journal of Biblical Literature* 100 (1981): 5–21. Reprinted in *A Companion to the Bible,* edited by Miriam Ward. New York, 1985.

———. *Understanding the Old Testament.* 4th ed. Englewood Cliffs, N.J., 1986.

———. *The Unfolding Drama of the Bible.* 3d ed. Philadelphia, 1988. Pp. 89–93.

———, ed. *Creation in the Old Testament.* Philadelphia, 1984. Pp. 1–24.

Barr, James. "Story and History in Biblical Theology." *Journal of Religion* 56 (1976): 1–17.

Barton, John. *Reading the Old Testament: Method in Biblical Study.* Philadelphia, 1984. A judicious discussion of various approaches to the Bible.

Battles, Ford Lewis. "God Was Accommodating Himself to Human Capacity." *Interpretation* 31 (1977): 19–38. John Calvin's interpretation of scripture with some discussion of that of the church fathers.

Birch, Bruce C., and Larry L. Rasmussen. "The Nature and Role of Biblical Authority." In their *Bible and Ethics.* Rev. ed. Minneapolis, 1989.

Brown, Raymond. *The Critical Meaning of the Bible.* Mahwah, N.J., 1981. Discussion of biblical criticism and Christian faith by a Roman Catholic biblical scholar.

Brueggemann, Walter. *Israel's Praises.* Philadelphia, 1988. A sociological appreciation of the Psalms. ——— *The Message of the Psalms.* Minneapolis, 1984.

Bultmann, Rudolf. "New Testament and Mythology: The Problem of Demythologizing the New Testament Proclamation" (1941). In *New Testament Mythology and Other Basic Writings of Rudolf Bultmann,* edited and translated by Schubert M. Ogden. Philadelphia, 1984.

Childs, Brevard. *Introduction to the Old Testament as Scripture.* Philadelphia, 1979.

———. *The New Testament as Canon: An Introduction.* Philadelphia, 1985.

Cone, James H. *A Black Theology of Liberation.* Maryknoll, N.Y., 1986.

Croatto, J. S. *Exodus: A Hermeneutics of Freedom.* Translated by Salvator Attanasio. Maryknoll, N.Y., 1981. A superb example of Latin American liberation theology.

Cullmann, Oscar. *Salvation in History.* New York, 1967. A New Testament theologian and church historian advocates a "history of salvation" (*Heilsgeschichte*) interpretation of scripture.

Cyris, Moon Hee-Suk. "An Old Testament Understanding of Minjung." In *Minjung Theology: People as the Subjects of History,* edited by the Commission on Theological Concerns of the Christian Conference of Asia. Rev. ed. Maryknoll, N.Y., 1983.

Fackenheim, Emil. *God's Presence in History: Jewish Affirmations and Philosophical Reflections.* New York, 1970. A philosophical discussion of Exodus and Sinai in Jewish tradition.

Fackre, Gabriel. *Authority: Scripture in the Church for the World.* Vol. 3 of *The Christian Story.* Grand Rapids, Mich., 1987. Discussion of the narrative mode of scripture by a systematic theologian.

Fishbane, Michael. *Text and Texture: Close Readings of Selected Biblical Texts.* New York, 1979.

Frei, Hans. *The Eclipse of Biblical Narrative: A Study in Eighteenth and Nineteenth Century Hermeneutics.* New Haven, 1974.

Frye, Northrop. *The Great Code: The Bible and Literature.* San Diego, 1982.

Frye, Roland Mushat. "Metaphors, Equations, and the Faith." *Theology Today* 37 (1980): 59–67.

Gottwald, Norman. *The Hebrew Bible: A Socio-Literary Introduction.* Philadelphia, 1985. A sociological approach to Israel's history.

Gutierrez, Gustavo. *A Theology of Liberation.* Maryknoll, N.Y., 1973.

———. *The Power of the Poor in History.* Maryknoll, N.Y., 1983. A fine example of Latin American liberation theology.

Habel, Norman. *Literary Criticism of the Old Testament.* Philadelphia, 1971.

Hanson, Paul. *The People Called: The Growth of Community in the Bible.* New York, 1986.

Herberg, Will. "Biblical Faith as *Heilsgeschichte:* The Meaning of Redemptive History in Human Existence."

In *Faith Enacted as History,* edited by Bernhard W. Anderson. Philadelphia, 1976.

Heschel, Abraham Joshua. *God in Search of Man: A Philosophy of Judaism.* New York, 1955.

Kane, Margaret. "Minjung Theology." *Theology* 90 (1987): 351–356.

Koch, Klaus. *The Growth of the Biblical Tradition: The Form-Critical Method.* Translated by S. M. Cupitt. New York, 1969.

Meeks, Wayne. *The First Urban Christians: The Social World of the Apostle Paul.* New Haven, 1983.

Muilenburg, James. "Form Criticism and Beyond." *Journal of Biblical Literature* 88 (1969): 1–18. An important essay on rhetorical or stylistic criticism.

Niebuhr, H. Richard. *The Meaning of Revelation.* New York, 1941. See especially chapter 4.

Osiek, Carolyn. "The Feminist and the Bible: Hermeneutical Alternatives." In *Feminist Perspectives on Biblical Scholarship,* edited by Adela Yarbro Collins. Chico, Calif., 1985.

Patte, Daniel. *What Is Structural Exegesis?* Philadelphia, 1976.

Perrin, Norman. *What Is Redaction Criticism?* Philadelphia, 1969.

Polzin, Robert M. *Biblical Structuralism: Method and Subjectivity in the Study of Ancient Texts.* Philadelphia, 1977.

Rad, Gerhard von. *Old Testament Theology.* 2 vols. Translated by D. M. G. Stalker. New York, 1962–1965. An Old Testament theologian advocates a "history of salvation" interpretation of scripture.

Rahner, Karl. "Poetry and the Christian." In *Theological Investigations,* vol. 4, *More Recent Writings.* Translated by Kevin Smyth. Baltimore, 1966.

Rothschild, Fritz A. "Truth and Metaphor in the Bible: An Essay on Interpretation." *Conservative Judaism* 25 (1971): 3–22. A Jewish scholar advocates taking seriously the "root metaphors" and "archetypal myths" found in the biblical text.

Sakenfeld, Katherine Doob. "Feminist Perspectives on Bible and Theology: An Introduction to Selected Issues and Literature." *Interpretation* 42 (1988): 5–18.

Sanders, James A. *From Sacred Story to Sacred Text.* Philadelphia, 1987. Illuminating essays on "canonical criticism."

Schüssler-Fiorenza, Elisabeth. *Bread Not Stone.* Boston, 1984. A fine example of a feminist scriptural hermeneutic.

Segundo, Juan Luis. *Liberation of Theology.* Translated by John Drury. Maryknoll, N.Y., 1976.

Sternberg, Meir. *The Poetics of Biblical Narrative: Ideological Literature and the Drama of Reading.* Bloomington, Ind., 1985.

Stroup, George W. "Between Echo and Narcissus: The Role of the Bible in Feminist Theology." *Interpretation* 42 (1988): 19–44.

Trible, Phyllis. *God and the Rhetoric of Sexuality.* Philadelphia, 1978. An exquisite example of rhetorical criticism in a feminist perspective.

Tsevat, Matitiahu. "Theology of the Old Testament: A Jewish View." *Horizons in Biblical Theology* 8 (1986): 33–50.

Tucker, Gene M. *Form Criticism of the Old Testament.* Philadelphia, 1971.

Wilder, Amos. *The Language of the Gospel.* New York, 1964.

Wilson, Robert R. *Prophecy and Society in Ancient Israel.* Philadelphia, 1980. An important sociological examination of the types of prophecy in ancient Israel.

———. *Sociological Approaches to the Old Testament.* Philadelphia, 1984.

Wright, G. E. *God Who Acts.* London, 1952. A discussion of Israel's witness to the revelation of God in history.

BERNHARD W. ANDERSON

Introduction to The Old Testament

THE OLD TESTAMENT is a collection of sacred writings preserved by the community of Israel and accepted as Holy Scripture by Jews and Christians alike. In the Jewish community, the collection is called the Bible and is sometimes referred to by the acronym *Tanach*, representing the first letter of the terms for the three divisions of the Hebrew Bible—Torah, Prophets (Nevi'im), and Writings (Kethuvim). The collection is not identical in the Jewish and Christian communities, since Christian churches early preserved many Jewish writings that did not find their way into the Jewish canon of Holy Scripture. Thirteen such writings (fourteen if 4 Ezra is counted), called deuterocanonical or apocryphal, were regularly included in the Christian scriptures among Roman Catholics and Eastern Christians, but were treated as of lesser or no authority by numerous Protestant bodies. Today most Christian Bibles include all of the Apocrypha, and frequently include other Jewish writings, such as 3 and 4 Maccabees and Psalm 151.

The collections were also arranged differently in the Jewish and the Christian communities. In the Jewish collection, five books made up the Torah (Genesis, Exodus, Leviticus, Numbers, and Deuteronomy), also called the Five Books of Moses. Four books were found under the heading Former Prophets (Joshua, Judges, 1–2 Samuel, and 1–2 Kings), and four books or collections were preserved under the heading Latter Prophets (Isaiah, Jeremiah, Ezekiel, and the Book of the Twelve Prophets). The final section bore the general designation Writings. It contained the Psalms, Proverbs, Job, and the festal scrolls Ruth, Song of Solomon, Ecclesiastes, Lamentations, and Esther, and also contained Daniel, Ezra, Nehemiah, and 1–2 Chronicles. These Writings were considered to number nine in all, since the five festal scrolls were counted as one book.

The Christian Bible arranged the Old Testament writings quite differently. As the Hebrew Bible had been translated into Greek prior to the Christian era, the works could now be grouped by content. The Torah, or Pentateuch (Genesis through Deuteronomy), was first, as it was in the Hebrew Bible. The Historical Writings included Joshua, Judges, Ruth, 1–2 Samuel, 1–2 Kings, 1–2 Chronicles, Ezra, Nehemiah, and Esther, as well as several of the apocryphal books (in the case of those Christian Bibles that included the Apocrypha). The poetic and wisdom writings included Job, Psalms, Proverbs, Ecclesiastes, and the Song of Solomon, plus several apocryphal books. And finally, the collection ended with the Prophetic Writings, Isaiah, Jeremiah, Lamentations, Ezekiel, Daniel, and the Twelve Prophets (arranged in a different order than that found in the Jewish canon).

Thus one sees that the term "Old Testament" has a variety of meanings. Christian scholars today often refer to the collection as the Hebrew Bible in order to avoid any suggestion that the Christian community has simply taken away from the Jewish community the latter's sacred writings. Others preserve the use of the term, both because of its familiarity and because it is centrally a part of the Christian Bible, even though it remains the Bible of the Jewish people independent of its Christian use.

The three parts of the Jewish Bible tell one sweeping story—the story of the beginnings of the world, of Israel, of the kingship and the continuing life of the people of Israel through invasions, exile, return from exile, and their precariously secured independence under the rule of the Maccabees following Judas' victory over the Syrians in 164 B.C.E. It is a story of almost unremitting hardship, with trial after trial, while God demands fidelity to the divine precepts and continues to renew the promise of blessing for the people of Israel and for their descendants. The entire sweep of this history is one grand promise on its way to consummation but never discerned as consummated.

THE TORAH

Promise on the way to consummation is clearly the theme of the first five books of the Old Testament, the Torah. A series of "firsts" dominates the early chapters of Genesis: the first week of the world's history, when God calls all things into existence by the divine word; the first human pair; the first sin; the first child; the first farmer (Cain) and the first shepherd (Abel); the first sacrifice, followed quickly by the first murder; the first and only flood; and the first selection of a single family through which blessing is to extend to all the families of the earth (Gen 12:1–3).

The story of Abraham, Isaac, and Jacob continues the concern with God's promise, showing the ways in which human initiatives and divine interventions act upon the realization of God's promise. Indeed, this story continues in yet more dramatic form as Joseph makes his way into Egypt, where he is preserved in order to preserve the lives of his family later on. And the drama mounts as Pharaoh turns against the Hebrew people living at peace in Egypt, oppresses them, and must finally be forced to free the oppressed

slaves while God remains faithful to the promise made to Israel's forebears.

Exodus and the other books of the Torah tell of the beginnings of Israel's institutional life. While a covenant was made between Abraham and God, and while circumcision already existed in Abraham's time, most of the institutional and legal life of Israel is placed in the literature associated with the Exodus from Israel, the gathering at Mount Sinai, and the wanderings in the wilderness. Thus the Torah basically provides for the entire life of the people of Israel. When Joshua leads the people into the land of Canaan to take possession of it, the people of Israel have been given all that they need to live a life that is faithful to God and just to one another and to their neighbors. They have the Sabbath, the covenant of grace and of obligation with its fixed demands, circumcision, knowledge of how to organize for holy warfare, and laws for daily life and for regular worship; and they have the assurance of God's accompanying presence.

One thing they do not have: they do not have possession of the land. The Torah comes to be the central part of the Hebrew Scriptures, and yet it ends with the people outside the Promised Land, as Moses the great prophet and leader dies and is buried by God in a grave whose site is known to no mortal. That is a remarkable way for the Torah to end. One sees that *torah* rests firmly on divine promise and on partial realization of the promise.

The literature found in the Pentateuch is of quite varied character, consisting of ancient sagas, myths, and legends, of songs and blessings and cursings and "last words," and of extended narratives telling the story of the "firsts" that occurred, including the remarkably graphic narratives concerning Abraham, Isaac, Jacob, and Joseph.

THE HISTORICAL WRITINGS

The Former Prophets
The materials in the Former Prophets continue the story of God's promise on its way to realization. The book of Joshua recounts the entrance into the land, giving stories of conquest, treaty making with the inhabitants, and settlement in the land alongside its Canaanite population. It also describes the tribal

allotments and Joshua's words of farewell to the tribal representatives. The entire book of Joshua was reviewed and edited by a person from the late seventh century B.C.E. now referred to as the Deuteronomistic Historian, who gave to this book and also to the books of Judges, 1–2 Samuel, and 1–2 Kings a distinctive character. The historian responsible for the current shape of these books made clear that God's word was the dominant reality in Israel's history, shaping the events, offering divine intervention when human affairs had gone out of control, disciplining and punishing the people when they had failed God, but also protecting and saving the people in their many perils. Again, it is God's promise of blessing and fulfillment of life that is on the way to realization, despite the many travails that the word of blessing confronted.

In the Book of Judges the situation is much clearer. Old, independent narratives of the particular judges and leaders of Israel prior to the kingship of David were already woven together in the period of the early kingship. The Deuteronomistic Historian recast these to express the conviction that God always intervened to raise up a deliverer at just the right time. It is clear that those collecting the stories of the judges had a double attitude toward the institution of kingship. It was for them an institution providing stability and some order in a chaotic situation. At the same time, kingship was a threat to the kind of society God was demanding that the Israelites exemplify. From earliest days, the people of Israel had been associated voluntarily with one another and with God, not under the thumb of a despot prince but in the care of a loving parent who also laid down firm and clear demands. This character of the deity as both just and beneficent, associated with the people as head of the family, and leading them onward toward the day of fulfillment of the promised blessing, did not accord well with the institution of kingship.

The fable related in Judges 9 by Jotham, a surviving son of the judge Gideon, is particularly telling. Jotham shouted out his fable to the people of Shechem on the occasion when Abimelech, another son of Gideon, had made himself king of the central hill country by murdering his brothers wholesale. Jotham told how the trees of the forest had desired a king and had tried in vain to persuade the most luxurious and valuable trees and plants of the field and forest to rule over them. Only the worthless bramble was willing to be their king, and the bramble agreed to do so only on the condition that all authority be handed over to him. Kingship is a worthless institution, according to this remarkable story.

1–2 Samuel

The books of Samuel contain some of the most marvelous literature in the Hebrew Bible. Stories of the young Samuel, of the capture of the Ark by the Philistines, of David's rise to the kingship, and of the struggles over who was to succeed David as king have become part of world literature and are familiar to millions. The books of Samuel end with the story not completed, for David, now old, has still not passed on the kingship to his heir.

1–2 Kings

The story is carried on in 1–2 Kings, which contain the account of David's death, Solomon's succession to the throne, Solomon's wisdom and achievements as well as his failings, and the division of the kingship into a northern part (called Israel) and a southern part (called Judah). The conflicts between the unhappily divided people of God claim a good part of the books of Kings, but these also relate conflicts with foreign peoples, providing an excellent source for the history of the period from the late tenth century to the beginning of the sixth.

Embedded within the history of Israel and Judah is the collection of stories about the prophets Elijah, Elisha, and Micaiah. The last-named prophet appears in but a single episode (1 Kgs 22), but he is marvelously portrayed; the story supplements the fine picture of ninth-century prophecy contained in the stories of Elijah and Elisha (the bulk of 1 Kgs 17 through 2 Kgs 12).

The theme of God's promise on the way to fulfillment well describes the entire account of the Former Prophets, Joshua through 2 Kings. The Deuteronomistic Historian worked in quite different ways in dealing with the story found in 1–2 Samuel and that found in 1–2 Kings. He incorporates large blocks of literature already at hand when telling the story of Samuel, Saul, and David. As he turns to Solomon and his successors, he is much freer in revising and recasting the available court records, annals, and other materials at his disposal. The result is that the first two parts of the Hebrew Bible (the Torah and the Former Prophets) come to an end with the people of Israel in Babylonian exile, their temple and capital city destroyed, awaiting the next step in God's drama of bringing blessing to them and through them to the families of the earth.

THE LATTER PROPHETS

The prophetic literature is, from many viewpoints, Israel's great literary, moral, and spiritual treasure. The four massive collections grew over a considerable period of time, but almost all of the collection had assumed its present form by the beginning of the fourth century B.C.E. Four of the prophets dominate the latter half of the eighth century (about 760 to shortly after 700 B.C.E.): Amos, Hosea, Isaiah, and Micah. The first two addressed the community of Israel primarily, while the last two seem to have worked exclusively in Judah and Jerusalem. Their message might be summed up as follows: The God who claimed the life and devotion of the people of Israel offered a rich prospect for this people—an abiding presence, protection from foes, productive soil, and abundant opportunity for a wholesome life on God's good earth.

But the price for such lavish care was high: Israel was indeed claimed by God as the people of God, required to live in accordance with the demands of God's covenant with them (while it is difficult to know just when the idea of the covenant became central, the idea is without doubt present in the thought of these eighth-century prophets), and such demands involved an exclusive loyalty to Israel's God. Also involved was fidelity to the kind and quality of life individual Israelites were to live with their neighbors, and to the life the people as a whole were to live before God and before the world of the nations.

These prophets were never satisfied with the quality of Israel's devotion to God. Much of their writings centers on departures from what the prophets understood true fidelity to God to demand. The prophets were unremitting in denouncing kings, leaders, and individual Israelites for their failures, frequently pointing back to the history of God's deliver-

ance of Israel from Egyptian bondage, God's guidance in the wilderness, God's preparation of a land for them to inherit. The prophets also insisted that religious devotion could not be separated from public life and its opportunities and demands. Worship had to be a reflection of the actual character and moral commitments of the people, or else it was loathsome to God.

These prophets set the character of Israel's religious understanding. God the creator was the guide of historical existence, the moral standard for kings and commoners alike, just in all dealings, compassionate, and especially sensitive to the situation and the needs of the oppressed and the lowly. God's favor could not be bought, neither by the most lavish gifts nor by the most self-giving service. But God was disposed to come to the aid of the needy, welcomed the prayers of the faithful, and took delight in the people of Israel, whom the deity had borne "on eagles' wings" (Exod 19:3) to the mountain of revelation.

THE WRITINGS

The third collection of the Hebrew Bible, the Writings, is miscellaneous in content. Two of the major collections contained here are the Psalms and the three chief wisdom writings of the Hebrew Bible, Proverbs, Job, and Ecclesiastes. In addition, the five scrolls associated with major Israelite festivals—the Song of Solomon (Passover), Ruth (Weeks), Lamentations (the ninth day of the month Av, commemorating the fall of Jerusalem), Ecclesiastes (Tabernacles), and Esther (Purim)—have an honored place among the Writings. Other materials from the Writings are of special importance for an understanding of the life of Israel after the return from Babylonian exile in 538 B.C.E.—Ezra, Nehemiah, 1–2 Chronicles, and Daniel. Daniel is in a class by itself: it is the only example in the Hebrew Bible of the literature called apocalyptic. Apocalyptic literature, arising relatively late in the biblical period, describes God's effecting a consummation on earth following upon a decisive series of acts of judgment in which the various nations of earth play a part. Prophets spoke about judgment from God falling upon Israel and other peoples for their sins. Apocalyptic literature speaks of cosmic judgment: the whole earth, by virtue of its sin, must fall and be succeeded by a new and transformed earth. The Book of Daniel contains stories about Daniel and other faithful Jewish exiles taken into the Babylonian and Persian worlds and of their protection there by God. These stories are set in the context of dream-visions of God's restoration of the people of Israel following upon the dreadful cosmic judgment that awaits.

As mentioned above, the great treasure in this collection is the Book of Psalms. There, individual and corporate laments, hymns of praise and thanks-giving, affirmations of trust and confidence in God, and praises of God's teaching (*torah*, often translated as "law") contain actual prayers spoken by the people of Israel over the centuries. The Psalms date from the time of David to the middle or late period following the return from exile (1000 to 350 B.C.E.), though most of them probably were composed prior to the return from exile in 538 B.C.E.

The wisdom writings contain large blocks of wisdom sayings, often in poetic parallelism, of the sort known from ancient Egypt, Babylonia, and many other cultures. The wisdom traditions reflect a prag-matic attitude toward the world and its problems, and they also rest upon a pragmatic conviction that divine wisdom is present in the world's structures, a part of the creation itself. The world's mysteries and enigmas may well testify to a hidden divine wisdom not readily accessible to mortals; even so, such a wisdom is there, and its location is known to God (see Job 28 and the apocryphal Book of Baruch).

Job and Ecclesiastes contain challenges to the notion of a just and orderly world in which wisdom's contributions are evident to all. The author of Job presses the question of life's meaning with such rigor and relentlessness that the question of meaning is set in the context of an all-encompassing divine/human mystery. The author of Ecclesiastes calls into question the existence of any discoverable meaning to life but does not fall into resignation or despair. Rather, Ecclesiastes calls for humankind to take delight in the goods of life, to claim the values that are present in the changing circumstances of life, even though the path to some ultimately meaningful world seemed to its author to be blocked—and blocked by God and no other!

RELATION OF OLD TESTAMENT LITERATURE TO ISRAEL

Clearly the collection that constitutes the Old Testament is only a selection from the writings pro-duced by ancient Israelites and preserved by the Jewish and Christian communities throughout the centuries. How was the selection made? Almost certainly, it was not gathered by some official body that set out to determine what was the "true" or the most valuable or the most reliable body of available literature.

The selection was made on the basis of usage, of retelling the stories, reusing the hymns and prayers, teaching and repeating the proverbs and the historical reports, until the community had come to recognize what belonged and what did not. No doubt the work of highly gifted narrators, scribes, Levites, and inter-preters of the laws was influential in sorting, editing, and recasting portions of the tradition. But eventually (probably by the second century B.C.E.) the growing collection was well established. There would have been full agreement, by that time, on the contents of the Torah and the Former and Latter Prophets. Most of the Writings would have assumed their given form as well.

It was not until the controversies with the Christians that the Jewish community was led to set aside the works that we now call the Apocrypha. As this happened, the remaining collection at once took on a double character. It remained a part of the Christian Old Testament, while at the same time it was more clearly defined as the Bible of the Jewish community. The Jewish authorities also recognized the oral traditions that soon would be collected to form the Mishnah and would be treated as having authority equal with the written Bible. These oral traditions would later be augmented with other tradi-tions and interpretations of the Torah to form the Babylonian and Palestinian Talmuds.

The literature of the Old Testament is, therefore, a part of the sacred writings of the Jewish people and a part of the sacred writings of the Christian communi-ty. It is also a part of the classical literary and religious heritage of the world, having been the subject matter for scrupulous and intensive study and interpretation through the centuries, not only by persons concerned with its religious message but also by persons and groups who have focused upon its ethical and legal content and addressed the literary qualities of the collection quite apart from its religious message. In this sense, the Old Testament, which is certainly the literary and religious story of the people Israel and a book of profound religious and theological import for Christians and Jews in particular, is also a literary collection of marvelous power and beauty, deserving attention by individuals and groups that have no commitment to explore its religious significance.

FORMS OF OLD TESTAMENT LITERATURE

The Old Testament collection is literarily quite diverse. Opening sagas or "myths" tell of the origin of things in ways designed to take the community back behind the historically known world to the prehistorical epochs, to the very beginning of things. Ancient stories of the creation have survived from many cultures. Many of these were regularly used in acts of worship, representing the creation and the flood as elements in a great religious drama that safeguarded the continuation of life on earth. Israel drew upon these ancient myths and legends, but it brought them into the service of the God who alone had called into existence everything that had being. The myths were tied closely to the story of God's dealings with humankind, and they were entirely unrelated to some time "before" the creation of heaven and earth.

Other literary materials of the saga sort told the story of the beginnings of the people of Israel. Such sagas were connected stories of the particular ancestors of Israel—Abraham, Isaac, Jacob, and the rest. These particular stories also had their very old parts—curses and blessings; taunt songs; songs commemorating victory in battle; prayers of thanksgiving for divine deliverance; pleas to God for deliverance from the power of sickness, from foes in time of battle, and from false accusers; and the wisdom utterances that were so popular in the ancient world. This vast literary collection also includes such magnificent stories of the struggles of judges and kings and prophets that readers can reenter the world they portray, feel the vital issues faced by Gideon (Judges

6–8) or Saul and David (1–2 Samuel) or Jeremiah (see especially chapters 36–45). And one can enter into the longings of the human heart so vividly portrayed in Psalms 42 and 43, Psalm 130, or Psalm 73, or into the confident faith of the psalmists responsible for Psalm 23 and Psalm 46.

The writings of the prophets and of the sages also contain their distinct literary forms. The prophets used available forms of speech drawn from the world of the law courts, from the courts of the kings, from procedures connected with warfare, and from family life, as well as from many features of community life. They also created their new forms to fit particular needs (for example, the summons to repentance, a good example of which is found in Hosea 14:1–3). Similarly, the author of the poetry in the Book of Job used proverbs, diatribes, personal laments, poetic analogies drawn from nature, and many other literary forms to express that book's great poetic meditation on life's meaning.

Other literary forms should not be overlooked. There is sophisticated recounting of historical events, with heavy emphasis upon matters of human motivation (see the story of David's rise to the kingship in 1 Samuel 16–2 Samuel 6 and the related story of the struggle over the question of who was to succeed David as king in 2 Samuel 9–20 and 1 Kings 1–2). There are the quite different ways of reporting Israel's history found in 1–2 Chronicles and in parts of 1–2 Kings. In addition, there are the marvelous short stories of Jonah, of Ruth, of Esther, of the prophet who appeared before King Jeroboam at Bethel (1 Kgs 13), of the prophet Micaiah (1 Kgs 22), and of Daniel and the three young men taken into captivity in Babylon (Dan 1–6).

Study of the literary forms has made possible the setting of much of Israel's literature into its appropriate place in the cultic and social life of the people. The result has been a recognition of the actual sweep of the religious and cultural life of the people—how they worshipped, how they governed themselves, how they related to their neighbors in warfare, in treaty making, and in times of peace.

Study of the literature of the Old Testament in other ways has also enabled students better to recognize and appreciate its universality and depth. Structuralist analysis of the literature shows such universal elements in the fresh light of depth perspective, indicating the way in which, for example, the Book of Ruth discloses a literary movement from emptiness to fullness, from bereftness to wholeness of life. Literary studies of the same book, or of the prophet Jonah, or of the magnificent narratives of 2 Samuel display the genius of narrative art in the ancient world and in Israel, placing this literature among the finest of the literary creations of the world. Few who have studied the story of Amnon's rape and contemptuous rejection of Tamar (2 Sam 13:1–9) can read of rape or incest in the same way as before.

METHODS OF INTERPRETATION

Since biblical times, the books of the Old Testament collection have required literary and religious interpretation. Stories from an early time are used to register moral or religious guidelines for a later time (see Jer 26:16–19 and Hos 12:2–9). Central features of the biblical record are used to hold under critical review other features that seem clearly not to be so central. This biblical record requires interpretation; it is not adequate simply to read the record and accept it as "literal" truth.

Some of the material is, of course, factual and should be accepted as factual, such as the reported birthdates of prophets and kings, their hometowns and their associates, or accounts of their family affairs and the chief events of their lives. But much of the biblical record calls for critical study and reflection. Indeed, few bodies of literature in the world have received more attention than has the Bible.

Critical analysis that enables one to place the writings in their social, historical, cultural, and cultic settings has been invaluable. Once this has been done, it is possible, from the literature of the Bible and from extrabiblical evidence, to order the literature chronologically and to trace roughly the development of Israelite religious thought and practice, from earliest times to the close of the biblical canon. Literary analysis also assists the reader in discerning the character of particular kinds of literature, how such literature functioned in the ancient world, and what overall and specific purposes it tended to serve. Comparative study of ancient Near Eastern religious communities and their ideas and practices in relation

to those of the Bible has placed the biblical material in close association with literature from Ugarit, Babylonia, Assyria, and Egypt. Such comparative work enables one to see both the similarities of the biblical material to the literatures of the neighbors and also the distinctive features of biblical literature.

Sociological analyses have helped to identify typical movements and features of the community of Israel in relation to neighboring societies. Such studies have greatly illuminated the dominant characteristics of biblical peoples and their religious understandings and practices. Throughout the centuries, however, the biblical record has been studied in particular for the way in which it discloses a view of human life in association with God, with essential and abysmal mystery being revealed. The Bible is first and foremost religious literature, proposing for human reflection a view of life that takes account of the religious claim that God is the ultimate source and creator of all that has being; that God is disposed toward the creation in a way that is gracious and life-enhancing; and that purposiveness underlies and shows through in the overall sweep of historical existence, for the people of Israel and for all the peoples of earth.

TRANSLATING THE BIBLE

In the twentieth century the Bible has been translated into contemporary languages throughout the world, largely through the efforts of various Bible societies to make the biblical record available to all peoples in their own languages. Translations into English are particularly numerous and particularly good. Beginning with the Revised Standard Version in 1946 (New Testament) and 1952 (Old Testament), scholars have produced excellent, idiomatic translations into English for the various English-speaking parts of the world and for the various religious communities. The New English Bible (1961, 1970) is an entirely fresh translation of the Bible, not tied to the preceding translations in the King James biblical tradition. The New Jewish Version, published under the title *Tanakh* (1985), is also an entirely new translation, not a revision of the 1917 Jewish edition that had been widely used previously in Jewish circles. The Jerusalem Bible (1966, 1967, 1968) and the New

Jerusalem Bible (1985), which depend upon the French edition produced by scholars of the École Biblique in Jerusalem and their collaborators, are also fresh and independent translations into English. Today's English Version (1976), also called the Good News Bible, is the product of the United Bible Societies and the American Bible Society. This translation employs the translation principle of "dynamic equivalence," an effort to render the biblical language and idioms into their modern equivalents, even if this requires a considerable departure from the form and word order of the Hebrew and the Greek. The same applies, but to a lesser extent, to the New International Version (1978), a fresh translation effort carried through by evangelical Protestants.

The New King James Version (1982, 1983), on the other hand, is a revision of the Authorized Version of 1611, an attractive effort to remove the obscurities of language in the King James translation and provide an accurate and up-to-date translation in the King James idiom.

The new edition of the Revised Standard Version, nearing completion in 1988, also continues the King James tradition present in the current Revised Standard Version, though it is a thoroughgoing revision into more idiomatic and less "biblical" English.

It is refreshing to note that divisions within the religious communities are not connected to particular translations of the Bible. The existence of fine scholarly translations of the Bible from so many different religious schools of thought has disarmed the criticism often focused upon particular translations.

It is also noteworthy that the two distinct principles of biblical translation are nicely complementary. Dynamic equivalency can help to make the biblical record much more understandable and readable by persons who lack wide knowledge of a given modern language, for these translations use contemporary idioms and also restrict themselves to a limited vocabulary. Idiomatic translations that stick more closely to the language and outlook of the biblical writers help to draw readers more nearly into the social and cultural world of the Bible—a most valuable gain for sound interpretation. Such translations also are better able to preserve the literary power and beauty of the biblical language.

Bibliography

Aharoni, Yohanan. *The Archaeology of the Land of Israel: From the Prehistoric Beginnings to the End of the First Temple Period.* Translated by Anson F. Rainey. Philadelphia, 1982. A brilliant essay on archaeological discoveries in Canaan and in Israel and on the importance of these discoveries for an understanding of the Hebrew Bible, literarily, historically, and religiously.

Alter, Robert. *The Art of Biblical Narrative.* New York, 1981. An excellent introductory study of the literary qualities and features of the Hebrew Bible.

Anderson, A. A. *The New Century Bible Commentary: Psalms.* 2 vols. Grand Rapids, 1972. A brief commentary on the entire book of Psalms, with a lucid and useful introduction to the Psalms and to Israelite worship.

Anderson, Bernhard W. *Out of the Depths: The Psalms Speak for Us Today.* Rev. ed. Philadelphia, 1983. A brief, cogent presentation of the religious life of ancient Israel reflected in the Psalms.

————. *Understanding the Old Testament.* 4th ed. Englewood Cliffs, N.J., 1986. The standard introductory study of biblical literature, history, and thought.

Bailey, Lloyd R., ed. *The Word of God: A Guide to English Versions of the Bible.* Atlanta, 1982. Essays offering critical treatments of each of the recent English translations of the Bible.

Blenkinsopp, Joseph. *A History of Prophecy in Israel.* Philadelphia, 1983. A fine study of the entire sweep of Israelite prophecy from its beginnings to the end of the canon of the Hebrew Bible.

Crenshaw, James L. *Old Testament Wisdom: An Introduction.* Atlanta, 1981. An excellent critical examination of wisdom literature, with brief essays on each of the biblical wisdom collections.

Gottwald, Norman K. *The Hebrew Bible: A Socio-Literary Introduction.* Philadelphia, 1985. A detailed and thorough literary and sociological study of the Hebrew Bible, amply illustrated.

Hanson, Paul D. *The People Called: The Growth of Community in the Bible.* San Francisco, 1986. An important and discerning study of the religious and social development of the people of Israel, carrying the story into the New Testament world.

Harrelson, Walter. *The Ten Commandments and Human Rights.* Philadelphia, 1980. A study of the importance of the Ten Commandments for social and ethical life, in ancient times and today.

Hayes, John H., ed. *Old Testament Form Criticism.* San Antonio, 1974. An excellent, detailed study and evaluation of form-critical studies of the Hebrew Bible.

Heschel, Abraham Joshua. *The Prophets.* New York, 1962. A discerning analysis of central themes in the literature and thought of Israel's prophets.

Koch, Klaus. *The Prophets: The Assyrian Period and The Babylonian Period.* Translated by Margaret Kohl. 2 vols. Philadelphia, 1983, 1984. Brief treatments of each of the major prophets, filled with discernment and original insights.

Ringgren, Helmer. *Israelite Religion.* Translated by David E. Green. Philadelphia, 1966. A lucid, comprehensive portrayal of the development of Israelite religion from earliest times to the Hellenistic period.

Vaux, Roland de. *Ancient Israel: Its Life and Institutions.* Translated by John McHugh. New York, 1961. Israelite cultural life, worship, and social-political institutions analyzed and summarized brilliantly.

WALTER HARRELSON

Genesis

THE TITLE *GENESIS* means "the beginning," and the Book of Genesis stands at the beginning of the Bible. For Jews and Christians, the Book of Genesis is an account of the beginnings that concern the life and faith of ancient Israel.

GENERAL CHARACTERISTICS

The Book of Genesis gives a narrative account of the two crucial beginnings for the Bible. On the one hand, the book gives an account of the genesis of the world in the creation narratives of chapters 1 and 2. On the other hand, Genesis 12 and the narratives that follow give an account of the genesis of Israel as a people of faith who are identifiable as a historical entity. The two narratives of the origin of the world (Gen 1–11) and the origin of Israel (Gen 12–50) are quite distinct and are arranged in intentional sequence, covering first the world and then Israel. The Book of Genesis seeks to articulate the relation between the two, so that the world and Israel stand in an intentional relation to each other. On the one hand, it can be argued that in this literature the creation of the world is intended for and aimed at the creation of Israel. That is, from the beginning, the point of creation is the emergence of Israel, for this narrative is Israel's account of its own decisive importance in the world. On the other hand, Israel is not an entity unto itself. It exists with reference to, in

relation to, and perhaps for the sake of, the whole world. Whether we read Genesis from Israel to the world or from the world to Israel, Israel's significance in the history of the world is peculiar, and this peculiar significance is of interest and moment not only for Israel but for the world. At the outset, we should be properly astonished that the narratives of Genesis boldly and unabashedly dare to link these unlikely partners, Israel and world, in a specific and imaginative way.

The matter of the origin of the world and of Israel can be understood historically, that is, as a descriptive account of what happened at the point of origin. But such a historical understanding is quite problematic. Most scholars conclude that the actual historical emergence of Israel is to be located, at the earliest, in the Book of Exodus, around the event of Exodus, the covenant at Mount Sinai, and the leadership of Moses. It is nearly impossible to conclude that the Genesis narratives reflect the actual appearance of a historically identifiable community we call Israel. Thus the narratives of the origin of Israel in Genesis 12–50 are better understood in a way other than as descriptive of a precise historical happening.

It is even more problematic to understand the narrative account of the origin of the world as historically descriptive. There are, of course, scientific hypotheses that seek to describe the way the created world was formed, but none of these "descriptive hypotheses" operates with the categories of the Genesis narrative. The accounts of Genesis are not and surely do not intend in any way to be a scientific characterization.

Since the narratives are not essentially historical or scientific, we need to investigate them as theologically affirmative and celebrative. They do not deal in the categories of empirical data in order to explain how things came to be. Rather, they serve to make an affirmation about the theological (God-related) character of the world and of Israel. This does not mean that the narratives are less true or less important, but only that they serve a very specific purpose. The purpose is very different from the historical and scientific purposes that are popularly imposed on these narratives. We must attend to the intention of the literature in order to understand what the literature sets out to do and what it does not attempt to do. In this narrative, both the world and Israel are referred to God, derive from God's action and will, have their life from God, and are accountable to God for doing God's purpose. The narrative of Genesis is saturated with references to God and thus marks itself as intentionally theological. Genesis insists that, in their very character and shape, neither the world nor Israel can be understood apart from the reality of God. The beginning of the world as creation and the beginning of Israel as a community of faith are both credited to the speech of God.

Both the world and Israel are "creatures of the Word" and exist only because God speaks. In Genesis 1, the world is summoned: "And God said." In Genesis 12, Israel (Abraham) is addressed: "The Lord said to Abraham." Such a presentation puts us on notice that we are dealing with a theological text that affirms a very particular theological claim. It is the primary claim of Genesis that the God of the Bible is a God who speaks, one whose speaking is so sovereign and magisterial that it functions as decree, summons, invitation, order, command, assurance, and promise. It is the word that brings into being that which is not (*cf.* Rom 4:17), that speaks in ways that create an object that can respond in obedience (*cf.* Ps 33:6). The speech of Yahweh, the God of the Bible, is the source of the world that is called to be. The speech of Yahweh is the source of Israel, through Abraham and

Sarah, who are called to be. Both the world and Israel are evoked by Yahweh's sovereign word, and both have their life in their capacity to answer the command in obedience and to trust the promise in faith.

The Book of Genesis is not literature that explains or justifies or argues. It does not give an account of Yahweh or explain why Yahweh's speech is so powerful. Rather, Genesis is "belief-full" speech, formed in a community of faith that already trusts in this God and believes this speech. Yahweh is thus a premise held in the literature and not a conclusion reached through the literature. This literature is testimony, affirmation, confession, and celebration that the speech of Yahweh is "originary," that is, has the power to originate. Derivatively, the communities of faith, Jewish and Christian, have also found this text to be originary; in each new generation this text is the speech through which God causes the world and Israel to be. Genesis is to be read, then, not to find explanations that are scientific or to find reports that are descriptive, but as an act of faith that participates once again in the originary power of the founding events, to which we have access only through this literature.

The Book of Genesis as a founding narrative does not exist by itself. Genesis needs to be read and understood in relation to the foundational literature of the other early books of the Bible, because the other literature articulates what eventuates from this beginning.

Two scholarly hypotheses have been important in recent interpretation of Genesis. First and most influential has been the work of Gerhard von Rad, who published his definitive proposal in 1938. Von Rad proposed that Genesis belongs, with theological intentionality, to the literature that runs from Genesis to Joshua as a single corpus. These six books he calls the Hexateuch. This literature is held together by the general, overarching theme of promise and fulfillment. The governing promise of Yahweh is made to Israel, in Genesis 12:1–4a, that Israel shall have a new land. Israel's life, as portrayed in this literature, is organized around the question of trust in that promise. As the literature now stands, the promise of land comes to fulfillment in the "conquest" stories of Joshua 1–12, in the division of the land in Joshua 13–21, and especially in the concluding theological summary of Joshua 21:43–45, which asserts that all of God's promises to Israel have been kept. According to this hypothesis, the entire body of literature is to be understood along the line that runs from the promise of Genesis 12:1–4a to the fulfillment of Joshua 21:43–45. If the literature be taken in that way, then the entire faith memory of Israel is clustered around the capacity of Yahweh to make and keep promises, the capacity of Israel to trust that promise and respond accordingly, and the peculiar character of the land as the object of the promise and the gift of Yahweh.

Von Rad is, of course, aware that originally the promissory narratives of Genesis and the land stories of Joshua had no relation to each other. Those narratives surely emerge out of different contexts, reflect very different literary genres, and exist in very different circles of tradition. Thus it is a major imaginative theological move (made somewhere in the process of shaping the literature into a theological statement) to bring together these different materials into a quite powerful, creative faith-statement. Von Rad and numerous other scholars agree that the articulation of promise and fulfillment sets the major theological issue of all biblical faith. This interpretation places much weight on the proposal that the normative theological statement presented in Genesis continues through the book of Joshua.

Martin Noth (1972), however, discerned a major literary problem with von Rad's hypothesis. Noth was a close associate of von Rad's in breaking new ground in the study of these ancient traditions, but he differed at a crucial point. In 1943, five years after von Rad presented his remarkable hypothesis, Noth proposed that the Book of Deuteronomy begins a very different literature and articulates a quite distinctive theological position. His most influential hypothesis (whose major claims are still held by a majority of scholars) is that Deuteronomy initiates a new literary-theological statement that continues through Joshua, Judges, Samuel, and Kings. This hypothesis makes a decisive break between Numbers and Deuteronomy and denies a relation of Genesis to Deuteronomy and Joshua, a relation that is indispensable to von Rad's thesis. Noth is left by default with a literary corpus of Genesis to Numbers, only four books, or a Tetrateuch. According to Noth's analysis, the normative story of Israel arrives at the edge of the land of promise, but

stops short of entry. At the most there is an abortive effort to enter the land, which fails (Num 13–14). The originary tale ends short of completion, and Israel is left waiting for the land and waiting to see if the promises will indeed be kept. According to Noth, the story is continued in the very different literature of the Deuteronomist (Deuteronomy–Kings), which is the story of receiving land and losing land. The normative story of the Tetrateuch is pre-land, and the promises still await fruition.

Von Rad has proposed a normative corpus of six books, a Hexateuch, which completes the arc of promise to fulfillment. Noth has proposed a corpus of four books, a Tetrateuch, which leaves the promises open and unresolved. These two dominant hypotheses seem to be mutually exclusive. Scholarly attention has been given to finding ways of making these hypotheses compatible, but the matter remains vexed. Scholars have suggested that there may have been an earlier form of the Pentateuchal tradition that carried Israel fully into the land (as in the Book of Joshua). But in the final form of the tradition as we have it, shaped by the priestly writers who wrote for landless people, exiles, the ending has been removed, only to be reclaimed for a new use in the new historical-theological narrative beginning with Deuteronomy. Such explanations may seem to be excessively complex. It is sufficient to observe that contemporary scholars have noticed in the tradition some ambiguity as to whether the tradition included the actual fulfillment in the land or stopped the account of the promise short of fulfillment.

It is not important for us to adjudicate these various hypothetical alternatives. It is enough to notice that the various alternatives are not mere scholarly guesses but point to difficult and important theological issues. What is most important is to see that the Book of Genesis cannot be studied by itself. It has important connections to the literature that follows, and these connections are to be understood in theological categories concerning the promises and gifts of Yahweh.

There is, however, a major problem with both the hypothesis of a Hexateuch (von Rad) and that of a Tetrateuch (Noth), no matter how we decide between them. The canonical form of the Bible does not recognize or present a corpus of either four or six books. As the canonical texts are presented, there is no clear break after Numbers, nor can it be argued that the narrative continues into Joshua. The normative presentation of Israel's memory has shaped the founding story around the magisterial person of Moses; this does not mean that Moses wrote this literature, but the tradition understands the literature as "the book of Moses," resting on his theological authority. For Jews and Christians alike, it is clearly the five books, Genesis through Deuteronomy, that constitute the normative corpus. Moreover, the end of Deuteronomy and the beginning of Joshua make a decisive break as leadership is transferred from Moses to Joshua.

Although much can be learned from the proposals of von Rad and Noth, neither is finally satisfactory. Von Rad has found it necessary to include the Book of Joshua in his notion of promise and fulfillment, with the Book of Joshua as fulfillment. Because he must include the Book of Joshua, which falls outside the Pentateuch, von Rad seems to disregard the theological statement made by the Pentateuch as such. Conversely, Noth has grouped the Book of Deuteronomy with Joshua through Kings; neither takes the structure of the Pentateuch seriously.

As a matter of canonical discipline, it is finally in the context of the five-book structure of the Pentateuch that Genesis must be understood. The Pentateuch ends at the conclusion of the Book of Deuteronomy, with Moses looking into the Promised Land (Deut 34:1–7), but Moses (and Israel with him) do not enter. They are left poised at the Jordan boundary, ready to enter into the place of fulfillment, not yet there, not yet permitted to be there.

It is this unresolved character of the literature that provides the literary context of the Book of Genesis. The Book of Genesis generates a historical memory that pushes toward fulfillment but does not finally arrive there. The literature (and the community linked to it) is utterly convinced of the power of God's promise and God's watchful attention to that promise, but nonetheless the promise still awaits fulfillment. The fundamental promise is of the land, but the story is set completely among people short of promise and without promise. The shaping memory of the biblical literature is peculiarly appropriate for a people who are waiting for land, passionately believ-

ing they will receive land, but in the meantime living their lives in landlessness. Indeed, it is this tension between actual landlessness and promise of land that provides the central dynamic of the Pentateuch. And what Israel knows about land, the Bible also knows about earth (Gen 1–11), for the cosmic attention to earth and the historical attention to land point to the same reality, most often rendered by the same Hebrew word, *erets*. Thus the land-earth (*erets*) motif is crucial in both Genesis 1–11 and 12–50.

The Book of Genesis is a decisive beginning, but it is not an ending, a completion, or a fruition. It leaves one waiting to see if God—in the narrative—will be willing and able to complete what has been stunningly begun there. If one stays inside the literary corpus of the Pentateuch, the answer to that question is not given. The Pentateuch invites Jews and Christians to wait in hope.

HISTORY OF SCHOLARSHIP

The conventions of tradition have affirmed that Genesis and all of the Pentateuch are authorized and authored by Moses. The connection of authorization to authorship is important and problematic. There is no doubt that the Pentateuch, the Jewish Torah, is the normative biblical document and is sanctioned and legitimated by the person of Moses, the human creator of biblical faith. One way in which the tradition asserted that important authorization is to claim authorship by Moses. As a result, it has been held that Moses wrote the Pentateuch in the sense that he transcribed the actual words of the text.

There are, however, two problems connected with such a notion of authorship. First, scientific study of the Bible, as summarized by Hayes and Clements, has affirmed that the five books are not a continuous, single document reflecting the style or substance of one writer. The Pentateuch is much more complex and complicated than single authorship would allow. Scholars have observed in the Pentateuch evidence of a long process of editorial activity, perhaps undertaken by influential persons, perhaps done through the community's telling and retelling the old memory. The evidence for such a complex process includes contradictions in detail, repetitions, different words used in parallel contexts, complex and problematic chronology, and historical anachronism. To be sure, there are those who conclude that none of this evidence is decisive against the authorship of Moses, but serious academic scholarship has largely agreed that the literary-historical evidences speak heavily against a single authorship. The evidence leads one to the judgment that to try to see the document in a modern sense as written by a single person simply ignores and misunderstands the nature of the material before us.

The second problem with the claim of Mosaic authorship has not received as much attention from scholars but in the long run is perhaps more important. In the ancient world, the notion of a single author writing an identifiable document is simply alien. Literature in the ancient world does not come to be in that way. Rather, it is the product of a community, one that emerges over a long period of time through the ongoing process of telling, transmitting, and reformulating stories again and again. Thus in describing it one can more accurately speak of the formation and emergence of an oral tradition than of the writing of a document. The argument is not that someone (or more than one) other than Moses wrote the document, but that the community over a long period of time formulated the actual words of the literature. As noted by Walter Ong, this is the process of Homeric literature and is the process in any community that relies on oral communication.

In the scholarly consensus, then, we must distinguish between authorization (a religious claim) and authorship (a literary designation). Our modern Western propensity is to connect the two intimately, so that authority follows authorship. But here the two are not so necessarily linked that we must hold to Mosaic authorship in order to claim Mosaic authorization. Indeed, it is precisely the claim of critical faith to affirm Mosaic authorization but to deny Mosaic authorship. The authority of scripture depends on a religious affirmation and is not tied to any particular literary designation. As a religious judgment, Jews and Christians firmly assert that this originary text claims Mosaic authority. Authorship, according to Michael Fishbane (1985), however, is the slow, sustained work of the entire community of faith in the process of tradition-building. Many hands and many voices had a part in formulating this literature that now stands under Mosaic authorization. As a religious judgment, we have no trouble concluding that the purposes and intentionality of God have been at work in that process of tradition-building. The purpose and intentionality of God at work are claimed in the authorization of Moses as God's agent in the Pentateuchal tradition.

For the last several centuries, critical scholarship has largely bracketed out the religious question of authorization and has been preoccupied with the literary-historical question of authorship. In important ways that season of scholarly analysis reflects the intellectual history of the modern period. It is important to be conversant with that scholarship in order to understand how the Book of Genesis is presently perceived. While digesting that scholarship, however, it is important also to hold in abeyance issues of religious authority. Our essay is here concerned with literary history, not with theological claim.

The modern effort to understand the literature of the Pentateuch begins with the assumption that the Pentateuch is a series of documents written at various times in the history of ancient Israel. It is important to recognize that eighteenth- and nineteenth-century scholars posed the question of literature in terms of written documents because they themselves in their own setting perceived the intellectual world in terms of written documents. (The same assumption of the text as document is made by the literalists who opposed these documentary analyses.) According to this early critical hypothesis, each such document "rewrote" the memory of ancient Israel and in so doing sought to be faithful to the normative memory of the tradition, but inevitably each recast that memory in the categories of its own time and in response to its own needs and perceptions.

While scholars proposed a variety of theories about the development of the Pentateuchal literature, a general consensus was reached at the end of the nineteenth century. This consensus, known as the Documentary Hypothesis, is especially linked to the name of Julius Wellhausen, who wrote the classic formulation of the hypothesis in 1883; thus it is often also called "Wellhausianism," even though many other scholars contributed to the hypothesis.

The classic formulation of the Documentary

Hypothesis proposes that there were four identifiable recastings of the normative memory:

(1) In the time of Solomon, there was a reformulation (called J for Jahwist, or Yahwist) that, as Wolff has described, articulated the faith of Israel in relation to the pride and power of the United Monarchy. The memory was shaped as a reflection on the richness of blessing with all of its attendant obligations and temptations.

(2) In the ninth century, during the period of Elijah and Elisha, there was a second, parallel recasting of the memory (called E for Elohist) that focused on the problem of religious syncretism and the temptation to compromise the claims of Israel's faith. This formulation asserted the importance of pure faith expressed as obedience.

(3) In the seventh century, during the period of King Josiah (or perhaps somewhat earlier), an important theological movement arose that represented Israel's memory in terms of covenant. That inventive formulation (called D for Deuteronomy) articulated the ancient memories in terms of a binding commitment between God and Israel, which offered great promises and imposed weighty sanctions on Israel.

(4) Finally, in the fifth or sixth century, the Pentateuch received its final casting by traditionalists assumed to be priests (hence called P). In the exile or just after, these traditions provided a displaced people with rootage, identity, and security by shaping the memory around cultic practices, ritual institutions, genealogies, and a symmetrical sense of the world that combated the sense of confusion and chaos present in the community.

The Documentary Hypothesis has been heavily criticized in the last two generations of scholarship. While not abandoned, it no longer commands central attention. There is no doubt that scholars were excessively preoccupied with the detailed assignment of biblical verses to particular "sources"; and there is no doubt that this literary proposal carried with it a theory of religious development that by the 1970s was seen to be highly doubtful. Yet there are important gains from that era of scholarship from which we may still benefit. First, it is clear that the Pentateuch is a historical document that has been formulated by a series of castings and recastings of the normative memory. As noted by James A. Sanders, that process

of recasting permitted the tradition to have continued vitality and pertinence.

Second, these recastings did not happen in a vacuum, but occurred in response to specific historical crises, cultural needs, and theological questions. The recastings were serious attempts to assert and articulate the contemporary authority and power of the memory. Each such recasting was done with theological seriousness and intentionality. In each case, it was assumed that the old memory must have a contemporary voice, but the contemporaneity of the voice is in the service of the enduring claims of the normative memory.

The documentary hypothesis was not simply an intellectual exercise or a game of "alphabet soup" (JEPD), but was an attempt to interpret a serious theological dynamic expressed in an ongoing community of faith. The gains of that era of scholarship are important because they have taught us to ask certain questions of the text, and those questions must be asked if we are to understand the text in its ongoing vitality. The documentary hypothesis assumes that serious theological literature is always articulated in the midst of a specific historical situation. The text is not a contextless absolute: we must understand how this literature has operated in and impinged upon the life of the community. Indeed, it would fail to notice the disclosing process that the community regularly found alive in the text over time.

At the beginning of the twentieth century, new scholarly questions emerged that reflected serious misgivings about the singular commitment of nineteenth-century scholarship to view the Bible only as a collection of documents. It was suggested that scholarship had been excessively preoccupied with scientific, technical questions of the text to the neglect of artistic, imaginative dimensions of the literature. The tension between technical analysis and artistic appreciation is always at work in interpretation. At the turn of the century, Hermann Gunkel turned critical scholarship in a fresh direction. He stressed that the biblical text is not the product of a group of ancient scholars who wrote documents much like nineteenth-century scholars but rather the outcome of a community reflecting imaginatively on its experience in the midst of its life. Appreciation of the creative work of the community led Gunkel to observe that every community develops characteristic ways of speaking and conventional formulations of speech that regularly carry certain kinds of content. As the progenitor of form criticism, Gunkel proposed a taxonomy of conventional forms of speech that he found in the Pentateuch, especially in the narrative literature of Genesis. His basic insistence is that one cannot discern the substance and intent of a passage in the text unless one notices the way it has been formulated, because certain forms are conventionally used as vehicles for certain kinds of substance.

While Gunkel and his colleagues in the form-critical enterprise identified many conventional forms, only a few of the most prominent will be listed here: myth, saga, legend, and fable (see Coats 1985).

Myth is the first category taken up by Gunkel. A great deal of confusion exists about this term. Gunkel meant it only as a literary category referring to tales told about action among the gods. This genre is utilized in texts of theophany (appearances of gods), in stories of angels, and in stories of conversations in heaven. In pure form, the genre of myths assumes a polytheistic religion.

Much more important is saga, which is rooted in historical experience but is rendered with great imagination and freedom. More recently sagas, as pointed out by Claus Westermann (1964), have been treated as "family stories." These narratives are the material out of which families and communities maintain continuity over generations and construct a world for their young. The sagas are bearers of the foundational commitments of a community. While such stories may have a religious dimension, that is not their main purpose.

Legend is a story providing religious legitimation for a variety of cultic practices. That is, the story may give a reason for keeping the Sabbath, for practicing sacrifice, or for having a certain priest. Legends help the community authorize the religious practices it has found workable, necessary, and significant.

Fable is a story that articulates the imagination of childlike fantasy. The story presents a world of wonders in which animals have voices and much is said to be possible that the reasonable world of adulthood has dismissed as impossible.

Gunkel's discernment is that the Pentateuch (and especially Genesis) largely consists of scores and scores of narratives; these embody and utilize various conventions of speech that in and of themselves carry specific meaning for the community. Gunkel's approach is aesthetic and deliberately pre-theological. That is, he was not interested in nor did he address theological questions. In reaction against the preoccupation with documents shown by earlier scholars, Gunkel focused attention on the actual modes and dynamics of communication reflected in concrete speech. In reaction against excessive preoccupation with historical questions, he focused on the artistic quality of the text.

Gunkel's contributions concern the artistic and sociological dimensions of the text. The artistic, dramatic dimension of his work noted the match between substance of speech and form of speech and led eventually to the awareness that what is said is related to how it is said, or, in more contemporary terms, that the medium is to some extent the message. The sociological dimension of his work led to the awareness that texts are embedded in and generated by real communities, which in turn continue to draw life from the texts. In inchoate terms, Gunkel had seen that the community behind the text uses the text in its social construction of reality. These two aspects of study, artistic and sociological together, permitted the articulation of a taxonomy of forms of speech that are fairly stable and predictable. From this perspective, the completed text of Genesis is not to be read as an endless series of distinctive texts, each to be understood on its own. Rather, one may identify habits and patterns of speech that show the community articulating the same claims and convictions in repeated but varied fashion.

Gunkel's work is, of course, not without its weaknesses. First, in his attention to aesthetic dimensions, Gunkel neglected to ask any theological questions of the text, a matter that had to await subsequent scholarship. Second, his attention to the smallest speech unit tended to atomize the text, even though he noticed reiteration of the same set of forms. One gets from Gunkel no holistic sense of the text. Nonetheless, he showed that one must not read Genesis texts simply to find their substantive message, but that the recognition of the form of the text itself will enable us to participate, albeit at a distance, in the life of the biblical community that generated, transmitted, and valued the text.

The interpretive methods of Wellhausen and Gunkel have been decisive for a critical understanding of Genesis. The next major advance came in the development of new hypotheses in the 1930s, especially through the work of Gerhard von Rad and, to a lesser extent, Martin Noth. This period of scholarship worked to recover the early period of Israel's tradition (the period before the Davidic monarchy) as the time when the tradition that became the Pentateuch was formulated with great theological intentionality. Von Rad assumed and accepted the methods and conclusions of Wellhausen and Gunkel, but he moved beyond them to offer a sense of theological coherence to the entire literature of the Pentateuch. He proposed that in the early period of tribal Israel there was a regular liturgical activity in which Israel convened as a covenant-making community to reenact its distinctive memory and to embrace its peculiar and radical ethical responsibility.

Von Rad identified three primal texts (Deut 6:20–25, 26:5–10, Josh 24:1–13) as examples and embodiments of the substance of early Israel's faith. According to his hypothesis, the people of Israel gathered regularly to recite these stylized memories, which are shaped by and for such liturgical use. The three liturgies tersely communicate the dominant themes of the faith and memory of early Israel. Von Rad noticed that the substance of this "credo" concerns three themes: an abbreviated mention of the ancestors (eventually Abraham, Isaac, and Jacob), the Exodus, and the settlement of the land. Noth, in parallel fashion, saw that the complete set of themes were five, von Rad's three plus the sojourn in the wilderness and the meeting at Sinai. These five themes constitute the normative memory of Israel, from which Israel received its identity as a distinct community, defined by the peculiar actions of God in its past and by its contemporary practices of covenantal obedience, in the form of a covenantal ethic.

Von Rad then made a remarkable interpretive move. He concluded that this credo structure of the normative theological themes became the organizing principle for the literature of the Pentateuch (Hexateuch). As concerns Genesis, the credo theme asserted in minimal fashion: "My father was a wandering Aramaean. He went down into Egypt." That brief allusion to Father Jacob (see Josh 24:2–4) became, so the hypothesis runs, the magnet to which all kinds of traditional matter was drawn. The theological substance in the credo is that the ancestors were led by the promise of God. Around the theme of God's promise there came to be clustered all kinds of material (Gunkel's sagas, legends, etc.) that originally had no theological intentionality and were not related to any theological conviction. These materials were simply available in the storytelling activity of the community. The traditioning process established a new and creative relationship between folk materials of all kinds and the theological theme of promise, so that the folk materials became vehicles for a theological affirmation they originally did not have. To read Genesis according to this hypothesis requires that one attend in each text to the theological theme that is present. That theme may be implicit or explicit, intrinsic or imposed. The presence of the theological theme in the text transforms the meaning of the text so that it becomes a vehicle for faith. In this way von Rad overcame Gunkel's lack of theological attentiveness by arguing that each text had now been drawn into the sphere of theological affirmation.

Thus, for example, Genesis 12:10–20 apparently was a saga about a "wife-sister," a common motif in folk literature. When the text is related to the credo theme of promise, however, as it is by its placement in the Genesis material, the story now asserts that Abraham was blessed by Pharaoh and that Sarah was kept safe to demonstrate a specific case in which God watched over the promise made to Abraham and Sarah. If this promissory motif is not included in our understanding of the text, we will have missed the point insofar as the text articulates the faith of Israel. In this text, the wife-sister tale originally had no relation to the promise, but now it has been made a vehicle and voice for that theme. Thus von Rad is able to argue that all of Genesis 12–50 functions to express the promissory faith of Israel, faith in which God is a promise-maker and Israel is a promise-truster. Von Rad has shown that all of Genesis is to be read as an articulation of the promissory character of God and Israel.

It is important, as it is in the case of other great scholars before him, to understand von Rad's scholarly contribution in his historical context (Crenshaw 1978). His hypothesis, published in 1938, was formed in the context of the Confessing Church in Germany, a group of German church people who dared to articulate theological resistance to Hitler and to the National Socialist movement. This community of faith needed to find theological authorization in order to stand against and criticize the dominant nationalist ideology. Their standing ground was found in a confessing posture in which the community asserted an alternative theological claim it judged to be normative—exactly the method von Rad used in developing his credo hypothesis. Thus his work both greatly advanced scholarship and served his own immediate theological situation.

Von Rad's hypothesis continues to be the dominant one among scholars and is the most theologically satisfying that we have. However, it can lead to reductionism. There is a propensity to interpret each individual text in Genesis as pointing to the theme of promise, which surely distorts the concrete character of each specific episode. Nevertheless, von Rad's great gift to us is that he has shown us how to ask a theological question that is appropriate to the text itself and not an alien question that is imposed from the categories of classical theology.

While German scholarship continued to move in a theological direction under the impetus of von Rad, the dominant trend of American scholarship moved in a very different direction. Under the influence of William Foxwell Albright (1955), two generations of American scholars attempted to answer historical questions through archaeology and comparative data from the ancient Near East. Albright and his students established a correlation between the historical hints of the book of Genesis and the archaeological discoveries of the twentieth century. That scholarship argues that the movements of the ancestors in Genesis can be correlated with the movements of people and the rise and fall of empires and cultures in the Middle Bronze and Late Bronze periods of the second millennium. During the 1940s and 1950s, quite specific and precise correlations were made (although that claim has more recently been relaxed), based in particular on specific social practices and the common uses of proper names in the ancient Near East. Through such comparative data,

the Albright school developed a coherent picture of ancient Near Eastern culture and history into which biblical materials could be placed. The general conclusion drawn from this work is that the Genesis materials reflect a high level of historicity.

The scholarship fostered by Albright assumed that establishment of the historicity of events in the text served the religious validity of the texts. There is in such an assumption a temptation to embrace historical positivism, reflecting a general tendency in that period of scholarship to trust the methods of positivistic history. Yet, remarkably, that mode of scholarship lost much of its vitality and support beginning in the 1970s.

Scholars have identified two very different kinds of problems in Albright's approach. First, it is increasingly doubtful whether biblical literature permits one to ask such historical questions, because the literature is essentially theological construction. It is ironic that Albright (1964) was so appreciative of Gunkel's work on Genesis (against Wellhausen), when Gunkel's artistic sense of the literature in fact precludes the historical questions so central to Albright. Second, even if the historical question is accepted as legitimate, it is now argued (van Seters 1975; Thompson 1974) that the alleged historical and archaeological parallels are problematic and unconvincing. Very likely some will continue to ask about the historical evidence supporting the text, or conversely will ask what historical certitude the text itself offers. On the whole, however, scholars in the 1970s began to question the legitimacy of such questions, arguing not that the material is "unhistorical" in the sense of being untrue or fictional but that this kind of literature cannot be comprehended in categories that reflect an epistemology alien to the text of Genesis; hence, questions about the historicity of the text are not very helpful in understanding the intentionality of the text.

The shift away from historical-archaeological investigation has been paralleled by a shift toward a new form of literary criticism (Clines 1978). This literary criticism, which is not unrelated to narrative theology and canon criticism, regards the text itself as the creative, constructive, imaginative presentation of an alternative life-world. The literature is intended not as a description of what is extant but as the evocation of a social possibility beyond discernible reality.

This literary approach places a high value on artistic imagination in the text and in the act of interpretation. Conversely, it minimizes the importance of positivistic, historical questions. In important ways this scholarship pursues the lines of investigation already anticipated by Gunkel. No doubt such a perspective, like the others I have cited, reflects the milieu of its practitioners. It has gained prominence at a time when positivistic social sciences have run their course and scholarship generally is moving to an awareness that texts are sociological proposals in which the form of articulation itself creates human possibility. The power and process of language and its creative, concrete symbolization constitute worlds for us. Such evocative power of speech to form worlds and create social possibilities is presumed in the Bible but clearly works against much recent interpretation that has been on the one hand rationalistic and on the other hand literalistic. The newer criticism enables us to reject categories of rationalism and literalism in order to let the text be heard as a live world. Interpretation in this way brings literary and theological concerns close together so that the actual words of the text are disclosures (revelations) of new reality.

Clearly each generation asks questions and pursues issues in interpretation that are distinctly appropriate to its own time and place. It is relatively easy for us to see the inadequacy of scholarly proposals from other cultural contexts, yet our task as interpreters is not to defend or refute such previous efforts but to find categories of interpretation that are responsible and appropriate to our situation. There are enduring interpretive questions, but we must formulate and practice interpretive strategies that are peculiarly our own.

THE SHAPE AND CONTENT OF GENESIS

The Book of Genesis readily falls into four roughly equal parts, consisting of chapters 1–11, 12–25:18, 25:19–36, and 37–50.

Genesis 1–11

The opening chapters now function to provide a cosmic setting for the story of Israel that is to follow. The texts purport to tell us not about Israel, but about God's governance of the whole world. They affirm that God has a relationship not only with this special people but also with the entire world.

Scholarly emphasis has demonstrated that the opening chapters of Genesis have ancient Near Eastern counterparts (Pritchard). The two major narratives of this section of Genesis, the creation stories and the flood story, are closely paralleled by the Enuma Elish and the Gilgamesh Epic and the account of Atrahasis, respectively. Those stories share many of the same dimensions of plot.

In its appropriation of these stories, of course, Israel has taken them up in a particular way for its own use. They are not merely borrowed, but in important ways have been transformed as vehicles for Israel's faith. First, Israel made selections that we may presume were intentional. Second, the borrowed materials were arranged in certain sequences and juxtapositions. This arrangement itself is a way of shaping a particular message. Third, Israel transformed the material through observations and affirmations that are peculiarly its own. The end result of the process of appropriation is a theological statement that is intentionally and distinctively Israelite. Judgment and discernment are required to determine the degree to which the biblical material is reflective of ancient Near Eastern religious traditions, and that to which the biblical presentation is peculiarly Israelite. Both factors are clearly evident and operative.

The materials taken up by Genesis 1–11 belonged to the great public liturgical traditions of the ancient Near East. Hence, we may at the outset dispel any notion that such texts intend to describe what happened, either scientifically or experientially. The liturgical texts do not intend to give accounts that we might regard as in any way explanatory. Thus to ask in Genesis about the historicity of Adam and Eve, or Noah, is a question quite remote from the social provenance of this material. These texts, both in the Near East and in Israel, address the issue of the meaningfulness and significance of human life as found in the inescapable awareness that life is to be referred to the gods and that human actions are to be taken seriously and responsibly. These narratives, cast in mythical, epic, and liturgical forms, reflect the religious dimension of life (the rule of the gods) and the political reality of human freedom and account-ability, an interface leading to the general affirmation that human life consists in the juxtaposition of grace and freedom, of sin and judgment.

Furthermore, because these traditions are residual from the great public liturgies of the Near East, they are not private, speculative reflections, nor are they statements from the margins of society. They have been preserved and used because they come from the great temple festivals and serve the dominant political ideology of priesthood and kingship. Therefore they are preoccupied with questions of order and account-ability. In sum, they are a probe and reflection of the ways in which the abiding shape of human interactions comes to visibility in concrete moments. The intellectual function of these materials is not unlike the reflections of the Book of Proverbs (Mendenhall).

The best-known example of the utilization of common cultural inheritance in Genesis is the text of chapters 1–4. These narratives are so well known because they have been incorporated into thematic theology among Christians under the rubric "creation and fall" (Bonhoeffer 1959) and because they contain narrative elements that are easily incorporated into the popular imagination (e.g., the forbidden fruit, the snake, and the mark of Cain).

The Bible begins with two creation narratives. The first, in 1:1–2:4a, in symmetrical, magisterial fashion portrays the creation by God's word of decree. In an ordered way (day by day), this creation by word culminates in (1) the emergence of humankind in God's image, (2) the verdict that the world is "very good," and (3) the practice of the Sabbath as the culmination of creation. This narrative, commonly assigned to exilic traditionists, asserts that the world is a reliably ordered habitat in which human persons have a place of dignity, freedom, and responsibility. The second creation narrative (2:4b–3:24) is less global and crafted in a very different style. It focuses only on the creation of humankind and portrays the problematic of human existence (Trible 1978). It seems more primitive theologically and is more candid in its portrayal of human life. While the two narratives are very different in style and reflect very different traditioning processes, together they articulate a theologically informed shape of creation and of human vocation in that creation. Note well that neither narrative seeks to explain in scientific ways the origin of the world; rather, both seek to articulate the ways in which the reality of creation concerns God and humankind in tension with each other. The narratives of expulsion (chap. 3) and of Cain and Abel (chap. 4) are closely parallel. Both bespeak the ways in which human life is distorted, the first in relation to God and the second in relation to human beings. These first four chapters of Genesis together present both the positive, life-giving shape of God's creation and the deep problematic of human life in that world that belongs to God.

The other great narrative in Genesis 1–11 is the flood story of 6:4–9:17. As noted, this story is also appropriated from a common epic tradition, which means that Israel did not "make it up." It is futile to ask about the historicity of the flood. Rather, we must ask how the flood narratives have become a vehicle for Israel's faith. A study of the text indicates that the story, contrary to popular notions, in fact is not interested in vast amounts of water. Rather, it concerns on the one hand the corruption of humankind (6:11–12) and the continuing prospect of human life, and on the other hand the grief of God (6:6–7), which culminates in God's resolve to be faithful even in the face of human corruption (8:20–22). Thus the narrative is a statement that God's faithfulness and resolve persist in the face of human recalcitrance. That persistence on God's part is what permits the human project to endure.

Read thematically, the narrative plot moves from the inundation that threatens to terminate creation (7:17–24) to the appearance of the rainbow (9:8–17). In theological terms, we witness the end of old creation and the resolve of God to begin a new creation, a resolve that is founded only in God's fidelity (Anderson 1978).

The narrative of Genesis 11:1–9 also warrants comment. Here too Israel uses a story current in the culture of its time to tell the story of its own faith. The tale of the tower likely reflects a Mesopotamian story about a ziggurat, a Babylonian earth mound function-ing as a temple. It is clear that the story functions as an etiology for why there are so many languages. But at the same time it has been transformed to serve as a vehicle for a statement about God's sovereign rule and the human recalcitrance that leads to social disorder.

Of the texts discussed, only Genesis 1:1–2:4a seems unambiguous in its presentation of life as fully ordered and without distortion. The other narratives (2:4b–4:16, 6:4–9:17, and 11:1–9) all portray the two-sidedness of human life as governed by God and distorted by human action and choice. Despite momentary narrative resolutions of the tension, there is no final resolution, because the narratives assert that the tension itself belongs to the character of human life. Von Rad (1972) has proposed in an influential interpretation that although the stories reflect older traditions, they have now been placed in this particular sequence in order to make a larger, more coherent statement. Each of the stories is about sovereignty and distortion. The distortion is not the last word, for God characteristically responds to the distortion with an act of graciousness and fidelity that permits human life to continue, even in the face of the distortion. But in contrast to the stories preceding it (as von Rad has noted), the text of 11:1–9 contains no such saving response on the part of God. This section of Genesis ends with a lack of resolution, a hard, anxious waiting to see if God will make a new move.

The materials of Genesis 1:1–11:9 trace the history and condition of the created world as a world deeply alienated from God. Those chapters, however, do not prepare us for the abrupt appearance of the family of Terah, which eventually leads to Abraham. We are not told why there is such attention in 11:27–32 to this particular family, but the story invites us to linger with them nonetheless. The focus becomes even more specific in verse 30b, naming Sarah and commenting on her barrenness. It is a remarkable and odd way to culminate a narrative that begins in creation, yet that culmination is a part of the dramatic intent of the whole.

Mention should also be made of the genealogies in chapters 5, 10, and 11. Each of them needs to be understood and studied separately, for they are very different and perform very different functions (Wilson 1977). The genealogies are in part borrowed from old royal lists that predate the Bible, which could help us to understand the great longevity attributed to various persons in chapter 5. That is, Israel simply took over these numbers from an older tradition that did not intend to be historical. As they now stand in Genesis, the genealogies seem to assert the continuity of all the generations. They help to bind the narratives together, showing that all humanity participates in one continuing story and that the entire narrative is under God's rule. The disruptions caused by human distortion (e.g., the Flood) do not finally violate the continuities of the human process, which these lists show to be remarkably resilient. The world does indeed hang together from generation to generation.

As a result of a complex traditioning process, then, Genesis 1–11 presents a coherent theological picture of human reality. The tradition focuses on two themes in deep tension with each other: moral coherence and God's sovereign fidelity. On the one hand, the world is morally coherent. Human choices are important and may be costly. Because the world is morally coherent, actions and choices lead to consequences (Koch 1983, Schmid 1984), and indeed there have been enough of the wrong choices to place the whole world under the power of curse, which will lead to death. Such a view is not magical, theologically primitive, or supernaturalist. It is simply a moral discernment that a density of wrong choices will bring deep trouble. Wolff has seen that, in various ways, the world of Genesis 1–11 is a world in which curse has decisive power (Wolff 1975, 41–66). Curse happens because of human recalcitrance and God's constancy in assuring consequences, which together will lead to death.

The countertheme, on the other hand, is that in the face of curse God maintains remarkable freedom to work newness. The move in the narrative from Genesis 1–4 to 6:4–9:17 shows that God suffers the distortion of creation but also powerfully works a newness. In 8:20–22 and 9:8–17, God begins again in the face of the incredible failure of creation. Thus there is more to life than its moral coherence. God's passion for the life and well-being of the world causes God to override the consequences of human distortion and to begin again. Although sin is real, curse is powerful, and death is close at hand, it is the power of God's fidelity that governs. In delicate ways, by the careful utilization of old tales with theological sensitivity and intentionality, the tradition arrives at the religious affirmation that God "will not always chide, nor will he keep his anger forever" (Ps 103:9). It is this reality about God, so crucial to the narrative, that permits human hope and gives the world a future.

Genesis 1–11 takes moral accountability very seriously. It is that point which causes the expulsion of Genesis 3, the exile of Genesis 4, the Flood (6–9), and the scattering of the tower (11:1–9). But these narratives show such categories to be penultimate. Only God's governance is ultimate. Genesis 1–11 ends, however, without resolution. The tradition is dramatically arranged so that the hearer of the text must wait, yet it is not even clear what the listener is to wait for. We learn eventually that the wait is for God's next act of fidelity, which is embodied in God's call to Israel, that is, in Abraham and Sarah. The traditionists in ancient Israel have utilized common Near Eastern texts in constructing their story, but the end result is a remarkably fresh and imaginative theological statement that focuses on Israel's peculiar theological categories. The text as we have it was likely completed in the exile. The text responds to the yearning and hopes and needs of exiles. In their guilt, they know that moral coherence requires that they suffer banishment (like Cain). In their displacement, they wonder about their chaos and learn that in the midst of chaos-exile God is yet at work making new promises that allow creation—and history—to begin again. The total narrative that eventuates in the story of Abraham and Sarah asserts that there is a new call and a new beginning wrought out of the loss. That is precisely the hope asserted in this completed tradition for exiles.

Genesis 12:1–25:18

The materials concerning Abraham, the first father of Israel's faith, and Sarah, the mother of promise, constitute a very different kind of material from chapters 1–11. These narratives are mostly family stories, rooted in a concrete particularity that is lacking in 1–11 (Coats 1983). Just as chapters 1–11 concern the sovereign rule of God over the world, so 12:1–25:18 concern the promise of God and the way in which Abraham and Sarah trust in that promise.

The beginning point of the narrative is in God's promise. The remainder of the narrative explores the question of whether the promise can be trusted. The promise is formally introduced three times, likely from three different layers of tradition. The originary statement is in 12:1–3, a passage that is commonly regarded as a peculiarly poignant and imaginative

piece of theology. The promise comes as an abrupt speech of Yahweh. We are not prepared for it. We do not know why it is spoken. We are not told how Abraham received the word. The substance of the promise is "land, great nation, great name." The promise culminates with the relentless sounding of the word "blessing," which will be given for Israel and for the nations. This family of Abraham is now the bearer of God's decisive promise in history.

The second articulation of the promise is in chapter 15. In 15:1–6, the promise is for a son who will be the heir. The promise of 12:1–3 did not mention a son and heir, but obviously everything depends on this gift. For if there is no next generation, there can be no promise to perpetuity. The long-range promise, then, depends on this immediate and concrete matter. As the life of the world begins in chaos (1:2), so the life of Israel begins in barrenness (11:30). But God promises (15:4), and Abraham believes the promise (15:6). In 15:7–21 the promise of son and heir is then extrapolated to the land and now becomes much more expansive and explicit than the terse initial announcement of 12:1–3. There will be an heir, and the heir will have an inheritance. Israel is now a people that waits for the promise to come to fruition. This narrative is the hopeful way through which Israel waits. Israel waits by telling and retelling the story of the promise.

The third presentation of the promise is in chapter 17, a long and stately decree in which Abraham, through the rite of circumcision, is bound into this promissory covenant. Again it is a struggle for the land (v. 8), wrought through the gift of a son (vv. 16–19) through whom a future will be given to Israel. These three versions of promise narrative articulate the governing categories of faith for Genesis and for much of the Bible that is to follow.

The story of Abraham and Sarah culminates in chapters 23, 24, 25:1–18, but the culmination is not an announcement that the promise has come to fulfillment. The promise does not hurry. Israel must wait. Israel knows that the interaction between the intent of God and the unresponsive reality of life processes is remarkably slow and cannot be rushed to resolution. Therefore the most that the narrators of this story are able to assert is not fulfillment or fruition, but that the promise is kept alive into the next generation. More than that Abraham and Sarah were not given. There is a son who will survive his parents. That is enough to keep the promise alive and visible for one more generation. More than that is never given to Israel, because assurance is given to only one generation at a time. Israel will walk by faith and not by sight.

The culmination of the Abraham-Sarah story is articulated in three different texts. In 23:1–10 we are given a laconic account of Abraham's provision for the death and burial of Sarah. This "mother of Israel," who had been at risk and danger (cf. 12:10–20), whom God finally made laugh in joy (21:6), is buried honorably and with dignity, making way for the next generation. In 24:1–67 we have a long, playful, artistic narrative about the securing of an adequate bride for Isaac, child of the promise. This new wife is so important because she is to be the next mother in Israel who must bear a son to keep the promise alive and visible. In addition to its contribution to the theme of promise, this narrative is of interest for its imaginative use of literary conventions in a way that makes the story suspenseful and humorous. Finally, in 25:1–18, Father Abraham dies and is buried honorably. The material of 25:1–18 is merely an index, but it yields important information. First, while there was a struggle for a true heir, a struggle resolved only with the later-born Isaac, Abraham is prolific and is indeed the father of many nations (cf. 17:6). Second, Isaac, child of the promise, and Ishmael, son of lesser promise, together supervise his burial (v. 9). For all its commitment to Isaac, this narrative is not narrow or exclusive in its spirit.

Thus the narrative of Abraham and Sarah is enveloped by beginning in promise and by culminating in ways that are hopeful, but do not yield a resolution. The Book of Genesis invites us to continue to wait, even as Israel must continue to wait.

The Abraham-Sarah narrative consists of a number of different materials, which have now been shaped into a thematic whole. Among the materials are the following:

First, there is a group of narratives concerned with the promise of a son, which is linked to the person of Sarah. Whether the barren woman can be a vehicle for the promise is a constant and recurring question in the narrative. These materials include parallel ac-

counts of "the danger to the ancestress" (12:10–20, 20:1–7; cf. 26:6–11) in which Abraham is portrayed as having lied to protect himself, even though the lie placed Sarah in jeopardy. This material gathered around Sarah also includes the two accounts of Hagar and Ishmael (16:1–16, 21:8–21), in which Abraham resorts to an alternative way to secure a son. These narratives utilize common social conventions, but are taken up by Israel in fresh ways to articulate its theology of promise.

Second, in chapters 13 and 18–19, there is a quite distinct set of traditions related to Lot, nephew of Abraham. These materials are concerned with the promise of land, and not at all with the matter of a son. The stories likely reflect on the relation of Israel and Moab and Ammon, rivals for land (19:30–38). But in their incorporation into the larger narrative, the old tales of land dispute are again made to serve the general theme of promise.

Third, in chapter 14, a most peculiar chapter that does not seem related to any of the strata of tradition elsewhere, the narrative seems to link Abraham to Jerusalem (Salem, v. 18), perhaps in preparation for the Davidic connection to that city (cf. 2 Sam 24:18–25). In any case, this narrative of the war of the kings is the clearest evidence that Israel (Abraham) is related to and involved with the larger political realities of the Near East. This story, however, has no evident connection to the main plot of the Abraham-Sarah tradition.

The corpus of 12:1–25:18 contains materials of many different kinds from many different circles of tradition. Not all of it is to be read in the same undifferentiated manner. Like every great literature, some parts of this account may be taken as more pivotal, warranting special attention. Here I shall comment on three narrative elements that are of special interest for the internal dynamic of this material as a whole.

Genesis 18:1–15 is of peculiar interest because it seems to be the most decisive announcement of a son to Abraham and Sarah. Westermann (1980) has suggested that this is the only narrative in which the promise of an heir is not extrinsic to the narrative but integral to the story itself. The birth of a son to this old couple is acknowledged as an impossibility (v. 14). But it is precisely this impossibility that concerns

Abraham and Sarah, and indeed the whole of biblical faith (Brueggemann 1982). Indeed, the work of God is the work of impossibility. The book of Genesis is a reflection on that impossibility. The faith of Israel consists precisely in adhering to that impossibility. Israel's faith is not a reasonable faith but one that embraces, narrates, and reflects upon the wonders that the world judges to be impossible. As the narrative is now arranged, this "impossible possibility" is indeed wrought by God. The son-heir is born (21:1–6). Sarah, the mother who laughed in incredulity (18:12), now laughs in delight and celebration (21:6). God does keep promises.

The theological reflection of 18:16–33 is one of the most remarkable in the Bible. It begins with an acknowledgement of Abraham's distinctive relation to God (vv. 17–19). Abraham is portrayed as utilizing this distinctive and preferential position to raise bold and risky issues with God (vv. 23–25). This narrative ostensibly relates to Sodom and Gomorrah. In fact, it is a remarkable theological reflection showing that Israel (and God) struggles with the question of justice and the problematic of punishment and rescue (Schmidt 1976). Dramatically what is astonishing is that Abraham, father of faith, seizes the initiative with God, instructs God, and bargains against God's immediate inclination. Theologically what is surprising is that God is willing to adjust the calculus of wickedness and righteousness and what it will take to warrant a rescue. The narrative exhibits the struggle of Israel and of Israel's God with the problem of grace in a religion of equity. The narrative leaves the issue unresolved, and the question lingers to resurface repeatedly in Israel's subsequent life with God.

The narrative of chapter 22 is perhaps the best known and most important in the Abraham-Sarah materials, continuing to be of special import for both Jews and Christians. The "testing of Abraham" likely originated as a story to explain why animals are sacrificed rather than sons, but in its present context the story has been transformed into a vehicle for Israel's faith. In the context of that faith, the motif of child sacrifice is subordinated to the larger question of faith. The issue of faith is resolved in verse 12, where the angel says to Abraham: "Now I know that you fear God." This story takes on peculiar poignancy because it follows immediately after chapter 21. There, after

such a long dramatic narrative of waiting, at last a son is given. The whole narrative drives toward the birth in 21:1–6. In chapter 22, immediately and abruptly, Abraham is called to give "your son, your only son Isaac, whom you love," the one for whom the entire narrative and the entire history of Israel have been waiting. Abraham is called to heed God's voice and trust God's promise of a future so fully that he will yield his son, who is the very pledge of that promise. Isaac is the visible token of God's fidelity, the visible indication that the future is still alive for Israel. It is Isaac as beloved son and as sign that is now to be surrendered for the sake of the promise. Finally, it becomes evident that "God will provide" (vv. 8, 14), but only when Abraham is radically faithful. Dramatically this narrative embodies the climax of the Abraham-Sarah story. The child is given, the promise is kept. The child is submitted, Abraham trusts, God is faithful, and Abraham is faithful. With such a conclusion, we are prepared for the next generation and the narrative moves on.

Finally we focus on the decisive decree of blessing and promise in 12:1–3. Von Rad and Wolff have considered this passage as a piece of remarkably inventive theology—a dramatic and crucial connection between chapters 1–11 and 12–25. The two clusters of material do not have the same subject matter and surely had no original connection to each other. The former deal with nations and the character of global human history. The latter deal with this particular family of Abraham and Sarah. It is not self-evident how the traditions are related to each other, just as it is not self-evident how Israel and the world are related to each other. But as the text of Genesis now stands, they are related to each other. That relation is established through the decree of 12:3, which is a remarkable and most imaginative intellectual act of connecting what had not been previously connected. Through this text, the ongoing relation between Israel and the world of the nations is decisively established for all that is to come. "By you" (i.e., by means of Israel), "all the families of the earth will bless themselves." The other nations are under curse (cf. Gen. 3:14, 13:17, 4:11, 5:29, 8:21, 9:25). Now the nations (and the earth) are given access to blessing through the life of Israel. Perhaps this is an invitation for the nations to heed Israel. More likely it is an assertion to Israel that Israel exists not only for itself, but that Israel's very existence is a vehicle and agent whereby other nations will be blessed.

This programmatic statement places Israel theologically in the scope and sphere of the other nations. There is no doubt, according to this tradition, that Israel is especially chosen. But this special status, borne by Abraham and Sarah in this narrative, is not in a vacuum. The promise to Abraham and Sarah is in some way a promise concerning all peoples. There is something grandly ecumenical about this narrative that places the whole world under the power of God's promise. That grand inclusive vision guards against the temptation in Israel to regard the promise of land and heir as a private possession to be held too narrowly and too closely.

Genesis 25:19–36:41

The materials clustering around Jacob are of a very different kind from those concerning Abraham and Sarah. It is likely that they represent a very different circle of tradition and initially had no relation at all to the Abraham-Sarah materials. We may identify three obvious differences between the two clusters. First, the Jacob materials are placed geographically in the north of Israel, in the region of Bethel and Schechem, whereas Abraham and Sarah are linked to southern cities and shrines. Second, the narrative of Jacob is preoccupied with the issue of God's blessing, whereas the Abraham-Sarah materials focus on promise. It is true that the promise motif is present (*cf.* especially 28:13–15, Rendtorff 1977), but it is greatly subdued in contrast to its prominence with Abraham and Sarah. In the Jacob narrative the question is, rather, will Jacob receive the blessing of well-being and security that has been announced over him? Third, whereas Abraham is portrayed mostly as a man of trustful, obedient faith, Jacob is presented as a man in deep conflict on every front. As the story is told, Jacob is variously in conflict with his brother, Esau, his father, Isaac, his father-in-law, Laban, and eventually even with the mysterious stranger at Jax Penuel. Moreover, Abraham is presented in the tradition as a morally respectable person, whereas Jacob can hardly be measured by moral criteria. All of these factors indicate that this is a very different kind of narrative, reflecting a very different origin and intentionality.

The Jacob materials are complex in their construction. Following Gunkel, we may suggest that the completed narrative is composed of three identifiable materials. First, the story is organized around two "stories of divine encounter" at Bethel (28:10–22) and at Penuel (32:22–32). These stories likely reflect older cult narratives that justify not only the name but also the legitimacy of the shrine. The founding of the shrine has no special bearing on the Jacob narrative, so we may conclude that these founding stories originally were not attached to Jacob, but have been appropriated for Israel's ancestor. A second kind of material (in 25:19–34, 27:1–45, and chaps. 32–33) concerns Jacob's problematic relation to his older brother, Esau. The story is cast as an intense interaction between actual persons, but in the end, the story seems to concern the relation between two peoples, Israel and Edom. There is a general development from personal interaction to tribal relationships. In the center of the narrative (chapters 29–31), the third cluster of materials offers accounts of the relationship between Jacob and Laban, no doubt again reflecting tribal relationships, this time between Israel and the Aramaeans. The "Laban connection" includes the drama of Jacob's two wives, Leah and Rachel, and the birth of twelve sons, who come to be the twelve tribes of Israel. Thus the Jacob materials contain narratives of powerful interpersonal relations, but each of these serves a tribal reflection concerning Edom, the Aramaeans, and twelve-tribe Israel.

It is remarkable that as the text is arranged these various clusters do not overlap. That is, Esau is not present in the middle section of 29–31, and the family of Laban is scarcely mentioned in the Esau narrative, though allusions to wives and children are necessary to the drama of 32–33. Presumably the traditioning process proceeded in quite separate communities and circles concerning these various persons and tribes. Finally, there are a few other incidental materials, including stories of Isaac (26), the interaction with Shechem (34), and concluding notes plus a genealogy (35–36), which fall outside the main drama of the present form of the narrative. It is especially noteworthy that Isaac seems to occupy no independent position in the Genesis narrative, but functions only as a transitional figure between the generations.

The dramatic beginning of the narrative is found in the twin stories of 25:19–34 and 27:1–45. These two are governed by the birth oracle of 25:23, which asserts that "the elder shall serve the younger." This is the premise and promise of the narrative, all of which is told to see whether and in what ways this decree can come to fruition. The decree immediately summons Jacob and Esau into the central problematic of the narrative. In 25:27–34 Jacob receives the birthright (*bekorah*) of Esau, not by trickery but by intensity and hard bargaining. In 27:1–45 Jacob receives the blessing (*birkāh*) of Esau by an elaborate deception. Chapter 27 merits careful attention because it is one of remarkable artistic power and pathos. The story is dominated by the intense speech concerning "my son" (vv. 8, 18, 21, 24, 26, 37) and "my father" (vv. 18, 31, 34, 38). The story culminates in the rage of Esau and the bitter anguish of Isaac, who had wrongly bestowed the blessing (vv. 38, 41, 33–34). But as the narrative is constructed, Isaac had no real choice, though he thought he did. The assignment of birthright and blessing to Jacob had already been decreed in 25:23. The trick concerning the blessing is simply a working-out of the decision of the decree.

Thus the story begins with familial relations inverted and distorted against conventional expectations, because Jacob embodies a decree that reorganizes family relations and keeps them in crisis. The narrative is constructed to show that the decree overrides human planning and human choice, because the purpose of Yahweh is so massively allied with the outcome of the life of Jacob. The power of the decree may be worked out through all kinds of doubtful and dubious procedures. The narrative does not shrink from that, however, because it is a tale of how the power of the decree comes to fruition. Everything else must be subordinated to that theme.

The dramatic ending of the narrative in 32:1–33:17 (33:18–36:43 falls outside the dramatic design of the narrative) returns to the problem of Esau, who has dropped out of the narrative after chapter 28. Jacob finally must meet his brother, Esau. He knows this meeting is ominous because the issues of birthright (25:27–34) and blessing (27:1–45) have never been resolved. The meeting is arranged according to a careful stratagem designed to protect what is most precious to Jacob, and to impress Esau (32:17–20,

33:1–3). The story includes a carefully wrought prayer showing that Jacob is still a tough bargainer, even with God (32:9–12). In the midst of the narrative of meeting is the other meeting at Penuel (32:22–32). That mysterious encounter ends with the enigmatic statement, "I have seen God face-to-face and yet my life is preserved" (v. 30). That statement is shown to be remarkably freighted in 33:10, where Jacob says to his feared brother, "For truly to see your face is like seeing the face of God." The face of Esau and the face of God are both seen, and the story is told so that the two ominous experiences surely overlap. The narrative asserts that Jacob's life is at risk on every front.

In the end Jacob is indeed reconciled to his brother (33:11). The decree of 25:23 has been vindicated, for Jacob seems preeminent. The narrative is remarkably honest about Jacob and dares to say that even in the marvelous moment of reconciliation, Jacob is dishonest with his brother one more time. He tells him he will follow, and promptly heads in the opposite direction (33:14–17). Nothing more is said of it, and the narrator leaves us to draw our own conclusion.

The Esau materials provide a literary frame for the completed story. The narratives of 25, 27, and 32–33 form an envelope. The two cultic encounters of Bethel and Penuel come next as we move toward the center of the story. At the center of the story is the continuous and uninterrupted account of Jacob-Laban-Leah-Rachel and the twelve sons. This narrative contains several traditional pieces of folk-storytelling, including the encounter with Rachel at the well, the bargaining for a wife, and the process of birthing and naming the sons. These various traditional materials are now put together to reflect the power of Jacob's unprincipled person as it is constructed by the narrator, and the indefatigable power of the initial decree, so that in spite of and through Jacob's cunning and wiles the blessing is effected. The story culminates in 30:25–43 with the assertion of and celebration of God's blessing to Jacob. In the total narrative it is as though the reception of blessing now prepares the way for Jacob to return to Esau. The one who left as an empty-handed fugitive now returns home, secure and prosperous (31:3). It is this reversal of the fortunes of Jacob that permits a very different conversation with Esau at the end.

The narrative of Jacob is a carefully and symmetrically shaped tale. In separate analyses, Fishbane (1979), Fokkelman (1975), and Gammie (1979) have shown that the narrative is arranged in a series of concentric circles. At the very center of the whole is 30:22 ("The Lord remembered Rachel and God hearkened to her and God opened her womb"). In that act the old promise to Abraham and Sarah is kept. The promise is assured continuity through the next generation through this child of the promise. This motif of the son of promise is in tension with the theme of blessing, but the two motifs converge through the power of the narrative and the person of Jacob. The outcome is that Israel has yet another witness to the powerful, resilient, and finally irresistible way in which God's intention is at work in the life history of this family. This is an intense and self-confident account of faith, which has seized upon narrative as its only adequate form of articulation.

Genesis 37–50

The Joseph narrative of chapters 37–50 is peculiar in the book of Genesis. While Genesis reckons the person of Joseph as the next in the sequence of "fathers of promise," Joseph is never listed in the formularies in that way (cf. Exod 32:13, 33:1; Deut 1:8, 6:10, 9:5; 1 Kgs 18:36; 2 Kgs 13:23). Indeed, in the narrative itself Joseph never receives the promises explicitly, and a case can be made that it is Judah and not Joseph who carries the promise. In the Joseph narrative the promise is reiterated to Jacob (46:14). Nowhere in the subsequent literature of the Old Testament is Joseph reckoned as a bearer of promise.

It is clear that the material of the Joseph narrative contrasts sharply with the stories of Abraham and Sarah and Jacob. First, this narrative seems in its major articulation to be one continuous story and is not a complex collection of old materials, as in the preceding materials concerning Abraham and Jacob. Second, the narrative does not present God as an active, visible agent in the story. This God is much more distant and removed, working silently if at all. This God is indeed hidden from view. Third, the intellectual climate of this material seems very different. The narrative seems to reflect an intellectually sophisticated context. Von Rad has proposed that this story reflects the cultural advances of the Solomonic

period, so that it has most in common not with the Abraham and Jacob materials but with the more literarily sophisticated accounts of David in 2 Samuel (von Rad 1966, 292–300). That is, the achievements of this literature are not historical but literary. Fourth, von Rad has suggested that this story seems not to serve the advance of the Genesis promise in any direct way, but reflects rather a sapiential understanding of social reality. That hypothesis (not unchallenged) suggests that the purpose of the narrative is to model wise behavior by those who serve in royal courts. Fifth, it is likely that this narrative is not concerned with the narrative life of the ancestors but serves to provide a transition to the Book of Exodus. That is, it offers a credible narrative account of why the community of Moses began in Egyptian bondage. As one prepares to read the Book of Exodus, one sees that the Bible is knowing and candid about imperial monopoly and what it will do to the life and faith of Israel. It is for that reason that Brevard Childs (1979) can judge Joseph to be a threat to the promises of Genesis.

If this general line of scholarly reasoning is correct, it shows how the traditionists in Israel were capable of taking up very diverse materials and forming them into a coherent literary and theological statement. As the Book of Genesis now stands, the Joseph narrative consists of urbane material placed with great literary finesse immediately alongside ancestral tales that lack that finesse and urbanity.

The beginning point of the Joseph narrative is the initial dream, which governs all that follows (37:5–11). It is the dream of "the little one" that he will be the preeminent one, that his brothers will bow down to him. The dream obviously functions as a literary device. But like the decree of 25:23, it is more than a literary device. It is a governing statement that continues to guide and shape the narrative, and to which all characters in the plot must be responsive, whether they wish it or not, whether they know it or not. The entire plot revolves around the issue of whether the dream will come to fruition. If it does, it does so through the governance of God, even though that governance is hidden and inexplicable. The hidden God works a purpose that the characters in the narrative do not know about and do not understand, but finally cannot resist.

The immediate response to the dream does not

surprise us. The brothers devise a plot to eliminate the dreamer. Their deception brings the father to deep and unresolvable grief (v. 35). The outcome is that Joseph has come to Egypt, the setting of the story.

The dramatic culmination of this dream narrative is given in two encounters, 45:48 and 50:15–21. These two statements are intentional theological comments in the mouth of Joseph that draw together the governing tensions of the narrative. In 45:48 Joseph surprisingly discloses himself to his brothers. But the central point, repeated three times, is that "God has sent me." This disclosure surprises us for two reasons. First, we do not expect such an explicit statement on the lips of Joseph, for his portrayal has not been noticeably religious. It is also a surprise because the narrator has not in fact placed much emphasis upon the rule of God, except for the framing statements of chapter 39: verses 2, 4, and 23. But the words of Joseph clearly allude back to the dream of chapter 37. The malevolent action of the brothers is simply a mode through which God does God's own intent. Contrary to what has been previously known, it is God and not the brothers at work in the life of Joseph (in order to bring the dream to fulfillment). All of Israel's history is read here from the perspective of God's providential governances. Even the evil intent of the brothers is a part of God's watchful care.

That same general point is made even more dramatically in the second theologically intentional passage, at 50:15–21 (Brueggemann 1983). At the end of the narrative, Jacob the father is dead. The sons must approach their brother, now the feared prime minister of the empire. It is an ominous meeting, not unlike that of Jacob with Esau in 32–33. But the narrative again has Joseph astonish his brothers. He refuses to deal with categories of sin and forgiveness, as they have requested. Then Joseph utters one of the Bible's great programmatic statements on God's providential care: "You meant it for evil, but God meant it for good." The good purpose of God has overridden and cancelled out any evil intent on the part of the brothers. What was designed by the brothers as a cynical plot against a troublesome younger brother turns out to be a way to organize Egyptian food supplies, in order to feed and save "many people." Worth noting is the fact that in verse 18, the brothers "fall down," thus completing the dream of chapter 37.

Joseph's narrative life proceeds on two fronts. First, in chapters 39–41 we are told of Joseph's life in the empire (Humphreys 1978). Joseph is cast as an important personage in the empire. The narrative traces the dangerous moves by which this imported slave, a nobody when he arrives in Egypt, is quickly established as the ruler there. The story presents the sequence as a general movement of humiliation and exaltation.

In chapter 39 the danger of courtly intrigue threatens Joseph, and through no fault of his own he is imprisoned. In chapter 40 we are introduced to the practice of dream interpretation, which prepares the way for Joseph to come to the attention of Pharaoh. In quick and dramatic moves, this man who is seen to be endowed with special gifts of wisdom is established at the center of the imperial government. He is acknowledged to be "wise and discreet" (41:33, 41:39). He immediately sets about organizing the wealth and produce of the empire. In the less positive portrayal of 47:13–26, we are told that Joseph's administrative prowess and cunning served to increase the number of lands under royal control. This policy of an increasing monopoly prepares the way for the crisis of the Exodus, toward which the narrative leads. The irony of Joseph's Egyptian role is apparent. This dreamer of a boy who could only anger his brothers becomes, by the force of his dream, the most powerful. What did not work with the Israelite brothers works with the Egyptian rulers.

The second front on which the story moves is in relation to the brothers and his father, Jacob. Chapters 42–44 present an elaborate and at some points confused narrative about the brothers. They came to Egypt to get food in the midst of the famine. The drama of the narrative is assured by the literary fact that Joseph recognizes his brothers and they do not recognize him. That gives him a great deal of freedom in the narrative that is not available to the brothers. Moreover, we as readers are privy to this unfair drama. The only reason the brothers are before Joseph is in order to get food. Joseph presides over the food monopoly. The play in the narrative happens because food becomes an instrument of Joseph's strategy in order to see his younger brother, Benjamin, and his father, Jacob. This textual material is marked by eloquent speech and the steady development of the plot until the brothers have no recourse but to conform to Joseph's hidden wish. The dream is at work in ways the brothers cannot even recognize.

After each of these two principal disclosures on the part of Joseph, the narrative moves to its conclusion. Joseph meets his brother Benjamin face to face (45:14) and Jacob learns of Joseph's survival in Egypt (45:26–28, 46:28–30). What follows are miscellaneous materials related to the settlement in Egypt, a narrative and a poem transmitting the blessing to the next generation (chaps. 48, 49), and a provision for the deaths, in turn, of Jacob and of Joseph. The narrative ends with the old promise still alive and in effect having been transmitted through one more troublesome generation. Here it may be noted that two elements, the narrative of chapter 38 and the poem of chapter 43, stand (perhaps in symmetrical relation to each other) outside the main flow of the story.

The narrative is constructed to move in an arc from the dream of 37:6–11 to its fulfillment in 50:18. The dream is a disturbance in the life of this family. The fulfillment is an amazement in the faith of Israel. The materials between, concerning empire (chaps. 39–41) and family (chaps. 42–44), are designed to trace the odd and unexpected ways in which the dream comes to fulfillment. But the dream per se is not of interest, and the narrative does not encourage any speculation on the phenomenology of dreams. Rather, the dream serves as a vehicle for the narrative presentation of God's providential care and governance. Providence is a strange theological notion. It offers the sense that God can plan ahead, see ahead, govern ahead, care ahead. There is no stress here on Israel being God's chosen people, but only the affirmation that God has already intended the outcome of the narrative. The outcome of the Joseph narrative, then, is a majestic statement about God's sovereign way in the world, a way that has been operative since God initially asserted the goodness of creation in 1:31. In this way we are able to see that the book of Genesis has an overall plan and dynamic to it that stretches all the way from creation to this moment in Israel, when the text awaits Moses and the liberation.

As the Joseph narrative is now placed, however, that general claim about providential governance is given a more particular ambience. The context makes it clear that God's governing care is not only to keep the dream but to bring the people of promise in Genesis to the wonder of deliverance in Exodus. The core historical memory of Israel is finally served by the narrative, a history that tells repeatedly of the last ones becoming the first ones.

ENDURING THEOLOGICAL SIGNIFICANCE

The Book of Genesis is not simply a historical memory. It is not primarily a record of what happened, and its linkage to historical facticity is variously loose and difficult to determine. Genesis, rather, is an authoritative text that keeps generating new meaning, new vitality, new truth, and new faith for the communities that attend to it. Jews and Christians have found this literature alive and authoritative in a number of ways.

In the Old Testament itself, the tradition of Genesis occupies a peculiar role. It is fair to say that the Book of Genesis has been more influential in subsequent Jewish and Christian reflection than it has been in the Old Testament itself.

The creation theme, sounded in Genesis 1–2, is of course much utilized in the Old Testament, especially in the Psalms, the poem of Job, and Isaiah 40–55. But with the important exception of Psalm 8, it is not clear that the Genesis version of creation has been especially influential. Moreover, the "stories of disruption" in chapters 3–4 and 11:1–9 have exercised no influence in the Old Testament. The flood story is only minimally visible (*cf.* especially Isa 54:9–11). For all the attractiveness of Genesis 1–11 for subsequent reflection and speculation, it is peculiar that the Old Testament itself does not treat these texts as in any way central.

The ancestors of the four generations have also not exercised great influence. The first three, Abraham, Isaac, and Jacob, have become names in a set formula articulating God's promise of land, to which God is faithful. The four ancestors figure variously in the genealogies. The most important theological use of Abraham is made in the exilic texts to assert that God's promise is indeed operative (van Seters 1975). In the traditions of Ezekiel (33:24) and 2 Isaiah (Isa 41:8, 51:2, and other allusions), Abraham is cited as

GENESIS

a bearer of continuity in a community that is deeply shattered by discontinuity. Thus the tradition functions to assert God's abiding and uninterrupted fidelity.

In general the Old Testament relies upon the book of Genesis to articulate the general themes of sovereignty and fidelity, but specific allusions are not as many as might be expected. It is the case that the Genesis materials fall outside the decisive credo events to which Israel regularly has recourse, events more directly associated with Moses than with any of these ancestors. It is odd that the Book of Genesis has more powerfully preoccupied Jewish and Christian theological reflection of later periods than it has the canonical text itself.

Subsequent Jewish use of the Book of Genesis is extensive. (On this topic, see Sarna 1966 and Plaut 1974.) The general affirmation of the literature is that God has made the world and that God has made an abiding promise to this people. Genesis provides a source for such an overriding conviction in Judaism.

Perhaps the most "usable" idea of Genesis for Judaism is the conviction that God has promised to Israel a quite specific land with identifiable borders. The notion of promise is theologically prior to every theory of land possession or any strategy for occupying the land. Just as that promise became a driving force for occupation in the Joshua traditions, so in postbiblical Judaism a driving force has been the conviction that Israel's possession of the land is not simply a historical accident or a political necessity but a theological fact willed in the purpose of God. Zionism is a dream of secure land that is more immediately rooted in the Jerusalem tradition of David than in the ancestral promises, but behind the Jerusalem claims is the more foundational dream of God's promise to the ancestors. It is worth noting that even Israel's most sensitive religious interpreters, such as Abraham Joshua Heschel and Martin Buber, take land as decisive for God's dealing with Israel. The promise thus operates to assure that Judaism is a thoroughly historical, this-worldly religion preoccupied with questions of faithful materiality.

On the other hand, the story of creation and fall that figures so prominently in Christian theology has not been a matter of great interest to Judaism. This

point is cited to support the observation that Jews and Christians are able to read and interpret this text in very different ways, largely shaped by very different and well-delineated traditions of interpretation. On the whole Jewish tradition is not overwhelmed by a sense of sin and sinfulness as Christian theology tends to be, so that "the fall" of Genesis 3 (as read by classical Christianity) is no central part of Jewish interpretation. An important exception is the pathos-filled reflection of 2 Esdras, which understands the human plight since Adam as an impossible situation of being judged for sin yet unable not to sin. Such use makes clear the marvelous plasticity of the text, which permits very different readings to meet different religious needs.

In some ways the Book of Genesis has figured more prominently in Christian theology than in Jewish tradition. Two uses of Genesis in the New Testament may be identified as having exercised enormous influence. First, Genesis 1–3 has become decisive for Christian theology through the interpretation given by Paul in Romans 5. More than any other part of the Old Testament, these chapters have been preempted for systematic theology under the rubric of "creation and fall" (Bonhoeffer 1959). Genesis 1–2 is taken as God's initial act of creation. Chapter 3 then is read as the singular event through which the world has become distorted for all time, until the Messiah comes. This way of reading the text has been taken as a context for the Christian gospel of redemption through Jesus (see Rom 5:12, 18). All historical critics agree that this influential and shaping exposition imposes upon Genesis 3 a theological intentionality that is not present in the text, for Genesis 3 and the Old Testament generally do not know of any "fall." Nonetheless this reading continues to be a predominant exegesis, thus indicating how freely interpretation can and does handle tradition.

The other primary usage from Genesis in the New Testament is the figure of Abraham, father of faith and the bearer of God's promise. We may cite two clusters of uses, though reference should also be made to Hebrews 11. In the Gospel of Luke, Jesus pays particular attention to the poor and dispossessed. Four times Luke invokes the figure of Abraham as a guarantee of God's special attentiveness to the poor (Dahl 1980). Mary's song of liberation is based on the promise to Abraham (Luke 1:55). The woman with the "spirit of infirmity" is called "a daughter of Abraham" (13:16). The poor man is carried by angels to the "bosom of Abraham" (16:22). Zacchaeus, the tax collector, is called "a son of Abraham" (19:9). These several uses indicate that Abraham now functions as a sign of God's care for the disqualified without reference to merit.

That same function of Abraham as the bearer of God's unconditional promise is given a theologically more intentional articulation by Paul in Romans 4 and Galatians 3–4. Paul's argument opposes Abraham, the bearer of God's grace, to "the law," which Paul takes as a cipher for the Judaism he means to critique. In Romans 4:13 Abraham is credited with "righteousness through faith." In Galatians 3–4 Abraham is the embodiment of the faith that saves. In Galatians 3:6 Paul quotes Genesis 15:6 and in Galatians 3:8 Paul quotes Genesis 12:3. These two texts, Genesis 12:3 and 15:6, become the interpretive key for Paul's understanding of the Abraham narrative and its relation to his gospel. Because Paul focuses on faith and promise, Abraham's blessing is termed "the gospel beforehand," that is, the anticipation of what is to be fully given in the Christian dispensation.

It is not to be argued that Paul has given the "right" interpretation of Genesis, or that Jesus is the fulfillment of Genesis. Rather our interest is in the generative power of the Genesis text, which has the rich capacity to fuel imagination and faith in the very different castings of Judaism and Christianity. Like every great piece of literature, Genesis can beget more than one interpretation. While each religious community arrives at its own normative (canonical) interpretation, the original literature itself is more free, more bold, and more energizing than any of its derivative interpretations.

Genesis belongs peculiarly to several religious communities of interpretation, but it is not limited to these. Genesis in powerful ways is a literary statement that belongs to all of humanity, including our contemporary human community. It speaks in grand themes that have repeatedly claimed the attention of those who stand outside the community of Jews and Christians but who seek resources for the great human issues.

Creation faith articulated in Genesis 1–11 permits us, living at the end of the Enlightenment period with its excessive confidence in technical modes of knowledge, to perceive the world differently. First, in this (scientifically) primitive narrative form, the world is presented to us as having a holy purpose outside itself. The world exists not for itself, not for its own ends, not under its own authority, but with reference to holy purposes that remain always elusive and beyond our capacity to dominate and control. Second, the world has a moral purpose and a moral coherence. It follows that human persons are held accountable for decisions and actions made in the world. Third, there is at work in the world a power resolved to heal and begin again that works against the power of distortion and destruction. This discernment of the world offered in the Genesis scenarios on creation, which is programmatic for all of the Bible, leads to a celebration of human freedom, human choice, and human responsibility. Such a claim militates against a mistaken sense of autonomy that would permit anyone to pervert and abuse the world, against a denigration of material reality in any pursuit of a more "spiritual" existence, and against a despair about what is possible in the world because we imagine ourselves the only agents at work. Creation faith in Genesis makes available to the world alternatives to the false notions of autonomy, spirituality, and despair. This becomes an articulation of a world characterized by faithful accountability, materiality, and hope.

Furthermore, the promise narratives of the ancestors make a statement that human life is a process of promise making and promise keeping. But intergenerational social reality is required in order to participate in the ongoing power of the promise. Jürgen Moltmann (1967, 102–112), building upon the seminal work of von Rad, has shown how the power of promise provides for a practice of hope in the world, because God hopes for the world relentlessly, against chaos and against barrenness. It is the promissory quality of life reflected in the Genesis narratives that stands as a criticism of every attempt at absolutism in the world, whether the presumed absolutism is political, theological, moral, intellectual, or whatever. The power of promise keeps life fundamentally open to what is new and what God has yet to give. That powerful promise, rooted in the character of God, becomes the foundation of human possibility and guards against every totalitarian regime that would distort the world and crush the human spirit.

These two themes of God's gracious, sovereign ordering of creation and God's free, powerful promise are the central theological claims of the Book of Genesis. The tradition of Genesis knows very well that the world has not yet been brought to obedience and that the promise has not yet been kept. Chaos still is powerful in the face of that gracious, sovereign ordering. Barrenness still prevails against the power of the promise of birth. But this common memory, shared by Jews and Christians, becomes a powerful, reassuring, and unsettling voice in a world that imagines itself as autonomous and absolutizes social processes as though there is not more still to be given. The Book of Genesis is not the whole of this story of faith, but it articulates the themes that decisively shape the faith story that is to follow.

Bibliography

Albright, William F. Introduction to *The Legends of Genesis,* by Hermann Gunkel, vii–xii. New York, 1964. A foremost Semitist identifies the contribution of Gunkel to the study of Genesis.

Alter, Robert. *The Art of Biblical Narrative.* New York, 1981.

Anderson, Bernhard W. "From Analyses to Synthesis: The Interpretation of Genesis 1–11." *Journal of Biblical Literature* 97 (1978): 23–39. A structural analysis of the flood narrative indicating the emergence of new interpretive methods.

Bonhoeffer, Dietrich. *Creation and Fall.* Translated by John C. Fletcher. New York, 1981. A theological interpretation of Genesis 1–3 according to the categories of classical Christian faith.

Bright, John. "Modern Study of Old Testament Literature." In *The Bible and the Ancient Near East: Essays in Honor of William Foxwell Albright,* edited by G. Ernest Wright. Garden City, N.Y., 1961. Pp. 13–31. A critical review of scholarly methods and assumptions in relation to Pentateuchal criticism.

Brueggemann, Walter. *Genesis.* Atlanta, 1982. A theological exposition.

Buber, Martin. *A Land of Two Peoples,* edited with commentary by Paul Mendes-Flohr. New York, 1983. Judaism's most important recent interpreter reflects on the meaning of land for Jewish faith.

Childs, Brevard. *Introduction to the Old Testament as Scripture.* Philadelphia, 1979. Pp. 136–160. A canon-ical proposal for Genesis, with a summary of critical scholarship and exhaustive bibliography.

Clements, Ronald. *One Hundred Years of Old Testament Interpretation.* Philadelphia, 1976. Chap. 20.

Clines, David J. A. *The Theme of the Pentateuch.* Journal for the Study of the Old Testament, suppl. 10. Sheffield, U.K., 1978. A theological exposition of the theme of promise.

Coats, George W. *Genesis, with an Introduction to Narrative Literature.* Grand Rapids, 1983. A splendid summary of what form criticism has taught us about Genesis narration; the standard reference on this subject.

———, ed. *Saga, Legend, Tale, Novella, Fable: Narrative Forms in Old Testament Literature.* Sheffield, U.K., 1985. The authoritative summary of the current state of form-critical scholarship in narrative.

Crenshaw, James L. "Method in Determining Wisdom Influence upon 'Historical Literature.'" *Journal of Biblical Literature* 88 (1969): 129–142. A programmatic critique of the propensity to find wisdom influences in narrative. The critique applies particularly to von Rad's treatment of the Joseph narrative.

———. *Gerhard von Rad.* Waco, Tex., 1978. Helpful in understanding von Rad's remarkable contributions in their context.

Dahl, Nils A. "The Story of Abraham in Luke-Acts." In *Studies in Luke-Acts,* edited by Leander Keck and J. Louis Martyn. Philadelphia, 1980. Pp. 139–158. An exegetical study of the use of old textual traditions in a new textual usage.

Davies, W. D. *The Gospel and the Land: Early Christianity and Jewish Territorial Doctrine.* Berkeley, 1974. A magisterial study of the land traditions of Judaism and Christianity in the New Testament period.

Fishbane, Michael A. *Text and Texture: Close Readings of Selected Biblical Texts.* New York, 1979. Pp. 40–62. A suggestive structural analysis of the Jacob materials.

Fokkelman, J. P. *Narrative Art in Genesis.* Assen, Netherlands, 1975. Pp. 85–237. A detailed structural analysis of several Genesis texts.

Gammie, John G. "Theological Interpretation by Way of Literary and Tradition Analysis: Genesis 25–36." In *Encounter with the Text,* edited by Martin J. Buss. Philadelphia, 1979. Pp. 117–134. Applies the newer methods of literary criticism to the Jacob narrative.

Gunkel, Hermann. *Genesis.* Göttingen, 1901. The classic study of literary genre, which put the study of Genesis on a new foundation.

———. *The Legends of Genesis.* Translated by W. H. Carruth. New York, 1964. An English translation of the introduction to Gunkel's great 1901 commentary on Genesis; the only part in English translation.

Hayes, John H. *An Introduction to Old Testament Study.* Nashville, 1979. Chaps. 4 and 5. A lucid and helpful summary of Pentateuchal scholarship.

Humphreys, W. Lee. "The Motif of the Wise Courtier in

the Book of Proverbs." *Israelite Wisdom: Theological and Literary Essays in Honor of Samuel Terrien*, edited by John G. Gammie et al. Missoula, Mont., 1978. Pp. 177–190. A survey of the role and significance of the bearer of wisdom in Israel's royal sociology.

Koch, Klaus. "Is There a Doctrine of Retribution in the Old Testament?" In *Theodicy in the Old Testament*, edited by James L. Crenshaw. Philadelphia, 1983. Pp. 57–87. First published in 1955, this classic essay is indispensable for a study of creation faith in ancient Israel.

Mendenhall, George E. "The Shady Side of Wisdom." In *A Light unto My Path*, edited by Howard N. Bream et al. Philadelphia, 1974. Pp. 319–334.

Moltmann, Jürgen. *Theology of Hope on the Ground and the Implications of a Christian Eschatology*. Translated by James W. Leitch. London, 1967. Of interest for this study because it is decisively informed by the promissory theme of Genesis as explicated by von Rad.

Noth, Martin. *The Deuteronomistic History*. Sheffield, U.K., 1981. Noth's classic proposal (1943) of a foundational literary division between Numbers and Deuteronomy, thus a Tetrateuch.

———. *A History of Pentateuchal Traditions*. Translated by Bernhard Anderson. Englewood Cliffs, N.J., 1972. Reprinted Chico, Cal., 1981. Noth's second classic, first published in 1948. Studying the five basic themes of the Pentateuch, Noth saw that Genesis 12–50 is organized around the theme of promise.

Ong, Walter J. *Orality and Literacy: The Technologizing of the Word*. New York, 1982. A programmatic criticism of the history of speech and technology.

Plaut, W. Gunther. *Genesis*. New York, 1974. An exposition of Genesis with particular reference to Jewish traditions of interpretation.

Pritchard, James B., ed. *Ancient Near Eastern Texts Relating to the Old Testament*. Princeton, 1955. The standard collection for textual parallels between the Old Testament and its cultural context.

Rad, Gerhard von. "The Beginnings of Historical Writing in Ancient Israel." In *The Problem of the Hexateuch and Other Essays*, translated by E. W. Trueman Dicken. Edinburgh, 1966. Pp. 166–204. Von Rad's suggestive recognition of the emergence of a new narrative art in Israel, which he judged to be related to the emergence of a new level of cultural sophistication.

———. "The Form-Critical Problem of the Hexateuch." In *The Problem of the Hexateuch*, pp. 1–78. Von Rad's classic proposal (1938) for the history and shape of the Hexateuch, which has decisively shaped all subsequent discussion.

———. *Genesis: A Commentary*. Translated by John H. Marks. Philadelphia, 1972. Still the most important commentary, now significantly supplemented by Westermann.

———. "The Joseph Narrative and Ancient Wisdom." In *The Problem of the Hexateuch*, pp. 292–300. A proposal that the Joseph narrative is shaped by sapiential thought and intentionality. The proposal has been severely criticized but continues to energize the discussion.

———. *Old Testament Theology* Translated by D. M. G. Stalker. New York, 1962. Vol. 1. A normative theological exposition, derivative from the approach outlined in "The Form-Critical Problem."

Rendtorff, Rolf. *Das überlieferungsgeschichtliche Problem des Pentateuch*. Beihefte zur Zeitschrift der alttestamentlichen Wissenschaft, no. 147. Berlin, 1977. A programmatic attempt to move Pentateuch studies beyond the categories of von Rad and Noth; it has met with mixed response.

Sanders, James A. "Adaptable for Life: The Nature and Function of Canon." In *Magnalia Dei: The Mighty Acts of God*, edited by Frank Moore Cross, Werner E. Lemke, and Patrick D. Miller, Jr. Garden City, N.Y., 1976. Pp. 531–560. A leading proponent of canon criticism interprets the dynamic and vitality of the Old Testament canon.

Sarna, Nahum M. *Understanding Genesis*. New York, 1966. A sensitive exposition of Genesis, utilizing the evidence of the Near East and giving attention to the ongoing Jewish tradition of interpretation.

Schmid, H. H. "Creation, Righteousness, and Salvation: 'Creation Theology' as the Broad Horizon of Biblical Theology." In *Creation in the Old Testament*, edited by Bernhard W. Anderson. Philadelphia, 1984. Pp. 102–117. An important study showing how and why creation faith is definitional and not marginal for the faith offered in the Old Testament.

Schmidt, Ludwig. *De Deo*. Beihefte zur Zeitschrift der alttestamentlichen Wissenschaft, no. 143. Berlin, 1976. A study of Genesis 18:16–32.

Seters, John van. *Abraham in History and Tradition*. New Haven, 1975. A vigorous argument against the historicity of the Abraham traditions.

Thompson, Thomas L. *The Historicity of the Patriarchal Narratives*. Beihefte zur Zeitschrift der alttestamentlichen Wissenschaft, no. 133. Berlin, 1974. A careful survey of the connections between archaeological-historical materials and the Genesis narratives. Draws conclusions that largely negate the powerful historical claims enunciated by the school of Albright.

Trible, Phyllis. *God and the Rhetoric of Sexuality*, chapter 4. Philadelphia, 1978. A remarkable exposition of Genesis 2–3 that relies upon literary and rhetorical methods to offer a feminist perspective.

Wellhausen, Julius. *Prolegomena to the History of Israel*. Translated by J. S. Black. Edinburgh, 1885. Reissued as *Prolegomena to the History of Ancient Israel*. New

York, 1957. The classic of nineteenth-century scholarship on the Pentateuch, giving the decisive formulation of the Documentary Hypothesis.

Westermann, Claus. "Arten der Erzählung in der Genesis." In *Forschung am Alten Testament*, 9–91. Theologische Bücherei, no. 24. Munich, 1964. Continues and advances the form-critical work of Gunkel on the Genesis narratives. Most helpful is the suggestion that the ancestral narratives are "family stories."

——. *Genesis 1–11: A Commentary*. Translated by John J. Scullion. Minneapolis, 1984.

——. *Genesis 12–36: A Commentary*. Translated by John J. Scullion. Minneapolis, 1985. The first parts of Westermann's comprehensive and exhaustive commentary, which follows in the train of von Rad but advances our understanding in important ways.

——. *The Promises to the Fathers*. Translated by David E. Green. Philadelphia, 1980. A summary statement of the promissory theme in Genesis.

Wilcoxen, Jay A. "Narrative." In *Old Testament Form Criticism*, edited by John H. Hayes. San Antonio, 1974. Pp. 57–98. A helpful summary of the form-critical work on Genesis, fully reporting on Gunkel and summarizing more recent developments.

Wilson, Robert R. *Genealogy and History in the Biblical World*. New Haven, 1977.

Wolff, Hans Walter, and Walter Brueggemann. *The Vitality of Old Testament Traditions*. Atlanta, 1975. See especially Wolff's article "The Kerygma of the Yahwist" (pp. 41–66), a study that has greatly influenced theological interpretation.

WALTER BRUEGGEMANN

Exodus

THE OPPRESSION OF the Israelites in Egypt and their liberation and escape into the wilderness of Sinai under the leadership of Moses constitute the major theme of the Hebrew Bible. These events are mentioned in that body of literature no less than 120 times, and they left an indelible impression on the institutions and teachings of the religion of Israel in many diverse, but always profound, ways.

THE TITLE

The work that narrates these experiences is known as the Book of Exodus, the second of the books of the Torah or Pentateuch, the five books of Moses with which the Bible begins. The English title derives from the Latin version of the Bible known as the Vulgate, which, in turn, was influenced by the Septuagint, the Greek translation of the Pentateuch made by the Jews of Alexandria, Egypt, in the third century B.C.E. The Septuagint, and later the Vulgate, became the official version of the early Christian church. The title "Exodus" is abbreviated from an originally longer title that was current among the Jewish communities of the Near East: "The Book of the Exodus [i.e., departure of the Israelites] from Egypt." In Hebrew the work came popularly to be known as *Shemot,* which literally means "Names," the first significant word in the book.

THE SEQUEL TO GENESIS

While Exodus constitutes a distinct literary unit within the Pentateuchal corpus and enjoys an integrity of its own, it also continues the story begun in Genesis, and it can be understood only against the background of the narratives contained in that book. There we learn of the highlights in the lives of the three generations of the founding fathers of the people of Israel: Abraham, Isaac, and Jacob. Each patriarch received divine promises of nationhood and national territory for his descendants. In Genesis 12:2 and 12:7, for example, Abraham is told by God: "I will make you a great nation. . . . I will give this land to your offspring," referring to the land of Canaan. This pledge is repeated several times in the course of Abraham's long life. His son Isaac received similar assurances: "I will give all these lands to you and to your offspring, fulfilling the oath that I swore to your father Abraham. I will make your descendants as numerous as the stars of heaven, and give to your descendants all these lands" (Gen 26:3–4; all citations are from the translation of the Jewish Publication Society, *Tanakh,* 1985). Isaac's spiritual heir was his younger son, Jacob. Jacob too received divine revelations affirming the continuity and reality of those blessings. He is promised: "Your descendants shall be as the dust of the earth; you shall spread out to the west and to the east, to the north and to the south" (Gen 28:14); Jacob's name was changed to Israel. When this took place, he was told by God:

> Be fertile and increase;
> A nation, yea an assembly of
> nations shall descend from you,
> . . . the land that I gave to
> Abraham and Isaac I give to you;
> And to your offspring to come
> Will I give this land.
> (Gen 35:11–12)

Aside from these bipartite promises of posterity and territory, another passage in Genesis crucial to the understanding of Exodus is 15:13–14. God made a covenant with the childless Abraham and besides promising him posterity also ominously warned him: "Know well that your offspring shall be strangers in a land not theirs, and they shall be enslaved and oppressed four hundred years; but I will execute judgment on the nation they shall serve, and in the end they shall go free with great wealth." The "land not theirs" turned out to be Egypt. The last fourteen chapters of Genesis relate how the Israelites came to migrate to that land in the culmination of a chain of events set in motion by the sale of Joseph, Jacob's son, into Egyptian slavery by his brothers. Just before starting out with his family on the journey to Egypt, Jacob was reassured by God: "Fear not to go down to Egypt, for I will make you there a great nation" (Gen 46:3). Finally, as Joseph himself lay dying, he uttered these words: "God will surely take notice of you and bring you up from this land to the land that He promised on oath to Abraham, to Isaac, and to Jacob" (Gen 50:24).

The Book of Exodus presupposes knowledge of the fundamental features of the ancestral narratives, and its own tale is predicated upon them. Thus the opening paragraph mentions the migration of the Israelite tribes to Egypt, the death of Joseph, and the particular fact that the Israelites were "fertile and prolific, they multiplied and increased very greatly." It is thereby implicitly affirmed that God's promises to the ancestors had by now been partially realized. The nation existed. In fact, the term "Israelite people"

appears here for the first time (Exod 1:9). The subjection of this people to slavery, vividly described in the first chapter, fulfills the above-cited prediction God made to Abraham. The liberation of Israel from Egypt and its settlement in its own promised land still remain to be effected. How the former is successfully achieved is carefully narrated in the first part of this book. The experiences, hardships, and disappointments that occur along the way to realizing the latter goal occupy the remainder.

THE NATURE OF THE NARRATIVE

It would be a mistake, however, to conclude that the Book of Exodus was intended to be a history. Its main purpose was certainly not simply to preserve the memory of a segment of Israel's past for future generations, although admittedly that tendency may have been present. The documentation is extremely sparse, given the time span involved. For instance, between the descent of Jacob to Egypt and the onset of the oppression, a considerable time must have elapsed, yet, other than a reference to the increase in population, the text is totally silent with regard to this period. In all, relatively few episodes and incidents are recorded, and it is quite clear that these have been carefully selected and artfully presented with certain didactic ends in mind. The biblical materials in general are essentially documents of faith and religious teaching, and Exodus exemplifies this characterization more than any other biblical work. History has been utilized to inculcate the norms of faith; hence a detailed examination of the structure and content of Exodus is needed for a deeper understanding and keener appreciation of its nature and function.

First, however, we need to consider how the material that makes up the book came to be put together in its present form. Even a cursory examination indicates a composite origin with a complex literary history. A widely held scholarly view is that the ultimate building blocks were stories, hymns, and oracles that were handed down from generation to generation in oral form. From the varied complexes of *tradition developed what has been called an Old Epic narrative. Over the course of time two narrative strands* are thought to have emerged, one originating in the northern kingdom, the other in the southern. These have respectively been given the sigla E (for Elohist) and J (for Y/Jahwist), the designations being based on the distinctive names for God (*Elohim* and *YHWH*) used by each. The two overlapping sources were eventually fused to form one continuous narrative. Onto this major text were grafted collections of laws and legal decisions, while priestly scribes contributed additional characteristic elements such as lists of names, genealogies, itineraries, and descriptions of ceremonial and ritual practices (Anderson 1986, 151–180).

THE STRUCTURE OF EXODUS

The Book of Exodus is thus made up of very diverse material that does not readily yield to classification. Several approaches are possible. For instance, some scholars have divided the material on the basis of geographic location. This approach isolates three main sections:

1. Israel in Egypt (1:1–12:36)
2. Israel in the wilderness on the way to Mount Sinai (12:37–18:27)
3. Israel's experiences at Mount Sinai (19:40)

Other scholars distinguish among several narrative components. Although there is no unanimity of opinion, the following arrangement may be the most satisfactory:

1. Israel in Egypt (1:1–12:36)
2. The departure from Egypt, the escape across the Sea of Reeds, and the wanderings in the wilderness (12:37–18:27)
3. The covenant of Mount Sinai and the laws (19:1–26:18)
4. Instructions for building the tabernacle and consecrating its functionaries (25–31)
5. The sin of the golden calf and the renewal of the covenant (32–34)
6. The construction of the tabernacle and its furniture (35–40)

The foregoing separation according to broad narrative blocks may be more informative than the geographic arrangement, but even so, it hardly does justice to the richness and great variety of the book's content.

The Oppression

Exodus opens with an introductory paragraph that establishes the connection with the Genesis narratives. Those texts dealt with the lives of individuals. A note about the phenomenal increase in the Israelite population in Egypt now effects the transition to the central topic of this book: the fortunes of the people as a whole (1:1–7).

A new king ascended the throne of Egypt. He perceived the presence of such a large alien population as a threat to the security of the country, and he proceeded to take harsh measures to counteract it. The Israelites were pressed into forced labor on state projects under degrading and brutal conditions (1:8–14).

When this repressive policy failed to achieve the expected result of diminishing the Israelite population, a royal order was given to the midwives to murder all newborn Israelite males. The midwives, being God-fearing, could not bring themselves to carry out the iniquitous decree, whereupon Pharaoh commanded that all newborn males be thrown into the river Nile (1:15–22).

The Exodus and History

It was pointed out above that the Book of Exodus was intended to be not a historical record in the sense in which this phrase is generally understood today but rather a theological, God-centered interpretation of historical events. Nevertheless it is pertinent to ask whether the events described can be fitted into the framework of recorded and datable history. Formidable difficulties await us, however, if we attempt to do so. The text never gives the proper names of the Egyptian kings but invariably refers to each one as "Pharaoh." The biblical text does not yield a single explicit correlation or synchronism with any datable event in Egyptian or Near Eastern history, nor do any archaeological finds attest unambiguously to the Exodus and to Joshua's conquest forty years later. The data given in the Bible do not permit reconstruction of a consistent chronology. We cannot make a calculation from the time of the patriarchs because we do not know how much time elapsed between the death of Joseph and the onset of the oppression of the Israelites. Even if we did, no scholarly unanimity exists as to when Abraham lived.

At first glance we ought to be able to use the information given in 1 Kings 6:1. King Solomon built the Temple in Jerusalem 480 years after the Exodus, in the fourth year of his reign. Since he came to the throne about 960 B.C.E., the Exodus should be placed around the middle of the fifteenth century B.C.E. However, this period presents many difficulties. Powerful kings reigned in Egypt at this time: Thutmose III (*ca.* 1490–1436 B.C.E.) and Amenhotep II (*ca.* 1436–1412 B.C.E.), both of the eighteenth Egyptian Dynasty, are known to have exercised firm control over Canaan and to have campaigned there periodically. It is hardly credible that the conquest of Canaan by Israel could have taken place in the course of their reigns, especially since Egypt is never mentioned as a factor in Joshua's wars of conquest.

Another complication with a fifteenth-century dating arises from Moses' purported dealings with various Transjordanic states (Num 21:21–35, Deut 1:4–5, and Deut 2–3), yet archaeological surveys show that these regions were largely uninhabited in this period and certainly had no settled states.

As to the 480-year span cited above, there is reason to conclude it was intended to be understood in a rhetorical rather than literal sense. It is the product of two factors, 12 and 40, each of which is a conventional or symbolic number in the Bible and the ancient Near East. It also happens that according to the biblical data, exactly 480 years passed between the building of the Temple by Solomon and the Cyrus Declaration of 538 B.C.E., which gave the Jews permission to return from the Babylonian Exile and rebuild the Temple at Jerusalem. It is likely, therefore, that by giving the figure of 480 years after the Exodus, the biblical writer wished to establish that the building of Solomon's temple was the central, pivotal event in the history of biblical Israel.

A good, though by no means decisive, case has been made for placing the Exodus more than two centuries later. The texts tell us that the Israel-ites' settlement in Egypt was in Goshen, a place widely accepted as having been located in the northeastern delta of the Nile. They also make clear that the then capital of Egypt was there or close by. This was true of the period of Ramses II (*ca.* 1290–1224 B.C.E.). This Pharaoh undertook ambitious building projects and needed a readily available supply of labor. The conscription of the Israelites for the purpose, as described in Exodus, fits this policy. One of the towns said to have been built by the Israelites was, in fact, named Raamses (Ex 1:11). The successor to Ramses II was Merneptah (*ca.* 1224–1211 B.C.E.), who spent much time and energy fighting an invasion of the mysterious "Sea People" and the Libyans. When he died, Egypt was plunged into anarchy. Not very long thereafter, Egyptian domination of Canaan came to an end.

Many great powers in the Near East were in eclipse. It was in the course of the thirteenth century B.C.E. that Troy was destroyed, the Hittite Empire collapsed, and a branch of the Sea People invaded the coast of Canaan. Canaanite civilization, as excavations show, was in an advanced state of internal disintegration. Several lesser peoples in the region established new states at this time, as for example the Arameans in Syria and the peoples of the Phoenician coast and Transjordan. Certainly the moment was propitious for the Israelite advance into the Promised Land. In fact, mention of the people of Israel in a stele of Merneptah points to their presence in the highland region of Canaan, but without as yet definite borders. Finally excavations reveal that some of the Canaanite city-states mentioned in the Bible as having been destroyed by Joshua's armies were violently devastated around this time. Thus, several lines of evidence converge to make a strong case in favor of the later dating of the Exodus (DeWit 1960; Bimson 1978).

The Birth of Moses

Irrespective of the actual date of the Exodus, there is no doubt that the central human role was played by Moses. His origin is related in the story of a couple from the tribe of Levi who managed to hide their newborn son for three months but were eventually forced to abandon him to the Nile. The mother placed the baby in a waterproof wicker basket and floated it among the river's reeds while the boy's sister, later identified as Miriam, watched discreetly from a distance. Presently an Egyptian princess appeared and, hearing the baby's cries, had him fetched. She recognized at once his Hebrew origin. At this point, the sister came forward and offered to fetch a Hebrew wet nurse. Pharaoh's daughter consented, and Miriam brought her mother. Thereupon the princess paid the baby's mother to nurse him, without knowing her true identity. In light of subsequent developments, it appears that Pharaoh's daughter had the baby brought to the palace once he was weaned. It was the princess who gave him the name Moses, which was actually Egyptian but was hebraized in the text and by means of wordplay can be interpreted to mean "drawn out from the water" (2:1–10).

The arrangements made between Moses' mother and the princess conform to Egyptian custom as well as to adoption contracts that have come to light in Mesopotamia. A woman in Egypt possessed full rights under the law and could be a party to a contract on her own. Cuneiform documents record agreements with wet nurses by adopters of foundlings. The provisions found in these contracts conform closely to the pact made in the birth story of Moses (Childs 1965).

The narrative itself has been subjected to scrutiny for its literary quality (Ackerman 1974) because of features it has in common with a literary genre known as the "abandoned hero motif" (Rank 1959; Redford 1967). It has been noted that many folkloric compositions about the birth and upbringing of national heroes feature similar themes: the abandonment of the infant, placing his life in jeopardy; his rescue and adoption by perfect strangers; the ultimate discovery of his origin and his rise from obscurity to power and fame. A particularly celebrated example of this genre is the account of the birth and upbringing of Sargon, ruler of Akkad in Mesopotamia and one of the world's earliest empire builders. However, while it is not impossible that the biblical narrator might have been influenced by such legends when giving literary form to his narrative, there are so many points of contrast with and departure from the common

pattern in the story of Exodus that the Sargon legend cannot have been its inspiration (Sarna 1986, 29–31).

Moses' Character

The biblical narrative is remarkably silent about Moses' childhood and adolescent years. Egyptian sources give us a glimpse of the education of an aristocratic youngster. Commencing school at the age of four, the student followed a curriculum mainly consisting of reading, writing, and arithmetic, with special stress on penmanship and memorization. The presence of non-Egyptians, especially Semites, in the court schools is well-attested.

Whatever type of education Moses received in the Egyptian palace, subsequent developments show that he remained conscious of his Israelite origins. Three episodes are related in the Book of Exodus that confirm this. It is told that one day while visiting the construction sites where the Hebrew slaves were laboring, he witnessed the beating of one of them by the Egyptian taskmaster. Moses instinctively reacted with righteous indignation, struck the Egyptian with a fatal blow, and then buried him quickly. The following day, attempting to intervene in a brawl that had erupted between two Hebrews, he reprimanded the aggressor. To his surprise, the offender referred to Moses' killing of the Egyptian. Before long, news of the deed reached the palace and Moses was condemned to death, but he managed to escape to the land of Midian in the peninsula of Sinai. There, by a well, he witnessed the maltreatment of the shepherdess daughters of the local priest and at once came to their aid.

Clearly, all three episodes are intended to establish Moses as a person who could neither tolerate injustice nor remain passive in the face of it. These qualities fitted him for leadership.

In the meantime, Jethro, the father of the shepherdesses, invited Moses to his home, where he married Zipporah, one of the daughters. A son was born of the union and was named Gershom, which in Hebrew can yield the meaning "a stranger there," a name symbolically descriptive of Moses' plight (2:11–22).

The Commissioning of Moses

Moses was employed as a shepherd to Jethro's flocks. One day he drove them far into the wilderness, where, at a mountain called Horeb, he was attracted by the remarkable spectacle of a bush on fire that was not consumed by the flames. As he came closer, he heard a voice twice calling his name. On responding, he was told to come no closer and to remove his sandals because he was standing on holy ground. The voice identified itself as the God of Abraham, Isaac, and Jacob. An awestruck Moses was informed that the time had come for Israel to be redeemed from Egyptian slavery and to inherit the Promised Land, described as "a land flowing with milk and honey." Furthermore, he was told that he, Moses, had been chosen to be God's instrument for the salvation of Israel and was to go and negotiate with Pharaoh. Moses at first shied away from the task, asserting his personal inadequacy, but God was insistent. Moses then asked how he was to identify to the people this "God of the Fathers"; what was this God's personal name? The reply was, "Ehyeh Asher Ehyeh" (I am who I am), which implies that God is ultimately beyond human understanding. It also indicates that the characteristic name of the God of Israel in the Hebrew Bible, which is consonantally spelled *Y-H-V-H*, was perceived to be connected with the verb "to be."

When Moses expressed his fear that the people of Israel would not accept his leadership, he was given three "signs" that he was to duplicate in their presence and that would validate his mission. Still Moses balked at the idea of becoming leader of Israel, claiming lack of eloquence, perhaps even a speech defect. This objection was overcome by the appointment of his elder brother, Aaron, as his spokesman. Moses finally accepted his inexorable fate, obtained permission from his father-in-law to leave Midian, and set out for Egypt accompanied by his wife and sons (2:23–4:20).

The Return to Egypt

A strange and enigmatic incident occurred at a night encampment on the way back. Moses appears to have become desperately ill, and his life was saved only by Zipporah's quick action in circumcising their son (4:24–26).

Moses then met with Aaron, and together they delivered God's message of the impending liberation. After they were accepted by the people, they proceeded to the palace to petition Pharaoh to permit the Israelites to leave Egypt in order to celebrate a religious festival in the wilderness. However, Pharaoh brusquely denied knowledge of the God of the Israelites and refused permission. Moses and Aaron then modified their request and asked for a three-day holiday for the same purpose. In light of Egyptian documents, this was not something unreasonable. One surviving record of the supervisor of a labor gang notes the absence of a worker because he was "sacrificing to the god," while another registers a four-day religious holiday for conscripts of the corvée (Kitchen 1975, 156–157). Nevertheless, this too was refused, and angrily so, while a royal directive was issued to intensify the burden imposed on the Israelites. Straw, an essential ingredient in the manufacture of bricks, formerly provided by the state authorities, was henceforth to be collected by the laborers themselves, who at the same time had to fulfill the same quota of bricks as before. This proved to be an impossible task, and the Israelite foremen were severely punished for their failure to maintain the production level. As a result they turned against Moses and Aaron, blaming them for the worsening of their condition. Moses himself became very discouraged (4:27–5:23).

At this low point, Moses received a divine revelation reiterating the message of liberation and the promises made to the patriarchs. He conveyed this to the people, but they, crushed by cruel bondage, were not receptive. Thereupon God told Moses once again to seek an audience with Pharaoh and to demand the right of the people to emigrate. He protested that this was a futile exercise, but to no avail.

This ends the initial phase of the struggle for freedom. The literary unit is rounded out with genealogies of the tribes of Reuben, Simeon, and Levi, leading up to the family of Moses and Aaron. This section and the opening verses of the book thus constitute a kind of envelope structure. The section concludes with a brief recapitulation of the developments thus far (6:1–30).

The Ten Plagues

Moses was now warned that Pharaoh would prove to be obstinate and unyielding until humbled by extraordinary measures. A drama, in which punitive calamities of increasing severity befell the Egyptians, was about to unfold. These events, popularly known as the "ten plagues," are introduced by a contest between Moses and Aaron and Pharaoh's magicians. The results were initially inconclusive, but the final outcome was a decisive augury of future developments (7:8–13). The ten plagues afflicted Egypt one after the other. The Nile turned to blood, swarms of frogs invaded the dry land, lice infested man and beast, masses of insects settled on the land, the livestock in the field were struck with pestilence, man and beast were smitten with boils, destructive hail ravaged the countryside, vast numbers of locusts swarmed over Egypt, and three days of darkness descended upon the land. The final, climactic plague was the death of all firstborn sons at midnight (7:14–11:10, 12:29–30).

The first nine plagues were all natural phenomena known to visit Egypt from time to time. The water turning to blood may be understood as a poetic description of an unusually heavy pollution of the Nile brought about by an excess of the tropical red sediment that is regularly discharged into the river at its source during its annual rise. This excess occurs when there is an abnormally heavy rainfall in the regions south of Egypt where the river originates (Hort 1957–1958). The plague of darkness may also be a metaphorical depiction of a phenomenon known as the khamsin, a hot southerly wind that sometimes blows into Egypt from the Sahara Desert, carrying with it sand and dust. The other plagues are easily recognizable as nature's periodic scourges. To the biblical narrator, however, it is their concentration, their timing, and their intensity that endowed these visitations with the stamp of the deliberate work of Providence. To emphasize this fact, the narrative, detailing the first nine plagues, has been cast in an elaborate literary mold that denotes design and purposefulness (Zevit 1976).

Each three plagues form a set, and within a set there are recurring patterns. Pharaoh was forewarned of the first two plagues of each set, but not of the third, which struck unannounced. The first plague of each set was announced to Pharaoh in a confrontation that took place "in the morning," but the others had no time indicator. Moses is instructed, "Station yourself before Pharaoh"; for the second, the formula is each time, "Come to Pharaoh"; the third has no common instruction formula. The entire first set of plagues was effected by Aaron, the entire last three through the agency of Moses; the middle three show no particular pattern. The climactic tenth plague falls outside of any possible "natural" explanation and was therefore directly executed by divine instrumentality (11:4–6, 12:29–30).

The Passover

Prior to the climactic finale, Moses gave the people careful instructions for their last days in Egypt. They were to demand from their Egyptian neighbors costly articles, perhaps as compensation for unpaid forced labor. Then, on the tenth of the month of Abib (Spring), each household was to put aside a blemish-free, year-old male lamb or kid, which was to be slaughtered at dusk on the fourteenth of the month. The Israelites were to daub some of its blood on the doorposts and lintels of their houses. This would designate the house as belonging to an Israelite and so save it from the impending plague. The flesh of the lamb was to be roasted and eaten together with unleavened bread and bitter herbs. Any part not consumed was to be burnt the next morning. The people were to be dressed, ready to depart. The lamb was to be a "Passover" or "protective" offering, and forever after this ritual was to be enacted on each anniversary of the night of the Exodus and was to be followed by a seven-day celebration of the Feast of Unleavened Bread. During this period, the house must be free of all leaven (12:1–28; Segal 1963).

The Exodus

Several times in the course of the preceding plagues, Pharaoh had made limited concessions to Moses' demands, only to withdraw them when the misfortune ended. Only with the tenth plague was

Pharaoh's obstinacy finally broken. Spurred on by his courtiers, and by public pressure, he summoned Moses and Aaron in the middle of the night and bade them quickly get the Israelites and all their possessions out of Egypt. The Israelites, fully prepared for this eventuality, assembled at the town of Succoth in the Nile Delta with their livestock. It seems that at the same time other, non-Israelite slaves took advantage of the confused situation to escape from Egypt (12:29–42).

At this point the narrative is broken by the insertion of some homiletical and exegetical material. The great events associated with the liberation of Israel from Egyptian bondage are briefly recapitulated to provide the historicization of the annual Passover offering and the feast of unleavened bread. The consecration and need for redemption of the male firstborns, and the sacrifice of animal firstlings, are explained in terms of the last plague, to which the Israelites and their livestock were immune (12:43–13:16).

The narrative resumes with the Israelites at the edge of the wilderness, having avoided the more direct coastal route from Egypt to Canaan. They then employed the stratagem of suddenly changing course in order to deceive Egyptian intelligence into thinking that the Israelites were hopelessly lost in the wilderness. In the meantime, it had dawned on the Egyptians that they had forfeited a most valuable labor resource. Thereupon, Pharaoh mustered his infantry and chariotry and set out in pursuit of the Israelites. A week after leaving Egypt, the erstwhile slaves suddenly found themselves hemmed in by the advancing enemy to their rear and the sea ahead of them, and they became so dispirited that they were prepared to return to Egypt there and then. However, Moses rallied the people and in the name of God encouraged them with these words: "Have no fear! Stand by, and witness the deliverance which the Lord will work for you today; for the Egyptians whom you see today you will never see again. The Lord will battle for you; you hold your peace!" (14:13–14).

The Israelites were ordered to march forward while Moses lifted his rod, the symbol of divine power. As he did so, a strong east wind drove back the sea, dividing the waters so that the people could march through to the other side. The Egyptians followed, but their horses and chariots became mired in the muddy seabed. At daybreak the wind let up and the sea returned to its normal state. The waters came crashing down upon the enemy forces led by Pharaoh, drowning them all. The deliverance of Israel was accomplished; the Egyptian menace was finally eradicated. Moses and the people burst into a triumphant hymn of praise to God, a composition now known as the "Song of the Sea" (13:17–15:20). It begins exultantly with:

> I will sing to the Lord,
>   for He has triumphed gloriously,
> Horse and driver He has hurled
>   into the sea.

It is the first lengthy piece of sustained poetry in the Bible.

The Tribulations in the Wilderness

The narrative now focuses on the trials and tribulations of the people as they made their way through the wilderness in the direction of Mount Sinai. For three days they experienced a shortage of water, and when they finally reached an oasis the waters were bitter. This led to much grumbling until God showed Moses how to make the waters potable. One month after the Exodus, food became scarce, evoking nostalgia among the people for the "fleshpots of Egypt," which exploded into criticism of Moses and Aaron. In response to their clamoring, God sent quail and manna, a fine, flaky, sweet substance that looked like coriander seed and could be boiled or baked (Bodenheimer 1947; Bates 1959–1960). Continuing their trek, the people again thirsted for water and again became quite unruly, whereupon God told Moses to strike a certain rock with his rod. When he did so, water gushed forth (15:22–17:7; Coats 1968).

The Attack by Amalek

It was at the encampment in the wilderness, called Rephidim, that Israel was subjected to a sudden and vicious assault by a bedouin tribe named Amalek.

In this moment of military crisis Moses called upon a certain Joshua to take charge of the Israelite forces. In a long day's battle Joshua was able to ward off the attack and wear down the enemy, who broke off the engagement and retreated (17:8–16). This unprovoked attack resulted in heavy Israelite civilian casualties. Moreover, the Amalekites controlled the valuable trade routes of Sinai and the Negeb. For these reasons the Israelites were enjoined always to remember the event, to be alert to their own vulnerability.

REORGANIZATION OF THE JUDICIARY

The quick succession of events now slowed down to permit a calming pause in preparation for the great theophany at Sinai. An interesting episode is related about a visit of Jethro and his daughter Zipporah, Moses' wife, and their two sons to the Israelite camp. The narrative is silent as to how and why Moses' family became separated from him. The day after his arrival, Jethro observed Moses acting as the sole magistrate in Israel, while those in need of adjudication had to wait hours on end for their turn. Considering this system of administering justice to be too exhausting for all concerned, he proposed a radical reorganization based on a multilevel, centralized judicial structure with Moses as the supreme judicial authority. The judges were to be drawn "from among all the people" and were to be "capable men who fear God, trustworthy men who spurn ill-gotten gain." Jethro's plan was adopted and instituted. He then returned to his native land.

The Revelation at Mount Sinai: The Covenant

The Israelites went forth again and reached Mount Sinai six weeks after their departure from Egypt. It should be noted that the location of that site and the route of the Exodus from Egypt to Canaan are to this day matters of scholarly dispute. There are so many unknowns in the biblical data that neither can be reconstructed with confidence (Davies 1979; Har-El 1983).

At Sinai the people made preparations for the culminating event of the Exodus—the establishment of a solemn, binding, public, national covenant with God, one that would create a special relationship between God and Israel and that would impose on the Israelites a distinctive way of life dedicated to the service of God (McCarthy 1963; Hillers 1969).

Moses instructed the people to purify themselves, to launder their clothes, and to abstain from sexual relations. On the third day they were to witness the theophany on Mount Sinai, for the duration of which the perimeter of the site would be cordoned off and be strictly out-of-bounds to man and beast.

The dawning of the third day was accompanied by peals of thunder and flashes of lightning. A dense cloud enveloped the mountain, and a loud horn blast was heard. The people, led by Moses, marched out of the camp and took their place at the foot of the site on level ground. The theophany itself consisted of the divine voice promulgating the Decalogue, or Ten Commandments. The awesome, terrifying nature of this unmediated experience prompted the people to beg Moses to act as the agent of divine communication on their behalf. Moses ascended the mountain and remained there in seclusion (chaps. 19–20).

The Book of the Covenant

The Decalogue, in the main, comprises the minimal moral imperatives essential to the maintenance of an ordered and wholesome society. These imperatives express general principles of right and wrong of eternal validity, but they contain no provisions for enforcement. No humanly imposed penalties for their violation are mentioned. Specific cases could not be adjudicated in a court of law simply on the basis of this document. So the Book of Exodus now continues with a body of detailed legislation governing various areas of day-to-day living. This literary unit, covering 21:1–23:19, has come to be known as the Book of the Covenant or the Covenant Code, based on the phraseology of 24:4–7, which states, "Moses then wrote down all the commands of the Lord" and "He took the record of the covenant and read it aloud to the people."

The Book of the Covenant consists of two

distinct sections. Exodus 21:2–22:16 falls within the realm of the judiciary, and the enforcement of these laws is the duty of the appropriate institutions of the state. The second part is mainly made up of various social, ethical, moral, and religious prescriptions that are left to the dictates of conscience (Paul 1970; Boecker 1980).

The first collection of laws, extensive as it is, is not a comprehensive code but represents a series of observations, amendments, and exceptions to what must have been an existing body of unwritten customs and common law. This is the best way of explaining the numerous important lacunae such as laws regulating marriage, sales, contracts, sureties, and pledges. The items that are included make up a miscellany of diverse legal topics that may be subsumed under five broad headings:

1. The rights of slaves (21:2–11)
2. Physical injury inflicted by persons (21:12–27)
3. The homicidal beast (21:28–32)
4. Damage caused to another's property (21:33–22:14)
5. The seduction of a virgin (22:15–16)

The foregoing laws are drafted in what is called the "casuistic" style. That is to say, instead of stating abstract legal principles that, as in Western law, may then be applied to specific cases, the laws are mostly formulated in terms of hypothetical concrete situations in life. A good example is 21:26, which reads: "When a man strikes the eye of his slave, male or female, and destroys it, he shall let him go free on account of his eye." Another is 21:33–34: "When a man opens a pit or digs a pit but has not covered it, and an ox or an ass falls into it, the one responsible for the pit must make restitution; he shall pay the price to the owner, but shall keep the dead animal."

This first section of the Book of the Covenant belongs to a venerable tradition of Near Eastern law collections that can be traced back to at least the middle of the third millennium B.C.E. Mesopotamia, the cradle of this legal tradition, has bequeathed us at least five sizable collections, and another important and large corpus has survived from the Hittite civilization of Asia Minor. Without doubt, it too owes its inspiration to Mesopotamia. All these collections share in common the casuistic formulation as well as many legal topics. The Book of the Covenant itself has numerous points of contact with the cuneiform traditions. All these correspondences and parallels are not to be explained on grounds of direct literary dependence. Rather, they result from the fact that the ancient Near Eastern peoples enjoyed a common legal culture of which Israel was a part. On the other hand, the biblical corpus exhibits several significant, distinctive features that will be discussed below (Greenberg 1960, 1986).

The second part of the Book of the Covenant, 22:17–23:19, consists of a mélange of religious, ethical, moral, and social prescriptions that, because they are presented as issuing from a divine source, have the force of law, even though their infraction may not always come within the purview of the courts. These laws are mostly framed in a style similar to that of the Ten Commandments. They are apodictic prescriptions, expressed concisely and authoritatively as absolutes. A few examples will illustrate the point:

Whoever lies with a beast shall be put to death (22:18).

You shall not wrong a stranger or oppress him, for you were strangers in the land of Egypt (22:20).

You shall be men holy to Me; you must not eat flesh torn by beasts in the field; you shall cast it to the dogs (22:30).

The collection of laws concludes with an epilogue exhorting the people to be faithful to their duties and obligations under the covenant; their reward was to be prosperous in the land they were to inherit (23:10–33).

This second part of the Book of the Covenant has no counterpart in the ancient Near Eastern collections mentioned above. Although many of its prescriptions are found in the nonjuristic literature of neighboring peoples, there they are the fruit of experience and prudential wisdom. The intermixing of religious, moral, ethical, and secular matters is part of the originality of the Book of the Covenant. Concomitant to the preceding is the assumption that all these legal prescriptions flow from the same source and possess the same imperative force. This leads to what is perhaps the fundamental individuality of biblical law, namely, its claim to issue from a divine source rather than royal proclamation or other human authority. Another singularity is the heavy emphasis on the concern for the unfortunates of society—the widow, the orphan, the poor, and the stranger. There are two more unique features of the corpus of law in Exodus. First, the laws are an integral part of the narrative, which thereby was endowed with legal sanction. Second, because the laws are presented as the stipulations of the covenant between God and Israel, they possess a public quality, and the knowledge and study of them became a universal religious obligation (Sarna 1986, 158–159).

With the completion of the legal material the narrative resumes with the description of the ceremony ratifying the covenant. Moses, Aaron and his two sons, and the seventy elders of Israel were in attendance. Moses repeated to the people all the commands just set forth, and they, in turn, unanimously responded: "All the things that the Lord has commanded we will do!" Thereupon Moses committed the laws to writing. The next morning he set up an altar at the foot of the mountain with twelve pillars, doubtless symbolizing the twelve tribes of Israel. Sacrifices were offered and certain rites performed with the blood of the animals. Moses then read aloud to the people the written record of the covenant, and once more the assembled throng affirmed its acceptance of its obligations. We are told that the representatives of the people then experienced a vision of the divine glory, after which a culminating ceremonial meal was held. Moses then ascended the cloud-covered mountain and remained there in prolonged communion with God. He was to receive two tablets of stone on which were inscribed the Ten Commandments (chap. 24).

Instructions for the Tabernacle

It was during his period of seclusion on the mountain that Moses also received elaborately detailed, lengthy instructions for the erection of the tabernacle. The people were soon to depart from Sinai to continue their journey to Canaan. The tabernacle, a mobile sanctuary, was to serve as a visible, concrete symbol of the enduring presence of God in the camp of Israel, irrespective of the increasing distance they were to place between themselves and the mountain of the revelation (Woudstra 1970).

The materials to be used for the construction of the tabernacle were the three basic metals of antiquity, gold, silver, and bronze; fabrics of various types and colors; hides; and acacia wood. The plan featured three successive zones, the Court, the Holy Place, and the Holy of Holies, all surrounded by an enclosure attached to upright posts inserted into bronze sockets. Covering the entire structure overhead were to be four layers: sheets of linen, goat hair, ram skins dyed red, and dolphin skins.

Each of the three divisions of the tabernacle was to have its own distinctive items of furniture. The outer Court was to contain an altar made of wood overlaid with bronze as well as a large bronze washbasin set on a bronze stand. Inside the Holy Place were to be a table for the "bread of display" and an altar for incense, both to be manufactured of wood and overlaid with gold, and a golden menorah, or lampstand. The Holy of Holies was to contain nothing but the two tablets of stone that were to be placed inside an ark, or chest, it too being of wood overlaid with "pure gold" inside and out and equipped with a lid of "pure gold" adorned at either end with golden cherubim (chaps. 25–31; Kennedy 1902; Cross 1961, 1981; Haran 1978; Hurowitz 1985).

The Golden Calf

During Moses' protracted absence on Mount Sinai an event of major importance with disastrous consequences occurred. Believing that Moses had disappeared, the people felt bereft of the exclusive mediator between themselves and God. About to depart from the mount of revelation, they had as yet nothing that would function as the material symbol of the invisible presence of the sovereign God on which to focus their spiritual strivings. They came to Aaron and demanded just such a symbol. Aaron asked for donations of gold jewelry, which he melted and fashioned into a golden calf. He built an altar before it and declared the next day to be a feast to the Lord. Early the following morning the people offered up sacrifices, sat down to feast, and then indulged in revelry.

Seeing this, the Lord ordered Moses to return quickly to the camp of Israel, for the people had committed apostasy. God asserted his willingness to destroy them and to rebuild the nation through Moses. Moses, however, pleaded with God not to destroy Israel, and the Lord renounced the punishment that he had planned.

Moses descended the mountain carrying the two tablets of stone, the symbol of the covenant between God and his people. As he approached the camp and observed the people engaged in what appear to have been orgiastic rites, he smashed the tablets, an act that in the Near East carried with it the force of legal symbolism, signifying abrogation of the covenant. He then seized the golden calf, burnt it, ground it to powder, and strewed it upon the water, forcing the Israelites to drink of the mixture. This last act is reminiscent of the bitter water ordeal administered to the suspected faithless wife described in Numbers 5:11–31. Moses confronted Aaron with having brought great sin upon Israel when he fashioned the golden calf. Aaron excused himself by blaming the people, who, he said, were "bent on evil." He also claimed that all he had done was to cast the gold into the fire; the calf had emerged all by itself!

By now, the people were out of control, and to save the situation Moses issued a call for all who had remained faithful to the Lord to rally to his side. The tribe of Levi immediately responded. They took up their swords and slaughtered 3,000 rebels.

The following day Moses pleaded with God to forgive Israel for its sin. He nobly stated that if Israel remained unforgiven, he would prefer to be no longer among the living. God yielded to Moses' entreaty to the extent that the punishment would be postponed until some indefinite future time (chap. 32; Bailey 1971; Loewenstamm 1967, 1975).

God now bade Moses lead the people to the Promised Land but warned that because of their faithlessness an angel, not God himself, would go before them. This is another way of saying that the sin of the golden calf had impaired the direct relationship between God and Israel. The people went into mourning and refrained from wearing any ornaments, a sign of their deep remorse.

Renewal of the Covenant

The narrative continues with Moses pitching a tent outside the camp, called the "tent of meeting," to which anyone who "sought the Lord" could go. It was there that Moses communed with God, and a pillar of cloud descended and placed itself at the tent entrance. That is to say, in contrast to the people, Moses' personal, unmediated, intimate relationship with God remained unimpaired. He therefore resumed his intercession on behalf of the people and succeeded in having the covenant with God renewed. The shattered tablets of stone were then replaced (chaps. 32–34).

The Tabernacle Constructed

A call went out to the Israelites to contribute the materials for the construction of the tabernacle, and they responded with lavish generosity. A master craftsman named Bezalel was designated to fashion the various components. The detailed description of all the materials and parts and repeated confirmation of conformity to Moses' instructions are the topics of the last chapters of the Book of Exodus. When the work was finished Moses assembled the tabernacle in accordance with the vision he had seen on the mountain. Aaron and his sons were consecrated and installed as the priests. As a sign of divine favor, a symbolic cloud covered the tent, and the presence of the Lord filled the tabernacle (chaps. 35–40). On this note the book ends.

Many critical scholars have been skeptical that any contemporary reality lay behind the story about the construction of the tabernacle in the wilderness. They called into question the availability of the needed construction materials and of the necessary skilled craftsmen under the conditions of the times. They claimed that the account in Exodus is a fictional retrojection of King Solomon's Temple into the period of the wilderness wanderings. Refuting these doubts is the evidence of the biblical text that before the Israelites left Egypt they "stripped the Egyptians" and obtained "objects of silver and gold" (Ex 11:2, 12:35–36; Ps 105:37). Furthermore, since Israelite males had long been subjected to the corvée in a country that was one of the most technically advanced in the civilized world, there is no reason why they should not have produced talented and experienced professionals in the various skills required for the construction of the tabernacle.

The evidence produced in recent years proves that portable shrines were in wide use in the ancient Near East. This practice is attested among Arab bedouin of the pre-Islamic period and among the ancient Phoenicians and Carthaginians, as well as among the Egyptians themselves. It appears on Egyptian bas-reliefs portraying the battles of Ramses II. Even more relevant is the discovery of early Egyptian use of the same prefabricated construction technique as is described in the tabernacle narrative. Actual samples have survived from the tombs of Queen Hetepheres (early 26th century B.C.E.) and King Tutankhamen (*ca.* 1350 B.C.E.) (Kitchen 1960, 7–13; 1977, 85–86).

The Tabernacle narrative in the Book of Exodus, the architectural plan, and its content and form all communicate certain inherently Israelite religious concepts. Conceptually, as was noted above, the tabernacle was meant to be an extension of Mount Sinai, always present wherever the people might be wandering in the wilderness. Its tripartite arrangement, with each successive zone featuring an increasingly higher degree of holiness, followed the pattern of the revelatory experience. The Holy of Holies corresponded to the mountain peak where Moses alone was privileged to be. The Holy Place, the middle zone, was the counterpart of the area at the mountain to which only the priests and elders had access. The Court was the equivalent of the level ground at the foot of the mountain where the laity stood. The tablets of stone, the focal point of the entire edifice, symbolized the content of the theophany, the proclamation of the Ten Commandments. They were housed in the Holy of Holies, and the cherubim above the Ark in which they were kept represented the ever-present divine spirit. Finally, the cloud that enveloped the completed tabernacle suggested at once the cloud-enveloped mountain at the time of the theophany.

There are still other ways in which the shrine projected national and religious values and aspirations. The narrative repeatedly emphasizes the all-Israelite nature of the enterprise. It also reiterates its harmoniously integrated sacred unity despite the large number and variety of its component parts (26:6, 11;

36:13, 18). This, together with the Holy of Holies, constructed as a cube, the symbol of perfection, represents the unity and perfection of the divine being.

A strange aspect of the narrative containing the instructions for the manufacturing of the tabernacle is that it closes with the law about the observance of the Sabbath (31:12–17), and the same law introduces the account of its actual construction (35:1–3). This juxtaposition of seemingly unrelated themes would appear to communicate one of the most profound biblical concepts, the one concerned with a human being's relationship to the holy. It sets up a relative scale of holy time and holy space, with the former taking precedence over the latter. The Sabbath, holy time, is in the Genesis cosmogony the consummation of creation, and as such is part of the cosmic order. The holiness of space finds no mention there.

THE RELIGIOUS TEACHINGS OF EXODUS

Just as the Exodus is the leading theme of biblical literature, the Book of Exodus is the seminal biblical text, since it recounts the epochal events that shaped the entire course and development of the religion of Israel, which in turn gave eventual rise to the other two great monotheistic religions of the world, Christianity and Islam. It is of critical importance, therefore, to dwell upon the major aspects of this book as a religious document, for it is as such, after all, that it had an impact on humanity.

First, it should be stressed that the underlying presupposition is the concept of God as creator of the world, as set forth in the opening chapters of Genesis. It is not the process of creation but the fact of God's creating that is dominant, for by virtue of this creating, God is sovereign over nature. He does not inhere in nature as the pagan gods were thought to do, but he is outside of it and wholly independent of the material world. Direct reference to this aspect of the divine being is to be found in the Ten Commandments with their rationalization of the Sabbath institution (20:11). The narrative about the plagues takes it for granted that God exercises control over nature and can manipulate it at will.

Next, it is taken as axiomatic that this creator God is not an otiose deity. Having created the world, God is not indifferent to its fate but is sovereign over history as well as nature. History, therefore, has direction, meaning, and purpose. What happens in Egypt and Canaan is the unfolding of the divine plan of history. Human beings may exercise their God-endowed freedom of will, as did Pharaoh in resisting God's demands, but human arrogance and defiance must inevitably bow to the superior and ultimately invincible will of God.

The story of the Exodus also defines the biblical understanding of God's personality. God is vitally concerned with injustice and oppression. This passion for justice manifests itself, above all, in the act of liberation of Israel from Egypt, and it translates into a demand on human beings to be especially sensitive to the needs of the unfortunates of society. The laws of the Book of the Covenant feature such imperatives as:

You shall not wrong a stranger or oppress him, for you were strangers in the land of Egypt. You shall not ill-treat any widow or orphan. If you do mistreat them, I will heed their outcry as soon as they cry out to Me, and My anger shall blaze forth. . . . If you lend money to My people, to the poor among you, do not act toward them as a creditor: exact no interest from them. If you take your neighbor's garment in pledge, you must return it to him before the sun sets; it is his only clothing, the sole covering for his skin. In what else shall he sleep? Therefore, if he cries out to Me, I will pay heed, for I am compassionate. . . . You shall not subvert the rights of your needy in their disputes. . . . You shall not oppress a stranger, for you know the feelings of the stranger, having yourself been strangers in the land of Egypt. (22:20–26 23:6, 9)

Another way in which the divine attributes of justice and mercy translate into legislation can be seen in the rules governing the relationship between master and slave. Although the institution of slavery is not expressly abolished, uniquely among the law collections of the ancient Near East it is humanized and transformed in favor of the rights of the slave as a human being. Thus, one day a week, on the Sabbath, the slave is entitled to the same rest as the master (20:9); the term of service is limited (21:2); a female slave cannot be sexually abused (21:7–11); slaves,

male and female, cannot be killed with impunity by their own master (21:20); and they automatically regain their freedom for the loss of a limb, even a tooth, as the result of maltreatment at his hands (21:26–27).

The definition of God's personality is more explicitly elaborated in Exodus 34:6–7. In this passage God is described as "a God compassionate and gracious, slow to anger, abounding in kindness and faithfulness, extending kindness to the thousandth generation, forgiving iniquity, transgression and sin." At the same time, he executes justice and "does not remit all punishment."

The most important and pervasive aspect of the Exodus experience is the covenant between God and Israel. This idea of the relationship between a people and God governed by a covenant is unparalleled outside the Bible in the ancient world. It is the most distinctive idea of the religion and it informs all subsequent biblical books. Flowing from the covenant is the idea that God demands exclusive allegiance and unwavering fidelity to its stipulations. The entire history of Israel is measured by the writers of scripture according to the people's fidelity or infidelity to this covenant, and the national weal and woe are considered to be consequent upon one or the other.

The Book of Exodus is also distinguished for its initiation of all the main institutions of Israel, except for the monarchy. The divine name, written in Hebrew by the tetragrammaton (YHVH), now became predominant. Other, earlier names fall into desuetude (3:12–14, 6:2–3). The battle against polytheism and idolatry, which is another major concern of the scriptures until the Babylonian exile, begins in Exodus with the idea of "judgments on all the gods of Egypt" (12:12) and the repeated prohibition against representing God in material form and against the use of images in worship (20:3–5, 23; 23:24; 34:13–17). The prophetic office, one of the most influential and persistent developments in Israelite history, has its origin in the person of Moses, the archetypal prophet, the messenger prophet, the guardian and monitor of the conscience of the people, and the intercessor before God on their behalf. The idea of a central shrine, the sacrificial system, and the priesthood similarly have their origin in this book. So does the religious calendar of Israel. The great pilgrimage festivals, originally seasonal celebrations rooted in the life of the soil, are here invested with an entirely new meaning and significance as they relate to the historical deliverance from Egypt. The religion thus became historicized. Last, but by no means least, the Egyptian bondage and God's liberation of Israel became the inspiration for moral tenets and ethical precepts, the stimulus for the promotion of human welfare (Daube 1963).

Bibliography

Commentaries

Cassuto, Umberto. *A Commentary on the Book of Exodus.* Translated by Israel Abrahama. Jerusalem, 1967.

Childs, Brevard S. *The Book of Exodus: A Critical Theological Commentary.* Philadelphia, 1974.

Clements, Robert Ernest. "Exodus." In *The Cambridge Bible Commentary on the New English Bible.* Cambridge, 1972.

Cole, R. Alan. *Exodus.* Tyndale Old Testament Commentaries. London, 1973.

Driver, S. R. *The Book of Exodus.* Rev. ed. Cambridge, 1918.

Hyatt, J. P. *Exodus.* The New Century Bible Commentary. Grand Rapids, 1971.

Background Studies

Ackerman, James S. "The Literary Context of the Moses Birth-Story." In *Literary Interpretations of Biblical Narratives,* edited by Kenneth R. R. Gros Louis with James S. Ackerman and Thayer S. Warshaw. Nashville, 1974. Pp. 74–119.

Anderson, Bernhard W. *Understanding the Old Testament.* 4th ed. Englewood Cliffs, N.J., 1986.

Bailey, Lloyd R. "The Golden Calf." *Hebrew Union College Annual* 42 (1971): 97–115.

Bates, Marston. "Insects in the Diet." *American Scholar* 29 (1959–1960): 46–49.

Bimson, J. J. *Redating the Exodus and Conquest.* Journal for the Study of the Old Testament, supplement series, no. 5. Sheffield, U.K., 1978.

Bodenheimer, F. S. "The Manna of Sinai." *Biblical Archaeologist* 10 (1947): 2–6.

Boecker, Hans Jochen. *Law and the Administration of Justice in the Old Testament and Ancient East.* Translated by Jeremy Moiser. Minneapolis, 1980.

Childs, Brevard S. "The Birth of Moses." *Journal of Biblical Literature* 84 (1965): 109–122.

Coats, George Wesley. *Rebellion in the Wilderness: The Murmuring Motif in the Wilderness Traditions of the Old Testament.* Nashville, 1968.

Cody, Aelred. "Exodus 18:12: Jethro Accepts a Covenant with the Israelites." *Biblica* 49 (1968): 153–166.

Cross, Frank Moore. "The Priestly Tabernacle." In *The Biblical Archaeologist Reader,* edited by G. Ernest Wright and David Noel Freedman. Garden City, N.Y., 1961. Pp. 201–228.

———. "The Priestly Tabernacle in the Light of Recent Research." In *Temples and High Places in Biblical Times,* edited by Avraham Biran. Jerusalem, 1981.

Daube, David. *Studies in Biblical Law.* Cambridge, 1947.

———. *The Exodus Pattern in the Bible.* London, 1963.

Davies, G. I. *The Way of the Wilderness: A Geographical Study of the Wilderness Itineraries in the Old Testament.* Cambridge Society for Old Testament Study Monograph Series, no. 5. Cambridge, 1979.

DeWit, C. *The Date and Route of the Exodus.* London, 1960.

Fensham, F. Charles. "Did a Treaty Between the Israelites and the Kenites Exist?" *Bulletin of the American Schools of Oriental Research* 175 (1964): 51–54.

Greenberg, Moshe. "Some Postulates of Biblical Criminal Law." In *Yehezkel Kaufmann Jubilee Volume,* edited by Menahem Haran. Jerusalem, 1960. Pp. 5–28.

———. *Understanding Exodus.* New York, 1969.

———. "More Reflections on Biblical Criminal Law." In *Studies in Bible.* Scripta Hierosolymitana, vol. 21. Jerusalem, 1986. Pp. 1–17.

Haran, Menahem. *Temples and Temple Service in Ancient Israel: An Inquiry into the Character of Cult Phenomena and the Historical Setting of the Priestly School.* Oxford, 1978.

Har-El, Menashe. *The Sinai Journeys: The Route of the Exodus.* Rev. ed. Los Angeles, 1983.

Hillers, D. R. *Covenant: The History of a Biblical Idea.* Baltimore, 1969.

Hort, G. "The Plagues of Egypt." *Zeitschrift für die alttestamentliche Wissenschaft* 69 (1957): 84–103; 70 (1958): 48–59.

Hurowitz, Victor. "The Priestly Account of Building the Tabernacle." *Journal of the American Oriental Society* 105 (1985): 21–30.

Kennedy, A. R. S. "Tabernacle." In *A Dictionary of the Bible,* edited by James Hastings *et al.,* vol. 4. New York, 1902. Pp. 653–668.

Kitchen, Kenneth Anderson. "Some Egyptian Background to the Old Testament." *Tyndale House Bulletin,* Cambridge, 5–6 (1960): 7–13.

———. *Ancient Orient and Old Testament.* Downers Grove, Ill., 1975.

———. *The Bible in Its World.* Downers Grove, Ill., 1977.

Loewenstamm, Samuel E. "The Making and Destruction of the Golden Calf." *Biblica* 48 (1967): 481–490; 56 (1975): 330–343.

McCarthy, Dennis J. *Treaty and Covenant: A Study in Form in the Ancient Oriental Documents and in the Old Testament.* Rome, 1963.

Nims, C. F. "Bricks Without Straw." *Biblical Archaeologist* 13 (1950): 22–28

Paul, Shalom M. *Studies in the Book of the Covenant in the Light of Cuneiform and Biblical Law.* Leiden, 1970.

Plastaras, James. *The God of Exodus: The Theology of the Exodus Narratives.* Milwaukee, 1966.

Rank, Otto. *The Myth of the Birth of the Hero.* Edited by Philip Freund. New York, 1964.

Redford, Donald B. "The Literary Motif of the Exposed Child." *Numen* 14 (1967): 209–228.

Sarna, Nahum M. *Exploring Exodus: The Heritage of Biblical Israel.* New York, 1986.

Segal, Judah Benzion. *The Hebrew Passover: From the Earliest Times to A.D. 70.* London, 1963.

Woudstra, Marten H. "The Tabernacle in Biblical Theological Perspective." In *New Perspectives on the Old Testament,* edited by John Barton Payne. Waco, Tex., 1970. Pp. 88–103.

Zevit, Ziony. "The Priestly Redaction and Interpretation of the Plagues Narrative in Exodus." *Jewish Quarterly Review* 66 (1976): 193–211.

NAHUM M. SARNA

Leviticus

THE BOOK OF Leviticus is more aptly described by its tannaitic, or early rabbinic, name, Torat Kohanim, the Priests' Manual. It is thematically an independent entity. In Exodus the Priestly code describes the construction of the cultic implements (the tabernacle and the priestly vestments); in Leviticus this static picture is converted into scenes from the living cult. The Book of Numbers that follows concentrates on the cultic laws of the camp in motion, for example, the military arrangement of the tribes, the censuses of the warriors, the transport of the sanctums, and their protection against encroachment. Since the latter is the function of the Levites, it is no accident that all the cultic laws pertaining to the Levites are in Numbers, and none are in Leviticus.

Although the Priests' Manual focuses on the priesthood, few laws are reserved for priests alone (Lev 8–10, 16:1–28, 21:1–22:16). Their role is defined in pedagogic terms: to teach the distinctions "between sacred and common, between the pure and impure" (10:10 [cf. 14:57], 15:31; Au. trans.). They must do this because Israel's moral sins and physical impurities are leading to the pollution of the sanctuary and the expulsion of Israel from its land. The priests, then, are charged with a double task: to instruct Israel not to cause defilement, and to purge the sanctuary whenever it is defiled. However, Leviticus is not just a collection of rituals. On the contrary, the ethical element fuses with and even informs the ritual so that one may seek a moral basis behind each ritual act.

The book comprises two Priestly sources, known as P (Priestly Code) and H (Holiness Code). They are not homogeneous; each betrays the work of schools. For example, two P strata are discernible in chapter 11 (a later P stratum in verses 24–38 and 47), as are two H strata in chapter 23 (a later H stratum in verses 2–3 and 39–43). Contrary to reigning scholarly consensus, H is a later source than P. This conclusion can be deduced from the interpolations (without considering the introductions and subscripts) in the main repository of P, chapters 1–16. These interpolations are 6:12–16; 7:22–27; 8:10–11; 10:10–11; 11:24–38, 39–40, 43–45; 14:33–53; 16:29–34. Whether they belong to P or H can be determined by two criteria: ideology and terminology.

The most important ideological distinction between the two codes rests in their contrasting concepts of holiness. For P, spatial holiness is limited to the sanctuary; for H, it is coextensive with the Promised Land. As for the holiness of persons, P restricts it to priests and Nazirites (cf. Num 6:5–8); H extends it to all of Israel. This expansion follows logically from H's doctrine of spatial holiness: since the land is holy, all who reside on it are to keep it that way. All adult Israelites are enjoined to attain holiness by observing God's commandments, and even the *ger*, the resident alien, must heed the prohibitive commandments, the violation of which threatens to pollute the land for all (for example, 18:26).

P's doctrine of holiness is static; H's is dynamic. On the one hand, P constricts holiness to the sanctuary and its priests. P assiduously avoids using the root *qdsh* ("holy") even in describing the Levites (compare their induction ceremony, Num 8:5–22, with the priestly consecration, Lev 8). H, on the other hand, though it concedes that only priests are innately holy, repeatedly calls upon Israel to strive for holiness. The dynamic quality of H's concept is highlighted by its resort to the same participial construction, *meqaddesh* (sanctified), to describe the holiness of the laity and the priesthood. Sanctification is an ongoing process for priests (21:8, 15, 23; 22:9, 16) as well as for all Israelites (21:8, 22:32). No different from the holiness of the Israelites, the holiness of the priests expands or contracts in proportion to their adherence to God's commandments.

The converse doctrine of pollution also varies sharply. P holds that the sanctuary is polluted by Israel's moral and ritual violations (4:2) committed anywhere in the camp (but not outside) and that this pollution can and must be effaced by the violator's purification offering and, if committed deliberately, by priestly sacrifice and confession (16:3–22). H, however, concentrates instead on the polluting effects of Israel's violations of the covenant (26:15), for example, incest (18, 20:11–24), idolatry (20:1–6), and depriving the land of its sabbaths (26:34–35). Pollution for H is nonritualistic, as shown by its metaphoric usage (e.g., 18:20, 24; 19:31) and by the fact that the polluted land cannot be expiated by ritual, which would irrevocably lead to the expulsion of its inhabitants (18:24–29, 20:22).

The difference between P and H is also discernible in their distinctive vocabularies, especially in their use of homonyms and synonyms. Examples of the former are *shiqes* and *time'*, which in P mean "defile (by ingestion)" and "defile (by contact)" respectively (11:8, 11), whereas in H they are used interchangeably (20:25). Examples of the latter are P's term for "law," which is always given in the feminine form *huqqa, huqqot* (e.g., 10:9), whereas H will also resort to masculine *hoq, huqqim* (e.g., 26:46), and the term "commit sacrilege," which in P is *ma'al* (5:21) and in H *hillel* (19:8).

On the basis of these two criteria, ideology and

terminology, which of the above-listed interpolations can be said to be P and which H? The blood prohibition in 7:22–27 applies to "all your settlements" (7:26), of interest only to H, since the violation pollutes the land, not the sanctuary (P). The passage in 10:10–11 contains the masculine plural *huqqim*, a characteristic of H. The dietary injunction, 11:43–45, uses *shiqes* and *time'* synonymously and enjoins Israel to holiness, both unmistakable signs of H. The law of the afflicted house (14:33–53) applies anywhere in the land, a concern only of H. Finally, 16:29–34 includes the *ger*, of relevance only to H.

These pervasive intrusions of H characteristics into the P text point to the strong possibility that H is not only subsequent to P but is also P's redactor. Furthermore, when notice is taken of H interpolations generously distributed throughout the books of Exodus and Numbers—e.g., the *ger* and the Passover offering (Exod 12:47–49, Num 9:14); the Sabbath law (Exod 31:12–17; note the reference to the "sanctifying" of Israel in verse 13); the *ger* and the sacrifices (Num 15:13–16, 22–31); the tassels law (Num 15:37–41 [note that Israel is enjoined "to be holy," in verse 41]); the subscript to the laws on vows (Num 30:17; note that the term for "law" here is *huqqim*)—the conclusion begins to form that H may also be the redactor of Exodus and Numbers, at least of their legal sections.

The Book of Leviticus divides into the main P text (1–16), comprising descriptions of the sacrificial system, the inaugural service at the sanctuary, and the laws of impurities; the H text (17–26), and a section on commutation of gifts to the sanctuary (chap. 27).

THE SACRIFICIAL SYSTEM (CHAPTERS 1–7)

In chapters 1–5 the sacrifices are characterized by donor: chapters 1–3 speak of sacrifices brought spontaneously (burnt, cereal, well-being); chapters 4–5, of sacrifices required for expiation (purification and reparation). Chapters 6–7 regroup these sacrifices in order of their sanctity. The common denominator of the sacrifices discussed in these chapters is that they arise in answer to an unpredictable religious or emotional need, and are thereby set apart from the sacrifices of the public feasts and fasts that are fixed by the calendar (chaps. 9, 16, 23; *cf.* Num 28–29).

The Burnt Offering
(Chapter 1)

The burnt offering is the only sacrifice that is entirely consumed on the altar (*cf.* Deut 33:10; 1 Sam 7:9). Verses 3–5 summarize the major concepts of the sacrificial system: imposition of hands, acceptance, expiation, slaughter, blood manipulation, entrance to the tent of meeting. The donor is an active participant in the ritual. The burnt offering must be chosen from male, unblemished, and eligible species of the herd, flock, or birds. It is probably the oldest and most popular sacrifice (*Tosef. Zev.* 13:1). Its function here is expiatory (v. 4; *cf.* 9:7, 14:20, Job 1:5, 42:8, and Ugaritic Texts [UT] 9:1, 7), but in P, whenever it is offered by an individual, the occasion is a joyous one (*cf.* Lev 22:17–21, Num 15:1–11).

The Cereal Offering
(Chapter 2)

In the non-Priestly texts this term connotes both "a present made to secure or retain goodwill" (Driver 1898; e.g., Gen 32:14–22 [EV 13–21]) and a tribute brought by subjects to their overlords, both human (Judg 3:15–18) and divine. This sacrifice may be brought in either animal or vegetable form (Gen 4:3; 1 Sam 2:17). In P, however, it is exclusively cereal, either choice flour (Lev 2:1–3) or cakes of choice flour (2:4–10) or roasted grain (2:14–16). Because leaven and honey (fruit syrup) ferment, whereas salt preserves, the first two are forbidden, and salt is required on the altar (2:11–13). Leaven, however, is permitted as a first-fruit offering to the priest (23:17; 2 Chr 31:5). The restriction to cereal emphasizes that man's tribute to God should be from the fruits of his labors on the soil. In daily life, however, the aspect of appeasing God may also have been present (1 Sam 26:19; *cf. ANET* [2d ed.], p. 439, l. 51). Because cereal was abundant and cheap, it became the poor man's burnt offering (Philo, *On the Special Laws*, 1.271; *Lev. Rabbah* 8:4).

The Well-Being Offering
(Chapter 3)

The well-being offering never serves as expiation (but *cf.* chap. 17). Its basic function is simply to permit the consumption of flesh. The motivation was usually spontaneous and occasioned by a sense of elation. The rules are similar to those of the burnt offering, except that the victims may be female but not birds. Also, being of lesser sanctity, its portions are assigned to the donor as well as to God. The choicest internal fats (suet) are turned to smoke.

The Purification Offering
(Chapter 4)

The purpose of the purification offering is to remove the impurity inflicted upon the sanctuary by the inadvertent violation of prohibitive laws. The brazen violation of these laws is punishable by death through divine agency (Num 15:27–31). Other instances specify the nature of the violations: defiling of holy days (e.g., Passover, Day of Atonement), contamination of sanctums (7:20–21), prohibited cultic acts (17:3–4, 8–9) and illicit sex (18:29).

Borderline Cases of the Purification Offering
(5:1–13)

Rabbinic tradition distinguishes between the purification offering of chapter 4 and that of 5:1–13, calling the latter "the scaled offering" geared to the financial means of the offender (not his status, as in chap. 4). This separate offering probably arises from the failure or inability to cleanse impurity immediately upon its incurrence.

The Reparation Offering
(5:14–26 [EV 5:14–6:7])

The reparation offering is prescribed for trespass upon the property of God or man, the latter through the use of a false oath. The sin to which it relates is desecration: the sanctums or the name of God have become desanctified (as opposed to cases of the purification offering in chapter 4, where the sin is contamination of sanctums).

Supplementary Instructions
(Chapters 6–7)

Since the well-being offering is eaten chiefly by the donor, the rules pertain mainly to him (7:11–34, esp. 7:23, 7:29). Otherwise they are the concerns of the officiating priest. The subjects are the altar fire (6:1–6 EV 8–13]); the manner and place for eating the cereal offering (6:7–11 EV 14–18]); the daily cereal offering of the high priest and the voluntary one of the ordinary priest (6:12–16 EV 19–23]); safeguards in sacrificing the purification offering (6:17–23 EV 24–30]); the ritual for the reparation offering (7:17, missing in chapter 5); the priestly share in the burnt and cereal offering (7:8–10); the types of well-being offering and their taboos (7:11–21); the prohibition against eating suet and blood (7:22–27); the priestly share of the well-being offering, set aside by the donor (7:28–36); the summation (7:37–38). The inclusion of the consecration offering before the well-being offering in this summation suggests that a section based on Exodus 29 originally preceded 7:11.

THE INAUGURAL SERVICE AT THE SANCTUARY (CHAPTERS 8–10)

In chapters 8–10, which follow logically and chronologically upon Exodus 35–40, the priests are inducted into service after the priestly vestments and the tabernacle are completed. It is not Aaron, however, but Moses who dominates the scene. He is the one who conducts the inaugural service, consecrates the priests, and apportions all tasks. Aaron is clearly answerable to him, as seen from their confrontation in chapter 10:16–20. Strikingly, the superiority of prophet over priest is insisted upon by the Priestly document.

The Consecration of the Priests (Chapter 8)

"To ordain you" (8:33) is literally "to fill your hands." In Scripture this phrase is used exclusively for the consecration of priests (Exod 32:29; Judg 17:5, 12; 1 Kgs 13:33), but in the archives of Mari it refers to the distribution of booty. Thus, the Hebrew idiom indicates that installation rites officially entitle the priests to their share of the revenues and sacrifices brought to the sanctuary. "As the Lord commanded Moses" concludes each phase of the consecration ceremony, a reminder that this chapter is a repetition of the instructions in Exodus 29.

The Priests Assume Office (Chapter 9)

On the eighth day following the week of consecration, the priests begin their official duties. They offer up special sacrifices for the people "that the presence of the Lord may appear" (9:6; also 9:4, 9:23). Indeed, the whole purpose of the sacrificial system is revelation, the assurance that God is with his people. However, God's presence is never assumed to be a coefficient of the ritual performed (in contrast to other religions); it is always viewed as an act of his grace.

The Sin of Nadab and Abihu (10:1–11)

The two sons of Aaron are consumed by an "alien" fire. That the fire was "alien" was the fault of either the offering or the offerer. Most likely the fire was taken from elsewhere, not from the altar (16:12, Num 17:11 [EV 16:46]).

The Consumption of the Initiatory Offerings (10:12–20)

This section continues the material from chapter 9. The cereal and well-being offerings are eaten by the priests in accordance with the injunctions of 6:9 [EV 6:16] and 7:28–34. But the procedure for the purification offering is switched from the individual to the communal form: the disposal of blood (9:9, 15; 10:18) has been carried out in accordance with 4:30 but not the disposal of its flesh (10:11), which follows 4:12 rather than 6:19 [EV 6:26] and despite 6:23 [EV 6:30]. The death of Nadab and Abihu has intervened. Aaron follows the more stringent procedure of destroying rather than eating the sacrificial meat because it has been doubly polluted by the sin and death of his sons. Its ingestion would not be "acceptable in the sight of the Lord," and it must be burned outside the camp.

THE LAWS OF IMPURITIES

Chapters 11–16 deal with four sources of impurity: carcasses (chap. 11), childbirth (chap. 12), scale disease (chaps. 13–14), and genital discharges (chap. 15). (A fifth source, the corpse, is dealt with in

Numbers 19.) The common denominator of these impurity sources is that they stand for death. Blood and semen represent the forces of life and their loss, that is, death. The wasting of the body, the characteristic of scale disease (chaps. 13–14), symbolizes the death process (*cf*. Num 12:12) as much as the loss of blood and semen. Carcasses (chap. 11) and corpses (Num 19) obviously are the epitome of death and therefore of impurity. Since impurity and holiness are semantic opposites, it is incumbent upon Israel to prevent impurity or, at least, to control its occurrence, lest it impinge upon the sanctuary, the realm of the holy God.

Animal Impurities
(Chapter 11)

The criteria for permitted animals have but one purpose: to limit Israel's access to the animal kingdom. The food and blood prohibitions form a united dietary code allowing humans to consume meat and not be brutalized in the process.

Land animals (11:1–8). Compare verses 3–4 with Deuteronomy 14:4–6, where the permitted quadrupeds are named. The classification is the result not of empirical medical knowledge (Albright) but of the universal need to classify the phenomena by establishing beneficent and destructive categories (Douglas).

Fish (11:9–12). That neither prohibited nor permitted fish are enumerated (either here or in Deuteronomy 14:9) may be explained by the relative absence of sea life in the Mediterranean prior to the construction of the Suez Canal. Fish—alone among the creatures—were not named by Adam (Gen 2:19–20).

Birds and winged insects (11:13–23). No classification is given for birds, probably because none was known. A number of the identifications (translations) are conjectural.

Impurity by contact with carcasses (11:24–40). This section is an insertion from another source, since it interrupts the fourfold classification (11:46) of creatures that may not be eaten. Nonporous articles are polluted by cadavers of the eight species listed in verses 29–30 and must be washed, but contaminated earthenware (porous and absorbent, 6:21 [EV 6:28]) may never be reused. Food and seed grain are immune

to impurity except when moist, since water is an impurity carrier.

Swarming things (11:41–42). Continues 11:23.

Israel enjoined to be holy (11:43–45). See the introduction above.

Summary (11:46–47).

The Impurity of Childbirth
(Chapter 12)

For seven days following the birth of a male child and fourteen days following that of a female child, no conjugal relations are allowed. For an additional period of thirty-three and sixty-six days respectively, contact with sanctums is proscribed. That sacrifices are brought only subsequently indicates that earlier ideas of demonic control of this period have been rejected. The rite certifies that passage of the prescribed time has removed impurity, and it is scaled to economic circumstances (5:7–13, 14:21–32).

The Impurity of Scale Disease
(Chapters 13–14)

The priest is instructed to identify and isolate those who are afflicted with scale disease, wrongly translated as "leprosy." It is a noncontagious condition, probably vitiligo or, less likely, psoriasis. Leviticus 13:47–59 describes the deterioration of garments probably because of mildew or fungus, and 14:33–53 describes the infection of houses because of the spread of saltpeter or moss, in which case quarantine procedures are also enforced. Unusual considerations for property are reflected in verse 36: the priest clears the house prior to his inspection so that the contents will not be condemned with the house.

The Impurity of Genital Discharges
(Chapter 15)

This chapter is composed of two sections: natural discharges of men and women (15:16–18 and 19–24, respectively), an impurity removed simply by bathing, and pathological discharges (15:2–15 and 25–30, respectively), which require sacrificial expiation.

The Impurities of Sanctuary and Nation
(Chapter 16)

According to verse 1, chapter 16 follows upon chapter 10. Thus, chapters 11–15 are an insert listing the specific impurities that will contaminate the sanctuary (15:31) for which the purification ritual of chapter 16 is mandated.

THE HOLINESS SOURCE (H)

The remainder of the Book of Leviticus, it is often held, consists largely of an independent code in which moral and ritual laws alternate, motivated by holiness. This, however, is questionable. Chapter 17, the alleged beginning of the code, is connected thematically and verbally with the preceding chapters. Chapters 25–26, which are often alleged to be the conclusion, form an independent scroll, to judge from the unique vocabulary (e.g., 25:18–19, 26:5), theme (25:8–13; 26:34–35, 43), and redaction (25:1, 26:46). Nonetheless, much of the language and some ideas in chapters 17–26 differ from the first part of Leviticus.

Killing for Food
(Chapter 17)

Whosoever kills a sacrificial animal outside the sanctuary is guilty of murder (17:3–4). Two ends are thus achieved: Sacrifice to "satyrs" is abolished (17:5–9), and expiation for killing the animal is assured through a ritual by which its lifeblood is returned to its creator, either upon the altar (17:10–12) or by being drained and covered by earth, in the case of game animals (17:13–14; cf. Deut 12:16). The inescapable conclusion to be drawn from the context is that verse 11 has nothing to do with the expiation of sin in general.

On Being Holy
(Chapters 18–20)

Though these three chapters were originally independent, they are thematically united: chapter 20 prescribes the penalties for the illicit relations and homicidal cult practices proscribed in chapter 18 (20:1–5) and for violating the ban on magic put into effect in 19:31 (20:6). Moreover, the entire unit is framed by a single goal: separation from the Canaanites and their idolatrous and immoral practices, which pollute the divinely chosen land (18:3, 18: 24–30, 20:22–24). The arraignment of Ezekiel 22 contains a mixture of ethical and ritual sins based solely on those chapters, indicating that their written formulation is preexilic.

The key word in this section is *holy*. This word clusters in the food prohibitions (Lev 11:44–47, 20:23–26) and only one other context, the rules concerning the priesthood, 21:6–8. This fact is significant. The priesthood, Israel, and mankind, respectively, form three rings of decreasing holiness about the center, God. The biblical ideal is that all Israel shall be "a kingdom of priests and a holy nation" (Exod 19:6). If Israel is to attain a higher sphere of holiness, it must abide by a more rigid code of behavior than that practiced by the nations, just as the priest lives by more stringent standards than those applying to common Israelites. Holiness, then, implies separation, and is so defined in chapter 20:26. The positive aspect of holiness is discussed in chapter 19.

Illicit sexual relations (chapter 18). The list of prohibitions is framed (18:1–5 and 24–30) by castigating the sexual mores of the Egyptians and the Canaanites. In contrast, Israel is charged with an exacting code of family purity whose violation means death (20:10–16). Only the Holiness Source proclaims the sanctity of the land of Canaan; hence the responsibility of both Israelites and resident strangers to maintain its sanctity (18:26–27, 20:2, 24:22). The moral justification for its conquest (18:27–28, 20:22) is also a warning: if guilty of the same infractions, Israel, too, will be "vomited out."

Imitatio Dei—positive holiness (chapter 19). For Israel, "holy" means more than that which is unapproachable. It becomes a positive concept, an inspiration and a goal associated with God's nature and his desire for humans to be holy: "You shall be holy; for I . . . am holy" (19:2). That which man is not, nor can ever fully be, but which he is commanded to emulate and approximate, is what the Bible calls "holy." Holiness means *imitatio Dei*—the life of godliness.

How can human beings imitate God? The answer of Leviticus 19 is given in a series of ethical and ritual commands, above which soars the commandment to love all persons (19:18), including aliens (19:34). Such love must be concretely expressed in deeds: equality in civil justice (20:2; 24:16, 22; Num 35:15), free loans (25:35–38, Deut 10:18, 23:20), and free gleanings (19:9–10).

Penalties for certain infractions (chapter 20). The penalties for illicit sexual relations are graded according to the severity: verses 9–16, death by man; verses 17–19, death by God; verses 20–21, childlessness. Since there had been such apparent and notable violators as Abraham (v. 17; *cf.* Gen 20:12) and Amram (v. 19; *cf.* Exod 6:20), the offender may only be reprimanded; God alone will settle with him. Of the idolatrous varieties, only Molech worship and oracles through mediums are singled out, the former because of its monstrousness and the latter because of its prevalence (Deut 18:9–12; 1 Sam 28:9; Isa 8:19). The absence of the lofty pronouncements of chapter 19 from this list is mute evidence that ethics are really unenforceable.

The Disqualifications of Priests and Sacrifices (Chapters 21–22)

Restrictions are placed upon the priests in order to guard against moral and ritual defilement, which might entail dire consequences for them and the people (22:9, 15–16; *cf.* 4:3, 15:31).

The Festivals (Chapter 23)

H's listing of the festivals is distinguished from Old Epic (JE) tradition (Exod 23:14–17, 34:21–23) and D (Deut 16) by emphasis on natural and agricultural data. Because Leviticus 23 addresses lay people, like farmers, rather than priests, the New Moon festival is omitted (on this day the Israelites have no special duties or prohibitions). Indeed, with the exception of verses 13 and 18–20, all requirements of the priestly, public cult are ignored, and only the offerings of individual farmers are enumerated.

Miscellany (Chapter 24)

The lamp oil (24:1–4). Since the lampstand stood inside the sanctuary, its greater sanctity required the use of pure oil and also required it to be lighted by the high priest (Exod 30:7, Num 8:1–4; "sons" in Exod 27:21 is a probable error).

The Bread of the Presence (24:5–9).

The law of blasphemy (24:10–14 and 23). Blasphemy means more than speaking contemptuously of God, for which there is no stated penalty (Exod 22:27

[EV 22:28]). It must involve the additional offense of uttering the tetragrammaton, and it is the combination of the two (24:15–16) that warrants the death penalty. The tetragrammaton's power affects not only the speaker but the hearers; their contamination is literally transferred back to the blasphemer by the ritual of the imposition of hands.

An appendage of civil-damage laws (24:15–22). The extension of *lex talionis* (Exod 21:23–25, Deut 19:21) to the stranger is one of the great moral achievements of P's legislation. Every distinction is eradicated not only between the powerful and the helpless but even between the Israelite and the non-Israelite. The interpolation of these civil statutes, with their emphasis upon the resident alien, is due to the legal status of the half-Israelite offender.

The Sabbatical and Jubilee Years (Chapter 25)

Each seventh year is a sabbath of liberating respite for Israelite slaves (Exod 21:2–6, Deut 15:12–18), debtors (Deut 15:1–11), and the land (Exod 23:10–11). In H, this "full" sabbatical is reserved for the jubilee, whereas the seventh-year sabbatical applies only to the land.

The Concluding Exhortation (Chapter 26)

The threat of total destruction and exile appears in three other books of the Bible: Deuteronomy, Jeremiah (while he was still a deuteronomic evangelist), and Ezekiel (whose eschatology is largely based on Leviticus 26). These books also share with this chapter the preprophetic view that cultic transgressions alone cause the nation's collapse; idolatry (26:1) and the neglect of the sabbatical system (26:2 and 34–35) are specified here. Since the events in chapters 25–26 are attributed to Israel's sojourn at Mount Sinai (25:1, 26:46), these may well constitute the text of the Sinaitic covenant according to the Holiness Source.

Commutation of Gifts to the Sanctuary (Chapter 27)

The following gifts are discussed: persons (27:1–8), animals (9–13), houses (14–15), land (16–25), firstlings (26–27), devotions (28–29), and tithes (30–33). The organizing principle of this chapter is that gifts offerable on the altar may never be desanctified, but nonofferable gifts (with the exception of devotions) may be desanctified by their sale or redemption.

Bibliography

Commentaries

Driver, S. R. *The Book of Leviticus: A New English Translation.* New York, 1898.

Elliger, K. *Leviticus.* Tübingen, 1966.

Hoffmann, David Z. *Das Buch Leviticus, übersetzt und erklärt.* Berlin, 1905–1906.

Kalisch, M. M. *A Historical and Critical Commentary on the Old Testament.* London, 1866.

Milgrom, Jacob. *Leviticus,* vol. 1. New York, 1989.

Snaith, N. H. *Leviticus and Numbers.* London, 1967.

Wenham, G. J. *The Book of Leviticus.* Grand Rapids, 1979.

General Works

Albright, W. F. *Yahweh and the Gods of Canaan.* New York, 1968.

Brichto, Herbert Chanan. "On Slaughter and Sacrifice, Blood and Atonement." *Hebrew Union College Annual* 47 (1976): 19–56.

Douglas, Mary. *Purity and Danger.* London, 1966.

Gray, George Buchanan. *Sacrifice in the Old Testament.* Oxford, 1925.

Haran, Menahem. *Temples and Temple Service in Ancient Israel.* Oxford, 1978.

Hurvitz, Avi. *A Linguistic Study of the Relationship Between the Priestly Source and the Book of Ezekiel.* Paris, 1982.

Janowski, Bernd. *Sühne als Heilsgeschehen.* Neukirchen-Vluyn, 1982.

Levine, Baruch A. *In the Presence of the Lord: A Study of Cult and Some Cultic Terms in Ancient Israel.* Leiden, 1974.

Milgrom, Jacob. "Priestly Terminology and the Political and Social Structure of Pre-Monarchic Israel." *Jewish Quarterly Review* 69 (1978): 65–81.

———. *Sancta Contagion and Altar/City Asylum.* Vetus Testamentum Supplements, vol. 32. Leiden, 1982.

———. "The Graduated Chattā't of Leviticus 5:1–13." *Journal of the American Oriental Society* 103 (1983): 249–254.

———. *Studies in Cultic Theology and Terminology.* Leiden, 1983.

Rendtorff, Rolf. *Studien zur Geschichte des Opfers im alten Israel.* Neukirchen-Vluyn, 1967.

Rodriguez, A. M. *Substitution in the Hebrew Cultus.* Berrien Springs, Mich., 1982.

Vaux, Roland de. *Studies in Old Testament Sacrifice.* Cardiff, Wales, 1964.

Vink, J. G. "The Date and Origin of the Priestly Code in the Old Testament." *Oudtestamentische Studiën* 15 (1969): 1–144.

Weinfeld, Moshe. "Social and Cultic Institutions in the Priestly Source Against Their Ancient Near Eastern Background." *Proceedings of the Eighth World Congress of Jewish Studies. Bible Studies.* 1983.

JACOB MILGROM

Numbers

HOW FAITHFUL IS God to promises made to an ungrateful and rebellious people? Does God give people a second chance? What does it mean to be a holy community, and how is that sanctity to be maintained? What kind of leadership does a journeying people need on its way between promise and fulfillment? How does God provide when the leaders struggle under their burden or even abandon their task? These are some of the important questions addressed in the Book of Numbers.

The Book of Numbers is the fourth of the five books in the Pentateuch or Torah, the first major division of the Hebrew Bible. The book opens with the people of Israel encamped at the foot of Mount Sinai, receiving instructions from God through the word of their leader, Moses. At the conclusion of the book, the people are encamped in the plains of Moab opposite Jericho, poised to enter the Promised Land west of the Jordan River. While an initial reading of the book may give the impression of a disorganized conglomeration of material, there is in fact some overall organization to the presentation. And while its confusing stories and ancient ritual legislation may at first seem strange and remote, even such obscure material takes on new meaning as its context is clarified.

THEOLOGICAL THEMES

Numbers is a book about a people on the road from bondage to freedom—people repeatedly complain about their lot, blame their situation on God and the leaders divinely chosen for them, and find the old days of captivity more enticing than the challenges of their journey toward the fulfillment of God's promises to them. The book incorporates some of a larger body of Pentateuchal legislation that guided this people in various periods as it sought to maintain its status as a holy community under the leadership of priests and prophets. When the burden of leadership becomes too great, God provides assistants to share the load; nonetheless, the leaders are required to lead the people rightly in reverence for God or risk revocation of their leadership responsibility. Numbers pays special attention to duties of the priests as representatives of the people before God.

Most basic, and undergirding all else, Numbers is a book about God, about the promised yet ever-surprising loyalty of the God who refuses to let go of the people, no matter how rebellious they may be. It is a book about God's provision of material sustenance and leadership, God's acts of intervention on behalf of the people, and God's sustaining blessing of the people as a new generation arises and stands poised at the edge of the Promised Land. As a book about God's care for a people who had a dream but often found themselves too tired or too afraid to move toward fulfillment of that dream, it is a book for such people in every age.

NAME

The English name "Numbers" is a translation of the title ascribed to this book in the Greek (*Arithmoi*) and later Latin (*Numeri*) translations of the Hebrew scriptures. This name derives primarily from the records of two occasions on which Moses takes a census of the Israelites (Num 1–4, 26). Some ancient Jewish traditions also look to the census in referring to Numbers as the "fifth of the numbering" (i.e., the one-fifth of the Torah that includes the counting of the people). Although these chapters concerning census-taking are an important key to understanding the organization of the book, they comprise only a minor part of its overall content. The alternative Hebrew name of the book, *Bamidbar* (in the wilderness), more clearly suggests the range and interest of the book as a whole.

COMPOSITION

Although there is a longstanding tradition that the entire Pentateuch was composed by Moses, this tradition has been called into question by careful studies of the text ever since the early centuries of the common era. Today most Christian and Jewish scholars believe that the Book of Numbers received essentially its present shape during the period of the Babylonian exile (586–539 B.C.E.), after the destruction of Solomon's temple and the city of Jerusalem by King Nebuchadrezzar of Babylon. At that time an anonymous individual or group usually referred to as the Priestly writers (because of their special interest in things pertinent to the priesthood of Israel) prepared an edition of Genesis, Exodus, Leviticus, and Numbers and incorporated older written and oral traditions of the Israelite community. Some of these traditions may go back to the time of Moses; others may have come into existence later and were projected back to the time of Moses. The Priestly writers were concerned with preserving the ancient narrative and legal traditions in such a way that they would have special relevance for the Israelite community in exile in Babylon and could serve as a blueprint for their life in years to come, whether in Babylon or back in their homeland of Judah.

A principal source incorporated by the Priestly writers was the so-called Old Epic tradition. This tradition probably took shape in oral storytelling

during the period of the Judges (*ca.* 1200–1000 B.C.E.) and then was committed to writing during the early period of the monarchy. There may have been two written versions, one (usually designated J) made in Jerusalem in the era of David and Solomon (1000–922) and another (usually designated E) in the independent kingdom of northern Israel that split off from Jerusalem after Solomon's death. In Numbers it is not generally possible to separate J from E, and some preexilic, non-Priestly materials from other independent traditions seem to have been worked into the text as well. Specialists are able to distinguish between Priestly (P) and non-Priestly materials with some precision, but further subdivisions are less certain.

Although the basic shape of the book was established during the Babylonian exile, it seems clear that various materials—sometimes whole chapters, sometimes a few verses or even just a phrase—were added to the text later, probably during the next 200 years. The Priestly transmitters of the tradition wanted to be sure that all the regulations of their own era concerning matters of worship and its leadership, as well as other important matters of community legislation, could be traced to the founders, Moses and Aaron. Unlike today, the custom of those times permitted and even honored such attribution of material to famous personages of the past.

STRUCTURE

All stages of composition described apply to Genesis through Numbers as a whole, although Leviticus and Numbers contain most of the postexilic additions. In Numbers, especially, this overall process resulted in a book with a seeming hodgepodge of material, jumping from one subject to another, often without a discernible reason for the change in topic. As Dennis Olson (1985) demonstrates in detail, the apparently miscellaneous character of the book has led to great diversity of opinion concerning the outline of Numbers, even in its broadest form. Outlines based on chronology, geography, or thematic considerations lead to various results, and many competing options are possible within each of these main categories.

There is broad agreement that a major break in the narrative occurs at 10:11, with the story of the Israelites' departure from the wilderness of Sinai. Recognition of this break poses, however, two major questions: First, why does the book itself begin in the middle of the Sinai material (which extends back through Leviticus all the way to Exodus 19)? And second, what corresponding division(s) should be identified in the subsequent chapters of Numbers?

With regard to the first question, some scholars have viewed the division between Leviticus and Numbers as purely arbitrary and without significance. But since the breaks between the other Pentateuchal books are fairly obviously related to a shift in content (Genesis/Exodus: the death of Joseph; Exodus/Leviticus: the dedication of the tabernacle; Numbers/Deuteronomy: the final speeches of Moses), it seems likely that ancient tradition did regard the first census-taking as a turning point, even though it lay within the traditions associated with Sinai. Olson (1985, 48–49) emphasizes that the material of Leviticus is summarized at its conclusion as God's word to Moses "on Mount Sinai," whereas the opening of Numbers presents God's command to Moses "in the wilderness of Sinai," a significant distinction in locale for the ancient hearer.

The question concerning subdivisions in the remainder of Numbers is more difficult to answer. Most have supposed that another major break corresponding to that at 10:11 comes either at 20:14 (departure from Kadesh in the wilderness) or at 22:1 (the arrival of the people in the Plains of Moab). The miscellaneous character of the material in the book as a whole has led to a proliferation of variations on this basic consensus; some scholars would even view an attempt to outline the book as an arbitrary imposition of order upon the miscellany of the book.

An alternative approach that cuts through much of the confusion is to concentrate on the two census texts in the book as the key to its structure and organization (Olson 1985). The opening chapter of Numbers enumerates all males of the first generation who are of military age (twenty and older) and ready to march toward the Promised Land. This is followed in chapters 3–4 by a special enumeration of the Levites (who are not counted in the census of the rest of the community). Chapter 26 provides a similar enumeration of adult males

ready for battle, followed by enumeration of the Levites. The concluding comment in chapter 26 makes clear that this new census is taken after the first generation has died out during the forty years' wandering occasioned by the people's disobedience:

These were those numbered by Moses and Eleazar the priest, who numbered the people of Israel in the plains of Moab by the Jordan at Jericho. But among these there was not a man of those numbered by Moses and Aaron the priest, who had numbered the people of Israel in the wilderness of Sinai. For the LORD had said of them, "They shall die in the wilderness." There was not left a man of them, except Caleb the son of Jephunneh and Joshua the son of Nun. (26:63–65; RSV)

The census itself shows that, while there had been some shifting in the total population of individual tribes, the grand total remained constant at approximately 600,000 persons counted, the traditional number of Exodus participants (aside from women, children, and camp followers) according to Exodus 12:37–38 and Numbers 11:21.

According to this analysis, chapters 1–25 present the story of the Exodus generation, which rebelled and refused to take the land, and the story of how this generation gradually died off, partly in the course of judgments for more rebellions. Chapters 26–36 present the story of the successor generation, which is under the same requirement of obedience and is to learn from the fate of its parents. While the first part of the book records the death of everyone except Moses and the two faithful spies Caleb and Joshua, in the second part of the book potential acts of disobedience on the part of the people are averted and no deaths are reported among the Israelites of the new generation.

Most significant of these events involving the second generation is the narrative in chapter 32 of Moses' warning to the Reubenites and Gadites who want to settle in Gilead and not participate with the other tribes in the taking of the land west of the Jordan. Moses reminds them of the dreadful fate (recounted in chapter 14) that befell the spies and indeed the entire previous generation because they failed to take the entire land at God's command. The Reubenites and Gadites swiftly promise to participate fully in the twelve-tribe operation before returning to Gilead. In this text the phrase "from twenty years old and upward" (32:11) is quoted from 14:29 to identify the generation that had been condemned to die in the wilderness for refusing to go up to the land at God's command. This key phrase, used here in a military context, refers explicitly to the group counted in each census, also "from twenty years old and upward . . . able to go forth to war" (1:3, 26:2; RSV).

OUTLINE

The preceding observations and a variety of lesser connecting points make it clear that the book should be seen in two parts, chapters 1–25 and 26–36. There are still many possibilities in the subdividing of each major part, however; it seems probable that various transmitters of the tradition viewed the emphases of the story differently, so that the text itself incorporates overlapping outlines.

The difficulties in further subdividing the story are threefold. First and most basic is the tension implicit in the tradition about where the "wilderness" ends and "the land" begins. The question is whether the Israelite territory in Transjordan is to be regarded as part of "the land." All adults of the generation who fled Egypt (except Joshua and Caleb) are supposed to die "in this wilderness" (14:29). According with the two-part division of the book based on the census lists, one would assume that the Israelites who die in the plague recorded in Numbers 25 are in fact the last of those adults counted in the first census (although the text never explicitly identifies their generation). Yet at the time of the plague the people are in the plains of Moab and have already taken the Transjordanian territories of Sihon and Og, which will subsequently be allotted to the tribes of Reuben and Gad and half of Manasseh. To reconcile the time of the ending of the first generation with the time of Israel's entrance into the land, one must assume that "the land" does not include Transjordan, but only the territory west of the Jordan River, even though Israelite tribes lived in Transjordan. This point of view is indeed presented in the boundary summary of Numbers 34, where the eastern boundary is given as the Jordan River; it is also conspicuous in other biblical texts (e.g., Jos 5:12, which records that the manna ceased after the people

had crossed the Jordan). Once the capture of Transjordan is thus eliminated from the "land" tradition and attached to the "wilderness" tradition geographically as well as chronologically, there remains no one geographical subdivision of singular importance between 10:11 and chapter 26. One may opt either for the beginning of the attempt to enter the land from the east (20:14 or 20:22), or for the arrival in the plains of Moab as a staging ground for taking "the land" (22:1). Alternatively, one may ignore geography altogether and organize chapters 1–25 around the theme of disobedience or around the theme of leadership.

The second major difficulty in outlining the text lies in the miscellaneous character and seemingly random location of the legal materials found in Numbers. As can be seen in the outline below, these laws are found in chapters 5–6, 15, 19, 27, 28–30, 35, and 36. Itinerary lists and instructions for priestly duties are also scattered through the narrative material in a way that seems to defy modern logic. A variety of explanations has been offered in rabbinic tradition and in modern scholarship, but all seem to be ad hoc.

Third, chapters 26–36 overall give the impression of a series of appendixes, despite the structure provided by the two-census pattern. The separation of the two narrative/legal texts concerning the daughters of Zelophehad (Num 27 and 36), the commissioning of Joshua (27:12–23) before the end of Moses' military leadership, the view of Balaam in 31:16, so different from his portrayal in chapters 22–24, and the disproportionate amount of legislative material all support the view that much of chapters 26–36 consists of additions to the basic core of the book.

In light of the many complications, the outline that follows offers just one of many possible approaches. Anyone who studies Numbers should take up the challenge of outlining the book, if only to discover the problems involved.

Part One: The First Wilderness Generation
(Those who left Egypt under Moses' leadership)

A. Preparation for journeying from Sinai
   (1:1–10:10)
   1. Census of all the congregation and

arrangements for order of encampment and order of march (1:1–2:34).

2. Special role of the Levites between the whole congregation and the Aaronic priests; census of the Levites (3:1–4:49).

3. Miscellaneous legislation covering skin diseases, restitution in damages cases, women suspected of adultery, Nazirite vows (5:1–6:21; the logic of this collection and its placement is not clear).

4. Aaronic benediction (6:22–27).

5. Review of offerings given at the dedication of the tabernacle (7:1–89; this dedication, recorded in Exod 40, took place prior to the census of Num 1–4).

6. Consecration of the Levites (8:1–26).

7. Concerning the Passover celebrated at the dedication of the tabernacle, prior to the census (9:1–14).

8. Anticipatory description of encamping and breaking camp by the sign of the cloud over the tabernacle; silver trumpets for official signals to leaders and people (9:15–10:10).

B. Journey from the wilderness of Sinai to the plains of Moab opposite Jericho (10:11–21:35).

1. The march commences according to the instructions of chapters 2–3 (10:11–27).

2. Old traditions concerning Moses' father-in-law, the ark of the covenant (10:29–35).

3. Stories about proper leadership (11:1–20:13).

(a) The people's desire for meat and the sharing of Moses' leadership with seventy elders (11:1–35).

(b) Miriam and Aaron challenge Moses' special relationship to God and are rebuffed (12:1–16).

(c) Spies sent into Canaan bring back a discouraging report, leading to rebellion of the people. God intends to disinherit the people completely, but Moses intercedes on their behalf. God forgives the community but declares that none of this generation "twenty years old and upward" shall enter the land, except the two faithful spies Caleb and Joshua (13:1–14:45).

(d) Miscellaneous legislation concerning various offerings, sabbath violation, tassels on garments as reminder of commandments (15:1–41; logic of collection and its placement not clear).

(e) Challenges to Aaron's leadership; Aaronic priesthood confirmed by almond blossoms on his rod; responsibilities of Aaronic priests and the Levites (16:1–18:32).

(f) Ritual of the red heifer: purification in cases of contact with dead bodies (19:1–22; logic of placement not clear).

(g) Death of Miriam; failure of good leadership on part of Moses and Aaron means that they cannot lead the people into the land but must die in the wilderness with the first generation (20:1–13).

4. Travel from Kadesh to the plains of Moab: death of Aaron and Eleazar's succession to priestly leadership; battle at Arad; fiery serpents; Sihon and Og (20:14–21:35).

C. End of the first generation in the plains of Moab opposite Jericho (22:1–25:18).

1. Balaam, hired by King Balak of Moab to curse Israel, can only bless Israel because God has blessed the people (22:1–24:25).

2. Israel's apostasy in contact with Moabites and Midianites leads to the death of the last of the first generation (25:1–18).

Part Two: The Second Wilderness Generation
(Those who will later enter the land under Joshua's leadership)

A. Census of the new generation, with indication that the census will be basis for land distribution; census of the Levites (26:1–65).

B. Miscellaneous collection of legislation and narrative covering all events prior to the final speeches of Moses and his death, which are reported in the book of Deuteronomy (27:1–36:13).

1. The daughters of Zelophehad and regulations concerning women's land inheritance (27:1–11).

2. Commissioning of Joshua as Moses' eventual

successor (27:12–23).

3. Miscellaneous legislation concerning offerings, festivals, validity of women's vows (28:1–30:16; logic of collection and its placement not clear).

4. War against Midian (following command given in 25:17) and distribution of booty (31:1–54).

5. Allotment of territory in Transjordan to Reuben, Gad, and half the tribe of Manasseh (32:1–42).

6. Summary of itinerary from Egypt to the plains of Moab (33:1–56).

7. Matters concerning land distribution (34:1–36:13).

    (*a*) Summary of the boundaries of the Promised Land and appointment of the leaders who will apportion the land to the tribes (34:1–29).

    (*b*) Instruction that the (landless) Levites shall be apportioned cities with pasturage (35:1–8).

    (*c*) Designation of cities of refuge for persons who commit homicide; regulations for use of these cities (35:9–34).

    (*d*) The daughters of Zelophehad and tribal marriage restriction for women who inherit land (36:1–13).

VALUE AS HISTORICAL SOURCE

Although scholars have questioned all parts of Numbers as reliable information for the period prior to the emergence of Israel in Canaan, many individual texts probably developed from historical circumstances in various periods of the people's past. Perhaps the most basic question is whether or not a twelve-tribe structure existed during the wilderness period. To answer this question the historical validity of the overall narrative structure of the Pentateuch must be assessed. Did one family (twelve sons, seventy persons; Exod 46:8–27) go down to Egypt in the time of Jacob and blossom to twelve full-scale tribes, 600,000 men, by the time of Moses? Did all these people leave Egypt to gradually die out over forty years in the wilderness, and did the successive generation arrive in equal strength opposite Jericho?

Scholars agree widely that the biblical account presents an idealized and generalized portrait of the background of the people of Israel in the land. Most do not accept the assumption of a twelve-tribe structure for the historical group that left Egypt and experienced the adventures of the wilderness. Indeed, some would question even whether the tribes came together formally in a group of twelve during the period of the Judges, suggesting instead that the twelve-tribe system was a construct developed for administrative purposes during the reign of King David (*ca.* 1000 B.C.E.). Thus neither the listing of the tribes in the two census documents nor the total population figures given reflect the wilderness situation. It seems more likely that some groups who made up Israel during the period of the Judges recalled stories of desert life and perhaps of battles engaged in, and that these stories became a part of the Old Epic tradition of the whole community. Even in the twentieth century anthropologists have found tribal groups who have forged a common identity through a process in which the stories of various individual clans and tribes are adopted as the stories of everyone in the community. It is somewhat like the way that people in the United States have adopted the Thanksgiving story of the Pilgrims as part of their own heritage, even though they come from many different ethnic backgrounds and arrived in the United States in different periods.

Although it is difficult to state with certainty what happened in the wilderness, it is reasonable to assume that a group of oppressed slaves fled Egypt under Moses, gained a new or renewed religious identity, and moved through the Sinai Peninsula to Transjordan. The date is difficult to fix precisely, and the tradition of forty years of wandering should probably not be taken as an exact figure. Sometime during the thirteenth century seems the most likely period in which to place the movement from Egypt to Canaan. It also seems reasonable to assume that Moses did play the key leadership role, despite the argument by some scholars (e.g., Noth 1972) that Moses did not have a significant place in the original events. The people who fled Egypt into the barren wastes of the Sinai Peninsula may have eaten manna (probably a sweet, sticky excretion of scale insects that can still be gathered today in the Sinai), perhaps quail also (the birds drop exhausted on the ground after migratory flight across the Mediterranean), and may have seen water come from a break in hard-surfaced limestone rock. It is possible that some of them participated in battles at places such as Arad/Hormah (21:1–3; *cf.* 14:45) or in the area of Heshbon (21:21–25), although archaeological work has not been able to confirm such events. It is possible that this group remained in the wilderness for a full generation, but it should be noted that the text itself suggests that most of this time was spent at the oasis of Kadesh, some fifty miles southeast of Beersheba. And yet establishment of such details, if it were possible, still would not bring one to the heart of the story. For it is most of all a story about a people and its leadership and its God, and how the three interact. Much of what the book is about is simply not verifiable by the methods of historical inquiry.

Many scholars believe that the text reflects traditions of two different groups who entered the land separately. One of these, associated especially with the name of Caleb and the area around Hebron, entered from the south. Its story, told in Numbers 14, now takes the form of an abortive effort, because the story of the arrival through Transjordan (chaps. 20–25) became normative for the later community.

The passages describing duties of priests and Levites probably reflect various stages in the development of Israel's priesthood, especially the late period. Likewise, the regulations concerning festivals and sacrifices show development through many phases, especially when studied in connection with related texts in Exodus, Leviticus, and Deuteronomy. Much on such subjects that appears in Numbers probably relates to worship in the second Temple after 515 B.C.E. and thus belongs to the "post-P" supplementation of the text. The other legislation scattered throughout Numbers is also likely to represent traditions of varying provenance.

Some of the disputes about leadership may go back to events of the wilderness period, but all have been extensively edited to reflect concerns of later generations. The story of the seventy elders and the prophesying of Eldad and Medad (Num 11:27–29), for example, focuses on the possibility of prophecy outside regular channels, an issue of great concern in the era of the monarchy. So also the story of Aaron and Miriam's challenge to Moses (Num 12) probably reflects controversies between competing religious groups during the monarchical period. The period(s) and nature of the controversies between the Levites and the priesthood of the line of Aaron are much debated, but, again, concerns reflected in the text seem to relate most directly to the Second Temple period, perhaps to some degree also to the reign of King Josiah (640–609 B.C.E.).

SELECTED CRITICAL ISSUES

Census Lists

The lists around which the book is structured have been the subject of scholarly inquiry from several perspectives. One concern has been to make some kind of historical sense out of the seemingly excessive numbers in the lists. The basic twentieth-century consensus has been that the totals are impossibly high. One solution lies in taking the Hebrew word *'elef* to mean not "thousand" but some non-numerical unit, perhaps a subgroup within a tribe. George Mendenhall (1958) observed that census lists are known from a variety of ancient kingdoms and that those known generally serve one of two purposes, either taxation or military registration. Given the explicit references to those "able to go to war" in the lists of Numbers 1 and 26, he has argued that the lists represent quotas (rather than the totality of fighting troops available from each tribe) and relate to specific occasions of military call-up. The term *'elef*, according to Mendenhall, represents the subsections of the tribes for purposes of military conscription. Thus, for example, the number of Reubenites, 46,500 (Num 1:21), was originally to be read as 46 units contributing a total of 500 men, or about 11 men per unit. On this hypothesis the number of men conscripted per unit varies greatly from one tribe to another, from a low of about 5 to a high of about 14. The lists are attributed to the period of the Judges, and their lack of symmetry is interpreted as evidence of historical validity. The Priestly writers who incorporated the ancient lists no longer understood the word *'elef* properly and took the list as simple numerical totals for the people.

Various questions can be raised about details of Mendenhall's interpretation, and variations on his analysis have been proposed; but the general direction of his work is widely accepted among those who believe that there was indeed an organized twelve-tribe structure during the premonarchic period. But the existence of a twelve-tribe league that regularly acted in concert in religious and military matters has been increasingly questioned in recent scholarship. No doubt subgroups of tribes coalesced from time to time to face particular emergencies, but if the twelve-tribe system belongs to the period of David or is only a later ideal construct, then some other interpretation of the census lists is needed. They may reflect traditions from the early part of the time of David, or they may be simply inventions of the Priestly writers. Scholars who accept the latter interpretation often assume that the seemingly random numbers are based on some symbolic system, but no convincingly satisfactory solution has been proposed. Compounding the difficulty in understanding the census lists is the dramatic shift in the population of some tribes, despite the stability of the overall total counted. Even Mendenhall's emphasis on quotas for different battle occasions cannot adequately account for all these differences.

Another problem of interpreting the census lists involves the difference in order of the tribes between these two lists, which must be considered in the context of the even greater variety that appears when all namings of the twelve tribes in Numbers and elsewhere in the Pentateuch are taken into account. Olson (1985, 56–70) offers a convenient summary of the evidence and major hypotheses. Most important for the perspective of Numbers is the fact that Levi is nowhere included among the twelve tribes but rather is always counted separately. Instead of Joseph and Levi as sons of Jacob, Joseph's two sons Ephraim and Manasseh are used everywhere here to make up the twelve. Despite the varied order of the names of the twelve, the census lists, and indeed the lists throughout Numbers, consistently distinguish between the tribes that do eventually inherit land and the Levites, who receive no portion of land but whose livelihood is to come from the offerings of the other Israelites (18:21–24).

Whatever the census events and their numbers may have meant historically or symbolically, their function as they are incorporated by the Priestly writers into Numbers is at least twofold. First, they organize the book into two major parts. Second, they indicate that the company of Israelites did not diminish during the wilderness period and the transition of generations; thanks to God's providence, the community is fully sustained. Those of the new generation ready to enter the land still total over 600,000 men, just as did those who left Egypt and lost their opportunity to enter the land because of their rebellious spirit.

The Priesthood

While Julius Wellhausen's classic treatment of the history of Israel's priesthood (1883, 121–151) continues to exercise great influence, important new studies have appeared in the last fifty years. The various contemporary reconstructions of the history of the Israelite priesthood offer differing bases from which to approach interpretation of a whole series of texts in Numbers. Although some of these texts themselves form part of the evidence for the history of the priesthood, the evidence involves texts from diverse parts of the Pentateuch, Samuel, Ezekiel, Ezra, Chronicles, and other books as well. Scholars identify three important problems in this biblical evidence. First, the relationship between Levites and Aaronic priests is unclear in the tradition as a whole and seems to have evolved especially between the seventh and fifth centuries. Second, the relationship of the Zadokite priesthood (established by David in Jerusalem and growing in power in the succeeding centuries) to the "line of Aaron" is not clear from the biblical text and must be reconstructed. Finally, there are hints of a priesthood related to the lineage of Moses that need to be explained.

The texts in Numbers of particular significance for this discussion include chapters 3–4, giving the lineage of Aaron, the census of the Levites, and their various sanctuary duties; chapter 8, describing the consecration ceremony for Levites (in contrast to a ceremony for Aaronic priests in Lev 8); chapter 12, Aaron and Miriam's challenge to Moses; chapters 16–18, Korah's challenge to Aaron, the confirmation of Aaronic authority, and the separate duties and rights of Aaronic priests and other Levites; chapter 25, the vindication of Phineas; and 26:57–62, the second Levitical census.

The reconstructions made by two scholars will

serve to illustrate the problems. Aelred Cody (1969) argues that neither Moses nor Aaron is depicted as a priestly figure in the Old Epic tradition. Moreover, in line with many other scholars, Cody believes that the Zadokites of the Jerusalem Temple had no historical tribal connection to Aaron or to the Levites; he views the connection portrayed in biblical texts as a late fiction created by the Zadokites to establish their claim to continuous authority. According to Cody's analysis, Aaron was a popular figure in southern Judah and some members of the tribe of Levi began to trace their ancestry to him. In the seventh century B.C.E., King Josiah centralized worship in Jerusalem and closed local shrines in the countryside. At that time some of the Levites who had functioned as priests at such shrines sought admission to the priesthood at the Jerusalem Temple but were rebuffed by the Zadokites. In the aftermath of the Babylonian exile, the traditional "preference" that all priests should be of Levitical extraction arose and prompted the Zadokites to claim the southern Levites' Aaron as their ancestor as well. Some Levites who had been local priests did become officiants at altar sacrifices along with the Zadokites, but most were relegated to secondary duties of care for the Temple equipment. These were called "levites"; the use of the lowercase in English indicates a change in the connotation of the Hebrew term: what had long designated tribal membership (Levite) comes to describe instead a person with particular temple duties (levite).

Frank Moore Cross (1973), by contrast, views Aaron as a priestly figure in the Old Epic traditions and regards Moses as the ancestral head of a priestly house as well. Cross argues that the Zadokites represent an ancient lineage of Aaronides centered in Hebron whom King David installed in Jerusalem alongside the Mushite (from Moses) line of Abiathar. Solomon's dismissal of Abiathar led to the gradual ascendancy of the Zadokite line. King Jeroboam of the schismatic northern kingdom imitated David's religious policies, according to Cross, by establishing a Mushite priesthood in Dan and an Aaronide priesthood in Bethel. (Cody regards the priesthood of Dan as Levitical but not Mushite, and rejects any historical connection of an Aaronide line with Bethel.) Since Cross's focus is on the early period, he does not detail the emergence of the postexilic picture of priests and

levites in the Jerusalem Temple. Clearly the process would be simpler than that pictured by Cody, since the Zadokites are regarded as Aaronides from the beginning.

On the model of either analysis, the Priestly material in the story of Korah's revolt (chap. 16) can best be understood as a Levitical protest overruled by priestly (Zadokite) interests in the period when the Zadokites were consolidating their claims and the "levitical" status of other temple functionaries was emerging. Both interpretations of the priesthood would recognize the postexilic distinction between Aaronic priests and subordinate levites in the duty and offering requirements detailed in chapter 18.

The alternative reconstructions of the priesthood make a significant difference, however, for the interpretation of chapter 12. Cody argues that the story shows no priestly traits in Aaron's behavior, since Aaron's intercession for Miriam is with his brother Moses, not with God, and since the shutting out of persons with skin disease is not restricted to the priesthood (p. 150). Cross, by contrast, offers no comment on such details but focuses instead on larger themes of the passage. He finds that the text highlights "(1) Moses' superiority to the house of Aaron as mediator of the divine command, and (2) the affirmation of the Mushite priesthood despite its 'mixed' blood" (p. 204).

Divergent interpretations of the genealogical information in chapters 3 and 26 are quite technical, and any study of this complex topic is somewhat speculative. On the whole, Cross's approach offers a better rationale for the preservation of stories such as Numbers 12 over centuries of tradition. Most important is to understand the general point that neither the narratives nor the more technical priestly information about the Levitical families can be interpreted apart from some comprehensive view of Israel's priesthood.

Moses, Aaron, and Miriam

The preceding section on the priesthood alluded to the likelihood of tension early in the era of the monarchy between priestly families tracing their ancestry to Moses and to Aaron. Various features in Numbers, especially when viewed in connection with certain texts in Exodus, point to a concern by late editors of the tradition to show that Moses and Aaron were equal in authority, with perhaps a very slight edge going to Moses. Miriam does not achieve the prominence of her male counterparts; yet her presence at two critical junctures indicates her importance in the tradition.

The two texts in which Miriam appears, Numbers 12 and 20, indeed recount the two most important incidents that portray the relationship between Aaron and Moses. The appearance of the leaders together in each of these texts is surely original, although some scholars have claimed that Aaron is a secondary addition. In chapter 12, Aaron and Miriam together challenge Moses' unique role. Here may be the vestiges of a historical dispute. In the narrative itself, however, the emphasis lies on the special character of Moses' relationship to God. It is he who "beholds the form of the LORD" (v. 8, RSV). While God may speak through others, like Aaron and Miriam (or the seventy prophesying elders of chapter 11), the manner of communication with Moses is unique. The point is made in another way in Exodus 4:14–17, where Aaron is introduced as Moses' brother and coleader, yet the special place of Moses is maintained. It is significant that Numbers 12 does not denigrate the leadership of Aaron and Miriam; the Lord's anger is kindled because they sought to usurp the role assigned to their brother.

Why is Miriam punished by a skin disease (the Hebrew word does not mean leprosy), while Aaron goes unscathed? The question cries out for an answer, especially in a time when scholars are giving special attention to the role of women in the Bible. And yet the text does not offer any direct help. Since priests had to be ritually pure, and any skin disease was considered a disqualifying defilement (Lev 21:20), perhaps it was inconceivable to the narrator that Aaron would be afflicted by God with such a condition. Perhaps Miriam is more dramatically judged because it is she, not Aaron, to whom the appellation "prophet" is attached in the tradition (Exod 15:20) so that she is perceived as a greater threat to the uniqueness of Moses' prophetic role. Whatever the reason for her special punishment, Miriam appears as a leader of great stature, yet not surprisingly she is more expendable than her brother Aaron.

The three appear together again in Numbers 20, although here they are not quite so directly connected. The chapter opens with the death of Miriam (v. 1) and concludes with the death of Aaron (vv. 22–29). By its very inclusion in the narrative, Miriam's death notice signifies her relative importance as a leader. At the same time, it reveals her relative unimportance compared with the two men, since the narrator does not even record a period of mourning for her. While the death of Moses takes place much later in the narrative, it is announced in this chapter and associated with the death of Aaron.

Verses 2-13 explain why both Moses and Aaron will die outside the Promised Land. This is the story of the leaders' disobedience when the people grumble against them because there is no water. The text exemplifies Moses' special role as the recipient of God's instruction, even though Aaron is present. While there are occasional examples in Exodus-Numbers of divine address to both Moses and Aaron, God generally speaks to Moses alone; only twice does God address Aaron apart from Moses (Lev 10:8; Num 18:1, 8, 20). This role of Moses is consistent with the picture given in Numbers 12 and Exodus 4:15–16, as well as that in Exodus 6:28–7:2. Despite Moses' particular role, Numbers 20:2–13 presents the two leaders as partners in their disobedience. The rod that Moses carries is clearly Aaron's rod, taken from "before the LORD" (v. 9; *cf.* Num 17). God's words of judgment are spoken to both Moses and Aaron: "Because you [plural in Hebrew] did not trust in me, to affirm my holiness in the sight of the Israelites, therefore you [plural] shall not bring this assembly into the land which I have given them." (v. 12; Au. trans.) The point is reiterated in the narrative of the death of Aaron in verse 24.

Exactly what Aaron and Moses did wrong is not made explicit in the text, but the overall sense, together with the reference to Moses' "rash words" in Psalm 106:33, points to the words spoken rather than the striking of the rock. The significant point is that the text explains why neither of the two men continues in leadership into the land. By attributing to both the same irrevocable failure, the Priestly writers place Moses and Aaron on a par at the tragic conclusion of their careers. Although they may have symbolized competing priestly houses in the early monarchy period, in the exilic literary tradition they represent prophet and priest as types of religious leadership. In a time of religious confusion, the writers emphasize the need for leadership that will affirm God's holiness. The story suggests that only such leaders will be qualified to guide the people on their return from Babylon to the land.

The balance between Moses and Aaron is carried through by the narrators into the succeeding generation, in the stories of the investiture of Eleazar (20:22–28) and the commissioning of Joshua (27:12–28). While the balance in the wilderness era seems tipped slightly toward Moses, in the second generation the final form of the story tips the balance slightly toward Eleazar and the priestly side. This can be seen especially in 27:21, where the actions of the Israelites under Joshua's leadership are to be decided by the results of Eleazar's inquiry of the Lord. Joshua, although invested with some of Moses' authority (27:20), is pictured more as a military commander (perhaps even as a prototype of the later monarchs as military leaders) rather than as a spokesperson for God in the line of Moses. Thus Joshua's consulting of priestly authority simply emphasizes that "civil" authorities need priestly guidance; it does not denigrate prophetic authority or the role of Moses.

The Land

Several sections of Numbers concern the taking of territory in which Israel will eventually settle. This discussion is linked with procedures for distributing that land among the tribes and clans. Within the first part of the book, chapters 13–14 are of crucial theological significance; much of the second part also relates to this topic.

The possibility exists that chapters 13–14 preserve a transformed tradition about a group, probably Calebite, who entered Canaan from the south and occupied the area of Hebron. For the purposes of understanding the present structure and the message of the book, however, it is far more important to interpret the story as it stands, namely as the record of an abortive attempt to enter the land, an attempt that failed because the people refused to go forward when first commanded to do so. The narrative is basically Priestly in its present form, although it incorporates earlier Old Epic and other material. Understanding the story is predicated on the reader's knowledge of

the promises made to Abraham and his descendants and reiterated to Moses, according to the final form of the Pentateuch. These promises included a numerous people (fulfilled in the large number leaving Egypt), the blessing of other peoples through Israel, and a land, Canaan, traditionally described as a land flowing with milk and honey.

In Numbers 13–14, the Israelites arrive at the southern edge of this promised land and send twelve spies (one per tribe) to investigate both its strength and its prosperity. The spies report that the land indeed abounds with agricultural riches, but that it is extremely well fortified and is inhabited by strong and large people. The Israelites panic and seek to choose a replacement for Moses and return to Egypt. They are unwilling to hear the counsel of the two faithful spies, Caleb and Joshua, who urge the taking of the land because "the LORD is with us" (v. 9). Angered by the people's distrust, God is ready to disinherit them, but in response to Moses' remarkable prayer of intercession decides to maintain the covenant relationship with the community. Punishment is exacted, however: the ten unfaithful spies die immediately, the people's belated attempt to take the land fails, and the rest of this first generation remains in the wilderness until their lives' end.

Within the structure of the Priestly Pentateuchal narrative, this story recounts the climactic sin of the people, comparable in scope to the failure of leadership by Moses and Aaron in Numbers 20. In rejecting the opportunity to enter the land, they reject God's promise and thereby show their lack of faith in God's power to fulfill the ancient promise to the community. In seeking to turn back to Egypt they abandon the very God who has delivered them from bondage. By comparison with this rebellion, their other complaints and rebellions against Moses, Aaron, and God pale into insignificance. It is only for the sake of reputation among the nations and because of a steadfast, forgiving loyalty to this people that God continues with them at all. The message is a powerful one to a community in the context of the Babylonian exile. God does not abandon the ancient promises even in the face of radical disobedience; judgment is not the final word. There is hope for a future in the land beyond the time of exile, even as there was hope for a second wilderness generation. That hope is grounded in God's faithfulness, yet it will require the people's willingness to move ahead at the appointed time.

The texts related to land apportionment in chapters 26–36 of Numbers center on two themes, the solidarity of the tribes and the need for regulation of inheritance. The first of these themes is highlighted in the narrative of chapter 32, in which Moses insists that the Reubenites and Gadites must participate with the other tribes in the military action west of the Jordan. He agrees that they may have the territory east of the Jordan that has already been conquered, and that they may leave their wives, children, and flocks in this territory for the time being. But they must cross the Jordan for battle and return only when all the land has been taken and distributed. The story reflects an underlying tension between these tribes and those settled west of the Jordan, which is expressed more fully in a companion narrative found in Joshua 22. Here the return of the Transjordanian tribal contingents to their homes is reported, with a dispute over an altar that they build on the bank of the Jordan River. The question whether Israelites living east of the Jordan can really be regarded as part of the people of God lies at the heart of that dispute, which is eventually decided in favor of those in Transjordan.

Various regulations for property ownership and distribution conclude the book of Numbers. The story of the daughters of Zelophehad (chaps. 27 and 36) offers a unique example of how general case law could be derived from a specific instance of legal appeal. The first part of the story turns on the need for territorial possession as a way to assure the preservation of a man's name. Zelophehad's daughters are allowed, in the absence of male offspring, to inherit a portion of the Promised Land so that his name will not be blotted out from the rolls of Israel. Although the possibility of women holding property in Israel should not be denigrated, and the general law makes explicit a daughter's right to inherit ahead of any male relatives except sons, the story is told primarily because it addresses concern for the father's name.

In the second part of the story, chapter 36, the other members of Zelophehad's tribe have realized that the women's property will move with them when they marry. Thus the point of the chapter is to restrict the marriage of women property holders to members of their own tribe, so that the overall tribal holdings will remain constant. This regulation brings the laws of inheritance into harmony with the regulations concerning the jubilee, in which every fifty years property reverts to those to whom it was originally allotted. Whether the jubilee principle was ever put into practice in Israel is doubtful, but its ideals of land held in trust and a sufficient agricultural base for family survival were basic to Israel's ethical outlook. The understanding that the size of land allotment is related to the size of a particular tribe (33:54) reflects this same goal of a community in which proportional distribution of resources prevails.

Finally, the provision of cities for the Levites (35:1–8) also upholds this ideal. The Levites were not counted among the twelve tribes in the tradition of Numbers, and they received no general territorial allotment. The idea that they were to depend for their livelihood on offerings made by the people probably was practical only in the very late period, when levites (lowercase) were temple functionaries. Earlier, it appears that they lived scattered among the other Israelites; to ensure arrangements for this, the tradition reports that they had specified city locations, with rights to the surrounding pasturage. As is true of the other traditions about territory, the historical background is difficult to trace. But the theme of provision for all members of the community remains consistently in the foreground.

Balaam

Chapters 22–24 tell the story of the summons issued by King Balak of Moab to the foreign diviner Balaam to curse Israel. The narrative itself is surely composite, although the present form of the text can be comprehended as a unity. Four poetic oracles spoken by Balaam are incorporated into the prose narrative; these oracles have been the subject of intensive scholarly inquiry.

The narrative opens with Balak's anxiety over the horde of Israelites encamped in the plains of Moab. His elders, together with the elders of Midian, send messengers to Balaam. Balaam receives them graciously but reports that the Lord refuses to let him go with them. Balak dispatches a second, more distinguished group of dignitaries, who are told again that Balaam can do only what God commands. This time, however, the Lord grants Balaam permission to accept the invitation. As soon as Balaam is on the road, however, the Lord becomes angry and an angel of the Lord goes to intercept Balaam. There ensues the magnificently told encounter between the angel and Balaam's ass, a story that should be read aloud to be fully savored and appreciated. In the end, Balaam is permitted to continue his journey, but with the reminder once again that he speak only what God commands. When the critical moment arrives, Balaam speaks only blessing on Israel, not curses. Balak is enraged; Balaam says he must speak what God tells him. After the second and third attempts produce blessing again, Balak commands Balaam to return home. Before he goes, Balaam offers a fourth oracle announcing future relations between Israel and Moab.

Two conspicuous levels of tension in the prose narrative can be identified. The first is apparent even in such a brief summary of the story line. If God permits Balaam to accept Balak's invitation, why the sudden burst of anger and attempt to stop him? Most commentators regard this unevenness (22:22) as a device to introduce an alternative version of how Balaam came to know that he should speak only the Lord's word. Second, does the story want to emphasize that Balaam is obedient to God (i.e., that he speaks whatever God commands him) or that God can control even the words of a foreign diviner (i.e., that Balaam has no choice in what he utters)? In 22:38, for example, Balaam says to Balak, "Have I now any power at all to speak anything? The word that God puts in my mouth, that must I speak" (RSV). But in 23:12 he says, "Must I not take heed to speak what the LORD puts in my mouth?" (RSV).

The narrative is essentially Old Epic, with no indications of Priestly material. Despite the tensions mentioned, efforts to identify independent, parallel versions of the story that have been combined have been less than convincing. It seems likely that overlapping motifs associated with the telling of the story in early times have been assimilated into the present text, either by the original writer or in the process of supplementary expansion.

Whether Balaam was a historical figure remains open to debate. The modern discussion has been fueled by the 1967 discovery of fragments of an inscription at Tell Deir 'Allā, in Jordan. This inscrip-
tion, written on plaster in red and black ink, appears now to be written in a dialect of first-millennium B.C.E. South Canaanite and is dated to the beginning of the seventh century (Hackett 1984). Though much is broken, the text is clearly about a vision of Balaam, son of Beor; the name is identical to that of the biblical Balaam, and he appears to announce a prophecy given him by the gods. Scholars infer from the lack of introduction to Balaam in the Deir 'Allā inscription that the tradition about him was well known to the writer and the community. That the biblical texts also refer to this same figure seems a very reasonable assumption. It must be recognized, however, that apart from the similarities that each Balaam receives divine messages and that each is possibly connected to the deity Shadday, no firm conclusions can be drawn. The finding of the inscription in Transjordan is suggestive, since the Israelites are in the plains of Moab as the biblical story unfolds, but this speaks at best for the locus of a tradition; it says nothing directly of the historical reliability of the biblical account.

The oracles of Balaam are of particular interest, both for their theological content and for their attestation of an earlier form of Hebrew spelling than that known to us in most of the Hebrew Bible. The oracles are notoriously difficult to translate and interpret, in part because they are in poetry and because their subject is inherently obscure, but also because erratic preservation of archaic spellings has led to misunderstandings of the text by ancient copyists and readers as well as by ancient and more recent translators. In ancient Hebrew writing short vowels were not represented at all, while some (but not all) long vowels were represented by alphabet letters. The alphabet letters used for these vowels also served as consonants (h, w, and y), so confusion was likely, especially when the conventions for representation of long vowels changed over time.

The classic study of the text of the oracles is that of W. F. Albright (1944). Albright proposed a late-tenth- or early-ninth-century date for the poems, based partly on archaic spelling conventions that he identified and partly on the content of the poems. A date early in the period of the monarchy has been accepted by many (but not all) subsequent studies.

Studies in literary aspects of the poems suggest

that at least the first two, possibly the first three, are related in structure. The first two poems (23:7–10, 23:18–24) emphasize God's sovereignty, God's intent to bless Israel, and the impossibility of a curse upon the people whom God has blessed. The third poem (24:3–9) reiterates themes of the second, notably the bringing of Israel out of Egypt and the devouring of Israel's enemies. The motifs of the lion and the wild ox appear in both. In the third poem, the necessity for Balaam to bless rather than curse Israel is no longer highlighted; yet the theme of blessing and cursing is retained (v. 9). The poem expresses in another way God's promise to Abraham that "I will bless those who bless you, and whoever curses you I will curse" (Gen 12:3; Au. trans.). The theme of the multiplication of the people promised to Abraham in the Genesis text ("I will make of you a great nation") is likewise manifest in this third Balaam poem, in which references are made to the extensive encampments of Israel, Israel's numerous offspring, and the exaltation of its king and kingdom.

The fourth oracle (24:15–19), addressed to Balak, concentrates on Israel's future ascendancy over Moab and Edom and includes the famous line "a star shall come forth out of Jacob, and a scepter shall rise out of Israel" (v. 17b; RSV). Both the star and the scepter are familiar symbols of kingship in the ancient Near East, and most scholars see the immediate reference of the poem to the reign of David and his victories in Transjordan. In the early years of the common era, however, the text was reinterpreted in a messianic sense by both the Jewish and Christian communities. The leader of the Jewish revolt against Rome in 132–135 C.E. was called Bar Kokhba, which means "son of the star"; and Jesus, descendant of David, is called "the bright morning star" in Revelation 22:16.

What is the overall point of the Balaam material? It is important to recognize that these chapters do not emphasize strongly any wrongdoing on the part of Balaam. The view of Joshua 24:10 that Balaam tried to curse Israel but did not succeed is at best latent in this text. Nor is Balaam blamed here for any apostasy of Israel, in contrast to Numbers 31:16. Yet it is not sufficient to say (as does Coats 1973, 28) that the story is only about a legendary hero who demonstrates the virtue of "radical dependency on God's word." The

theme of the sovereignty of Israel's God is present in prose as well as poetry. Israel's God can and does overrule any force that seeks to stand over against Israel. Thus Balak is overcome, and Balaam not only is obedient but also recognizes that he has no choice in the matter.

Most remarkably, Israel itself plays no role in the narrative, except the completely passive one of being viewed by Balaam as he prepares to pronounce the oracles. The story as a whole tells of the God of Israel providing protection for the community even when the people are unaware of the danger that besets them. The story of their life in the wilderness is full of their grumblings about imagined dangers; here when the danger is real they are portrayed as quite unaware of it. Thus the theme of God's care and guidance is highlighted as they arrive in the plains of Moab, and the story of their apostasy that follows in chapter 25 is rendered all the more tragic.

The Aaronic Benediction

A brief text of blessing is regularly used in worship services in both Jewish and Christian traditions:

> The LORD bless you and keep you:
> The LORD make his face to shine upon you,
> and be gracious to you:
> The LORD lift up his countenance upon you,
> and give you peace.
>
> (6:24–26; RSV)

God instructs Moses to have Aaron and his sons use these words in blessing the Israelites. This setting suggests that the blessing has been incorporated into the text by the Priestly writers; but the wording of the blessing has been dated as early as the tenth century or as late as the sixth. While certainty is impossible, a preexilic date is most widely accepted. The emphasis of the text is on the wording and on the perpetual right and responsibility of the Aaronic priests to pronounce the blessing. The act of blessing itself is not instituted here; Leviticus 9:22 recounts Aaron's blessing of the people at the conclusion of the first occasion of communal worship and sacrifice after his ordination. The act of blessing is thus firmly set in the context of public worship, and especially at the conclusion of the service.

The meaning of the blessing is bound up in its highly charged theological terms, such as "bless," "keep," "be gracious," and "peace." Each of these has been the subject of major independent studies; only brief comments on themes in the blessing as a whole may be given here. First, the repetition of the divine name at the beginning of each line emphasizes that God rather than any human agent is the dispenser of blessing, a theme expressed in a different way in the Balaam material discussed above. Although the priests proclaim the blessing upon the people, it is God who blesses. The divine command that this blessing be proclaimed underscores God's readiness to support and succor the people.

Second, the references to the countenance or face of God point in Hebrew tradition to the very presence of God; in fact the Hebrew word "face" is sometimes best translated into English as "presence" (as, for example in the Lord's promise "my presence [Heb., face] will go with you," Exod 33:14; RSV). The specification of this presence as God's shining countenance makes clear that this presence is for positive help, protection from enemies, provision of what is needed for the matrix of daily life lived near to God (*cf.* Pss 31:16, 67:1). Ancient Israel had a very high view of the holiness and majesty of God; it was believed that no one could look on the face of God and live. Nonetheless, the face of God may turn toward the people in blessing, and God indeed commands that such gracious turning be invoked in the words of the Aaronic blessing.

Third, the blessing should be understood in the larger theological context of a distinction between salvation and blessing as two differing modes of God's positive presence in human life. While the two belong together, blessing emphasizes God's work manifested not in "mighty acts" of intervention but in continuing activity of growth, maturation, taking root and bearing fruit, the prospering of life in all realms (Westermann 1978). The Hebrew word for "peace" (*shalom*) underlines this theme of preservation and growth, for the Hebrew word means far more than the absence of conflict. The gift of God's peace means health, safety, and contentment, material as well as spiritual welfare, and thus appropriately

climaxes, summarizes, and concludes the blessing as a whole.

This understanding of the meaning of blessing also provides an appropriate conclusion to this essay on Numbers as a whole. Of course the book includes narratives of specific acts of divine rescue and intervention, and indeed instances of divine judgment as well. But the larger setting testifies to God's steady and gracious "keeping" of the people in a very concrete and this-worldly way. As one generation succeeds another, as the people find themselves undiminished after forty years in the wilderness, Numbers bears witness to the steadfast faithfulness of the God who both saves and blesses Israel.

Bibliography

Commentaries

Budd, Philip J. *Numbers.* Waco, Tex., 1984. Gives attention to history of scholarship on individual texts, with special attention to form and redaction criticism, plus extensive bibliography.

Gray, George Buchanan. *A Critical and Exegetical Commentary on Numbers.* New York, 1903. A classic exposition in the source-critical tradition of scholarship.

Mays, James L. *The Book of Leviticus, The Book of Numbers.* Richmond, Va., 1963. A nontechnical treatment emphasizing the place of Numbers in the larger Pentateuchal context.

Noth, Martin. *Numbers: A Commentary.* Translated by James O. Martin. London, 1968. Focuses on the growth of the tradition in its oral and written stages.

Vaulx, Jules de. *Les Nombres.* Paris, 1972. Balances traditio-historical and theological interpretation.

General Monographs

Fritz, Volkmar. *Israel in der Wüste: Traditionsgeschichtliche Untersuchung der Wüstenüberlieferung des Jahwisten.* Marburg, 1970. Identification of texts from the Yahwistic (J) source, along with a traditio-historical study of them, with a review of results and implications for geography, history, and theology.

Gressmann, Hugo. *Mose und seine Zeit.* Göttingen, 1913. A classic form-critical treatment of many passages from Numbers.

Haran, Menahem. *Temples and Temple Service in Ancient Israel: An Inquiry into the Character of Cult Phenomena and the Historical Setting of the Priestly School.* Oxford, 1978. Argues that the Priestly material of Pentateuch reflects a utopian vision set forth during the reign of Hezekiah (*ca.* 715–687).

Noth, Martin. *A History of Pentateuchal Traditions*. Translated by Bernhard Anderson. Englewood Cliffs, N.J., 1972. A rigorous application of traditio-historical methodology to the Pentateuch, with special focus on Exodus and Numbers.

Olson, Dennis T. *The Death of the Old and the Birth of the New: The Framework of the Book of Numbers and the Pentateuch*. Chico, Calif., 1985. The census texts in chapters 1 and 26 are seen to provide a key to the outline of Numbers and to a theological interpretation of the book as a whole.

Wellhausen, Julius. *Prolegomena to the History of Israel*. Translated by J. S. Black. Edinburgh, 1885. Reissued as *Prolegomena to the History of Ancient Israel*. New York, 1957. A classic presentation of the history of Israel's religion in relationship to the themes and dates of Pentateuchal sources.

Archaeology and Geography

Davies, G. I. *The Way of the Wilderness: A Geographical Study of the Wilderness Itineraries in the Old Testament*. Cambridge Society for Old Testament Study Monograph Series, no. 5. Cambridge, 1979. Uses Jewish, Christian, and Arabic sources, together with basic principles of toponymy, to identify sites and routes in the Sinai Peninsula and Transjordan.

Wright, George Ernest. *Biblical Archaeology*. Rev. ed. Philadelphia, 1962. Pp. 53–68. Archaeological evidence for the wilderness route, dating, and features of desert life.

Census Lists

Gottwald, Norman Karol. *The Tribes of Yahweh: A Sociology of the Religion of Liberated Israel, 1230–1050 B.C.E.* Maryknoll, N.Y., 1979. A study of the emergence of Israel in Canaan, with special attention to anthropological evidence for tribal structures.

Mendenhall, George E. "The Census Lists of Numbers 1 and 26." *Journal of Biblical Literature* 77 (1958): 52–60. Mendenhall argues that the word for "thousand" originally meant a tribal subunit.

The Priesthood

Cody, Aelred. *A History of Old Testament Priesthood*. Rome, 1969. Argues for a late fictional connection of the Zadokites to Aaron.

Cross, Frank Moore, Jr. *Canaanite Myth and Hebrew Epic: Essays in the History of the Religion of Israel*, esp. 195–215. Cambridge, Mass., 1973. Cross proposes that priestly families descended from Aaron and Moses were in competition at the beginning of the monarchy.

Moses, Aaron, and Miriam

Lohfink, Norbert. "Die Ursünde in der priesterlichen Geschichtserzählung." In *Die Zeit Jesu,* edited by Günther Bornkamm and Karl Rahner. Freiburg, 1970. The sin of Moses and Aaron symbolizes the sin of the religious leaders of the exilic period.

Sakenfeld, Katharine Doob. "Theological and Redactional Problems in Numbers 20:2–13." In *Understanding the Word: Essays in Honor of Bernhard W. Anderson,* edited by James T. Butler, Edgar W. Conrad, and Ben C. Ollenburger. Sheffield, England, 1985. An argument for balance between the roles of Moses and Aaron in the final form of the Pentateuch.

The Land

Brueggemann, Walter. *The Land: Place as Gift, Promise, and Challenge in Biblical Faith*. Philadelphia, 1977. A theological survey of the land theme in Hebrew scripture.

Klein, Ralph W. *Israel in Exile*. Philadelphia, 1979. Theological responses to the Babylonian exile in various parts of the Hebrew scriptures, with special attention in chapter 6 to the Priestly writers.

Sakenfeld, Katharine Doob. "The Problem of Divine Forgiveness in Numbers 14." *Catholic Biblical Quarterly* 37 (1975): 317–330. A critical and theological analysis of the spy narrative.

Balaam

Albright, W. F. "The Oracles of Balaam." *Journal of Biblical Literature* 63 (1944): 207–233. A technical study of orthography, poetry, and vocabulary, with comments on historical allusions.

Coats, George W. "Balaam: Sinner or Saint?" *Biblical Research* 18 (1973): 21–29. Coats argues that the genre of the Balaam story is legend, emphasizing the virtue of its hero, not the mighty acts of God.

Hackett, Jo Ann. *The Balaam Text from Deir 'Allā*. Chico, Calif., 1984. A linguistic and orthographic study of an ancient inscription referring to "Balaam Son of Beor," with discussion of earlier treatments of the inscription.

Wharton, James A. "The Command to Bless." *Interpretation* 13 (1959): 37–48. Wharton cites the power of God's word and the obedience of the prophet as themes present in the Balaam narrative.

Aaronic Benediction

Miller, Patrick D. "The Blessing of God." *Interpretation* 29 (1975): 240–251. A brief treatment of theological themes, emphasizing the providence of God.

Seybold, Klaus. *Der aaronitische Segen: Studien zu Numeri 6:22–27.* Neukirchen-Vluyn, 1977. Discusses the use of the name of God, the possible liturgical setting of the blessing, and its overall theological meaning.

Westermann, Claus. *Blessing in the Bible and the Life of the* Church. Translated by Keith R. Crim. Philadelphia, 1978. Considers the larger context of blessing in the Old and New Testaments and in church rituals.

KATHARINE DOOB SAKENFELD

Deuteronomy

THE SO-CALLED Fifth Book of Moses is named Deuteronomy because of the title *deuteronomos*, meaning "second Torah" or less precisely "second Law," given it in the Septuagint, a pre-Christian Greek translation of the Hebrew scriptures (Old Testament). Christian Bibles use the Septuagint titles and generally follow the Septuagint order of books of the Bible. It is in any case an imprecise title. The title in Hebrew is taken from the first noun in the first verse of the scroll, *devarim*, meaning "words" or "things." It is common in Hebrew and other Semitic languages to refer to a scroll, a book, or any literary composition by the first salient word or words in the first sentence of the text. Though the reference in context is clear, it is not strictly speaking a title in the Greek or European sense of title and is no more precise than "Deuteronomy."

The first full clause of the first verse of the book reads, "These are the words which Moses spoke to all Israel beyond the Jordan." This clause could also be rendered as, "These are the things that Moses said" (Au. trans.). It signals what in large measure ensues in the book, namely, a long speech delivered by Moses on the east bank of the Jordan in the plain of Moab. He himself would not be crossing over into Canaan, the Promised Land (1:37, 3:25–27, 34:1–4), so that this occasion of the last campsite before the crossing is Moses' last opportunity to instruct his "people come out of Egypt" (or the next generation thereof) before

he departs from them and they embark upon a totally new existence.

The words or things he said to them include a narrative review of their peregrinations since they had gathered for the giving of the law at Mount Horeb (Sinai), numerous sermons and exhortations, a clear statement of the ethic of election by which they had become the people of God, the conditions entailed therein and how it would work for them, as well as a new giving of the law (chaps. 12–26) and apparently a new sealing of the convenant to supplement the one sealed at Horeb (28:56 [EV 29:1]), and finally a theological poem (chap. 32) followed by Moses' blessing of the tribes before his death (chap. 33). The speech runs through the first thirty-three chapters with interruptions only for third-person editorial remarks about how Moses went about delivering his address. The last chapter then tells of Moses' death and burial and the thirty-day mourning period the people observed, and finally a eulogy is offered that seals Moses' unique relation to God and to the people for all time to come.

Deuteronomy's influence on Judaism and Christianity has been immense. The heart of all Jewish liturgy, the Shema' (Hear, O Israel), is taken from Deuteronomy 6:4ff.; it was one of the three most important biblical books discovered at Qumran (site of the Dead Sea Scrolls) if the number of copies found indicates its place there; it is one of the three most cited Old Testament books in the New Testament; and Jesus passed all three of the tempter's tests (Matt 4:1–11, Luke 4:1–13) by citing passages from Deuteronomy (8:3, 6:13, 6:16) about utter dependence on the one God of all creation who alone must be worshiped.

DEUTERONOMY'S PLACE IN THE LAW AND THE PROPHETS

Deuteronomy is a discrete book in itself, different in significant ways from what precedes it and from what follows. It had been suggested already in antiquity (Nestle 1902) that the scroll found in the Temple in Jerusalem in 621 B.C.E. (2 Kgs 22:8–10) was essentially the Book of Deuteronomy or at least an early form of it, perhaps chapters 12–28 (more or less) or an early form of chapters 5–28 (Lohfink 1976). It has a literary style that is easily recognizable and distinct from the rest of the Pentateuch and Joshua, though one can detect editorial traces of the same style elsewhere. The theological outlook is distinct, as are the vocabulary and the rather simple grammar (except for chapters 28, 32, and 33). Furthermore, one could skip from the end of Numbers (Num 36:13) to the beginning of Joshua and sense no hiatus or disruption.

Such observations, scholars generally agree, raise, in a rather acute way, the question of the place of Deuteronomy in the running narrative that begins in Genesis and ends at the close of 2 Kings. English translations, following the lead of some ancient Greek translations, insert Ruth after Judges; otherwise the order of the books from Genesis to Kings is the same as it is in the Hebrew manuscripts. (It is after Kings that the order of books of the Bible varies considerably between the Jewish and Christian canons.) There is in both versions a sense of history, beginning with creation and moving through the episodes about the great patriarchs and matriarchs of Genesis to the exodus from Egypt, the giving of the law and sealing of the covenant on Mount Sinai (Horeb in Deuteronomy), the forty years' sojourn in the wilderness, the trek around Edom, the victories over Sihon and Og, the story of Balaam, and the gathering east of the Jordan River (the site of Moses' discourse in Deuteronomy). Next comes the story of the entrance into Canaan and the conquest and settlement,

followed by the response to the Philistine threat, the crucial role played by Samuel in that era, and the anointing of Saul and then David as king. The story continues with the golden age of Solomon, followed by the split of the kingdom into Israel in the north and Judah in the south, and ultimately the defeat of both in the eighth and sixth centuries B.C.E., respectively. Finally there is the exile of Judah and the beginning of the great dispersion at the end of 2 Kings, which describes the surviving Judahite king, Jehoiachin, under house arrest in the palace of the Babylonian king Evilmerodach.

Deuteronomy is situated in the middle of the story that stretches from Genesis to 2 Kings. Both the Masoretic text and the Septuagint trace the story outlined above through Kings. The Septuagint inserted Ruth after Judges, thereby stressing that the Bible up to that point is indeed a history, since the Ruth story is set in the period of the judges. The Septuagint, incidentally, went even further in focusing on the Bible as largely story or history by putting Chronicles, Esdras, Ezra-Nehemiah, Esther, Judith, Tobit, and the books of the Maccabees (in that order in many manuscripts) after Kings; the Septuagint thus presents a "history" that goes from creation through to the Hellenistic period just before the Roman domination. In the Hebrew canon Chronicles, Ezra-Nehemiah, Esther, and Ruth are in the distinct third section that follows the books of the great prophets. It is not that the Masoretic text was less aware of the history involved; on the contrary, it was perhaps even more aware of the peculiar significance of that history in that it placed the books named for prophets right after Kings. This order focuses on the apparently failed history of the whole venture by cutting the story line at the end of 2 Kings, which tells of the destruction of Judah and Jerusalem and the beginning of the exile under Babylonia. Then the prophets—Isaiah, Jeremiah, Ezekiel, and the Minor Prophets—present in sharp particulars the case that the historians make in Deuteronomy to Kings. Deuteronomy is indeed at the center of the biblical story to that point.

This is so much the case that the four books that follow Deuteronomy in the Masoretic text—Joshua, Judges, Samuels, and Kings—are often called the

Deuteronomic history. How so? Much of the material in those four books comes from earlier ancient sources, to be sure, but the books seem clearly to have been edited with a distinct point of view that is present in the book of Deuteronomy itself. If the story of the call of Abraham is going to end in the apparently resounding defeat recounted in Kings, then manifestly a convincing explanation is in order. The Deuteronomic history, without apparently violating its sources, is so shaped as to make clear the following points: (1) it is not God who let us down, rather (2) it is we who had let God down well before the destruction took place; (3) God has sent prophets often and betimes to warn us of what would happen; but (4) God has promised that if we take it all to heart there will be restoration.

Some prophets appear early on, beginning with Samuel, who was perhaps both the last judge (as in the Book of Judges) and the first of the prophets, at least prophets in the sense that Deuteronomy speaks of prophets. Joseph Blenkinsopp (1977) has shown that the title "prophet" was so revered during the exile as to be attributed to even earlier figures than Samuel. But the prophets whose names are associated with specific books of the Bible, like Isaiah, Jeremiah, and Ezekiel, and the Twelve (Hosea, etc.), that follow directly on Kings in the Masoretic text argue the case with devastating clarity: God had indeed sent messengers early and betimes to tell Israel about the divine ethic and about how God operates in specific historical moments. The prophetic corpus, seen in this light, substantiates the claim of the Deuteronomic history.

Moses, in his long speech on the plains of Moab, as recorded in Deuteronomy, predicts future events. He also illuminates what had transpired earlier, how things had gone up to that point since the call of Abraham and the freeing of the slaves in the Exodus, and especially the various laws promulgated on Mount Horeb (Sinai) and in the wilderness. Deuteronomy may be seen as the key to an understanding of the apparent failure of the venture (just as the New Testament Gospels may be seen in part as an explanation of the crucifixion).

Deuteronomy casts light forward and backward, as it were, in many ways. In its light the Ketuvim, or third section of the Hebrew canon, might be seen as Judaism's attempt to live with and live out a monotheistic faith by offering a review of history and an extension of it that would give hope to those who felt called to the service of God and believed Judaism to be the right expression of that service. In the great Tiberian Masoretic manuscripts (Leningradensis and Aleppensis), Chronicles is the first book of the Ketuvim. It provides a sympathetic review of the sacred history from Adam to the exile, with the addition of a notice regarding the edict of Cyrus, which permitted the Jews to return home from Babylonian captivity. Chronicles differs from the Genesis-to-Kings story in many ways but notably in allowing that certain leaders had been more obedient to the divine will than the earlier account had reported; hence if it does not yet provide models for obedience, it at least begins the new view of human capacity that will eventually issue in praise of the ancestors in the faith (Sir 44–50). This is quite a new development indeed (Mack 1985).

The story/history is resumed in the last two books of the Ketuvim (Daniel and Ezra-Nehemiah), which attest to God's continuing activity on the side of righteousness during the horrors of exile, the physical restoration of Jerusalem, the rebuilding of its walls with Persian financial assistance, and the promulgation of the definitive editing of the Torah (Pentateuch) by Ezra in the Water Gate (Neh 8). After Chronicles comes the Psalter (in the Leningradensis manuscript immediately on the same column) with its monotheistic manner of praising God in obedience to the law (Torah), on the one hand, or engaging in lament over the darker aspects of life, on the other (Brueggemann 1984). Thereupon follows Job with all the honest questions and doubts it contains—questions that are of necessity raised by belief in one God. Just as Deuteronomy focuses on God's grace in providing humanity with clear legal guidance so that people might serve God, be obedient, and either avoid disasters or live with and through them, so the Book of Proverbs, which follows Job, offers simple wisdom regarding those areas of life not encompassed by the legal codes and on daily ways to please God. There follow the Five Scrolls, to be read at the special feasts and fasts that relate Israel's faith to the joys and sorrows of existence under one God. Finally, at the end of the codex the story/history is resumed (Daniel, Ezra-Nehemiah).

There are numerous duplications of the laws in the Pentateuch as it was finally shaped. These doublets and triplets have been the subject of many studies. The best tabular comparison is in S. R. Driver's commentary (1902, iv–vii, 299). Although simpler listing of the laws of both the Book of the Covenant (Exod 20–23) and Deuteronomy may be found in Gerhard von Rad (1966, 13), it is equally important to see the fuller comparison with laws in Leviticus and Numbers as presented by Driver. It has been the view of scholars that the latter laws derive from the later sources referred to as P (Priestly) or H (Holiness) sources. Some of them are surely still more ancient; even so, as the Pentateuch is composed, which is the way believing communities have received it ever since, Deuteronomy is seen as the epitome of all, not as a text that preceded some. And it is necessary, therefore, to see them all in that light in order to be able to understand the role of Deuteronomy within the entire history.

According to the history presented in these books, God made known his will as to how Israel should live as God's people, clearly governing nearly every aspect of life at the time, even stipulating certain rules to be followed after the departure from Sinai. Moses summarized these rules, omitting some but adding many more in his farewell address in Deuteronomy. Israel disobeyed time and time again, until God had no choice but to carry out the threats and curses that had been so clearly stated in conjunction with the laws (Exod 23:21, Lev 26:14–39, Deut 28:15–68). One has but to read these sections (in that canonical order) to gain a sense of increasing emphasis on the horrors that await disobedience. The half verse in Exodus 23 increases to twenty-five verses in Leviticus and fifty-four in Deuteronomy, which then makes clear the point that the destitution and exile in which Israel came to find itself after 587 B.C.E. had been acutely described well in advance. Israel had been warned.

If that were not enough, the shapers of "The Law and the Prophets," in what the Masoretic text calls the Early Prophets (Joshua to Kings) and the Latter Prophets (the Three and the Twelve), provide one case study after another of disobedience and rebellion. The Early Prophets constitutes a continuous story in prose (with a few hymns included), while the Latter Prophets is both superscribed and interjected with clear dates and occasions on which to place the mostly verse-form prophetic indictments and sentences that fill the pages of the prophetic corpus. Israel had indeed been warned.

But following the warnings of consequences for disobedience there follow conditions set, in Leviticus 26:40–45 and Deuteronomy 30:1–10, for reinstatement after the disasters have befallen the people. The ground for reinstatement in both is clearly God's grace. Leviticus promises that when Israel has been driven into the lands of her enemies God will remember the covenants with the patriarchs in Genesis and with the people through Moses at the time of the Exodus. Deuteronomy 30 promises the Israelites' return from the Diaspora to the Promised Land if they remain faithful to their religious traditions. God will gather them back into the land and make them even more prosperous than before the disaster, and God will circumcise their heart as well as the heart of their offspring to come so that they will indeed love God as they were supposed to have done in the first place (Deut 30:6; *cf.* Deut 6:5 and 10:16). Nothing could be clearer than Deuteronomy's theology of history, both as it is stated in the book and as it is worked out in the history that follows through Kings. The story of the man of God from Judah who confronts Jeroboam I in 1 Kings 13 is referred to in 2 Kings 23 precisely during the great reformation instigated by the most Deuteronomic of all the kings, Josiah himself.

The metaphor of God as the great physician, or surgeon, who wounds in order to heal (Deut 32:39), or who signifies the adversity of destruction, exile, and diaspora as in effect circumcising the heart of his people himself (Deut 30:6) and not leaving the circumcision to them (as in Deut 10:16 and Jer 4:4), begins with Hosea (Hos 6:1) and is developed further in Jeremiah (Jer 30:12–17) and Ezekiel (Ezek 36:26–27). Though there are good reasons to believe that those three prophets antedate the composition of Deuteronomy 30–32, the canonical order of reading puts the prophetic books in the position of elaborating and working out what Deuteronomy promises in 30:6. Moses anticipates those prophets' explication of how God would signify the adversity. And they had indeed issued their warnings, indictments, and sentences well in advance of the actual disasters.

Deuteronomy, positioned at the juncture of

Torah and Prophets, throws light on the Prophets' words in their time—Hosea just before the fall of the northern kingdom in the eighth century B.C.E., Jeremiah just before the fall of the southern kingdom early in the sixth century B.C.E., and Ezekiel at the time of the exile reflecting on the cause of that fall from the vantage point of a Diaspora already established. But the metaphor of surgery is one that not only gives meaning to pain as part of an operation performed by God himself; it gives hope to the future. When the restoration takes place it will include a factor not there before: a divinely circumcised heart.

One might well ask whether the restored people, once eased of pain and again prosperous, might not revert to their sinful ways. These passages, and others, suggest that God, as the author of the operation, will see to it that they obey (Ezek 36:27) in that the operation was on their very heart, the seat of thinking itself, on which God's own Torah will have been sutured (Jer 31:31–34, Isa 51:7). As Abraham Heschel wrote, Torah is made up of both Haggadah and *halakhah*, story and stipulation (1972; Sanders 1972 and 1975). Deuteronomy fully affirms such a view, as its literary structure makes clear.

DEUTERONOMY AND TORAH

If it is true that the core of the Book of Deuteronomy dates to the seventh century B.C.E. and was the scroll found in the Temple in 621 B.C.E., and if it can be rightfully maintained that one can pass over this book without disturbing the story line of the Hexateuch (i.e., the Pentateuch plus Joshua), then how and why did Deuteronomy come to intrude there and how does it function in its present literary position between Numbers and Joshua? Gerhard von Rad (1938) showed clearly that the story line of the Hexateuch as found elsewhere in the Bible in short recitals of the story (e.g., 1 Sam 12:8, Deut 26:5–9, Josh 24:2–13 *et passim* in Prophets and Psalms) was the core of the faith of Israel throughout biblical times. Some of these recitals were very short and some quite detailed (Neh 9:6–37; Pss 78, 98, 105), but all included the core of the story of the Hexateuch. Von Rad was interested in why none of the accounts include the sojourn at Mount Sinai and the giving of

the law save for those of the postexilic period (such as Neh 9; von Rad 1966A). But an equally interesting question arises when comparing the recitals with the Hexateuch itself. Since they all include the entrance into or conquest of the land, one must ask why the Book of Joshua is not included in the Pentateuch (Sanders 1972). Why does it end where it does, that is, with Deuteronomy? Why does it leave the Israelites out in the plains of Moab mourning the death of Moses?

The question is canonically critical inasmuch as it is an observation about the function of Torah (Pentateuch) in the worship of believing communities, especially in the synagogue service. All indications are that beginning soon after Ezra brought the Torah back to Jerusalem from Babylon, where it had received its final shape in the exilic community (Ezra 7:6–10, Neh 8), the Torah was recited in full either in annual cycles or in triennial cycles. Just so is it recited today in annual cycles of *parashiyyot* (lectionary readings), beginning with the reading of Genesis 1 during the fall festival of Simchat Torah, immediately upon the conclusion of the reading of the last *parashah* in Deuteronomy. In other words, Joshua is not an integral part of Israel's or Judaism's basic Torah but is read in portions of *haftarah* (lectionary readings in the Prophets) just like other scattered portions of the Prophetic corpus, in conjunction with the *lectio continua* (continuous reading) of the Pentateuch. The basic function of both Torah and canon is to provide identity for believing communities who find themselves year after year and generation after generation in ever-changing situations; equally important is its function of providing guidance for obedience. In other words, generation after generation Torah continually provides Jews with refreshed and renewed understanding of their identity and of how they should conduct themselves in everyday life. Who are we, and what are we to do? Faithful reading and rereading of Torah year after year provides ever-fresh and relevant answers to those two essential questions of life.

Two important questions arise about the position of Deuteronomy in those continuing recitals. How does it function as the last book of the Torah, and why did it come to usurp the rightful place of the Book of Joshua? Why could the Torah not include Joshua too?

A six-book Torah that begins with Genesis and ends with Joshua would make a lot of sense. The Torah does not begin with Moses; why should it end there? If the whole story of Moses (that of emancipation and law-giving) were complemented by the book of promise to the patriarchs (Genesis) before it and the book of fulfillment of the promise (Joshua) to conclude it, as the short recitals all seem to indicate a full and proper Torah should be complemented, no such questions would have arisen.

It has been observed that the Pentateuch as it stands appears to be a "life of Moses" (*vita Mosis*) with Genesis as its introduction (Knierim 1985). Moses, the agent and instrument of the (near-) fulfillment of the promises of Genesis, becomes in such a view the central focus of the Torah. Moses is without question presented as the liberator and mediator of the covenant about whom biographical data are supplied stemming from various ancient sources; but as in the case of material supplied about other "prophets" or personages, such data are subordinated to a much larger purpose than the presentation of a biography (Baltzer 1975, 38). The principal character and actor of the Torah, indeed of the whole of the Torah and the Prophets, as of most of the rest of the Bible, is neither Moses nor any human whatever; it is God. Canonical hermeneutics must always begin and end with God; the Bible educes in itself, and must be read by, a theocentric monotheizing hermeneutic. In this sense the Gospel, God's story, begins with Genesis and the creation of all that is, and reaches its climax in the promise of re-creation; just so, the prophets and Deuteronomy assert that God can signify pain and adversity in creating the new Israel, whose heart is to be inherently circumcised, and on whose heart the Torah is to be sutured permanently.

The Torah cannot, in a final sense, be seen as a "life of Moses," though it indeed appears so in a literary structural analysis of the books from Exodus to Deuteronomy. The Bible perhaps also contains the elements, as George Mendenhall (1973) has suggested, for sketching a biography of God (*cf.* Sanders 1979). Even Moses' death does not in the final analysis belong to him: it is a death summoned by God, as Deuteronomy so poignantly makes clear. After Moses has sung his song (chap. 32) and pronounced his blessings on the tribes (chap. 33), he climbs Pisgah's lofty heights. And there God shows him the land that he, God, had promised to the ancestors in Genesis (34:4). Then God summons him to die: "And Moses the servant of the Lord died there in the land of Moab at the summons of the Lord; and he buried him . . ." (34:5–6a). This was God's man; there had been none like him. He had indeed lived by all that proceeds out of the mouth of the Lord (Deut 8:3). Yet the focus of the text is not on Moses but on God. God summoned Moses to death and then buried him. Because of earlier rebellion (*cf.* 32:51), Moses is denied going with his people into the Promised Land despite his continuing vigor (34:7). Nay, this is God's story, and the human focus is shifting already, though with full reverence for Moses' ministry (34:10–12), to Joshua the son of Nun and all that must yet happen.

Deuteronomy affirms and assures the theocentric point of view as the hermeneutic by which the whole story must be read. If it is right that a core of Deuteronomy was the scroll discovered in the time of Josiah as recorded in 2 Kings, one must note that Moses is mentioned only once (2 Kings 23:25), and then in a paragraph praising Josiah, not Moses. Indeed, Moses had very little authority in the late seventh century. The preceding passage indicates that the festival of Passover had not been observed since the days of the Judges (2 Kings 23:22), and the chapter preceding indicates that the scroll discovered had to be verified by Huldah, the prophetess (2 Kings 22:14–20), who in authenticating the scroll says not a word to Josiah about Moses but instead praises Josiah for perceiving the validity and relevance of the contents of the scroll for his day. The name of Moses appears only twice in the preexilic prophetic literature and seldom in the prophetic corpus after the Book of Joshua. Moses' authority increased considerably in the exilic-postexilic period after the failure of the monarchy, largely because of the crucial role Deuteronomy undoubtedly played in raising Judaism out of the ashes of the old kingdoms of Israel and Judah. Furthermore, the Pentateuch as well as the distinctly later biblical literature reflects the stature Moses had in early Judaism and has had for centuries since. But the Pentateuch as Torah ends with Deuteronomy not because it concludes a biography of Moses but because of the needs of those communities scattered in the Diaspora as described in Deuteronomy 29–31 and in the Deuteronomic history.

THE SHAPE OF DEUTERONOMY

Though scholarly views regarding the sources and dates of Deuteronomy are in considerable flux (Preuss 1982), the literary structure of the book is basically rather simple. It begins with a superscription (1:1–5) giving the date and place of the following address. Then follow two introductory speeches (1:6–4:40 and 4:44–11:32), interrupted by an account of Moses' appointing three cities of refuge in the Transjordanian area (4:41–43). Actually 4:44–49 provides a second superscription, which seems to serve as introduction to what follows right on through the exposition of the law (chaps. 5–26). After the giving of the Ten Commandments (5:6–21) there follows a hortatory address (chaps. 6–11) developing the implications of the First Commandment and how it should guide and govern the very life of the community for all time (Driver 1902, ii; Lohfink 1963). There is perhaps no section of the Bible that has as specific a discourse on the meaning of monotheism as this second hortatory speech, which includes the Shema', the heart of Jewish liturgy and worship.

Concluding the legal section is chapter 26, a rather remarkable climax to chapters 5–26 and undoubtedly the climax to the whole book. It has three parts. The first gives instructions on how to conduct a service of thanksgiving at "the place the Lord God will choose to have his name dwell" (26:1–11) and includes the famous confession of faith and identity (26:5–9); the second lists instructions on how to conduct a service of confession of obedience in the third year, the year of tithing (26:12–15; *cf.* Luke 18:9–14); and the third consists of a concluding hortatory speech by Moses, bringing the giving of the law to a close (26:16–19).

Immediately following the legal section, chapter 27 presents editorial remarks in the third person rather than in the form of a speech by Moses. This chapter prescribes a ceremony, to be conducted near Shechem on Mounts Gerizim and Ebal, in which the whole people are involved in the acceptance of the Deuteronomic laws. The chapter concludes with a series of curses to be declaimed from Mount Ebal.

Chapter 28 resumes the Moses speech and seems to be the proper conclusion to the treaty or covenant form begun at the beginning of the book. Moses (not Levites as in chap. 27) pronounces a series of blessings that will follow obedience (28:1–14) and curses that will be brought on by disobedience (28:15–68). As noted above, these pronouncements are very explicit, especially the horrors attendant on disobedience. Recent studies of various treaties in the ancient Near East (Mendenhall 1955, McCarthy 1963, Weinfeld 1972) indicate that the basic shape of the core of Deuteronomy would have included at least some of the review of history given in the first introduction (1:6–3:29) and perhaps some of the hortatory sections that follow it in the first and second introductions (chaps. 4–11).

Most of what we have seen so far in the book could plausibly be argued to date—with later editorial shaping, of course—to the late preexilic period and to have had its sociological setting in the Josianic reformation (2 Kings 22–23:27) as a reaction to the policies that had obtained through most of the seventh century B.C.E. to accommodate Assyrian hegemony and domination. Chapter 28 seems to have been composed in the exilic period by the School (tradents) of Deuteronomy in various efforts to make the preexile scroll relevant to the Diaspora situation. It has affinities with the Deuteronomic prose sections of the Book of Jeremiah that follows.

Chapter 28:69 (EV 29:1) seems to suggest a covenant made in the plains of Moab as a supplement to the Horeb (Sinai) covenant that is so often referred to in the book, but distinct from it. Chapter 29:1–8 (EV 29:2–9) provides yet another review of history, from the sufferings in Egypt through the victories in Transjordan (the major review in chaps. 1–3 had started only with the departure from Horeb). The passage in 29:9–14 (EV 29:10–15) seems to describe the setting of the sealing of the covenant, while the rest of the chapter again describes the curses that will result from disobedience (10–27 [EV 11–28]) but this time seems to reflect what actually happened in the exile itself (*cf.*, e.g., Ezek 5:13–17).

Chapter 30 is crucial to understanding Deuteronomy in its exilic setting. Despite the dire warnings already declaimed, and even in the midst of their fulfillment in exile, another chance is offered if "you call them to mind among all the nations where the Lord your God has driven you, and return to the Lord your God, you and your children, and obey his voice in all that I command you this day, with all your heart and with all your soul" (30:1–2; RSV). Here the adversity of defeat and destitution is interpreted as a curative operation performed by God as surgeon (30:6). This second chance, right in the situation of judgment, is a firm reality and need not be sought with great effort: it is in their mouth and in their heart, for it has been given by God. Life or death, blessing or curse: those are the choices. To choose life is to love and obey God as set forth in this book. The blessings will ensue once more and the restoration to the land will be effected. But if they abandon the monotheistic faith (30:17), everything will be forfeited.

Chapter 31 contains Moses' and God's final exhortations to the people and to Joshua; they are largely words of encouragement anticipating the sorts of encouragement God will eventually give before they cross the Jordan River (31:7–8, 23; Josh 1:6–9). Arrangement is made for renewal and rereading at the Feast of Booths. This is followed by words of comfort by God to Moses, preparation for his death, and a sad recounting of the rebellion and exile to come. But it is also an introduction to the song of Moses that follows in chapter 32. The chapter ends with instructions to the Levites about where to place the book, along with another mournful description of the rebelliousness to come.

The song in chapter 32 concludes with the statement by Moses that the song is their life itself (32:47). God then instructs Moses to ascend Mount Nebo and prepare for death. One could go straight from chapter 32 to chapter 34 to read of Moses' compliance with the divine instruction about his death. But here chapter 33 intrudes, offering the blessings of Moses, God's man, upon the children of Israel. They are in the form of the blessings uttered by a dying man upon his children (*cf.* Gen 49). In verse form, they include, after a short review of God's epiphany with and for his people (33:2–5), blessings on Reuben, Judah, Levi, Benjamin, Joseph, Zebulun, Gad, Dan, Naphtali, and Asher. The longest are those upon Levi and Joseph, and the latter includes Ephraim and Manasseh to make twelve. The book concludes with the account of

God's summoning of Moses to death and his burying of his servant.

The text of 34:6 has disturbed readers through the ages. The Septuagint reads, "And they buried him" rather than the Hebrew "And he buried him." Indeed, some modern translations make the verb passive: "And he was buried." These renderings miss a point that none of the other ancient translations have missed (including Jerome). The God who had made a pastoral call on his first parishioners in Eden's bower (Gen 3:8) and even had sewn garments of skins for them before dismissing them from the garden (Gen 3:21), and who later paid another call on Abraham and Sarai (Gen 12:1), that same God buried his friend Moses after summoning him still in a state of youthful vigor. No disease or physical limitation took Moses: it was his longtime intimate companion (Exod 34:29) who had also been friend to Abraham (Isa 41:8), the God of death as well as of life (Deut 32:39), who summoned him. And Moses, as might be expected, was obedient to the end.

THE LAWS

There seem to be two collections of legal material in Deuteronomy, chapters 12–18 and 19–26, although it is difficult to see quite how the laws are arranged (Rendtorff 1986; *cf.* Kaufman 1979). They seem to be made up of earlier subcollections. The first grouping (12–18), which has been called Yahweh's law of privilege (Horst 1961, 17–154), has roughly five sections: the demand that there be but one cultic center in the land (12:1–28); prohibitions against any form of foreign worship and warnings about false prophets of polytheism (12:29–14:21); various offerings required, Sabbath or jubilee-year legislation, and various social obligations (14:22–15:18); regulations about the firstborn and certain festivals (15:19–16:17, 16:21–17:1); and finally strictures on those who hold certain positions in society, including kings, and those who would practice various forms of divination (16:18–20, 17:2–18:22). The second collection, if one can call it that, includes regulations concerning the community as a whole (chaps. 19–21) followed by legislation about individual conduct (chaps. 22–25). Chapter 26, as noted above, stands by itself as the climax of the whole.

THE DEUTERONOMIC LAWS

4:16–18, 4:23, and 7:25	Against images	21:22–23	Burial of a criminal who under death penalty is hanged on a tree
5:6–18	The Decalogue		
6:8 and 11:18	Phylacteries		
6:14 and 11:16	Against polytheism (cf. chaps. 13 and 18)	22:1–4	Lost animals or other property
6:20–25	Instruction for future generations	22:5	Against transvestitism
7:2–5,16 and 12:3	Against Canaanitic pact or practice	22:6–7	Release of mother bird taken with young
7:6; 14:2, 14:21, 26:19, 28:9	Israel to be a "holy people"	22:8	Requirement of roof parapet: liability
10:19	Love of stranger	22:9–11	Against mingling of kinds
12:2–28	Place for sacrifices restricted	22:12	Garment tassels required
12:16, 12:23, 15:23	Against eating blood	22:13–21	Concerning the virginity of a bride
12:29–31	Against imitating Canaanites		
13	Against idolatry and polytheism	22:22–27	Against adultery
14:1–2	Against certain mourning practices	22:29	Seduction of a virgin
		23:1 (EV 22:30)	Against incest with stepmother
14:3–20	Clean and unclean animals	23:2–9 (1–8)	Strictures on admittance to community
14:21	Against food improperly killed or prepared	23:10–15 (9–14)	Cleanliness in the camp
14:22–29	Tithes	23:16 (15)	Protection of escaped slave
15:1–11	Jubilee year	23:18–19 (17–18)	Against cult prostitution
15:12–18	Hebrew slaves	23:20–21 (19–20)	Against usury
15:19–23	Firstborn animals	23:22–24 (21–23)	Regulations concerning vows
16:1–17	Three annual festivals in Jerusalem	23:25–26 (24–25)	Limits on gleaning neighbors' crops
16:3	Against leavened bread at Passover		
16:3–4, 8	Unleavened bread lasting a week thereafter	24:1–4	Regulations governing divorce
		24:5	One-year honeymoon
16:4	Passover meal to be eaten before morning	24:6, 10–13	Regulations on pledges taken on loan
16:13, 15	Festival of Booths (seven days)	24:7	On kidnapping
16:18	Appointment of judges	24:8–9	On leprosy
16:19–20	Justice in judgment	24:14–15	Timely wages
16:21–22	Against Asherahs and cultic pillars	24:16	Protection of the family of a criminal
17:1	Sacrifices to be without blemish	24:17–18	Protection of a stranger, orphan, widow
17:2–7	Against polytheism		
17:6, 19:15	Need for two or three witnesses	24:19–22	On leaving some of crop unharvested for the poor
17:8–13	High court		
17:14–20	Strictures on kingship	25:1–3	Restriction to forty stripes' punishment
18:1–8	Rights of Levites		
18:9–22	Further strictures on prophets and polytheism; promise of a prophet like Moses (18:15, 18)	25:4	Ox not to be muzzled when treading grain
		25:5–10	Law on levirate marriage (widow to brother-in-law)
19:1–13	Three cities of refuge	25:11–12	Stricture on a woman fighting a man
19:14	Against removal of boundary markers		
		25:13–16	Regulations on weights and measures
19:15–21	Regulations on bearing witness in court	25:17–19	"Remember Amalek"
19:21	Lex talionis	26:1–11	Service of thanksgiving and confession of faith
20	Holy War legislation		
21:1–9	Expiation rite for an unknown murderer	26:12–15	Service of confession of obedience
21:10–14	Treatment of women taken captive	27:5–6	Altar to be of unhewn stone for sealing of covenant
21:15–17	Rights of firstborn		
21:18–21	Legal limits of a rebellious son		

The accompanying table indicates the extent of the laws in Deuteronomy. (Compare the synopsis in S. R. Driver [1902, iv–vii and 299].) As one can discern, these are mainly cultic, civil, and criminal laws with some ethical regulation mixed in; the purely ethical issues seem to be stressed mainly in 4–11, where the Decalogue is lodged as well. But the emphasis is on the cultic, the acceptable way to worship the Lord, the one true God, with special emphasis on the prohibited ways. The latter include any form of divination, not only because there were so many such practices in Babylonia, the center of the exile, but mainly because they deny the freedom of God.

Deuteronomy stresses not only the freedom of the grace of God (7:6–11) but also the freedom of God to bless and to judge as God sees fit. To be able to divine through mechanical means what will take place in the future suggests that God is rigidly tied to an agenda which God cannot change, and that certain humans can read the agenda, understand it, and claim that God is bound by it. Deuteronomy 18:9–11 might today be read to prohibit those who misuse Scripture by seeking an exact declaration of the timetable God is committed to for the fulfillment of the divine purpose in history. Like sooth-sayers, augurs, sorcerers, charmers, mediums, wizards, and necromancers (18:10–11), the literalists turn the Bible to their own ends in a manner comparable to ancient diviners, who used the tricks of their trade to deny the freedom of God's actions. While Deuteronomy presents God as faithful to his promises, it also insists that God will fulfill those promises in God's own surprising ways in God's own time. This perspective helps one under-stand the astounding honesty of the Bible in retaining in the text various prophets' statements about what would happen in their time, or shortly thereafter, that never actually happened (Lindblom 1962, 199).

THE COMPOSITION OF DEUTERONOMY

The language of Deuteronomy is quite formulaic; indeed some formulas recur with regular frequency. Much of Deuteronomy seems to reflect the language of the court and a good bit of it the language, rhetoric, and style of liturgical as well as legal texts. Others have noted that it seems to be composed in the language of a ruling class in Jerusalem. Deuteronomy 28:28–33 may reflect neo-Assyrian legal texts for solemn occasions, which would have been well known in court circles during the Assyrian hegemony of the seventh century B.C.E. in Judah (Weinfeld 1972).

And while much of Deuteronomy may have been actually composed in court circles in the decades before its "discovery" in 621 B.C.E. in the Temple, there is evidence as well of editing of older works, such as what scholarship calls Old Epic tradition, that is, the amalgamation and conflation of some northern (E or Ephraimitic) and southern (J or Judean) traditions after 722 B.C.E., when the northern kingdom was destroyed by Assyria and many in Samaria apparently sought refuge in Judah. Precursor texts important to Deuteronomy would also have included the cultic decalogue of Exodus 34:10–26 (*cf.* Exod 23:13–33), the great decalogue of Exodus 20:1–17, and the Book of the Covenant (Exod 20–23). Deuteronomy 16 as well as other passages seem to be based on the cultic decalogue of Exodus 34.

The great decalogue seems eventually to have had a decisive effect on the present shape of Deuter-onomy, especially the first commandment, which in Deuteronomy, and eventually in Scripture as a whole, must be called the main commandment or the commandment par excellence (*Hauptgebot*; Lohfink 1963). This is the all-pervasive commandment where-in the believer is called upon in every way conceivable to monotheize, to pursue the oneness of God with all one's heart (thinking), self (very being), and might (power or control over any of God's gifts as steward); see Deuteronomy 6:4–5 *et passim*. One could inter-pret Deuteronomy 5, 9–11, and 28:69 (EV 29:1) to mean that God gave only the great decalogue at the ratification of the covenant on Mount Horeb but gave the rest of the laws to Moses alone, which the latter then proclaimed until shortly before his death in Moab (precisely those in the book of Deuteronomy). Deuteronomy 18:15–18 could be read to mean that the prophets' later statements are but commentary on the Decalogue, which is quoted almost literally in Deuteronomy 5:6–21. Note that Hosea "will" say that by a prophet God brought Israel up from Egypt and by a prophet sustained Israel (Hos 12:13— even though Hosea antedates Deuteronomy by at least a century, and even a theoretical late-eighth-century B.C.E. core of it by some decades).

On the other hand, there appear to be a number of exilic additions to the Josianic Deuteronomy, such as chapters 1–3 and 29–32 (esp. chap. 30), but also much of chapters 4 and 7–9. Some of chapters 5 and

9–11 also seem dependent on the subsequent Deuteronomic history. Deuteronomy 4, 7, and 9 seem to resonate with P (Priestly) portions of the Pentateuch; likewise, Deuteronomy 4 resonates with Deutero-Isaiah, as does Deuteronomy 7 with Ezekiel and Deuteronomy 30 with Jeremiah (Lohfink 1975). Deuteronomy 32 has been called a summary of "prophetic theology"; that claim has also been denied in asserting that it dates from preprophetic times (Wright 1962). In its canonical position it seems to "anticipate" much of what the prophets will say in their specific case studies in demonstration of the Deuteronomic ethic of election. Numerous phrases seem to come right out of the prophetic corpus. In the major Masoretic manuscripts of the Old Testament Exodus 15 and Deuteronomy 32 alone are copied in poetic stichs or colons. These are the two great anthems of the Torah (Pentateuch), the one the Song of the Sea, sung in massive celebration of the crossing of the Re(e)d Sea, the moment of redemption and salvation in which God created a people for himself; and the other sung by Moses himself after the conclusion of his great speech in the plains of Moab just before his last will of patriarchal blessings on the tribes and not long before his divinely summoned death. The latter is a monotheizing hymn par excellence. It affirms, as Hannah "will later" reaffirm (1 Sam 2:6), and as Scripture as a whole testifies, that God, the one God of all creation and redemption, is the God of death as well as of life who can resurrect his people corporately from a form of national death (Deut 30:3ff., Ezek 37; *cf.* Hos 13:14) because he is the God both of death and of life. Early Judaism in the exilic-postexilic period will be able thereupon to affirm that the same God can also resurrect individuals (e.g., Isa 26:19), a doctrine that later became central to the Pharisaic faith and to Christianity.

THE THEOLOGY OF DEUTERONOMY

Deuteronomy is perhaps the most patently theological book of the Bible (Rendtorff 1986, 155). It develops the theology of monotheism more thoroughly than any other. It is indeed the book that contains the great Shema' (Deut 6:4ff.), preceded by a reformulation of the great Decalogue (Deut 5:6–21; *cf.* Exod 20). The first commandment becomes in Deuteronomy the governing concept through which all others are understood.

The Book of Deuteronomy seems to be a product of several compromises: between priestly groups, prophetic groups, and Wisdom schools; between the great traditions of the north, Israel, and those of the south, Judah; between royal theology and prophetic theology (Weinfeld 1972). It restricts the authority and activity of kings (chap. 17) and of prophets (chaps. 13 and 18) but not of the wise. This is especially interesting in view of Jeremiah's many challenges to the thinking of the wise, especially after the reign of Josiah (e.g., Jer 8:8ff.). Jeremiah, according to most scholars (*pace* Holladay 1986 and others), earlier supported the Deuteronomic-Josianic reform but then turned against it and challenged it as inducing false thinking and false hope. This has led some to suggest that the seventh-century core of Deuteronomy was composed by a group called "the wise" (*hokchamim*). It may well have been a newly formed group that drew on both priestly and prophetic traditions and thinking but was too young to yet come under stricture.

Deuteronomy urges a revival of Mosaic traditions, theology, and thinking. It presents a serious challenge to royal theology by which Manasseh, who had been king in Jerusalem for most of the years the seventh-century Assyrian domination lasted, was able to find a flexibility of policy toward the Assyrians. Many Assyrians conducted trade, business of various sorts, and financial dealings in Jerusalem, even though Judah was nominally independent in the sense that it had not been crushed and disintegrated as had northern Israel in 722.

Deuteronomy "mosaized" some of the old royal or Davidic traditions, which with the triumph of Deuteronomy were now relegated to the books of Samuel and Isaiah and the Psalter. Everybody knew and continued to recite the traditions that called Jerusalem the "city of David" (the city that he had taken from the Jebusites; 2 Sam 5) as well as the psalms attributed to him, but in Deuteronomy the claim is made that it had been Moses who "authorized" the one site where the one Temple should stand, the one place where God would cause his name to dwell. (Is Deuteronomy's failure to name that place evidence of a sensitivity to the Davidic claims?)

In Deuteronomy the concept of God as the one God of all creation is somewhat more spiritualized than in earlier traditions. At the same time the sacrificial or sacerdotal system appears also to be spiritualized. God's claim on Israel is stressed, while Israel's claims on God are minimized, even denied. God keeps God's promises, to be sure, but solely on God's own schedule and according to God's agenda. The concept of remembrance is stressed, as is identity on the part of the reciting community of faith with the generation of the Exodus and wanderings.

No other book of the Bible so focuses on the oneness of God, the legitimacy of only one cult or mode of worship, one Torah, one Temple in which true worship can take place, and one people or nation. Some survivors of the debacle in the north in 722 are now integrated into the surviving kingdom of Judah. Purity of worship is as great a concern as its unity. Never again should such a terrible catastrophe fall on the people, now unified into Judah.

And yet it did; and chapters 29–31 look ahead to the results of the second catastrophe that is to take place in 586 B.C.E. and the possibility of restoration if all that is laid forth in Deuteronomy be taken to heart. The people addressed in the plains of Moab are a generation different from those who came out of Egypt, and yet the covenant with its promises and obligations holds for them and each new generation in ever-changing circumstances. The first generation, that of the Exodus, had sinned greatly by refusing to enter the land (1:34), but the new one now being addressed will cross over and possess it (1:39). Still beyond these there will be yet future generations who will become corrupt in the land (4:25ff.), will experience exile and destitution, but in it, if they come to their senses and take all this to heart, they will be able once more to enter the land and possess it (30:2–3).

All this is set forth in a framework of looking back and looking ahead, both to the people's transgressions and to God's faithfulness. Deuteronomy actualizes the past and brings it into the present, then looks to the future (5:3). In doing so it reshapes many of the old laws, giving hermeneutic hints and clues for Israel to emulate in future in order to keep the covenant ever-fresh and vital in both faith and obedience, no matter how much life and history change (von Rad 1953; Childs 1979, 214ff.). Deuteronomy cements itself, as it were, both to Israel's past (Genesis to Numbers) and to her future (Joshua to Kings and beyond). The fact that the Septuagint manuscripts extend that history, as noted above, into Roman times bears out the point.

Read in the totally different context of the Diaspora to come, Deuteronomy creates its own problems. Its ethic of election is so clear, and its challenge to the policies of the monarchy and government of the seventh century B.C.E. so sharp, that even when there was no more such government or unified nation it would be misreading the text to say what it did not earlier say. Its ethic of election had three parts: God's grace and election of Israel are prevenient and undeserved (7:7–9); but Israel must be faithful and obedient to the stipulations of the covenant; and if not, the consequences will be abrogation of the covenant as well as the curses attendant on disobedience, but if so, blessings will ensue. This was unfortunately misread in the later period as suggesting a meritocracy in which obedience would bring blessings to the individual and disobedience, curses; this was further distorted to mean that those who were blessed must have been obedient and righteous but those upon whom suffering or deprivation fell must have sinned. This misreading is challenged sharply by the Book of Job as well as a great deal of Wisdom literature and the New Testament (Sanders 1987, 180ff.). This is one of the many instances in which the Bible must be read critically and historically lest it be badly misread.

Deuteronomy, on the other hand, provided the clues as to how early and formative Judaism could develop the oral law in a way that would keep it as relevant as possible to ever-changing situations. If Moses could remember all the laws he promulgated in Deuteronomy, forty years after the giving of the Law on Horeb, on the east bank of the Jordan, then surely he could also have remembered the many more that make up the oral law (Mishnah, Talmud). Deuteronomy (mishneh torah, "second Torah"), written and designed to meet the needs of the people in the seventh and sixth centuries, showed the way to keep alive the past in the present, but far more than that, showed how Judaism was to continue and re-present the covenant and its obligations for all time to come (Sanders 1976, 1979; see 1987, 9–39, 125–151).

But Deuteronomy also provides a way to understand faith in God's eternal oneness or integrity as well as faith in God's enduring purposes. Deuteronomy shows as perhaps no other book in the Bible, Jewish or Christian, what covenantal love means (Moran 1963), both for the individual and for the people ("church"). It provides a way of understanding how they would be able to "hear" the basic tenet of the faith for all time to come, that is, the oneness of God, or the ontological and ethical integrity of Reality (6:4ff.). Whether or not there would always be one cult or way to worship God, or one Temple, or one system of sacrifices, or even one Torah, there would always be everywhere and forever, for over two and a half millennia to come, the integrity of Reality (oneness of God) at the heart of the faith, whether Jewish or Christian: "Hear, O Israel, the Lord our God is ONE." The first commandment remains perhaps the greatest challenge to the human mind history has ever known, and Deuteronomy makes that challenge both explicit and mandatory. Deuteronomy is surely one of the major reasons these diverse texts became canon for two great faiths, for it gives them the shape and clarity and adhesiveness that would render them adaptable for ages to come (Sanders 1972, 1976). Deuteronomy forever broke the grip of Israel's and, indeed, humanity's claims on God, and it sealed for all time the basic shape of Torah, hence canon, as God's story in and for all generations.

Bibliography

Alt, Albrecht. "Die Heimat des Deuteronomiums." In *Kleine Schriften zur Geschichte des Volkes Israel*, vol. 2. Munich, 1953. Pp. 250–275.

Baltzer, Klaus. *The Covenant Formulary in Old Testament, Jewish, and Early Christian Writings*. Translated by David F. Greene. Philadelphia, 1971.

———. *Die Biographie der Propheten*. Neukirchen-Vluyn, 1975.

Blenkinsopp, Joseph. *Prophecy and Canon: A Contribution to the Study of Jewish Origins*. Notre Dame, Ind., 1977.

Brueggemann, Walter. *The Message of the Psalms*. Minneapolis, 1984.

Carmichael, Calum M. *Law and Narrative in the Bible: The Evidence of the Deuteronomic Laws and the Decalogue*. Ithaca, 1985.

Childs, Brevard S. *Introduction to the Old Testament as Scripture*. Philadelphia, 1979. Pp. 202–225.

Christensen, Duane L. "Prose and Poetry in the Bible: The Narrative Poetics of Deuteronomy 1:9–18." *Zeitschrift für die alttestamentliche Wissenschaft* 97 (1985): 179–189.

Clements, Ronald Ernest. *God's Chosen People: A Theological Interpretation of the Book of Deuteronomy*. London, 1968.

Craigie, Peter C. *The Book of Deuteronomy*. Grand Rapids, 1976.

Driver, S. R. *A Critical and Exegetical Commentary on Deuteronomy*. The International Critical Commentary. Edinburgh, 1902.

Halbe, Jorn. *Das Privilegrecht Jahwes: Ex. 34, 10–26*. Göttingen, 1975.

Heschel, Abraham. "A Time for Renewal." *Midstream* 18 (1972): 46–51.

Holladay, William Lee. *Jeremiah: A Commentary on the Book of the Prophet Jeremiah*, edited by Paul D. Hanson. Philadelphia, 1986.

Horst, Friedrich. *Das Privilegrecht Jahwes*. Göttingen, 1930. Reprinted in his *Gottes Recht: Gesammelte Studien zum Recht im Alten Testament*. Munich, 1961. Pp. 17–154.

Kaufman, S. "The Structure of the Deuteronomic Law." *Maarav* 1:2 (1979): 105–158.

Knierim, Rolf P. "The Composition of the Pentateuch." *Seminar Papers*. Society of Biblical Literature, Denver, 1985. Pp. 393–415.

Lindblom, Johannes. *Prophecy in Ancient Israel*. Philadelphia, 1962. Pp. 311–375.

Lohfink, Norbert. *Das Hauptverbot: Eine Untersuchung literarischer Einleitungsfragen zu Dtn 5–11*. Rome, 1963.

———. "Deuteronomy." In *The Interpreter's Dictionary of the Bible: Supplementary Volume*, edited by Keith Crim. Nashville, 1976. Pp. 229–232.

———, ed. *Das Deuteronomium: Entstehung, Gestalt und Botschaft*. Leuven, 1985.

Mack, Burton L. *Wisdom and the Hebrew Epic: Ben Sira's Hymn in Praise of the Fathers*. Chicago, 1985.

McBride, S. D., Jr. "Policy of the Covenant People: The Book of Deuteronomy." *Interpretation* 41 (1987): 229–244.

McCarthy, Dennis J. *Treaty and Covenant: A Study in Form*. Rome, 1963.

McConville, J. G. *Law and Theology in Deuteronomy*. Sheffield, England, 1984.

Mendenhall, George. *Law and Covenant in Israel and the Ancient Near East*. Pittsburgh, 1955.

———. *The Tenth Generation: The Origins of the Biblical Tradition*. Baltimore, 1973.

Minette de Tillesse, Georges. "Sections 'tu' et sections 'vous' dans le Deuteronome." *Vetus Testamentum* 12 (1962): 29–87.

Mittmann, S. *Deuteronomium 1:1–6, 3: Literarkritisch und traditionsgeschichtlich untersucht*. Berlin, 1975.

Moran, W. L. "The Ancient Near Eastern Background of the Love of God in Deuteronomy." *Catholic Biblical Quarterly* 25 (1963): 77–87.

Nestle, E. "Das Deuteronomium und 2 Könige 22." *Zeitschrift für die alttestamentliche Wissenschaft* 22 (1902): 170–171, 312–313.

Nicholson, Ernest Wilson. *Deuteronomy and Tradition.* Philadelphia, 1967.

———. *God and His People: Covenant and Theology in the Old Testament.* New York, 1986.

Noth, Martin. *The Deuteronomistic History.* Sheffield, England, 1981.

Perlitt, Lothar. *Bundestheologie im Alten Testament.* 1929.

Plöger, Josef Georg. *Literarkritische, formgeschichtliche und stilkritische Untersuchungen zum Deuteronomium.* Bonn, 1967.

Preuss, Horst Dietrich. *Deuteronomium.* Darmstadt, 1982.

Rad, Gerhard von. *Das Gottesvolk im Deuteronomium.* Stuttgart, 1929.

———. *Studies in Deuteronomy.* Translated by David Stalker. Chicago, 1953.

———. "The Form-Critical Problem of the Hexateuch." In *The Problem of the Hexateuch and Other Essays.* Translated by E. W. Trueman Dicken. Edinburgh, 1966. Pp. 1–78.

———. *Deuteronomy: A Commentary.* Translated by Dorothea Barton. London, 1966.

Rendtorff, Rolf. *The Old Testament: An Introduction.* Philadelphia, 1986. Pp. 150–156.

Rofe, A. "The Monotheistic Argumentation in Deuteronomy iv 32–40: Contents, Composition, and Text." *Vetus Testamentum* 35 (1985): 434–445.

Sanders, James A. *Torah and Canon.* Philadelphia, 1972.

———. "Torah and Christ." *Interpretation* 29 (1975): 372–390.

———. "Adaptable for Life: The Nature and Function of Canon." In *Magnalia Dei: The Mighty Acts of God,* edited by Frank Moore Cross, Werner E. Lemke, and Patrick D. Miller, Jr. Garden City, N.Y., 1976. Pp. 531–560.

———. "Text and Canon: Concepts and Method." *Journal of Biblical Literature* 98 (1979): 5–29.

———. *From Sacred Story to Sacred Text.* Philadelphia, 1987.

Seitz, Gottfried. *Redaktionsgeschichtliche Studien zum Deuteronomium.* Stuttgart, 1971.

Skehan, Patrick W. "The Structure of the Song of Moses in Deuteronomy (Deut. 32:1–43)." *Catholic Biblical Quarterly* 13 (1951): 153–163.

Weinfeld, Moshe. *Deuteronomy and the Deuteronomic School.* Oxford, 1972.

Wright, G. Ernest. "The Lawsuit of God: A Form-Critical Study of Deuteronomy 32." In *Israel's Prophetic Heritage: Essays in Honor of James Muilenburg,* edited by Bernhard W. Anderson and Walter Harrelson. New York, 1962. Pp. 26–67.

JAMES A. SANDERS

Joshua

WHEN READ THROUGH in one sitting, the Book of Joshua exhibits both unity and disunity. An analysis of each is intrinsic to modern attempts to understand the finished work in the context of the ancient setting in which it was composed.

Much of the unity of Joshua comes from two discrete sections which together account for the bulk of the book—a narrative of Israel's conquest of Canaan west of the Jordan in chapters 1–12, and an account in chapters 13–21 of the distribution of the land thus taken among the various tribes of Israel. Both these sections contain introductory, concluding, and summary passages (1:1–18, 10:40–43, 11:16–23, 12:1–24, 13:1–7, 14:1–5, 18:1–10, 19:51, and 21:43–45) that tie the sections together and help to orient the reader. The relationship between taking the land and allotting it is articulated already in chapter 1, which also prepares the reader for Joshua's leading role in both functions.

Apart from these two sections on the conquest and the allotment of the land, and the passages that organize them, the Book of Joshua appears to disintegrate into a diversity of constituent parts in which unity and organization are much less obvious. A series of appendixes ends the work. Chapter 22 narrates the departure of the Transjordanian tribes who live east of the Jordan River and a dispute between them and the Cisjordanian majority west of the river over an altar

built at the river's edge. Cast as the farewell speech of Joshua, chapter 23 seems to conclude what was begun in chapter 1. Undeterred by this apparent finale, the Book of Joshua in its present form continues on to chapter 24, which contains an account of a covenant at Shechem, partially parallel to chapter 23, and ends with a series of burial notices.

JOSHUA AS PART OF THE "DEUTERONOMISTIC HISTORY"

In the last half century, attempts to understand the unities and disunities within the Book of Joshua have led to the conclusion that it was composed as but one part of a larger whole. A growing consensus of biblical scholars believes that the books of Deuteronomy, Joshua, Judges, 1 and 2 Samuel, and 1 and 2 Kings were written in their present form as a "Deuteronomistic History"—a single entity intended to be read as such.

Earlier treatments of this larger "history" followed the pioneering lead of Martin Noth (1943, 1981) and sought to relate it to the experience of the exiles in Babylon in about 550 B.C.E. Since the first chapters of Deuteronomy introduce a work that concludes with the release of King Jehoiachin from a Babylonian prison in 2 Kings 25:27–30 (ca. 560 B.C.E.), Noth reasoned, the Deuteronomistic History as a whole was written in and for the period immediately following this event. Some scholarly work on the Book of Joshua continues in this vein, on the assumption that older literary materials showing a wide diversity of origins, genres, and modes of preservation were edited together as a Deuteronomistic History for the first time during the exile.

Following Frank Moore Cross (1973), a growing number of scholars now believe that the Deuteronomistic History was composed essentially in the manner posited by Noth, but in at least two stages. The earlier and major composition occurred before the exile, during the reign of Josiah (640–609 B.C.E.), this being the only context that can account for many of the characteristics of the work.

Even a sketch of this hypothesis can suggest something of its explanatory power. In the whole of the Deuteronomistic History, for example, Josiah is unique in having the particulars of his kingship prophesied some three centuries in advance (1 Kgs 13). The account of his reign in 2 Kings 22:1–23:25a not only narrates the self-conscious and detailed fulfillment of this prophecy but also pictures him as the only king ever to comply in full with the laws found in chapters 12–26 of Deuteronomy. These laws stand as a frontispiece for the Deuteronomistic History and establish the standards by which it evaluates the events and careers it recounts.

Together with other evidence, such data suggest that a major "first edition" of the Deuteronomistic History ended at 2 Kings 23:25a, with the account of Josiah's "reform" as the climax of the piece. The motive for this work was to undergird and legitimate Josiah's policies. If these political dynamics shaped Joshua as a part of a larger entity, then the basics of Josianic history are of utmost significance for understanding the book.

Before examining this point more closely, however, the parts of the Deuteronomistic History not belonging to the main, Josianic edition must be accounted for. The need for a "second edition" arose not only because of Josiah's death at the hands of Pharaoh Neco (2 Kgs 23:29) and the failure of his "reforms," but because of the subsequent destruction of the Judahite state by the Babylonians and the exile of its upper classes to Babylon.

These events necessitated an addition to the Josianic Deuteronomistic History that completed the story down to a mildly positive event for the exiles, the release of King Jehoiachin from prison and his elevation to pensioner at the table of the king of Babylon (2 Kgs 23:25b–25:30). But the same events mandated more than an appendix, for the "first edition" had spared few pains in preparing the reader for Josiah's reign as its goal and culmination.

The explanation for Josiah's death and the nation's fall given by the addition—that the sins of Josiah's grandfather, Manasseh, were so great as to require the destruction of Judah as punishment (2 Kgs 23:26–27)—was therefore foreshadowed in a series of glosses inserted earlier in the History. A clear case in point within the account of Josiah is the exilic recomposition of 2 Kings 22:15–20. In its current form, this passage explains that Josiah, because of his penitence and humility, will be "gathered to his fathers," lest he be forced to witness the destruction of Judah.

The clearest example of such exilic insertions in Joshua occurs in 23:13b and 23:15–16, which mute the climax in 23:14 and interrupt a rhetorical sequence similar to 21:43–45. Although it contains much older material, Joshua 24:1–27 may be the work of the exilic editor as well (Nelson 1981a, 94–98). Alternatively, chapter 24, with its partial parallel in 8:30–35 (cf. Deut 11:29–30; 27:2–8, 11–26; 31:9–13, 24–29), can be understood as an insertion still later than the main exilic editor (Mayes 1983, 49–52).

Other traces of the exile in Joshua are possible, but attempts (Boling 1982; Peckham 1985) to find extensive evidence of an exilic Deuteronomist in the book have not as yet attracted a wide following. Since the entire book (apart from 8:30–35, 23:13b, 23:15–16, and 24:1–33) is intelligible as part of the larger Josianic work, it will be explicated here as such.

CONTEXT AND DYNAMICS OF THE JOSIANIC "REFORM"

Discussion of Josiah's "reform" can be organized under six rubrics, but these are merely facets of the same systemic reality. The focus here will be upon their interaction and mutual reinforcement, for that potent combination defined the "force field" that shaped the contours of the Book of Joshua within the larger literary context of the Deuteronomistic History.

The "reform" of Josiah involved a reassertion of Judahite national independence in the context of declining Assyrian power. Since the time of Ahaz of Judah (*ca.* 734–715 B.C.E.) and the mighty Tiglath-pileser III of Assyria (745–727), the small state of Judah had moved mostly in the orbit of imperial Assyria, the dominant superpower of that time. Hezekiah (*ca.* 715–687) challenged Assyrian suzerainty, but paid dearly for the attempt. During most of the long reign of Manasseh (*ca.* 687–642), Judah was of necessity an obsequious vassal of Assyria. As is typical in such situations, a measure of cultural imperialism accompanied the political domination, with citizens of the vassal state affecting aspects of the suzerain's "superior" culture.

Late in the reign of Asshurbanapal of Assyria (668–627) and following his death, Assyria went into steep decline. After a century under the Assyrian heel, the petty states of western Asia—including Judah—struggled to regain at least some measure of freedom. These independence movements were strongly nationalistic and anti-Assyrian.

Josiah's repair of the Temple in Jerusalem is to be understood in the light of these political realities. The Temple was a national shrine, the dynastic chapel of the Davidic monarchy. When the Davidic king became an Assyrian vassal, symbols of that subservience were displayed in his state temple and its forms of worship (2 Kgs 16:10–18, 21:3–7). Removal of the foreign cultic artifacts, conversely, was a consummately political act, a powerful declaration of independence from Assyrian control.

Temple repair, moreover, was the mark of a successful king in the ancient Near East. Symbolically, it was the equivalent of temple-building, one of the strongest assertions of power a monarch could make. Since a century of subservience to Assyrian superpower had discredited the Judahite monarchy among its subjects, such symbolic acts were important if Josiah was to recover the king's authority.

The reassertion of royal prerogatives addressed another problem as well. Not only had Assyrian superpower discredited the Davidids (kings of the Davidic dynasty), it had also served to further divide the local ruling factions in Judah. Josiah's father,

Amon, had been killed in the course of factional fighting (2 Kgs 21:19–26), bringing Josiah to the throne when only a child of eight. National independence and resurgent Davidic kingship required the suppression of these factions to mold national identity and unity, with the Temple in Jerusalem as its center.

Territorial expansion was a major part of Josiah's program. Three centuries before his time, at the death of Solomon, the "ten northern tribes" had seceded from the rule of the Davidids to form the separate monarchic state of Israel (1 Kgs 11–13). Two centuries thereafter (722–721), that same state fell to Assyria. For a hundred years prior to the climax of Josiah's "reform" (622–621), therefore, the land and population of what had previously been the northern kingdom had been parceled out among various provinces of the Assyrian empire. With the crumbling of that empire and its effective control over its western provinces, Josiah reasserted Davidic hegemony over the north.

However, he faced several impediments to his perceived "manifest destiny" there. Solomon's social and economic policies had pushed the northern peasants to the brink of rebellion. When his son, Rehoboam, arrogantly promised more of the same, the northerners rebelled against what they saw as Davidic tyranny (1 Kgs 12:1–20). In Josiah's time, even the intervening centuries had not quieted all northern suspicions of the Davidic dynasty.

Assyrian imperial policy also bequeathed Josiah an obstacle to his policies that outlived Assyrian control in the area. The Assyrians had deported the ruling elite of the fallen northern kingdom to other parts of the empire, thereby severing the roots from which they drew their power to resist. Conversely, they had also moved defeated elites from other portions of the empire into northern Israel. When Assyrian power receded, the descendants of those foreign elites were left in the area as rivals to Josiah's authority.

Against all these impediments, Josiah pursued his objectives with a combination of "carrot and stick." Specifically, he and his officials effected a "lamination" of the Mosaic and Davidic traditions. Much of what was nearest and dearest to the hearts of northern villagers had its traditional fountainhead in the figure of Moses. Josiah's reform appealed to the northerners by adopting Mosaic law and tradition as its legitimating constitution. Mosaic law and tradition were used to support the current Davidid (Josiah) in his claim to be the sole legitimate executor of that law and tradition. This Josianic integration of the Davidic and Mosaic traditions found full elaboration in the Deuteronomistic History.

According to 2 Kings 22:3–14 and 23:1–3, Josiah's repair of the Temple occasioned the finding of a legal document, which he then solemnized as the law of the land in a covenant ceremony. Speculation that this book was some form of Deuteronomy 12–26 is one of the longest-standing pillars of modern scholarship. Most of the policies and actions attributed to Josiah in 2 Kings 23:4–24 find unique sanction in the legal section of Deuteronomy. This section, in turn, is cast as part of the farewell speech of Moses just before Israel's entry into the promised land. As numerous parallels from ancient western Asia demonstrate, however, Josiah's promulgation of the Mosaic law amounts to an assertion of royal authority.

Centralization was the keystone of the Josianic "reform." Politically, the reform involved reassertion of the prerogatives of the monarch and his national government at the expense of the landed nobility, made binding in Josiah's home territory of Judah and in the portions of the north he captured.

Josiah's centralization of religious worship was of a piece with his political policies. Legislation in chapter 12, requiring that Israel worship only at "the place which Yahweh your God will choose, to make his name dwell there" (12:11; RSV emended), heads the laws of Deuteronomy 12–26. In the context of Josiah's rule that place could only be the Temple in Jerusalem.

The elimination of cultic installations other than the central sanctuary, mandated in Deuteronomy 12, plays a major role in the Deuteronomistic account of Josiah's "reform" (2 Kgs 23:4–20). This narrative reaches its climax in the destruction of Bethel (23:15–20; *cf.* v. 4). From a Josianic perspective, Bethel—a royal cult site established by Jeroboam I (*ca.* 931–910) to rival Jerusalem and legitimize his secessionist state in the north—epitomized all that was evil and all that impeded national unity under a rightful heir to the Davidic throne. As previously mentioned, the Deuteronomistic account of Jeroboam's establishment

of the Bethel sanctuary (1 Kgs 12:26–33) is followed by an extended prophecy of its destruction (1 Kgs 13), which mentions Josiah by name (v. 2).

Finally, Josiah emphasized the Passover festival (2 Kgs 23:21–23). This carrier of the Exodus traditions had been prized at the grass-roots level, particularly in the north. By giving it new prominence and claiming that "no such Passover had been kept since the days of the judges . . . or during all the days of the kings of Israel or of the kings of Judah" (2 Kgs 23:22, RSV), Josiah presented himself as the champion of popular sentiment. By insisting that the observance of Passover be centralized at Jerusalem according to the provisions of Deuteronomy 16:1–8, however, he disenfranchised all other cult sites and their personnel and enlisted the Passover in the service of his centralization program.

STRUCTURE OF THE DEUTERONOMISTIC HISTORY

Cast as the swan song of Moses, the ultimate authority figure for northerners, Deuteronomy provides the legal mandate for the specifics of Josiah's "reform." It also enunciates the norms in terms of which the entire history becomes a series of object lessons, leading up to and legitimating the policies of Josiah.

Seen in this light, the Book of Joshua becomes an extended, positive object lesson, illustrating how the Josianic objective of territorial expansion can be properly and successfully achieved. The people of Israel must be fully united under one leader who is the sole legitimate successor of Mosaic authority. The policies and actions of this leader must conform to Mosaic law in strict detail, and he must see to it that the people do so as well. All foreign influences are to be expunged, lest they constitute a temptation.

As presented in the finished form of the book that bears his name, Joshua is the historical prefigurement of Josiah. Against northern suspicions of Josiah, the Deuteronomistic book of Joshua argues tacitly but eloquently that the model for Josiah's behavior is none other than a northern hero, Joshua, the Ephraimite. Just as Joshua was successful in capturing and distributing the land because he adhered strictly to the law of Moses, so, too, will Josiah succeed in capturing and distributing the land in his time because he treads in Joshua's footsteps.

Judges and 1 Samuel, which are bracketed together in the Deuteronomistic History, present the opposite side of the same coin. In that period of the "judges"—among whom the Josianic writer includes Saul—Israel was oppressed by foreigners in its own land because of its disobedience to Mosaic law, particularly because of the decentralized and syncretistic forms of worship and the lack of unitary leadership and stability of succession. Historical paradigms for Josiah's opponents and rivals, in other words, are presented as both leading to disaster and breaching the fundamentals of Mosaic law.

Beginning in 2 Samuel 1:1, "after the death of Saul," an ideal Davidic king is presented as the sole means of salvation from such ills. From that point on in the "history," each of the Davidids is judged by how closely he adheres to the Deuteronomic ideal. Several provide positive models, but none measures up to Josiah. "Before him there was no king like him, who turned to Yahweh with all his mind, with all his being, and with all his strength, according to all the legal instruction of Moses" (2 Kgs 23:25a; Au. trans.).

The kings of the north, on the other hand, are without exception judged to be evil. Because they sundered the unity of state and religion, their history can only serve as a negative object lesson. The eventual fall of this evil nemesis moves the Deuteronomistic historian to a peroration on the significance of the event (2 Kgs 17:7–18), just in case the reader still has any doubts.

JOSHUA AS A JOSIANIC BOOK

The preceding analysis of the Deuteronomistic History and its multiform address to the dynamics of the Josianic "reform" helps to explain certain features of the Book of Joshua. Chapters 1 and 23—both written almost entirely in formulas that the Deuteronomistic historian uses elsewhere in framing passages and speeches—bracket the diverse materials in chapters 2–22 and shape them to portray Joshua as a legitimating model for Josiah. Chapter 1 obtains this end so effectively that it may serve as a lens to focus and organize

further discussion of the Josianic Book of Joshua.

The phrase with which Joshua opens, "And it happened after the death of [Moses]," also appears in Judges 1:1 with the name of Joshua and in 2 Samuel 1:1 with that of Saul. Part of an obvious pattern here, but rare elsewhere, this formula directs attention to the basic structure and concerns of the Deuteronomistic History. The era of Moses was unique, a time when laws and norms were set down for all time to come. Because of his obedience to those laws and norms, Joshua, in his time, was chosen to lead Israel toward the fulfillment of God's promise of land. After his death, however, Israel transgressed the law of Moses and as a consequence became unable to withstand its enemies (cf. Judg 2:6–15). Such was the case until Saul's death cleared the way for David—the founder of Josiah's dynasty—to rule a united, enlarged, and powerful Israel.

Following the introductory formula, Joshua 1:1–9 reports Yahweh's charge to Joshua. The form of this charge indicates the installation of officeholders, while its emphasis upon obedience to the law reveals that the office in question is royal. Joshua's assumption of power immediately upon Moses' death also conforms to the royal pattern of dynastic succession, and distinguishes it from the charismatic practice of judges or prophets. These same elements appear together in 1 Kings 2:1–4, a passage whose parallels to Joshua 1:1–9 offer trenchant commentary upon the latter's form and purpose.

Portrayed in the Deuteronomistic History as the sole legitimate successor to Moses, Joshua undergoes a double investment—once by Moses (Deut 31:7–8; cf. 1:38; 3:21; 31:3, 14–15, 23), and once by Yahweh (Josh 1:1–9). This succession of authority is repeatedly reinforced in the Book of Joshua. As part of his charge to Joshua, Yahweh promises, "As I was with Moses, so I will be with you" (1:5). In Joshua 1:17, the Transjordanian tribes echo the sentiment from below: "As in everything we obeyed Moses, so we will obey you; only may Yahweh your God be with you, as he was with Moses!" When Joshua is about to lead Israel across the Jordan to dry ground—a parallel to Moses at the Sea (cf. 4:23)—Yahweh assures him, "This day I will begin to magnify you in the sight of all Israel, so that they will know that, as I was with Moses, so I will be with you" (3:7). After the people have crossed, the narrator reports, "Yahweh magnified Joshua in the sight of all Israel; and they stood in awe of him, as they had stood in awe of Moses, all the days of his life" (4:14). There are dozens of similar references in Joshua where Moses is mentioned by name and his authority invoked to sanction Joshua's —therefore Josiah's—actions.

This explicit, Mosaic sanction of Josiah in the person of Joshua is reinforced at the implicit level as well. Joshua's theophanic encounter with the commander of Yahweh's army (5:13–15) recalls Moses' "burning bush" experience (Ex 3:1–6), with verbal parallels between Joshua 5:15 and Exodus 3:5.

From the perspective of more recent literary criticism, moreover, Robert Polzin argues that the rhetoric of Joshua 1:2–9 and its parallels accomplishes by implication two additional purposes:

> First, it presents the narrator as one who can report God's word directly just as Moses habitually did. Our narrator had already prepared us for his practice of directly quoting God in Joshua–2 Kings by beginning to quote God in direct discourse five times toward the end of the Book of Deuteronomy. . . . Thus, the narrator immediately assumes his authoritative role here in Joshua, a role patterned after that of Moses as he is portrayed in Deuteronomy. Second, if the content and context of God's reported utterance exalts now the role of Joshua as the successor of Moses immediately following Moses' death, the phraseological composition of reported and reporting speech in Joshua 1:2–9 impresses upon the reader rather the role of the Deuteronomic narrator as successor to Moses vis-à-vis those readers whom he addresses. (Polzin 1980, 76)

Polzin himself does not place the composition of the Deuteronomistic History in a particular historical context. But his analysis of how the narrative structure transfers to the narrator Moses' role as God's definitive spokesperson reveals a dimension of the text that fits Josiah's policies perfectly. The Deuteronomistic Historian's interpretation of history and current events is authoritative because, implicitly, he in his time speaks directly with God, just as Moses did in his time.

Applied to the explicit links between Moses and Joshua in Joshua 1:5, 1:17, 3:7, and 4:14, such an analysis of the implicit dimension of the text reveals a technique similar to that of the Deuteronomistic

narrator. Although referring to a different passage, Polzin's words describe the phenomenon exactly: "We see the authorial voice emphasizing a particular theme by placing it in the mouth of now one, now another, authoritative personage in his story" (p. 79). Note that in this particular series, however, the culminating version of the theme (4:14) is voiced by the narrator.

The theme of the authoritative leader is linked with the unity of the whole nation. In 1:2 a singular "you," referring to Joshua, is joined to "all this people." Expressed in the phrases "all the Israelites," "all Israel," "all the men of Israel," and "all the nation," this national unity punctuates the book of Joshua like a drumbeat (Josh 3:1, 7, 17; 4:1, 11, 14; 6:5; 7:3, 23, 24, 25; 8:15, 21; 10:15, 21, 24, 29, 31, 34, 36, 38). In its larger literary context, the emphasis in chapters 3–4 on twelve men and twelve stones representing the twelve tribes of Israel functions the same way. This internal unity, in turn, is matched by enmity toward foreign nations and peoples (4:24; 7:9; 10:21, 42).

Joshua 1:2 sounds another theme central to both the Deuteronomistic History and the "reform" of Josiah—the declaration that Yahweh is giving the land to Israel (Deut 1:20, 25; 2:29; 3:20; 4:1, 21, 40; 5:16, 31; 11:17, 31; 12:9; 13:12; 15:4, 7; 16:5, 18, 20; 17:2, 14; 18:9; 19:2, 10, 14; 20:16; 21:1, 23; 24:4; 25:15, 19; 26:1–2; 27:2–3; 28:8; Josh 1:11, 15; cf. 1:13; 5:6; 9:24; 11:23; 18:3; 21:43; 23:5). This land is repeatedly referred to as "the land which you are entering [crossing over Jordan] to possess" (Deut 4:5, 14, 22, 26; 6:1; 7:1; 9:1, 5; 11:8, 10–11, 29, 31; 23:20; 28:21, 63; 30:16, 18; 31:13; 32:47; Josh 1:11).

In giving further expression to this "manifest destiny" and the Mosaic mandate for it, Joshua 1:3–5ab is modeled almost verbatim on Deuteronomy 11:24–25. The declaration of these passages to the Israelites that they shall possess "every place upon which the sole of your [plural] foot shall tread" sets the remainder of the book into the context desired by the Deuteronomistic historian (cf. 14:9) and anticipates the role of the priests' feet in the crossing of the Jordan (3:13, 4:18).

In its repetition of "No man shall be able to stand before you" from Deuteronomy 11:25, Joshua 1:5 (cf. 10:8) changes the "you" from plural to singular and adds "all the days of your [singular] life." This concentration of Yahweh's promise to the people upon one individual and his military success evinced a royal ideology exactly fitted to Josiah's policies.

Josiah's "historian" had to walk a tightrope in depicting the territory taken by that royal figure. On the one hand, he needed to stake Israelite land claims at their most optimistic and extensive, and picture Josiah's forerunner, Joshua, as virtually irresistible in his drive toward realizing Israel's territorial aspirations. The ideal boundaries as outlined in Joshua 1:4—modeled, in turn, on Deuteronomy 11:24 (cf. Deut 1:7)—served this purpose, as did generalizing statements, as in Joshua 11:23.

On the other hand, the territory actually incorporated into Josiah's realm was decidedly less extensive, and he faced both internal and external rivals for its control. Along with not raising unachievable expectations, the narrator therefore needed to caution his readers against rival leaders and ways, if he was to prepare them for a negative object lesson regarding alien influences in Judges and 1 Samuel. For these reasons, he framed his composite and relatively modest traditions of allotment in Joshua 13:14–21:42 with the motif of the land and peoples that remained as a test and challenge (Josh 13:1–13, 23:4–13a; cf. Judg 3:1–6).

Opinions vary regarding what territory Josiah actually controlled. It appears likely, however, that his primary domain and attempts at expansion lay in the Cisjordan. Deuteronomy 2:5, 9, and 19 make clear that the Transjordanian lands of Edom, Moab, and Ammon, which had been part of the Davidic empire, were not included in the "land grant" presupposed by the Deuteronomistic History.

This geopolitical reality may account for a pervasive feature in the Deuteronomistic Book of Joshua— the division of the land at the Jordan between the two and one-half Transjordanian tribes and the nine and one-half Cisjordanian tribes (Josh 1:12–18; 4:12–13; 12:1, 6–7; 13:7–12, 15–32; 14:2–4; 18:5–7; 21:5–6, 27; 22:1–34; cf. Deut 3:12–22; 29:7–8). The lands of the former are portrayed as having been taken and distributed by Moses. Only Cisjordan is conquered by Joshua and then allotted to the people. Was such a division intended by Josiah's court historian to voice Israel's historical claims to Transjordan, while at the same time relieving Josiah from pressure to move into

territory that he had no realistic chance of taking or holding?

Another note significant for Josiah is struck in Joshua 1:5c–7a and 1:9, with the obvious, often literal adumbration in Deuteronomy 31:6–8. Joshua is urged repeatedly to "be strong, be resolute, do not tremble, do not be dismayed" (cf. Deut 1:21, 3:28, 31:23; Josh 1:18, 8:1, 10:8, 10:25, 11:6). At first glance, this rhetoric may appear to protest too much. Why was this repetitive encouragement and reassurance necessary? As Nelson (1981a, 122) explains, Josiah's policies would have faced opposition from many quarters: (1) the newly unemployed provincial clergy; (2) the average peasant, whose familiar, local rituals were being abolished; (3) town and city officials—many in the north were foreigners, brought in by the Assyrians—who saw the prestige and influence of their localities being diminished as their sanctuaries were destroyed; (4) the more extreme reformers, who felt that Josiah had not gone far enough; (5) pro-Assyrian elements, who had supported Manasseh's policies; and (6) ardent northern nationalists, who refused to accept a Davidic king.

Against this opposition, the historian urges that Josiah should be resolute, for he, like Joshua his prototype, has been chosen by Yahweh to secure Israel's inheritance of the land promised of old (cf. Josh 1:6 with 11:23, and Deut 1:38, 3:28, 12:10, 19:3, 31:7). His authority to partition the land reflects the king's right to divide his realm into districts and distribute it to loyal followers (1 Kgs 4:7–19).

By emphasizing that success depends upon scrupulous observance of Mosaic law, Joshua 1:7bc–8 further underscores Joshua's royal role in prefiguring the program of Josiah. These lines are modeled on the "law of the king" in Deuteronomy 17:18–20. In Deuteronomy, torah, "law, legal instruction," is always referred to as "this law," stressing its pertinence for the current (Josianic) context. Such is the case not only in the "law of the king" (Deut 17:18–19), but in the introduction (Deut 1:5; 4:8, 44) and various appendixes to the book (Deut 27:3, 8, 26; 28:58, 61; 29:21 [Masoretic text 20], 29 [MT 28]; 31:9, 11–12, 24, 26; 32:46.)

This Mosaic torah becomes, in turn, the mandate for all of Joshua's actions and his legacy to future generations (Josh 1:7, 8; 8:31, 32, 34, 35; 22:5; 23:6; 24:26). *Torah* is not mentioned again in the Deuteronomistic History until David's deathbed instruction to Solomon to keep it (1 Kgs 2:3). Solomon, it should be remembered, was the founding builder of the Temple that Josiah repaired and placed at the center of national life. In this regard, note Solomon's long, dedicatory prayer in 1 Kings 8:12–45, which reflects the spirit of the Deuteronomistic historian. *Torah* next appears in 2 Kings 10:31, which states that Jehu, though a tool of Yahweh's judgment against the dynasty of Omri, shares with every single northern king the onus of breaking the law. One Davidid (Amaziah) is praised (2 Kgs 14:6) for keeping a specific provision of Deuteronomic law (Deut 24:16). Apart from two passages deriving from the exilic editor (2 Kgs 17:37, 21:8) and the chapters regarding Josiah, the only other mentions of *torah* in the Deuteronomistic History concern the fall of Samaria (2 Kgs 17:13) and the unlawful syncretism of those left or placed in the north after its fall (2 Kgs 17:34). Even without the culminating treatment of *torah* in the account of Josiah, the specific relevance of each of these passages for Josianic policies is patent.

The Deuteronomistic historian, of course, did not leave the matter at that, but presented Josiah's discovery and implementation of the Mosaic *torah* as the climax of his work (2 Kgs 22:8, 11; 23:24–25a). That he portrayed Joshua as a unique prototype for Josiah's strict obedience to Deuteronomic law is shown by the distribution of the admonition found in Joshua 1:7 regarding that *torah:* "Turn not from it to the right hand or to the left." This admonition to keep to the legal straight and narrow is used four times in Deuteronomy (5:32; 17:11, 20 [the "law of the king"]; 28:14), and again in Joshua's farewell address to Israel (Josh 23:6). It does not recur in the Deuteronomistic History until Josiah is said to have fulfilled it (2 Kgs 22:2).

Similarly, Joshua "left nothing undone of all that Yahweh had commanded Moses" (Josh 11:15). No such report of complete obedience to Mosaic law occurs again in the Deuteronomistic History until the account of Josiah reaches its climax in 2 Kings 23:25a.

In addition to these references to the Mosaic *torah* as a whole, Joshua contains many examples of events that fulfill or violate specific injunctions in

Deuteronomy. Most remarkable among these is the "holy war" mandate of Deuteronomy 20:16–18 (*cf.* 7:1–5) that all previous inhabitants of the land given to Israel be "utterly destroyed" or "put to the ban." Explicit references to this statute are found in Joshua 2:10; 6:17–18, 21; 7:1, 11–13, 15; 8:26; 10:1, 28, 35, 37, 39–40; 11:11–12, 20–21; 22:20 (*cf.* 6:19, 24; 8:2, 8, 24–25, 27–29; 9:24; 10:20, 30, 32–33; 11:6, 9, 14, 17, 22). The "nations" so to be exterminated are listed in Deuteronomy 20:17 by a formula that is repeated in Joshua 3:10, 9:1, 11:3, and 12:8 (*cf.* Judg 3:5). The kings of certain of these vanquished peoples are treated (Josh 8:29, 10:27) in strict adherence to the regulations of Deuteronomy 21:22–23 governing the exposure of the bodies of executed criminals.

Few portions of the Bible so offend many moderns as this grisly tale of divinely mandated genocide. As has been seen, however, this narrative of conquest is not an "objective history" of Joshua's time, but one "historical" object lesson among many legitimating the cause in which the Josianic composer believed so fervently in his own time. Although notions of holy war and putting to the ban are not restricted to this author or his context, the application of the ban to an entire population as ordered in Joshua occurs only in passages that bear every indication of Deuteronomistic composition.

The rhetorical thrust of what seems to amount to a mandate for genocide is to give expression to the pent-up national anger felt by a small state whose identity and integrity had been compromised by decades of domination by foreign superpowers. Viewed from the subjectivity of the rage of the oppressed and the passionate hope for national independence and purity, the only good foreigner was a dead foreigner. (Before dismissing such rhetoric as unworthy, citizens of modern superpowers might well ponder if they are ever the objects of such legitimate anger from the smaller nations that serve as their pawns and surrogates.)

Alongside the need for the public expression of unqualified rage against foreign influences, regimes such as Josiah's face the practical necessity of subtly legitimating certain "good foreigners," whose services are essential to the regime. Rahab (Josh 2:1–24; 6:17, 22–23, 25) fits this description, as do perhaps the Gibeonites (Josh 9:3–27), for they, like Rahab, are exempted from the strictures of Deuteronomy 20:16–18. Nor can such "creative interpretation" of Deuteronomic law be an unintentional oversight by the narrator, as Polzin has demonstrated on literary grounds (1980; 84–91, 117–123). Rahab is, after all, the very first "Canaanite" encountered by representatives of Israel, and the explicit law of the ban is bent by authoritative interpreters—including both Joshua and the narrator—to spare the lives of her family.

This tension between strict and "creative" application of Deuteronomic law to specific cases has been noted by Polzin throughout the Deuteronomistic History as a dialectic between a voice of "authoritarian dogmatism" and one of "critical traditionalism." While Polzin's analysis is ahistorically literary, the dialectic it reveals fits Josiah's policy needs perfectly. When Josiah needed the mandate for his "reforms" to be unyielding and absolute against opponents or subordinates, it was the very law of God delivered to Moses. When administrative exigencies required a certain freedom of royal interpretation, the paradigm of "critical traditionalism" was invoked.

The taking of cattle and spoil as booty in Joshua 8:2, 8:27, and 11:14 may constitute another case of such "creative interpretation," for it would seem to violate a literal application of Deuteronomy 20:16. Alternatively, these passages are perhaps to be read in light of Deuteronomy 20:14, which allows spoils to be taken from distant cities. (Ai and Hazor, the cities in question, were both in the north.)

Be that as it may, the location of the extensive narratives of Joshua 7–8 in the immediate vicinity of Bethel cannot have been lost on a Josianic audience (cf. 2 Kgs 23:4–20). The story of Achan—a Judahite—reinforces a royal claim to all treasure goods and metals (cf. Josh 6:19, 24) taken in Josiah's campaign against Bethel, while allowing his Judahite troops to appropriate certain livestock and agricultural goods for themselves. Finally, Joshua's rending of his clothes when he discovers that Mosaic law has been breached at Ai near Bethel (Josh 7:6–9) prefigures Josiah's reaction to the discovery and reading of that same law (2 Kgs 22:11–13).

The Deuteronomistic historian's use of the Passover traditions in Joshua 5:10–12 is even more subtle. Although this old material is not Josianic in composition, its mere inclusion in the larger work adds Joshua's authority to the centralized Passover prescribed by Moses in Deuteronomy 16:1–8 and effected by Josiah in 2 Kings 23:21–23.

JOSHUA AND HISTORICAL RECONSTRUCTION

This essay has emphasized the relationship between the Book of Joshua and the historical dynamics of Josianic Israel, in and for which it was composed in nearly its present form as part of the much larger Deuteronomistic History. This emphasis is not intended to deny that the Josianic author(s) incorporated previously extant materials—some of considerable antiquity, extent, and cohesion. The exact shape of these pre-Deuteronomistic materials and their relationship to the history that generated and shaped them, however, present a great quandary. The two major attempts in twentieth-century scholarship to address this hornet's nest of issues now stand under heavy—and probably decisive—criticism.

The so-called "nomadic infiltration model" for Israel's origins, associated with such scholars as Alt, Noth, and Weippert (Chaney 1983, 41–44), assumes that most of the stories incorporated into the Deuteronomistic narrative of "conquest" were etiologically generated, that is, composed to explain some physical artifact such as an unusual heap of stones beside the Jordan (see, e.g., Josh 4:5–7, 20–24). The assumption regarding the type of these materials made by scholars of this school denies their usefulness as historical sources. More recent analyses by Seeligmann, Childs, and Long (Chaney 1983, 44), however, demonstrate that the etiological element in the Joshua narratives belongs to the latest, not the earliest, stages of the tradition.

A second scholarly model for Israelite origins, often called the "conquest model," is championed by such scholars as Albright, Wright, and Lapp (Chaney 1983, 44–48). In polemical reaction to the nomadic infiltration model, it has sought to demonstrate the "essential historicity" of the Joshua narrative, without insisting that every detail is literally true. During the middle decades of the twentieth century, when this school reached its flood tide, the fledgling discipline of Palestinian archaeology appeared to many to have shown that numerous sites mentioned in the Bible as taken by Joshua were in fact destroyed in the thirteenth century B.C.E. More recent and fuller archaeological research proved an embarrassment for this point of view, since more and more of the sites said by the text to have been captured by Joshua have been shown to have been uninhabited in Joshua's time.

Mendenhall, Gottwald, and Chaney (Gottwald 1979; Chaney 1983) have still more recently explored a model of "peasant and frontier revolt," which begins with an extensive critique of the two previously regnant paradigms. While preliminary analyses of some of the pre-Deuteronomistic materials in Joshua have been undertaken by these scholars, no commentary on the book exists that works consistently from their methodological stance. Coote and Whitelam (1987) take their point of departure from this model of peasant and frontier revolt, but bracket the biblical text methodologically in order to place Israelite origins in a much larger chronological and geographical context.

The major scholars espousing each of these models all see the Book of Joshua in its present form as a Deuteronomistic work. Few seem to have grasped fully the relationships between that text and Josianic society. Only a beginning sketch of those relationships is offered here, but the detailed and rigorous pursuit of such investigation is surely prerequisite to any more certain delineation of the pre-Deuteronomistic materials in the Book of Joshua and their possible relationship to any given set of historical dynamics.

Bibliography

Boling, Robert G. *Joshua.* Anchor Bible, vol. 6. Garden City, N.Y., 1982.

Butler, Trent C. *Joshua.* Waco, Tex., 1983.

Chaney, Marvin C. "Ancient Palestinian Peasant Movements and the Formation of Premonarchic Israel." In *Palestine in Transition: The Emergence of Ancient Israel,* edited by David Noel Freedman and David Frank Graf. Sheffield, England, 1983. Pp. 39–90.

Coote, Robert B., and Keith W. Whitelam. *The Emergence of Early Israel in Historical Perspective.* Sheffield, England, 1987.

Cross, Frank Moore. "The Themes of the Book of Kings and the Structure of the Deuteronomistic History." In *Canaanite Myth and Hebrew Epic: Essays in the History of the Religion of Israel.* Cambridge, Mass., 1973. Pp. 274–289.

Gottwald, Norman K. *The Tribes of Yahweh: A Sociology of the Religion of Liberated Israel, 1250–1050 B.C.E.* Maryknoll, N.Y., 1979.

Mayes, Andrew D. H. *The Story of Israel Between Settlement and Exile.* London, 1983.

Nelson, Richard D. *The Double Redaction of the Deuteronomistic History.* Sheffield, England, 1981. (1981a)

——. "Josiah in the Book of Joshua." *Journal of Biblical Literature* 100 (1981): 531–540. (1981b)

Noth, Martin. *Das Buch Josua.* 2d, rev. ed. Tübingen, 1953.

——. *The Deuteronomistic History.* Sheffield, England, 1981. A partial translation of Noth's *Überlieferungsgeschichtliche Studien* (1943).

Peckham, Brian. *The Composition of the Deuteronomistic History.* Decatur, Ga., 1985.

Polzin, Robert. *Moses and the Deuteronomist: A Literary Study of the Deuteronomistic History.* New York, 1980.

Soggin, J. Alberto. *Joshua: A Commentary.* Translated by R. A. Wilson. London, 1972.

MARVIN L. CHANEY

Judges

BECAUSE OF RENEWED scholarly interest in Israel's "conquest" of the land of Canaan, Judges is one of the most discussed biblical books today. It is an exciting book to read because it is so colorful; at the same time its diversity makes it somewhat difficult to understand. In the first place, the book is a composite, which accounts for its repetitions and inconsistencies. Also, in the recounting of Judges, not one but several literary forms are used; for example, folklore, sagas, and historical fragments are mixed throughout the book. The contents of Judges can be divided into three main sections: the exploits of military and civilian leaders (chaps. 3–16), the migration and relocation of the Danites (chaps. 17–18), and the civil war between the Benjaminites and the rest of the tribes of Israel (chaps. 19–21).

Judges is extremely valuable for understanding the origins of Israel; it is the only biblical source for the twelfth and eleventh centuries B.C.E., the turbulent era between the death of Joshua and the institution of the monarchy. Although this period continues to be a dark age, with few hard facts available, Judges is helpful for reconstructing the social, political, and religious life of early Israel.

HISTORICAL BACKGROUND

With allowance for an overlap of 200 years, the Late Bronze Age came to an end and the Iron Age began about 1200 B.C.E.; iron, however, was not commonly used in Canaan until the tenth century B.C.E. Egyptian domination over Canaan was beginning to wane at that time as new people, including the Israelites and the Philistines, were making their appearance. The settlement patterns began to change at the beginning of the Iron Age; the fortified cities of the Late Bronze Age were destroyed, and small village settlements began to spring up in the central hill country, in Galilee, and in Transjordan (modern Jordan). The Israelites settled these regions in the era of the judges and led a sedentary agricultural life.

The earliest written reference to Israel outside the Bible is found on the Merneptah stela, also called the Israel stela; it reads: "Israel lies desolate; its seed is no more." Merneptah, the son and successor of Pharaoh Rameses II, ruled Egypt from about 1212 to 1202 B.C.E. This victory stela commemorates his defeat of Syria-Palestine. About 1175, Sea Peoples known as the Philistines began to settle along the southwestern coast of Canaan. For the next several centuries the Israelites and the Philistines were locked in bloody conflict, both contending for the same land.

Concerning religious practice, Yahweh—to use the cultic name of the God of Israel—was not worshiped exclusively. Baal stood alongside the God of Israel. The Israelites also adopted some of the religious customs of the neighboring peoples; several centuries later the prophets were still inveighing against the syncretism of Israel. Nonetheless, it was not political but religious unity that bound together the Israelite tribes.

CONQUEST OR SETTLEMENT?

Scholars are uncertain about how Israel came to control Canaan. The nature of the historical evidence does not permit a straightforward answer. The problem is not a new one; it was already present when the books of Joshua and Judges were taking shape. Each book has a different view about how Israel came into possession of the land: Joshua speaks of a unified conquest conducted with great speed, whereas Judges describes a gradual infiltration of Canaan.

In the attempt to explain how Israel gained control over the land of Canaan, scholars have suggested three models or hypotheses. The conquest model, which accords with Joshua 1–12, supposes an invasion, with armed conflict resulting in the destruction of Canaanite cities. Archaeology, however, does not support this explanation, especially in the cases of Jericho, Ai, and Gibeon. In the late thirteenth century, Jericho in the Jordan Valley was an insignificant settlement, hardly more than a fort. Ai, to the east of Bethel, had been destroyed and unoccupied from about 2250; at the time when the Israelites are alleged to have conquered Ai, it was still uninhabited. Gibeon (modern el-Jib), five miles northwest of Jerusalem, shows no evidence of settlement in the Late Bronze Age (1550–1200). The fact that the early Israelites settled in unpopulated regions indicates that their extensive occupation of the land of Canaan was not accomplished by military conquest.

The second explanation, the immigration model, accords well with the portrayal in Judges. Described as a long process of peaceful infiltration, it runs counter to the swift campaign depicted in Joshua. The evidence of archaeology does support the more gradual operation of Judges. For example, Lachish, thirty miles southwest of Jerusalem, was not conquered until 1150 or later, while the major fortified Canaanite city of Hazor, ten miles north of the Sea of Galilee, was already destroyed by the end of the thirteenth century. The decline and eventual destruction of the Canaanite cities, which cannot be attribut-

ed to a single historical event, took place over fifty years. The fact that the culture of the Early Iron Age (1200–1000) shows dependence upon Late Bronze Age culture rules out the conquest hypothesis and points to a process of settlement over a long period of time.

The third model, based on social reorganization, is called by some a "peasants' revolt." It may have been perpetrated by oppressed people composed of indigenous Canaanites and Israelite (?) infiltrators (Gottwald 1985). Instead of "revolt," some would describe the process as "withdrawal" by the indigenous Canaanite farmers from the lowlands and their ascent to the highlands (Stager 1985). Each of these models has its problems and cannot be accepted without modification. A definitive conclusion will have to await additional textual and archaeological evidence.

Meanwhile, the following evidence from Early Iron Age villages is useful in understanding the manner of Israelite settlement in Canaan. Village layout, pillared houses, slope terracing, and other features of these villages reflect a sophisticated technology. The Israelite settlers were not simply pastoral nomads from the desert; it would seem that the Israelites were well settled in the land and had been living as agriculturalists for a considerable time.

DEUTERONOMISTIC HISTORY

Judges is not an independent book but is part of a larger literary corpus known as the Deuteronomistic History, which includes Deuteronomy, Joshua, Judges, 1 and 2 Samuel, and 1 and 2 Kings. The Deuteronomistic History is so called because it is heavily influenced by the teachings of Deuteronomy 5–28, with their emphasis on the Mosaic covenant. Completed during the exile, around 550 B.C.E., the Deuteronomistic History has its own theological point of view, consisting of the following four-point pattern: rebellion, punishment, cry for help, deliverance (Judg 2:11–19). In summary, it is a theology based on divine retribution, maintaining that the fortunes of the Israelites rose and fell with their fidelity to Yahweh's covenant. Loyalty to the covenant merited blessing; disobedience was deserving of divine judgment. This four-point cycle is best exemplified in the account of Othniel, the first of the judges (3:7–11).

JUDGES

The biblical term "judge" (Hebrew *sopet*) is ambiguous and consequently often misunderstood. The Hebrew verb "to judge" may also be rendered as "to rule." "Judge" certainly designated one who dispensed justice, as in the Mosaic era. In the period of the Book of Judges, however, the word described a military deliverer rather than one who rendered juridical decisions. The judges who succeeded Joshua were charismatic leaders; for the most part, they were local rather than national figures. Unlike the kings, the judges were temporary and not hereditary rulers.

The Book of Judges includes, perhaps arbitrarily, six major and six minor judges. All the major judges, with the exception of Samson, delivered the Israelites from their enemies. With the exception of Deborah, who is described as a prophetess, all were military leaders. Little is known about the minor judges, who may have been tribal chieftains. With the exception of Shamgar, the minor judges functioned in civil and not military roles. Shamgar is reminiscent of Samson: he saved Israel by killing 600 Philistines with an oxgoad (a long, metal-tipped pole) (3:31). The remaining minor judges are Tola of Issachar (10:1–2), Jair of Gilead (10:3–5), Ibzan of Judah or Zebulun (12:8–10), Elon of Zebulun (12:11–12), and Abdon of Ephraim (12:13–15).

PRELUDE

The prelude (1:1–2:5) is a summary statement that overlaps the Book of Joshua but voices discrepancies regarding the occupation and settlement of Canaan. In contrast to Joshua 1–12, with its description of complete conquest under Joshua, Judges 1 indicates clearly that the western hill country was gained only after a long struggle on the part of individual tribes. These annals appear to be written from the southern point of view, especially that of Judah, at the expense of the northern tribes, who were less successful in conquest. The prelude closes with a theological interpretation of Israel's military failures, attributing them to the infidelities of the Israelites (2:1–5).

INTRODUCTION

A kind of second introduction to Judges is presented in the form of a theological interpretation based on Deuteronomistic History (2:6–3:6). The deuteronomistic conception of history consisting of the four basic principles (defection, oppression, cry for help, deliverance) is stated succinctly in 2:11–19; herein lies the key to Judges. The appearance of judges at that time was Yahweh's way of extending deliverance expressed in historical terms. However, Israel's fidelity continued to be "tested" by the presence of foreign nations in its midst.

NARRATIVES

The section consisting of narratives and annals (3:7–16:31) is the longest in Judges. It deals with the military victories of the major judges over their hostile neighbors, including the Canaanites, Moabites, Ammonites, Midianites, and Philistines.

Othniel

The story of Othniel, the first of the judges, is fragmentary and vague. He has the distinction of being the only southern judge and is depicted as an ideal leader. Before the account in 3:7–11 that focuses on Othniel, it is related in 1:11–13 that he captured the city of Debir, earlier named Kiriath-sepher, a Canaanite royal city in the southern Judaean hill country (it is identified with modern Khirbet Rabud, a large tell southwest of Hebron). Othniel defeated Cushan-rishathaim, a king of Upper Mesopotamia whose identity is uncertain. This king, whose name *rishathaim* means "double wickedness," oppressed Israel for eight years and may have been Israel's first conqueror. The Israelites' sin was their practice of the cult of the Canaanite Baal and his female consort Asherah. Asherah can also denote a cult object representing the goddess; it may be in the form of a wooden pole or a living tree.

Ehud

The saga of Ehud is humorous and rich in detail. Called a "deliverer," Ehud was a left-handed (literally, "restricted in his right hand") Benjaminite who by a ruse killed the Moabite king Eglon (3:12–30). The

Moabite territory is situated on the plateau east of the Dead Sea; it is bordered on the north by the Arnon River and on the south by the Zered River. Before Ehud's victory over them the Moabites had oppressed Israel for eighteen years through invasion and occupation of the land. Eglon had crossed the Jordan River and established his camp at Jericho, "the city of palms," situated in the Jordan Valley six miles north of the Dead Sea. When presenting the required tribute to the king of Moab, Ehud secured a private audience ostensibly to convey a secret message to the king, who was sitting in a room on the second floor of the palace. He seized the opportunity to assassinate the obese ruler by thrusting a short, double-edged sword, which he had girded to his right thigh (because he was left-handed), into the royal belly. Making his escape before his crime was detected (for the royal servants thought the king was off relieving himself), Ehud cut off the escape of the Moabite army and annihilated them before they could return to their homeland east of the Jordan River.

Deborah and Barak

Israel's ultimate conflict with the indigenous Canaanites is described in this episode; subsequent battles were fought only against foreign invaders. Deborah and Barak led Israel to victory over the Canaanites, who were under the command of Sisera, in the Plain of Esdraelon. Although Barak was Israel's general, Deborah is described as the "inspiration" behind him. As a consequence of this victory after twenty years of oppression at the hands of the Canaanites, Israel won the Plain of Esdraelon from the Canaanites.

The story of Deborah and Barak appears in two forms, with some differences between them: Judges 4 is a late account in prose; Judges 5 is a vivid description in poetry. The poetic version, a victory song composed shortly after the event, is one of the oldest examples of extant Hebrew literature, dating to the twelfth century B.C.E. Some scholars consider Judges 5, commonly called the Song of Deborah, to be an eyewitness account because of its vivid detail.

Deborah, described as "mother in Israel" (5:7), functioned in several capacities: she was a prophetess, a military leader, and a judge who rendered legal decisions. Barak, who led the Israelites against the Canaanites, refused to go into battle without Deborah. Six tribes (Ephraim, Benjamin, Manasseh, Zebulun, Issachar, and Naphtali) participated in battle alongside Deborah and Barak; four tribes (Reuben, Gilead, Dan, and Asher) failed to do so. There is no mention of Judah and Simeon, the more distant tribes.

The Canaanite general Sisera had 900 iron chariots under his command when he did battle with Israel for control of Esdraelon. Also known as the valley of Jezreel, Esdraelon is the name of the plain lying between Galilee to the north and Samaria to the south; it also includes the Plain of Megiddo. The poet records that the battle took place "at Taanach, by the waters of Megiddo" (5:19). Taanach, on the southern edge of the Esdraelon Plain, is five miles southeast of Megiddo. According to archaeologists, Taanach was destroyed about 1125 B.C.E.; this destruction may be related to the battle under discussion. Megiddo, another important city in the Esdraelon Plain, was situated at modern Tell el-Mutesellim, twenty miles southeast of Haifa. Strategically located on the military routes, Megiddo figured prominently in many battles in the course of biblical history. In the last quarter of the twelfth century B.C.E., Megiddo was not extensively populated. The Kishon Brook is a stream that drains the Esdraelon Plain and the adjacent mountains. During the rainy season it becomes a marsh, as Sisera learned too late. He was defeated by the Israelites at this spot when his chariots became mired in mud. Prior to the confrontation between the Israelites and the Canaanites in the Esdraelon Plain, Barak had mustered his forces on Mount Tabor, 1,850 feet high and twelve miles from Megiddo in the northeast sector of the Esdraelon Plain. Descending the mountain, the Israelites routed the enemy.

Sisera escaped and fled, only to be transfixed with a tent peg shortly thereafter at the hands of Jael, wife of Heber the Kenite, with whom he sought refuge. Originally the Kenites were a tribe of smiths from northern Sinai; apparently they came into Canaan with the tribe of Judah and maintained a close association with Israel. The subtlety of Deborah's prediction to Barak before the battle should not be missed: "The road on which you are going will not lead to your glory, for the Lord will sell Sisera into the hand of a woman" (4:9; RSV). When Sisera died at the hands of Jael the prediction was fulfilled. Nothing was more ignominious for a man than to be killed by a woman. As Deborah was superior to Barak, so Jael was superior to Sisera—a powerful statement in a society that treated women as inferior to men.

The Sisera episode, as related in chapter 5, ends on a poignant note: His anxious mother awaited his return from battle. Assuming he had been victorious, she became a bit apprehensive over his delay in returning despite the assurances of her attendants. The poet appears to gloat over the fact that the great general was already dead.

Gideon

In the Gideon episode, the longest narrative in Judges, Israel is oppressed by the Midianites. The fact that the story is composed from two traditions accounts for inconsistencies that make it somewhat difficult to follow. The judge who finally expelled the invading Midianites is Gideon from the tribe of Manasseh. His name may mean "he who casts down" or "he who cuts off"; he also had the name Jerubbaal, meaning "let Baal contend." The second name was acquired when he destroyed his father's altar honoring Baal. The fact the altar was destroyed indicates that Baal did not "contend," that is, Baal was defeated.

The story opens with the account of the annual Midianite raids on Israelite land. These marauding bands invaded at harvest time, encamped, and plundered the produce. The Midianites were a semi-nomadic people who came from the region south and east of Moab and Edom. Archaeologists have not yet excavated or surveyed thoroughly the northwestern part of the Arabian peninsula and little is known about the region. The Midianites are thought to have intimidated the Israelites particularly because they were camel-mounted raiders. (The domestication of the camel dates to as early as the third millennium, but Israel's first contact with camels was at the end of the second millennium, at the close of the Late Bronze Age.) The Amalekites also accompanied the Midianites on their incursions west of the Jordan River. Nomadic people wandering in northern Sinai and the Negeb, the Amalekites were the perennial enemies of Israel, as early as the Israelite exodus from Egypt.

The Deuteronomistic theologian emphasizes that the Israelites were suffering devastating attacks by the Midianites because they had failed to adhere to the Mosiac covenant. Despite Yahweh's beneficence, especially at the time of the Exodus, Israel continued to be recalcitrant.

The dialogue between "the angel of the Lord" (a manifestation of God) and Gideon (6:11–18) follows a pattern typical of "announcement" narratives in the Bible, as with the angelic annunciation concerning the births of John and Jesus in the Lucan infancy narrative. Such narrations follow a general pattern: apparition of Yahweh or an angel, confusion on the part of the recipient of the announcement, communication from the divine messenger, objection by the recipient, and confirmation of the message by a divine sign.

As a sign, Gideon's sacrifice was consumed by fire. Before destroying the Baal altar, Gideon built an altar to Yahweh-shalom ("the Lord is peace"), recalling the Lord's greeting to him, "Peace be to you," to commemorate the sign (6:17–24).

Gideon then summoned the militia from among the various tribes and camped at Harod (Ain Jalud), the site of a copious spring at the foot of Mount Gilboa, before the battle against the Midianites. The 32,000 troops he had mustered were too large a contingent, since Yahweh was fighting on the side of Israel, so Gideon reduced the number by the ordeal of drinking water. Some scholars think the test was a purely arbitrary way of discriminating; others suggest that those who "lapped, putting their hands to their mouths" (numbering 300), showed signs of being more alert and vigilant than those who "knelt down to drink water." Gideon and his small band of 300, equipped only with trumpets and lighted jars, were victorious over the Midianites when they threw them into panic by a noisy surprise attack at night.

Pursuing the Midianites across the Jordan River, Gideon and his force, on the verge of exhaustion, rightfully expected support and sustenance from the Israelites resident in Succoth and Penuel, but relief was not forthcoming, perhaps out of fear of Midianite reprisal. Succoth, situated in the Jordan Valley close to the east bank of the Jordan, was an important city. It may perhaps be identified with modern Tell Deir Alla, two miles north of the Jabbok River (the modern Zerqa). Penuel, located apparently near a ford of the Jabbok River, is identified with modern Tulul edh-Dhahab. Gideon retaliated brutally by sacking these cities. Having defeated the Midianites, he executed their two kings.

After his victory over the Midianites, the people wanted to crown Gideon king. However, he declined to institute hereditary rule over Israel, because Yahweh alone was king; to have a human king would compromise God's exclusive role. Instead Gideon asked for gold from the spoils of the Midianites for an "ephod" to be erected in his native city of Ophrah. "Ephod" has several meanings, so it is not certain what it connotes here; usually it designated a priestly garment shaped like an apron, with a breastplate in front containing the Urim and Thummim used for divination. The ephod may have served to bring the wearer into contact with the deity. In the Gideon narrative the ephod was more likely an image or idol, a statue of the deity.

Abimelech

The tragic story of Abimelech ("my father is king") serves as a supplement to the Gideon narrative. Son of Gideon by his Schechemite concubine, Abimelech became the local king, ruling for three years over the Shechem area; ultimately he destroyed Shechem (1150–1125) in reprisal for the people's revolt. (Archaeological evidence points to the destruction of Shechem in the mid twelfth century B.C.E.) The treacherous Abimelech was made king after he had arranged the murders of his seventy half brothers; the only one to escape the bloody purge was Jotham, the youngest of Gideon's sons.

Shechem (Tell Balatah) was an important city in biblical history from the time of Abraham, who built an altar there; it was also the scene of renewal of the covenant under Joshua (Josh 24). It is located forty miles north of Jerusalem and one mile northwest of modern Nablus in the hill country of Ephraim, in the strategically important pass between Mount Gerizim to the south and Mount Ebal in the north.

Ascending the heights of Mount Gerizim, Jotham uttered the famous fable about the trees and their king, an indictment of the Shechemites for their injudicious choice of king. The highly respected and serviceable olive, fig tree, and vine all declined the proffered kingship, but when it was offered by default to the despised bramble, it accepted arrogantly. The

implication is obvious: the trees of value represent Gideon; the useless bramble stands for Abimelech. The Abimelech story manifests an antimonarchic tendency in Israel's history.

While besieging Thebez, a town in the vicinity of Shechem, Abimelech suffered a fractured skull when a woman deliberately let a millstone drop from the wall. Chauvinist to the end, he ordered his armor bearer to dispatch him lest it be recorded that he had been slain by a woman.

The story of Abimelech has significance for the history of the twelfth and eleventh centuries. In addition to portraying the conflict between the Israelites and the Canaanites, it illustrates that the Canaanites had not been driven out of the land during earlier conflicts. Also, the Canaanites and the Israelites appear to have merged: Abimelech was the offspring of an Israelite father and a Canaanite mother; Shechem, a Canaanite city, was governed by Israelites.

Jephthah

Israel's continued apostasy occasioned a new oppression, this time at the hands of the Ammonites. When Israel repented, Yahweh raised up Jephthah as deliverer, the only major judge from Transjordan. Jephthah, a Gileadite warrior who led an outlaw band in the manner of Robin Hood, delivered Israel from the domination of the Ammonites, who did not become a threat again until the time of Saul. Gilead, a hilly and wooded country, extends from the Sea of Galilee in the north to the Dead Sea in the south. The Ammonite territory, east of the Jordan, on the north bank of the Jabbok River, bordered the Arabian Desert. With their capital at Rabbath-Ammon (modern Amman), the Ammonites settled the land at the beginning of the thirteenth century. When the Ammonites invaded Gilead, the Israelites in Transjordan appealed to Jephthah to lead the attack. He agreed on condition that he would continue as chieftain after peace was restored. Before taking up arms against the Ammonites, the diplomatic Jephthah tried to negotiate the boundary dispute but was unsuccessful.

Before going into battle, Jephthah vowed to offer a holocaust ('olah) in return for victory, promising, "Whoever comes forth from the doors of my house to meet me, when I return victorious from the Ammonites, shall be the Lord's" (11:31). The first to greet him on return was his only daughter. A vow was considered irrevocable, so Jephthah did the inevitable. Abraham had been prevented from sacrificing Isaac by divine intervention; this time there was none. Human sacrifice was not condoned, but it happened occasionally.

Achieving victory over the Ammonites, Jephthah had to battle the Ephraimites, who resented their exclusion from Israel's war against the Ammonites. He defeated the Ephraimites in Gilead and slew them at the fords of the Jordan River as they tried to return west to their own land. To identify the retreating Ephraimites, Jephthah's sentries required them to pronounce the word *shibboleth*, which may mean "ear of corn" or "torrent." Because of differences of dialect east and west of the Jordan, the Ephraimites could pronounce only *sibboleth* (*s* instead of *sh*). The mispronunciation meant death for the Ephraimites.

Samson

The Samson episode of Judges, a cycle of stories composed of folklore, riddles, hyperbole, and assorted literary forms, is colorful and entertaining. Samson, a hero of the Danite tribe, is identified as the last of Israel's judges, but he was quite different from his predecessors. He did not lead an army, nor did he function as a deliverer; he conducted a vengeful private war against the Philistines. He is often described as a legendary hero, but that is not to deny a historical basis to the person and his exploits. If Samson resembles heroes in Greek mythology, it is not surprising; Samson's neighbors, the Philistines, apparently were a seafaring people with roots in the Aegean region, perhaps Crete. Samson, whose name is related to the Hebrew *semes* ("sun"), was an unlikely Nazirite, but he had been consecrated (*nazir*) from the womb. The Nazirite vow included abstinence from intoxicating drink, from use of the razor, and from contact with the dead (Num 6). Samson was not the most exemplary of Israel's judges, but most people in moments of truth can identify with his frail humanity. It may be difficult to recognize Samson as the hero of faith in the New Testament: "For time would fail me to tell of Gideon, Barak, Samson, Jephthah . . . who through faith conquered kingdoms, enforced justice, received promises, stopped the mouths of lions" (Heb 11:32–33).

The stories that constitute the Samson saga are valuable for the information they convey about life on the border between the Israelites and the Philistines at the time of Judges. They lived side by side, intermingled on each other's land, intermarried, and fought on occasion, not unlike people in modern times.

Despite the importance of the Philistines in biblical history, much about them is still unknown. Archaeologists excavating intensively at Philistine sites are clarifying Philistine daily life as they recover material culture, especially pottery, from the twelfth and eleventh centuries. But until they uncover documents and inscriptions in the Philistines' language, many uncertainties will remain.

The five major Philistine cities (Pentapolis) on the coast of southern Canaan are Ashdod, Ashkelon, Gaza, Gath, and Ekron. With the exception of Gath, archaeologists are now certain of the location of these cities. Another Philistine town mentioned in the Samson saga is Timnah, situated in the northern Judean plain and under excavation since 1977. Timnah changed hands several times between Israel and Philistia.

Dagon (16:23) was the principal deity of the Philistines. Temples to this god were located in Gaza and Ashdod. The god's name may be related to the Semitic word *dagan* ("grain"), suggesting that Dagon was a vegetation or grain god.

APPENDIXES

The final section of Judges (chaps. 17–21) consists of two appendixes in the form of narrative supplements: the Danites migrate to the north, and en route kidnap a Levitical priest (chaps. 17–18); a Levite's concubine is raped and murdered at Gibeah, and measures are taken to save the tribe of Benjamin from annihilation (chaps. 19–21). The narratives in these last four chapters belong to the period of the judges but do not concern the office of judge. The appendixes underscore the increasing anarchy of the period that resulted from the lack of a strong central government. The final verse of Judges says it all: "In those days there was no king in Israel; every man did what was right in his own eyes" (21:25).

THE DANITES AND THEIR SANCTUARY

Micah (chaps. 17–18), from the hill country of Ephraim, north of Jerusalem, played a part in the account of the Danites' migration northward. His story is told presumably to explain the origin of the Danite sanctuary. He stole a large sum of money from his mother but, fearful of being cursed, restored it. To expiate his crime, she in turn established a private shrine equipped with idol, ephod, and teraphim. The teraphim were cultic objects that in this context may have been used for divination. These practices were contrary to the Mosaic law proscribing the use of images (Ex 20:4–6). At first Micah appointed one of his sons as priest for the shrine; later he engaged the services of a Levite from Bethlehem as priest. When the Danites stole Micah's cultic paraphernalia and induced the Levite to serve as priest in their new sanctuary, he pursued the felons, but was no match for them and had to retreat. Thus ends the story of Micah!

The tribe of Dan originally occupied a small parcel of land west of Benjamin in southwest Canaan. Pressured by the Philistines, they migrated north and settled in a fertile area close to the source of the Jordan River, ten miles north of Lake Huleh. It became the northernmost Israelite city, as indicated in the phrase "from Dan to Beersheba" (Judg 20:1). Before the newly acquired territory was called Dan, it was known as Laish, identified with modern Tel Dan, a fifty-acre site, where excavation began in 1966. The settlement goes back to the Early Bronze Age II (2900–2700); it was destroyed by fire in the eleventh century but was soon rebuilt. The Danites set up their stolen cultic objects there; later, King Jeroboam I of Israel (922–901) built a temple at Dan, making it one of the two important sanctuaries of the Northern Kingdom.

INTERNECINE WARFARE AGAINST THE BENJAMINITES

A second appendix (chaps. 19–21), featuring the shameful Benjaminites is a combination of fact and fiction. Small in territory, Benjamin was strategically located on the central ridge between Jerusalem and Bethel. The Benjaminites had a reputation for bravery and skill in warfare. Their outrage, described in this final section of Judges, is placed at Gibeah, a Benjaminite city located at modern Tel el-Ful, five miles north of Jerusalem. Not only did the residents of Gibeah withhold hospitality from the Levite and his concubine, but they brutalized her to death. To galvanize the tribes to action against such a heinous crime, the Levite distributed twelve pieces of the concubine's corpse throughout Israel. (Readers must judge this macabre action and several others in Judges in the context of a violent era.) The other tribes went to war against the Benjaminites to avenge the atrocity, and in the course of a bitter intertribal struggle Gibeah was destroyed.

As a result of the war against Benjamin, the tribe was threatened with extinction. To maintain the integrity of the overall tribal structure, the Israelites assured the continuity of Benjamin by providing wives seized from Jabesh-Gilead and Shiloh. The people of Jabesh-Gilead, a town east of the Jordan River in Gilead, had refused to participate in the war against Gibeah. As a punishment all were slain except 400 young virgins who became the wives of Benjaminites. In addition, women were abducted from Shiloh, the religious and administrative center of the tribes, ten miles north of Bethel.

The internecine division and general disarray rampant in the period of the judges prepared the way for the institution of monarchy in the time of Samuel. In the perspective of the Deuteronomistic historian, it was a time of trial, when the people's faith in God was put to the test in various situations of conflict.

Bibliography

Aharoni, Yohanan. "The Israelite Occupation of Canaan: An Account of the Archaeological Evidence." *Biblical Archaeology Review*, 8 (1982): 14–23.

Boling, Robert G., ed. *Judges*. Anchor Bible, vol. 6A. Garden City, N.Y., 1975.

Coogan, Michael. "A Structural and Literary Analysis of the Song of Deborah." *Catholic Biblical Quarterly*, 40 (1978): 143–165.

Freedman, David Noel, and David Frank Graf, eds. *Palestine in Transition: The Emergence of Ancient Israel*. Sheffield, England, 1983.

Fritz, Volkmar. "Conquest or Settlement? The Early Iron Age in Palestine." *Biblical Archaeologist*, 50 (1987): 84–100.

Gottwald, Norman K. *The Hebrew Bible: A Socio-Literary Introduction.* Philadelphia, 1985. Pp. 229–288.

King, Philip J. "The Contribution of Archaeology to Biblical Studies." *Catholic Biblical Quarterly,* 45 (1983): 1–16.

Malamat, Abraham. "How Inferior Israelite Forces Conquered Fortified Canaanite Cities." *Biblical Archaeology Review,* 8 (1982): 24–35.

Mendenhall, George. "The Hebrew Conquest of Palestine." *Biblical Archaeologist,* 25 (1962): 66–87.

Stager, Lawrence. "The Archaeology of the Family in Ancient Israel." *Bulletin of the American Schools of Oriental Research,* 260 (1985): 1–35.

Ussishkin, David. "Lachish: Key to the Israelite Conquest of Canaan?" *Biblical Archaeology Review,* 13 (1987): 18–39.

PHILIP J. KING

Ruth

THE BOOK OF Ruth bears the name of a widowed and childless Moabite woman who chose to accompany her Judean mother-in-law to Bethlehem, and whose faithfulness led to remarriage, a son, and a place in the genealogy of David, king of Israel.

THE STORY OF RUTH

According to Jewish tradition, the Ruth scroll belongs in the third section of the Hebrew canon (Writings); however, most English Bibles follow the Septuagint in placing it after Judges. Verse 1 locates the story "in the days when the judges judged" (*ca.* 1200–1020 B.C.E.), but the situation in Ruth differs markedly from that found in much of the book of Judges. Whereas the latter work ends in a morass of lawlessness, violence, and self-indulgence, the story of Ruth is bereft of villains, and its societal setting is relatively tranquil. Absent, too, are miracles that turn events to their proper conclusions. Rather, the scroll presents us with caring characters whose difficulties are overcome through acts of extraordinary loyalty and exemplary behavior.

Scene 1

The novella begins with a brief but eventful introduction (1:1–7). A famine in the land of Judah forces a Bethlehemite named Elimelech, his wife Naomi, and their two sons, Mahlon and Chilion, to migrate to Moab. There, Elimelech dies. The sons marry Moabite women, Orpah and Ruth; but at the end of ten years Mahlon and Chilion perish as well. Bereaved of both husband and children, Naomi decides to return to Bethlehem, since the famine there has ended.

The three women set out together, but Naomi soon urges each of her daughters-in-law to return to "her mother's house." Eventually, Orpah obeys; but Ruth steadfastly refuses to go back to "her people and her gods." On the contrary, Ruth insists, "Your people shall be my people, and your God my God." The two continue on to Bethlehem and are greeted by towns-women, who marvel at the change in their old friend. In response to their queries, Naomi rejects her former name (meaning "pleasant") for a new one, Mara ("bitter"). Attributing her misfortunes to God, Naomi complains that although she went away "full," Yahweh has brought her back "empty." Her words anticipate important themes within the work as a whole: for want of food, she and her family had left Bethlehem ("house of food") for Moab. There both husband and seed (progeny) were lost. Now Naomi's homeland is fertile, but she is empty. Will Yahweh make her full once more? Chapter 1 ends on a hopeful note, for the two widows arrive in Bethlehem "at the beginning of barley harvest" (1:22).

Scene 2

Chapter 2 opens with yet another indication that Naomi's situation may not be as hopeless as it seems. The storyteller informs us that she has a kinsman, a member of Elimelech's family, a man of wealth and reputation named Boaz.

With Naomi's consent, Ruth sets out to glean in the cultivated land around the town. Israelite law provided for gleaning (gathering stalks of grain that the reapers left behind) by the poor and homeless [Lev 19:9–10, 23:22; Deut 24:19].) "By chance," the narrator tells us, she comes to the field of Boaz, where her diligence draws the attention of both servants and master (2:3–6). Boaz instructs Ruth to remain in his field and authorizes what one commentator has called "a little generous cheating on her behalf" (2:15–16). Blessing her in Yahweh's name, Boaz commends Ruth for her faithfulness to Naomi and ensures that she receives adequate food and protection for the duration of the harvest. When Naomi realizes in whose field Ruth has been gleaning, she in turn blesses Boaz in the name of Yahweh, "whose kindness has not forsaken the living or the dead!" (2:20).

Scene 3

Naomi determines to relieve the barrenness of her family line and of Ruth (3:1). She tells her daughter-in-law to bathe, anoint herself, and dress in her finest clothing, then go to the threshing floor, where Boaz is spending the night. There, she is to "uncover" the feet of Boaz, lie down, and await his instructions (3:3–5).

Ruth prepares herself accordingly. Her toilet suggests bridelike behavior (although such acts are not unique to brides; *cf.* 2 Sam 12:20), and other sexual nuances are woven into the scene as well. Note, for example, the repetition of the verbs "to lie down" and "to know," which in Hebrew may mean "to have sexual intercourse with" in some contexts. The word for "feet" is a common euphemism for sexual organs. Furthermore, Ruth's request that Boaz "spread your skirt over your maidservant, for you are next of kin" (3:9), echoes similar language in Ezekiel's metaphorical description of the betrothal between Yahweh and Jerusalem (Ezek 16:8). The scene is provocative; however, the notion that Boaz and Ruth engage in

sexual intercourse at the threshing floor goes beyond what the text states and runs counter to the story as a whole, which everywhere depicts both Ruth and Boaz as persons of extraordinary virtue and propriety.

It seems clear, at any rate, that Ruth's words constitute a request that Boaz enter into a levirate marriage with her, that is, a union that may produce an heir for her deceased husband (see also Gen 38, Deut 25:5–10). As the following scene shows, the redemption of a field that belonged to Naomi's deceased husband also is an issue. The Book of Ruth apparently presupposes that the responsibilities of levirate marriage and land redemption (i.e., caring for the land and the dependents of its former owner) go together, although no existing legal code within the Hebrew scriptures juxtaposes them. Boaz agrees to Ruth's request, but he also introduces a new complication into the plot: there is a nearer kinsman than he, whose right to redeem has priority over his own.

Early in the morning, Ruth slips unnoticed from the threshing floor. Before she leaves, Boaz gives her food, for she "must not go back empty-handed" to her mother-in-law. Naomi's words tell of her confidence in Boaz: "Sit tight, my daughter . . . the man will . . . settle the matter today!" (3:18).

Scene 4

Arriving at the town gate (the conventional site for transacting business and dispensing justice in ancient Israel), Boaz catches sight of the nearer kinsman. He calls the unnamed man aside and gathers together ten elders to witness their exchange. Boaz apprises his kinsman of Naomi's situation and asks whether he wishes to redeem her land. The man responds immediately, "I will redeem it" (4:4). However, Boaz speaks again, introducing both Ruth and the possibility of a future heir for Mahlon into the matter. Textual problems, coupled with our incomplete knowledge of legal transactions in ancient Israel, make it difficult to determine precisely the content and the import of Boaz's words. Clearly, however, the nearer kinsman of Naomi decides not to redeem the land because Ruth's presence threatens to diminish his estate. Should she have a son, he would someday claim the plot of land as his inheritance.

His refusal frees Boaz to act as redeemer; their agreement is sealed when one man (probably the unnamed kinsman) removes his sandal and gives it to the other. (Verse 7 presupposes that this old custom was outmoded and unfamiliar to the storyteller's audience.) The elders and others at the gate, who witness Boaz assuming the responsibility for the redemption of the land, invoke a marriage blessing upon Ruth and Boaz (4:11–12).

Scene 5

In one swift sentence, we learn of the marriage of Boaz and Ruth and the conception and birth of a son. According to the text, Yahweh "gave her conception" (4:13). (The belief that Yahweh works in the wombs of women, bringing about pregnancies, fashioning the fetus, and enabling delivery, appears frequently in Hebrew scripture; see, for example, Gen 30:2; 1 Sam 1:19–20; Job 10:18, 31:13–15; Jer 1:5; Isa 66:9.) Their fertility stands in stark contrast to Ruth's ten childless years of marriage to Mahlon. The townswomen speak to Naomi in praise of Yahweh, for God "has not left you this day without next of kin." Ruth, too, is singled out for praise: she is more to Naomi than seven sons (an ideal number; see Job 1:2). Naomi's initial complaint, "I went away full, but Yahweh has brought me back empty" (1:21), here finds a resolution of sorts. No explanation is given for the loss of her husband and sons; however, her emptiness is relieved by a grandson, Obed (so named by the townswomen), and his mother. Verse 17b, possibly a later addition, identifies Obed as the grandfather of David, Israel's future king. The book concludes with a secondary genealogy (4:18–22) that provides Boaz with a "patriarchal pedigree" (Campbell 1975).

QUESTIONS RAISED
BY THE BOOK OF RUTH

Although the story of Ruth is beautifully constructed, it nonetheless leaves a number of questions unanswered: First, if Naomi owned a piece of property in Judah, why did Ruth have to glean for their food? Did women require male assistance to reclaim land that had belonged to their families (a possibility suggested by the story recounted in 2 Kgs 8:1–6)? Second, is it likely that the nearer redeemer knew nothing about Naomi's return from Moab and

his obligation to her prior to his conversation with Boaz at the town gate? Third, what was the precise content of the exchange between Boaz and the nearer kinsman? The Revised Standard Version translates Boaz' words as follows: "The day you buy the field from the hand of Naomi, you are also buying Ruth the Moabitess" (4:5). However, the text is difficult. It is possible that Boaz states his *own* intention to marry Ruth and raise an heir for Mahlon, thereby thwarting the nearer kinsman's hopes of benefiting from his role as redeemer.

Such questions may arise, in part, because our knowledge of ancient Israelite customs and legal practices is incomplete. However, the storyteller undoubtedly exercised freedom to shape events in ways that would advance the plot.

THE ROLE OF GOD
IN THE BOOK OF RUTH

There is merit in the frequent observation that God's activity takes place behind the scenes in the Book of Ruth. This is not to suggest that Yahweh is absent from the story. On the contrary, the divine name is invoked in a number of contexts: the narrator asserts that Yahweh relieved both the famine in Judah (1:6) and the barrenness of Ruth (4:13); Naomi attributes her troubles in Moab to Yahweh's doing (1:20–21; the divine name Shaddai also is used); characters bless others and are, in turn, blessed in Yahweh's name (1:8b–9a; 2:12, 19–20; 3:10; 4:11b–12, 14–15). The audience will no doubt attribute to God's providence the fact that Ruth "happened" to glean in the field of Boaz (2:3). However, the problems and tensions within the story are resolved, for the most part, through the exemplary actions of faithful Yahwists rather than by miraculous divine interventions.

DATE OF COMPOSITION

According to the Talmud (B.T., B.B. 14b), Samuel authored Judges and Ruth, as well as the book that bears his name. However, most commentators attribute Ruth in its canonical form to a postexilic author. In the period following the Babylonian Exile (i.e., after 538 B.C.E.) the Jewish community in

Palestine struggled with questions of inclusiveness (see, e.g., the heartbreaking account in Ezra 10). The Book of Ruth, with its depiction of a righteous Moabitess who, with her descendants, played a significant role in the history of Israel, appears to address this concern in powerful, albeit nonpolemical, fashion. Other factors, including the place of the scroll within the canon of Hebrew Scripture, and authorial explanations of archaic practices (see 4:7), strongly suggest a postexilic date (fifth–fourth centuries B.C.E.). However, it is unlikely that the author simply made up David's Moabite ancestress; and the story of Ruth may have circulated orally for some time prior to assuming its written form. (1 Sam 22:3–5 places David's parents in Moab during his "outlaw" period.)

One of the five scrolls, or *megillot* (see also Song of Solomon, Ecclesiastes, Lamentations, and Esther), read at various Jewish festivals, Ruth is appropriately associated with Shavu'ot, the Feast of Weeks, which celebrates the end of the grain harvest. The same period is traditionally identified as the time when the Torah was given at Mount Sinai—a gift intended for all people, according to the rabbis. Ruth, with its inclusive perspective, is appropriate to this observance.

Bibliography

Beattie, D. R. G. *Jewish Exegesis of the Book of Ruth.* Sheffield, England, 1977. See especially pp. 155–202, in which the author shares rabbinical reflections on the story of Ruth.

Campbell, Edward F., Jr. *Ruth: A New Translation with Introduction, Notes, and Commentary.* Garden City, N.Y., 1975. A lucid, well-written commentary in which the author argues that the book of Ruth dates from about the tenth to eighth centuries B.C.E.

Green, Barbara. "The Plot of the Biblical Story of Ruth." *Journal for the Study of the Old Testament* 23 (1982): 55–68. A readable essay that explores the themes of barrenness and fertility in the book of Ruth.

Hals, Ronald M. *The Theology of the Book of Ruth.* Philadelphia, 1969.

Smith, Louise Pettibone. "The Book of Ruth: Introduction and Exegesis." In *The Interpreter's Bible.* Vol. 2. Nashville, Tenn., 1953.

Trible, Phyllis. "A Human Comedy." In *God and the Rhetoric of Sexuality.* Philadelphia, 1978. Trible's reading of the story of Ruth and Naomi uncovers countless literary insights.

KATHERYN PFISTERER DARR

I and II Samuel

I Samuel

THE FIRST BOOK of Samuel tells the story of a crucial period of transition in the history of Israel. Threatened by the Philistines, Israel moved from tribal federation to monarchy. Because Israel understood itself as a community in covenant with Yahweh, the rise of kingship recounted in 1 Samuel causes theological as well as political tensions. Traditions within the work that reflect differing points of view at the time of this transition have been combined with the comments and reflections of later editors to yield a narrative that is notoriously complex and difficult to interpret. It is, therefore, necessary to understand the literary history of 1 Samuel before the contents of the narratives can be examined.

Although the two books of Samuel are dealt with separately in this essay, in the original Hebrew manuscripts they were one book. The division into two comes from the Greek and Latin versions; the length of the Samuel text made it more convenient to divide it in two. Since a number of important biblical books end with the death of a major figure, it seemed natural to make the break after the death of Saul.

The text of 1 Samuel differs substantially from one translation to the next, because recent developments in textual studies have greatly altered our reconstruction of the text. It had long been known that the Greek version of 1 Samuel, in the Septuagint (LXX), was much longer than the surviving Hebrew texts, thus it included many details not found in the Hebrew. Subsequent translators generally thought that the Greek translator was the source of the additions, and so based their work on the shorter Hebrew text. But the discovery in 1952 of three ancient manuscripts of the Books of Samuel at Qumran proved the existence of an ancient Hebrew text that was much closer to the longer text of the Septuagint. Older English translations are based upon the shorter Hebrew text, but several recent English translations (NAB, JB, NIV) reflect the new value placed on the longer Greek text and have included much of it as new material in their translations.

LITERARY HISTORY OF 1 SAMUEL

Until the 1960s most of the commentary on 1 Samuel distinguished two sources: an early, historically valuable source that was close in time to the events reported and generally positive about the kingship and Saul; and a later and therefore unreliable, sixth-century source dating to the time of the exile, which was negative toward kingship in general and Saul in particular. Following the groundbreaking work of Martin Noth (1957), most scholars have identified the late source as the work of a Deuteronomistic historian commenting on the rise of kingship from the perspective of its failure centuries later. This earlier consensus on two sources, however, has been widely questioned. Critical views of kingship must already have existed at the time of the establishment of the monarchy in the mid eleventh century and need not be seen as the product of an exilic historian. Increasingly, evidence also suggests that the stories of this period had already been put into their present shape by an editor long before the exile.

A widely held view now sees 1 Samuel as the product of a three-stage literary development:

(1) Early traditions witnessing the dramatic events of the Samuel and Saul period were collected into connected narrative complexes. At least three of these old narrative units can be discerned in 1 Samuel. An Ark Narrative (4:1b–7:1) tells the story of the capture and return of the ark by the Philistines. A cycle of stories about Saul centers on the tale of how Saul went to find his father's lost asses and instead found a seer who revealed to him his future kingship (9:1–10:16) and on an account of Saul's heroic leadership in the rescue of Jabesh-gilead from the Ammonites (11:1–15). This Saul cycle may also have included the various stories of exploits against the Philistines by Saul and his son Jonathan (13:2–7a, 13:15b–23, 14:1–46). Most scholars also believe that the story of Samuel's birth in chapter 1 was originally a story of Saul's birth that was appropriated in order to heighten the importance of Samuel's prophetic stature. If so, the birth story would also be a part of the Saul cycle. Finally, most of the material in 16:14–31:13 was part of a connected narrative of David's rise to kingship in place of Saul, a narrative that continues through the first five chapters of 2 Samuel and ends with David securely on the throne.

(2) The present shape and perspective of 1 Samuel evidences the work of a prophetic historian who took the older narrative complexes, reworked them, added new material, and arranged them in the order we now have them. The basic theological perspective of this prophetic history holds that kingship is sinful and unnecessary, but that since the people have insisted upon a king, God has chosen one. However, the king is subject to the authority of God's prophet. As a result of this perspective, the role of Samuel as prophet is greatly enhanced in this history. Saul and David are both understood to have

been chosen by God, anointed by Samuel, and measured by their fidelity to God's will. Eventually, Saul comes into conflict with God's will as mediated by Samuel and is rejected from kingship and dynasty. David appears in 1 Samuel as God's anointed through Samuel and rises to replace Saul on the throne. This rise to the throne is completed in 2 Samuel: David, having shown himself faithful to God and respectful of God's prophets, is confirmed in kingship and dynasty by the prophet Nathan (2 Sam 7).

The prophetic history seeks to understand the new system of governance introduced by kingship as one conditioned by accountability to the prophets, who are God's spokesmen. The prophets elect, reject, and instruct the kings in the name of Yahweh. This view of kingship was long associated with the northern kingdom, yet the prophetic history also clearly seeks to understand and legitimate the election of the Davidic dynasty in the south. This suggests that the prophetic history of Samuel, Saul, and David was written near the end of the eighth century, after the collapse of the northern kingdom. Northern in its views of prophetic and royal authority, it nevertheless sees the continuity of David's dynasty as the expression of God's will and as the future of Israel.

(3) A final stage of development incorporated the prophetic history discussed above into the larger work of the Deuteronomistic historian, which, scholars agree, stretches from Joshua through 2 Kings. This history, written and edited at the time of Josiah in the late seventh century and supplemented during the exile, stressed allegiance to the Davidic king and the primacy of the Jerusalem Temple. It understood much of Israel's history in terms of Yahweh's opposition to idolatry and was generally sympathetic to prophetic interests. In the Books of Joshua and Kings this Deuteronomistic historian extensively shaped, revised, and added to older material. By contrast, in 1 Samuel the Deuteronomistic reworking is minimal. It seems apparent that the prophetic history already in existence gave the traditions an interpretive shaping that met with the approval of the Deuteronomistic historian. This historian shapes Samuel's farewell speech in chapter 12 into one of the full speeches by major figures with which the Deuteronomistic History divides the epochs of Israel's story. He adds notes that anticipate the dynastic oracle of 2 Samuel 7 (e.g., an

addition to Abigail's speech in 25:28–31) and adds archival notes common in the Books of Kings to mark Saul's kingship (13:1–2, 14:47–51). Additions to the stories of Samuel and Eli and the note on idolatry in 8:8 are used in Samuel to show a pattern similar to the cycle of idolatry and redemption used by the Deuteronomistic historian to organize the Book of Judges.

With this brief overview of the literary history in mind we can look at the content of 1 Samuel as it now stands. Many sections are informed not by just one point of view but by diverse attitudes that characterized the rise of kingship and subsequent attempts to interpret these crucial events in the life of Israel.

SAMUEL: PROPHET AND JUDGE

Samuel is introduced as one whose very birth destined him for leadership in Israel. His mother, the devout Hannah, prays to Yahweh for release from her barrenness, a condition of hardship and ridicule, and her prayer is answered (chap. 1). The child Samuel is a gift of God, and Hannah dedicates him to service with Eli, the priest of Yahweh's sanctuary in Shiloh. The prayer of Hannah, which opens chapter 2, is an eloquent psalm of thanksgiving emphasizing God's concern for the powerless and the dispossessed. (It is an obvious model for the Magnificat of Mary in Luke 1:46–55.)

The remainder of chapters 2 and 3, which speaks of Samuel's upbringing in the household of Eli, is testimony to the interests of the prophetic editor. As noted above, many think the birth story originally referred to Saul, the child of destiny who was to become Israel's first king. The naming in chapter 1:20 (*cf.* 1:28) is a wordplay on the meaning of Saul's name, not Samuel's. In any case, these chapters are designed to impress us with the importance of the prophet's role as a gift of God to Israel at a crucial time in its life. The integrity of the young Samuel is contrasted to the depravity of Eli's sons, whose greed leads them to corrupt the worship of Yahweh (2:12–17). Even as a child Samuel becomes the vehicle of God's word when Yahweh reveals to him, in a nighttime encounter, the end of the house of Eli (3:1–18). Difficult times are coming to Israel, but in the view of this account God's prophet will provide the leadership

needed for God's people: "And Samuel grew, and the Lord was with him and let none of his words fall to the ground. And all Israel from Dan to Beer-sheba knew that Samuel was established as a prophet of the Lord" (3:19–20; RSV).

Into this story of Samuel's childhood the Deuteronomistic historian inserts a long addition in 2:27–36 and uses the fall of Eli's priestly house as an occasion to anticipate the building of the temple in Jerusalem and the establishment there of the priestly house of Zadok.

There follows in chapter 4 the story of the disastrous military engagement with the Philistines and the capture of the Ark. The Ark Narrative will be fully discussed in the next section. This story of the Ark's capture and return, with its implication of continued Philistine threat, is followed in chapter 7 by the story of Samuel as the deliverer, recounted in the style of the stories of the heroes of the Book of Judges. Samuel calls on the people to renounce idolatry (7:3–4, perhaps Deuteronomistic); when the Philistines attack, they are routed from the field by the confusion sent from Yahweh. The extravagant claim of 7:13—"So the Philistines were subdued and did not again enter the territory of Israel. And the hand of the Lord was against the Philistines all the days of Samuel"—is motivated by the desire of the prophetic historian to make clear that prophetic leadership was all the people needed even in the face of the Philistine threat. When, in chapter 8, the people insist on a king, it must be seen as a lack of trust in Yahweh and Samuel.

THE ARK NARRATIVE

It was Leonhard Rost (1926) who first called attention to the uniqueness of chapters 4–7:2. Unlike the rest of 1 Samuel, the focus is not on any human character but on the Ark of Yahweh and its fate.

The account reflects events that took place around 1050 when the Philistines, Israel's neighbors on the western coastal plain, decided to attack Israel and expand their territory. After an initial defeat at Ebenezer, the Israelites decided to bring the Ark of the Covenant to the battlefield (4:1b–4).

The Ark of the Covenant was a wooden chest in which were said to be deposited the two tablets of the law that Moses had received on Mount Sinai (Deut 10:5; 1 Kgs 8:9). Fashioned above the Ark were two winged cherubim, which flanked and supported God's invisible throne. Thus, the Ark was Yahweh's footstool (1 Chr 28:2; Pss 99:5, 132:7; Lam 2:1) and the chief sign of Yahweh's presence in the midst of Israel. In battle the Ark was the visible sign that God was fighting for Israel. When it arrived the men of Israel raised a ritual shout and a divine panic spread to the enemy; but the Philistines steeled themselves for battle, defeated Israel, and captured the Ark. The sons of Eli, Hophni and Phinehas, bore the Ark and were killed (4:5–11). When news of this disaster reached their father he fell over and died (4:12–18). Thus the house of Eli and its corruption ended, as had been revealed to the boy Samuel.

Chapter 5 is an extended account of the calamities that befell the Philistines from the presence of the Ark in their cities. The idol of their god Dagon was destroyed, and the inhabitants of the Philistine cities were afflicted with diseases and tumors. In chapter 6 the leaders of the Philistines, wanting to appease the wrath of Yahweh, decide to send the Ark back to Israelite territory on a cart drawn by cows and accompanied by golden objects. It comes first to Bethshemesh, where fear of its great holiness causes it to be sent on to the Gibeonite village of Kiriathjearim. It remains there, relatively unknown for twenty years, until David finds it and brings it to Jerusalem (2 Sam 6).

Since the work of Rost, most scholars have seen these chapters (4:1b–7:2) as belonging with 2 Samuel 6 and as comprising an originally independent Ark Narrative. The point of the narrative was understood to be an attempt to justify and explain how the Ark of Shiloh came to Jerusalem, in order to establish the legitimacy of the Jerusalem shrine and its priesthood.

The monograph of Patrick D. Miller, Jr., and J. J. M. Roberts (1977) has revised our understanding of this material. It describes an extensive body of ancient Near Eastern literature on the capture of an enemy's gods and convincingly shows 1 Samuel 4:1b–7:2 to be an example of such literature. The focus of these chapters is not on how the Ark got to Jerusalem but on how Yahweh could have allowed Israel's defeat and the capture of the Ark. In the ancient literature

the victors always describe the capture of an enemy's gods as evidence of the superiority of their own gods. The enemy's gods might even later be magnanimously returned. In accounts by defeated armies, the capture of the images is always described as being ordained by gods angry with their own people. The return of images was, of course, the gods' magnanimous return to the defeated people. Stories of the defeated often included reports on the terrible calamities that befell those who carried off their gods' images.

It seems obvious that 1 Samuel 4:1b–7:1 as it now stands is a story of this type, concerned with reaffirming Yahweh's power at a time of defeat. The actual beginning of the Ark episode is in the reports of corruption in the house of Eli. Probably written at a time when the Philistines were still a threat (i.e., before David's kingship), the account affirms that Yahweh was in control all along and used these events to bring about the downfall of the house of Eli for the shame it had brought on the worship of Yahweh. Placed now by the prophetic editor between materials favorable to Samuel as leader and God's prophet, the Ark story reinforces the case that even the Philistine threat does not justify the establishment of kingship. This view would exclude the older position that saw 2 Samuel 6 as part of the original Ark Narrative. It should be seen instead as an independent, later narrative that no doubt built upon the earlier stories of the Ark and its importance as a cultic symbol.

SAUL: ISRAEL'S FIRST KING

The section of 1 Samuel dealing with King Saul (8:1–15:35) often is confusing: Saul seems to become king on three separate occasions (9:1–10:16, 10:17–26, 11:14–15). He is rejected by Samuel twice (13:8–15, 15:1–35). Some of the stories seem very positively inclined toward Saul, whereas others treat the very concept of kingship as sinful. These tensions in the text no doubt reflect tensions over the establishment of kingship at the time of the events themselves. In spite of these tensions the prophetic editor has arranged the materials in a manner that discloses the importance of the theological perspective of these events.

In chapter 8 the elders meet with Samuel to insist on a king to "govern us and go out before us and fight our battles" (8:20). They want to be "like the nations" in spite of Samuel's strong leadership. Samuel prays to Yahweh, who tells him that the people have rejected Yahweh's own kingship in making this demand. Nevertheless, after warning them of the dangers, Samuel grants their request and chooses a king for them. There is no mention of a Philistine threat that would make the request for a king urgent and necessary. Samuel has himself already dealt with this threat (chap. 7). Thus, the attitude here is negative toward kingship. It is attributed to the people's willful desire to copy the nations. The dangers described in verses 10–18 are often thought to reflect the actual abuses of royal power that characterized later reigns. In spite of the view that kingship is equated with rejection of Yahweh, the chapter makes clear that if kingship is to come, the monarch will be one of God's choosing, through the mediation of God's prophet.

The story of the young Saul going out to find his father's lost asses and finding instead a kingdom follows in 9:1–10:16. Considered alone, the tone of this story is very positive toward Saul as God's chosen king; his role is to save Israel from the hand of the Philistines (9:16, 10:1). This hopeful and enthusiastic view of Saul is then tempered by the story's placement after chapter 8, which presents kingship as a rejection of Yahweh.

This episode has the quality of a folktale. The youthful Saul and his companion set out in search of lost asses and come upon a strange city where they encounter a seer who reveals to Saul his destiny to become prince (*nagid*; the Hebrew for "king" is not actually used in this episode) of Israel. This old story of Saul has been reshaped a bit by the prophetic historian, who identifies the seer as none other than the great prophet Samuel. Samuel anoints the young Saul and commissions him to his task (10:1). As a sign of his status as God's anointed one, Saul then experiences the spirit of Yahweh coming mightily upon him in the presence of a band of prophets. He is empowered by the spirit into joining with them in their ecstatic prophesying. According to the perspective of the prophetic historian, both anointing by a prophet and possession of Yahweh's spirit are regarded as essential elements in legitimating a king. Although Saul's prophesying is observed (10:11–12), its meaning is not yet revealed to the people. The youthful

Saul returns home to await the later fulfillment of his commission to lead Israel (10:14–16).

The narrative continues with the gathering of an assembly at Mizpah to choose a king by lot (10:17–27). The lot falls upon Saul, who is hiding in the baggage. He is found by the assembly, and when people see that he stands a head taller than any of the others, he is confirmed as God's choice by shouts of "Long live the king" (10:24). This may be an old tradition reflecting divine choice of Saul, but in the story's present form and placement it serves to confirm the choice made much earlier when Saul was anointed by Samuel. Even in this story of casting lots the role of Samuel is heightened. Samuel calls the assembly and in a prophetic judgment speech admonishes Israel for its insistence on a king (10:17–19). When Saul is acclaimed king Samuel tells the people the "rights and duties of the kingship" (10:25; this passage is perhaps better translated as "the justice of the kingdom") and writes them in a book to be placed before Yahweh. The clear implication is that the king's authority is not absolute but limited by divinely sanctioned laws, which the prophet Samuel promulgates and no doubt enforces, as later events make clear.

It then falls to Saul to prove himself a worthy recipient of God's spirit and the office of king. Chapter 11 serves this purpose by recounting Saul's heroic leadership in rescuing the city of Jabesh-Gilead from Nahash the Ammonite. This is undoubtedly an old story from a cycle of favorable Saul stories. The story shows little awareness of Saul as king until the people seem to spontaneously install him as king after his heroic victory (11:15). By making this a "renewal" of kingship, the editor is probably attempting to harmonize his account with that of chapter 10. Indeed, Saul is out working in the fields when the summons for help comes. The spirit of the Lord comes upon him exactly as it had come upon an earlier hero, Samson (Judg 14:6, 14:19, 15:14). He then delivers those in danger much in the manner of earlier judges of Israel. In its present position in the text, this old story serves as a public manifestation of God's spirit, which had already come upon Saul at the time when he was anointed by Samuel. Saul, then already proclaimed king as well, begins his career with a heroic deed of the spirit.

With a king established in Israel, Samuel's farewell address in chapter 12 serves to redefine the relationship between prophet and king that is to pertain in Israel's new order. Samuel begins by asking the witness of the people if he has exercised leadership in a just manner, and they affirm this to be true. Since Samuel had earlier warned the people of the unjust ways of kings (8:10–18), this speech serves to contrast the leadership of prophets and kings in a manner that denigrates kingship. Verses 16–19 demonstrate the prophet's power, which is drawn directly from Yahweh. Samuel calls upon Yahweh and commands the elements of nature, causing the people to confess that they sinned when they requested a king (v. 19). It is, however, too late. The new order of kingship is in place. Samuel's final words are to redefine the role of the prophet. The implication is that the prophetic historian responsible for much of this chapter saw that the prophet lost some of the leadership responsibilities to the office of the king. In this new era of kingship Samuel promises to intercede for the people with Yahweh and to "instruct you in the good and the right way" (12:23). The prophet's chief tasks become intercession and moral admonition.

Although most of chapter 12 comes from the hand of the prophetic historian, the Deuteronomistic historian inserted the great historical summary in verses 6–15, and made a few other minor additions. It is part of the structure of this type of history to mark the end of major historical epochs with speeches by major figures in which they look both backward and forward in a summary fashion. Samuel's speech serves admirably as the end of the era of judges and the beginning of that of kings.

Furthermore, the usual Deuteronomistic formula for beginning the reign of a king appears in 13:1. Material that narrates the exploits of Saul and his son Jonathan against the Philistines follows (13:2–7, 15b–23, 14:1–52). It becomes obvious that most of the land is under Philistine domination and that Saul's early kingly tasks were largely military.

Tension between prophet and king breaks out in two episodes (13:8–15, 15:1–35), both shaped by the prophetic historian, in which Saul is denounced and rejected by Samuel. Although these have often been treated by commentators as doublets of the same incident, they serve separate and distinct purposes, at least as used by the prophetic editor.

In 13:8–15 Saul waits impatiently for Samuel, who is late in arriving to offer proper sacrifices before battle. Seeing military opportunity slip away, he offers the sacrifices himself, only to have Samuel arrive and condemn him for taking cultic matters into his own hands. The language of the rejection is very specific: "The Lord would have established your kingdom over Israel forever. But now your kingdom shall not continue; the Lord has sought out a man after his own heart" (13:13b–14a). It is David whose rise is foreshadowed as the man after God's own heart, and it is David whose kingdom is later established forever (2 Sam 7). Saul is denied the privilege of a dynasty, whereas David, unlike Saul, is succeeded by his sons.

Chapter 15 concerns the conflict with Samuel over Saul's failure to carry out Samuel's instruction to take no spoils from a war with the Amalekites but to devote the spoils to Yahweh by destroying them. Saul saves the Amalekite livestock and brings their king, Agag, back as a prisoner. Samuel is enraged at Saul's disobedience of the sacrificial ban (herem), a practice of ancient holy war, and himself kills Agag on the spot (vv. 32–33). Refusing Saul's explanations, Samuel gives a bitter speech of judgment in which he declares to Saul, "You have rejected the word of the Lord, and the Lord has rejected you from being king over Israel" (15:26). Not only will Saul have no dynasty, but he is himself rejected as God's anointed. In 16:14, following the anointing of David, the spirit of Yahweh leaves Saul and he is plagued by an evil spirit. The end of this segment of 1 Samuel is clearly punctuated by the comment "And the Lord repented that he had made Saul king over Israel" (15:35b).

THE RISE OF DAVID

If there is to be a king in Israel, then it will be a man of God's own choice. That man is David, and the remainder of 1 Samuel (16:1–31:13) chronicles the rise of David's fortunes, paralleling them with the simultaneous collapse of Saul's. In this section the prophetic historian incorporates an older collection of traditions on the rise of David that sought to present him as the legitimate successor of Saul. The prophetic editor added little to this collection except to preface it with the story of David's anointment by Samuel while yet a boy. This serves to heighten the point that David was God's own choice to succeed Saul. The opening of David's story now parallels that of Saul. He is anointed by a prophet and the spirit of the Lord comes immediately upon him (16:13). He makes a public debut as a musician in the court of Saul (16:14–23). He then performs a heroic act defeating the Philistine champion, Goliath (17:1–58), through which he demonstrates the power of the spirit. In the extended narrative that follows, David's rise is contrasted with Saul's decline, until David's ultimate confirmation in kingship and dynasty, an outcome that reaches fruition in 2 Samuel.

David's rise is not, however, without its trials and difficulties. The chief concern of the old collection of stories seems to be to show that he came to his kingship legitimately. He did not act callously or unjustly, and, most especially, he acted with respect toward Israel's first king. By contrast Saul is pictured as a man who loses control, perhaps suffering from mental illness. Although David is entrusted with great responsibility by Saul, marries Saul's daughter Michal, and is bound to Saul's son Jonathan in sworn friendship, Saul becomes jealous of David and seeks to kill him (chaps. 18, 19; *cf.* chap. 20).

Saul neglects his royal duties to pursue the fleeing David and the men with him in the desert. In an act of apparent madness, Saul massacres the whole community of priests at Nob (22:6–23) for giving aid to David. By contrast David spares Saul's life when he has a clear chance to kill him (23:14–24:22, 26:1–25). When David is forced to work for the Philistines as a mercenary commander he does not attack Israelite cities and even shares spoils with the elders of Judah (27:1–28:2). When a Philistine army is assembled to put down Saul, David and his men are mustered but spared at the last minute from doing battle against the army of Israel and his own friend Jonathan (29:1–11). In all of this Yahweh is with David. The old history of David's rise presents David as the man of God's own choosing, whereas Saul is presented as a man who has fallen from God's favor.

The final chapters of 1 Samuel offer a last glimpse of Saul as a broken man. Facing a crucial battle with the Philistines, he secretly consults a

medium. He seeks a favorable sign but instead encounters the shadow of Samuel, who condemns him again from beyond the grave (28:3–25). When, on the next day, Saul sees his army defeated on the plain below Mount Gilboa and his son Jonathan killed in battle, he tragically takes his own life (chap. 31; also 2 Sam 1:1–16).

As they stand, these chapters on the rise of David seek to legitimate both the kingship and the dynasty of David as being in accordance with God's will. It remains for 2 Samuel to carry on the story. Saul, Israel's first king, is dead. Can David assume the throne of Israel and avoid the forces that brought Saul to grief?

II Samuel

The Second Book of Samuel is a continuation of traditions on the establishment of kingship in Israel that began in the first book. As noted above, the two books were originally one book that was later divided into two scrolls. Whereas 1 Samuel revolves around the interactions of three great figures, Samuel, Saul, and David, 2 Samuel is dominated entirely by the personality of David. The book opens as David receives word that Saul and his son Jonathan, David's friend, have died. Its narrative then recounts the events that make David king as well as other important stories of David's public and private life. The result is one of the most profound portraits, of both the strengths and weaknesses, of any biblical character. It is a remarkably thorough and honest portrayal, but one that shows clearly the greatness of David, celebrated throughout generations of later biblical and other Jewish literature. The book ends not with David's death but with the last of the stories that portray him in full health and action. It is the first Book of Kings that opens with David on his deathbed and the story of the power struggle that is resolved with Solomon's accession to the throne following his father's death.

As with 1 Samuel, it is necessary to look briefly at the literary history of the materials that make up the book. Since the kingship of David is so important in Israel's history, its significance has been reexamined and re-presented numerous times. Thus, 2 Samuel contains various tellings of the David stories, which reflect the concerns that prevailed during several different periods in Israel's history.

LITERARY HISTORY OF 2 SAMUEL

Since the work of Martin Noth (1957), scholars have generally agreed that 2 Samuel is part of a larger Deuteronomistic History stretching from Deuteronomy to 2 Kings. This work, compiled around the time of Josiah's reform in the late seventh century and reedited after the destruction of Jerusalem in 587, sought to reevaluate Israel's history to accord with the theology of Deuteronomy. This theology included a view of David as the ideal king, a negative view of other kings measured against the Davidic ideal (except for Josiah), a positive view of the role of the Temple in Jerusalem, and a deep concern for idolatry as chief among Israel's sins. Unlike other books (e.g., Judges) that show extensive evidence of Deuteronomistic editing, only a few places in 2 Samuel betray such evidence. This is probably because the historian found already in existence a comprehensive history for the Davidic period and was in essential agreement with its perspective. Thus, the Deuteronomist added or commented upon only a few items in 2 Samuel. He is probably responsible for the editing of chapters 5:1–8:18, which served to highlight the importance of Jerusalem by giving prominence to the stories of the city's capture (5:1–10) and the establishment of the Ark there (chap. 6). Additions were also made to the important dynastic oracle in chapter 7 so that it would not seem anti-Temple.

Many scholars now believe that the basic shaping of 2 Samuel in chapters 1–5 and 9–20 was accomplished by a prophetic editor in the late eighth century (McCarter 1984). This prophetic edition begins in 1 Samuel and tells the stories of the rise of kingship in Israel. Its distinctive perspective regards kingship as an inherently sinful institution, unless the kings are held accountable to Yahweh by prophets. In 2 Samuel the work of this prophetic editor is most clearly visible in the stories featuring Nathan, the prophet to David's court. These stories of the dynastic oracle (chap. 7) and of David's sinful relationship with Bathsheba and confrontation by Nathan (chaps. 11–12) are both shaped by the prophetic hand and placed prominently as turning points in the history of

David's kingship. (A fuller discussion of this prophetic edition appears earlier in this essay in the discussion of 1 Samuel.)

The prophetic editor utilized older narrative sources dating from the time of David or shortly thereafter. The first of these is the conclusion of a history of David's rise to kingship found in 2 Samuel 1–4. (This history, which began in 1 Sam 16, has been considered in the discussion of 2 Samuel.) The second narrative source incorporated into the prophetic and later the Deuteronomistic histories is a long block of stories called the Succession Narrative. Leonhard Rost (1926) proposed the hypothesis that 2 Samuel 9–20 and 1 Kings 1–2 were a unified narrative organized around the question of who would succeed David on the throne. Gerhard von Rad (1944) turned Rost's hypothesis into an almost universal consensus by treating these chapters as the first example of genuine history writing to show the full play of human motives and actions as the arena of God's work.

Until the 1960s, Rost's hypothesis of a Succession Narrative was accepted by those who treated 2 Samuel. But unlike von Rad, many saw this narrative not as idealistic history writing but as political propaganda. For those scholars, the question was not so much who would succeed David on the throne as why Solomon succeeded him. According to this view, the Succession History is a pro-Solomonic narrative.

The notion of a unified Succession Narrative in 2 Samuel 9–20 and 1 Kings has been increasingly challenged. Although there is no clear consensus, the view of Kyle McCarter (1984), who contends that only 1 Kings 1–2 is concerned with justifying Solomon's succession to the throne, can be taken as representative of this trend. The rest of the material serves different ends. For example, 2 Samuel 13–20, the story of Absalom's revolt, is a pro-Davidic attempt to understand and interpret the tempestuous events that almost toppled David from power. It is royal apologetics, presenting David as human and fallible, but essentially sympathetic and admirable. McCarter understands 2 Samuel 11–12, the story of David and Bathsheba, as the work of the prophetic editor, who inserted this account before the difficulties that will plague David's family in chapters 13–20 in order to give them theological justification. In their present shape these materials of 2 Samuel take on the function of a court history. Although held accountable by the prophet Nathan for his sin, David, as is Solomon later, is treated as justified in his actions in the crisis narrated in the stories.

Although many scholars continue to see a non-unified Succession History in 2 Samuel, a growing body of opinion suggests a more varied history for this material (e.g., McCarter 1984). The following discussion of 2 Samuel will treat the book in its present, final shape but will point out some of the more obvious instances of earlier editorial viewpoints that appear in the text.

DAVID AS KING

Second Samuel opens as David receives the news of Jonathan's death in battle and Saul's death by his own hand. David then sings an eloquent lament over Saul, the first king of Israel, and over Jonathan, Saul's son and David's friend: "Thy glory, O Israel, is slain upon thy high places! How are the mighty fallen!" (1:19; RSV). Although Saul had attempted to kill him, David honors the dead king as God's anointed. David understands that kings may reign over Israel only by God's authority and not just by political authority.

Following Saul's death David goes to Hebron and is there anointed king by the men of Judah (2:1–4). While David had been working for the Philistine king of Gath, he actually protected the cities of Judah with his own military force, and used portions of the tribute intended for the Philistine king as gifts to the elders of Judah (1 Sam 27:8–12, 30:26–31). It is, therefore, little wonder that Judah is ready to act independently of the rest of Israel and make David king over Judah alone.

In the north, Abner, Saul's general, installs Saul's son Ish-bosheth on the throne, but he must operate from Gilead in the Transjordan since all territory west of the Jordan was in Philistine hands (2:8–10). Ish-bosheth's original name was Ishbaal (man of the lord; 1 Chr 8:33, 9:39) but an editor concerned with idolatry (perhaps the Deuteronomist) has removed the part of his name that is the same as the Canaanite god Baal and substituted the word for shame, *boshet*.

Border disputes along the Benjamin-Judah frontier escalate into open hostility between Judah and the Israelite kingdom (2:12–3:1). The conflict between the supporters of David and those of the surviving house of Saul involves Joab, David's general, in a blood feud with Abner, general of Israel. These events make the prospect remote that David could ever become king over all Israel.

After a falling out with Ish-bosheth, Abner decides that he will cast his lot with David and Judah (3:6–11). Abner and David agree on a pact to bring all of Israel under David's rule. David will receive back his wife, Michal, the daughter of Saul, and in this way will once again be related to the household of Saul (3:12–20). Unfortunately the smooth flow of events is interrupted when Joab kills Abner in revenge for the death of a relative. It now appears that David has acted treacherously against the general of the northern tribes. To counter this impression David orders and participates in elaborate mourning over the death of Abner and accords him full burial honors. He swears his innocence formally and calls for the blood of Abner to fall on Joab alone (3:21–39).

The elders of Israel are convinced of David's innocence. Opportunists kill Ish-bosheth, hoping to earn David's favor; but David instead deals harshly with them (4:1–12). Lacking king or general, knowing David's past deeds, and believing that he had not acted with treachery toward them, the elders of Israel anoint David king over Israel (5:1–3), David is now king over all Israel and Judah, holder of two kingships.

The Second Book of Samuel then recounts David's initial efforts to consolidate his reign and deal with the various challenges before him. First, he must establish his capital. To reign from a city either of the northern tribes or of Judah would leave him open to charges of favoritism and bias. Hence, 5:5–10 reports that David and his own men (not the tribal militia) capture the centrally located city of Jerusalem from the Jebusites. Its capture is by stealth rather than destruction so David is able to occupy it immediately and make it his capital, quite literally "the city of David." Since Jerusalem was probably a city with its own king, David in effect also becomes king of Jerusalem. This story marks the beginning of the rise to central importance for the role that Jerusalem is to play in the history of Israel.

David then turns his attention to the Philistines and their continued hold on most of the land. For their part, the Philistines now also see David as a threat, and 5:17–25 tells of several military encounters between the Philistines and David's forces. In these David, supported by the Lord's presence, is the decisive victor. Other stories of David's exploits in the war with the Philistines appear in appendixes to 2 Samuel, which will be treated below (21:15–22, 23:8–39). Philistine expansion is halted by these Davidic victories; and although their territory itself is not conquered the Philistines are never again a force to be feared. The period of the Israelite kingdom has begun.

A final issue is the relation in David's reign between kingdom and faith. Saul came to grief because he angered God's prophet Samuel: he found himself rejected by the chief representative of the Israelite religion and its God, Yahweh (2 Sam 15). David seems determined not to risk conflict between religion and kingdom. In chapter 6 he brings the Ark of the Covenant to Jerusalem. The Ark, which had been captured by the Philistines, was returned to Israelite territory but had remained lost for many years (1 Sam 4–6). Indeed, it had been accepted among scholars that 1 Samuel 4–6 and 2 Samuel 6 belonged together as an original Ark Narrative until the work of Miller and Roberts (1977) challenged the belief (see discussion above at 1 Samuel). Although the writer of 2 Samuel 6 knows of the earlier stories of the Ark's capture, his purpose is to detail how David restored the Ark of the Covenant, the most sacred symbol of Yahweh's presence in the midst of Israel, and gave it an honored place. Psalm 132, a liturgical celebration of this event, suggests that David could not rest until he had searched for and found the Ark. The account in 2 Samuel focuses on the bringing of the Ark to Jerusalem. David's personal joy is so great that he strips off his clothing and dances unashamedly before the Ark in procession. The message of this story is clear: kingship and the worship of Yahweh are not in conflict under David. The king is a personal patron of the cultus, and Jerusalem is both royal capital and chief sanctuary of Yahweh. From this seed grows one of the pillars of Davidic theology, namely that Jerusalem is Yahweh's permanent dwelling place: "For

the Lord has chosen Zion. . . . This is my resting place for ever; here I will dwell" (Ps 132:13–14; RSV).

THE DYNASTIC ORACLE

Chapter 7 not only is a crucial chapter in the structure of 2 Samuel, it is also of central importance to the whole history of Israel that stretches from Joshua to 2 Kings. It lays the foundation for a Davidic royal theology that remains central to the southern kingdom's (Judah's) perspective on Israel's faith down to the Babylonian exile.

With peace and security established in the kingdom, David expresses to Nathan, the prophet, his desire to build a house (temple) for Yahweh even as the king now has a secure house (palace). Nathan is initially very positive about this prospect (7:1–3). But later that same night the word of Yahweh comes to him: David will not build a house (temple) for Yahweh.

Yahweh's long oracular speech (7:5–17) seems to express a sense of offense at the very notion that God should need a house: such a structure could almost be considered a restriction of divine freedom when compared with the worship of Yahweh that was not confined to one place but that moved in a tent as the people moved in the wilderness (7:5–7). Then the divine speech makes a great reversal: David will not build a house (temple) for Yahweh; rather, Yahweh will build a house (dynasty) for David. Yahweh reminds David that he sits upon the throne by virtue of divine initiative and that he will make David great among his people (7:8–11)—a promise that extends beyond David himself: "Your house and your kingdom shall be made sure for ever before me; your throne shall be established for ever" (7:16). Though David's sons may commit iniquity and be chastened by God, the kingdom shall not be taken from the house of David as it had been from Saul (7:14–15). This remarkable promise builds cleverly on the various meanings of the Hebrew word for "house."

Curiously, after seeming to be offended at the idea of a temple, Yahweh almost in passing reveals that a change is coming. David may not build a house for Yahweh, but "I will raise up your offspring after you. . . . He shall build a house for my name" (7:12–

13)—an obvious reference to Solomon and the building of the Solomonic Temple. What started out as an anti-Temple oracle is changed into divine acquiescence at least as concerns the Temple.

This chapter is such an important turning point that all editors responsible for shaping its material have left their imprint on it. Its original form was probably hostile to the notion of a temple but positive toward David. The prophetic editor probably heightened the emphasis on divine chastisement of kings (a chief prophetic role) while accepting Davidic dynasty as divinely blessed. The Deuteronomistic historian softened the anti-Temple bent by making God's response only a delay of fulfillment until the time of Solomon. Each took an element of the tradition and heightened its role, so that all are heard with a strong voice in the final form of the text.

In verses 18–29, David, in response to the great oracular promise, prays to Yahweh. He humbly speaks of his own insignificance and Yahweh's graciousness and then petitions God for faithfulness to the divine promise of dynasty and eternal blessing through that dynasty.

With this brief description in mind, some comment must be made on the far-reaching significance of these themes for Israel's faith. In Jerusalem and the southern kingdom of Judah, it became the belief that the secure, ongoing dynasty of David and the Temple as God's dwelling place were the chief evidences of God's presence in Israel and blessing of its people. They were new acts of divine salvation alongside the redemptive events of Exodus, Sinai, and the wilderness. But unlike the covenant with Moses, the covenant with David is unconditional, a sign of the permanence of divine blessing in the midst of Israel. King and Temple are to be the visible signs of God's grace. Chapter 7 is the story of the establishment of this promise, as mediated directly by Yahweh's prophet Nathan. It is, then, a foundation for understanding much of later Israelite tradition, whether it assumes the viewpoint of royal theology (Isaiah and many of the psalms) or reacts against it (Hosea, Jeremiah). It is also only against the backdrop of the central importance of the Davidic royal promise that we understand how thoroughly catastrophic the Babylonian exile was, when both king and Temple were swept away.

EVENTS IN THE DAVIDIC KINGDOM

In keeping with the theme of David's bringing the kingdom to rest and security so that his son can later build the Temple, these chapters show David expanding the borders of the empire, sometimes by diplomacy and sometimes by the defeat of enemies. In chapters 8 and 10 certain notes reflect the establishment of David's administrative, military, and trade arrangements. He is portrayed here as an ideal and just king: "David administered justice and equity to all his people" (8:15).

Tucked into the middle of this section (chap. 9) is the story of David's benevolence toward Jonathan's surviving son, the lame Mephibosheth (originally Meribbaal). Through Saul's old servant Ziba, David finds Mephibosheth and gives him land and a place at the royal table. Although this is presented as an act of kindness and respect for the house of Saul, it is possible that this episode belongs with the story in 21:1–14, in which seven sons of Saul are given over to death at the hands of the Gibeonites to atone for the wrongs done them by Saul. If chapter 9 originally followed 21, as many believe, it would show that David acted graciously toward Mephibosheth not only because of his friendship with Jonathan but also because he wanted to counter the negative public opinion that seems to have been generated by the hanging of Saul's seven sons.

THE COURT HISTORY

Verses 1–20 and 26 in chapter 11 form the heart of what is usually treated as the Succession History. Most would see its natural ending in 2 Kings 1–2.

It is immediately apparent in chapter 11 that this encounter is a different tradition. No longer an account of the ideal and heroic David, this is the story of David's sin in the matter of Bathsheba— of David's most blatant misuse of royal power, with its deadly consequences for an innocent and loyal subject. But chapter 11 must be read in tandem with chapter 12, for the final word of this story is that such abuses do not escape divine notice. The prophet Nathan confronts David with his sin, and the king must face its consequences.

Chapter 11 opens with the scene of a bored

David, while his army is away on a campaign. He is pacing on his roof when he spots Bathsheba bathing nearby. With the exercise of whim possible to royal power he simply "sent" for her, "took" her, and "lay" with her (11:4). Bathsheba has no role in the story as told except that of victim of royal power. She conceives a child and sends word of it to David (11:5).

David now compounds his sin by attempting to cover up what he has done. He sends for Bathsheba's husband, Uriah the Hittite, who has been with David's army laying siege to Rabbah. He encourages Uriah to spend the night with Bathsheba, but Uriah refuses, out of loyalty to the vow of chastity taken by soldiers while on campaign. David then sends Uriah back to the front lines with a letter for Joab ordering Uriah be sent into battle under circumstances that ensure his death (11:14–21). When Uriah is killed David takes Bathsheba for his wife and she bears a son (11:27). The text says simply, "But the thing that David had done displeased the Lord" (11:27b).

In chapter 12 Nathan comes before David and tells a parable of a rich man who takes the only ewe lamb of a poor man to feed to his guest. David, acting in the king's capacity of rendering judgments, declares that such a man deserves to die—only to be told, "You are the man!" (12:1–7). Nathan then pronounces an oracle of judgment that foreshadows violence in David's own family because of the violence he has committed against Uriah. As the text now stands, chapters 11–12 serve to prepare the ground for the prophetic viewpoint of the tragic and violent events, narrated in chapters 13–20, that are characteristic of David's later years.

Nathan's oracle is followed by the poignant story of the death of the child born to David and Bathsheba and David's grief over the child (12:15–24). Bathsheba, however, bears David another child, whose name is Solomon (v. 24). The final outcome of the succession to David's throne is now foreshadowed.

A persuasive case has been made (McCarter 1984) that chapters 13–20 existed as a narrative of the revolt of Absalom prior to their incorporation into the larger court history. Seen from this point of view, the chief function of this narrative was as royal apologia. In spite of these events that seem to show David as weak and vacillating, he is nevertheless defended as God's anointed one and more worthy of the throne than his scheming, violent sons. In his grief over Absalom he shows himself a compassionate and loving father in spite of his son's treachery.

These stories are rich and detailed; only their bare outline can be suggested here. The detail rings so true that it has often been remarked that these narratives must be from the hand of an eyewitness.

Chapter 13 opens with the tragic story of the rape of Tamar, Absalom's sister, by her half brother Amnon. Amnon's lust, having achieved its goal by deceit, turns to hatred toward the violated Tamar, and he turns her out in disgrace. Violence begets further violence when Absalom kills Amnon in revenge (13:23–29). But since this takes place two years later, it would seem to reflect more than a passionate rage over the violation of Tamar. Absalom has eliminated his older brother, the main contender for the inheritance of David's throne, leaving himself now in the chief position.

In chapter 14 Joab intervenes to reconcile David and Absalom. Perhaps David is too gullible and indulgent, for immediately afterward, in chapter 15, unfolds the story of Absalom's treachery against David himself.

Absalom cannot wait to inherit the throne. He gathers a following from among those disgruntled with David (15:1–6). Absalom is described as handsome and charismatic; by contrast, the aging David does not seem the decisive man of action of the earlier traditions. He soon finds himself faced with open revolt and decides to retreat from Jerusalem lest he be trapped there (15:13–14). The account of David's retreat is filled with remarkable episodes and vignettes too numerous to detail. Friends and enemies, advisers and commanders are all forced to take sides for either David or Absalom. One loyal counselor ends up as a spy in Absalom's camp. Another adviser betrays David to stay with Absalom. Some come out to curse David, others to offer help. Zadok and Abiathar are sent back to Jerusalem with the Ark. Ziba comes to report the betrayal of Mephibosheth but later is discovered to have betrayed Mephibosheth for his own gain. The retreat narrative is a tapestry of human relationships and struggle for power (15:13–17:28).

The battle is finally joined in chapter 18, and David's men, led by the experienced Joab, win the victory. Absalom is caught in a tree by his hair (18:9) and then killed by Joab, in direct violation of David's order that his son's life be spared. The account of David grieving over Absalom's death is one of the most moving passages of mourning in ancient literature: "O my son Absalom, my son, my son Absalom! Would I had died instead of you, O Absalom, my son, my son!" (18:33).

In all of this, David, though often weak and indecisive, is somehow sympathetic. The account is at pains to note the mitigating circumstances of David's failures and human shortcomings. After the death of Absalom, the grief-stricken father is unable to attend to the affairs of the kingdom until he is roused to action by Joab's rough admonition (19:1–8).

The final episode of the court history is the story of Sheba, a Benjaminite, who attempts to foment a revolt of the northern tribes in the aftermath of Absalom's rebellion. It is quickly put down by men of Judah loyal to David (20:1–22).

Although it lies beyond 2 Samuel, brief mention must be made of 2 Kings 1–2, which many believe to be the conclusion of the Succession History. The passage relates the events that bring Solomon to the throne, even as David lies on his deathbed. If 2 Samuel 13–20 serves as a defense of David in spite of his weaknesses, then 1 Kings 1–2 can be also seen as royal apologia, this time in defense of Solomon. He came to the throne in a bloody purge that is presented as regrettable but justified. As these two pieces of royal apology have now been edited together they serve as a defense of the Davidic dynasty, and of the father and son who are the founders of the dynasty. (Nevertheless, the fact that 1 Kings 1–2 builds on the earlier elimination of possible rivals to the throne does not necessarily mean that these chapters come from the same author who composed 2 Sam 13–20.)

MISCELLANEOUS TRADITIONS

Chapters 21–24, sometimes called appendixes to 2 Samuel, seem to be collected here in a way that interrupts the flow of the account of the succession to David's throne. They are all stories occurring earlier in David's reign and seem very much out of place. Why have they been collected here? The best explanation seems to be that in the final editing of the

book, 2 Samuel 1–20 was basically fixed in its present form as an integral narrative history. Chapters 21–24 contain other stories of David, which the editor thought should also be preserved. The natural place for them was just before the hero's death, that is, just before 1 Kings 1, when David is dying. This same principle is seen in the collection of miscellaneous poems and other materials just before the death of Jacob in Genesis (chap. 49) and Moses in Deuteronomy (chap. 34).

There is a curious symmetry to the arrangement of these miscellaneous materials. At the beginning and end are stories of great disasters that occur during the reign of David: 2 Samuel 21:1–14 tells of the Gibeonites' revenge against the house of Saul, and 24:1–25 tells of the census of David, which angered Yahweh so that he sent a plague upon the people. This latter story ends with the erection of an altar on the threshing floor of Araunah, later to become the site of Solomon's Temple.

In the center of this section are two poems attributed to David: 22:1–51 is a hymn of praise also found as Psalm 18; 23:1–7 is another hymn of praise, sometimes referred to as the last words of David. It includes reference to the "everlasting covenant" of dynasty made with the house of David (23:5). Between the poems and the two narratives are sections listing heroes in the service of David and some of their exploits (21:15–22, 23:8–39).

With these additions the Book of 2 Samuel ends; but before they were divided into books, the early manuscripts were intended to lead directly into 1 Kings 1–11, to the story of Solomon, David's successor. The two Books of Samuel recount the turbulent events that established an Israelite kingdom. It now remained for Israel's historians to chronicle the fate of the kingdom in the two Books of Kings.

Bibliography

Albright, William F. *Samuel and the Beginning of the Prophetic Movement*. Cincinnati, 1961.

Birch, Bruce C. *The Rise of the Israelite Monarchy: The Growth and Development of 1 Samuel 7–15*. Missoula, 1976.

Carlson, R. A. *David the Chosen King: A Traditio-Historical Approach to the Second Book of Samuel*. Translated by J. Sharpe and Stanley Rudman. Stockholm, 1964.

Flanagan, James W. "Court History or Succession

Document? A Study of 2 Samuel 9–20 and 1 Kings 1–2." *Journal of Biblical Literature* 91 (1972): 172–181.

Gunn, David M. *The Story of King David: Genre and Interpretation.* Sheffield, England, 1978.

Hertzberg, Hans Wilhelm. *I and II Samuel: A Commentary.* Translated by J. S. Bowden. London, 1964.

Knierim, Rolf P. "The Messianic Concept of the First Book of Samuel." In *Jesus and the Historian,* edited by F. Thomas Trotter. Philadelphia, 1968.

McCarter, P. Kyle, Jr. *I Samuel.* Garden City, N.Y., 1980.

———. *II Samuel.* Garden City, N.Y., 1984.

McCarthy, Dennis J. "The Inauguration of Monarchy in Israel: A Form-Critical Study of I Samuel 8–12." *Interpretation* 27 (1973): 401–412.

Mettinger, Tryggve N. D. *King and Messiah: The Civil and Sacral Legitimation of the Israelite Kings.* Lund, Sweden, 1976.

Miller, Patrick D., Jr., and J. J. M. Roberts. *The Hand of the Lord: A Reassessment of the "Ark Narrative" of 1 Samuel.* Baltimore, 1977.

Noth, Martin. *Überlieferungsgeschichtliche Studien: Die sammelnden und bearbeitenden Geschichtswerke im Alten Testament.* Darmstadt, 1957. Translated as *The Deuteronomistic History.* Winona Lake, Ind., 1981.

Rad, Gerhard von. "The Beginning of History Writing in Ancient Israel." In *The Problem of the Hexateuch and Other Essays,* translated by E. W. Trueman Dicken. Edinburgh, 1966.

Rost, Leonhard. *Die Überlieferung von der Thronnachfolge Davids.* Stuttgart, 1926.

Weiser, Artur. *Samuel: Seine geschichtliche Aufgabe und religiöse Bedeutung: Traditionsgeschichtliche Untersuchungen zum 1. Samuel 7–12.* Göttingen, 1962.

Whybray, Roger N. *The Succession Narrative: A Study of II Samuel 9–20 and I Kings 1 and 2.* London, 1968.

BRUCE C. BIRCH

I and II Kings

THE BOOKS OF Kings open with the last days of David, most of his reign and that of his predecessor, Saul, having been covered in the Books of Samuel. The story continues with the rule of Solomon, describes the disruption of the kingdom after his death, and presents a dovetailing account of the sometimes rivalrous, sometimes allied kingdoms of Judah in the south and Israel in the north. Following the demise of Israel in 722 B.C.E., the narrative follows events in Judah through the monarchy's collapse and the subsequent exile of the people in 587 B.C.E. The books conclude with reports about those of royal connection who remained among the ruins of Judah and the reversal of the exiled Judean monarch's misfortune.

Beginning with the waning years of David, the larger story is divided into regnal periods, virtually all of which are introduced and concluded with formulaic information. The writer identifies each monarch, and evaluates him from a religious and moral point of view; the conclusion cites other sources of information, reports the king's death and burial, and mentions his successor. Between these conventional limits, the writer presents details of the particular reign (see, e.g., 1 Kgs 14:21–31; 2 Kgs 18:1–20:21).

This organizational principle, also found in Herodotus, runs counter to the modern taste for a sustained narrative leading to a dramatic climax. The Books of Kings offer, instead, a chainlike series of royal epochs, arranged chronologically as blocks of tradition. Each regnal period is reckoned as something unto itself, except in the case where events in the northern and southern kingdoms are juxtaposed (1 Kgs 12–2 Kgs 17). Then, the years of one monarch are aligned with those of his counterpart in the opposite kingdom (e.g., 1 Kgs 22:41).

A conceptual unity is achieved mainly by analogies between personages and events, which overcome the constraints of serial presentation and strict chronology of the narrative. For example, each king is measured by how well he upheld the primacy of God (Yahweh) and God's Temple in Jerusalem or, more typically, how he utterly failed in this responsibility. Northern kings stand condemned for following the ways of Jeroboam, who had in his own time turned away from the standard embodied by David (cf. 1 Kgs 11:38 with 12:25–33). Similarly, with the exception of Hezekiah and Josiah (2 Kgs 18:1–7, 22:1–2), all southern rulers departed from David's example (e.g., 2 Kgs 14:1–4). From this system of moral comparisons arises an important sense of unity. David's reverence toward God flows through the narrative like a tracer mineral, exposing weaknesses in the arteries, and yet sustaining the physician's promise of health—God's promise of unbroken dynasty (e.g., 2 Sam 7 + 1 Kgs 11:38–39).

The writer further adds to the books' sense of unity by inserting interruptions into the regnal history (e.g., 1 Kgs 2:12b–46 2 Kgs 17:7–23) that emphasize certain didactic themes and assert a theological connectedness among events. Trajectories from prophecy to fulfillment also help create a sense of conceptual unity. The writer speaks with the voice of God and so demonstrates on numerous occasions that a prophet's word, once uttered, comes to pass (e.g., 1 Kgs 11:11–13, 31–39 + 12:1–24) and that God's word presses for order, meaning, and explanation in the chaos of time.

In these and lesser ways, 1–2 Kings achieves a unity in rhetorical suasion, for although the subject of the books is royal history, the theme is the moral and religious failure that led to the eventual loss of national identity and autonomy. Accordingly, the narrative, which to a secular historian suffers from omissions and religious bias, keeps this didactic, moral, and theological purpose uppermost in mind.

ORIGINS OF THE WORK

At the time of Christian origins, 1–2 Kings were regarded as one book, a continuation of the Books of Samuel, and thus part of a consecutive account of ancient Israel's monarchy. The Septuagint, a Greek translation of the Jewish Bible used in the same period, grouped Samuel and Kings together as 1–2 and 3–4 Kingdoms (Basileiai). Even though adhering to a fifteenth- or sixteenth-century division into two parts, the present-day Hebrew Bible reflects a traditionally religious sense of the books' contents and literary context. Joshua, Judges, Samuel, and Kings constitute the Former Prophets and together present a religiously inspired account of the ancient Israelites' life in the Land of Israel from settlement until exile.

Scholars of the history of the Bible generally agree that the present form of 1–2 Kings is the result of a long process of collection, editing, writing, and revising of diverse materials, some of which could at one time have been transmitted orally. One widely held hypothesis suggests that the preserved text is a preexilic history of the monarchy that was revised after 587 B.C.E. in light of the Judean exile, when the hopes vested in King Josiah (640–609 B.C.E.) had come to nothing. Another opinion holds that the Books of Kings belong to a series of writings by a single author (possibly having undergone successive revisions), which include Deuteronomy, Joshua, Judges, Samuel, Kings, and a vignette of Judah's last king in Babylonian exile (2 Kgs 25:27–30). Adherents of both views assume that an author (or authors) unified this work with theological ideas reflected in, and derived from, the Book of Deuteronomy.

This "Deuteronomistic historian," as well as later revisers, emphasize throughout that proper worship may be offered only in Jerusalem, in the manner that God demands, and in the Solomonic Temple, the place where God's name rests. The unfolding events are seen as fulfilling old prophecies, and the accounts of political and personal strivings thus become merged in a morally directed narrative of the faithful and the miscreant. The nation's leaders are condemned for their failure to rule within God's covenant, that is, in conformance with God's *torah,* or teaching. The ancient historian forges a literary unity in the work with the aid of (1) epitomizing digressions in the narrative (e.g., at Josh 12; Judg 2:11–3:6; 2 Kgs 17:7–23); (2) long speeches by God and heroic leaders at pivotal moments (e.g., Josh 1:2–9, 23:2–16; 1 Sam 12; 2 Sam 7; 1 Kgs 8:14–61); (3) specially constructed narratives that convey favorite didactic themes (e.g., 1 Kgs 3:3–15, 9:1–9; 2 Kgs 22:3–23:20); (4) a schematic chronology of 480 years running from Moses and the flight from Egypt (Deut 1:3) to the building of the Jerusalem Temple by Solomon (1 Kgs 6:1).

Whether or not one accepts this hypothesis of one author or perhaps several editors of the larger Deuteronomistic work of history, this composition as it now appears in the Bible is a necessary context for understanding the Books of Kings. After investigating origins, we must take into account the key images, literary patterns, and connective motifs that define 1–2 Kings as part of the wellspring of religious thought for Jews and Christians.

The diversity of the material in Kings suggests a variety of sources, as indicated by repeated references to other works: the "Book of the Acts of Solomon" (*sefer divrei shelomoh;* 1 Kgs 11:41), the "Book of the Chronicles of the Kings of Israel" (*sefer divrei hayyamim lemalkhei yisra'el;* 1 Kgs 14:19), the "Book of the Chronicles of the Kings of Judah" (*sefer divrei hayyamim lemalkhei yehudah;* 1 Kgs 14:29). Whether these were in fact sources, what their literary character was, and what information they contained have been matters of research and dispute. Many scholars assume that these books contained basic formulaic information and narratives about the various kings, perhaps along the lines of certain Assyrian and Babylonian chronicles. Another source is supposed to have been an extensive narrative, now deposited in 2 Samuel 5–1 Kings 2, of the reign of David. Also available were popular narratives about kings and prophets, as well as stories of individual prophets, such as Elijah and Elisha (1 Kgs 17–19; 2 Kgs 1–9). Some scholars have claimed to find traces of an account of the Jerusalem Temple: its construction (1 Kgs 6–9), loss of wealth (e.g., 1 Kgs 14:26–28; 2 Kgs 12:18), reform (e.g., 2 Kgs 12:5–17 [4–16; RSV]), and degradation (e.g., 2 Kgs 16:10–18, 25:13–15).

However plausible such hypotheses may be, they remain unsupported by concrete evidence. Unfortunately, the raw material from which 1–2 Kings were created exists only as a hypothetical possibility. But it is useful for grasping the sense of the work to consider how the various types of material contained therein contribute to the narrative shape and implied purposes of the composition, and how their arrangement accords with models of literary composition known elsewhere in the Bible and the ancient Near East. For these tasks, modern modes of historical and literary analysis prove especially helpful.

LITERARY STYLE OF 1–2 KINGS

The most important materials in the Books of Kings are lists, reports, prose narratives, and evaluative commentarial summaries. Contained within these organizing categories are many other types of ordinary discourse, stylized speech, poetic fragments and prayers, and a range of narrative styles that are also found in other biblical writings.

Lists

Most simply, a list recounts items without any discernible principle of order. In more developed examples, intentionality plays a larger role, with items arranged systematically by a main idea, common element, or purpose. In the Books of Kings, lists order aspects of the past in ways that have special relevance to a writer whose purposes and perspective must be inferred by the reader. In this context, lists serve as literary and informative tools of historiography and persuasion.

For example, there are two separate tabulations of Solomon's royal officials in 1 Kgs 4:2–6, 8–19. Each carries a brief subject heading or superscription (vv. 2a, 8a), and the names are listed in series, like an administrative register. However, within the larger literary context, the lists gain special nuance. They are linked by a common word, "officers" (RSV) or "prefects" (JPS), in verses 5 and 7, which suggests that we read the second list (vv. 8–19) as spelling out the grand significance of Azariah's position "over the officers" (v. 5). This in turn lends weight to the statement at the head of the chapter that "King Solomon was king over all Israel" (v. 1). A concluding remark, near the end, notes again that these "officers supplied provisions for King Solomon (5:7 [4:27; RSV]). The result of this play on a common word, "officers," is to urge the reader to take this massive bureaucratic mechanism as part and parcel of the writer's praise of Solomon's fantastic stature (see 4:20–5:6 [4:20–26; RSV]).

Obviously, not all royal officeholders are listed, but some seem to have been chosen for their importance to the wider narrative of the rule of David and Solomon. Despite the puzzling duplication and naming of Abiathar, who according to 1 Kings 2:35b had been removed from office by this time, the mention of priests (1 Kgs 4:2, 4a) expresses a common ancient Near Eastern idea that the king's first religious duty is to support the cult of the national God (see, for David, 2 Sam 7; 8:17, 18). This idea finds extensive expression in Solomon's royal-religious and priestly character. He prays for an "understanding mind" to govern the people (1 Kgs 3:5–14), builds and dedicates the first Temple in Israel (1 Kgs 6:1–8:66), and in a dream sees it accepted by Israel's God as a munificent offering (1 Kgs 9:1–3). Other people listed establish continuities with earlier and later events. Benaiah (1 Kgs 4:4) was party to Solomon's accession (1 Kgs 1:8, 10, 26, 32–44) and carried out the executions by which the new king consolidated his power (1 Kgs 2:25, 34–35). The sons of Nathan (1 Kgs 4:5) evoke the memory of the father who was important to David's rule, the beginnings of Solomon's, and the God-given basis for the Davidic dynasty in Jerusalem (2 Sam 7, 12; 1 Kgs 1). The position of supervisor of forced labor (1 Kgs 4:6b) of David's time (2 Sam 20:24) is accorded renewed significance due to the need for slaves to manage Solomon's building program (1 Kgs 5:27–32 [5:13–18; RSV], 9:15–23; *cf.* 1 Sam 8:12–17). Among the "officers" responsible for provisioning the king, two are singled out for having married daughters of Solomon (1 Kgs 4:11, 15), a note about political connections that mirrors Solomon's own actions (1 Kgs 3:1, 11:1–8).

In context, then, these lists amount to a system of cross-references to other parts of the account of the Israelite monarchy. The administrative continuity between the reigns of David and Solomon suggests conceptual links to the theological themes that underlie the inception of the monarchy. These themes are couched in paradigmatic terms and symbols of rule under God. Behind Solomon's accession to the throne is Yahweh's special love (2 Sam 12:24–25), the force of divine destiny (2 Sam 7:4–17; 1 Kgs 1:37, 48; 2:4), and the trusteeship of sovereignty under the *torah* of Moses (1 Kgs 2:3–4).

Therefore, the second list (1 Kgs 4:8–19) gives evidence of the blessings that accrue to a ruler who walks in the ways of God. The "prefects" mentioned in verses 7 and 27 (5:7; MT) provide a framework for offering unabashed praise for the king who controls the kingdom's wealth and prosperity: Solomon, "king over all Israel," takes on legendary proportions (4:20–27 [4:20–5:7; MT]). Continuity in administration, the interlocking of twelve disparate regions in obligation to the king's daily needs, and the fabulous wealth of the kingdom all attest to the continuance of God's promise that he would establish the house of David forever (2 Sam 7:16). Shielded by a shade tree of divine benevolence, alive to history and promise, all "Judah and Israel dwelt in safety, from Dan even to Beer-sheba" (1 Kgs 4:25; RSV).

Reports

A report is a brief prose narrative, usually in third-person style, about a single event or situation. It has no plot or character development. Reports vary in length from succinct notices (e.g., 1 Kgs 3:1) to longer, even composite, accounts that link together several reports of diverse content (e.g., 2 Kgs 13:22–25; 1 Kgs 6:1–7:51). They are often integral parts of longer narratives. As tools of historiography, reports efficiently convey diverse information, rapidly survey varying spans of time, construct analogies and other connections between parts of the larger literary work, and afford an opportunity to comment on passing events. Reports are also easily adaptable for didactic purposes.

The Books of Kings contain reports of royal construction projects (1 Kgs 6:2–6, 8–10; 7:2–8; 12:25; 16:24, 34), military campaigns and battles (1 Kgs 14:25–26; 2 Kgs 8:20–22, 24:10–17, 25:1–12), conspiracies against the crown (1 Kgs 15:27–30; 16:9–13; 2 Kgs 15:10,14, 25, 30; 21:23), and diplomatic concordats (1 Kgs 15:17–20; 2 Kgs 12:17–18, 16:5–9, 18:13–16). There are also reports of prophetic visions (1 Kgs 22:19–22), oracles (1 Kgs 6:11–13, 12:22–24, 16:1–4; 2 Kgs 19:6–7, 20–28; 20:1, 16–18; 21:10–15), and a deathbed farewell (1 Kgs 2:1–9).

The range of topics, however, is less instructive than the use to which reports are put in the Books of Kings. For example, David's last words to his son Solomon (1 Kgs 2:1–9), composed of originally separate pieces of tradition, follow a typical sequence: (1) reference to advanced age or impending death, (2) admonitions, (3) directives to those gathered nearby. The model is widely used in the Bible and attests to a long-lived literary tradition: Joshua 23:2b–16, Genesis 49: 29–32, 1 Maccabees 2:49–70, Acts 20:18–35. On the other hand, 1 Kings 2:1–9 is also similar to Deuteronomy 31:23, Joshua 1:2–9, and 2 Chronicles 32:7–8; all three reports mark the transfer of a clearly defined leadership position from one person to another. David's words of encouragement to Solomon, "Be strong, and show yourself a man" (1 Kgs 2:2; RSV), and his assurance of divine aid in the exercise of power (vv. 3–4) are typical of these investiture speeches.

The report of David's final words has overtones of other transitional moments in Israelite historiography: the shift from the ancestors who bore a promise of destiny to Moses, who received the *torah* in the liminal world between Egypt and the Land of Israel (Gen 47:29–49:33); from Moses to his servant Joshua, who entered the Promised Land and sacralized it with *torah* (Deut 31:14–23, Josh 1:1–9); from

Joshua to the quasi-royal "rulers" (RSV "judges") who brought order to the land and guarded its *torah* holiness (Josh 23:2–16).

These solemn moments are fraught with historic significance that is best captured in the evocative imagery of national beginnings. Genesis 49 stresses the relations between the twelve root tribes, and Joshua 23, the giving of land in fulfillment of the ancestral covenant. In the monarchical history, 1 Kings 2:4 alludes to the theological underpinnings of David's dynasty: "If your sons are scrupulous in their conduct, walking before me in faithfulness with all their heart and with all their being, [then] a man of yours shall never be cut off from the throne of Israel" (Au. trans.; *cf.* 2 Sam 7:12–16; 1 Kgs 1:35–36, 48; 2:45; 11:34, 36). This newly formulated covenant cemented divine selection of kings to mutually defined obligations (see 2 Sam 7:1–29, 23:2–5) and established David as the model for the kings in Judah. This Davidic covenant was a reservoir of hope from which an ancient reader of Kings, weighted by exile and loss of national identity, might draw some measure of encouragement at the end of the book (2 Kgs 25:27–30).

Moreover, the directives issued by David (1 Kgs 2:5–9) pointedly look back to incidents in the remote past of his reign: Joab's murder of two army commanders (2 Sam 3:22–27, 20:4–10), the loyalty shown David by Barzillai (2 Sam 17:27–29), and the curse pronounced over David by Shimei (2 Sam 16:5–13). At the same time, these final instructions anticipate the murder of Joab and Shimei (1 Kgs 2:28–34, 39–46), the unfinished business that occupies Solomon in the first days of his reign.

The deathbed testament marks a paradigmatic transition by suggesting analogies with other heroic leaders of the past. David and Solomon are viewed within a theological framework: the continuity of Solomon's posterity is to be realized as a function of the mutuality of God's covenant with the Judahite Davidic dynasty.

Several times, the writer of 1–2 Kings includes brief reports of successful conspiracies to overthrow a reigning monarch, mostly in the north (1 Kgs 15:27–30, 16:9–13; 2 Kgs 15:10, 25, 30; 21:23 [a Judean king]). These reports follow a similar schematic sequence by mentioning "conspiracy," the "striking down" and death of the king, and a statement that the conspirator "reigned in his [the murdered king's] stead." Similar reports are to be found among Babylonian chronicles and king lists.

These reports in the Books of Kings consistently underscore the justness of the historian's negative evaluations. Violent death at the hands of a usurper, it is suggested, is a fitting fate for kings who "did not turn away from the transgressions of Jeroboam," that archetypal apostate who established a shrine in the north to rival the Temple in Jerusalem (2 Kgs 15:9, 24, 28). Similarly, Amnon, the one Judahite king who comes to a similar end (2 Kgs 21:23), is condemned for walking in the ways of his father, Manasseh, who had sullied the inner reaches of the Jerusalemite sanctuary (2 Kgs 21:4–9). The text presses this causal link between moral failure and throne conspiracy even for one particular reign of twenty years' duration (2 Kgs 15:27), when the final murderous deed is the *only* event recorded.

In two other cases (1 Kgs 15:27–30, 16:9–13) reports of palace conspiracies are elaborated to draw an explicit moralizing conclusion and, moreover, to make thematic connections with other regnal periods. Using formulaic language indicating that these events occurred in fulfillment of prophecy (15:29b, 16:12b), the writer explains that the murderous conspiracy was really divine judgment for the king's misdeeds (15:30, 16:13; *cf.* 16:15–19). With transgression and punishment, the warp and woof of the north's first dynasty, one may weave a garment of all the kings from Jeroboam to Zimri. Jeroboam's son, Nadab, is murdered by Baasha (15:27–30), in fulfillment of an earlier prophecy (15:29, 14:10). In the separate account of Baasha's reign (15:33–16:7), a connection is made between a prophecy of punishment for Baasha's house and those treacherous deeds against Jeroboam's dynasty (16:1–4, 7). This prediction later comes true in another treachery when the son of Baasha loses his throne to Zimri (16:9–13), and Zimri, uneasy about his ill-gotten gains, takes his own life (16:17–19) when challenged by a rival military commander. Again, misdeeds against God (16:19) lead to an ignoble end.

Thus, when reports of throne conspiracy are linked one to another for didactic purposes, they turn a skeletal summary of successor kings into a cross-generational tale of turmoil and dissolution. Matter-of-fact reports convey an object lesson, prophecy is fulfilled, and moral flaws are exposed.

Prose Narratives

This material in the Books of Kings develops dramatic plot and a cast of characters. Background events pose a problem; action builds to a climactic turning point, which then leads to resolution of the matter; and narrative tension is relieved. Throughout such a trajectory, the narrator creates a rich account of a real world populated with psychologically plausible personalities. All such narratives in the Books of Kings are historical in tone: they present plot and characters realistically and purport to recount and explain past events. This does not, however, preclude the use of fictional elements to heighten drama, explore the paradigmatic or archetypal proportions of personages, and manipulate the reader's experience. Many such narratives feature individual kings, prophets and kings, or prophets alone as central characters.

Prose narratives are a primary medium to convey a sense of regnal epochs, especially the Omride period in the north (1 Kgs 16:23–2 Kgs 10:36) and the time of Hezekiah and Josiah in Judah (2 Kgs 18:1–23:30). These narratives often appear designed to persuade the reader of certain moral or religious values and sometimes to counter simplistic ideological responses. The writer's rhetorical skill thus renders particular events while suggesting associations with other parts of the monarchical account.

For example, 1 Kings opens with a narrative about how Solomon, and not his elder brother Adonijah, came to succeed David as ruler over all Israel. The matter could have been presented in straightforward fashion, like God's command to Moses that assured that Joshua would lead the post-Mosaic generation into the Promised Land (Deut 31:14–23). Instead, through manipulation of time, a fuller sense of the succession is created. In the rush of events charged with emotions, the reader's allegiance and sympathy are not so definitively directed to Solomon as they are to Joshua in Deuteronomy, as examination of 1 Kings 1 shows.

A framework of repeating motifs (1 Kgs 1:1, 4 and 1:15b) marks out a section of narrative that conveys information relevant to two ongoing series of contemporaneous events: Adonijah's feast at En-rogel (1 Kgs 1:9, 41ff.) and the palace intrigue in Jerusalem (1 Kgs 1:15–40). The framework itself suggests that David's infirmity is some kind of precondition for all subsequent events. Inside this framework, many temporal complications arise. Adonijah's feast precedes other events, such as Nathan's crafty proposal (vv. 11–14). From verse 41 one learns that his feast is contemporaneous with other events in the story, such as the representations made to David in verses 15–31. Furthermore, Adonijah's celebration loses something of its unique character by being reported as regularly repeated acts of self-importance. The prince (had been) exalting himself, (had) prepared chariots as kings do, and (had) gathered supporters to his cause (vv. 5, 7) while the ailing David lay shivering and unmoved to passion in the palace. Nevertheless, as explained in verses 6, 8, and 10, Adonijah's actions have some justification. David had never protested his son's overreach, and Adonijah was "a very handsome man . . . born next after Absalom" (RSV). In brief, this son of David meets the physical requirements of a future king (see 1 Sam 10:23, 16:12; 2 Sam 14:25–26); and since Absalom is dead (2 Sam 18:17), he is the natural heir.

With this background information and assorted conflicting impressions, the reader can now follow Bathsheba to David's room (v. 15), where the main action is about to unfold. It is not easy to take sides at this moment. One recalls the vigorous and passionate monarch of the Books of Samuel and contrasts that image with the now infirm David who must deal with the aggressive, dashing, and self-important Adonijah, whose claim to the throne is not without legitimacy. The worn-out, tired, older generation is thus contrasted with the vigorousness of youth—seeking to mold what is or what may be. Then there is Nathan conjuring up yet another specter: Solomon, seated on the throne vouchsafed him by an oath forgotten—or never made—by King David (vv. 11–14). In granting legitimacy to Adonijah's actions and suggesting at the same time that the position of the older son may have been undermined by an oath, the narrator makes it impossible to reach any facile judgment of these events.

Thus, the Books of Kings open on a note of ambiguity, as though the author wanted to undermine any straightforward response by offering a counter-point to the formulaic condemnations and praises of kings that characterize introductions to other regnal periods (e.g., 1 Kgs 14:21–24). Never in this "history" of the kings does the epoch of David lend itself to easy judgments.

Narratives involving prophets are also important to the Books of Kings, since these figures tend to voice themes that seem fundamental to the writer's point of view. For example, stories about Elijah and his successor, Elisha, span the Omride dynasty from Ahab (1 Kgs 16:29) to Jehoram (2 Kgs 3:1), through its overthrow by Jehu (2 Kgs 9–10), until the reign of Jehu's grandson, Jehoash (2 Kgs 13). Throughout this long stretch, unencumbered prophetic devotion is pitted against royalty's continuing defection from Yahweh.

This didactic point emerges unmistakably in Elijah's grandly staged opposition to the Baal worshipers in Ahab's kingdom (1 Kgs 17–19), a moment captured in Felix Mendelssohn's oratorio *Elijah*. God's protagonist demands single-minded obedience to Yahweh; King Ahab, the antagonist, worships Baal, and with Queen Jezebel seeks to rid the kingdom of Yahweh's troublesome prophets. Against this background, Elijah and Baal's prophets compete for a sign from the heavens. Elijah, alone against the many (18:22, 25), taunting, mocking their vain attempts (18:26–29), deliberately sets impossible conditions for Yahweh to overcome, should he respond to this test of the gods and their believers (18:30–35). In the end, there is no contest. The "fire of the Lord" consumes the altar, and the people fall prostrate in awe and reverence, purged of their limping disbelief (vv. 21, 38–39). The triumph, however, seems incomplete. Jezebel, now a kind of villainous stand-in for Ahab, continues her relentless persecution (19:1–2) and Elijah, God's lone defender, becomes disheartened and complains to God—or to the desert emptiness (19:10, 14). The enigmatic response is described as a "still small voice" (RSV) or a "soft murmuring sound" (v. 12; JPS) and offers little consolation. Elijah is told to anoint the king's successors, and through *them* the virulent conflict between Yahweh and Baal, Elijah and the Baal worshipers, will find its just resolution (19:15–18).

The predicted outcome (1 Kgs 19:15–18, 21:21–24) is finally realized in Jehu's conspiracy, inspired by

Elisha, to take the Omride throne (2 Kgs 9:1–14). Jehu writes to supporters, "Know then that nothing of the word of the Lord which the Lord spoke concerning the house of Ahab shall fall to the ground; for the Lord has done what he announced through his servant Elijah" (2 Kgs 10:10; Au. trans.). And after the tumult quiets, the historian directly addresses the reader: "Thus Jehu wiped out the Baal from Israel" (2 Kgs 10:28).

However, the prophets act not only as the narrator's agents but also as ideologues in temporal matters, as attested in 1 Kings 20:12–30, where an unnamed prophet imposes an ideological stamp on what might have been presented more blandly as a simple account of a battle between Ahab (the Israelites) and the Aramaeans. In a variation on a commonly used literary device of consulting a priest or prophet about the outcome of an impending conflict (see Judg 1:1–2; 1 Sam 23:1–5, 10–12; 2 Sam 5:19), King Ahab's oracles arrive unsolicited, as though by divine initiative, and offer more than the conventional assurances of victory. His triumph will demonstrate to Ahab (v. 13), all Israel (v. 28), and the reader that Yahweh is present in these events. Just this theological claim seems at issue in verses 23–25, 28. The Aramaean advisers rest their counsel on an assumption that the power of Yahweh the mountain God is ineffectual in the valleys. Given that point of view, Aram acts with cunning when he challenges Israel to a second battle on the plain near Aphek. But to an Israelite reader, who already is convinced of Yahweh's universal power, this strategy must have seemed amusingly lame. Read in this way, the prophet's words have turned the military opponents into ideological combatants, one of whom, ironically, is a victim of misguided premises.

Moreover, the prophetic words are enclosed within repeated descriptive motifs, thus enhancing the characters of the combatants. Aram's muster of drunkards (vv. 12 and 16) is contrasted with Ahab, who in the mind's eye drinks soberly from God's cup. The clarity of guidance offered Israel is etched against the Aramaean muses of confusion, as is divine protection against flawed human initiative. The second oracle (v. 28) similarly nests within descriptive clauses that present a once-defeated Aramaean army as reconstituted, man for man, chariot for chariot, horse for horse, into a mighty band that "filled the country-side," whereas Israel is encamped opposite these hordes "like two little flocks of goats" (vv. 25–27, 29a). With these unequal opponents poised opposite one another, the prophet's pronouncement causes yet another confusion in Aram. His armies falter this time because of foolish presuppositions. For the reader, therefore, it is not simply a matter of overwhelming numbers threatening the small force of Israel, but rather, of foolishness and impotence arrayed against the underdog's sober reliance upon Yahweh's power, which will, so says the prophet, reveal itself to all.

Narratives that feature a prophet as one of their main characters offer particularly rich possibilities to further the aims of didactic historiography, as in the case of 2 Kings 5:1–27. Interlocking pulses of narrative energy roll along, each generating from within itself the power for another. One trajectory carries the action from leprosy to its cure; a "great man," Naaman, flawed only by his unsightly illness, finds such a miraculous cure that his flesh becomes like that of a "little child" (v. 14). Yet, there is a second generative impulse within. The reader's knowledge that it was the God of Israel who has given Naaman his successes among the Aramaeans (v. 1) contrasts sharply with Naaman's intransigent arrogance toward Yahweh's prophet Elisha and the land set aside for God's people. The expectation of reversal in Naaman's attitude is fulfilled when, having been healed, Naaman "turns back" (the word also means "repent") to Elisha and speaks like a convert to Israel's God (vv. 15–19). A third narrative movement arises out of this second one. Gehazi, a servant of Elisha, witnesses Naaman's humility and sullies the moment of repentance by turning it to his own material advantage. For this he stands accused, as Elisha asks him, "Was it a [suitable] time to accept money and garments . . . ?" (v. 26). The remark that Gehazi went away "a leper, as white as snow" (v. 27b) turns this tale of reversals and contrasts into a circle of ironic twists. Naaman, who at the beginning of the story was a leper, unaware of Yahweh's power, becomes a healed and converted devotee who urgently presses reward on Yahweh's prophet. And Gehazi, who enters as healthy but opportunistic, wanders away afflicted with Naaman's disease, suitably rewarded for his treachery.

Through this flow of power, Elisha retains his dominance, dispensing rewards and punishments as befits those who deal with God's prophet in truth or deceit. The prophet's role contrasts sharply with that of the Israelite king, who, in his ineptness, nearly thwarts the fulfillment of prophetic mission in his own realm (vv. 6–8). The writer depicts King Jehoram unfavorably and illustrates the overall negative assessment of the king given at the beginning of the account of his reign (2 Kgs 3:3). In due time it becomes clear (2 Kgs 5:8) that a successor to Elijah is authorized to carry on the defense of Yahweh amidst the political disarray and godlessness of the northern kingdom (*cf.* 2 Kgs 3:13–14). The dramatic struggle, begun in Elijah's time, to obliterate the voice of Yahweh in the kingdom moves inexorably to a resolution during Elisha's life (2 Kgs 9–10).

Evaluative Commentarial Summaries

These summaries interrupt the narrative at strategic points, offering explanations, illustrations, or appraisals of personages and events. A note that an earlier prophecy has been fulfilled (e.g., 2 Kgs 10:17) is a regularly used device. More frequent is a theological evaluation—couched in formulaic language—of the king in the introduction to virtually all regnal periods (e.g., 1 Kgs 16:25–26). Judahite rulers are introduced with general information about the dates of their accession, the length and place of their rule, and the name of the king's mother, followed by a statement such as: "And [royal name] did what was upright [or evil] in the eyes of Yahweh," or "[he] walked in all the ways [all the transgressions] of his father [royal name]" (see 1 Kgs 15:11, 15:3). Often these general appraisals are substantiated by more specific allegations of misconduct, or, less often, citations of instances of faithfulness to God. The language used is characteristic of that of the Book of Deuteronomy. Israelite, or northern, kings tend to receive negative evaluations throughout. Typical is the statement "And he did evil in the eyes of Yahweh," followed by various formulaic references to the king's failure to turn away from the ways of Jeroboam, the archetypal transgressor of the northern kingdom (see 1 Kgs 15:26; 2 Kgs 3:2–3).

According to these summaries, the kings, virtually without exception, yielded to personal and national temptations and thus failed in their devotion to Yahweh and destroyed the preeminence of the Temple in Jerusalem. Such untiring censure, which characterizes the account of each reign, is offered as explanation for the monarchy's ultimate fall.

The comments also provide cross-references within the Books of Kings: the praiseworthy kings Josiah and Hezekiah in Judah are favorably linked to the unique merits of David, whereas others, like Solomon (1 Kgs 11:6), are found wanting. The northern kings are encumbered by the original transgression of Jeroboam, whose infamy stemmed from missing an opportunity to be like David (1 Kgs 11:38) and establishing a center of worship in the north to rival the Temple in Jerusalem. Even responsibility for the final demise of the Judahite kingship is likened to this curse on the northern kingdom. Among other sacrilegious acts, King Manasseh erected non-Jerusalemite cultic objects just as Ahab had done, following the path of Jeroboam (2 Kgs 21:3). Only Hezekiah and Josiah among the successors of David deserve praise (2 Kgs 18:3–7, 22:2), but even Josiah's merits prove insufficient to erase the stain of Manasseh (2 Kgs 21:6, 23:26–27). This web of guilt that covers both the northern and southern kingdoms ultimately originates in some form of deviance from David's ways, and the formulaic condemnation turns the history of the Israelite kings into an epic of willful failure.

In a longer excursus in 2 Kings 17:7–22 about the rise and fall of the northern kingdom, the narrator pauses to reflect on the reasons for the catastrophe, reaching into the dimly lit innocence before monarchy to the apostasies of the time when God had brought the young nation into a strange land (vv. 7–8). The range of temporal vision of this excursus also extends into the future, when Judah, too, will be exiled (vv. 19–20). Finally, the story time resumes its normal forward movement and the writer returns to the reader's time: "Israel was exiled from their own land . . . *until this day*" (v. 23b). With this remark, the present of moral application swallows the past of history. By exploiting the supratemporal consciousness—as in those omniscient formulaic appraisals of the kings—the writer achieves unity of vision and literary connection.

A SENSE OF THE WHOLE

The Books of Kings must be seen as part of a five-part account of the monarchy in ancient Israel. The tale begins with Saul and David, whose destinies —the one downward to disgrace, the other upward to unrivaled fame—seem inseparable (1 Sam 7:15–2 Sam 4:12). David rules free of Saul's shadow, but not those of his own sons (2 Sam 5:1–1 Kgs 2:12a). Solomon follows (1 Kgs 2:12b–11:43) and then, in the wake of his reign, comes a divided and contentious kingdom, the spoiled fruit of his turning from God (1 Kgs 11:9–13), which in turn wastes away in exile (1 Kgs 12:1–2 Kgs 17:41). The fifth and last phase follows the remnant of Judah until its own destruction and offers a glimpse of several survivors— the nobility, the people of Judah under Babylonian rule, and the exiled King Jehoiachin (2 Kgs 18:1–25:30).

In the system of cross-referenced regnal years for the divided kingdom, the writer starts and finishes each particular reign before beginning another. This means that in some cases the reader is carried far ahead chronologically and then thrown back in time for the discussion of the monarch in the adjoining kingdom. See, for example, how Baasha, an Israelite, strides into view during the reign of Asa, a Judahite (1 Kgs 15:16–22), long before his own reign appears in the larger narrative in proper formulaic garb (1 Kgs 15:33–16:7). In this story world, time flows ahead, then back again, until it finally achieves a kind of rest in the exile of Judah, presumably close to the actual time of the writer.

In short, the literary form of Kings is an extended parataxis, a series of regnal epochs, each covered separately with no linguistic markers of logical or temporal subordination. Within particular epochs, this mode of composition is also evident. Even where transitional phrases, such as "in those (his) days," "then," or "at that time," are used, the relationships amount to little more than juxtapositions. Sometimes such expressions do not convey any clear temporal sense, despite the temporality implied in the words themselves. In 2 Kings 14:8, for example, "then" has no precise function other than joining material that may originally have been separate (*cf.* 1 Kgs 16:21; 2 Kgs 10:32; 15:16, 37; 16:5, 6). Elsewhere, the linkage is made with simple, but essentially vague, connectors such as "after these things" (1 Kgs 17:17, 21:1) or *ve*, rendered into English variously as "and," "but," "so," "therefore," or "now" (e.g., 1 Kgs 12:25, 17:1; 2 Kgs 2:1, 11:1, 14:5). Evidently the Books of Kings reflect in narrative the paratactic style that is lodged in the syntax of the Hebrew language itself.

Given these stylistic characteristics, the conceptual unity is usually achieved by analogy, the juxtaposition of remote or proximate narrative elements. Repetition of a word or phrase, for example, can connect otherwise independent traditions and suggest some parallels between them. The words "to his house resentful and sullen" (1 Kgs 20:43, 21:4) are such a case. The repeated motifs in 1 Kings 12:33b and 13:1b, which link the tradition of Jeroboam's "sin" (12:26–32) with the story about the old prophet from Bethel (13:1–32), are typical in this respect.

The stereotyped regnal summaries also suggest analogies with non-Israelite literature and ideas about kingship. On the one hand, the writer reckons each ruler according to Hebrew chronology (only near the end of the entire story are the kings placed into the scheme of "Babylonian time"; see 2 Kgs 24:12, 25:8). On the other hand, the parade of Hebraic kings, synchronistically arranged as self-sufficient items, suggests the similar pattern of Assyrian and Babylonian chronicles and king lists. This likeness to a foreign neighbor, despite the time-bound particularities of any given Hebrew ruler, was already expressed in the birth cry of kingship, "Appoint for us a king to govern us like all the nations" (1 Sam 8:5). The attempt to make common cause with the nations posed a theological dilemma, for it meant spurning the God-king who had rescued the people from Egyptian slavery (1 Sam 8:7–8). In the Books of Kings, the comparable case was the building of Solomon's Temple, which obviously resembled undertakings in neighboring kingdoms: it was a concerted enterprise (1 Kgs 5:15–26, 32 [5:1–12, 18; EV]) necessitating importation of skilled workers to produce the opulent decorations (1 Kgs 7:13–44). Elsewhere the writer of 1–2 Kings implies that the analogy should not be pushed too far lest the particularities of Israel's Temple be cheapened by copying a foreigner's altar design (2 Kgs 16:10–16).

The writer further qualified the Temple analogy by setting its foundation in a suprahistorical "Yahwistic" time and thus freeing it from the constraints of narrative time. According to 1 Kings 6:1, construction began 480 years after the Exodus from Egypt. Unconstrained by the temporal limits of monarchy, one can imagine the span of 480 years between the Mosaic Exodus and the Solomonic Temple as a bridge between Egypt and Jerusalem. Thus, discrete time periods merge into a single flow from Moses to Solomon, which takes its significance from the theologically resonant hero-places of Moses-Egypt (oppression and deliverance) and Solomon-Jerusalem (Temple, Davidic dynasty, and the promises of Zion; see 2 Sam 7:1–29; 1 Kgs 1:48, 2:45, 6:11–13; 2 Kgs 19:14–31). Therefore, when Solomon dedicates his Temple, he offers it as a gift to God in accordance with ancient Near Eastern practice (1 Kgs 8:12–13), and the narrator invokes this Hebraic time-space-hero matrix from which blessings seem to flow: "There was nothing in the ark except the two tables of stone which Moses put there at Horeb, where the Lord made a covenant with the people of Israel when they came out of the land of Egypt" (1 Kgs 8:9; *cf.* 8:15–21).

The same interplay between the singularity of history and the paradigmatic world of didactic historiography is evident in other portions of the regnal summaries. A king is always bound by concrete circumstances—a time and place of rule, a mother who may assume a dramatic role in events (e.g., 2 Kgs 11:1–16), an infirmity of the feet (1 Kgs 15:23), an ignoble end (2 Kgs 23:29), and the like. Yet every king is measured according to certain standards of theological appraisals: how well he upheld—or, more usually, failed to uphold—the primacy of Yahweh and Temple in Jerusalem. Once subjected to moral evaluation, details of a monarch's reign become less important than the way in which he was like or unlike his predecessors.

The evaluations contained in regnal summaries yield a scale of values by which to measure the performance of the kings. For example, Jeroboam's rise is closely tied to Solomon's fall. His rule is foretold by a prophet who simultaneously condemns Solomon (1 Kgs 11:29–39), and his accession is noted as fulfilling that oracle (12:15). Yet it is Jeroboam's subsequent patronage of sanctuaries and cults at Dan

150

Dan and Bethel (12:26–32) that make him a patriarch of infamy, whose transgressions are replicated far beyond his days. His successor Ahab is judged worse in degree but not in kind (1 Kgs 16:29–22:40); the incidents that selectively cover his reign actually etch his apostasy on a canvas of heinous opposition to God and God's prophet Elijah (see 1 Kgs 18:17–18, 20:42, 21:20–24, 22:38). The virulent infection lived on among Ahab's successors. Even the demise of the kingdom did not still its outrages, as two centuries later the settlers at Bethel continued to affront Yahweh with worship of rival gods (2 Kgs 17:24–41). The miscreant in the southern kingdom was Manasseh, who, through Ahab, carried the "sin" of Jeroboam into the Davidic line (2 Kgs 21:3).

Jeroboam then is David's demonic counterpart. As the former infects regnal time with the burden of guilt, the latter infuses it with "awe," "reverence," "fear," and spirituality toward God. The promise of unbroken dynasty was predicated on David's intrinsic merit (2 Sam 7) as a model of piety (e.g., 2 Sam 8:6–14, 12:7–23, 22:1–23:7). This standard was carried over into Kings as the ultimate standard for *all* kings. Jeroboam began his reign by departing from *David's* ways and thus became a curse on the non-Davidic kingdom (1 Kgs 11:38, 14:8) in the north. The basic paradigm held for the fall of the Davidic kingdom as well: at fault was Manasseh, who was like Ahab and hence like Jeroboam (2 Kgs 21:3). In other words, God accepts David and rejects all those who go their own way. Yet the paratactic assemblage of regnal epochs ends with a suggestion of David's residual power. The Babylonian king who elevated Jehoiachin, the last of the successors to David, "spoke kindly to him, and gave him a throne above those of other kings who were with him in Babylon" (2 Kgs 25:28; JPS).

Besides these wide-ranging associations, the writer exploits a few opportunities to speak directly to the reader. Normally the transition from one reign to another passes without comment. Sometimes, however, the narrative flow is interrupted by the insertion of reflections, legend, comments, and evaluations. Consider 2 Kings 17:7–22, for example. In lieu of the usual concluding summary for Hosea, the last of the infamous northern kings, one reads—the writer addresses the reader directly—that the exile of the northern kingdom is really the punishment for Jeroboam's transgression. Like a poison in the blood, the ancient offense has at last overwhelmed the body politic. At the same time, the writer looks ahead in time to the analogous demise of Judah, as yet untold. This pausal moment deflects the attention from regnal time to the timeless realm of omniscience, in which analogies explain events and instruct the pious.

Or, again, consider 2 Kings 2:1–25, a filled gap between the reigns of Ahaziah (2 Kgs 1:17–18) and Jehoram (2 Kgs 3:1–3). The story of Elijah's leave-taking occurs outside of ordinary time, despite its movement through well-known places (see 2 Kgs 2:1, 2, 4, 6, 15, 18, 23, 25). In the uncanny strangeness of that space beyond the Jordan River, Elijah departs this world, winnowed from his earthly chaff by fiery chariotry (2 Kgs 2:7–12). His mantle, a symbol of prophetic otherness, touches the earlier time and place of another king's reign, when this same mantle was cast upon Elisha and stirred those passions that turn people from simple pursuits to a higher calling (1 Kgs 19:19–21). Further, Elisha—now the empowered successor—becomes the heroic predecessor: he strikes the water (2 Kgs 2:14) as his master Elijah had done (v. 8), and the river parts, as it had for Elijah and for Moses before him (Exod 14:21, 26–27). The transition from Elijah to Elisha is suggestive of the Moses-Joshua archetypes. Just as Joshua was a deputy or "minister" to Moses (Exod 24:13, 33:11; Num 11:28), so Elisha "ministered" to Elijah (1 Kgs 19:21). As Joshua had been marked as successor with "spirit" (Num 27:18; Deut 31:7–8, 14–23) and was confirmed in this role after Moses' death (Josh 1:1–9), so Elisha takes his master's position, spirit, and trappings of power and is confirmed by divine vision (2 Kgs 2:9–15). Just as Moses died without a trace (Deut 34:6), and Joshua, "full of the spirit of wisdom" (34:9), quickly parted the Jordan River waters (Josh 3:11–17), so too Elijah disappears in whirlwind and fiery vision, and his successor parts those same waters to take his place as leader among the prophets (2 Kgs 2:14). The pausal moment is filled with ghosts of successions past and so it is, as in the story of Moses-Joshua, paradigmatic, metahistorical, beyond time. As Moses and Joshua embodied constancy in faithfulness to Yahweh, so too do Elijah and Elisha in a northern kingdom bedeviled with the curse of Jeroboam.

There are other pausal moments as well (1 Kgs 2:12b–46; 12:1–20; 15:32; 16:7, 21–22; 2 Kgs 11:1–21; 13:14–25; 15:12; 24:7). Although not all of these passages are of special consequence to the whole of the Books of Kings, enough are of sufficient significance to suggest that these interpolations were deliberately used to elucidate the deeper meaning of events.

The fulfillment of prophecies is another device employed by the writer of Kings to escape the temporal confines of regnal epochs. Indeed, prophecy-fulfillment is a rhetorical strategy by which the writer speaks with God's voice and so persuades the reader of the authority out of which his work comes. The writer not only knows God's inner feelings and motivations (e.g., 1 Kgs 3:10; 11:9; 2 Kgs 13:3, 19), but he also knows what God's role has been in the twists and turns of historical events (e.g., 2 Kgs 5:1, 7:6, 10:32). He demonstrates that prophecy, once uttered, comes to pass (*cf.* 1 Kgs 11:11–13, 31–39, with 12:1–24). God has revealed his commands through the "book of teaching" (*torah*; 2 Kgs 22:11; Au. trans.), through the prophets' words (2 Kgs 21:10–15), and through the words of a narrator who, like a prophet, knows the mind of God. In the structural coherence of stories (e.g., 1 Kgs 17:8–16), in formulaic observations (e.g., 1 Kgs 16:1–4, 22:38), and in associative links (*cf.* 1 Kgs 21:19, 13:2 with 2 Kgs 22–23; 1 Kgs 19:18 with 2 Kgs 10:28), the divine word works its power and will in the world of the monarchs. Those who proclaim that word, the prophets, are confirmed in that role in the writer's commentary (2 Kgs 17:13). These harbingers of crisis warn Israel and summon it to repentance (1 Kgs 11:11–13, 38–39; 2 Kgs 22:14–20). But when warnings go unheeded, disaster follows —even if deferred to subsequent generations. Thus the final catastrophe of Judah's exile finds its rationale in a metahistorical viewpoint: God's word emboldens prophets, chastises kings, destroys the unrepentant, and makes order out of chaos through the simple acts of fulfilling prophecy, rewarding the obedient, and punishing the wayward.

Even when Judah is no more, it may be that the reader, having been prepared through numerous correspondences across the reigns, will conclude once again that prophecy speaks in the rehabilitation of Jehoiachin (2 Kgs 25:27–29). The day may yet come when turning (recommitment) to Yahweh will be accomplished, and the ancient dream of a kingdom set under a God who chooses Israel for covenant, and commands a partnership of deeds in the world, will be realized. Such at any rate seems to have been the aim of this grand experiment in realizing individual and national self through historical memory.

Bibliography

Cogan, Mordechai, and Hayim Tadmor. *II Kings*. New York, 1988.

Cross, Frank, Jr. "The Themes of the Book of Kings and the Structure of the Deuteronomistic History." In his *Canaanite Myth and Hebrew Epic*. Cambridge, Mass., 1973.

DeVries, Simon. *1 Kings*. Waco, Tex., 1985.

Freedman, David N. "Deuteronomistic History." In *Interpreter's Dictionary of the Bible*. Supplementary vol. Nashville, 1976.

Gray, John. *I and II Kings*. Philadelphia, 1970.

Grayson, Albert K. *Assyrian and Babylonian Chronicles*. Locust Valley, N.Y., 1975.

Gunn, David. *The Story of King David*. Sheffield, England, 1978.

Hobbs, T. R. *II Kings*. Waco, Tex., 1985.

Kenik, Helen. *Design for Kingship: The Deuteronomistic Narrative Technique in 1 Kings 3:4–15*. Chico, Calif., 1983.

Klein, Ralph W. *Israel in Exile: A Theological Interpretation*. Philadelphia, 1979.

Long, Burke. *1 Kings with an Introduction to Historical Literature*. Grand Rapids, 1984.

McCarthy, Dennis. "II Samuel 7 and the Structure of the Deuteronomic History." *Journal of Biblical Literature* 84 (1965): 131–138.

Mayes, Andrew D. H. *The Story of Israel Between Settlement and Exile*. Birmingham, England, 1983.

Montgomery, James. *A Critical and Exegetical Commentary on the Books of Kings*. New York, 1951.

Nelson, Richard D. *Double Redaction of the Deuteronomistic History*. Sheffield, England, 1981.

――――. *I and II Kings*. Atlanta, 1987.

Noth, Martin. *The Deuteronomistic History*. Sheffield, England, 1981.

Peckham, Brian. *The Composition of the Deuteronomistic History*. Atlanta, 1985.

Rad, Gerhard von. "The Deuteronomic Theology of History in I and II Kings." In *The Problem of the Hexateuch and Other Essays*. Translated by E. W. Trueman Dicken. New York, 1966.

Rost, Leonhard. *Succession to the Throne of David.* Sheffield, England, 1981.

Seters, John van. *In Search of History: Historiography in the Ancient World and the Origins of Biblical History.* New Haven, 1983.

Würthwein, Ernst. *Die Bücher der Könige.* 2 vols. Göttingen, 1977, 1985.

BURKE O. LONG

I and II Chronicles
Ezra
Nehemiah

THE CHRONICLER'S CORPUS

THE BOOKS OF of 1–2 Chronicles, Ezra, and Nehemiah comprise what is known as the Chronicler's work. It was written on two scrolls, 1–2 Chronicles on one, and Ezra-Nehemiah on the other. This body of literature traces the history of Israel from the reign of King David to the return of the Jews from the Babylonian exile and the rebuilding of the Temple and walls of Jerusalem. While there is no consensus about the date of the compilation and completion of the Chronicler's work, scholars have identified four phases in the development of this literature. The first phase may be dated to the time of Hezekiah (ca. 715–687 B.C.E.). The preexilic Chronicler was interested in Hezekiah, whom he considered the embodiment of the Davidic ideal (2 Chr 29–31). The chronicles of the kings of Judah were undoubtedly used as source material, but they were fashioned in a way distinct from what is now subsumed under the Deuteronomistic History.

The second phase in the development of these books occurs around 520–515 B.C.E., when the earlier work was expanded by continuing the history of the kings of Judah on the basis of the Deuteronomistic History but with the addition of material from other sources. Appended to this combination of materials is an account that picks up the story of the return

approximately fifty years after the fall of Jerusalem in 587, with the significant and stirring events from the decree of Cyrus in 538 until the rebuilding and dedication of the Temple in 515. The return, restoration, and renewal kindled old hopes for a reestablishment of the Davidic monarchy. The prophets 2 Isaiah, Haggai, Zechariah, and Malachi appeared to proclaim the new age, and a new narrative was produced to bring the history of the kingdom up to date. This narrative included 1 Chronicles 10 through Ezra 6, excluding Ezra 4–5.

The focus on the kingdom of Judah, the house of David, the city of Jerusalem, and the Temple in the prophetic literature indicates the hope for a return to the glory days of David. Zerubbabel, of royal lineage, was the prospective scion. This hope is absent from what we call the Primary History (Genesis–2 Kings; see Freedman 1976a and 1976b), which ends before the beginning of the Persian era and contains no mention of this extraordinary development. Instead it may be dated by its last entry, a note stating that thirty-seven years after the captivity of King Jehoiachin, Judah was still in exile.

The third phase in the compilation of the Chronicler's work occurs sixty years later, around 460, when the scribe Ezra wrote his memoirs (Ezra 7–10) and added important archival data to the account of the restoration of Jerusalem (Ezra 4–5). He is generally credited with attaching this new material to the corpus already compiled and with editing the whole. By Ezra's time, however, the political situation had changed, and the thrust of his memoirs reflects the new realities. Judah was administered by a high priest of the house of Aaron and a governor of Judahite descent, both of whom reported to the Persian satrap and, ultimately, the emperor. Although Zerubbabel served as governor of Judah and Jerusalem in the initial phases of the return, he never became king, and any connection of the governorship with the house of David vanished after Elnathan, a possible successor who may have been the son-in-law of Zerubbabel. There was no place for even a puppet king in the Persian organization, so the hopes for the reestablishment of the monarchy were dashed or at least had to be put off to a more distant time. Later governors, like Nehemiah, had no royal claims or pretensions.

As a result, Ezra changed the focus in his account from David to Moses, the latter being the supreme prophet and lawgiver. Ezra exalted the rule of law and the role of Moses as mediator of the covenant by which the people were to live. Since Moses was not a king and founded no dynasty, his name and fame posed no threat to the Persian authorities. With the elevation of Moses to a model of faith, the hope for the renewal of the monarchy under a second David, or at least a descendant of the royal line, diminished. Nevertheless, the significance of David as king and founder, if not builder, of the Temple, especially of its liturgy and music, was greatly enhanced. The redirected work now focused on the intimate relationship of the people with its God, mediated by Moses, a relationship that predated nationhood and kingship, and outlasted both.

The fourth and final Chronicler may well have been Nehemiah, who wrote his memoirs and appended them to the work around 432, in the thirty-second year of the reign of Artaxerxes I. Nehemiah's memoirs are linked with Ezra's and the rest of the work through the account of Ezra's reading of the law in Nehemiah 8–9. Aside from the struggle to rebuild the walls of Jerusalem, the focus remains the same: Moses and the Torah. Nehemiah was, after all, Ezra's contemporary and collaborator.

THE ROLE OF THE CHRONICLER IN THE EDITING OF THE BIBLE

When we reach the end of Nehemiah, we find that the Hebrew Bible is more than the story of Israel; it also contains within it the story of the Bible. We begin with the Torah, and we end with the Torah. The final phase of the Chronicler's work, the memoirs of Ezra and Nehemiah, not only sheds light on the life of the postexilic community, but also gives a new emphasis to the canon by enhancing the prominence of the Mosaic law and playing down the house of David.

The first edition of the Hebrew Bible was most likely compiled between 560–540 B.C.E. It included the Primary History (Gen–2 Kgs) and the prophetic corpus associated with that history (1 Isa, Jer, Ezek, and the first nine books of the minor prophets). The last date recorded in this material is the thirty-seventh year of the exile of Jehoiachin, or the first year of the reign of Evil-merodach (Awil-Marduk), king of Babylon (*ca.* 561 B.C.E.). This is possibly the actual date and place of publication. The first Bible contained the story of God and his people from the beginning to the fall of the kingdoms and the exile of the people. The supporting prophetic corpus holds hope, however, for a return and restoration.

To the first Bible were added 2 Isaiah, Haggai, Zechariah, and Malachi in the prophetic corpus, and 1 and 2 Chronicles and Ezra 1–3, 6, taking the story to the resumption of work on the Second Temple and its completion in 515. The decree of Cyrus in 538 kindled new hopes for a restoration of the kingdom and the Davidic dynasty, as these writings reflect. Their purpose was to support the community in its efforts at rebuilding the city and Temple. This part of the Chronicler's work, and the accompanying prophetic literature (Hag 1–2, Zech 1–8), deals with new situations arising in the postexilic community. The Book of Psalms, Proverbs, Ruth, and Song of Solomon, all associated with the house of David, accompanied the Chronicler's work in the section called the Writings.

The third Bible, primarily the work of Ezra as compiler and editor and his contemporary Nehemiah, includes the memoirs of those two men added to the Chronicler's work and the rest of the Writings (Job, the other *megillot*, and Lamentations), with the possible exception of Ecclesiastes and Esther. The project was completed during the reign of Artaxerxes I (465–425), probably around 432, the last date recorded in Nehemiah. More important, Ezra redirected the Hebrew Bible's focus. He separated the Torah (Gen–Deut) from the rest of the Primary History and designated that part as the primary and central authority within the Bible. What was left of the Primary History became the Former Prophets (Josh–2 Kgs) in an enlarged prophetic collection.

Thus, with the hopes of reestablishing the Davidic dynasty postponed until a later time, Ezra's hand in the Chronicler's work can be noticed in the emphasis on the Mosaic law and de-emphasis of the house of David. This approach can be seen in the whole Hebrew Bible as well and can also be attributed to Ezra, who revived and renewed the Mosaic covenant as the legal authority for the postexilic community.

AUTHORSHIP AND DATE

The authors of both the first and second phases in the development of the Chronicler's work are unknown. We know, however, that phases three and four comprise the memoirs of Ezra and Nehemiah, contemporary leaders in the postexilic community of Jerusalem. Scholars have generally agreed that Ezra had a prominent role in the editing of both books of Chronicles and in appending his memoirs to them.

Ezra was the religious authority, a priest and scribe in the community around 458. But since religion was defined by the law of Moses, he was a legal and judicial authority as well. Nehemiah was governor of Judah around 445–432. The fact that he was not of Davidic lineage confirms the decline in status and function of the royal house of David, which survived in the progeny of Jehoiachin and Zerubbabel as recorded in 1 Chronicles. The Davidic dynasty is barely mentioned in Nehemiah's memoirs, where the focus is on the rebuilding of the city and the formation of a community based on values, ethics, and heritage.

Scholars have long differed on not only the date of the books of Ezra and Nehemiah but also the sequence of events presented in them. Of particular interest is whether it was Ezra or Nehemiah who returned to Jerusalem first and whether or not they were contemporaries. Regarding Nehemiah there is scholarly consensus. According to the text in the twentieth year of King Artaxerxes' reign, Nehemiah requests and is granted permission by the king to return to Judah (Neh 2:1–8, esp. v. 1). Scholars agree that the king is Artaxerxes I (465–425), and thus the twentieth year is 445. Disagreement arises over the date of Ezra's return to Jerusalem.

According to the material in the book of Ezra, Ezra returned to Jerusalem in the seventh year of Artaxerxes, the king of Persia (Ezra 7:1, 7–8), that is, in 458, assuming that it is the same king, Artaxerxes I. Thus, Ezra preceded Nehemiah. Some scholars, however, find it difficult to believe that Nehemiah followed Ezra to Jerusalem, for the following reasons:

(1) In Nehemiah 13:23–27, Nehemiah seems to view marriage between Jews and foreigners as undesirable but legal, and he attempts to solve the problem of mixed marriages with measures far less severe than those of Ezra (chaps. 9–10). Only later did Nehemiah, possibly influenced by Ezra, lay down stricter prohibitions against mixed marriages. Many scholars assume that the warnings of Nehemiah were unsuccessful, which necessitated sterner prohibitions when Ezra arrived.

(2) Very few passages in the books of Ezra and Nehemiah mention the two men together. This lack of evidence regarding their contemporaneity and cooperation leads some scholars to presume that the two men did not reside in Jerusalem at the same time.

(3) Jerusalem was thinly populated in the days of Nehemiah (Neh 7:4), but in the time of Ezra there were many Jews living in Jerusalem (Ezra 10:1). It is reasonable to suppose that the population of the city grew during those years and, therefore, that the passage in Ezra probably refers to a time later than that of Nehemiah.

(4) Scholars argue that Nehemiah completed the wall around Jerusalem before Ezra returned and read the book of the law, assuming that the relevant texts in Nehemiah are in chronological order. The completion of the wall appears in Nehemiah 6:15, and the episode of Ezra's reading of the law occurs in Nehemiah 8:1–8.

(5) Finally, according to the evidence in Ezra and Nehemiah, Nehemiah was a contemporary of the

high priest Eliashib (Neh 3:1), and Ezra of the high priest Jehohanan (in Ezra 10:6 = Johanan in Neh 12:22 = Jonathan in Neh 12:11). Since Jehohanan was the grandson of Eliashib (see the genealogy of high priests in Neh 12:10–11), Ezra would have had to follow Nehemiah to Jerusalem. Furthermore, Johanan (Jehohanan) appears in an Elephantine papyrus (AP 30; A. Cowley 1923), which dates his ministry to 410–407. On the basis of this information some scholars date Ezra to the reign of Artaxerxes II (405/404–359), that is, after Nehemiah.

Scholars who accept the theory that Ezra came to Jerusalem after Nehemiah assign either 398/397 or 428/427 B.C.E. as the date for his return. Proponents of the former date identify the king of Persia in Ezra 7:1, 7–8 as Artaxerxes II, not Artaxerxes I as in Nehemiah 2:1–8. The seventh year of Artaxerxes II would have been 398/397. Other scholars claim that a conjectural emendation of the text is required. They claim that "the seventh year" should be changed to "the thirty-seventh year," in which case the king in question would be Artaxerxes I, the same king mentioned in Nehemiah and Ezra. The year of Ezra's return would then be 428/427.

The traditional view of the order and dates of the two men is preferable, for several reasons:

(1) The differences in the ways in which they handle mixed marriages were determined not by the order of their arrival in Jerusalem but by their respective roles in society. Nehemiah's main concerns were political and social stability, the rebuilding of the city, and the securing of the community against outside intervention. Ezra, on the other hand, was a religious leader whose primary concern was the maintenance of the integrity and solidarity of the Jewish community as the people of God. With the destruction of the nation Israel, the political identity of the people was gone. Their identity rested not only on their common allegiance to the law of Moses but also on their claim to be lineal descendants of the citizens of the old kingdom of Judah, including Levites and priests. Mixed marriages were therefore a threat to their religious and ethnic identity. For this reason, elimination of mixed marriages, while a matter of importance to both men, weighed more heavily with Ezra, the religious leader, than with Nehemiah, the civil ruler.

(2) Also weighing against the contemporaneity of Nehemiah and Ezra is the lack of evidence regarding their interaction as leaders of the community. The only instance in which both are present is found in Nehemiah 8:1–12, especially verse 9. Yet if Ezra resided in Jerusalem at a time when a governor other than Nehemiah was in office, as in 398/397, then the same argument can be made; that is: Why was that governor not mentioned by Ezra? It seems more reasonable to assume that they were contemporaries, that their paths did cross—as is evidenced not only by Nehemiah 8:9 but also by Nehemiah 12:26—but that generally they tended to their own distinct interests and activities.

Nehemiah the governor and Ezra the priest and scribe had different responsibilities, and the material that tells their stories reflects that divergence. An analogous situation occurs in the material of the eighth-century prophets, Hosea and Amos in the north and Micah and Isaiah in the south. Although their ministries overlapped, the accounts of their activities contain no evidence that they had contact with one another. The same situation occurs with Jeremiah and Ezekiel, who do not seem to have known each other although their careers overlapped for more than a decade. Jeremiah wrote at least one letter to the exiles, and Ezekiel addressed many oracles to the people in Jerusalem. We would expect, despite the fact that they were in different places, that they had heard of and possibly knew one another. If there was such a relationship, however, it is not reflected in their writings.

With regard to Nehemiah and Ezra, it is clear that Nehemiah was not in residence at Jerusalem all the time. He arrived in Jerusalem in 445, but he returned to the royal court and came back to Jerusalem in 432 (Neh 13:6–7). There would have been extended periods when of the two only Ezra was in Jerusalem. Thus, for the thirteen years from 458 to 445, Ezra was present in Jerusalem during Nehemiah's absence, and then, for a period of about a year (433–432), Ezra again was the only one in Jerusalem. The time when both were in Jerusalem extended from 445 to 433.

(3) The argument that the city grew in size between the time of Nehemiah and the time of Ezra is based on a misreading of Nehemiah 7:4 and Ezra 10:1. The passage in Nehemiah states that the city was large

but that few people were living within its confines. Ezra does not state that the population of Jerusalem had increased but that a large number of people from throughout Israel had gathered at the Temple in Jerusalem. Since the city had been destroyed and left abandoned over a century earlier, the returning exiles probably chose to live in the countryside with farming as their basic mode of subsistence. Only over a long period of time was the city gradually restored to a semblance of its former glory, slowly attracting people to settle within its limits.

(4) It is misleading to assume that the materials in Ezra and Nehemiah were arranged in chronological order. A cursory glance at datable material in the books of the prophets shows that thematic and other literary constraints often override the chronological order. This is also the case in Ezra and Nehemiah. However, the arrangement of the books in the Hebrew Bible, with Ezra first and Nehemiah second, seems correct.

(5) Frank Cross (1975) has reconstructed the genealogy of high priests in Nehemiah 12:10–11 and argues for the traditional view that Ezra arrived in Jerusalem before Nehemiah. In the Samaria papyri, Cross found evidence for papponymy, the practice of naming a son after his grandfather, among the descendants of Sanballat. Assuming that this was also a practice in the families of high priests, Cross changed the genealogy in Nehemiah 12:10–11 from

1. Jeshua
2. Joiakim
3. Eliashib
4. Joiada
5. Johanan (Jonathan)
6. Jaddua

to

1. Jeshua
2. Joiakim
3. Eliashib I
4. Johanan I
5. Eliashib II
6. Joiada
7. Johanan II
8. Jaddua

The doubling of names more accurately fits the number of generations needed to cover the time span

from Jeshua to Jaddua, and the omission of Eliashib I and Johanan I from the genealogy can be explained by haplography, the repetition of names. Thus, Ezra, a contemporary of Johanan I, came to Jerusalem before Nehemiah, who was a contemporary of Eliashib II. The association of Ezra with the Johanan of the Elephantine papyrus (Johanan II, who ministered during the reign of Artaxerxes II) is therefore invalid.

THE VARIOUS TEXTS

It can be argued that in final form 1–2 Chronicles, Ezra, and Nehemiah were one work, as the repetition of 2 Chronicles 36:22–23 at Ezra 1:1–3a suggests. The Chronicler's work, too long to fit on one scroll, was written on two (1–2 Chronicles on one, Ezra-Nehemiah, originally titled Ezra, on the other); the repetition, then, integrates the "books" originally written on separate scrolls into one work. (Others have regarded the repetition as a conscious attempt on the part of a late editor to link what were previously unrelated works.)

In the Hebrew Bible the Chronicler's work appears in the section called the Ketuvim (Writings), where the two "books" are separate. In the tenth-century-C.E. Aleppo Codex, widely regarded as the oldest and best of all the medieval manuscripts of the Hebrew Bible, Chronicles is placed at the beginning of the Ketuvim, while Ezra-Nehemiah remains in its place after all the other books in the Hebrew Bible. Since nine books come between the two parts of the Chronicler's work, the repetition of the last paragraph of Chronicles in the first paragraph of Ezra serves an important purpose—to remind the reader that the story has been resumed at a critical point. Similarly, the Chronicler's work forms an envelope around the rest of the Ketuvim, thus reinforcing its own distinctive emphasis in contrast to that of the Primary History. In addition, the story is told in chronological order, which seems preferable to the somewhat inverted order that obtains in the case of the Leningrad Codex (eleventh century C.E.) and other standard texts.

In fact, in the Leningrad Codex, on which the standard text editions of Kittel's *Biblia hebraica* and the *Biblia Hebraica Stuttgartensia* are based,

1–2 Chronicles, immediately preceded by Ezra-Nehemiah, closes the codex. The effect is stunning and significant. Chronicles ends with the proclamation of Cyrus, the king of Persia, allowing and encouraging the Jews to return home and rebuild the Temple destroyed by the Babylonians in 587 (2 Chr 36:22–23). Ezra 1:1–3a repeats this proclamation. Thus, the placement in the Leningrad Codex encloses the entire work of the Chronicler within an envelope-like structure: the opus, while not in chronological order, begins and ends with the proclamation of Cyrus. Since the Deuteronomistic History (or the Primary History) makes no mention of this epochal decree in the story of Israel, the double announcement in the Chronicler's work serves to set that work apart from the other in a dramatic way.

Taken a step further, the fact that Chronicles ends the Hebrew Bible produces an envelope-like construction around the entire Hebrew Bible as well. "In the beginning God (Elohim) created the heavens (*hashamayim*) and the earth (*ha'arets*)" (Gen 1:1; RSV) is echoed in 2 Chronicles 36:23, where Cyrus proclaims, "All the kingdoms of the earth (*ha'arets*), he, Yahweh the God (*elohei*) of the heavens (*hashamayim*), gave to me" (Au. trans.). It is not coincidence but an important theological statement that the words for "heaven" and "earth" as well as divine names both begin and end the Hebrew Bible. The entire Hebrew Bible recaptures the relationship between a people on earth and their God on high—his promises and their long suffering, their struggle to be faithful and their ultimate collapse and rebirth. It is fitting, therefore, that their story should begin and end with words that bring to mind that relationship.

The Greek and Latin text traditions (represented by the Septuagint and the Vulgate) preserve a larger corpus of Ezra literature than the Hebrew Bible and what we know as the English Bible. Included with Ezra (Esdr B in the Septuagint, 1 Esdr in the Vulgate) and Nehemiah (Esdr C in the Septuagint, 2 Esdr in the Vulgate) are 1 and 2 Esdr (Esdr A and Esdr the Prophet in the Septuagint, 3 and 4 in the Vulgate).

First Esdras (or Esdr A or 3 Esdr in the versions) is not an independent work but a compilation and translation of material found throughout 2 Chronicles, Ezra, and Nehemiah. It covers the events from the celebration of Passover by Josiah to the reforms of Ezra; the work of Nehemiah is less emphasized. Most of the work duplicates 2 Chronicles 35–36 and Ezra—only a few verses of Nehemiah appear—but the author does not follow the historical sequence. The date of this work is generally placed around the same time as the composition of Daniel (second century B.C.E.). Nevertheless, the contents and arrangement of materials in this text support the traditional view of the dates and order of Ezra and Nehemiah.

The book of 2 Esdras (or Esdr the Prophet or 4 Esdr in the versions) purports to be the "second" book of Ezra, and its three major parts deal with Ezra's commission (chaps. 1–2), a series of seven visions (chaps. 3–14), and prophetic material (chaps. 15–16). Although this work exists only in the Greek and Latin manuscripts, the consensus is that it was originally composed in Hebrew or Aramaic and dates from the first to the third century C.E. The main themes of 2 Esdras are God's mercy and love and the hope for the coming of a messianic age.

THE CHRONICLER'S WORK

The books of Chronicles, Ezra, and Nehemiah were meant to be both supplements to the Primary History (Gen–2 Kgs) and authoritative interpretations or rereadings of Samuel and Kings with regard to the history of Judah. In the Primary History, the Elohist (E) writer considers Abraham the primal figure at the beginning of Israelite history; the Priestly (P) source begins in Genesis 1:1; and the Jahwist (J) source begins in the Garden of Eden with Adam. The story in the Deuteronomistic History (D) begins with the farewell addresses of Moses. For the Chronicler, however, the story begins with the death of Saul and the enthronement of David, who is the hero of the book of Chronicles.

To the Chronicler, the survival of the Davidic dynasty has been guaranteed since the beginning of time. Thus, emphasis is placed on those institutions and characters that preserve David's kingdom: Judah, Jerusalem, and the Temple, on the one hand; David and his descendants and the priesthood, on the other. David and his descendants are presented as the sole legitimate possessors of royal authority in Israel. Emphasized are only those institutions and characters that relate to the monarchy and David himself. These relationships, not the Mosaic law or the Abrahamic covenant, are the symbols of the permanent bond between God and his people, the divine commitment. The northern kingdom of Israel is not discussed because it broke away from the Davidic dynasty and went its own way.

The Chronicler's work portrays not only the events of the monarchic rule but also those that occurred after the fall of Jerusalem, during the period of the return from Babylonian exile, the rebuilding of the Temple, and the repair of the walls of Jerusalem—during the century or so from 539 to 432. Thus, it provides a different literary emphasis from that of the Primary History. The Primary History ends with the fall of Judah and the destruction of Jerusalem. The last date recorded in 2 Kings refers to the thirty-seventh year of the Babylonian exile, which was the first year of the reign of Evil-merodach, king of Babylon in 562. We would claim, then, that the Torah and the Former Prophets were completed between 560 and 550. The Chronicler's work is of a later period, however. With the aid of hindsight, it portrays the destruction and exile as a temporary disruption, a serious but reparable lapse. There was little doubt that the perpetuity of the kingdom and the dynasty of David was guaranteed and that God would restore his kingdom. In the new age, God's commitment to his chosen—the people of Judah and Jerusalem—remains.

The tragedy of the fall of Judah set the tone for much of the Old Testament, reflecting shattered hopes and loss of identity. In contrast, the return from exile revived a sense of hope, as is evidenced in the Chronicler's work. Eager anticipation accompanies the rebuilding of the Temple, which was initiated by Sheshbazzar and completed by Zerubbabel, direct descendants of David and Joshua, the high priest. There is even some expectation of a restoration of the monarchy. The Chronicler's last word (2 Chr 36:22–23) is one of hope and promise. Continuity is emphasized over discontinuity; restoration over destruction. It is a new word for a new day, as is demonstrated in the works of the Chronicler's prophetic contemporaries: 2 Isaiah, Haggai, and Zechariah.

The new community formed its identity through ties to the past, as is evidenced in the genealogies, lists, and institutions that link the present group to their forefathers of the monarchic period. For example, 1 Chronicles 1–9 is a collection of genealogies, beginning with Adam and including the line of descent through Judah to David, and down to the Chronicler's own day. It draws a thread of continuity through Israelite history and sets the stage for emphasis on the kingdom of Judah and, particularly, David, the man at the center of the Chronicler's theology. In addition to the background information about the lineage of David, it also presents the genealogical data on which the returnees could stake their own claims to the community and test the validity of others. The postexilic descendants of all the tribes are included (1 Chr 3:10–24, 9:10–34; cf. Ezra 2, 8:1–20; Neh 7:5–73). This genealogy, prefixed to Chronicles later in the editorial process, extends to the time of Ezra-Nehemiah.

Other lists include the names of David's warriors and supporters (1 Chr 11:10–12:40), singers and musicians (15:16–24, 25:1–31), Levites (23:1–23), priests (24:1–31; cf. the genealogy of Ezra in Ezra 7:1–5), gatekeepers (1 Chr 26:1–19), and military and civil leaders (26:29–27:34). This material must also have been used to confirm the descendants in their posts in postexilic times and to screen out impostors and those whose claims could not be verified. The notion of legitimacy was just as important for such posts as for the monarchy. The Chronicler's work is truly the books of descents, of genealogies and the legitimization of claims to the land and a place in the holy community.

Ezra follows closely 2 Chronicles, as is made apparent by the repetition of 2 Chronicles 36:22–23 in Ezra 1:1–3a. The focus of the second phase of the Chronicler's work (with the addition of Ezra 1–3, 6) is the return and the rebuilding of the Temple. The historical period covered by Ezra and Nehemiah begins in 538, with the decree of Cyrus, the Persian, allowing the Jewish community to return to Jerusalem and to rebuild the Temple (Ezra 1:1–4, vv 1–3, repeating 2 Chron 36:22–23, and Ezra 6:2–5, in Aramaic). Although some scholars are skeptical about specific points, there is general agreement about the authenticity of the decree of Cyrus, which is given in two forms: one in Hebrew (already mentioned), the other in Aramaic (Ezra 6:2–5), the official language of the western Persian empire (this version is regarded as closer to the original and more reliable in its details). The authenticity of this decree is furthermore confirmed by other documents of a general Persian policy of allowing peoples in exile to return home, to restore their sanctuaries, and to reinstitute the worship of their gods (see, for example, Pritchard 1955, 316). Ezra 1 presents Cyrus' decree and details the preparations for the return home. We should note, however, that not all Jews elected to go back. As the Murashu archives from Babylon indicate, a number of Jewish families had become quite wealthy while in exile, and certainly those and others with ties to Babylon would tend to remain.

The return was led by Sheshbazzar, the prince (perhaps the same as Shenazzar, one of the younger sons of Jehoiachin mentioned in Chronicles), and Joshua, the high priest. After Sheshbazzar, Zerubbabel, a grandson of Jehoiachin, became the governor of the district and apparently became the focus of the community's hope for a new kingdom under a Davidic monarch. The dreams and promises of the Second Isaiah and the prophecies of Ezekiel were no doubt remembered by the exiles and nourished their hopes for glorious national renewal.

The altar was rebuilt and dedicated (Ezra 3:1–7), and the rebuilding of the Temple was begun (3:8–13). The latter enterprise, however, met with intense opposition, and work stopped until the second year of Darius (520; Ezra 4). The reasons for the opposition were probably twofold: (1) the Samaritans and others considered the rebuilding of the Temple a political threat—that is, the beginning of a Jewish state in a region they claimed to control; and (2) the Samaritans and others were forbidden access to the Temple on the grounds that they were not authentic Israelites but a mixed group. (The Samaritans were the descendants of those inhabitants of the northern kingdom who had either remained after its destruction in 722 or returned after having been deported. The group may also have included non-native Assyrians. The Samaritans were considered a mixed group ethnically, religiously, and politically by the postexilic Jewish community. Therefore they were ostracized.) As a result of all these conflicts, the Jewish community, in an attempt to remain firm and consistent in its faith, inserted a wedge between itself and others in the land.

The friction aroused strong opposition and brought work on the Temple to a halt.

When the prophets Haggai and Zechariah chastised the new community for its failure to finish the Temple (Ezra 5:1–2; see the books of Haggai and Zechariah), a renewed effort was undertaken by Zerubbabel and Joshua. The opposition took its case to King Darius (5:3–17) but lost. The original decree of Cyrus, or a copy, was found in the royal archives, and on that basis Darius gave permission to rebuild the Temple (6:1–12). The Temple was completed in 515 (6:13–15) and then dedicated (6:16–18). It is important to note that Ezra 4:8–6:18 (the section dealing with the rebuilding of the Temple and opposition to it) and Ezra 7:12–26 (the letter of King Artaxerxes to Ezra regarding his commission) are preserved in the lingua franca of the Persian empire, Aramaic. No doubt the correspondence between the governors of Palestine and the Persian king, as well as Ezra's commission from the king, were originally written in Aramaic, not Hebrew. The legitimacy of the construction project is enhanced in Ezra's memoirs by the presentation of the material in its original language.

Historical reality did not entirely fulfill the hopes and expectations of the people, for the restoration was modest. Although the prophets contemporaneous with the Chronicler who influenced him called Zerubbabel "the signet ring" of Yahweh (Hag 2:23) and "the Branch" (Zech 6:9–14, with the restoration of Zerubbabel in the text), he was not a second David. Thus, years later, in the period depicted in the memoirs of Ezra (chaps. 4, 5, 7–10) and Nehemiah (458–432 B.C.E.), the focus has shifted drastically: from David and the monarchy to the rebuilding of the walls of Jerusalem. David and his dynasty are important only in that they provide the stamp of authority for the reestablishment of the cult (Neh 12:45–46). Although the Persians had placed descendants of David in the governor's seat in the beginning, that practice had long since been abandoned, and Nehemiah was an ordinary civil servant with no royal background or pretensions.

The Chronicler's emphasis on prophecy, which is an integral part of monarchic political life, disappears in the memoirs of Ezra and Nehemiah. The prophetic adviser and confidant of kings is absent here. The writer of Chronicles was no doubt a contemporary of Haggai and Zechariah and was greatly influenced by them. Nehemiah, however, quickly disassociates himself from prophets and the royalty gambit after he is accused of trying to designate himself king (Neh 6:6–8).

The story told is one of survival and persistence, not glorious restoration. Continuity and identity are preserved through the Mosaic law and the Davidic cult tradition. Lacking a national structure through which to reassert a political identity, the community has to find an alternative way of gaining and maintaining unity in the face of the various pressures that threatened to destroy it. Although the deportations had taken away the elite of Judean society, a number of poor farmers and others had been left behind in the devastated land. These, along with Samaritans and peoples from other areas exiled to Israel by the Assyrians, resented the Persian-authorized encroachment of the returning Jews on the territory they had come to consider theirs. This group opposed the establishment of a new Jewish community (e.g., Ezra 4). In addition, the city of Jerusalem was in ruins and did not offer any opportunity for economic growth to the returning exiles, who themselves were poor and disorganized.

Thus, strong emphasis is placed on true worship and the legitimacy of the priesthood and functions as well as ethnic integrity and social solidarity as pillars in support of the preservation of the uniqueness of the people in difficult times. To this end, the memoirs of Ezra-Nehemiah highlight the Mosaic tradition of Exodus, wanderings, and settlement, not the monarchy. The focus in Ezra and Nehemiah is on the new community in Jerusalem and its struggle for survival and community identity in the midst of pressures—religious, political, and economic—that would destroy its existence and purpose.

The memoirs of Ezra (chaps. 7–10) depict his work in the Jerusalem community. Half of the material describes Ezra's ancestry, the commission from Artaxerxes, and his journey to Jerusalem (Ezra 7–8). The focus on heritage is noted not only in Ezra's genealogy, traced back to Aaron (7:1–5), but also in the list of the returnees, among them the Temple servants, who accompanied him (8:1–20).

The other half of Ezra's memoirs deals with his handling of religious problems of the community in Jerusalem. Foremost is the common practice of intermarriage by returning exiles with people who had either remained in Judaea or had been transported there. Ezra considers these mixed marriages an abomination to Yahweh and an act of disregard for the ancient law (9:10–15). His listing of the priests, Levites, and prominent Israelites "who had married foreign women" (Ezra 10:18–44; RSV) demonstrates the intensity of his anger.

Nehemiah focuses on the rebuilding of the walls of Jerusalem and social reforms, based on religious doctrine, with the goal of solidifying the Jewish community in Jerusalem. His emphasis in these matters arises from his position as governor of Judaea and its environs. Nehemiah is a politician concerned about the social and economic welfare of his people. He is not a professional cleric; nevertheless he exhibits a strong and abiding faith in the God of Israel and in the fundamental requirements of that faith, as defined by the laws of Moses.

In the 440s, during the middle years of Artaxerxes' reign, rebellions and revolts broke out in many parts of the far regions of the empire. Palestine was no exception. The friction between the Jewish community and the Samaritans, as well as increasing pressure from Edom and Arabia, created an unstable political situation for the Jerusalem community, without an effective defense. Jerusalem, particularly its walls, was still in ruins. Thus, when Nehemiah, cupbearer to King Artaxerxes, heard that the inhabitants of Jerusalem were in trouble, he requested permission to go to Jerusalem and rebuild the walls (Neh 1:1–2:8).

Nehemiah went to Jerusalem and inspected the walls (2:9–16); he also encountered strong opposition from the governors of the surrounding areas (2:17–20), who undoubtedly considered the rebuilding of the walls of Jerusalem a military threat and an act of rebellion against the Persian empire (6:6–7). The rebuilding began nevertheless, and chapter 3 lists a number of workers who were responsible for the construction of various portions of the wall and its gates.

The trials and troubles accompanying the rebuilding of the wall are the focus of Nehemiah's memoirs through chapter 6. Sanballat, Tobiah, and the Arabs continued to oppose the work (Neh 4, 6), and threatened armed intervention (4:11, 6:2–9). They went so far as to hire false prophets to persuade Nehemiah to abandon his project (6:10–14). Nehemiah responded by gathering the people, arming them with swords, spears, and bows and arrows, and positioning them at strategic places along the wall (4:13–23). The work continued, but the laborers were ever vigilant, with weapons at their sides.

The work on the wall was also complicated by famine, which threatened the health and security of the Jerusalem community (5:1–6). Although Nehemiah was troubled by the people's complaints, he was even more distressed by another age-old problem: the exploitation of the poor by the rich. People were forced to mortgage their farms to pay the interest on loans illegally charged by the nobles and the rich (5:1–13; see the books of Amos and Isaiah, in particular, which severely condemn oppression of the poor by the rich). Nehemiah denounced the practice (5:6–13) and held himself up as an example of one who made sacrifices for the good of the entire community (5:14–19).

In spite of internal problems and external threats, the wall was finally finished (6:15–19). Nehemiah's task was completed, and the first part of his memoirs ends with his return to the Persian capital of Susa in 433 (13:6–7).

Chapters 8–10, an interlude between Nehemiah's memoirs, recount the work of Ezra the scribe during Nehemiah's governorship. Since the focus is on cultic and religious matters rather than on social reforms, it is likely that these chapters represent phase three of the Chronicler's work and were not originally a part of Nehemiah's autobiography, which dates to phase four.

Nehemiah 8–10 includes Ezra's reading of the book of the law of Moses before an assembly at the Water Gate (8:1–12); a celebration of the Feast of Tabernacles, which was reinstituted when he found a description of the law (8:13–18); and a renewal of the covenant, which involved a day of fasting (9:1–5), a lengthy prayer by Ezra (9:6–38), and the ratification of a written covenant by the heads of families, including Nehemiah (9:6–27). A summary of the covenant appears in 10:28–39. Those who signed took an oath of obedience to the law of Moses and, more particularly, committed themselves to forbid

their children to engage in mixed marriages, to observe the sabbath, and to fulfill other obligations of the covenant.

Nehemiah 11–13 represents the second part of the memoirs of Nehemiah. Its relationship to the first part (chaps. 1–7) is demonstrated by the dedication of the completion of the wall, which was announced in 6:15. These links to the early chapters also argue in favor of the hypothesis that Nehemiah 1–7 and 11–13 once constituted a whole that was subsequently split up to connect the missions of Ezra and Nehemiah.

Nehemiah 11:1–24 and 12:1–26 record genealogies of community leaders in Jerusalem and of the priests, Levites, and Temple servants, respectively. These lists and genealogies, like those elsewhere in the Chronicler's work, again emphasize heritage, family, and links to the past. Although 11:1–24 draws much from 1 Chronicles 9, it and 12:1–26 are reminiscent of Nehemiah's earlier genealogies in 7:5–69. However, the genealogies in 7:5–69 move from a select list of those who returned, to priests and Levites, and so forth. The genealogies in 11:1–24 (those now residing in Jerusalem) and 12:1–26 (priests, Levites, etc.) are broken up by a short list of inhabited villages outside Jerusalem (11:25–36).

Just as the restoration of the Temple and the arrangement of its cult and servants were Ezra's main concern, so are the reconstruction of the walls of Jerusalem and their dedication Nehemiah's prime interest. This is brought out not only in lengthy reports of the problems encountered along the way but also in detailed discussion of the elaborate dedication ceremonies (12:27–43) and the appointment of gatekeepers and others (12:44–47). Because of Nehemiah's preoccupation with the construction of the wall, it was not sufficient to note in his memoirs that the wall had been completed (6:15); the dedication ceremony was also reported.

This completes the task set by second Isaiah (chaps. 44–45), who speaks of the rebuilding of the Temple and the restoration of the city. It is also an important step on the way to autonomy (at least with respect to neighbors) and the possibility for future fulfillment of a greater dream. So the final editor could not lay down his pen until the city was completed, that is, the wall as well as the Temple. This really interweaves the themes of prophecy, promise, fulfillment, and realization, however, without bringing the story to an end.

When Nehemiah's first term as governor of Jerusalem was over in 433, he returned to Susa. The last chapter of Nehemiah (chap. 13) is undoubtedly a postscript to the author's memoirs, when he again returned to Jerusalem "after some time" (13:6; RSV). Having left Jerusalem on a positive note, he must have been shocked to find the religious practices and identity of the community in a state of deterioration. The Temple had been desecrated by conversion of one of its chambers into the living quarters of Tobiah, an outsider who originally had opposed the building of the walls (13:4–9); provision for the Levites had been neglected, and they had returned to farming for subsistence (13:10–14); commercial transactions were conducted on the Sabbath (13:15–22); and marriages between Jews and foreigners, considered to erode the identity of the community, were commonplace (13:23–29). Nehemiah addressed each of the problems, in his words, "cleansing them from everything foreign" (13:30).

DIFFERENCES BETWEEN CHRONICLES AND SAMUEL-KINGS

The narrative of 1 Chronicles begins in chapter 10 with a brief description of the death of Saul, who was removed from kingship, according to the Chronicler, because of unfaithfulness to the Lord (10:13–14). Conspicuously absent in 1 Chronicles is a historical account of the development of the monarchy in Israel. Samuel, the prophet who anointed and deposed rulers at the bidding of God, and who was the conscience of kings, is nowhere mentioned in Chronicles. His rejection of Saul and his anointing of the boy David also do not appear. Instead, David, who has popular support among the inhabitants (11:1–9), is made king by the elders of Israel. And nothing is said about the death and removal of Saul's heir, Ishbaal, who ruled in the north for a while.

Unlike the Primary History, the narrative in Chronicles begins at 1 Samuel 31 with the death of Saul, because the Chronicler is interested only in setting the stage for David, not in a full history of the development of the monarchy. Thus the Chronicler omits the familial intrigues that plagued Saul and his

son-in-law David. Much of this is found in 1 Samuel 18–30. Saul becomes jealous of David's success and seeks to kill him. David flees and, with a band of men, becomes a mercenary for the Philistines. But these mercenary activities are only hinted at in 1 Chronicles (12:19), and a parenthetical statement is immediately added to clear David of collusion with the enemy, so as not to taint the reputation of this central character.

After Saul's death, civil war breaks out between the armies of David and Saul (2 Sam 2:8–4:12), ending in victory for David's forces and the death of Abner, Saul's general, and Ish-bosheth (in Primary History; Chronicles reads the original form, Ishbaal), Saul's son and heir to the throne. The Chronicler ignores this part of the story and in doing so suggests a smooth transition from the death of Saul (1 Chr 10:13–14) to the anointing of David (11:1–3). In fact, according to Chronicles (12:38), "All the rest of Israel were of a single mind to make David king."

The Chronicler chose to ignore as well a whole series of events recorded in 2 Samuel 11–23, including chapters devoted to David's adultery with Bathsheba, the murder of her husband, Uriah, and the subsequent troubles resulting from those sins (in the historiography of the writer of Samuel-Kings): the death of the child conceived in their sin, the rape of Tamar by Amnon, the defection of Absalom, the years of civil war between the followers of David and those of Absalom, the death of the latter, and the revolt of Sheba the Benjaminite. By eliminating the intrigues and familial infighting at the royal court, the Chronicler presents a more peaceful and pious account of David. For the Chronicler's purposes, David's defects—his human weakness—would only detract from the glory of his achievements in areas of religious development. Thus, the problems of David's accession to the throne and the subsequent difficulties in the succession are not dealt with in the Chronicler's account.

The only one of David's sins recorded by the Chronicler is the census of Israel he allowed to be taken (1 Chr 21). Even in this story, however, Chronicles varies from 2 Samuel 24 in a significant way. Although Satan is introduced in Chronicles primarily to relieve Yahweh of responsibility for leading David astray, he also serves to mitigate David's guilt.

For the most part 1 Chronicles 22–29 represents David's cultic activities. According to the Chronicler, the arrangements for material and manpower needed for the building of the Temple were made by David, not Solomon. Although David, in his old age, appointed Solomon as regent (1 Chr 23:1), the Chronicler states specifically that it was David himself who made the preparations for the Temple—presumably because Solomon was "young and inexperienced" (1 Chr 22:5; RSV). David's contribution to the Temple included not only purchasing and storing the building materials (22:5) but also decreeing the divisions of responsibilities among the Levites (chap. 23), priests (chap. 24), musicians (chap. 25), gatekeepers (26:1–19), treasurers (26:20–28), and officers and judges (26:29–32). Military and civilian officials were also appointed by David before his death, and he enjoined Solomon and the people to support the project.

In the Primary History, David is barred from building the Temple because he is a warrior; the Temple had to be constructed by a "man of peace" (a play on the name Solomon, from the root shlm, "be complete, sound, safe"). This ban apparently even extended to the preparations for the construction since there is no mention of David's contribution in this area. In the Chronicler's work, however, although the record also reflects the importance of having a man of peace build a permanent place of worship, the writer obviously does not feel that preconstruction preparations are included in the ban; therefore David, not Solomon, receives credit for them. These chapters enhance David's image as a pious man, elevate his stature, and link the three major focuses of Chronicles: David and his dynasty, the Temple, and Jerusalem.

The formal proclamation of Solomon as king (29:22b–25) and the death of David (29:26–30) bring 1 Chronicles to its end. Although the Chronicler's account portrays a rather formal transfer of kingship from father to son, the process was more dramatic and its legality not uncontested (1 Kgs 1–2). Again, the Chronicler eliminates material that might reflect adversely on David and his house.

In summary, Chronicles portrays David in a favorable, idealized light. His major sins and family troubles are ignored, while his contributions to the establishment of Jerusalem as the center of the kingdom and to the building of the Temple are underscored and even exaggerated. There is enough of his exploits on the battlefield to maintain his status as a great warrior and to justify God's decision not to allow him to build the Temple, but the bulk of the story focuses on his love of music and religious worship. The Chronicler brings back the erstwhile talented musician whose playing had brought him to the attention of King Saul and set him on the path to kingship. As king he uses these and other skills in preparing and organizing the Temple orders and religious practices.

The material in 2 Chronicles parallels much of 1 Kings 3 to 2 Kings 25, omitting, however, practically everything relating to the northern kingdom and its kings and dynasts. It constitutes a history of Judah from the glorious years of Solomon to the eventual destruction of the kingdom, of Jerusalem, and of the Temple, and the exile of the people to Babylon.

For the Chronicler, Solomon is a mere extension of David, and the same themes are present. After a brief description of the wisdom and wealth of Solomon (chap. 1), the Chronicler takes up the building (chaps. 2–5) and dedication (chaps. 6–7) of the Temple. Again, to demonstrate the cultic responsibilities of the Davidic line, as well as its piety, is among the Chronicler's foremost concerns.

This part corresponds with minor variations to 1 Kings 3–9:9. Omitted are the judicial decisions that demonstrate the wisdom of Solomon (1 Kgs 3:16–28), Solomon's appointing of court officials (1 Kgs 4:1–19), and the iteration of his daily provisions (4:20–28). The construction of the Temple, including measurements and equipment, is similar in both accounts, with the exception that the Primary History places greater emphasis on details of the dimensions of the Temple precincts and their accoutrements.

The practice of omitting material that denigrates the king again becomes apparent with regard to Solomon. After a detailed account of Solomon's role in the construction and dedication of the Temple, the Chronicler briefly discusses his reign, citing his wealth, wisdom, and fame, the latter convincingly demonstrated by the visit of the queen of Sheba. The writer ignores the details of Solomon's love of non-Israelite women, and his subsequent building of altars so that his wives might worship their gods (1 Kgs 11:1–13), a sin for which other kings are ruthlessly condemned. However, as punishment for his infidelity, God threatens to rend the kingdom from Solomon's son (1 Kgs 11:13), and Solomon is plagued by Edomite and Syrian incursions into Israel as additional punishment (1 Kgs 11:14–25). At the end of Solomon's reign, the prophet Ahijah predicts that Jeroboam will lead ten of the twelve tribes in a successful revolt and rend the kingdom in two (1 Kgs 11:26–40). Solomon subsequently attempts to kill Jeroboam, who, however, escapes and flees to Egypt.

All this does not appear in the Chronicler's account of Solomon's life, and Solomon is thereby made to appear as pure and pious as David. The emphasis is again on the religious objects and the Temple. Peace and prosperity are important aspects and are briefly mentioned in the Chronicler's work, but nothing derogatory is said about the son of David.

The rest of the book of 2 Chronicles (chaps. 10–36) details the history of the kingdom of Judah from Rehoboam's accession to the throne of his father, Solomon, to the end of the kingdom. Although the work covers the same time span as 1 Kings 14 to 2 Kings 25, it differs significantly from its counterpart in the Primary History.

First, 2 Chronicles is a briefer account of the years following Solomon's reign because it eliminates those parts of 1 and 2 Kings concerned with the northern kingdom of Israel. For the Chronicler, the true center of the worship of Yahweh is the Temple in Jerusalem, in the kingdom of Judah. The hope of the returning exiles lies in the revival of the traditional forms of worship, to be brought about by one of Davidic lineage. The northern kingdom, having forsaken the divine promises by separating itself from the Temple, from Jerusalem, and from the Davidic line, is thus unimportant to the Chronicler—except when the history of Judah is linked to it, either as an adversary or as an ally in war.

Second, the history that appears in 2 Chronicles can be described as a series of biographies or character sketches of Judah's kings. Those regarded as unfaithful to the divinely decreed responsibilities of leading the nation and maintaining the purity of the cultic tradition receive only brief mention. And those who attempt to restore and maintain purity of faith are dealt with in glowing terms and generally receive more attention than in Kings. For the Primary History, the ultimate embodiment of the Davidic ideal is Josiah; for the Chronicler, it is Hezekiah. In both accounts, not one of the northern kings passes muster. But the Primary History uses the northern kingdom as an example of a people and its leaders gone wrong, whereas the Chronicler virtually ignores it altogether.

Third, the account in the Primary History generally focuses on the political and military struggles of the nations. For instance, although Hezekiah initiated a major religious reform, the focus of the narration in 2 Kings 18–20 is the siege of Jerusalem by the Assyrian king, Sennacherib, in 701 B.C.E. (*cf.* Isa 36–37). Out of religious zeal, the king attempts to make changes in the political and social sphere, changes that lead almost to disaster. In contrast, the siege of Jerusalem receives little attention in 2 Chronicles 29–32. This event is overshadowed by the account of Hezekiah's religious reform and his personal piety. For both the Chronicler and the Deuteronomist, religious and political events interact, the one affecting the outcome of the other. But the way these factors influence the outcome and the degree of importance each receives vary considerably in the two treatments.

The reign of Asa covers three chapters (14–16) in 2 Chronicles. The first ten years of his forty-year reign were peaceful, and during that time he initiated a reform movement, aimed at purging the land of idols, altars, and high places dedicated to foreign gods and demanding that the people follow Yahweh (14:1–5, 15:1–19). Unfortunately, he is also remembered for less favorable reasons. When Israel closed off Judah and threatened war, Asa paid for the support of Aram (Syria; RSV) by raiding the Temple of its silver and gold. Although Aram responded by attacking and taking over parts of Israel, thus eliminating the threat to Judah, Asa's personal faith in Yahweh was questioned, and his actions were condemned (16:1–10). Another similar example can be found in 16:11–14: when Asa becomes sick, he relies on physicians rather than Yahweh to heal him; as a result, he dies.

In contrast, the account in 1 Kings 15:9–24 is shorter. Its major interest is in the war between Asa and Baasha of Israel, and Asa is not condemned for seeking Aramaean help. Regarding Asa's religious reform, 1 Kings notes that "the high places were not taken away" (15:14; RSV), and the reforms are not discussed in as great detail as in Chronicles. Finally, the death of Asa is not linked to his lack of faith in Yahweh; in this account he has a disease and eventually dies of it.

King Jehoshaphat is mentioned only briefly in 1 Kings 15:24 and 22:41–50. He is referred to as a righteous king, who exterminated the "male cult prostitutes . . . from the land" (22:46) but who, like Asa, did not do away with the high places (22:43). The book of 2 Chronicles treats this king much more extensively, devoting four chapters (17–20) to Jehoshaphat and his godly life. His religious reforms included removing the altars to foreign gods (17:6), providing seminars on the teachings of the book of the Law (17:7–9), and initiating a comprehensive judicial reform throughout the land (19:4–11). His personal piety, the subject of chapter 20, inspired the devotion of the people. To exemplify his faith, an account is given of a miraculous deliverance from a joint Moabite, Ammonite, and Edomite invasion. In particular, Chronicles records a prayer of Jehoshaphat to Yahweh, seeking divine help in the face of the advancing armies (20:5–12).

In the case of both Asa and Jehoshaphat, 1 Kings (the Primary History) focuses on the contemporaneous developments in the northern kingdom of Israel —on King Ahab and the prophet Elijah. Only briefly does it mention the leadership in Judah. Whenever Jehoshaphat appears in chapters 15–22, it is as a reference for dating the northern kings at times when the political and military fortunes of the two kingdoms are woven together.

As with Jehoshaphat, four chapters (29–32) are devoted to the reign of Hezekiah. They focus on Hezekiah's religious reforms, which include cleansing the Temple (29:1–11), sanctifying the Levites and the Temple servants (29:12–19), and reestablishing the proper rituals and religious ceremonies (29:20–36, 31:2–19). A Passover celebration, encouraged by Hezekiah, is chronicled in great detail (chap. 30), and further reforms (e.g., destruction of the high places) are mentioned (31:1). Hezekiah's personal piety is praised (31:20–21), and an example of it

appears in the abbreviated account of the siege of Jerusalem (32:1–23, esp. 7–8).

The account of these events in the Primary History works to the opposite effect: 2 Kings 18:1–20:21 is almost entirely devoted to the siege of Jerusalem by Sennacherib, including details such as Hezekiah's prayer (19:15–19), Yahweh's response through the prophet Isaiah (19:20–28), and the sign of the shadow during Hezekiah's illness (20:8–11). The religious reform of Hezekiah is mentioned only briefly in the summary of his reign (18:1–7).

Two other kings deserve mention for the distinct ways in which the two accounts portray their reigns. Manasseh is described briefly in 2 Kings 21:1–18 as a thoroughly evil king who is blamed in the Primary History for the eventual destruction of Jerusalem and the captivity of Judah (vv. 10–15). For leading the kingdom away from Yahweh and to the worship of Baal and Asherah and the practice of human sacrifice, he goes down in the annals as one who seduced the nation "to do more evil than the nations had done whom the Lord destroyed before the people of Israel" (v. 9). The destruction of Jerusalem is prophesied because of his lack of devotion to Yahweh (vv. 10–15).

Chronicles also details Manasseh's faithlessness and his offering of human sacrifices (here identified as his sons) to false gods (2 Chr 33:1–9), and the account notes, as did 2 Kings, that he did more evil than the nations. Yet it is also recorded that because of his sins, Manasseh was taken into exile to Babylon, where he repented and prayed God for forgiveness (33:10–13; see the apocryphal book the Prayer of Manasseh). After his repentance he is said to have returned to Judah and is credited with the removal of the altars and images of the false gods, and with the restoration of proper ritual to Judah (33:14–17). In this manner the Chronicler explains Manasseh's long and ultimately peaceful reign: having repented, he is not held responsible for the fall of Jerusalem.

The account of Josiah's reign is interesting in that the Primary History focuses in greater detail on his religious reforms than Chronicles. In 2 Chronicles, his achievements include the removal of idols and high places (34:1–7), the restoration of the Temple (34:8–13), and the discovery of the book of the Law (34:14–28). The latter resulted in a public reading of the Law and a national renewal of the covenant (34:29–33). A detailed and spectacular account of Josiah's celebration of Passover (35:1–19) follows.

The 2 Kings version also records the restoration of the Temple (22:3–7), the finding of the book of the Law (22:8–13) and its public reading (23:1–3), and the celebration of Passover (23:21–23), although the latter is recounted in less detail. Because of Manasseh's evilness, the prophecy of the destruction of Judah cannot be reversed. But the Primary History notes, through the prophecy of Huldah, that because of his piety, Josiah himself will not see the destruction (22:14–20). His religious zeal delays the disaster. Kings also describes in detail Josiah's removal of altars and images of the false gods, including the long-standing altar at Bethel, as well as the killing of the high priests serving those altars (23:4–20). The latter events go unmentioned in Chronicles.

These examples demonstrate the Chronicler's overwhelming interest in religion, ritual, the Temple and its servants, and Jerusalem and Judah. The Primary History focuses on the fluctuating fortunes of the nation, sparing no figure from blame, and charging the nation with responsibility for slow, but inexorable, progress towards its own destruction. Unfaithfulness was a major reason for the nation's demise, which is demonstrated in its conduct of domestic and foreign affairs as well as in worship of foreign gods. The Chronicler, however, tends to emphasize the positive and focuses on the highlights of the religious life of the nation. Discussions of politics and military operations are limited and generally connected to the faithfulness of individual kings, while events of religious significance find broader treatment.

Furthermore, the contrasting evaluations of Hezekiah, Manasseh, and Josiah indicate differing theological and historical perspectives that underly the two works. Josiah is the Davidic ideal of the Primary History, as reflected in its enlarged account of his religious reforms; Hezekiah is the embodiment of the Davidic ideal for the Chronicler. The difference in the treatment of Manasseh is clearly the result of a differing historical perspective. The Primary History explains the political background for the rise and fall of the nations of Israel and Judah. Even more, it provides the exiles, before the decree of Cyrus, with a rationale for what had happened. The blame is placed on Manasseh, the epitome of false worship and religious perversion. By contrast, the Chronicler's history emphasizes the religious high points of the past upon which the returning exiles can rebuild a thriving religious community. Political stability is contingent upon adherence to the ancient religious traditions, with the Davidic hope ever present. Since the Primary History, with which all exiles were familiar, used Manasseh as the scapegoat for the fall, the return, restoration, and renewal are predicated upon Manasseh's repentance, which changes the course of history and permits Yahweh to renew his covenantal relationship with his people (as Judah had been spared in 701 by the actions of Hezekiah). In this way, despite the temporary fall, the dynastic hope is kept alive until the time of Zerubbabel and the prophecies of Haggai and Zechariah.

Bibliography

Ackroyd, Peter R. *Exile and Restoration: A Study of Hebrew Thought of the Sixth Century B.C.* Philadelphia, 1968. An important study of the changes in Hebrew thought after the fall of the monarchies and the exile.

——. *The Age of the Chronicler.* Auckland, New Zealand, 1970. Ackroyd focuses on the historical situation and its effect on the Chronicler during the composition of Chronicles, Ezra, and Nehemiah.

——. *I and II Chronicles, Ezra, Nehemiah.* London, 1973. A brief, readable commentary for those who are beginning their study of the books of Chronicles.

Avi-Yonah, Michael. "The Walls of Nehemiah: A Minimalist View." *Israel Exploration Journal* 4 (1954): 239–248. An archaeological study of the ancient walls around Jerusalem that expresses the view that the walls were not all that imposing a structure.

Bickerman, Elias. "The Edict of Cyrus in Ezra 1." *Journal of Biblical Literature* 65 (1946): 249–275. A detailed review of the wording of the Hebrew and Aramaic edicts of Cyrus. Bickerman concludes that Ezra 1 preserves the genuine edict, which was promulgated in the same mode as the Roman edict.

Bright, John. "The Date of Ezra's Mission to Jerusalem." In *Yehezkel Kaufmann Jubilee Volume*, edited by Menahem Haran. Jerusalem, 1960. Arguing that the reading in Ezra 7:7 should be "thirty-seven" not "seven," Bright places the return of Ezra in 428 B.C.E., during the reign of Artaxerxes I.

Cowley, A. *Aramaic Papyri of the Fifth Century B.C.* Oxford, 1923.

Cross, Frank Moore. "A Reconstruction of the Judean Restoration." *Journal of Biblical Literature* 94 (1975):

4–18. Focusing on the genealogy of the high priests in Nehemiah 12:11–12, Cross argues for the traditional view that Ezra preceded Nehemiah to Jerusalem. His argument is based on the practice of papponymy in the family of Sanballat, which was found on the Samaria papyri.

Emerton, J. A. "Did Ezra Go to Jerusalem in 428 B.C.?" *Journal of Theological Studies* 17 (1966): 1–19. A refutation of Bright's position that Ezra 7:7f. should read, "the thirty-seventh year" and that Ezra and Nehemiah overlap, with Ezra following Nehemiah in 428 B.C.E. Emerton argues for a date of 398 B.C.E., during the reign of Artaxerxes II, for Ezra.

Freedman, David N. "The Chronicler's Purpose." *Catholic Biblical Quarterly* 23 (1961): 436–442. Freedman notes that the purpose of the Chronicler was to "establish and defend the legitimate claims of the house of David to preeminence in Israel, and in particular its authoritative relationship to the Temple and its cult." The books of Ezra and Nehemiah were added to update the work and adapt it to the new situation that existed in the fifth century.

———. "Canon of the Old Testament." *The Interpreter's Dictionary of the Bible.* Supplementary Volume 1976a. A general article regarding the formation of the Old Testament canon.

———. "The Deuteronomic History." *The Interpreter's Dictionary of the Bible.* Supplementary Volume 1976b. A general article regarding the formation of the Deuteronomic History and, in particular, its relationship to the Primary History.

Galling, Kurt. *Die Bücher der Chronik, Ezra, Nehemia.* Göttingen, 1954. A classic commentary on the books of Chronicles, Ezra, and Nehemiah in the best tradition of German scholarship.

Japhet, Sara. "The Supposed Common Authorship of Chronicles and Ezra-Nehemia Investigated Anew." *Vetus Testamentum* 18 (1968): 330–371. Japhet analyzes the Chronicler's literary corpus from a linguistic point of view and concludes on the basis of linguistic opposition, technical terms, and stylistic peculiarities that there is wide diversity of language between Chronicles and Ezra-Nehemiah. She further suggests that Ezra-Nehemiah is *earlier* than Chronicles.

Koch, K. "Ezra and the Origins of Judaism." *Journal of Semitic Studies* 19 (1974): 173–197. Koch's article presents the argument that Ezra is one of the greatest figures of the Old Testament. He bases that discussion on the following: (1) that Ezra's "march" (return) to Jerusalem was a second Exodus, a cultic procession; (2) that Ezra was a real high priest of the family of Aaron; and (3) that Ezra was sent to create a holy seed among the people "beyond the river," even the Samaritans.

McCullough, William Stewart. *The History and Literature of the Palestinian Jews from Cyrus to Herod: 550 B.C. to 4 B.C.* Toronto, 1975. A history of the Jewish community in Jerusalem. McCullough chronicles that history from the return of Cyrus until long after the period of Ezra and Nehemiah.

Morgenstern, Julian. "The Dates of Ezra and Nehemiah." *Journal of Semitic Studies* 7 (1962): 1–11. This article supports the traditional view that Ezra returned to Jerusalem in 458 B.C.E. and Nehemiah in 445 B.C.E.

Myers, Jacob M. *I and II Chronicles.* 2 vols. Garden City, N.Y., 1965. At present, the most detailed commentary in English on the Books of Chronicles. Each volume includes an introduction, a new translation with notes, and a selected bibliography.

———. *Ezra, Nehemiah.* Garden City, N.Y., 1965. Again, the most complete commentary in English on the books of Ezra and Nehemiah. The new translation with notes is accompanied by an introduction and selected bibliography.

———. *I and II Esdras.* Garden City, N.Y., 1974. A commentary, with introduction, notes, and a selected bibliography, on the apocryphal works that complete the Ezra literature. The discussion of the literature and text tradition in the introduction is invaluable.

Newsome, James D., Jr. "Toward a New Understanding of the Chronicler and His Purposes." *Journal of Biblical Literature* 94 (1975): 201–217. Newsome presents four thematic focuses of the Book of Chronicles—the Davidic king and prophet, Judah, its theology of history, and its emphasis on prophetic discourse—to suggest that Ezra-Nehemiah is a later work than Chronicles.

North, Robert. "Theology of the Chronicler." *Journal of Biblical Literature* 82 (1963): 369–381. The theological thought of the Chronicler is placed into four categories: legitimacy, short-range retribution, the Mosaic cultus, and Davidism.

Olmstead, Albert T. *The History of the Persian Empire.* Chicago, 1948. The classic history of the Persian empire, which presents the background for understanding the historical situation within which Ezra and Nehemiah worked.

Pritchard, James B., ed. *Ancient Near Eastern Texts.* 2d ed. Princeton, 1955.

Rowley, Harold H. "The Chronological Order of Ezra and Nehemiah." In *Ignace Goldziher Memorial Volume,* edited by Samuel Löwinger and Joseph Somogyi. Pt. 1. Budapest, 1948. This lengthy discussion of the date of Ezra's return to Jerusalem concludes that Ezra and Nehemiah did not overlap and that Ezra came to Jerusalem after Nehemiah, in 397 B.C.E.

———. "Nehemiah's Mission and Its Background." *Bulletin of the John Rylands Library* 37 (1955): 528–561. Because of the problems with the narrative concerning the rebuilding of the walls of Jerusalem, Rowley concludes that Nehemiah preceded Ezra to Jerusalem and that Nehemiah's ministry was during the reign of Artaxerxes I, while Ezra's was during the reign of Artaxerxes II.

————. *The Rediscovery of the Old Testament.* Philadelphia, 1964. The author describes the framework within which the community recaptured the law of Moses and the cultic ritual. A beautiful description of the ethos of the Jewish community is presented in chapter 7.

Rudolph, Wilhelm. *Esra und Nehemia.* Tübingen, 1949. Rudolph maintains that the Chronicler wrote the books of Ezra and Nehemiah as well as Chronicles.

————. "Problems of the Books of Chronicles." *Vetus Testamentum* 4 (1954): 401–409. A general discussion of the theology of the Chronicler in the light of previous scholarship.

————. *Chronikbücher.* Tübingen, 1955. The companion volume to Rudolph's *Esra und Nehemia.*

Snaith, Norman H. "The Date of Ezra's Arrival in Jerusalem." *Zeitschrift für die alttestamentliche Wissenschaft* 63 (1951): 53–66.

Stern, Ephraim. *The Material Culture of the Hand of the Bible in the Persian Period, 538–332* B.C.E. (in Hebrew.) Jerusalem, 1973. A detailed discussion of the archaeological remains from fifty Palestinian sites during the Persian period.

Torrey, Charles C. *The Chronicler's History of Israel.* New Haven, 1954. The last in a series of works that represent a half-century of writing on the Chronicler and his work.

Wright, John S. *The Building of the Second Temple.* London, 1958. A study that focuses on the rebuilding of the Second Temple, which was finished in 515 B.C.E. Archaeological evidence is considered.

DAVID NOEL FREEDMAN

BRUCE E. WILLOUGHBY

Esther and Additions to Esther

When Mordecai saw that evil was abroad,
    and Haman's edicts were proclaimed in Shushan,
he put on sackcloth and arranged for mourning, ordained
    a fast and sat in ashes.
"Who will arise to atone for error
    and win forgiveness for our ancestors' sins?"
A flower blossomed from the palm tree,
    Hadassah arose to stir those asleep.
Her servants hastened to give Haman wine
    that he might drink the venom of serpents.
He rose through his wealth and fell through
        his wickedness;
    upon the gallows he built he himself was
        hanged.
All the world was struck with amazement
    when Haman's *pur* became our Purim.

(Gordis 1974, 95)

    The lines above, part of an acrostic (alphabetical) hymn, are recited by Jews each year during the festival of Purim. The origin of that festival, as well as authorization for its annual two-day observance, is set out in the book of Esther.

THE STORY OF ESTHER

    With an eye to action rather than characterization, the author tells of two Jews, Esther and Mordecai, whose courage and cunning save their people from destruction in the days of Ahasuerus, king of Persia (=Xerxes I, 486–465 B.C.E.). Theirs is a story filled with suspense, drama, and ironic twists of fate. Conspicuously absent, however, are references to Yahweh, the God of Israel.

    Scene 1. Well into a second lavish, lengthy banquet (lit., a "drinking"), Ahasuerus is enraged by Queen Vashti's refusal to parade her beauty before his guests. After deposing her and ordering that all women honor their husbands, the king seeks a new wife among the loveliest young women of his provinces. His extensive search ends with the crowning of a beautiful Jewess, Esther (called Hadassah, "myrtle," in 2:7), who conceals her origins at the advice of Mordecai, the cousin who had raised her (2:10, 20).

    Scene 2. As a minor official in the royal court at Susa (the phrase "sitting at the king's gate" [2:19, 21] is likely a technical term; note that Ahasuerus uses it in 6:10), Mordecai not only keeps apprised of Esther's welfare but also learns of a plot to assassinate the king. He notifies the queen of the danger, and she informs Ahasuerus in Mordecai's name. The charge is substantiated, the guilty servants are hanged, and Mordecai's deed is recorded in the king's daily record.

    Scene 3. Haman, an Agagite, is appointed grand vizier, and lesser officials must bow before him (3:2). However, Mordecai refuses to do so. His obstinacy does not reflect Jewish unwillingness to bow before any save God, for it is clear that Jews bowed to kings and others of high rank (Gen 42:6). Rather, a reader familiar with Israel's traditions would realize that Mordecai, who traced his ancestry back to Kish (2:5), a Benjaminite and the father of Saul, would never prostrate himself before a descendant of Agag, the king of Amalek, who was Saul's enemy (1 Sam 15; see also Num 24:7, 20).

Enraged by Mordecai's insubordination, Haman devises a plan to kill all the Jews. A *pur*, or lot, is cast for every day of the year until, at last, a day (the thirteenth, according to the Septuagint; see 3:13) in the twelfth month, Adar (February–March), is judged favorable for the slaughter. Haman then persuades Ahasuerus that "a certain people" within his empire (the Jews are not specified) threatens the welfare of the rest, and the ruler consents to their massacre. Ahasuerus politely refuses Haman's bribe of ten thousand talents of silver (although he may have expected his vizier to pay the sum, despite his apparent refusal!) and gives him the signet ring that will seal Haman's plan. Word of the massacre is broadcast throughout the empire, and the scene ends with a grim contrast: "And the king and Haman sat down to drink; but the city of Susa was perplexed" (3:15b; RSV).

Scene 4. When Mordecai appears in public wearing sackcloth and ashes, Esther learns of Haman's scheme. Her cousin urges her to intercede with Ahasuerus on behalf of her people, but Esther is afraid since approaching the king unbidden is a potentially fatal violation of Persian protocol. Her response, "I have not been called to come in to the king these thirty days" [4:11], raises a question in the reader's mind: has some rift in the relationship of the royal couple rendered such action on Esther's part especially dangerous?

Mordecai's reply is an artful example of persuasion, for it combines an appeal to self-interest ("Think not that in the king's palace you will escape any more than all the other Jews") with assurance of success ("For if you keep silence at such a time as this, relief and deliverance will rise for the Jews from another quarter") and a challenge to participate in the high task of assisting providence ("And who knows whether you have not come to the kingdom for such a time as this?" [4:13–14]). Esther rises to the occasion, determining to go before the king in three days and ordering a preparatory fast among all the Jews in Susa.

Scene 5. When Esther approaches the king's hall, he greets her with a hyperbolic expression of his willingness to grant virtually any request (5:3). Rather than entreat on behalf of her people, however, Esther invites both Ahasuerus and Haman to a banquet. The latter is quickly located; and while they are drinking, the king inquires again about Esther's petition. Once more, she demurs, asking simply that both men return for another dinner the next day, when she will reveal the request. The king is filled with curiosity and the reader with suspense regarding the delay. Will Esther's opportunity to intercede on behalf of her people be lost if she continues to evade the king's questions?

As he returns home, Haman's exuberance is diminished only by Mordecai's obstinancy. The advice of his wife, Zeresh, and his friends cheers him, however: construct a gallows and secure the king's permission to hang Mordecai upon it before the dinner the next day.

Scene 6. Unable to sleep, Ahasuerus asks that excerpts from the record be read to him, whereupon he discovers that Mordecai was not rewarded for uncovering the plot against his life. Ironically, it is Haman, early to court and seeking permission to kill his enemy, whom the king asks for advice: "What shall be done to the man whom the king delights to honor?" (6:6). Thinking himself the most likely candidate for royal favor, Haman specifies the reward dearest to his own heart: that the man be dressed in royal robes, mounted upon a horse that wears a royal crown, and conducted through the city square while a courtier shouts his praise. His dreams of glory dissolve in bitter irony, however, when Haman realizes that he must lead Mordecai through the streets of Susa. The ordeal done, Haman returns home with covered head. There Zeresh and his friends, sounding "for all the world as if they were a Greek tragic chorus" (Clines 1984, 14), confirm ancient predictions of Israelite supremacy over the people of Agag (6:13; also see Exod 17:16, Num 24:7, 24:20).

Scene 7. At the second banquet, Esther reveals her petition to the king, who flies into a rage when Haman is identified as the one who has marked Esther and her people for destruction. While Ahasuerus struggles with his temper in the palace garden, Haman begs Queen Esther for his life. Reentering the chamber, the king mistakes Haman's position of

174

entreaty upon the couch for a physical threat to the queen. Haman's face is covered, this time by the attendants who will lead him to death upon the gallows he constructed for Mordecai. Here, the author relishes a reversal that will reappear within the next scene: the villain suffers the fate of his intended victim.

Scene 8. Although Haman is dead, his evil lives on in the unchangeable law of the Persians and Medes (a feature first introduced in 1:19). Ahasuerus cannot revoke Haman's edict; however, he permits a second edict, which supplements the first and allows the Jews to defend themselves against attackers, slaughter the families of their enemies, and plunder their goods. In these admittedly harsh words we again see a reversal in the fates of intended victims and perpetrators: that which Haman wanted done *to* the Jews will instead be done *by* the Jews to those seeking their harm (note that 8:11 is almost an exact quotation of Haman's words in 3:13).

Susa rejoices and Mordecai is clothed in royal attire. Throughout the provinces his people feast, and many gentiles claim to be Jewish, since "the fear of the Jews had fallen upon them" (8:17). (Commentators disagree about the significance of this phrase, since "fear" may refer to dread or to awe. In this context, either meaning is possible.) The conflict between Mordecai and Haman, a major element in the plot of Esther, ends amid Jewish "light and gladness and joy and honor" (8:16), for Mordecai enjoys the power and prestige that formerly belonged to his foe. Some scholars argue that the story of Esther originally ended with 8:17; and it is true that 8:15–17 sounds like a concluding paragraph. In its canonical form, however, the scroll goes on to detail the second major element in the plot of Esther—the fate of the Jews in the face of Haman's unchangeable decree and the celebration and authorization of Purim.

Scene 9. The day Haman chose for the massacre arrives; however, the situation differs somewhat from that described in preceding chapters. A lone foe (Haman) has become many "enemies of the Jews." Even though no one is able to make a stand against them and they are assisted by government officials who fear the power of Mordecai (9:2–4), the Jews "did as they please to those who hated them" (9:5), slaying them all. Scholars who argue that the Esther

scroll originally ended with 8:17 attribute such differences to another author or authors, who adopted the story in chapters 1–8 but changed and expanded it to suit their purposes. Those who defend the unity of Esther, however, explain such apparent discrepancies in other ways. For example, they assert that the widespread growth of anti-Jewish sentiments presupposed in chapter 9 reflects the tragic human tendency toward hatred that is motivated by greed and stereotyping (Anderson 1954, 828–829, 867).

A "historical" reason for the two-day celebration of Purim is detailed in 9:11–19, although Lewis B. Paton is surely correct when he observes that "history here arises from custom, not custom from history" (p. 288). On the thirteenth of Adar, the Jews in the provinces slay 75,000; those in Susa slay 500. The former rest from battle, feast, and celebrate on the fourteenth of Adar; however, Esther receives permission for the latter to engage in a second day of slaughter. Three hundred additional men are killed, and the Jews of Susa celebrate on the fifteenth. At no time do the Jews take plunder from their victims, although the second edict endorsed by the king permits them to do so (8:11). This thrice-repeated observation (9:10, 15, 16) probably serves two purposes. Not only does it make clear that Jewish actions were not motivated by greed for their neighbors' goods, but also it echoes the story of Saul's disobedience in sparing Agag and the best of the spoils of war (1 Sam 15). Mordecai and his people pass over such booty as led to the undoing of their ancestor.

Scene 10. In a letter recording recent events (not the book of Esther, however, since the writing of the letter is recorded in the book), Mordecai enjoins upon Jews the celebration of both days, such celebrations to consist of feasting and gladness, exchanging of choice portions, and gifts to the poor (9:20–23). A brief recital of the book's plot (9:24–25) is followed by a statement verifying that the Jews accepted the festival and determined to observe it throughout their generations (9:26–28), not only because of their own experience but also because of Mordecai's letter. Commentators are correct in observing that the emphasis upon writing, coupled with the legal style of verses 26–28, functions to stress that Purim observance, which has no basis in Torah, is nonetheless legally binding upon all Jews. Mordecai's letter is

175

further confirmed by a second letter, written by Queen Esther and conferring her full authority upon Purim observance (here characterized by fasting and lamentation). According to the Masoretic text, Mordecai, too, had a hand in this second letter. However, the verb in verse 29 is feminine singular ("she wrote"), and the phrase "along with Mordecai the Jew" should probably be regarded as a gloss anticipating verse 31.

Conclusion

The story ends as it began, extolling the riches and power of King Ahasuerus, who is joined by Mordecai, the Jew whom the king favors and who continues to be a source of *shalom* (peace) for his people. The author invites any who wish to learn more about these two great men (there is no mention of Esther) to consult the Book of the Chronicles of the Kings of Media and Persia (10:2). In the biblical books of Kings and Chronicles, similar references to royal archives appear (e.g., 2 Kgs 23:28; 2 Chron 24:27). The author of these verses no doubt cites the Persian chronicles in order to reinforce the book's claim to historical credibility.

ORIGIN OF PURIM AND ITS RELATION TO THE STORY OF ESTHER

The non-Hebraic origin of Purim is suggested by the name given to the festival itself (9:26, 28, 32), since *pur* ("lot"; hebraized pl., *purim*) is a loanword that the author must explain by providing its Hebrew synonym. In the Book of Esther, the name ostensibly derives from the lot cast for Haman to determine a favorable day for the massacre of the Jews (3:7, 9:24).

Scholars generally agree that Jews of the Diaspora adopted a pagan festival and explained its "origin" in the story of a great deliverance of Persian Jewry wrought by Esther and Mordecai. However, there is no consensus regarding the nascence of the festival itself; and various attempts have been made to trace it to a Babylonian myth (in which case, the names Esther and Mordecai may derive from the names of two deities, Ishtar and Marduk) or to a Persian festival (either a festival of the dead or a New Year ceremony). Our sources do not permit a conclusive identification of this festival, which the Jews adapted to their own

distinctive purpose. In fact, we do not know whether or not it was known as "Purim" outside Jewish circles, and we are uncertain about when it came to bear that name within them. The deuterocanonical work 2 Maccabees (first or late second century B.C.E.) refers to a "Mordecai's Day" (15:36), but not to "Purim."

The question of the relationship between Purim and the story of Esther is equally complex. Many scholars confirm that providing "historical" grounds for the observance of Purim among Jews is the *raison d'être* for the entire work. Others, however, insist that Purim is scarcely central to the story and that the essential plot of Esther is already resolved by 8:17, prior to the chapter that details both the events of 13, 14, and 15 Adar and the letters enjoining annual observance of the two-day festival among all Jews.

Persuasive evidence may be marshaled in defense of both these viewpoints. Undoubtedly, portions of the material following chapter 8 were either added or reworked at a later time. On balance, however, it seems best not to sever the institution of Purim altogether from the story as it appears in chapters 1–8, although the author may have adapted an earlier story to suit a particular purpose. Not only is the plot less satisfactorily "concluded" at 8:17 than some scholars would argue, but also the narrator employs certain literary techniques throughout the book that contribute to its appearance of unity. Note, for example, the frequent occurrence of pairs of events: Esther entertains Ahasuerus and Haman at two banquets; she appears before the king unbidden on two occasions; the Jews of Susa do battle for two days, after which a two-day celebration is authorized; and so forth (Berg 1979, 40).

HISTORICITY

Esther purports to be an accurate account of certain events that took place within the court of Xerxes I with serious consequences for Jews living in the Persian empire. The author begins the book in a way that is characteristic of biblical histories and concludes with a reference to certain royal archives wherein additional information may be found. The selection of an actual historical personage (Xerxes I), of a plausible setting (Susa, an Elamite citadel that served as Xerxes' winter residence), and the choice of certain details and words in the book reveals the narrator's familiarity with Persian administration, protocol, and terminology.

Accuracy in detail cannot be equated with historicity, however, since ancient storytellers were quite capable of enriching their tales with facts known firsthand or received from tradition. Furthermore, many details in the book refute evidence gleaned from other sources. For example, the author apparently labors under the misconception that Xerxes' reign (486–465 B.C.E.) followed soon, if not immediately, after that of the Babylonian king, Nebuchadrezzar II (605/604–562 B.C.E.). Yet if Mordecai was indeed among those exiled by Nebuchadrezzar in 597 B.C.E. (2:5–6), he would have been about 120 years of age at the time of our story (and his cousin could scarcely have been a beautiful young virgin). Again, Xerxes' wife was named Amestris, not Vashti; and there is no evidence that a Jewess named Esther replaced her or, indeed, that Amestris lost her crown for refusing to obey the king. Furthermore, at the time when the king in the Book of Esther was searching for a new bride, Xerxes was actually waging an unsuccessful invasion of Greece. Even the notion that Persian law was unchangeable (a feature crucial to the development of our story, which ancient authors sometimes used to introduce plot complications; see also Dan 6:15) seems unlikely, since ruling an empire under such a limitation would be virtually impossible.

These objections do not rule out the possibility that the story of Esther and Mordecai has some historical veracity. However, the account is not corroborated by any outside sources. An inscription referring to a certain Mordecai (Marduka), who was an official during the reign of Xerxes (and perhaps earlier, at the court of Darius I), scarcely invalidates this point, since the author may knowingly, or unknowingly, have supplied a fictional character with the same, perhaps common, name. Thus, it is probably best to bracket such historical issues and to regard the book as the polished product of a master storyteller who combined suspense, irony, and drama in order to ground a popular Jewish festival in events of universal significance.

DATE OF COMPOSITION

Scholars agree that the Book of Esther existed in its canonical form by the close of the second century B.C.E. From internal evidence it is obvious that the book postdates the reign of Xerxes; and some scholars argue that historical inaccuracies point to a time far removed from its Persian setting. The reign of Antiochus IV Epiphanes (175–163 B.C.E.) commends itself to a number of commentators, since persecutions of the Jewish people at that time could easily have sparked a tale in which Jewish defenders "did as they pleased" to their enemies.

External sources, too, fail to provide evidence for a date of composition. Jesus ben Sirach's omission of Esther and Mordecai from his "praise to the fathers" (Sir 44–49, ca. 180 B.C.E.) may be due to other factors and cannot be taken as proof that Esther did not exist in his day (Ezra, too, is missing from Ben Sirach's list). We are left, then, with a span of possible dates from the fourth to the second century B.C.E., although probability points to a period late within this span.

CANONICITY AND THE ADDITIONS TO ESTHER

Throughout the centuries, Esther has enjoyed tremendous popularity among Jews. So beloved was the story that some medieval Jewish artists relaxed the prohibition against depicting human figures in order to beautify the Purim scroll with lavish decorations and portraits of its central characters (Gordis 1974).

Evidence suggests, however, that the work was not always so popular among all Jews. Of the books of the Hebrew Bible, Esther alone is missing from the Dead Sea Scrolls and fragments found at Qumran. Josephus, a first-century C.E. Jewish historian, apparently regarded the book as canonical; and Esther appears among the twenty-four books of the Jewish canon listed in *Bava' Batra'*, a second-century C.E. rabbinical work. Nevertheless, two passages in the Talmud demonstrate that questions about Esther's status persisted as late as the third or fourth century C.E.

Perhaps some Jews rejected Esther because Purim observation violated the principle (stated in Lev

27:34) that Israelites should observe Mosaic festivals only. The absence of references to Yahweh or to any aspect of Israel's religious life and traditions probably raised questions about the book as well. Possibly the author omitted matters religious in order to suggest that in times of danger, Jews must save themselves rather than await divine intervention. Alternatively, the readers may have been expected to discern God's providential care behind the scenes and in the courageous acts of the story's heroine and hero. Certainly, Jews throughout history have read the book in the second of these two ways.

Early Christians knew Esther primarily through the Septuagint (LXX), the Greek translation of the Old Testament and the Apocrypha. In the Septuagint, the Book of Esther contains six major additions. Incorporated at various points in the narrative, these Additions (totaling 107 verses) constitute later attempts to enhance the story's historical credibility, dramatic impact, and religious tenor.

The Additions to Esther have no counterpart in the canonical Hebrew text, and they are not represented in either the Talmud or the Targums (Aramaic versions of the Old Testament). Because Jerome (*ca.* 331–419/420 C.E.) knew of no Hebrew text that contained them, he collected the Additions from their original locations in the Septuagint and placed them at the end of the Book of Esther.

The first and last Additions serve as "bookends" for the story of Esther. Addition A introduces Mordecai, describes his dream about a conflict between two dragons, and tells how he uncovered a court intrigue, thereby saving the life of King Xerxes and incurring the hatred of Haman. At the end of the book, Mordecai offers an interpretation of his dream (Addition F). Both the dream and its explanation cast the Hebrew story of Esther in a new light. Far from being the result of Haman's pride, or of an ancient rivalry between Amalekites and Jews, the struggle between Haman and Mordecai bears cosmic significance, with God intervening to rescue the Jews from nations seeking to destroy them.

Additions B and E purport to be the texts of letters that Xerxes distributed throughout his empire (see 3:12, 8:9–14). The first "letter" authorizes Haman to massacre the Jews; the second denounces Haman and orders the king's subjects to ignore the

first edict, assist those Jews who must defend themselves, and permit them to live under their own laws. Composed in embellished, diplomatic style, these letters allowed their authors the opportunity to place their own theological affirmations upon the lips of a Persian king. In the second letter, for example, Xerxes proclaims that "the Jews . . . are not evildoers but are governed by most righteous laws and are sons of the Most High, the most mighty living God" (Add Esth 16:15–16).

Addition C contains the prayers of Mordecai and Esther prior to Esther's initial unbidden appearance before Xerxes I. These prayers, which refer to Yahweh's universal sovereignty and unique relationship with Israel, give to the Greek Esther a deeply religious tone that is lacking in the Hebrew text. For example, the Addition concludes with the following words from Esther's prayer:

> From the day that I arrived here until now, your servant has not delighted in anything except you, Lord, the God of Abraham. God, whose might prevails over all, hear the voice of the despairing, and save us from the hands of the wicked! And, Lord, protect me from my fears! (Add Esth 14:18–19; trans. by Moore 1971, 107)

Finally, Addition D gives a dramatic account of Esther's audience with the king. According to this text, Xerxes was furious when the queen appeared before him, and his angry expression caused her to faint! However, God changed the king's ire to gentle concern.

Most scholars believe that the Additions to Esther were conceived and written in Greek, although a minority viewpoint holds that Additions A, C, D, and F may have been composed, at least in part, in a Semitic language. We know that Additions B, C, D, and E existed by about 90 C.E., because Josephus paraphrased them in his *Jewish Antiquities*. Less is known about the dating of A and F. A colophon at the end of Addition F, which claims that the preceding Greek translation of Esther is by Lysimachus and is authentic, probably dates from 114 B.C.E. However, we do not know whether this translation included all, or any, of the Additions.

Early Christians who read Esther (with Additions) in the Septuagint encountered no lack of religious references. Nevertheless, some branches of the early church were reluctant to accord it canonical status. For a number of Christians, the book seemed excessively nationalistic and hostile toward gentiles (characteristics that receive even greater emphasis in the Greek Esther). Too, the book explained the origin of a festival for which there was no Christian counterpart. The authors of the New Testament made no reference to it. Despite such objections, the church eventually affirmed the canonicity of Esther as it appears in the Hebrew Bible. For Roman Catholics, the Additions to Esther are also considered inspired writings, although they are "deuterocanonical." Protestants, on the other hand, follow both the Jewish canon and Luther in regarding them as apocryphal.

Bibliography

Esther

Anderson, Bernhard W. "The Book of Esther: Introduction and Exegesis." In *The Interpreter's Bible*, vol. 3. New York, 1954. Pp. 821–874. Excellent commentary and exegetical notes in a readable format.

Berg, Sandra B. *The Book of Esther: Motifs, Themes, and Structure.* Missoula, 1979. A technical discussion of major issues in the study of Esther.

Clines, David J. *The Esther Scroll: Its Genesis, Growth, and Meaning.* Journal for the Study of the Old Testament Supplement Series, no. 31. Sheffield, England, 1984. A fascinating technical study of the development of the story, as well as of the textual history of the book.

Gordis, Robert. *Megillat Esther.* New York, 1974. Briefly addresses important issues in the history of Esther scholarship in a nontechnical commentary.

Moore, Carey A. *Esther.* Garden City, N.Y., 1971. A readable, information-filled commentary.

———, ed. *Studies in the Book of Esther.* New York, 1981. A collection of seminal essays, prefaced by the editor's prolegomenon and including an extensive bibliography.

Paton, Lewis B. *A Critical and Exegetical Commentary on the Book of Esther.* New York, 1908. Still an immensely valuable commentary in a series characterized by impressive scholarship and extensive text-critical notes.

Additions to Esther

Bickerman, Elias J. "Notes on the Greek Book of Esther." *Proceedings of the American Academy for Jewish Research* 20 (1950):101–133. A discussion of Greek editions of Esther and the additions they contain.

Moore, Carey A. *Daniel, Esther, and Jeremiah: The Additions.* Anchor Bible, vol. 44. Garden City, N.Y., 1977. An interesting, readable examination of the Additions, with bibliography.

———. "On the Origins of the LXX Additions to the Book of Esther." *Journal of Biblical Literature* 92 (1973): 382–393. A technical discussion of the Additions, which addresses such questions as their dates and languages of composition.

KATHERYN PFISTERER DARR

Job

THE BOOK IN ITS PRESENT FORM

CONTRARY TO THE practice of most biblical scholarship, the working method of this chapter will be to begin by studying the present form of the Book of Job and attempting to understand the book as a coherent whole. Only afterward will the other questions generally raised about the origins and original setting of the book be examined. However tentative may be our assessments of the meanings of the book in its present form, at least we are dealing with a piece of literature that actually exists; by contrast, studies of origins, influences, authorship, date, and purpose, no matter how technically accomplished, are to a large extent necessarily speculative.

Shape

The shape of a book, as of anything, is not an intrinsic property of the object itself but a design in the mind of the observer. Without any arbitrariness, different readers of the book may discern different shapes in it, esteeming and highlighting this part or that part in varying degrees. Even a single reader may see more than one way of grasping the overall shape of the work. Here are three ways of seeing shape in the Book of Job.

Framework and core. We may distinguish between the framework of the book and its core or center, using the image of a painting surrounded by a frame. The book itself suggests this view of its shape through its use of prose and poetry. The framework of the book is prose, the core is poetry; and since the framework is naive (or so it seems) and the core is sophisticated, the distinction between the relatively cheap and unimportant frame of a painting and the painting itself sounds a convincing analogy. We can also distinguish framework from core by noticing that the framework of Job is narrative and the core is didactic poetry. The book as a whole is thus both a narrative and an argument, or, more precisely, an argument set within the context of a narrative, as shown in the accompanying table.

Framework (1:1–2:13)	prose	narrative
Core (3:1–42:6)	poetry	argument
Framework (42:7–17)	prose	narrative

Exposition, complication, resolution. Let us pay closer attention to the narrative thread that runs through the whole book. The analysis of shape given in the previous paragraph, though valid in general, ignores the fact that there is a certain amount of prose narrative within the poetry, and it pays little attention to the content of the narrative. But we can now discern a somewhat different structure if we emphasize the narrative elements, noting especially the marks of closure embedded in the narrative.

The narrative begins with God afflicting Job in order to discover whether Job's piety depends only upon his prosperity: Will Job still worship God loyally if God deprives Job of all his possessions? By 2:10 we find that Job is unshakable in his piety. "In all this Job did not sin with his lips" (RSV), says the narrator. So, to all appearances, the story is over. It requires no further development of the plot, and we have reached a point of closure.

The narrative continues, nevertheless. We learn that Job feels more than he has said, and we soon find him "curs[ing] the day of his birth" (3:1; RSV). This more aggressive behavior will continue for many chapters, with Job demanding that God cease his unjust treatment. Thereafter Job challenges God in a lawsuit to justify his actions legally. When he has finally delivered his challenge and his oath that he is innocent of any cause for which God could be punishing him, we reach a second point of closure, the narrator's sentence "The words of Job are ended" (31:40; RSV).

In the third segment of the book, God responds to Job—not by answering Job's challenge but by issuing a challenge of his own: What right has Job to dictate how the universe should be run? Job admits in the end that he has no right to question God's actions, and he withdraws his case against God (42:3). God shows he is free either to afflict or to bless by showering Job with wealth and extending his life. The final point of closure comes with Job's death, "an old man, and full of days" (42:17; RSV).

These three segments of the book, which we have identified from the story line and from the marks of closure, may now be analyzed as the three basic elements that are to be found in every story: exposition, complication, resolution. In the exposition the scene is set, the characters are introduced, and all the necessary conditions for the plot are established. In the complication, the characters encounter difficulties or dangers, and tensions emerge that excite the reader's curiosity as to how they can possibly be resolved. The resolution portrays how the narrative problem posed by the story is solved.

The three segments are further distinguished from one another by another device of the narrative:

new characters are introduced at the beginning of each of the segments. In the first it is Job (1:1–3). In the second it is the three friends who come to commiserate with Job (2:11–13). In the third it is the fourth friend, Elihu, who is angered by the speeches of the others (32:1–5). Even though the third of these introductions is surrounded by speeches in poetry, it is itself a prose account, which encourages the reader to connect it with the previous introductions of characters and to see it as a structuring device. The shape of the book from these perspectives is outlined in the accompanying table.

Action	Technique	New Character
God afflicts Job (1:1–2:10)	exposition	Job
Job challenges God (2:11–31:40)	complication	3 friends
God challenges Job (32:1–42:17)	resolution	Elihu

Prologue, dialogue, epilogue. Yet another way of viewing the shape of the book follows the indications given by the book itself about the speakers. The whole book may be seen as speech, the narrator speaking in the prologue and epilogue, and the characters in the dialogue. Thus:

Prologue (1:1–2:13)
  Narrator
Dialogue (3:1–42:6)
  First Cycle: Job and the three friends
      (3:1–11:20)
    Job (3:1–26)
     Eliphaz (4:1–5:27)
    Job (6:1–7:21)
     Bildad (8:1–22)
    Job (9:1–10:22)
     Zophar (11:1–20)
  Second Cycle: Job and the three friends
      (12:1–20:29)
    Job (12:1–14:22)
     Eliphaz (15:1–35)
    Job (16:1–17:16)
     Bildad (18:1–21)
    Job (19:1–29)
     Zophar (20:1–29)
  Third Cycle: Job and the three friends
      (21:1–31:40)

  Job (21:1–34)
        Eliphaz (22:1–30)
  Job (23:1–24:25)
        Bildad (25:1–6)
  Job (26:1–14)
  Job (27:1–28:28)
  Job (29:1–31:40)
Elihu (32:1–37:24)
      Elihu (32:1–33:33)
      Elihu (34:1–37)
      Elihu (35:1–16)
      Elihu (36:1–37:24)
  Yahweh and Job (38:1–42:6)
      Yahweh (38:1–40:2)
        Job (40:3–5)
      Yahweh (40:6–41:32)
        Job (42:1–6)
Epilogue (42:7–17)
    Narrator

This analysis alerts us to different realities in the book. First the narrator's words enclose those of all the characters, predisposing the reader to how all of the speakers in the dialogue are to be heard and at the end leaving the narrator's perspective uppermost in the reader's mind. Second, it is Job who for the most part initiates conversation: he speaks and the friends reply. Indeed, after Bildad's third speech the friends do not speak again, but Job speaks three times without any intervention by them, as if they have faltered and he has gained new energy. Elihu speaks four times, without receiving any reply from Job, as if Job is no longer listening: Is he waiting for someone else to speak? When Yahweh speaks, it is he and not Job who takes the initiative. Although Job has summoned Yahweh to speak, Yahweh's speeches are less a reply than a new approach. Third, all the speaking moves toward silence. Job, who has done most of the talking, in the end lays his hand on his mouth (40:4–5); the friends run out of arguments and do not even finish the third cycle of speeches.

The question has to be raised: What has all this talk achieved? Is the real resolution to the problem of the book a verbal one at all? Or perhaps does the resolution come only when Yahweh too stops speaking and actually does something about Job's suffering by "restor[ing] Job's condition" (42:10; NJB)?

Argument

We have distinguished between the narrative of the framework of Job and the argument of the poetry that forms the core of the book. But this distinction is not wholly valid. For we have been able to speak of the narrative of the book as a whole, that is, of a narrative that not only frames the book but runs through it as well. And we can now speak of the argument not just of the speeches in which the characters are obviously arguing with one another but of the book as a whole, narrative and speeches included.

What is the "argument" of the book? It is the view the book takes of the principal issue it is addressing. We may either suppose, with most readers, that the major question in it is the problem of suffering, or we may suggest that the chief issue is the problem of the moral order of the world, of the principles on which it is governed. Each of these issues provides us with a different perspective from which to consider the book.

The problem of suffering. To understand the book well, it is first of all important to know what exactly *is* the problem of suffering.

Many think that the question is: Why suffering? Or what is its origin and cause? Or why has this suffering happened to me? These are serious questions, but the Book of Job gives no satisfactory answer to them. It is true that the question is ventilated in the book, and partial answers to it are given by the friends. They say that suffering comes about sometimes as punishment for sins, sometimes as a warning against committing sin in the future, and sometimes, as in Job's case, for no earthly reason at all, but for some inscrutable divine reason. But in the end, readers are not left with any one clear view about what the reason for their own particular suffering may be. Nor will they discern any view about the reason for human suffering in general. For the book is entirely about the suffering of one particular and unique individual.

A second problem about suffering is whether there is such a thing as innocent suffering. The intellectual background of the book is obviously one in which cut-and-dried theologies of guilt and punishment have prevailed; for all the friends of Job, in their different ways, insist that if Job is suffering he must in some way be deserving of his suffering. It is still a natural human tendency to ask in time of suffering: What have I done to deserve this? The Book of Job, of course, does not deny the possibility that sometimes suffering is richly deserved, but it speaks out clearly against the idea that such is always the case. Job is an innocent sufferer. His innocence is asserted not only by himself (6:30, 9:15) but by the narrator (1:1) and above all by God (1:8, 2:3, 42:7–8). But even this question and its answer are not the primary element in the problem of suffering.

The third, and essential, problem of suffering in the Book of Job is a more existential one: In what way am I supposed to suffer? Or: What am I to do when I am suffering? To such questions the book gives two different but complementary answers. The first is expressed in the opening two chapters. Here Job's reaction to the disasters that come upon him is a calm acceptance of the will of God; he can bless God not only for what he has given but also for what he has taken away (1:21, 2:10). Fortunate indeed are sufferers who can identify with Job's acceptance of his suffering, neither ignoring the reality of suffering by escaping into the past nor so preoccupied with present grief as to ignore past blessing. The patient Job of the prologue is a model for sufferers.

But Job does not remain in that attitude of acceptance. Once we move into his poetic speeches, from chapter 3 onward, we encounter a mind in turmoil, a sense of bitterness and anger, of isolation from God and even persecution by God. Job makes no attempt to suppress his hostility toward God for what has happened to him; he insists that he will "speak in the anguish of [his] spirit" and "complain in the bitterness of [his] soul" (7:11; RSV). What makes this protesting Job a model for other sufferers is that he directs himself constantly toward God, whom he regards as the party responsible, both immediately and ultimately, for his suffering. It is only because Job insists on a response from God that God enters into dialogue with him. Even though Job's intellectual questions about the justice of his suffering are never adequately answered, he is in the end satisfied as a sufferer by his encounter with God.

Viewed as an answer to the problem of suffering, then, the argument of the Book of Job is: By all means

let Job the patient be your model so long as that is possible for you; but when equanimity fails, let the grief and anger of Job the impatient direct itself and yourself toward God, for only in encounter with him will the tension of suffering be resolved.

The moral order of the world. Another statement of the argument of the book can revolve around another question: Is there any moral order in the world? That is, are there any rules whereby goodness is rewarded and wickedness is punished? The belief that there is an exact correspondence between one's behavior and one's destiny is known as the doctrine of retribution. In one form or another it is shared by most human beings, not just religious people, since it is typically the foundation of one's childhood upbringing: certain behavior will earn you rewards, whereas certain other behavior will bring pain or disaster. There is indeed a mismatch between this principle, which we seem to require in some form or other for the world to have coherence, and the realities that contradict the principle. And to this mismatch both the narrator and the characters of the Book of Job turn their attention. Each has a distinctive standpoint on this question of retribution, or the moral order.

1. The *narrator* in fact founds the whole story upon the doctrine of retribution. Job, the wealthiest of all Orientals, is equally the most pious; there is no coincidence here, the narrator means to say. "That man was blameless and upright, fearing God and turning away from evil" (1:1; Au. trans.). That is deed. And here is consequence: "And there were born to him seven sons and three daughters [the perfect family], and he had 7,000 sheep, 3,000 camels," and so on (1:2; Au. trans.). Here then in the first two sentences is the doctrine of retribution wearing its more acceptable face: piety brings prosperity. Into that prosperity there breaks in one day the most terrible of calamities: Job loses all he has—not only his children and his wealth but, worse than that, his social significance, and, worse still, his reputation as a righteous man. For the other, and more unlovely, side of this principle of world order is that suffering is caused by sin.

Up to this moment Job has believed in retribution, but, now, unshakably convinced that he has done nothing to deserve his misery, he launches on a quest for another moral order. The doctrine has failed the test of reality, reality, that is, as he experiences it. Job's three friends, too, find their dogma challenged by Job's experience, for they have always taken Job at face value, as a pious man. After all, he is a conspicuous testimony to the validity of the dogma: His exceptional piety has brought about his exceptional wealth, has it not? It does not take them long, however, to decide against Job and in favor of the dogma, though each restates it differently.

What the friends have in common is their unquestioning belief that suffering is the result of sin. Their doctrine of retribution, that sin produces punishment, is also reversible: see a man suffering and you can be sure he has deserved it. There is no doubt in their minds of the order: Job's misery is by the book. But there is room for difference of opinion over what precisely Job's sufferings signify.

2. *Eliphaz*, the first friend, starts from the assumption that the innocent never suffer permanently: "What innocent man ever perished, where were the upright ever annihilated?" (4:7; Au. trans.). For him Job is essentially one of the innocent, so whatever wrong Job has done must be comparatively trivial, and so too his suffering is bound to be soon over. Eliphaz asks:

> Is not your piety your source of confidence?
> Does not your blameless life give you hope?
> (4:6; Au. trans.)

Job is blameless on the whole, pious in general. Eliphaz's search for order to explain the mismatch between theory and experience leads him to nuance the concept of innocence in this way. Even the most innocent of humans, like Job, must expect to suffer deservedly on occasion.

3. *Bildad*, the second friend, is if anything even more convinced of the doctrine of retribution, having just now seen a compelling exemplification of it. Job's children have died, cut off in their prime, the classic picture of the fate of the wicked:

> Your sons sinned against him,
> so he has abandoned them to the power of their guilt.
> (8:4; Au. trans.)

The very fact that Job still lives is proof that he, unlike his children, is no gross sinner. However serious his suffering, it is not as bad as it might be; his own sin is not as serious as he may fear.

4. Now whereas Eliphaz has set Job's suffering in the context of his whole life (his suffering is just a temporary pinprick), and Bildad has set it in the context of the fate of his family (the children are dead, but Job is not), *Zophar*, the third friend, perceives no such context for Job's pain. He would say that suffering is inevitably the product of sin. To contextualize Job's suffering and try to set it in proportion is ultimately to trivialize it. Zophar holds for principle rather than proportion: when all is said and done, Job is a sinner suffering hard at this moment for his sin.

Job refuses to acknowledge his sin, claiming:

> My doctrine is pure,
> I am clean in your sight, [O God.]
> (11:4; Au. trans.)

It follows that he is a secret sinner. Were the truth known, it would no doubt transpire that Job is a worse sinner than anyone suspects:

> If only God would speak,
> if only he would open his lips to you
> if only he would tell you the secrets
>   of his wisdom . . .
>   you would know that God exacts of you
>   less than your guilt deserves.
> (11:5–6; Au. trans.)

For all his talk about divine secrets, "higher than heaven—what can you do? Deeper than Sheol—what can you know?" (11:8; RSV), Zophar holds a theology of the essential knowability of God. God's wisdom is not of a different kind from human wisdom. But he knows more about humankind than anyone realizes, and that means more about their sins. Where there is suffering for no apparent reason, we can be sure, says Zophar, that God's wisdom holds the reason. What is more, it will not be some mysterious, ineffable, transcendental reason, but a reason that could easily be comprehended by a human being "if only God would open his lips." So although we cannot always be sure why God is punishing people, we can be sure that those who suffer are being punished by him for some reason or another, never without cause or gratuitously.

Zophar has as well a more distinctive contribution to make concerning the role of God's mercy in working out the principle of retribution. Job might be tempted to think that even though there is doubtless no escape from the workings of the law of retribution, perhaps he could appeal for mercy to soften its blows. But what you must know, says Zophar, is that "God has already overlooked part of your sin" (11:6; Au. trans.). Any mercy that God is going to allow to temper justice has already been taken into account when the law of retribution comes into play. Discounts for mercy's sake are included in the price you pay.

5. Another participant in the dialogue enters only after the first three friends have completed all they have to say. *Elihu*, the young man, is at first "timid and afraid to declare [his] opinion" (32:6; RSV). But in the end he intervenes, realizing that "it is not the old that are wise" but rather "it is the spirit in a man, the breath of the Almighty, that makes him understand" (32:8–9; RSV). He makes the point about retribution that it is not some balancing mechanism in the universe that operates ruthlessly and inescapably; rather it is a channel by which God speaks to humans. Suffering is not so much a mystery; it is more a revelation.

Sometimes, for example, God speaks in visions of the night, in terrifying nightmares, to warn people against committing sins they are contemplating. At other times, like Job, a person may be "chastened with pain upon his bed,/and with continual strife in his bones" (33:19; RSV).

The purpose of such suffering is not retribution. It aims to stimulate confession on the part of the sinner, leading to one's restoration by God and one's public praise of God (33:27). The other friends and Job as well have had too narrow a view of retribution as a process of tit for tat. Look to its design, says Elihu, and you will find that it is an instrument of divine communication.

For these four theologians, the retribution principle stands unshaken by Job's experience. Eliphaz has allowed a redefinition of "innocent" to mean "well,

hardly ever wicked"; Bildad has stressed that the law of retribution has a certain sensitivity (if you are not extremely wicked, you don't actually die); and Zophar has declared that the principle of retribution is not at all a rigorous quid pro quo, for a percentage of the punishment that should light upon you has already been deducted for mercy's sake. Even Elihu, while recognizing that there are more important theological truths than strict retribution, still affirms its validity.

6. In contrast to the friends' single-minded and static positions, *Job*'s mind is confused, flexible, and experimental. In every one of his eleven speeches he adopts a different posture, psychologically and theologically. In the end he admits that he has nothing to rely upon, not even God—nothing except his conviction of his own innocence.

His first, religious instinct is to accept what has happened to him as God's doing and to bless God even for calamity: "Yahweh has given, and Yahweh has taken away; blessed be Yahweh's name" (1:21; *cf.* 2:10). But his second thoughts are more reflective and theological, as he realizes that order has collapsed about him. His wish, expressed in chapter 3, that he had never been born is not mainly a result of his suffering from physical illness and from the grief of bereavement. It is a psychic reaction to disorder. Since it is too late now to strike his birth date from the calendar—the first thought that occurs to him (3:6) —in his second speech he cries out for God to kill him and so put an end to his disorientation:

> O that it would please God to crush me,
> that he would let loose his hand and cut me off!
> (6:9; RSV)

When nothing makes sense any longer, and especially when the principle of retribution, the most fundamental moral order of all, is subverted and disproportion reigns, there is nothing to live for:

> Am I the sea, or a sea monster? . . .
> I loathe my life, I would live no longer.
> (7:12, 16; Au. trans.)

Even so, to have nothing to live for, and to live without order, does not mean for Job that he can have no desire. In his third speech he openly desires what he lacks: a declaration that he is innocent. Although impossible to fulfill, it is his desire all the same:

> How can a man be declared innocent by God?
> If one took him to court [to prove one's innocence]
> one could not answer one in a thousand
> of his questions.
>
> (9:2–3; Au. trans.)

The problem with God is not just that he is super-wise and super-powerful (9:19); it is rather that he is by settled design hostile to his creation. As Job puts it, sardonically, "Being God, he never withdraws his anger" (9:13; Au. trans.). The ancient myths were right, thinks Job, when they recounted that the first thing God ever did was to create the world by slaying the chaos monster in a primeval act of aggression (9:13). Not only toward creation at large but also toward Job in particular God's attitude has been, since Job's conception, one of perpetual hostility and cruelty, albeit one masked by an apparent tender concern:

> Your hands fashioned and made me;
> and now you turn about to destroy me.
> (10:8; Au. trans.)

It is hopeless to seek vindication, he says, so he will not do it. But in the very act of saying to God that it is hopeless to ask for what he deserves, Job is in reality demanding what he believes he is entitled to.

Something has happened to Job in expressing his hopelessness. For in his next speech (chaps. 12–14) he has moved to a decision. He will nevertheless present his case to God:

> No doubt he will slay me; I have no hope;
> yet I will defend my ways to his face.
> (13:15; Au. trans.)

His decision is more startling than that, however. He cannot defend himself against the pain that God is inflicting on him; he can only defend himself verbally. But since God is not saying anything, Job can defend himself verbally only by creating a scenario in which both he and God are obliged to speak, each on

his own behalf. In short, Job initiates a lawsuit and summons God to a tribunal. He challenges God to give an account of himself—to explain what Job has done to deserve such suffering. But of course since Job believes he has done nothing wrong, implicitly he challenges God to confess that he and not Job is the criminal.

This is a case that must be heard promptly, for Job does not believe he can have much longer to live, considering how God is buffeting him about. If Job's name is not cleared now it never will be, and certainly not in any afterlife:

> For a tree there is hope,
> that if it is cut down it will sprout again,
> that its fresh shoots will not fail.
> Though its root grows old in the ground
> and its stump begins to die in the dust,
> yet at the scent of water it may bud
> and put forth shoots like a plant new set.
> But a man, when he dies, loses every power;
> he breathes his last, and where is he then?
> Like the water that has gone from a vanished lake,
> like a stream that has shrunk and dried up,
> Man lies down and will not rise again,
> till the heavens are no more he will not awake,
> nor be roused out of his sleep.
>
> (14:7–12; Au. trans.)

In the midst of uncertainty, what is now certain is that his word of challenge to God, having been uttered, cannot be unsaid. Once written into the heavenly record, it stands as his witness to himself in heaven. It is to his own assertion of innocence that Job refers in his fifth speech (chaps. 16–17):

> Even now, my witness is in heaven
> my advocate is on high.
> It is my cry that is my spokesman;
> sleeplessly I wait for God's reply.
> (16:19–20; Au. trans.)

And in his sixth speech (chap. 19) he speaks of the same affirmation of innocence as his "advocate": "I know that my advocate lives" (19:25; Au. trans.). He has in mind here no heavenly figure who will defend his cause before God, since there is none— least of all God himself, who has proved to be nothing but an enemy. He is compelled to undertake his own defense, to let his own affidavit speak in his behalf.

The climax to Job's self-defense and his demand that God explain why he has tormented Job comes in the last of Job's speeches (chaps. 29–31). Here Job reviews his past life in a final attempt to discover whether there can be any cause in himself for the suffering he has been enduring. But in every area of his life he considers, he judges himself blameless. He concludes his speeches with a mighty oath affirming his righteousness. Still working within the metaphorical scenario of the lawsuit, he imagines himself signing a declaration:

> Here is my signature [to my oath of exculpation];
> let the Almighty answer me!
> Oh, that I had the bill of indictment written
> by my adversary!
>
> (31:35; Au. trans.)

So brief would any bill of charges against Job be and so trivial his faults that Job would be proud to have all the world see how little he had offended against God and how greatly he had fulfilled the ideal of human piety:

> Surely I would carry [the indictment] on my shoulder;
> I would bind it on me as a crown.
> I would give him an account of all my steps;
> like a prince I would approach him!
>
> (31:36–37; RSV)

Job's impressive and convincing protestation of innocence poses a desperate problem for the moral order of the universe, however. For if Job is innocent, the doctrine of retribution is false. And there is no other principle available to replace it.

7. Only *God* can address the problem. He is compelled to enter the conversation by Job's metaphor of the lawsuit and by the logic of the author's narrative. But what divine word can both defend Job's innocence—to which God committed himself in chapter 1—and at the same time affirm the working of a moral law in the world?

In reality, God's speeches in chapters 38–41 are remarkable as much for what they omit as for what they contain. First, there is not a word of the retributive principle, either affirming it or denying it.

It must therefore not be so fundamental to understanding the world as all the previous characters of the book have thought. If God were passionately in favor of it or violently against it, would he not have mentioned it?

Second, the divine speeches are notorious for their insistence on asking questions rather than giving answers, quite apart from the seeming irrelevance of the questions themselves to the fundamental issues of the book:

> Where were you when I laid the foundation of the earth?
> . . . .
> Have you entered into the springs of the sea?
> . . . .
> Do you know when the mountain goats bring forth?
> . . . .
> Is it by your wisdom that the hawk soars?
>
> (38:4, 16; 39:1, 26; RSV)

Amazingly enough, those, and suchlike excursions into cosmology and natural history, are the substance of the divine speeches. The purpose of God's parade of unknown and unknowable features of the natural world can hardly be to browbeat Job with dazzling displays of his power and intelligence. For Job has not for a minute doubted that God is wise and strong, too wise and strong indeed for human comfort and for God's own good. Rather, God invites Job to reconsider the mystery and complexity—often the sheer unfathomableness—of the world that God has created.

God's questions to Job are arranged in three distinct sequences. First is the series that focuses on Job's nonparticipation in creation, such as: "Who shut in the sea with doors?" (38:8; RSV). Job, in other words, is not qualified to hold views on the nature of the universe. Second is the series on the management of the world, among which we find:

> Have you ever in your life ordered the morning forth?
> . . . .
> Can you bind the chains of the Pleiades
> or loose the cords of Orion?
>
> (38:12, 31; Au. trans.)

Job has never organized the appearance of a new day. How then can he speak about the governance of the universe? Third is the sequence of questions about the

188

animals, lion and raven, mountain goat and hind, wild ass, ostrich, war-horse, hawk, and eagle. Through these questions Job's gaze is deliberately fastened upon animals that serve no purpose in the human economy but are, instead, useless to humans, their habits mysterious to us. These chapters make no mention of those domesticated animals, sheep, ass, and camel, that Job possessed in abundance and whose ways he knew. The subject here is wild animals; the purpose of their existence is unintelligible to humans. By the end of the second divine speech (40:7–41:34) the focus has come to rest upon two animals, Behemoth and Leviathan, hippopotamus and crocodile. Symbols of primeval chaos, they, of all the animal creation, are the supremely wild and terrible ones.

The point must be that hippopotamus and crocodile, however alarming, are part of God's creation. God expects Job to realize, and Job is not slow at grasping the point, that the natural order—the principles on which the world was created—is analogous to the moral order—the principles according to which it is governed. In both orders there is much that is incomprehensible to humans, even threatening to their existence. But all of it is the work of a wise God who has made the world the way it is for his own inscrutable purposes. Innocent suffering is a hippopotamus. It makes sense only to God, for it is not amenable to human rationality.

Job has no right to an explanation for his suffering any more than he has a right to an explanation of the purpose of crocodiles. He is not even entitled to be told whether he is being punished for some wrongdoing he has committed or whether he is indeed the innocent sufferer he believes himself to be. The order of creation sets the standard for the moral order of the universe: God knows what he is doing and is under no obligation to give any account of himself.

What does this viewpoint expressed by the character God do to the doctrine of retribution? It neither affirms nor denies it but relegates it to a marginal position. In Job's case, at least, the doctrine of retribution is irrelevant. We, the readers, have known from the beginning of the book that Job is innocent, for both the narrator and God have affirmed it (1:1, 8; 2:3); and Job himself, though suffering as if he were a

wicked man, is unshakable in his conviction that he is innocent. We and Job know, therefore, that the doctrine of retribution is not wholly true. But Job never learns what God's view of the doctrine is, for God never tells Job that he accepts Job's innocence. All that Job learns from God is that retribution is not the issue; the issue is, instead, whether God can be trusted to run his world.

Job capitulates. The religiously reverential instinct that prompted his initial acceptance of his misfortune (1:21, 2:10) had been overwhelmed by his more intellectual and theological search for meaning. But now suddenly his religion and his theology coalesce. He replies to God:

> Who is this that darkens the [divine] design by words without
> knowledge?" [So you have rightly said, Yahweh.]
> You are right: I misspoke myself, I was beyond my limits
>
> I had heard of you by the hearing of the ear but now my eye sees you.
> (42:3, 5; Au. trans.)

Which means: I knew you but did not know you; what I knew of your workings (through the principle of retribution) was real knowledge, but it was not the whole truth about you. The whole truth is that you are ultimately unknowable; your reasons are in the last analysis incomprehensible.

> Therefore I melt in reverence before you and I have received my comfort, even while sitting in dust and ashes.
> (42:6; Au. trans.)

Job finds this position religiously acceptable, even comforting: to bow in awe before a mysterious God he cannot grasp, perceiving only the "outskirts of his ways" (26:14; RSV). This is the Job of the prologue, but with a difference: the religious instinct is now supported by a theological realignment. Now he not only feels but also has come to believe that it makes sense that God should not be wholly amenable to human reason. He was convinced by the theology of wild animals, the inexplicability of whole tracts of the natural order, the apparent meaninglessness of creatures useless to humankind but created by God nevertheless. Now he knows that was a paradigm for all knowledge of God.

8. The book does not conclude at this point, however. The *narrator* has yet to tell of the reversal of Job's fortunes. There is more to this happy ending of the book than at first appears, for the issues of the moral governance of the world and the doctrine of retribution are still on the agenda. Surprisingly, this concluding episode reinstates the dogma of retribution as the principle according to which the world operates. For at the story's end, just as at the beginning, the righteous man Job is also the most prosperous. Job is here described as the "servant" of the Lord, who has spoken of God "what is right," unlike the friends (42:7–8); and when he has prayed for forgiveness of the friends' "folly" he is rewarded with twice the possessions he had at first (42:10).

It must be admitted that the ending of the book undercuts to some extent the divine speeches of chapters 38–41. For although the Lord has implied that questions of justice and retribution are not the central ones, the narrator's concluding word is that after all the principle of retribution stands almost unscathed by Job's experience. By rights, according to the principle, the innocent Job should never have suffered at all; so the principle was partially defective. Yet in the end the principle becomes enshrined in the history of Job, and he functions as a prime witness to its general validity. Even if in every instance it does not explain human fates, in the main it is affirmed by the Book of Job as the truth about the moral universe.

Readings

All readers of biblical texts, as of any other texts, bring their own interests, prejudices, and presuppositions with them. While they would be wrong to insist that the Bible should say what they want it to say, they would be equally wrong to think that in reading the Bible it does not matter what they themselves already believe. For in no activity, and certainly not in reading the Bible, can one hide or abandon one's values without doing violence to one's own integrity. If one is, for example, a feminist, a pacifist, or a vegetarian, it will be important to oneself to ask what the text has to say, or fails to say, about these issues. One will recognize that the text may have little

concern with such matters, but if they are of serious concern to the reader they may be legitimately put on the agenda for interpretation, that is, the mutual activity that goes on between text and reader.

What usually happens when we bring *our* questions to the text instead of insisting always that the text set the agenda is that the text is illuminated in unpredictable ways. Furthermore, one need not be a feminist or a Christian, for example, to find readings from these perspectives interesting. The more readings, the more stereoscopic our picture of the Book of Job.

A feminist reading. A feminist reading of any text begins from the premise that in the history of civilization women have been regarded as inferior to men and have been excluded from positions of public influence. Assuming that we are right to reject these historic attitudes, we are now in a position to examine what effect the suppression of women has had upon literature, to what extent literature has abetted their subjection, or to what extent it contains materials subversive of a social order that has been unjust to women. Biblical texts come, of course, from male-dominated societies and reflect male interests. A feminist reading focuses both on the presence of women where they do occur in texts and on their absence from texts where we would have expected them to occur.

The feminist reader of Job notes first that in this great work of literature all the six principal characters (including God!) are male. The book, not surprisingly, thus subserves the outlook of an unthinkingly male-oriented culture that weighty matters of intellectual and theological inquiry are the preserve of males and that women have no place in such discussions. The outstanding stature of the Book of Job among world literature only reinforces the influence of its view of women.

The role of the one woman in the Book of Job fits exactly with the overall pattern. Job's wife functions in the narrative almost entirely as a foil to the male friends. Whereas they deliver themselves of formal, rationally argued speeches, she bursts out emotionally with a question and an imperative: "Do you still hold fast your integrity? Curse God, and die" (2:9; RSV). The last time we heard such words in the book was on the lips of Satan, who predicted to God that when Job lost his possessions he would indeed "curse you to your face" (1:11). At least the impression is given that Job's wife stands in relation to Job in much the same way as Satan stands in relation to God. Is it not worse, however, that anyone should encourage another to "curse" God? And furthermore what can she be thinking to incite her husband to a course of action that can only result in his death? It is little wonder that Job's wife has often been seen as a counterpart to Eve, the ancestral "temptress."

Job himself responds to her with a statement of his piety, which the narrator certifies to be valid: "In all this Job did not sin with his lips" (2:10; RSV). Job is calm, reasonable, and praiseworthy in his mild-mannered reproof of his wife. He does not reject her invitation to curse God for the blasphemy it is, but merely invokes her sense of dignity as he comments upon her suggestion as words like those of "the foolish women," whoever they may be. She is put in her place again with an unanswerable rhetorical question: "If we receive good at the hand of God, should we not also accept harm?" (2:10; Au. trans.).

This is not all that may be said about her intervention, however. If in the second half of her speech she echoes Satan's words, in the first half she uses God's: her husband, Job, is "hold[ing] fast his integrity" (cf. 2:3). It is not clear whether she is casting doubt on the reality of Job's claim to integrity, but she obviously questions the wisdom of maintaining it when the evidence of the great disasters that have befallen them is that God accounts Job a most dreadful sinner. Since she, Job himself, and all the friends have been unquestioning believers in the doctrine of retribution, it is nothing strange if she too should draw the obvious conclusions from recent events.

A feminist approach alerts us to a further aspect of her attitude also. Although the androcentric narrator has excluded her from parts of the narrative where she rightly belongs, as when he notes that "there were born to [Job] seven sons and three daughters" (1:2; RSV)—as though such were possible in her absence—by introducing her at all, even as a minor character, he opens the way to our rereading the whole of the narrative from her perspective. It must be said that, from her point of view, despite her husband's somewhat excessive scrupulosity (rising early in the morn-

ing after his children's birthday feasts to offer sacrifices in case any of them had inadvertently blasphemed God [1:5]), the net result of his way of life has been overwhelmingly negative. She has now been robbed of her ten children, of her income, of her social standing. And for the foreseeable future she must live with a husband afflicted with "loathsome sores" all over his body (2:7).

Indeed, no one—not even Job—disputes that he is to blame for the calamities that have befallen the homestead. God has sent the harm, but the husband has incurred it.

To the best of her knowledge, therefore, she has been terribly wronged by her husband but must go on maintaining her loyalty to him despite the guilt by association that now attaches to her. And although the family income has been reduced to zero, she is not exempted from the responsibility of managing her household and providing hospitality for leisured friends of her husband who come to "console" him—but ignore her and her quite comparable degree of suffering (2:11–12). Her only hope of release from a life of penury and disgrace is the death of her husband and a return to the security of her parents' family.

Job's wife is not again explicitly mentioned in the book, which has led many nonfeminist readers to suppose that she has been banished to the margins on the grounds of her misguided intervention in chapter 2. Yet her presence is indispensable in the narrative of the restoration of Job's fortunes in chapter 42. There he acquires a new family of seven sons and three daughters, and not—we must assume, though the narrator does not mention it—without the cooperation of his wife (there are no other wives or concubines in the story). We may therefore speak of the reconciliation of Job and his wife and of her intellectual development, no less necessary than her husband's, from a blind faith in the doctrine of retribution to an acceptance of the possibility of innocent suffering.

There are several other points in the book that catch the attention of the feminist reader. For example, the picture of domestic felicity with which the book opens has the daughters of Job being regularly invited to birthday feasts in the houses of their brothers, "to eat and drink with them" (1:4; RSV), a token of recognition of females by males not always encountered in the ancient world. It is noticeable, however, that the daughters do not have feasts of their own to which they invite their brothers. The more impressive feminist notation of 42:15 that the second set of daughters inherited property "along with" their brothers (a unique occurrence in the narrative world of the Hebrew Bible) is somewhat undercut by the immediately preceding remark that "in all the land there were no women so fair as Job's daughters" (RSV). It is implied, if not explicitly stated, that they gain their inheritance principally because they are beauties, not because they are the equals of their brothers as the offspring of Job.

The major feminist question for the book, however, is whether its principal concern is in any way gender-determined. If it is at all difficult to imagine an alternative version of the book in which all the protagonists were female and in which at the same time the principal issue arising from the loss of family, social standing, and reputation was the doctrine of retribution and the justice of God, then to that extent the book, however sublime a literary work, may be defective, as yet another expression of an uncritical androcentricity.

A vegetarian reading. Like feminism, vegetarianism is an ideology that manifests itself in various attitudes and practices. A simple vegetarianism may eschew the eating of meat on purely aesthetic grounds, or even as a matter of taste or preference; but a more principled vegetarianism takes as its starting point the nature of animals as living beings and develops a philosophy of the responsibility of humans to fellow inhabitants of the planet. By turning the everyday matter of diet into a set of ethical decisions associated with larger questions about human relationships with the environment generally, vegetarianism is for its adherents a powerful philosophy that influences many aspects of life, including reading. A vegetarian reader will be concerned to see whether the text under consideration uncritically adopts the attitudes of a carnivorous culture toward animals or whether in any way the text undermines those attitudes by a more positive estimation of animals.

There are three places in the Book of Job where animals are significant. In the first, Job is depicted as the owner and guardian of large flocks of animals: 7,000 sheep, 3,000 camels, 500 yoke of oxen, and 500

she-asses (1:3). After the restoration of his fortunes he has exactly double the number in each category (42:12). His wealth is measured almost exclusively in terms of his animals. Kept for reasons of the agricultural economy in which Job is engaged, the animals are involved in a relationship of mutual dependence with him. The text invites us to view Job as the center of a network of relationships: his family of wife and children immediately surrounding him, his "very many servants" standing between him and the animals that they tend, and these vast herds of animals on the periphery. The catastrophe that befalls Job begins on the fringes of this network, as oxen, asses, sheep, and camels progressively fall prey to disaster before his own children are struck down (1:14–19). Further, the purposes for which these animals are kept are equally instructive. The flocks (including both sheep and goats) are kept for their wool and their milk; the oxen for plowing (they are enumerated as "pairs" or "yoke" of oxen); the camels for riding or for carrying loads; the she-asses for milk, for riding, and for various kinds of farm work. There is no eating of meat or "flesh" in the narrative world of the book. This means, of course, not that the author is preaching or assuming vegetarianism, but that an affirmative attitude to animals sits comfortably with the outlook of the book.

Animals next appear in the narrative as the material of sacrifice. After every birthday celebration by his children Job offers "whole burnt offerings," whether of bulls, sheep, or goats, as a sin offering. He fears that his children may in the excitement of their partying have inadvertently spoken lightly of God and so makes the sacrifice that would have been required if they had in fact sinned (1:5). Corresponding to these animal sacrifices at the beginning of the book are the whole burnt offerings of seven bulls and seven rams that God commands Eliphaz to offer on behalf of himself and his two friends at the end of the book. The three friends have "not spoken of [God] what is right" and have thus acted "foolishly" (42:8); they need to offer a sin offering to atone for their wrongdoing. Unlike most other animal sacrifices, the sin offering was wholly consumed by fire, and no part of it was eaten by the offerer. Symbolically it represented the transfer of property from the realm of humans to the realm of the divine, the burning of the slaughtered animal being the means of removing the material of the animal from the earth to the sky, where the Deity lived.

The concept of animal sacrifice is of course aesthetically, if not also religiously, disagreeable to most people today, whether or not they are vegetarians. But within the cultural codes of the book we may at least allow that the animal is not being devalued by the practice but esteemed as a mechanism for communication between the earthly and heavenly worlds. From a vegetarian perspective, however, the point of most interest is that the convention of sacrifice, which is taken for granted by the book, is also called into question by the book. For the net effect of Job's sacrifices on behalf of his children is zero. Despite the sacrifices, they are cut off in their youth by a whirlwind, a clear sign of God's displeasure. The question is therefore implicitly raised whether the sacrifices of the friends in chapter 42 have any more efficacy than Job's sacrifices in chapter 1. Is it perhaps Job's prayer on behalf of his friends (42:8, 10) rather than their sacrifices that ensures their forgiveness?

The third major reference to animals is the most important of all. In the divine speeches of chapters 38–41, the existence of animals proves to be the essential clue to the meaning of the universe. It is not the domestic animals of chapters 1–2 that are here spoken of but the wild animals that serve no purpose in the human economy. Their existence prohibits a wholly anthropocentric view of the world and confirms to humans that the world does not exist solely for the benefit of humankind. In a sense, wild animals are even more valuable for humans than are domesticated animals: although tamed animals may serve to magnify humans' sense of their own importance and mastery over their environment, wild animals serve to impress humans with the fundamental inexplicability of the world as it has been created. The significance of wild animals is even more pointed in the context of the divine speeches, however. For there they function as an analogy to the existence of equally inexplicable elements of the moral order of the world, namely the existence of innocent suffering and of evidence that the principle of retribution is not wholly valid. God has created the world the way it is for his own inscrutable purposes. We can only presume that *he* knows what he is doing, for there are many things in

the world we experience that make no sense to *us*. In sum, in the view of the Book of Job a proper estimation of the animal creation is essential for coping with certain of the riddles of human existence. This is a far cry from an attitude that ignores animals except as food or as pets for humans.

A Christian reading. There have of course been many Christian readings of the Old Testament throughout the Christian centuries, most of them building on the assumption that the Old Testament conveys essentially the same teaching as the New Testament, but in a coded form. In traditional Christian interpretation of the Old Testament, for example, attention has often been focused on predictions or hints of a messiah and even on texts that did not ostensibly speak of a messiah but could be read in reference to Christ.

It is arguably a more appropriate Christian approach to the Old Testament to forswear an exclusively christological reading and to allow the Old and New Testaments to confront one another, with the possibility being entertained that they may be in conflict with one another over quite important matters. The legitimacy of a Christian reading will then be on a similar footing to that of a feminist or a materialist reading. Such a reading represents the personal ideological position of many readers, and it takes their concerns seriously by asking how they impinge upon the reading of the text.

A Christian perspective on the Book of Job first attends to the very first sentence of the book, which depicts Job as "blameless and upright," the first of these epithets also being conventionally translated as "perfect." For a Christian reader, such language, if meant literally, is inappropriate for any human being. Christian theology and culture take for granted that no one is perfect and that even the best of people can never be wholly free of sin. This perspective is part of what has been called the "introspective conscience of the West," fueled by the Pauline convictions that "none is righteous, no, not one," and that "all have sinned" (Rom 3:10, 23; RSV). Jesus himself is said to have refused the description "good" of himself on the grounds that "no one is good but God alone" (Luke 18:19; RSV). The point is not trivial, for it is fundamental to the story of Job that Job should be a perfectly innocent person who deserves nothing of what happens to him. For the reader who believes that such a man has never existed, Job is not merely a nonhistorical figure but a fictive and unrealistic character whose experiences lie outside the realm of normal human experience.

Since no one wants to regard the Book of Job as a kind of science fiction, the Christian reader is obliged to qualify Job's righteousness as not moral perfection but an innocence that deserves better treatment than has been meted out. Nevertheless, the Christian conscience remains unhappy at Job's total refusal to consider the possibility that he is in some way to blame for his misfortunes; it asks whether a person so unaware of his proclivities to sinfulness can properly be regarded as a righteous person at all. In short, a Christian reading relativizes the terms in which the problem of the book is posed.

A second major point at which a Christian ideology runs somewhat counter to the book is that Job's quest for *meaning* differs from the essentially Christian quest for *salvation*. If the fundamental truth about the human condition is that people are sinners alienated from God and in need of redemption from that state, Job's concern for order in God's governance of the universe is a secondary matter. If Job cannot see that human sinfulness, his own or others', should be the first item on his agenda, it may be argued that he has no right to question the way the universe is run. The book could then be read as an extended account of Job's attempt to evade the real question about suffering, which is human responsibility for human suffering.

Another, more charitable, Christian reading could agree to differ with the program of the Book of Job and allow that the issue of guilt and responsibility, however primary, is not the only issue and that the question of theodicy may legitimately be raised. In some Christian traditions (such as the mystical), some value might be allowed even to Job's perception that the alienation of humankind and God is God's doing rather than humans'. But however one handles the cleavage between a Christian orientation and the orientation of the book, it becomes clear that a Christian perspective calls into question some unexamined tenets of the book and suggests its own distinctive evaluation of the significance of the book.

A Christian reading will not by any means always

find itself in tension with the book, however. It will be particularly noticed by the Christian reader, for example, that the book, in dealing with the issue of innocent suffering, establishes an indispensable prerequisite for Christian theology. For if the Christian reader feels unhappy with the unselfcritical Job, such a reader can only be delighted with the way the book breaks the causal nexus between sin and suffering. If Jesus is to be judged by the conventional doctrine of retribution, he is the chiefest of sinners; it is only when the conception of innocent suffering propounded by the book can be invoked that any theological significance can be attributed to the death of Jesus. From a Christian perspective, moreover, the hints of a salvific quality to Job's suffering are doubly interesting: Job is able to pray for his friends, it appears, because of his experiences (42:8, 9). And the restoration of his fortunes is associated with, if not actually the consequence of, his intercession for the three friends (42:10).

A final point at which a Christian reading of Job is illuminating is over the issue of the rationale by which God governs the world. A Christian perspective identifies this as the issue of the principles of the kingdom of God, which is the central theme in the preaching of Jesus. Although the character of the kingdom of God is not a high-profile issue in contemporary Christianity, it is interesting that the parables of Jesus are at pains to show that God's rule is not always amenable to human rationality. Although Jesus never says that God acts unjustly, he does insist that the operation of the Kingdom defies many of the rules of human justice.

In the parable of the workers in the vineyard, for example, everyone is paid the same wage even though some workers have worked much longer hours than others (Matt 20:1–16). In other parables, as in that of the self-producing grain (Mark 4:26–29), the growth of the Kingdom is hidden and mysterious, just as in Job the principles of God's rule are hidden from the world of humans. Jesus' conviction of the presence of the kingdom of God despite appearances and his call for faith in a partly unknowable and partly self-communicating God resonate with the program of the Book of Job. A Christian perspective, in some ways alien to the Hebrew book, engages the reader in critical but associative thinking and opens up a rich new set of significances for the book.

A materialist reading. A materialist reading of a text typically has a double focus. The first is upon the material, that is, the socioeconomic conditions that have produced it, especially the existence of opposed social classes, which may be presumed for every society. The second is upon the material realities presupposed or supported by the narrative world of the text. The former consideration is a historical one that depends to some extent upon the questions of the book's origin (which will be discussed in the second section of this essay).

If we make only the simple and uncontroversial assumptions that the society in which the book originated was composed of rich people and poor people, or that some groups in the society held power and others were relatively powerless, or that some persons lived from the profits on their capital and others from wages earned from their daily labor, we have established two possible socioeconomic locations for the book. Whichever location we determine as the place of origin of the book will provide an important interpretive key for understanding not so much the verbal meaning of the book as its total significance.

That Job is a wealthy man does not of course prove that the book originated among the privileged classes, for poor people often tell stories about the rich. But the fact that he is both wealthy and pious, indeed, the *most* wealthy and the *most* pious, suggests it strongly. For, from the perspective of the poor, it is in general hard to believe that the rich deserve to be rich or can be both honest and rich. Equally, in the world of the rich it is assumed that the poor are dishonest or deserve to be poor. It is an interesting exception to say, "She was poor *but* she was honest." Indeed, the very problem of the book—the truth of the doctrine of retribution—may be said to be a rich person's problem. The rich fear that their reputation for piety may be as fragile as the prosperity that attests it. The poor, by contrast, cannot afford to believe in the doctrine of retribution because they know all too many examples of piety that does not lead to prosperity.

Furthermore, if we accept the scholarly consensus that the Book of Job forms part of the wisdom literature of ancient Israel and that such literature arose in court circles or in the educational establish-

ments that were attached either to the court or to the religious centers, then there is historical evidence for connecting the book with the powerful rather than with the powerless in society.

A materialist approach argues that literature is written, to a greater or lesser extent, to support the interests of the social class of its author. It makes a difference to our understanding of the Book of Job if we read it not just as a literary work or as a debate among theologians but as a work promoting the position of the privileged. In this reading, the book functions to support those of the wealthy classes who are temporarily impoverished or powerless; it assures them that if they have once been in a position of privilege, that remains their entitlement. At the same time it reassures those whose position is currently secure against the fear of calamity. The story of Job is after all one of a wealthy man who deserves his wealth and who, although he loses it through no fault of his own, regains it in the end—twice over. Readers who are wealthy will likely believe that they deserve their wealth and will identify with Job. Readers who are poor and have never been wealthy will find it difficult to identify with Job even in his poverty, not only because he once was wealthy and in that way more advantaged than the poor but also because he is destined to become wealthy again—which is more than the poor in general can even hope for.

If we turn now to the second focus, the world of the text as distinct from the external world in which the text was produced, we can make some observations concerning the material realities supposed or promoted by the text. We first note that the text shows little awareness of the realities of poverty. It never questions how Job and his wife and his domestic servants survive now that their means of livelihood, the livestock, has been lost. There had been feasting in plenty in the days before disaster struck (1:4, 13, 18), and there will be again after the restoration of Job's wealth (42:11). But even in the period of Job's calamity no one goes hungry. We know well enough (though the author never alludes to the fact) that his visitors, who sit with him for a week in silence (2:13) and thereafter engage in lengthy argument with him, need feeding. So too do his clients, servant girls, personal manservant, and wife, who are still dependent on him (19:15–17).

Moreover, when he contrasts his former privileged existence (chap. 29) to his present unhappy state (chap. 30), it is striking that his principal concern in both pictures is with his status, as though he is not suffering at all from erosion of his means of existence. He actually depicts the group of the homeless poor, who "through want and hard hunger . . . gnaw the dry and desolate ground," collect brushwood to warm themselves, and live in caves (30:3–7; RSV); but he does not identify with them. Rather he insists—still striking the patronizing stance of the rich—on regarding them as "a senseless, disreputable brood" (30:8; RSV) and complains that even they despise him. The overwhelming concern of the character Job with status rather than survival betrays a narrator (and, no doubt, behind the narrator, an author) who knows nothing of real poverty and therefore cannot envisage poverty as a moral criticism of wealth. Job's mental and physical suffering is "real" enough and is realistically portrayed; for rich people can suffer pain as badly as poor people. But rich authors cannot truly imagine poverty, and the depiction of Job's poverty is as a consequence unrealistic and unconvincing.

Another interesting attitude to material reality in the world of the text is expressed in the narrative of Job's restoration. We learn in chapter 42 that, after his time of poverty, Job regains all his wealth, or rather double his original wealth. If we ask how this comes about—a vital question for those who identify with Job in his poverty and who also wish to escape from poverty—the answer is disappointing but not entirely surprising: "The Lord restored the fortunes of Job. . . . The Lord gave Job twice as much as he had before" (42:10; RSV). To the poor, this can of course mean that anyone can be made rich by God. But it more likely means: if you are poor, there is no way of ceasing to be poor, short of a miracle. Since in general such miracles of divine enriching are thin on the ground, the story of Job means: even if you are as pious as Job, there is no way of clambering out of poverty; there is nothing you can do about it.

The story knows of no mechanism by which Job's stolen oxen and dead sheep can be regained. It serves to rub in the point made in 42:11 that only *after* God has restored Job's fortunes is he visited by all his friends and relatives, who bring him a piece of money. To him that hath is given. But when he is in need, even wealthy acquaintances do not want to know. The narrator knows his social class well and takes for granted that no one backs a loser. There is not a lot of encouragement for losers here.

Finally, a materialist perspective yields an important consequence for an interpretation of the book in the conclusion of the story of Job: the narrative of his material restoration. Many readers of the book have faulted it for the so-called naiveté of its "happy ending"; after the penetrating intellectual argumentation and psychological depictions of the dialogue, it seems to lower the tone of the book to return to an externalized description of the newfound wealth of the protagonist. Job has in 42:2–6 pronounced himself satisfied with God's answers. He has withdrawn his demand that God give an account of himself, and he declares himself "comforted" (so the second verb of 42:6 should probably be understood) even while still among dust and ashes. But for the narrator the story must not end, and justice will not be satisfied, until Job is lifted from his ash heap and has restored to him the goods that he has been wrongfully deprived of.

Translated into more ideological language, the plot implies that questions of divine justice and human suffering cannot be adequately answered on the intellectual level alone but demand affirmative action. Job requires not just the mental assurance that God knows what he is doing but a public testimonial from God that, despite the evidence, he, Job, is a righteous man. In a culture in which a dogma of divine retribution is pervasive and material prosperity has long been regarded as the most obvious sign of divine approval, Job must regain his wealth for his own sake and for God's. At this point the interests of rich and poor come nearest to coinciding. Neither group will allow that the possession of goods is a matter of no moral or religious importance, and each will argue that the divine justice cannot be fully and properly displayed when wealth among humans is unfairly distributed. The Book of Job thus resists a purely existentialist or theological interpretation; that is, the restoration of the hero's possessions is as needful as the divine speeches for the resolution of the book.

JOB IN HISTORICAL PERSPECTIVE

For the most complete understanding of any piece of literature, we need to consider all that may be known about its background, its author, and the circumstances of its composition. Unfortunately, in the case of the Book of Job, there is little hard evidence of this kind, and we must rely largely on speculation.

Origins

Most scholars today would date the composition of the Book of Job to some time between the seventh and the second centuries B.C.E., with the probability that a prose folktale of a pious sufferer existed long before the largely poetic book itself was written.

The story of the Book of Job is set in the patriarchal era depicted in Genesis, not in the era of its composition. Like Abraham's, for example, Job's wealth consists of his animals and his servants (1:3, 42:12; cf. Gen 12:16), and he himself as head of his family offers sacrifices without the intervention of any priest (1:5; cf. Gen 15:9–10). Like the patriarchs of Genesis, who live 175, 180, 147, and 100 years (Gen 25:7, 35:28, 47:28, 50:26), Job lives 140 years (Job 42:16).

In a search for the date of composition of the book, many have observed that the theme of the suffering of the innocent is found also in Jeremiah and in the poems of the suffering servant of the Lord in Second Isaiah, both of these prophetic texts stemming from the sixth century. Some have thought that the inexplicable suffering of Job may have been intended to be symbolic of the suffering of the Jews in Babylonian exile in that century and therefore to have been composed at about that period. But the author has so convincingly located his narrative in the patriarchal world that there are no clear contemporary allusions of any kind to the period contemporary with the author.

The earliest reference to Job outside the book is found in Ezekiel 14:14, 20, where Job is mentioned along with Noah and Danel (probably not Daniel) as an ancient hero. This sixth-century reference may well be, however, not to the Book of Job but to a more ancient folktale; so no inference about the date of the book can be drawn.

There can be little doubt that the author of the book was an Israelite. Although Job's homeland is depicted as northern Arabia or possibly Edom, and in most of the book Job himself does not know God by the Israelite name Yahweh, and although the book never refers to any of the distinctive historical traditions of the Hebrew people, these facts only mean that the author has succeeded well in disguising his own age and background in his creation of the character of his hero.

The History of the Book of Job

There are a number of indications in the book that it was not all written at one time but went through a history of composition. Some of the major elements that have been thought earlier or later than the main body of the book are the following:

The prologue and epilogue. Since the prologue (chaps. 1–2) and the epilogue (42:7–17) form a reasonably coherent prose narrative, and since there is some evidence that a folktale about Job existed earlier than the composition of our Book of Job, it has often been argued that the prose framework of the book existed in writing for some time before the poetic speeches were composed. It has been argued that some of the differences between the prose and the poetic sections of the book might be more easily explained if they are attributed to different authors. Thus, for example, Job is portrayed as a patient sufferer in the prologue but as a vehement accuser of God in the dialogues; in the prologue (and epilogue) God is known by the name Yahweh, not in the dialogues; and the cause of Job's misfortunes is recounted in the prologue but unknown in the dialogues.

All these differences between the prose and poetry of the book can be better explained, however, on literary grounds. Thus, it is dramatically satisfying that Job should change from his initial acceptance of his suffering to a violent questioning of it. And since the friends of Job are not represented as worshipers of Yahweh, it is only natural that in the dialogues the name of Yahweh should be avoided. It is also not surprising that the dialogues should proceed in ignorance of the events in heaven that have brought about Job's misery, for if the ultimate cause had been known, there would have been no problem for the friends to discuss. Furthermore, it is improbable that the prose narratives ever formed an independent whole: the narrative of the arrival of the three friends in 2:11–13 is plainly designed to preface the speeches, and Yahweh's closing address to the friends (42:7–8) makes no sense unless the friends had been speaking words for which God could reproach them. If they had merely sat in sympathetic silence with Job—which is all they do according to the prose narrative (2:13)—they would not have needed to offer sacrifices to atone for their foolish words (42:8). Even if these paragraphs of narrative should be regarded merely as editorial links between the prose and the poetry, it is hard to believe that any prose tale about Job could have moved directly from Job's patient acceptance of his suffering (2:10) to Yahweh's restoration of his fortunes (42:10) without some intervening events. It is therefore more probable that the author of the prologue and the epilogue is also the poet of the dialogues and wrote the prose framework deliberately for its present place in the book. This is not to deny, of course, that the story of Job may be much older than the book.

The speeches of Elihu. The great majority of critics regard the four speeches of Elihu (chaps. 32–37) as an addition to the book after its original composition. The main reason for this judgment is the absence of Elihu from both the prologue and the epilogue. While it might be replied that it could have been to the author's dramatic advantage to have a fresh interlocutor enter after the conversation of Job and his friends seems to have concluded (*cf.* 31:40: "The words of Job are ended" [RSV]), it is hard to explain why Elihu should not be mentioned in the epilogue. The first three friends have spoken "folly" about God and Job has spoken "what is right" (42:7), but no judgment is made on the wisdom or otherwise of Elihu's speeches. It is strange also that although Elihu's speeches intervene between those of Job and of God, God makes no allusion to Elihu when he replies to Job. The evidence that the Elihu speeches are secondary is quite strong, but it is nevertheless something of a difficulty to understand how an author wishing to expand the Book of Job would have inserted Elihu's speeches as chapters 32–37 but failed to insert Elihu's name in chapter 42. Whatever the origin of the Elihu material, the interpreter of the book must of course come to terms with the shape of the book as we have received it, and must, if at all

possible, explain the significance of Elihu's intervention (see page 183 above).

The poem on wisdom. The poem of 28:1–28 on the theme that wisdom is hidden from humans, who must content themselves with living according to the divine commandments (28:28), has also commonly been thought to be a later addition. It is somewhat strange in the mouth of Job because he subsequently arrives at a similar position only by dint of lengthy divine argument. It may be in fact that the third cycle of speeches (chaps. 21–31) has suffered some dislocation in the course of scribal transmission; for, as the text stands, Bildad delivers an uncharacteristically short speech in 25:1–6, and Zophar makes no speech at all. But even if the poem on wisdom was originally uttered by Zophar, as some suggest—and it is interesting that Zophar has already made similar points, though more prosaically, in 11:7–20—it still seems that the poem on wisdom lessens the effectiveness of the divine speeches when they come. In that case, the solution to the problem may be that Zophar is speaking only about the impossibility of knowing the particular cause of a particular misfortune, whereas God is speaking about the impossibility of humans' knowing whether a misfortune was due to any human cause at all. However the issue is resolved, we must acknowledge the possibility that the Book of Job has been subject to expansions at various times.

Job as Ancient Near Eastern Literature

The discovery in the present century of many works of ancient Near Eastern literature enables us to view the Book of Job within a wider context than that of the Hebrew Bible. Many individual motifs of the Book of Job are to be found in this nonbiblical literature, but no text can with any probability be regarded as a source or ancestor of the biblical book.

From the realm of Canaanite culture, we have the poetic epic of Keret, a king who loses all his family, including his wife, in a series of natural disasters. He himself is in danger of death, but at the command of the god El he finds a new wife and, like Job, begets a new family.

From Egypt, a text with some analogies to Job is the "Dispute over Suicide," otherwise known as the

"Dialogue of a Man with his Soul," in which a man debates with himself whether in his present misery suicide is not to be preferred to life: "To whom can I speak today? I am laden with wretchedness for lack of an intimate. . . . Death is in my sight today like the odor of myrrh, like sitting under an awning on a breezy day." Like Job, the man expresses his longing for someone who will take up his case in the heavenly council. Another Egyptian text, the "Protests of the Eloquent Peasant," contains the appeal of a man, who is suffering social injustice, for his wrongs to be righted by the chief steward. Like Job, he would prefer death to being oppressed by injustice, but unlike Job he is not making his plea to heaven.

From Babylonia, the most interesting parallel to the Book of Job is the work known as "I Will Praise the Lord of Wisdom" (*Ludlul bēl nēmeqi*), in which a pious man is struck down by disease. He is mocked by his friends as a wrongdoer, and his family has become hostile to him. He himself believes that he must have committed some sin, even if only inadvertently, to be so punished by God. He is troubled by his human inability to understand the gods: "What seems good to one, to a god may be evil. . . . Where have mankind learned the way of a god?" He describes his suffering in excruciating detail and appeals for deliverance from it. In the end he is restored to health. An older text, from Sumer, called by its translator "Man and his God," differs from the Book of Job on several fundamental points, but it has many elements, especially of wording, in common with Job. The sufferer here is complaining that he is being made to suffer by God and is being scorned by his friends: "You have doled out to me suffering ever anew. . . . My friend gives the lie to my righteous word." He begs God for mercy: "My god, you who are my father who begot me, lift up my face." Unlike Job, this man acknowledges that he has sinned, and the outcome is that God "turned the man's suffering into joy."

The Hebrew tale of Job, which we may suppose to have existed before the book came into being, may be indebted to such texts or at least to the traditional story material that they themselves draw upon. But the Book of Job itself seems to be a fresh and independent creation. Nevertheless, the other Near Eastern texts do remind us that the issues raised by the Book of Job were not unique to Israel.

Job as Biblical Wisdom Literature

Among modern students of the Hebrew Bible, Job is reckoned as belonging to a group of books known as wisdom literature. These are the books of Proverbs, Ecclesiastes, and Job, to which may be added two other wisdom books appearing only in the Greek Old Testament and now included in the Apocrypha or among the deuterocanonical books: the Wisdom of Solomon and Sirach (or Ecclesiasticus). They are so called because of their didactic content: they deliberately set out to be instructional about right living or right thinking.

These books are generally thought to have had their origin among the circles of "the wise" in Israel, who have been identified as a class of intellectuals or bureaucrats. Some of the "wise" will have been engaged in the education of the young, and others in the administration of government. In the Book of Proverbs, the narrator addresses the reader as "my son," in the manner of an ancient schoolmaster addressing his pupils, and Proverbs can easily be understood as a textbook for students in a scribal school. It would be a mistake, however, to limit the term "the wise" to professional wise men—in Israel as much as in any society today. So we cannot assume that Job or Ecclesiastes is the work of some professional wise man or that either reflects the views of a particular class or circle. Everything about the Book of Job as also about Ecclesiastes suggests that the authors were unique and somewhat unorthodox individuals. The Book of Job is such an intensely intellectual work that it is hard to imagine that it had a very much wider appeal to its ancient readers than it has to readers of the present day. Its presence in the canon of the Hebrew Bible may be as much due to happy accident as to any deliberate preservation of the book by a class of intellectuals or administrators for whom it spoke.

Even though there may be no common social background for the books of Proverbs, Job, and Ecclesiastes, it is instructive to compare them theologically, since Proverbs and Ecclesiastes are intellectually the nearest neighbors of the Book of Job. Next to Deuteronomy, the Book of Proverbs is the most stalwart defender of the doctrine of retribution in the Hebrew Bible. Its underlying principle is that wisdom —which means the knowledge of how to live rightly

—leads to life, and folly leads to death (e.g., Prov 1:32; 3:1–2, 13–18; 8:36). It is everywhere asserted or else taken for granted that righteousness is rewarded and sin is punished (e.g., 11:5–6). And the world of humans is divided into two groups: the righteous (or wise) and the wicked (or foolish). The group to which a particular individual belongs seems to be determined by upbringing and education, and there is little hope or fear that a person may move from one group to another. Thus there is a determinism about the outlook of Proverbs, and a rather rigid notion of cause and effect, which is reasonable enough in material designed for the education of the young but is lacking in intellectual sophistication and, it must be admitted, in realism.

Job and Ecclesiastes introduce that needed element of sophistication and realism into the philosophy of wisdom, calling into question as they do so the universal validity of the tenets of Proverbs. Ecclesiastes does not doubt the value of the quest for wisdom: "Wisdom excels folly as light excels darkness" (Eccl 2:13; RSV). But the author insists on raising the question: What happens to one's wisdom at death? Since death cancels out all values, not excepting wisdom, life cannot be meaningful if it is made to consist of gaining something that is inevitably going to be lost. However valuable the pursuit of wisdom, it is even better for a human being to regard life as an opportunity for enjoyment: "There is nothing better for humans than to eat and drink and find enjoyment in all their activity" (Eccl 2:24; Au. trans.). For enjoyment is not a cumulative possession or a process leading to a goal that can then be destroyed. Enjoyment exists in the course of living along with the activity that produces it. Having already been acquired and used up, it cannot be lost. Ecclesiastes thus inscribes a challenging question mark in the margin of Proverbs.

Job also confronts the ideology of Proverbs, but in a different manner. As we have seen, the Book of Job is an assault on the general validity of the doctrine of retribution. In the framework of the thought of Proverbs, the man Job is an impossibility. If he is truly righteous, he finds life, and wealth, and health. If he is in pain, he is one of the wicked and the foolish. In the end, of course, the Book of Job does not completely undermine the principle of retribution, for Job ends up pious *and* prosperous. But once the principle has been successfully challenged as in the Book of Job, even in a single case, its moral force is desperately weakened. For, once the case of Job becomes known, if a person who has a reputation for right living is found to be suffering the fate Proverbs predicts for wrongdoers, no one can point a finger of criticism.

The Book of Job has established that the proper criterion for determining whether people are pious or not is the moral quality of their life and not the accidental circumstances of their material existence. At the same time, the book maintains that a truly religious attitude does not consist of passive resignation to misfortune, but includes the courage to enter into confrontation with God. Even though the Book of Job dissents from the leading theological statement of Proverbs on retribution, it more than earns its place beside it within the corpus of wisdom literature for its implicit instruction on how to live rightly when one is suffering.

Bibliography

Commentaries

Andersen, Francis I. *Job*. London, 1976.
Clines, David J. A. "Job." In *The New Layman's Bible Commentary*, edited by G. C. D. Howley. London, 1979. Also in *The International Bible Commentary*, edited by F. F. Bruce. Grand Rapids, 1986.
———. *Job 1–20*. Waco, Tex., 1989.
Dhorme, Édouard. *A Commentary on the Book of Job*. Translated by Harold Knight. London, 1967.
Gordis, Robert. *The Book of Job: Commentary, New Translation, and Special Studies*. New York, 1978.
Habel, Norman C. *The Book of Job*. Philadelphia, 1985.
Janzen, J. Gerald. *Job*. Atlanta, 1985.
Pope, Marvin H. *Job*. 3d ed. Garden City, N.Y., 1973.
Rowley, Harold H., ed. *Job*. London, 1970.
Terrien, Samuel. "The Book of Job: Introduction and Exegesis." In *The Interpreter's Bible*, vol. 3. Nashville, Tenn., 1954.

Other Works

Barr, James. "The Book of Job and Its Modern Interpreters." *Bulletin of the John Rylands Library* 54 (1971–1972): 28–46.
Clines, David J. A. "The Arguments of Job's Three Friends." In *Art and Meaning: Rhetoric in Biblical Literature*, edited by David J. A. Clines, D. M. Gunn, and A. J. Hauser. Sheffield, England, 1982.
———. "False Naivety in the Prologue to Job." *Hebrew Annual Review* 9 (1985): 127–136.

———. "Belief, Desire, and Wish in Job 19:23–27: Clues for the Identity of Job's Redeemer." In *Beiträge zur Erforschung des alten Testaments und des antiken Judentums,* edited by M. Augustin and K.-D. Schunk. Vol. 13. Frankfurt, 1988.

———. 'Job: A Deconstruction." *Semeia* (1988).

Cox, Dermot. *The Triumph of Impotence: Job and the Tradition of the Absurd.* Rome, 1978.

Duquoc, Christian, and Casiano Floristan. *Job and the Silence of God.* London, 1983.

Glatzer, Nahum H., ed. *The Dimensions of Job: A Study and Selected Readings.* New York, 1969.

Gordis, Robert. *The Book of God and Man: A Study of Job.* Chicago, 1965.

Gray, John. "The Book of Job in the Context of Near Eastern Literature." *Zeitschrift für die alttestamentliche Wissenschaft* 82 (1970): 251–269.

Habel, Norman C. "Only the Jackal Is My Friend: On Friends and Redeemers in Job." *Interpretation* 31 (1977): 227–236.

———. "The Role of Elihu in the Design of the Book of Job." In *In the Shelter of Elyon: Essays on Ancient Palestinian Life and Literature in Honor of G. W. Ahlström,* edited by W. Boyd Barrick and John S. Spencer. Sheffield, England, 1984.

Terrien, Samuel. *Job: Poet of Existence.* Indianapolis, 1957.

Tsevat, Matitiahu. "The Meaning of the Book of Job." In *The Meaning of the Book of Job and Other Biblical Studies.* New York, 1980. (First published in *Hebrew Union College Annual* 37 [1966]: 73–106.)

Westermann, Claus. *The Structure of the Book of Job.* Philadelphia, 1981.

Whedbee, W. "The Comedy of Job." *Semeia* 7 (1970): 1–39.

Ancient Near Eastern Literature Cited

Gibson, John C. L. *Canaanite Myths and Legends.* Philadelphia, 1978.

Lambert, W. G. *Babylonian Wisdom Literature.* Oxford, 1960.

Pritchard, James B., ed. *Ancient Near Eastern Texts Relating to the Old Testament.* 3d ed. Princeton, 1969. Pp. 142–149, 405–410, 434–437, 589–591.

DAVID J. A. CLINES

Psalms

THE LONGEST BOOK of the Bible, the Psalms, contains some of the best-known and best-loved of all the pages of Scripture. Psalms have been used regularly in liturgy and sung as hymns of church and synagogue, and have provided form and words for personal piety and devotion. Few parts of the Bible have been taken more into the memory of the mind or into the literature of the culture. Because each psalm is generally a literary unit tied loosely if at all to the other psalms around it, it is possible for readers and singers to appropriate individual psalms for whatever purpose without having to be as concerned about the literary context as one must be with most of the rest of the books of the Bible. (The wisdom literature, such as Proverbs, functions in much the same way, Job being a notable exception.) If one uses a work of fiction, history, or biography as an analogy, the Psalms would seem to have little of the character of a book; one senses more a collection of individual pieces. A better analogy would be a hymnbook or a book of poems in which individual pieces have been brought together in some order. One's primary focus is upon the individual piece. There is also a sense that the arrangement of the pieces may have some meaning worth taking account of, and that is indeed the case.

The popularity of the Psalms is also due to the way in which they give expression to the deepest of human feelings and experiences—loneliness, shame, guilt, fear, hatred, joy, sickness, and the threat of death. In various forms the Psalms express the reality of human life before God and give us words to address God about those matters that threaten and enhance human existence. Even more important, they give permission to address the Lord of life. While much of the Bible is understood to be words from God, the Psalms are largely words to God, prayer and praise from the worshiping congregation and the individual believer. Many of them are meant to exalt the deity (praise) as much as or more than to express human feelings or give vent to human needs (prayer). More significantly, prayer and praise are frequently linked together: prayer heard and received by God stimulates in turn praise of the God who has heard and responded.

The gamut of deep human feelings in the psalms on the one hand invites the hearer to identify with the psalmist in the prayer but on the other hand serves as a barrier to the devout reader when those feelings express a sense of God's abandonment or a strong hatred toward other persons (e.g., Ps 137). Their popularity in corporate worship, individual piety, and other modes of the life of faith arises in part out of the simplicity and beauty of their expression, but this beauty and simplicity are somewhat deceptive. The imagery and language of the psalms, with their figurative and stereotypical character, often obscure the specifics of the situation out of which a particular psalm arises. Much of the study of the Psalms, particularly in this century, has been aimed at a better understanding of the who, what, and why of the individual psalms in order better to comprehend their nature and function then and now. The ensuing pages will look at some of those questions as a way of getting a grasp on what the individual psalms are about and then examine the content of the book as a whole.

THE TITLE

The English title of the book is derived from the title of the Greek translation, *psalmoi*, which means "songs." The singular form of the word is found in the superscription of many of the psalms and reflects both their origin in song and their subsequent use in liturgical singing. The musical context is further reflected in the various musical terms (the precise meanings of which are sometimes unclear) that appear in some of the superscriptions at the beginning of individual songs. An alternative title, Psalter, also derived from a Greek term referring to a stringed instrument, is occasionally used, especially when referring to the Book of Psalms as a whole collection.

The Hebrew title of the book is *Tehillim*, a term meaning "hymn," which is a particular type of song or psalm, that is, a song of praise. In a more specific way than the Greek and English titles, the Hebrew title gives the book a particular characterization: a collection of songs in praise of God. This is indeed an accurate description of many of the individual psalms and an appropriate way of viewing the collection as a whole. But, as is true of contemporary hymnbooks, not all of the psalms are true hymns set to exalt God in praise; many are addressed to God as prayers. Whether all of these prayers were couched in song is uncertain, although many of them are so labeled in the Psalter. All of the psalms, however, are poetic in form, and appreciating and understanding them depend upon some awareness of this dimension of their composition.

THE POETIC CHARACTER OF THE PSALMS

The principal characteristics of Hebrew poetry are the presence of balance or symmetry within lines of poetry and the heavy use of figurative language. Both of these characteristics can be found in prose texts, but they exist to a heightened and more consistent degree in poetry such as the psalms (Kugel 1981; Miller 1986, chap. 3). The balancing feature is seen in the fact that a line of poetry is normally composed of two or three parts (usually designated "colon," or "cola" in the plural) that to a large degree match or balance each other. This balancing tendency is found in rhythm through meter (which seems to exist in some fashion in Hebrew, though not in the strict fashion that one finds in other poetic systems); in length, as evidenced in the number of syllables in the paired cola; and in meaning, as evident in the parallelism of words and phrases between the cola of a line.

Parallelism is in some sense the most noticeable thing about the poetry of the psalms and other parts of the Hebrew Bible. The second and third cola of a line of poetry complement the first and second cola respectively, in some fashion. The latter cola may underscore the word that is given in the first colon by saying essentially the same thing in different language, thus reiterating the point and giving the speaker or reader further language and imagery to make the point. (All translations are from the Revised Standard Version, except as noted.)

> The heavens are telling the glory of God;
> and the firmament proclaims his handiwork.
> (19:1)

> In thy strength the king rejoices, O Lord;
> and in thy help how greatly he exults!
> (21:1)

In both of these cases, the second colon makes essentially the same point while bringing out aspects less clearly stated in the first colon: for example, the notion of the heavens and firmament as God's handiwork, and the move from strength to help, which is similar to but not precisely the same thing as strength. The second example illustrates another type of movement from the first colon to the second, that is, an intensifying. The king *greatly* exults. One finds the frequent use of *all* to intensify, as for example in Psalm 92:7,9 where reference to the wicked and the enemies in each case is balanced and intensified by reference to "*all* evildoers." A line of poetry may consist of two parts that express the balance or complementarity by countering each other, as for example in 34:10:

> The young lions suffer want and hunger;
>> but those who seek the Lord lack no good thing.

Within a line of poetry there may be a move from the more general to the more specific. In 1:1 the general and most common term for the unrighteous, "the wicked," appears first and is followed in the second colon by a roughly parallel term, "sinners," and then in the final colon by a much more specific term, "scoffers." Not infrequently the second part of a line may simply carry on the thought of the first part to completeness, in much the same way as one would find in a sentence of narrative prose:

> The angel of the Lord encamps
>> around those who fear him, and delivers them.
>>> (34:7)

The use of imagery is not confined to poetry, but its extensive use is characteristic of the poetic books and certainly of the Psalms. Indeed much of the affective power of the Psalms comes from this poetic feature. One has only to turn to Psalm 1 to encounter three powerful images that are the primary vehicles by which the content or message of the psalm is carried. The dominant or structural image is that of the way. The psalm is commonly known as the psalm of the two ways. The image of the way conveys both the notion of a mode of life or behavior and the sense of destiny or fate. Within this primary image, the psalm draws on two even more vivid similes, a tree that has been transplanted from the arid desert to the bank of a stream and wheat chaff that is blown away in the wind. The former is spelled out in three lines that convey an image of strength, fertility, durability, and usefulness. The comparison of the wicked to chaff occurs in a single line. All there is to say about chaff is that it is gone—it is insubstantial, ephemeral, useless. The concrete, vivid, pictorial language of the similes conveys the point of the psalm far more force-

fully and pleasingly than straightforward explanatory statements.

Personification of abstractions and forces of nature is common in the psalms. One of the most beautiful is the transformation of the abstract concepts "righteousness" and "peace" into lovers who meet and kiss, a poignant image of the harmony that the psalmist believes God will give to land and people (85:10). The personification in this psalm is an extended one. In one verse, the covenantal virtues of steadfast love and faithfulness, righteousness and peace, are lovers who meet and kiss; in the next verse, forces of nature sprouting up from the earth or looking down from heaven like the sun; and in the last verse, heralds who point the way that the mighty and victorious God will march:

> Steadfast love and faithfulness will meet;
>> righteousness and peace will kiss each other.
> Faithfulness will spring up from the ground,
>> and righteousness will look down
>>> from the sky. . . .
> Righteousness will go before him,
>> and make his footsteps a way.
>>> (85:10–11, 13)

Whether in explicit comparisons or in metaphors that describe persons and situations in evocative and sometimes surprising images, the plight of the petitioning psalmist is often described in very picturesque language. The "enemies" of the psalmist (that is, whoever sings or prays the psalm, originally or later) are often seen as animals moving in for the kill:

> Many bulls encompass me,
>> strong bulls of Bashan surround me;
> they open wide their mouths at me,
>> like a ravening and roaring lion. . . .
> Yea, dogs are round about me;
>> a company of evildoers encircle me.
>>> (22:12–13, 16)

The hurtful power of the words of the psalmist's adversaries is described in vivid terms by the use of simile and metaphor in Psalm 64:

> who whet their tongues like swords,
>> who aim bitter words like arrows,

shooting from ambush at the blameless,
    shooting at him suddenly and without fear.
                       (64:3-4)

The experience of being almost physically hurt by words can hardly be conveyed more directly or clearly. The comparison of the tongue to a sharp razor in 52:2 has a similar effect. Equally picturesque and almost horrifying is the image in 5:9, "Their throat is an open sepulchre."

The personal plight of the psalmist in trouble is described with many images: drowning in deep waters (69:1–2), caught in a net or snare (10:9, 18:4–5, 31:4, 91:3), cast into a deep pit (88:4–6, 130:1), plowed under (129:3), or besieged by an army (27:3). One of the most common of the images is that of sickness or physical disintegration of the body. In 6:2 the psalmist prays:

Be gracious to me, O Lord, for I am languishing;
    O Lord, heal me, for my bones are troubled.

Psalm 22:14–15 carries the image of bodily degeneration even further:

I am poured out like water,
    and all my bones are out of joint;
my heart is like wax,
    it is melted within my breast;
my strength is dried up like a potsherd,
    and my tongue cleaves to my jaws;
thou dost lay me in the dust of death.

Some of these vivid pictures of the body in various stages or modes of decay may reflect actual cases of sickness that evoke prayers for God's healing (e.g., Ps 38). Yet the language is so vivid and the imagery so universal and apt as a description of personal undoing that we may be confident that such pictures were used to express the plight of all sorts of persons.

In comparable fashion, an array of metaphors and images depicts the divine response to the human situation. Some of these convey a sense of solidity and firmness in an uncertain world, the most common of them being the rock as a metaphor for God (18:2, 31). Other images point in the same direction but speak more explicitly of God's care and protection:

the shepherd (23:1), the fortress (18:2), the shield (18:2), the wings of a bird (91:4). Still others see the power of God as a mighty warrior (68:1–2, 7–8, 11, 17, 21–23), a great king (24:7–10, 29:10, 68:24, 93:1, 95:3, 96:10), and a righteous judge (50:1–23; 82:1–8; 94:2; 96:10, 13).

Like the depiction of God as shepherd in Psalm 23, other extended images express the activity of God in dynamic fashion. Psalm 33:7 speaks of the Lord gathering the waters of the sea into a heap (or "bottle" in the Greek translation) and putting the deeps of the ocean in storehouses. Psalm 90:2 speaks of God as bringing forth the creation like a woman in childbirth, though most translations do not show this imagery very well. Psalm 104:1–4 displays images of the creator God like colors on an artist's palette: wearing the light like a garment, stretching out the heavens like a tent, laying the foundations of the divine abode on the waters, and riding on the clouds and winds as a chariot.

No summary can ever convey the power of poetry, in the psalms or anywhere else. The reading of them is an aesthetic experience as much as it is a theological one. The capacity of the psalms to touch the emotions and speak from the heart and to the hearts of persons across the ages and in every kind of situation is due in no small part to the poetic form in which they are couched.

TYPES OF PSALMS

If the poetic character of the psalms is inescapable to any sensitive reader, equally obvious is the fact that the psalms fall into certain categories or types, suggesting that even in their individuality they may have served the same aim. Some are clearly petitions to God for help, uttered by persons in some kind of trouble. Others are songs of thanksgiving to God for deliverance, or expressions of jubilant praise, extolling the greatness of God as revealed in the creation and in the Lord's dealings with humanity, particularly Israel. Some speak in the voice of a single individual, unidentified except by the account of his or her troubles or deliverance, while others sound the voice of the community in complaint to God for disasters that have come upon them. Several psalms speak about the king of Israel. Others echo each other in praise of the king of creation.

Such similarities in form and content have been the principal focus of attention in the modern study of the psalms, beginning especially with the formative work of the great German scholar Hermann Gunkel (1967), who recognized that the psalms—at least many of them—were originally oral expressions that grew out of life situations and had their appropriate use by others in similar settings in life. The psalms, then, were not spontaneous, free, individual works but expressions that arose out of particular moments, occasions, or acts of Israel's worship. Different occasions or acts of worship would obviously require different forms, so the task of the interpreter is to try to discern what those forms and occasions were. Gunkel thought that many of those psalms that speak in an individual, highly personal voice were composed privately by pious Israelites. But the type of psalm they exemplify had its origin in worship. The extant examples, Gunkel argued, were loosed from this setting in worship and were expressive of a more personal and private piety than the original setting afforded.

Although many of the psalms in their present form are the result of a history of compositional development, Gunkel's insight that the psalms fall into certain types that were appropriate expressions for typical kinds of experiences and human situations has been followed by most interpreters of the psalms, even if often modified in various ways. The relation to occasions of worship is a point of debate, some arguing an even closer connection to the public occasions of worship (e.g., Sigmund Mowinckel 1962) and some arguing a looser relation to such formal activities (e.g., Claus Westermann 1981). The basic categories that Gunkel discerned, however, still make sense. An awareness of those categories or types, together with possible modifications of the way that Gunkel laid them out, will help the reader of the psalms gain a sense of what the psalms are about as well as provide a handle for ordering, relating, and holding together the psalms in what otherwise might seem to be a quite large collection of totally separate and unrelated pieces. A glance at virtually any contemporary hymnbook will show a similar effort to group the songs according to certain categories, usually on the basis of

content. In discerning the types of the psalms, one must pay attention to both form and content and the way in which they come together.

The primary types of psalms in Gunkel's analysis are the individual lament (or complaint, as it is often called, because of the spirit and presence of complaint and also to distinguish these psalms from lament for the dead, or dirge), the song of thanksgiving, the communal lament, and the hymn of praise.

The Individual Lament

The individual lament is the most common type of psalm in the Psalter. Most of Psalms 3–17, for example, are of this type. This type of psalm expresses the petition of an individual in some sort of trouble. The individual lament, good examples of which may be found in Psalms 13 and 22, typically begins with an invocation or address to the deity (13:1, *cf.* v. 3). Some form of complaint or lament about the petitioner's dire situation is uttered (13:1–2, 3b–4; see also 10:2–11; 12:1–4; 22:6–8, 14–18). This will vary considerably, but the stereotyped language and imagery make it difficult to determine what situation might originally have evoked the psalm. Indeed the use of such language and imagery suggests that the psalm was created as a vehicle of complaint to God that would be appropriate in varying situations (and therefore more readily usable by those who sing or pray the psalm in other times and places).

There is a great deal of reference to sickness and physical disintegration (e.g., 6:2, 22:14–15), suggesting that such laments would have been appropriate in times of illness. One must be careful, however, about assuming that the language of sickness should be understood literally. The depiction of a body wasting away can be a powerful image for all sorts of human trouble. There are many indications that the lament psalms expressed the anguish of persons who were oppressed or put to shame by others. These may reflect situations of economic oppression, slander in the community, or false accusations in the court. Some of the lament psalms are strong protestations of innocence of whatever act or crime the psalmist has been accused of (e.g., Pss 5,7,17,26,139).

Westermann has suggested that on the whole the complaints of these psalms have three dimensions. They are directed to God as a complaint or accusation against God (13:1), to oneself as a self-accusation or description of inner shame and humiliation (13:2), and to others as a complaint against an enemy (13:2b). Not all of these three dimensions are present in every lament psalm, but they are generally characteristic and show that the laments deal with the whole person in relation to self, others, and God. One's individual life, one's standing and place in the community, and one's relationship to God all come into play and are in some sense threatened in the situation that evokes the psalm.

The frequent reference to enemies or evildoers is one of the most notable features of the psalms of lament or complaint. The one who prays seems powerless in the face of these enemies, who are characterized in many ways but especially as wild beasts surrounding the petitioner, warriors who come in battle against him or her, or persons who set a trap to ensnare the one who is praying. These enemies seem not to trust God or fear God's wrath in the face of their oppression and injustice; they mock the one who does and seek to do him or her in. We cannot be sure at all who these enemies or evildoers are. They may have been specific groups within the community at a particular period when the fabric of the community was breaking apart (Westermann 1980, 66–67). But such stereotypical expressions as we encounter in reference to the enemy can be appropriate in almost any situation.

Nor can we assume that the fact that the ones who threaten the petitioner in the psalms are usually described in plural terms means that the opposition always came from a group of people. That can be so, as seems to be the case with regard to Jeremiah, to whom several complaints are ascribed (11:18–12:6, 15:10–21, 17:14–18, 18:18–23, 20:7–18) and who was clearly threatened by groups of people in Judah, including members of his own family (11:21). At times the petitioner may have felt totally alone and threatened by everyone else, but we may assume that in some cases the opposition came from particular individuals. The story of Hannah's barrenness and the mockery of her rival wife Peninnah offers a good example (1 Sam 1). The story shows a woman in great distress who prays to God to ask for a son. The story indicates that God has closed her womb—thus the divine dimension in the story—and that Peninnah,

who has had children by their common husband, Elkanah, taunts her and causes her great vexation. Such taunting and vexation are typical of the attitude of the enemies of the psalmist in the individual laments. Hannah's prayer in the sanctuary is not preserved, but we may assume that it would have been something like one of the individual laments, perhaps like what we find in Psalm 6 (Miller 1986, 56–57).

At the heart of the individual lament is the petition. It may occur anywhere in the psalm and more than once. Often it is at the very beginning as a part of the initial address to God (12:1). Not infrequently it appears after the complaint proper (13:3; 22:11, 19–21). It may include a call to God to hear in the face of the often-expressed sense of absence or silence on the part of God (see the frequent references to God hiding the face). It may also contain a plea for help or deliverance, the overthrow of the enemies (if they have been mentioned), and the extrication of the psalmist from the present plight.

The petition may be accompanied by what have been called "motivation clauses" to urge God's intervention. The category is somewhat nebulous, but there seem to be various ways in which God can be pressed to respond. This may include references to God's compassion or righteousness on the assumption that once reminded of the Lord's character as a righteous God, the Lord will act accordingly (e.g., 25:6, 7b, 8, 11). The expression "for thy name's sake" (25:11) and similar expressions, such as "according to thy righteousness" (35:24), "for the sake of thy steadfast love" (6:4), all function to call upon God to act according to what the petitioner knows is God's nature and character and thus to fulfill God's avowed purpose to provide righteousness and steadfast love. In some cases a form of the complaint serves as a ground for the petition and thus as a kind of motivation. This is usually signaled when there is a petition followed by a reason for it (6:2). The very insignificance or humiliation of the petitioner, his or her state as one who is too weak to endure in this situation, can be a motivating factor (86:1), as can also the fact that the petitioner has sought to do right and has trusted in God. Such grounding of the pleas assumes what we find elsewhere in the Bible—that God responds to the small and the weak and will vindicate the way of the righteous.

A significant feature of the individual laments is the presence of some assertions of trust or confidence on the part of the petitioner. This may be a general statement of trust (13:5, 22:9–10) or an explicit claim that God has heard the prayer of the petitioner (6:8–9). Such assertions may represent turning points in the psalm: the petitioner has received some indication of the divine response, as for example in 6:8–9 and 22:21b (translated as "You have answered me from the horns of the wild oxen"; cf. 35:3b). Sometimes this confidence leads to a concluding vow of praise (7:17, 13:6). Some psalms are virtually entirely expressions of trust and confidence in God (e.g., Pss 11, 16, 23, 131).

Several suggestions have been made regarding the difficult question of what were the typical occasions or settings in which such individual prayers were used. Noting the frequent references to sickness in the psalms and the indications in some cases of a sense of connection between sin and guilt and sickness (32:1–4, 38:1–11), some interpreters have suggested that many of the individual prayers or laments belonged to occasions of sickness and possible ritual acts associated with the healing process or even to occasions of thanksgiving when there was recovery. Others, noting the number of psalms in which the petitioner seems to be wrongly accused of something (e.g., Pss 4, 5, 7, 17, 26), have suggested that these psalms belonged to occasions when such persons came to the sanctuary and lifted their petitions to God and asked to be exonerated. Explicit biblical references from outside the psalms to the handling of legal cases at the sanctuary (e.g., Exod 22:8–9; Deut 17:8–13; 1 Kgs 8:31–32) give plausibility to such a suggestion. In a more general fashion, the story of Hannah's prayer for a child in 1 Samuel 1 shows an occasion in which an individual in trouble and great distress went into the sanctuary during one of the public occasions of worship and prayed for God's help. Her weeping is consistent with a note that is frequently sounded in these prayers. The response of the priest Eli and Hannah's consequent vow are also consistent with elements discernible in these individual complaints to God.

It has been suggested by some that such prayers may not have belonged to the sphere of the sanctuary and public worship at all but took place within the context of the family or clan. Persons threatened by any of a wide range of problems went to a ritual expert within the family and participated in a ritual of healing that involved both words and acts. Healing involved rehabilitation of the individual and thus restoration of clan solidarity and harmony. Whether or not this proposed setting can be claimed with full certitude, the proposal does remind us that these prayers did not necessarily have to take place in the sanctuary or in the context of public worship, although they may have done so. Moreover, since the prayers were used by the community over a period of time, we cannot be certain that they had any fixed setting at all. Walter Brueggemann (1984) has observed that many of the psalms reflect aspects of the human experience common to all. They move between the extremities of orientation, when life is settled and one's existence proceeds in essentially harmonious and satisfactory fashion, and disorientation, when life is troubled and one's own activities or the acts of others threaten the self with disintegration. God's help in the process of recovery leads to a reorientation, a renewal, and extravagant thanksgiving and praise to God. Such a construct may not tell us much about the original settings in which the psalms were used, but it is quite consistent with the continuing use of the psalms throughout the centuries as they have become loosed from particular cultic settings.

Songs of Thanksgiving

The Psalter also contains songs of thanksgiving that were probably sung by persons who had prayed to God for help in situations of distress. The long concluding part of Psalm 22 (vv. 22–31) shows the one who has been in the very depths and cried out to God now making confession and thanksgiving before others. Psalm 122 (v.4) tells of persons coming to the sanctuary in Jerusalem to give thanks. In Exodus 18:10, 1 Samuel 25:32, and 1 Kings 1:48, individuals offer brief expressions of thanksgiving to God for having acted in their behalf. Psalms 30 and 116 are examples of songs of thanksgiving that share attributes in common, especially initial declarations of praise and thanksgiving (30:1, 116:1–2), which often are repeated at the end of the psalm and may occur elsewhere within; some narrative account of what God did to deliver the psalmist (30:6–12a, 116:3–11); acknowledgment of the Lord's deliverance from trouble (30:1b, 2b, 3b, 11; 116:1b, 2, 6–8); and at times a declaration of intention to present offerings of thanksgiving in fulfillment of vows made when the prayer for help was uttered (66:13–15, 116:12–19). The narrative of the past situation will usually tell something of the plight as well as what God did to extricate the petitioner from it. Because of the characteristic reporting of the past trouble and because the ultimate aim of the song of thanksgiving is to praise God, Westermann has called this type of prayer narrative praise. In Brueggemann's categories these psalms are expressions of that reorientation which comes from having experienced God's power and presence just as all had seemed lost.

The Communal Lament

While most of the prayer or petition psalms are couched in first-person or other individual terms, there are some psalms that are explicitly couched as the words of the community, which cries out to God in complaint because of the trouble that has come upon it. These are like the individual psalms of complaint or lament except that the complaint against God is even stronger; moreover, the community appeals to the covenantal relationship as a basis for expecting God's help. Whatever may have been the disaster or its cause, such prayers, of which the clearest examples are Psalms 44, 60, 74, 79, 83, and 89, do not represent confessions of sin. They are, rather, prayers that assume that God, whose own fate and reputation are wrapped up in the fate of the people, would not want to let the people be oppressed forever. These prayers seek to remind God of the Lord's past activity in their behalf and of the relationship that has always existed (with frequent references to "your" people, heritage, right hand, arm, etc.) and to affirm and insist upon the relationship that is the ground of the appeal. Noticeable in these psalms is the absence of much expression of trust or confidence of a hearing. A positive outcome is not assumed; one may speculate that the experience of oppression, exile, destruction of the city, and the like has led to a thorough questioning of God and to a belief that the people's cries may go unheard. These communal laments may have taken place on an occasion such as

that mentioned in 2 Chronicles 20 (without presuming the historicity of this particular narrative).

Hymns of Praise

The experiential corollary to complaint and petition in the psalms is praise and thanksgiving. In addition to those psalms that seem to be individual expressions of thanks to God for deliverance from trouble, thanks that is at one and the same time praise, there are many psalms that are straightforward hymns of praise that do not necessarily reflect a particular moment of deliverance as their motivating impulse. Instead they characterize and exalt God, describing the Lord's power and compassion in creation and history. The characteristic or paradigmatic song of praise, and one that shows that praise and thanksgiving ultimately are one and the same act, is the two-line stanza that appears a number of times in the Psalter and also elsewhere in the Bible (2 Chr 5:13, 7:3, 7:6, 20:21; Ezra 3:10–11; Jer 33:10–11; Pss 106:1, 107:1, 118:1, 118:29, 136:1–3):

> O give thanks to the Lord, for he is good;
> his steadfast love endures forever.

The essential structure of the hymn and its theological nature are here indicated. It begins with a call to praise that is directed toward an audience unnamed or named (Israel in Ps 118:2–4, the individual singer in Ps 103:1, all the earth in Ps 96:1, the natural elements in Ps 96:11–12) with directives to sing a new song, praise the Lord, give thanks, shout for joy, and the like. Sometimes the hymn begins with a declaration of praise by the one(s) singing rather than a call to others (Ps 145:1–2; cf. Exod 15:1 and Ps 145:21), but the function is the same. Such a call to praise usually begins a hymn, though not always. It frequently also appears elsewhere in the psalm, particularly at the end, as a return to the starting point and the chief intention of the psalm, that is, to call forth the praise of God (8:9, 103:20–22, 107:43, 113:9, 118:29).

The other primary feature of the hymn is the presence of a reason or reasons for praising. That is, praise is understood to be an appropriate, if not indeed a necessary, response to who God is or what God has done. The reasons are articulated primarily in terms of descriptions of God and sometimes more specifically of the divine activity. God's creative power and purpose are a frequent focus of attention (e.g., Ps 33:6–7, Ps 104), but not exclusively so. One of the themes that appears in the hymns is exaltation of God's transformation of the human situation, God's reversal of the way things are so that the poor and the weak will be lifted up and the mighty put down (1 Sam 2:1–10; Pss 113, 146). Aspects of God's character (see, for example, Ps 145) and God's beneficent activity for Israel or the human community in general are grounds for praise in the hymns of the Psalter, which enumerate aspects of God's work in the past, present, and future.

The structure of the hymn is well-represented in the shortest of all the psalms, Psalm 117. It begins and ends with the call to praise, in this instance addressed to all the nations, and gives as a reason for such praise the steadfast love and faithfulness that God has shown to Israel in the past and future. The basic themes of the hymn are well exemplified in Psalm 147; the structure of the hymn includes calls to praise (vv. 1a, 7, 12), which are followed three times by extensive reasons for manifesting such praise. These include God's creative work (v. 4) and providential care (vv. 8–11, 13–18), the specific deliverance and rule of Israel (vv. 2, 19–20), aspects of the divine character (vv. 4, 5, 11), and the reversal of the assumed order of human society (v. 6).

There are some psalms that seem to belong to this general category in terms of their basic character and function, but which display particular emphases that allow us to see them in some special relation to each other. Several psalms (46, 48, 76, 87, 122) serve to exalt and glorify God by focusing on Jerusalem as the abode of God and the locus of divine blessing and rule.

An even more obvious type of hymn is what has come to be called, whether accurately or not, the enthronement hymn. This category includes Psalms 47, 93, 96, 97, 98, and 99. Its primary identifying feature is the expression "the Lord reigns" or "the Lord has become king." This expression and the psalms in which it occurs have been associated with a presumed annual New Year's feast in which the Lord was ritually enthroned, celebrating God's victory over the forces of chaos and death and the present rule of

God in Zion. The hypothesis of an enthronement festival of this sort, which is most identified with the Norwegian scholar Sigmund Mowinckel (1962), is an uncertain one and not generally accepted among Old Testament scholars.

Whether or not there was such a major festival, the songs may well have belonged to some aspect of the public worship of God that affirmed and celebrated the Lord's rule. These psalms, as much as any other, voice the clear conviction that God is sovereign in the divine world, that is, over the gods, and in the human world, that is, over all the earth and its peoples. They announce the coming reign and judgment of God and so came to be seen in an eschatological light as they were sung in the community. The call to praise God in response to the glory, majesty, and power of God is everywhere apparent in these psalms, as it is in the hymns generally.

The uncertainties about the enthronement ceremony as a setting for the use of these particular hymns leaves open the question of what generally was the setting in which hymns were sung. We cannot be certain, but it is likely that the hymns were primarily used in a communal setting, presumably on any occasion when the congregation of Israel gathered for the worship of God. In the postexilic period during the time of the Second Temple, Temple singers sang praise and thanksgiving whenever the people gathered at the sanctuary for festival and celebration. We even have one of their hymns preserved in 1 Chronicles 16; it is a catena, or anthology, of three of the hymns of the Psalter (105, 96, 106). The contemporary use of hymns of praise in the public and corporate worship of God probably corresponds to their original function.

On the basis of the categories proposed by Brueggemann and mentioned above, the hymns belong primarily to the experience of orientation, to the sense of God's power and provision for life, to the awareness of the order of the creation, and the steadfast love and faithfulness of God. It must be recognized, however, that psalms that may have arisen out of the experience of the calmness of life, its prosperity and predictability, could also function as songs of reorientation for the individual who experienced in some fashion the radical and transforming deliverance of God after having descended to the depths and having sensed the absence of God and the terror and contingency of life. The same words and thoughts would be appropriate in both cases. It is what would have happened in between that is different and significant.

Royal Psalms

There are a number of psalms that may fit one or the other of the categories or genres set forth in the preceding pages but share a common focus on the king of Israel. For this reason, these psalms (2, 18, 20, 21, 45, 72, 89, 101, 110, 132, 144) have come to be known as royal psalms. They relate to various events and experiences of the king, among them coronation or enthronement (2, 132, and possibly others), prayer for victory in battle (20), deliverance from enemies (89, 144), thanksgiving after battle (18, 21, unless the latter psalm had a more general usage at a coronation), and marriage of a king (45). A number of other psalms, especially those that seem to have an individual speaking in the context of a national threat, may have something to do with the king even though they do not refer to him explicitly. The stereotypical language of the psalms and the elusiveness of many of the references make it difficult to be certain whether other psalms were clearly meant to be songs and prayers for and about the king. Psalm 18 is a good example of a psalm that in many ways is typical of lament and thanksgiving psalms but is also a psalm of a king, as confirmed by its use in the David story in 2 Samuel 22.

Those psalms that are clearly related to the king provide praise of the king; descriptions of God's favor toward him; words about how the king is chosen, anointed, and enthroned; and descriptions of his character and responsibilities. Psalm 2 is a typical example of a psalm for a coronation. Its central themes are the choice of the king as the Lord's anointed who rules on Zion and the king's claim to power and sovereignty over the other kings and nations of the earth. This is an example of the court style of the ancient Near East but one that had large implications for Israel's self-understanding and its view, in a later, postmonarchical time, of the claims and power of the anointed who would come to redeem Israel, the Messiah. This theme of the dominion of the king over the nations also appears prominently in Psalm 72. There it is linked to, indeed dependent

upon, the king's maintenance of justice and peace among his subjects. The psalms show a conviction that the ruler's maintenance of the rights of the weak, the poor, and the oppressed was the key to internal prosperity and well-being and external power and security. They also declare, even as they proclaim the Lord's eternal covenant with David and his dynastic line, that the king's failure to keep the instruction of God, to maintain the rights of the oppressed, and to obey God could bring about punishment and downfall (Pss 89 and 132). Presumably the explicitly royal psalms were composed during the time of the monarchy. They likely belonged originally to a collection of royal psalms. Their present scattering throughout the Psalter, in some cases framing larger collections (specifically Pss 2 and 89) and in other cases being inserted here and there (one notes, for example, a grouping of royal psalms, that is, Pss 18, 20, and 21, close together in the first book of the Psalter), points to their loosening from a specifically royal usage. They became a part of a collection that functioned generally in the life of the community after the monarchy, and the efforts to revive it, had disappeared. In that way, they came increasingly to function as eschatological or messianic psalms anticipating the rule of God's chosen one in the future and the universal reign of peace under the leadership of the anointed (that is, Messiah) of God.

Other Types of Psalms

Beyond these larger categories of psalms identifiable by structural or thematic features (that is, individual and corporate petitionary prayers or laments, songs of thanksgiving and praise, and royal psalms) there are other psalms that do not fit easily into the genres described above. Sometimes such psalms, though belonging to a larger category, are distinctive enough to call particular attention to themselves.

Wisdom psalms. A number of psalms (e.g., 1, 37, 49, 73, 112, and possibly 128) are distinguished by their reflection of the interests and themes of the wisdom literature and thus are usually designated simply wisdom psalms. They show a high regard for the law, or instruction, of God (e.g., Ps 1) and focus on the contrast between the righteous and the wicked. They hold at times to the conviction that the way that is chosen will earn its appropriate reward or punishment (e.g., 1, 37, 112, 128) and at other times to the sentiment found in Job and Ecclesiastes that those matters are not so clear and that sometimes it seems that the wicked are praised and prosper and the righteous fall (73), but death is the fate of all (49). Some of these psalms share features associated with other types, and psalms in the other categories discussed will manifest sapiential themes. See, for example, in Psalm 14, the castigation of the fool who says there is no God and whose activities and thoughts are those of the wicked as described in Psalm 10; or see the perspective of the wise that has manifested itself in the final editing of Psalm 107. The reader of the Psalter, in any event, will frequently hear both an affirmation of the wisdom of fearing God and the condemnation of the way of unrighteousness as a way that ends in death.

Liturgical psalms. There are some psalms that seem especially liturgical in their character, such as the short Psalm 134, which calls "servants of the Lord" to stand at night in the house of the Lord and lift their hands to the holy place. Two psalms (15 and 24) have been characterized as entrance or *torah* liturgies. They pose questions about the requirements for entering the place of worship (15:1, 24:3). The answer identifies the moral requirements necessary for standing in the presence of God (15:2–5, 24:3–6), requirements that arise out of the instruction, or *torah*, of God that is found in the legal literature of the Old Testament. It is quite possible that behind such psalms lay an actual ritual of question-and-answer involving priest and worshiper at the entrance of the sanctuary.

Torah psalms. A particular focus on the *torah*, or law, of God is also found in three psalms that belong to other categories but are often considered together because of their concern for the law: Psalms 1, 19, and 119. The latter is in some respects the most unusual of all the psalms because it is two to three times as long as any other psalm and is a kind of chain or anthology of verses and groups of verses exalting the statutes, ordinances, commandments, and precepts of God and expressing the psalmist's total devotion to these expressions of God's will. The psalm is also noticeable because it, like several other psalms (9, 10, 25, 34, 37, 111, 112, 145), is an acrostic, that is, the paragraphs (or verses in most cases) begin with

words whose first letters in sequence are the letters of the alphabet in sequence.

Penitential and imprecatory psalms. There are two types of psalms within the larger category of the lament or complaint psalms that should be singled out for comment. These are the penitential psalms and the imprecatory or cursing psalms. Here again we encounter features of prayer that may constitute a whole psalm or may be an aspect of a more general lament. The term "penitential" has been applied for many centuries to seven psalms (6, 32, 38, 51, 102, 130, 143) because they seem quite directly to be the prayers of a person who knows that he or she has sinned before God and prays for God's forgiveness. Some of these psalms have the reality of sin and the need for forgiveness and pardon at the center of their content and intention, for example, Psalms 51 and 130. Others in this traditional category may be more typically general laments that demonstrate the fact that the relationship with God is, as stated earlier, a basic aspect of the problem or trouble that is experienced by the one praying. Equally important in this regard is to recognize that the problem of sin is not a major one in the laments. The petitioner is as likely to protest innocence as to confess sin (e.g., Ps 7). Somewhat more surprising is the absence of a strong confession of sin in the communal or corporate laments that may grow out of a situation in which the people have experienced some military disaster or destruction, more specifically the destruction of the Temple (e.g., Ps 74 and 79), which was understood prophetically as the judgment of God for the sin of the people. Psalm 106 opens as a hymn of praise and thanksgiving, and not a communal lament, but then becomes an extended confession of the people's sins throughout their history and a prayer for God's deliverance in the present.

It is in relation to those protestations of innocence that one often encounters the rage and anger of the psalmist expressed in strong imprecations against his or her enemies and prayers to God to destroy them in no uncertain terms (e.g., 35, 59, 69, 109, 137, 139:19–22, and 140). The term "imprecation" is a little misleading. These are not curses that have some effect by their being spoken, but rather prayers for God's vindication, both of the Lord's own righteous purposes and of the psalmist who utters the petition.

Such prayers arise out of the rage of one who is truly oppressed. They express that deep anger in the dialogue with God, an anger that often comes out in strong and hyperbolic language. Emotionally, they are quite understandable and make very good sense. Theologically, however, they make sense only as prayers for God's overthrow of *God's* enemies and not just of the petitioner's adversaries. Psalm 139:19–22 exemplifies this well:

O that thou wouldst slay the wicked, O God,
    and that men of blood would depart from me,
men who maliciously defy thee,
    who lift themselves up against thee for evil!
Do I not hate them that hate thee, O Lord?
    And do I not loathe them that rise up against thee?
I hate them with perfect hatred;
    I count them my enemies.

The psalmist speaks as one who is unalterably opposed to those who have set themselves solidly against God's righteous and just purposes, a state of affairs that is made transparent by their unjust deeds against the psalmist.

The various types presented here do not account for all the psalms, and many of the psalms do not fit easily into one category. But most of the psalms are related in some fashion to these types in form and content.

SUPERSCRIPTIONS OF THE PSALMS

Most of the psalms begin with a superscription. These superscriptions, or titles, as they are sometimes inaccurately called, serve several functions. They include musical notes that are often enigmatic but may have to do with the type of psalm (song or maskil or psalm), or the person(s) who were responsible for singing and playing the song (e.g., the choirmaster or the sons of Korah or Asaph), or possibly notations about the melody or tune for the psalm (e.g., "the hind of the dawn" in Ps 22). In a few cases (Pss 38, 92, 100), the superscription says something about the liturgical occasion for the psalm. Most often, the superscriptions contain what look like historical references, particularly to David, although others are mentioned also (e.g., Moses in Psalm 90 and Solo-

mon in Psalm 127). The precise intention of these references is not altogether clear. The identification of David with music suggests the possibility that they were notes referring to authorship. On the other hand, they may have been intended to suggest that the songs were "for" David or "concerning" David.

A number of the psalms (e.g., 51–60 *passim*) have more extended historical notes giving the occasion on which the psalm was believed to have been composed or the occasion in David's life that would be an appropriate context for understanding it. A good example is the association of the anguished penitential Psalm 51 and its deep sense of David's sin, when he reacts to the visit of the prophet Nathan, who condemned him for murder and adultery. These historical notes can provide a point of reference that helps to make the psalm concrete even if it was not composed for the occasion identified. The superscription says, in effect, "Read the psalm as appropriate to such an occasion and you will grasp its meaning."

These superscriptions thus provide a glimpse at an early stage in the interpretation of the psalms and particularly in the continuing effort to relate them to the history of Israel and its leading figures. The assumption that such superscriptions have to do only with authorship, and thus are of no significance if they do not correctly identify the author, is a modern tendency that ignores their place and usefulness in the history of the exegesis of the psalms. Scholars have had little success in trying to locate the psalms in an original historical context. The superscriptions do provide a way of reading the texts "as if" they belonged to the occasion described. In such a manner they are particularized and concretized but also universalized by being connected with figures such as David, Solomon, and Moses, who are in many respects representative figures with whom the reader or singer of the psalm can identify.

THE PSALMS AS A BOOK

More than anything else in the Bible, with the possible exception of the Book of Proverbs, the psalms are generally read as individual works unrelated to their literary context. This is generally the case with hymnbooks, but the psalms do in fact exist in a book, and it is clear that some care has been taken in the process of collecting and editing the Psalter toward its present shape. Along the way, the editors, now unknown to us, have provided some clues for how the psalms should be read and have created some resonances and relationships that might not be perceived apart from their careful and conscious activity. A reading of the psalms as literature involves a reading of the book as a whole as well as the individual psalms.

While it is not so stated, the Psalter clearly has an introduction and a conclusion. There is no superscription before Psalm 1, nor is there one before Psalm 2. It may have been that Psalm 1 was meant to be the introduction to the Psalter as a whole and Psalm 2 an introduction to the first book of the Psalter, which is a Davidic collection. As one reads them now, however, they function as a combined introduction to the Psalter as a whole and as such give some direction for understanding what the book is about. The joining of the two psalms into a single prologue is indicated by several features: the absence of a superscription at the beginning of Psalm 2, despite the fact that virtually all the rest of the psalms in Book 1 (see below) have superscriptions, excepting only Psalms 10 and 33, which, like Psalm 2, seem now to function in some direct relation to the psalms preceding them; the beginning of Psalm 1 with a blessing sentence matched by the ending of Psalm 2 with a similar such sentence, creating a kind of envelope construction around the whole; the use of the image of the way in both psalms (Ps 1 *passim*, 2:11); and some significant shared vocabulary, discernible in the Hebrew text if not always in translations.

The presence of these two psalms as an introduction gives the reader some important clues about what lies ahead and how one is to approach the book as a whole. The first psalm sets forth two "ways," the way of the righteous and the way of the wicked. It pronounces one of these a way that is admired and envied by others ("Blessed is the one . . ."), fruitful and enduring in character (the image of the tree), and known and directed by God (v.6). The other way, by contrast, is insubstantial and useless (the image of the chaff) and leads to destruction. The psalm exalts the way that is instructed by God and suggests that in the psalms that follow one will find direction toward such a way.

The horizon of interest and the plane of action

are broadened with the continuation of the introduction to the Psalter in Psalm 2. The concern of the Lord of Israel, as identified in these psalms, includes the political affairs and the social life of all the peoples. Social justice and peace among the peoples, as well as personal and moral conduct, is the concern of this book. The attentive reader hears that it is not just the way of the individual that is of concern in these psalms but the ways of nations and empires, kings and rulers of all sorts. And indeed that is the case. The Psalms have much to say about the wicked and the pain they inflict as well as about the joy that belongs to those who live by the Lord's way. The first psalm instructs the reader to find in the whole Psalter not only a hymnbook for the worshiping community but a guide for true piety and the moral life.

The Psalter as a whole is divided into five books: 1–41 (assuming Psalms 1 and 2 are an introduction to the whole), 42–72, 73–89, 90–106, 107–150. The division is evident in that Psalms 41, 72, 89, and 106 each end with a doxology. The Psalter as a whole ends with a magnificent hallelujah hymn of praise in Psalm 150, and Book 4 (90–106) concludes with hallelujah hymns (104–106) as well as a final doxology. A tradition as old as the Midrash on the Psalms has compared this division into five books with the five books of the Torah, or Pentateuch. The rationale for the fivefold division is not altogether clear. It has been suggested that it reflects a three-year lectionary cycle for the reading of the Psalms in connection with the Pentateuchal readings, but this interpretation has not commanded a lot of support. Gerald Wilson (1985) has proposed that the Psalter was shaped in its final form to address the failure of the Davidic covenant in light of the exile, the Diaspora, and the oppression of Israel by the nations after the exile. In this construction the use of royal psalms at the "seams," that is, the beginnings and endings of the books, is important. Psalms 2, 72, 89, and possibly 41 may be construed as royal psalms. The first three books relate the failure of the Davidic covenant. The basic elements of the covenant, including God's choice of the Davidic king and the promise of protection against all enemies, is laid out in Psalm 2 and confirmed in Psalms 41 (Book 1) and 72 (Book 2). The conclusion of Book 3 (89:38–51), however, indicates that the covenant has failed. Wilson argues that "the Davidic covenant introduced in Psalm 2 has come to nothing and the combination of three books concludes with the anguished cry of the Davidic descendants" (1985, 213). Books 4 and 5 present the answer to the problem that has been documented in the earlier books by pointing especially to the kingship of God and the fact that God is the only ruler who can be trusted in every situation.

Such a reading of the final editorial shaping of the Psalter is quite plausible. It depends especially on how the five books begin and end. It also assumes that Book 4, which has fewer "titled" psalms, was subjected to more editorial shaping than the other books in order to formulate the essential response to the new situation in which the monarchy had failed: Israel's only hope is in the Lord, who is both king over all and Israel's refuge. Such an understanding obviously does not fully account for all aspects of the psalms; nor need one assume that the arrangement and ordering of all the psalms would have been controlled by such a purpose. Clearly some of the psalms existed in earlier collections, and other editorial procedures may have served to bring certain psalms into association with one another (e.g., catchword association of two psalms that have similar unusual words or phrases or share beginnings or endings). In any event it is appropriate in light of the book form of the Psalter to observe the contents of the five books in order to get some sense of what the Book of Psalms looks like as a whole.

Book 1 (Pss 1–41)

After the first two psalms, which serve to introduce the Psalter as a whole and also in some sense to introduce the first book, there is a collection of psalms that are almost entirely ascribed to David. They are largely psalms of complaint or lament interspersed with praise and thanksgiving (e.g., Pss 8, 19, 32–34) and moments of wise instruction (Pss 1, 19, 37). A number of the psalms that are not themselves psalms of complaint or petition are related to these types (e.g., Pss 14, 23, 25, 27:1–6). Although we cannot always be certain whether a psalm was originally intended for use by an individual or a group, most of the psalms in Book 1 are couched as "I" psalms of an individual.

There is a kind of core to the book in Psalms 15–24. Whether or not they reflect an editorial chiastic structure, as has been suggested (Auffret 1982, 407–438), they do begin and end with the two *torah* or entrance liturgies declaring the appropriate "credentials" for coming into the presence of God. At their center is Psalm 19, which underscores the place of the *torah* in the life of every individual and the community and also declares the praise of God in creation. A focus is placed upon the king: three psalms (18, 20, 21) speak for or about the king in words of petition and thanksgiving. By being personalized as David psalms, these royal psalms express both the heart of this universal human being and also the thoughts and wishes of the people for their king. Here we see clearly the movement back and forth from David as a representative human being whose prayers are appropriate petitions for all later readers of the psalms and David as God's agent manifesting the divine rule over the nations and kingdoms of this earth. The David of these psalms has a dual nature. He is always an individual before God; in trouble and joy he anticipates in his psalms the cries and petitions, the joys and praises, of all others who take up these psalms. But the David of these psalms is never just a person but is also and always God's chosen one, in whom all the hopes of corporate Israel are embodied.

This core also gives testimony to the movement from petition (22:1–21) to praise and trust (22:22ff., 23) that is characteristic of the king and of every member of the community who is beset by trouble and foes. It reaches its conclusion and in some sense a climax as the entrance liturgy of Psalm 24 becomes in its second half not only a psalm for the entry of an individual who has tried to walk the way described in Psalm 1 and is so measured, but also a psalm for the entry of the Lord of Israel, who is appropriately declared to be the king of glory. So while the human king is more prominent in this first book (four royal psalms, including Psalm 2) than in the other books of the Psalter, it is made clear that Israel's true king, the one who overcomes all other powers and gives to the human ruler protection and deliverance, is indeed the Lord of Israel, the king of glory. From this climactic word, then, we move on to hear again the petitions of those who trust in this Lord, the prayers of David and all those who are like David. In the midst of such prayers and thanksgiving the exaltation of God as king of all the world and its creator sounds again (Pss. 29 and 33).

Book 2 (Pss 42–72)

As one discerns from the superscriptions, the singers of these psalms are primarily the Korahites and David. There appear in this book and the following one a number of psalms ascribed to Levitical singers from the postexilic period. These singers are known to be specifically the Korahites (1 Chr 6:22) and Asaph, Ethan, and Heman (1 Chr 15:17–19). Psalms 42–43 —in actuality a single psalm—open the book with an individual's cry to God. This person could be the king (see the reference to "an ungodly people" in 43:1) but is not necessarily so. Psalm 44 follows with the community's cry of complaint. After a royal psalm for the wedding of a king Psalms 46 and 48 follow to exalt Zion as the city of God's dwelling, and Psalm 47 proclaims again the rule of God over all the earth.

Psalm 51 initiates a sequence of David prayers, a number of which have been associated by their superscriptions with specific incidents in David's life (51–60, 63). These are essentially prayers for God's help and expressions of trust and confidence in its reality. While the relation of any of them to David's life is historically very uncertain, the superscriptions are very suggestive of the kinds of situations out of which such psalms might spring. They range from a response to the threat of enemy forces facing either the individual or the community to the penitent plea for forgiveness of one who has sinned greatly (51).

Expressions of thanksgiving and praise to God for historical deliverance and the provision of blessing for life (65–68) are followed by further petitions to God for help (69–71) typical of the individual laments described above. The book closes with a royal psalm, one that is related in its superscription to Solomon, probably because of the reference to "the royal son" in the first verse (72:1). The book ends with a doxology (72:18–19), to which is added a note that all the prayers of David are now ended (72:20). That is not technically true, for there are others in the last three books. But the note may reflect a stage in the composition of the Psalter when the Davidic collection was indeed at an end, that is, before the Psalter was extended by the addition of further psalms or collections of psalms. It is the case that in the next two books only Psalms 86, 101, and 103 are ascribed to David, whereas in the long final book (Pss 107–150), which clearly seems to be an addition to the Psalter, more David psalms have been collected and brought into the work.

Book 3 (Pss 73–89)

The beginning of this book is not unlike the beginning of Book 2. Both open with the words of an individual in trouble who yet maintains that God is a refuge in whom the psalmist can trust (*cf.* Pss 42–43). The book then moves to a communal lament arising out of the exile that has a number of literary links to Psalm 73. The communal lament provides the context for reading the psalms that follow: it speaks of the experience of exile from the perspective of one who faces injustice and the apparent triumph of the wicked but still hopes in God as a strong refuge. Indeed, a large number of community psalms appear in this book; only Psalms 86 and 88 of the ones that follow are clearly individual petitions. The experience of God's judgment against Jerusalem and the subsequent exile is reflected in Psalms 74, 79, 80, 83, 85:1–7, and 89:38–51, which shows how much those events and their impact shape this part of the Psalter.

Various psalms recall God's past mighty deeds in Israel's behalf (e.g., Pss 76, 77:11–20, 78, 81) or exalt God as judge over all (75, 76, 82). These serve to establish the legitimacy of the claim that the very God who has punished Israel remains the only, and indeed the proper, hope of this people for the future. The songs that exalt Zion (84, 87) and affirm the divine promises to David (78:67–72, 89:1–37) also remind the people of God's faithfulness in the past. Nevertheless, the wider context of Book 3 gives rise to a tension about David and Zion that has not been as sharply focused in the previous books (although it can be discerned as one reads through Psalms 42–48, and hears the community lament of Psalm 44 alongside the songs about Zion in Psalms 46–48, which teach that it is not Zion but the Lord who dwells in Zion who is Israel's true refuge). Here the placement of Psalm 78:67–72 in between the story of God's care for faithless Israel (78:1–66) and the community's cry to God after having seen Jerusalem destroyed serves to highlight ambiguities. God's promises regarding the Davidic line and the city of Zion (Jerusalem) seem at odds with reality. Although the covenantal promises continue to play a major role in the psalms that follow, this context necessitates some reorientation, as is emphasized at the end of the third book. Psalm 89, a royal psalm, expresses the tension most clearly: it affirms the Davidic covenant in the strongest of terms in verses 1–37 but ends with the lament of the people because their experience has indicated that indeed the Davidic king has been rejected by God.

Book 4 (Pss 90–106)

This book begins with the only psalm ascribed to Moses. As in Deuteronomy 33:1 and Joshua 14:6, he is here called "the man of God," a characterization that is consistent with the intercessory role found in the portrait of Moses in the Pentateuch. Book 4 also picks up in some sense where the last book left off. The prayer ascribed to Israel's earliest leader acknowledges the people's sin and the appropriateness of God's judgment, but it also declares that the Lord, who has been the refuge of God's people throughout all the generations (vv. 1–2), is still Israel's only hope and the one to whom all its prayers are to be raised (vv. 12–17). By its language, the psalm is a prayer about the human condition in general, but in the light of the literary context in which it is set it is also a prayer about the specific condition of a people that has undergone the judgment of God.

The reliability of God's protecting care is then affirmed in the two psalms that follow, both of which can be read as psalms of an individual, as prayers of the leader of the people, or even as prayers reflecting the trust and thanksgiving of the whole community. The theme of God as refuge in Psalm 90 is picked up in Psalm 91, and the prayers of Psalm 90 for God's steadfast love and the manifestation of God's work are seen as answered and grounds for praise in Psalm 92.

The core of this book is the group of enthronement psalms that appears in Psalms 93–99. Psalm 94 does not belong to that category but reiterates the theme of God as refuge, a dominant theme anticipated in the introduction to the Psalter (2:12). In its declaration of God as judge of the earth, however, Psalm 94 anticipates a basic declaration of the enthronement psalms (96:13, 97:6–9, 98:9, 99:4): the

affirmation of the Lord's rule over all the earth and all the gods. These psalms are in some sense the foundation stone of the Psalter, anticipated in the introduction (Ps 2), in which the manifestation of that rule centers in the chosen king. The prayers of the king are still present in Book 4 in the words of Psalm 101, although there is no explicit reference to the king. That psalm is a kind of code of conduct for Israel's ruler, set in contrast to the actual failure of many of Israel's kings to rule with justice and obedience. But in the enthronement psalms there is no word of any human king.

It is not surprising that these psalms have often been seen in relation to the oracles contained in Isaiah (40–55). Like the prophecies of the anonymous prophet of the exile they declare, against the misleading evidence of history, that the Lord, the God of Israel, is indeed the one who controls history, judging the nations of the earth and the world of the gods. All the claims of the gods of the nations to power in history are considered as naught in these psalms. Whatever Israel's present experience may suggest, it is the Lord who reigns. An appropriate doxology to the claims of these psalms is then sounded in the familiar Psalm 100.

A further development in the movement of thought of the Psalter is to be noted as one moves through Book 4. That is the gradual shift from the dominant mood and word of complaint or supplication in the psalms of petition to a note of praise that grows increasingly louder. That note has not been absent in the previous books, and the prayers of complaint and petition will not disappear, as is indicated by Psalm 102, a general "prayer of one afflicted, when he is faint and pours out his complaint before the Lord" (v. 1). But the enthronement psalms themselves are hymns of praise, as are the psalms that follow in Book 4 (103–106); they praise God's providential care and deliverance in time of trouble (103), God's creative work (104), God's great deeds on behalf of the people (105), and God's judgment of them (106). The fourth book closes, like Book 3, with the experience of exile and the judgment of God and a prayer for God's delivering power to be manifest once again in the life of this people (106:40–47). The growing note of praise is accented in the final verses of the book (106:47–48).

Book 5 (Pss 107–150)

The direction signaled in the preceding book continues in the final book of the Psalter. The book begins with both the note of praise and the assumption of the experience of exile and return from exile (107:1–3). The prayer at the end of Book 4, "and gather us from among the nations" (106:47), is answered at the beginning of Book 5:

> Let the redeemed of the Lord say so,
> whom he has redeemed from trouble
> and *gathered in from the lands,*
> from the east and from the west,
> from the north and from the south.
> (107:2–3; emphasis added)

As with the beginning of Book 4, the opening psalm of Book 5 speaks in two ways: out of the particular experience of Israel in exile and return from exile and also as a song of thanksgiving for the great variety of situations in which people have known God's delivering power. The focus on God's steadfast love and the manifestation of God's work that was prominent in the opening psalms of Book 4 is echoed here also in the refrain "Let them thank the Lord for his steadfast love,/for his wonderful works to humankind" (Au. trans.). The refrain's fourfold repetition in verses 8, 15, 21, and 31 accentuates the two realities of God's steadfast love and God's work as the grounds for the praise of Israel.

Psalms 108–118 are primarily songs of praise. The exceptions are Psalm 109, which may be read as growing out of the experience of defeat at the hands of enemies described in Psalm 108, and Psalm 110, a royal psalm. The note of praise is so dominant in these psalms that even the wisdom psalm 112 is brought under its control with its opening, "Praise the Lord," and its linguistic and literary affinities with Psalm 111. It echoes some of the themes of the first psalm and anticipates the same in the great centerpiece of this book, Psalm 119. The sequence of Psalms 113–118 has come to play a role in Jewish liturgical tradition in association with the annual festivals.

The carefully worked out, long Psalm 119 echoes and develops the themes of Psalm 1, particularly the delight in the law of the Lord on which it meditates (e.g., vv. 97–104). The similarities between the two psalms are so striking that it has been plausibly suggested that Psalm 119 once concluded a form of the Psalter in a similar but more developed way than Psalm 1 began it. This hypothesis is strengthened by the fact that the psalms that follow it (120–134) clearly constitute a separate collection that has been put in at this particular point. In the present form of the Psalter, of course, Psalm 119 does not conclude, but it nevertheless stands as a giant beacon that declares the *torah* of the Lord, in all its forms, to be the highest good and the greatest joy for human existence. Whether or not the Psalter ever ended here, there is a clear trajectory that runs from Psalm 1 through the entrance liturgies of Psalms 15 and 24 and the various wisdom psalms of the preceding books to this massive structure that elevates the law of the Lord to its highest level. The reader knows now with a surety that studying and living the instruction of God is the goal of life; the Psalms encourage such study and living as well as themselves instructing in the way.

Psalms 120–134, commonly known as the "songs of ascents" from the superscription that begins each of them, are the clearest and in many ways the most beautiful of all the collections of psalms now brought together in the Psalter. In addition to their superscriptions, other indications that they form a collection are their general shortness; their being bracketed by the longer Psalms 119 and 135–136; the use of formal blessings, confessions, or hymnic sentences as endings; frequent references to Israel and Zion; and the repetition of the same element or line in different psalms. The language and imagery of these psalms reflect the milieu of simple folk, the family, farming, the craftsman, a mother (Psalm 131, probably written by a mother, compares her quieted soul to the child quieted at her breast). Psalm 132, a royal psalm, does not fit this general picture except in its quite important focus on Zion (Jerusalem) and in its liturgical character. Although these psalms may come largely from a lay milieu, they do have cultic or liturgical associations in specific content and form (e.g., 122:1–4, 132, 134) and probably in the superscription as well. Klaus Seybold (1978) has suggested that there is a kind of order to the collection, a progression from Psalm 121, the blessing for a journey at the beginning (still often read at the beginning of journeys), to the conclusion in Psalms 133 and 134, in which the pilgrims are in the sanctuary and experience the blessing of God. Not all the psalms fit stages of a pilgrimage, but the sense of movement to the Temple and return is present. Thematic considerations also account for some of the ordering, as for example, in Psalms 127 and 128, both of which deal with the realm of family and work. Even here a focus on Jerusalem is implicit in the words about building the city in Psalm 127.

The psalms of this collection thus function both as individual psalms and as communal psalms. They present themselves as a kind of handbook for pilgrims with prayers and songs and even texts for meditation (e.g., Pss 120 and 131). Regular pilgrimages to Zion are rooted in and connected with the great return to Zion after exile (Seybold).

Psalms 135 and 136 flow out of this collection quite naturally. Psalm 135 is a catena of lines from other psalms and has a number of affinities with Psalm 134. Psalm 136 is a grand litany that echoes the last of the songs of praise and thanksgiving before the songs of ascents, that is, Psalm 118. The two psalms together serve to identify a kind of paradigmatic song of thanksgiving in the words:

> O give thanks to the Lord, for he is good,
>   for his steadfast love endures for ever.
>   (118:1, 136:1)

The rationale for the placement of the imprecatory Psalm 137 is not entirely clear, although one hears again the note of exile and the cry of rage to God, pleading for violent vindication against the enemies of Israel.

Norman Gottwald (1985) has aptly described the final collection in the Psalter:

Eight Davidic psalms are joined in Psalms 138–45, the only such extended "run" in Books IV–V: the first two strike the note of trust, the next five lament, and the last breaks into hymnic praise which introduces five concluding Hallelujah ("Praise Yahweh!") hymns to climax the work. The last of these Davidic psalms is called a tĕhillāh, "psalm," which is the singular of the title of the book, tĕhillîm, "Psalms." It is the sole usage of the term in a psalm superscription and seems intended as a concluding echo of the title given the entire collection. (pp.536–537).

As one moves from Psalms 145 to 146 and 147, one cannot help noticing their thematic interrelationships in terms of the Lord's justice and transformation of society, more particularly the power of God to reverse the human situation (145:14, 146:7–8, 147:6). All three psalms reiterate the theme that the Lord lifts up the downtrodden and preserves those who love the Lord while putting down or destroying the wicked (145:20, 146:9, 147:6).

The Psalter comes to a conclusion with a loud, universal, and unending ripple of praise to the Lord, who is the principal subject and focus of this book. All the elements of the universe, all the peoples of the earth, are called to the praise of the God who has redeemed and preserved Israel. The last psalm is itself a doxology concluding the Psalter. It is customary in hymns to call for the praise of the Lord and give reasons why such praise is appropriate and necessary. In Psalm 150 the reasons nearly disappear in an extravagant call for "everything that breathes" to praise the Lord with every kind of musical instrument possible. All the proceding hymns and songs of thanksgiving have given the reasons for praise. Nothing is left now but to render that praise: "Hallelujah! Praise the Lord!"

Bibliography

Poetry of the Psalms
Alter, Robert. The Art of Biblical Poetry. New York, 1985.
Geller, Stephen. Parallelism in Early Biblical Poetry. Missoula, 1979.
Kugel, James L. The Idea of Biblical Poetry. New Haven, 1981.
Miller, Patrick D., Jr. Interpreting the Psalms. Philadelphia, 1986.
O'Connor, Michael. Hebrew Verse Structure. Winona Lake, Ind., 1980.
Watson, Wilfred G. E. Classical Hebrew Poetry. Sheffield, England, 1984.

Types of Psalms
Anderson, Bernhard. Out of the Depths. Philadelphia, 1983.
Brueggemann, Walter. The Message of the Psalms. Minneapolis, 1984.
Gerstenberger, Erhard. "Psalms." In Old Testament Form

Criticism, edited by John H. Hayes. San Antonio, 1974.

——. *Der bittende Mensch*. Neukirchen-Vluyn, 1980.

Gunkel, Hermann. *The Psalms*. Translated by Thomas M. Horner. Philadelphia, 1967.

Westermann, Claus. *The Psalms: Structure, Content, and Message*. Translated by Ralph D. Gehrke. Minneapolis, 1980.

——. *Praise and Lament in the Psalms*. Translated by Keith R. Crim and Richard Soulen. Atlanta, 1981.

The Psalms as a Book

Auffret, Pierre. *La Sagesse a bâti sa maison: Études de structures littéraires dans l'Ancien Testament et spécialement dans les Psaumes*. Göttingen, 1982.

Childs, Brevard. "The Psalms." In *Introduction to the Old Testament as Scripture*. Philadelphia, 1979.

Seybold, Klaus. *Die Wallfahrtspsalmen*. Neukirchen-Vluyn, 1978.

Westermann, Claus. "The Formation of the Psalter." In his *Praise and Lament in the Psalms*, (see above).

Wilson, Gerald H. *The Editing of the Hebrew Psalter*. Chico, Calif., 1985.

General Works

Becker, Joachim. *Wege der Psalmenexegese*. Stuttgart, 1975.

Brueggemann, Walter. *Praying the Psalms*. Winona, Minn., 1982.

Eaton, John H. *Kingship and the Psalms*. Naperville, Ill., 1976.

Gottwald, Norman K. *The Hebrew Bible*. Philadelphia, 1985.

Keel, Othmar. *The Symbolism of the Biblical World: Ancient Near Eastern Iconography and the Book of Psalms*. Translated by Timothy J. Hallett. New York, 1978.

Kraus, Hans-Joachim. *Theology of the Psalms*. Translated by Keith Crim. Minneapolis, 1986.

Kugel, James L. "Topics in the History of the Spirituality of the Psalms." In *Jewish Spirituality: From the Bible to the Middle Ages*, edited by Arthur Green. New York, 1986.

Lewis, C. S. *Reflections on the Psalms*. New York, 1958.

Mowinckel, Sigmund. *The Psalms in Israel's Worship*. Translated by D. R. Ap.-Thomas. Oxford, 1962.

Prothero, Rowland E. *The Psalms in Human Life*. New York, 1904.

Commentaries

Allen, Leslie. *Psalms 101–150*. Waco, Tex., 1983.

Anderson, Arnold A. *The Book of Psalms*. 2 vols. London, 1972.

Calvin, John. *Commentary on the Book of Psalms*. Translated by J. Anderson. Grand Rapids, 1949.

Craigie, Peter. *Psalms 1–50*. Waco, Tex., 1983.

Dahood, Mitchell. *Psalms*. 3 vols. Garden City, N.Y., 1966–1970.

Stuhlmüller, Carroll. *Psalms*. 2 vols. Wilmington, Del., 1983.

Terrien, Samuel. *The Psalms and Their Meaning for Today*. Indianapolis, 1952.

Weiser, Artur. *The Psalms*. Translated by Herbert Hartwell. Philadelphia, 1962.

PATRICK D. MILLER, JR.

Proverbs

ALONG WITH JOB, Ecclesiastes, Sirach, and Wisdom of Solomon, the Book of Proverbs belongs to what is called wisdom literature. Except for a few traditional sayings in other books of the Bible, the closest parallels to Proverbs occur in extrabiblical texts. Sumerian and Babylonian proverbs from Mesopotamia, Egyptian "Instructions," and the Aramaic "Teachings of Ahiqar" constitute a substantial literature of this type. Remarkable agreement between a discrete unit in Proverbs (22:17–24:22) and the Egyptian "Instruction of Amenemopet" points to a direct link between biblical and extrabiblical texts. In this instance the biblical text dates from a later period than the Egyptian material.

The Hebrew title of Proverbs, *Mishlei Shelomoh* (proverbs of Solomon), signifies several different types of literature, including similitudes, popular sayings, literary aphorisms, taunt songs, bywords, allegories, and discourses. The Greek and Latin titles, *paroimiai* and *proverbia*, are less ambiguous than the Hebrew. The essential meaning of the root *mshl* implies likeness, hence similitude. Some interpreters think the verb also connotes power, thus an authoritative saying. Both etymology and usage suggest a wide range of meanings for *mishelim*.

Several distinct collections make up the Book of Proverbs. Superscriptions identify seven collections:

1. The proverbs of Solomon, David's son, king of Israel (chaps. 1–9)
2. The proverbs of Solomon (10:1–22:16)
3. The sayings of the wise (22:17–24:22)
4. More sayings of wise men (24:23–34)
5. More proverbs of Solomon transcribed by the men of the Judean king, Hezekiah (chaps. 25–29)
6. The sayings of Agur, Jakeh's son, from Massa (30:1–9 [or 1–4 or 4–14])
7. Maternal instructions to Lemuel, king of Massa (31:1–9)

Two other divisions, 30:10–33 and 31:10–31, lack external identification. In the Septuagint the sequence beginning at 22:17 differs from the order of the Hebrew; in the Greek one finds 22:17–24:22; 30:1–14; 24:23–34; 30:15–33; 31:1–9; 25–29; 31:10–31.

Do these nine divisions require further fragmentation? A separate prologue (1:2–6) and a thematic statement (1:7) introduce the initial collection and the entire book. Stylistic differences between chapters 10–15 and 16:1–22:16 (antithetic parallelism in the former, a balance of synonymous, antithetic, and synthetic parallelism in the latter) invite hypotheses about distinct origins. Peculiarities in 14:26–16:15 such as decreasing use of antithetic parallelism, and frequent references to the Lord and to the king, as well as the presence of a cluster of sayings about hearing in 15:29–32 led Patrick Skehan (1971) to propose a suture at this point. Curiously, the Hebrew text of chapters 14 and 16 has more mistakes than usual.

On the basis of the Egyptian "Instruction of Sehetepibre," Glendon Bryce claimed to have discovered another book in 25:2–27. Topical and structural considerations (the king and the wicked, announcement of the topics [vv. 2–5], development of the topics [king, vv. 6–15; wicked, vv. 16–26], and rubrics [glory, 2:27b; honey, vv. 16, 27a]) supported the hypothesis.

Udo Skladny (1962) divided chapters 25–29 into a vade mecum or mirror for peasants and laborers (chaps. 25–27) and a mirror or program for rulers (chaps. 28–29). He, too, argued on the basis of content and style. In Skladny's view, chapters 25–27 focus on nature, stress the intellectual aspect of folly rather than its moral deficiency, maintain reserve toward rulers, and contain few prohibitions and parallelisms while abounding in comparisons. In contrast, chapters 28–29 concentrate on judicial and social problems, employing an antithetical structure 82 percent of the time.

The existence of at least nine collections in the book suggests a random arrangement. Do signs of intentional structure overcome that general impression? Skehan has endeavored to discern the "architecture" of Proverbs by attending to numerical and alphabetizing "clues." He argues that the numerical equivalent of what he identified as the key words in 1:1 (Solomon, David, Israel = 930) closely approximates the number of sayings in this corrupt Masoretic text of chapters 1–9 and that a variant spelling of Hezekiah (yḥzqyh) has the numerical value of 140, the number of lines in chapters 25–29. Skehan discerned signs of an alphabetizing principle throughout chapters 2–8, both in the number of lines per chapter (twenty-two or twenty-three; the Hebrew alphabet has twenty-two characters) and in various strophes (e.g., in his view 2:1–4 begins with *alef*, the first letter of the Hebrew alphabet, as do vv. 5–8, 9–11; the fourth [2:12–15], fifth [2:16–19], and sixth strophe [2:20–22] begin with *lamed*, the letter that begins the second half of the Hebrew alphabet). Skehan arranged chapters 2–7 into seven columns of text of twenty-two lines that develop the topics in chapter 2. He claimed that the structure of the book resembles a tripartite house with a front porch, nave,

and back room (chaps. 1–9, 10:1–22:16, 22:17–31:31). The liberties he took with the Hebrew text, however, cast grave suspicion on his entire enterprise.

With the exception of chapters 1–9, 22:17–24:22, and 31:10–31 the individual sayings appear to be complete in themselves. Coordination of subject matter does occur (16:12–15, 25:1–7, 26:13–16), and several sayings have the same introductory letter or word (*bet* in 11:9–12; *lev* [heart] in 15:13, 14; *ish* [person] in 16:27–29). Otto Plöger (1981–1983) believed that chapter 11 reveals an intentional design, with verses 3–8 stating the topics (just and wicked), verses 9–14 (17) specifying the effects of conduct on neighbors and society, and verses 18–20 repeating the themes outlined. Hans-Jürgen Hermisson (1968) made a similar claim that chapters 10–15 juxtapose sayings in a manner that forms true contexts so that larger units are discernible.

In the instance of 26:4–5, the juxtaposition of opposites creates a context of complementarity. Ordinarily sayings stand on their own even where they are linked with adjacent aphorisms by the use of key words. Considerable duplication of sayings within a single collection and between collections points to a haphazard arrangement. The appearance of randomness seems to derive to some extent from editorial glosses, for the epigrammatic character of the book invites supplementing.

The superscriptions offer information about the origin and transmission of the various collections, but their reliability is open to question. Three collections boast association with Solomon (chaps. 1–9, 10:1–22:16, 25–29), reinforcing the tradition of 1 Kings 4:29–34 (MT 5:8–14) that this king composed 3,000 proverbs and 1,005 songs. The description of these putative royal sayings suggests onomasticons, noun lists, of the sort discovered in Egypt. They contain a type of nature wisdom, that is, insights derived from studying the phenomena of nature, that differs sharply from other material comprising the Solomonic collections. This implies that if Solomon uttered proverbs of type mentioned in 1 Kings, they have not survived. More probably, the references to Solomon in the three collections indicate royal patronage. Even this concession stretches credulity with respect to chapters 1–9, perhaps also chapters 25–29, which add the more probable name of Hezekiah as royal patron. Many aphorisms from 10:1–22:16 may derive from the period of the monarchy, and a few may have appeared during the Solomonic era.

Two collections originated outside the land of Israel (30:1–14, 31:1–9). A superscription credits Agur with the first of these. Who was he? If one reads Massa instead of "oracle," then the son of Jakeh lived in Edom. Skehan proposes another explanation of the superscription: Agur poses a riddle about Israel and its God. The meaning of Agur, sojourner, points to Jacob-Israel (Gen 28:12–13, 47:9), as does also the question about going up to heaven and coming down. If Agur represents Israel, then Jakeh stands for God. The name alludes to a formula, *Yahweh qadosh hu'* (the Lord, blessed is he). The second foreign collection has a superscription that locates Lemuel, a royal recipient of a mother's instruction, in the territory of Massa. Egyptian parallels exist for instructions to the crown prince, although neither Amenemhet nor Merikare received formal instruction from his mother. Lemuel thus occupies a unique position in the literature of the ancient Near East. The content of this brief text also departs from the usual conventions, especially in its abstemiousness about the use of wine at the royal court.

At least two technical expressions occur in these superscriptions: *hakhamim* (wise men) and "Hezekiah's men." Although most other uses of the adjective "wise" lack a technical sense, here they connote a professional class, the wise. A similar use occurs in Ecclesiastes 12:9, which identifies the author of the book, Qohelet, as a professional teacher, a *hakham* (sage). The expression "Hezekiah's men" designates courtiers who had the responsibility to pronounce learned insights and hence reflect positively on the patron king.

These superscriptions probably represent a later stage of reflection than the actual period of composition of the several individual proverb collections. The information they contain may not accurately reflect the earlier stage of development. Precisely when *hakham* assumed a technical meaning remains obscure, although the author of Ecclesiasticus, Ben Sira, uses the word in this special sense toward the beginning of the second century B.C.E. Presumably, the reference to Hezekiah's men rests on reliable histori-

cal memory, whereas the tradition about Solomon's authorship or, more likely, patronage does not.

Several factors complicate all efforts to date the collections of Proverbs. First, because they lack specific historical allusions, the aphorisms have the appearance of timelessness. Their teachings have universal application and transcend spatial and temporal boundaries. Nothing connects them with any specific Israelite event or institution. Second, it is almost impossible to determine whether certain expressions are to be understood in a literal or an extended sense. For example, "my son" came to mean "my student" in the discourse of the sages, just as "father" assumed the technical meaning "teacher." Which connotation do the words have in Proverbs? The dating of the aphorism depends on whether the language describes a setting in a school or in a family. Third, differences in form and content suggest the possibility that simpler forms and very particular emphases developed into complex essays and poems over the years, and the various collections of Proverbs bear witness to this growth. Fourth, the likelihood of editorial revision along ideological lines should not be ruled out. Fifth, one would expect proverbs that originated in the royal court to reflect and perhaps promote the king's interests. Biblical proverbs do not, and hence may come from a period after the monarchy.

Dating the independent collections, then, poses great difficulty. One can hazard a relative sequence for them, but scarcely with much conviction: 10:1–22:16, chapters 25–29, 22:17–24:22, 31:1–9, 30:15–33, 24:23–34, chapters 1–9, 30:1–14, 31:10–31. Some of the proverbs probably originated within family settings at an early stage of Israelite history. Their compilation may have occurred in the period of the monarchy, perhaps during the late eighth century. This judgment applies to the first three collections. The final three collections may have been compiled in postexilic Israel, possibly as late as the fifth or fourth centuries B.C.E. The other three collections most likely arose in this late period as well, but they are too brief to suggest a more definite time frame.

Within the individual collections, proverbs from various historical periods stand alongside one another. This feature of juxtaposing multiple time periods characterizes chapters 1–9, which has inspired modern interpreters to argue that older proverbs were consciously subjected to theological revision. Several scholars have discovered ten "books" in this collection and claim that later theologians altered the original sayings.

R. Norman Whybray (1972) identified the following books:

1. Avoidance of evil company (1:8–19, except v. 16)
2. Avoidance of the strange woman (2:1, 9, 16–19)
3. Duties toward God (3:1–2, 3bc, 4–10)
4. Duties toward one's neighbor (3:21b–24, 27–31)
5. The traditional character of wisdom (4:1–4, 5bβ)
6. Avoidance of evil company (4:10–12, 14–19)
7. Importance of vigilance (4:20–27)
8. Avoidance of the strange woman (5:1–2 [+ 2:16 or 7:5], 3–6, 8, 21)
9. Avoidance of the strange woman (6:20–22, 24–25, 32)
10. Avoidance of the strange woman (7:1–3, 5, 25–27)

Whybray used six criteria in isolating these books: (1) all begin with the address "my son"; (2) all contain commands to "hear," "receive," "do not forget," and the like; (3) all assert the personal authority of a teacher; (4) all either assert or imply that the teacher's words have immense utility and value; (5) none contains references to an authority other than the teacher; and (6) all use wisdom with reference to ordinary human capacity, not as a personification. In Whybray's view, later editors made two types of additions to these older books. During the preexilic prophetic period they introduced wisdom and equated it with the teacher's views. After the exile editors identified wisdom with God and personified it as a divine attribute.

R. B. Y. Scott (1965) isolated the following units largely on the basis of subject matter: (1) 1:8–19; (2) 2:1–22; (3) 3:1–12; (4) 3:21–26, 31–35; (5) 4:1–9; (6) 4:10–19; (7) 4:20–27, 5:21–23; (8) 5:1–14; (9) 6:20–21, 23–35; and (10) 7:1–27. For Bernhard Lang (1972), the summons to hear functioned to identify the ten books, according to the following division: (1) 1:8–19; (2) 2:1–22; (3) 3:1–12; (4) 3:21–35; (5) 4:1–9; (6) 4:10–19; (7) 4:20–27; (8) 5:1–23; (9) 6:20–35; and (10) 7:1–27. Lang identi-

fied three characteristics of these instructions. They stressed the deed's inherent power to produce an appropriate result, advocated motifs of personal spirituality like those in the Psalms, and warned against the "strange woman."

Although the three interpreters differ over the exact scope of the ten books, they agree that material from different periods makes up the present initial collection. Poems about wisdom and scattered sayings supplement the original discourses. This underscores the necessity for distinguishing between date of origin and actual composition or compilation.

Such distinct points of view throughout the nine collections suggest different originating circles of tradition as well as various historical contexts. Who formulated the individual sayings and instructions? Where did these unknown authors carry out their peculiar task? Scholars have reached no consensus on these important matters, for the biblical text fails to provide adequate clues about the setting in which the book was produced.

The decisive issue—the extent of the authors' professionalism—remains obscure. Did they belong to a professional class of sages? Although many interpreters answer the question affirmatively, Whybray has challenged their response, opting for an intellectual tradition among the wealthy class instead of an elite group, "the wise." The distinction, more semantic than substantive, underlines the complex problem facing modern readers.

At least three settings seem likely: the family, the royal court, and the school. In the clan, parents instructed their children about ways to cope, warning them about hazards of all kinds, and admonishing them to behave in a certain manner. Naturally, the father (and mother) who instructed a son did not belong to a professional class. Once a royal patron appointed learned scholars to the court and entrusted them with official administrative responsibilities, that situation changed. Now a professional class like that in foreign courts began to gather preceptive texts and to foster advanced learning.

Eventually the setting for this activity collapsed, prompting the learned class to search for a new context. That quest led to the formation of a school, perhaps in the third century B.C.E. Around 190, Ben Sira (Sirach) invited young men to attend his house of instruction (*bet hamidrash*). Although André Lemaire's hypothesis (1981) that schools played the decisive role in canonizing the Hebrew Bible rests on a shaky foundation, he has posed a significant question: Who preserved the religious traditions, and why? Lemaire's answer: teachers used the literary traditions as textbooks.

Presumably, literary features representing the distinctive style and ideologies of the three groups exist in the present form of Proverbs. But the royal court has not shaped the material to any extent. A fundamentally agrarian perspective permeates the sayings and instructions. Perhaps the emphasis on eloquence derives from the needs of the court. An ability to speak the right word, a sense of timing, restraint, and truthfulness, equipped a young courtier for almost every eventuality. These qualities also ingratiated children with their parents and students with teachers.

A few of the sayings stand out because of their neutral stance. They describe reality without judgment. (All translations are from the Revised Standard Version.)

> One man pretends to be rich, yet has nothing;
> another pretends to be poor, yet has great wealth.
> (13:7)

> The poor use entreaties,
> but the rich answer roughly.
> (18:23)

> "It is bad, it is bad," says the buyer;
> but when he goes away, then he boasts.
> (20:14)

William McKane has claimed that, unlike prophets, professional courtiers could not afford the luxury of religious convictions. Their decisions resulted from an assessment of political realities, justifying the adjective "secular." Perhaps these neutral sayings constitute fragments of sayings from the royal court. But this proposal would encounter resistance from many interpreters who consider the sayings' objectivity an indication of their antiquity.

The distinction between objective and didactic sayings introduces the problem of literary genre. The primary literary types in Proverbs, sentence and instruction, possess easily distinguishable features. The sentence, or saying, consists of a single line, ordinarily in two equal halves, which relate to one another synonymously, antithetically, or synthetically. The instruction or admonition uses an imperative mode and reinforces the command with motive clauses containing threats or promises. Egyptian parallels to the instruction derive from the pharaoh's court, with two probable exceptions, Ankhsheshonk and Papyrus Insinger, which address ordinary citizens. In the Book of Proverbs instructions appear only in chapters 1–9, 22:17–24:22, and 31:1–9.

Individual sentences often combine to form larger units, particularly where numbers are involved. Numerical proverbs (6:16–19; 30:15–16, 18–19, 21–31) and additive sayings (6:12–15) approximate what William O. E. Oesterley (1929) labeled "small essays." Similarly, a group of sayings introduced by "There is" forms a larger cluster (30:11–14). Sometimes the unit resembles autobiography, a technique that enables a teacher to draw on personal observation to present an example of folly (7:6–13, 24:30–34). Occasionally a distinct type of sentence achieves prominence even if it stands alone. An example, the comparative saying, registers a value judgment about which of two things is the better. ("Better is a man of humble standing who works for himself than one who plays the great man but lacks bread" [12:9].)

Underlying all these literary forms is one fundamental conviction: the universe operates according to a principle of order established by its creator. Astute observers of nature draw analogies for the benefit of humankind:

> Like clouds and wind without rain
> is a man who boasts of a gift he does not give.
> (25:14)

> Three things are too wonderful for me;
> four I do not understand:
> the way of an eagle in the sky,
> the way of a serpent on a rock,
> the way of a ship on the high seas,
> and the way of a man with a maiden.
> (30:18–19)

These guardians of the public trust also examine society, and fashion lessons for the instruction of impressionable youth. Their eyes miss very little, for the characters these teachers portray strike readers as

227

entirely realistic: student and teacher, farmer, prostitute, gossip, nagging wife, thief, traveling businessman, adulterous wife, drunkard, simpleton, courtier, and so forth.

Belief in order contributed to optimism concerning one's ability to secure existence by wise conduct. Human beings believed they held their future in their own hands, and were assured a long life, fortune, health, and renown. To be sure, imponderables always lurked on the horizon, but these occasional incursions of the inexplicable did not destroy the optimism of the sages responsible for Proverbs ("An inheritance gotten hastily in the beginning will in the end not be blessed" [20:21]). The only exception is Agur, whose "human revelation" that there was no God, and that this intellectual position left Agur powerless or weary, challenged the premises of their thinking. But none of these sages elevated order above God, its guarantor and also the one who could set it aside if the occasion called for decisive action.

The sages' optimism gave way at one important point, if one can trust their rhetoric. They believed the fool posed a threat to society's well-being. The sage and the fool stand at opposite ends with hardly an intermediate category. These terms referred to moral attributes rather than to intellectual qualities. The distinctions among fools left little to the imagination, for at least eight Hebrew words describe members of the opposition party as untutored, innately stupid, obstinate, persistently foolish, crude, depraved, irrational, and inclined to scoff.

Such rich language found expression in other ways too. At least three units, wisdom poems, describe wisdom as a woman and a divine attribute. In 1:20–33 her language resembles prophetic harangue —judgment speech, seeking and not finding, calling and not being heard. Like Israel's prophets, she confronts people in the midst of their daily activities. But 8:1–36 has its closest affinities with divine speech. Christa Bauer Kayatz (1966) recognized Egyptian influence in this depiction of Wisdom as a goddess. Unlike the first-person style of Exodus 3:4–10 or Isaiah 43:1–7, which affirms God's revelation and divine intention, Wisdom boasts of preexistence in Proverbs 8. Like the goddess Ma'at, she loves those who love her (8:17) and gives them life and protection

(8:35). Egyptian officials wore an image of Ma'at (3:3, 6:1), who was portrayed with an ankh sign for life in one hand and a scepter, symbolizing riches and honor, in the other hand (3:16). Bernhard Lang has emphasized the polytheistic background of this myth; his approach lends plausibility to an older theory that the polemic against the foreign woman grew out of resistance to a vigorous fertility cult devoted to the worship of the Mesopotamian goddess Ishtar. But the Egyptian Ani warned against the foreign woman, implying that such language may have been a literary convention.

Roland E. Murphy (1981), although he grants Egyptian influence, explains the personification of wisdom and its erotic language as a way to gain and hold students' attention. In 9:1–6, Wisdom builds a house and invites guests to a feast of bread and wine. But she must compete with Folly (9:13–18), who excels in rhetoric: "Stolen water is sweet, and bread eaten in secret is pleasant" (9:17). For young unmarried men, this suggestive language had instant appeal, and even married men were open to such eroticism ("This is the way of an adulteress: she eats, and wipes her mouth, and says, 'I have done no wrong'" [30:20; cf. 5:15-20]).

Considerable controversy surrounds the nature of this imagery. Does the language extend beyond poetic metaphor to actual divine attribute? Many scholars think the grandiose claims in 8:22–31 that a heavenly creature was present at creation and brought God genuine pleasure require a real personification. Gerhard von Rad (1972) stresses personification in nature, which he understood as the self-revelation of God. In all probability, this text in Proverbs laid the groundwork for further speculation about a preexistent divine being who chose to reside on earth (Sir 24) and who was a divine hypostasis (Wis 7).

This praise of wisdom represents an advanced stage in Israelite thought, a kind of theologizing that placed its distinctive stamp on earlier wisdom. But this theological impetus found expression in other ways also. The idea of the fear of the Lord embedded itself in several aphorisms and instructions. The best translation, religious devotion, acknowledges the scope of this concept. The sages believed religion was both the first principle and the essence of knowledge.

A further step in the direction of theological interpretation of earlier wisdom was taken when the teachers linked parental discipline and divine chastisement. Obedience to the Torah thus found an echo in the language of teachers, whose warnings and exhortations gained in authority. Whereas older wisdom depended on the power of an insight to capture the imagination of those who heard it, later instruction reinforced its message by invoking divine warrants.

In the process a decisive change occurred. A sentence was self-validating, because a truth statement had universal application. That is, a truth statement was inherently authoritative. Those who heard it acknowledged the accuracy of the observation, for it rang true:

> Like a gold ring in a swine's snout
>   is a beautiful woman without discretion.
> (11:22)

> A bribe is like a magic stone in the eyes of him
>   who gives it; wherever he turns he prospers.
> (17:8)

> The words of a whisperer are like delicious morsels;
>   they go down into the inner parts of the body.
> (18:8)

Instructions imply a distancing of teacher and student, a gap that required rhetoric to reinforce their content. But these instructions occasionally used proverbial sayings as their crowning argument (1:17, 6:27–28, 9:17). Thus the authority of sentences surpassed that of instructions, despite the opposite impression.

The Book of Proverbs is not a complete moral or spiritual guide. Its maxims belong to a specific approach to life, an ethos that governs everything. For this reason, modern interpreters find it difficult to fill in the gaps resulting from what is left unstated. Like Job and Ecclesiastes, Proverbs is silent on the celebrated deliverances of Israel and its particular history—exodus, Sinai, election, covenant, David—and concentrates instead on things that were not peculiarly Israelite. The religion receives little attention (3:9), and institutions such as prophecy and priesthood elicit no significant comments. The teachers focus on lazy persons, fools, drunkards, gossips, sexually irresponsible individuals, ungrateful children, and the like ("As a door turns on its hinges, so does a sluggard on his bed" [26:14]). Or they emphasize the way to life, honor, friendship, and prosperity.

Their silence on polygyny deserves notice. The sages presupposed monogamy, even providing a handbook for bridegrooms (31:10–31). This description of the ideal wife places a premium on industry and charity, introducing a religious dimension almost incidentally. How should one understand this allusion to fear of God? As a natural climactic observation: "Of course, she worships God!"? Or as a religious editing of an older secular attitude? This question remains unanswered. The evidence does not permit an exact determination of when the religious dimension entered the several collections. Did it exist from the very beginning? Perhaps, but the religious emphasis probably grew more dominant as the years passed. A comparison of Sirach, from the early second century B.C.E., with Proverbs strengthens this hypothesis, for in his day the sage has become a worshiper, and prayer intermingles with sentences and instructions. In Proverbs, Agur's skepticism evokes vigorous criticism that includes citations from Deuteronomy and Psalms (30:5). The prayer that follows soars to unaccustomed spiritual heights (30:7–9).

This practical dimension of the book does not mean that Proverbs lacks theological profundity. The centrality of creation gives its contents a refreshing buoyancy, encouraging individuals to face life squarely and enthusiastically. The heart may have known its own bitterness, but individuals find comfort in the knowledge that God's spirit searched the inner being like a lamp (20:27; cf. 13:9; 15:3, 11; 20:20; 21:4). In addition, this conviction actually cancels distinctions between rich and poor, both of whom acknowledge the same maker. Most important, the book insists that faith precedes knowledge, indeed, that the ultimate goal of all understanding resides in God.

Bibliography

Alonso-Schökel, L., and J. Vilchez. *Sapenciales*. Vol. 1, *Proverbios*. Madrid, 1984.

Barucq, André. "Proverbes (livre des)." *Supplément au Dictionnaire de la Bible*, vol. 8. Paris, 1972.

Bryce, Glendon E. *A Legacy of Wisdom*. Lewisburg, Pa., 1979.

Camp, Claudia V. *Wisdom and the Feminine in the Book of Proverbs*. Winona Lake, Ind., 1985.

Crenshaw, James L. *Old Testament Wisdom*. Atlanta, 1981.

Hermisson, Hans-Jürgen. *Studien zur israelitischen Spruchweisheit*. Neukirchen-Vluyn, 1968.

Kayatz, Christa Bauer. *Studien zu Proverbien 1–9*. Neukirchen-Vluyn, 1966.

Lang, Bernhard. *Die weisheitliche Lehrrede*. Stuttgart, 1972.

————. *Wisdom and the Book of Proverbs*. New York, 1985.

Lemaire, André. *Les écoles et la formation de la Bible dans l'ancien Israël*. Brescia, 1981.

McKane, William. *Proverbs*. Philadelphia, 1970.

Murphy, Roland E. *Wisdom Literature: Job, Proverbs, Ruth, Canticles, Ecclesiastes, and Esther*. Grand Rapids, 1981.

Nel, Philip. *The Structure and Ethos of the Wisdom Admonitions in Proverbs*. Hawthorne, N.Y., 1982.

Oesterley, William O. E. *The Book of Proverbs*. New York, 1929.

Plöger, Otto. *Sprüche Salomos (Proverbia)*. Neukirchen-Vluyn, 1981–1983.

Rad, Gerhard von. *Wisdom in Israel*. Nashville, Tenn., 1972.

Scott, Robert B. Y. *Proverbs, Ecclesiastes*. Garden City, N.Y., 1965.

Skehan, Patrick. *Studies in Israelite Poetry and Wisdom*. Washington, D.C., 1971.

Skladny, Udo. *Die ältesten Spruchsammlungen in Israel*. Göttingen, 1962.

Toy, Crawford H. *A Critical and Exegetical Commentary on the Book of Proverbs*. New York, 1902.

Whybray, R. Norman. *Wisdom in Proverbs*. London, 1965.

————. *The Book of Proverbs*. Cambridge, 1972.

————. *The Intellectual Tradition in the Old Testament*. Hawthorne, N.Y., 1974.

Williams, James G. *Those Who Ponder Proverbs: Aphoristic Thinking and Biblical Literature*. Winona Lake, Ind., 1981.

JAMES L. CRENSHAW

Ecclesiastes

OF MAKING MANY Ecclesiasteses there is no end, and much scholarship is a weariness of the flesh. This play on the epilogue of the book (12:12b) captures its haunting tone and tantalizing power to evoke diverse interpretations. Is the treatise Hebraic or non-Hebraic in outlook, orthodox or heretical, pro-wisdom or anti-wisdom? Does it offer gloom or joy, resignation or celebration? Throughout history commentators have proposed every meaning under the sun. Their weary labor bespeaks the elusiveness of the text: affirmation undercutting affirmation; negation contradicting negation; description countering prescription; absolute opposing relative. If all literature be indeterminate, how much more the Book of Ecclesiastes.

TITLE AND AUTHOR

Qohelet, the Hebrew name, is an active feminine participle unique to this book. Scholars relate it to the noun *qahal*, meaning assembly or congregation. Hence, the term designates a functionary, an assembler, gatherer, or convoker. Linkage to the rare word *qehillah* provides another nuance. In context (Neh 5:6–13) *qehillah* implies argumentation. Thus *qohelet* may signal an arguer or haranguer. Despite grammatical gender, the functionary in question is male. Masculine verbs used for *qohelet* plus the analogy of similar participial forms (e.g., Ezra 2:55, Neh 7:57)

secure sexual identity. Occasional use of the definite article (Eccl 12:8; *cf.* 7:27) suggests an office, though absence of it may signify a proper name or nickname. In Ecclesiastes 1:12 the speaker identifies himself as "I, Qohelet." The Greek Bible translates the word *ekklesiastes*, from which derives the English title. It specifies a member of a congregation. He is called the speaker (1:2), the teacher (12:9), or, ineptly, the preacher.

The author to whom the title witnesses eludes identification. Tradition has named him King Solomon, the symbolic fountainhead of wisdom, but nowhere does the text make this claim. Language, date, and content render it impossible. To be sure, the superscription describes Qohelet as "the son of David, king in Jerusalem" (1:1), and Qohelet speaks of himself as "king over Israel in Jerusalem" (1:12; *cf.* 1:16), but the references confound. They may be a literary device to enhance authority; they may indicate royal lineage; or they may allude, in exaggerated fashion, to a governmental position. If not a political ruler, Qohelet is surely a sovereign of wisdom. He seeks (*drsh*) and searches out (*tur*) wisdom (e.g., 1:13, 2:3, 7:25), giving his mind (*lev*) to know (e.g., 1:13, 1:17). The search brings him recognition as professor, collator, aesthetician, and author (12:9–10). In addition, he is probably an astute businessman, skilled in economic transactions (*cf.* 1:3, 2:4–11, 5:10). He ponders gain and loss, invests in land and slaves, and accumulates wealth of gold and silver. He has leisure and resources to indulge his interests. Most likely, he belongs to the upper class, and yet his public persona hides him well.

Qohelet's personal history eschews investigation. Though he uses the first-person-singular liberally, perhaps more than any other character in scripture, he tells little about himself. The few clues are ambiguous. Some commentators think he was a bachelor (2:18–21, 6:2). Others believe he was embittered in marriage (7:26) and had no children (4:8). Still others declare he was happily married (4:9–12). To all such speculation, Qohelet might well reply, "This also is vapor." The sage knows the wisdom of privacy even as he reports on life lived.

COMPOSITION, CONTENT, AND FORM

If Qohelet the author eludes identification, his book resists organization. Overall structure consists of an editorial superscription (1:1) and three epilogues (12:9–10, 11–12, 13–14) surrounding the text proper. It begins (1:2) and ends (12:8) with a motto that may be an editorial flourish. Within this *inclusio* the body defies compositional analysis.

To meet the challenge, scholars have "sought out many devices" (7:29). Four positions illustrate the disparity. The first maintains that the document lacks unity and is a collection of independent sections, similar to Proverbs. The second posits a logical or linear outline while acknowledging digressions from it. The third proposes a literary structure. It emphasizes correspondence between content and rhetorical devices such as repetition and numerical patterns. Or it focuses on polar thought as the key to design. The fourth view mediates between compositional unity and diversity. Though the book may derive from a collection of individual sayings, it manifests topical coherence and wholeness of perspective. In these and other proposals, enigmas persist (*cf.* Crenshaw 1987).

Readers who follow the order of the text find its content moving forward, backward, and sideways. They encounter confusion, contradiction, and delay. The tracing of a single motif illustrates the difficulty. At the start, the motto "All is vapor" (1:2) precedes the question, "What does the individual gain by all the toil at which it toils under the sun?" (1:3). Where

all is vapor, a question of gain seems oddly out of place. Yet "all the toil" from which gain derives may counter the all that is vapor. If the relationship of question and motto is unclear, then surely one expects an answer in succeeding verses. But the words that follow sidestep the issue to introduce other ambiguities (1:4–11). By the close of the section, virtually the entire cosmos has been invoked, from sun to earth to wind to sea, as well as time past, present, and future; and still the question posed about gain and toil remains unresolved.

Thereafter the text presents an extended first-person testimony about wisdom before returning to the question (1:12–2:9). Even then, the long-awaited answer is slippery. Qohelet cites pleasure as the reward for toil only to dismantle the assertion immediately by an appeal to the vapor of everything (2:10–11). He continues to tease the topic, switches to other subjects, and returns to speak ambivalently. In Ecclesiastes 2:18–22 he despairs of toil, claiming that it yields days full of pain and nights without rest. On the other hand, there is nothing better than to find enjoyment from toil; that is a divine gift (2:24, 3:13). Nevertheless, death and lack of heirs (4:8, 5:15–17) deprive toil of pleasure, making it a grievous evil. Again, however, to find enjoyment in toil is God's gift (5:18). Yet toil never satisfies (6:7); it derives from envy (4:4). But enjoyment makes the difference (8:15, 9:9). Round and round goes Qohelet, and on his words Qohelet returns (*cf.* 1:6b). At the end, readers sputter.

Sampling the appearance, disappearance, fluctuation, and reversal of toil as subject shows the myriad movement of the text. Qohelet is on a quest that defies ordered progression, neat formulation, and assured conclusion. He sees in bits and pieces, first here and then there. His mind associates and jumps, mirroring experience that is messy, fragmented, and contradictory. The composition of the book reflects the struggle of the man.

If there be linear movement, it is the chronology of the life line (Kugel 1985). The early chapters (1–2) describe youthful endeavors: enjoying pleasure, building a career, acquiring property, and obtaining fame. Perhaps the middle chapters show a maturing vision. Interest extends to power structures, social justice, and cultic activities (e.g., 5:1–17). Interpersonal issues weigh heavily: corrupt business deals, lack of descendants, and gender disputes (4:7–8, 6:2, 7:26–28). In the background looms death (6:3). For certain, the last chapters (11–12) depict an individual approaching death. An allegory portrays old age as a deteriorating house (12:1–7). The keepers are arms that tremble; the strong men, legs that are bent; the grinders, teeth that are few; the windows, eyes that are dimmed; and the doors on the street, ears that are shut (von Rad 1972). Physical powers diminish and sexual desires fail as darkness grows. At the end Qohelet dies (12:7). Others attend to his obituary (12:9–10).

Out of many struggles the book produces a testimony. Some scholars compare the literary form with an ancient Egyptian genre called a royal testament. It offers observations on the human situation. The adjective *royal* fits well such allusions within Ecclesiastes (e.g., 1:12). Other critics find a single genre impossible to identify, though they recognize subgenres: proverb (e.g., 1:15, 4:6, 9, 10:8–9), example story (9:13–16), poem (e.g., 3:1–8), allegory (12:1–7), and extended reflection (e.g., 2:1–11, 12–17, 18–26). All together this varied material yields a document of complexity and confusion that fits the pilgrimage of Qohelet himself.

To comprehend his tortuous quest is to know the futility of ordering the text. "What is crooked cannot be made straight, and what is lacking cannot be numbered" (1:15; RSV). This proverb also indicates the difficulty of interpretation. Yet if for everything there is a season (3:1), then even a foolish commentary may testify to wise words.

INTERPRETATION

All Is Vapor

Within Qohelet. The word *hevel* sounds a dominant theme, though it does not cover the entire book. Throughout scripture the term connotes the insubstantial and transitory (e.g., Isa 57:13; Prov 21:6; Job 7:16; Ps 39:6, 12 [English version 39:5, 11]). It signifies breath and nothingness; it bears the negative import of worthlessness and deceit (Ps 62:10, Zech 10:2). The sum total is zero. Within Ecclesiastes the word describes diverse matters that lead some scholars to assign it a distinctive, if not idiosyncratic, usage.

Irony, the incongruous, is one suggestion; absurdity, the irrational, another; futility and mystery, yet others. The common rendering "vanity," while not incorrect, skews the basic meaning. No single translation can cover all connotations, but the word "vapor" suffices here as shorthand.

At the beginning (1:2) and end (12:8), *hevel* appears in the superlative, "Vapor of vapors, all is vapor." As the word permeates the book, it moves from topic to topic and back again. Toil and pleasure, wisdom and folly, wealth and poverty, sorrow and laughter, righteousness and wickedness, risk and assurance, power and powerlessness, talk and silence, justice and oppression, youth and age—these and other subjects come under the perspective of *hevel*. The theme manifests itself in envy of neighbor (4:4), lack of heirs (4:7–8), reversal of fortune (10:5), and impermanence of fame (4:13–16). Occasionally *hevel* parallels evil (*ra'ah*; 2:21, 6:1–2) and often the futile activity of striving after wind (e.g., 1:14, 2:11, 26, 6:9).

These negative meanings lead inexorably to fate (*miqreh*) and death. They enter the discussion in a comparison of wisdom and folly (2:12–17). Qohelet values the former. "Wisdom excels folly as light excels darkness." Immediately, however, he devalues it because of *miqreh*: "Yet I perceive that one fate comes to all of them." The signs of fate are no enduring remembrance and death. "How the wise man dies just like the fool!" (RSV). Concluding this section comes the refrain "All is vapor and a striving after wind."

If in the first instance *miqreh* removes any distinction between the wise and the foolish, on a second occasion it jettisons any advantage of human beings over animals. "The fate of humans and the fate of the animal is the same. As one dies, so dies the other . . . for all is vapor" (3:19). A third reference returns to the negation of value distinctions between human beings. "To all, one fate (*miqreh*): to the righteous and the wicked, to the good and the evil, to the clean and the unclean, to the sacrificer and the nonsacrificer. As the good, so the sinner; as the swearer, so the nonswearer" (9:2). *Hevel* is missing in this conclusion; evil (*ra'ah*) has replaced it. "This is the evil in everything that happens under the sun, that one fate comes to all. Also the hearts of people are full of evil, and madness is in their hearts while they live, and after that they go to the dead" (9:3; *cf.* 2:21, 6:1). For Qohelet, *miqreh* is arbitrary and uncontrollable. It does not result from how one lives or thinks. Yet it is predictable because all die.

Reflections on death also occur apart from fate, and everywhere the verdict is mixed. On the one hand, death threatens. It erases knowledge, memory, and life. Thus "a living dog is better than a dead lion" (9:4; *cf.* 12:1). Although there is a time to die (3:2), "why should you die before your time?" (7:17). On the other hand, "better is the day of death than the day of birth" (7:1). After all, death obliterates hate and envy (9:5–6). In a world of oppression, "the dead who are already dead [are] more fortunate than the living who are still alive" (4:2). But even then Qohelet fails to bury the subject. The merits of death over life are relative to a third possibility: "Better than both is the one who has not yet been and has not seen the evil deeds that are done under the sun" (4:3; *cf.* 6:3f.).

Wherever Qohelet looks, he sees *hevel* on earth under the sun. The incongruous, irrational, and vaporous pervade human existence, encompassing fate, evil, and death. His vision becomes a voice sounding a unique theme in scripture.

Qohelet and Proverbs. If his views appear to place Qohelet on the fringes of faith, nevertheless they evoke comparison with other biblical texts. Representing orthodoxy, the sages of Proverbs sound a different note. They seek to understand existence through the pursuit of knowledge, and, on the whole, they express optimism about their quest. Wisdom is obtainable and those who obtain it live long and well. "Happy is the one who finds wisdom. . . . Long life is in her right hand; in her left hand are riches and honor" (Prov 3:13–18). Moreover, to the wise belongs righteousness. They live blamelessly and reap good things. To the foolish belongs wickedness. They get into trouble and fall by their own deeds (Prov 11:5,8). Reward and punishment correlate precisely with wisdom and folly. Life is ordered and rational.

Over against this orthodox perspective the sage Qohelet takes his stand. Whereas Proverbs names life the supreme good and ignores the threat of death for the wise, Qohelet reports the terrors of life and sees death ever impending for the wise as well as the foolish. He dismantles the neat correlation of the righteous with long life and the wicked with destruction. "In my vain life," he says, "I have seen everything. There is a righteous one who perishes in righteousness and there is a wicked one who prolongs life in evildoing" (7:15; *cf.* 8:10–13). Qohelet knows that the wise may not be rich and famous (8:14–15) and that fools may destroy good deeds (9:17–18). He disavows an ethical system of reward and punishment. "Again I saw that under the sun the race is not to the swift, nor the battle to the strong, nor bread to the wise, nor riches to the intelligent, nor favor to the people of skill; but time and chance happen to them all" (9:11).

Repeatedly, Qohelet emphasizes the limitation of wisdom. He exploits what Proverbs at best hints (*cf.* Prov 16:1, 2, 9; 19:21; 20:24; 21:30–31). Thus his stance undercuts the exuberance of wisdom to yield the irony of *hevel.* By giving negative value to the positive, vapor deconstructs orthodox thinking. Wisdom becomes vexation (1:18), knowledge increases sorrow (1:18), work produces pain (2:23), justice brings wickedness (3:16, 8:14), and money yields dissatisfaction (5:10). In this hermeneutical move *hevel* saves wisdom from idolizing itself and thereby serves faith.

Qohelet and Genesis 2–3. The perspective of *hevel* likewise engages creation texts. Ecclesiastes 7:29 captures Genesis 2–3 *in nuce.* "Behold, this alone I found, that God made *haadam* upright, but they have sought out many devices" (*cf.* Eccl 3:11a). Divine creation is marred by human disobedience. In expanding his insight, Qohelet concentrates on the second half, the many devices that characterize life under the sun. With variations, such existence reflects the judgments described in Genesis 3. Five topics make the connection: work, animals, exile, sexuality, and death.

Even as God intended the first human creature (*ha adam*) to till and keep the garden and eat freely of its trees (Gen 2:15–16), so Qohelet perceives a similar plan. "There is nothing better for *adam* than to eat and drink and find enjoyment in toil. This also, I saw, is from the hand of God" (Eccl 2:24; *cf.* 3:13, 5:18). Contrary to the divine intention, however, humankind disobeyed in the garden of Eden. Fulfilling work became alienated labor. To the man (*adam*),

234

God said, "Cursed is the ground because of you; in toil ['*itstsavon*] you shall eat of it all the days of your life" (Gen 3:17). Qohelet too knows alienated labor. "What has a man (*adam*) from all the toil ('*amal*) and strain . . . ? For all his days are full of pain, and his work is a vexation" (Eccl 2:22–23; *cf.* 5:10, 6:7). Profit is like thorns and thistles, yielding no satisfaction (*cf.* Gen 3:18a). "This also is vapor." Human devices pervert the fulfilling work that came from the hand of God.

The perversion includes the animal world. If in creation humankind ruled over the animals (Gen 2:19–20), in disobedience the harmony of the hierarchy was lost. Perpetual enmity between the serpent (*nahash*) and the seed of the woman (Gen 3:15) continues in Ecclesiastes. "A serpent (*nahash*) will bite the one who breaks through a wall" (10:8b; *cf.* 10:11). The birds also betray. "Even in your thought, do not curse the king, . . . for a bird of the air will carry your voice, or some winged creature tell the matter" (10:20). Yet Qohelet goes beyond the primeval judgment to deny even a hierarchy. People themselves "are but beasts" (3:18). Humans and animals have the same breath and the same fate, namely death, "for all is vapor" (3:19). Ironically, this leveling recalls the serpent eating human dust all the days of its life (Gen 3:14b, 19b). What Genesis hints, Ecclesiastes proclaims.

Awareness of human frailty once led Qohelet to entertain alternatives for existence. He desired to "see what was good for the children of *adam* to do under heaven during the few days of their life" (2:3b). So he tested pleasure (2:1–11). Though many of his activities reflect urban life, some suggest the garden (*gan*) of Eden. Qohelet planted vineyards, made gardens (*gan*) and parks, and put in them all kinds of fruit trees (Eccl 2:5; *cf.* Gen 2:8–9). He made himself "pools from which to water the forest of growing trees" (Eccl 2:6), an evocation of the river that "flowed out of Eden to water the garden" (Gen 2:10). Every attempt to construct a place of pleasure ended, however, in disappointment and futility. In effect, the sage learned that he could never return to the primeval garden in which God "placed the cherubim and a flaming sword which turned every way, to guard the way to the tree of life" (Gen 3:24). Thus Qohelet sounds his refrain on exiled existence. "All

is vapor and a striving after wind and there is nothing to be gained under the sun" (Eccl 2:11b).

The topic of human sexuality further links Genesis and Ecclesiastes. God decrees that it is not good for the human creature to be alone. Two together mean fulfillment and joy (Gen 2:18, 23–25). Qohelet declares, "Two are better than one. . . . If they fall, one will lift up the other. . . . Again, if two lie together, they are warm; but how can one be warm alone?" (Eccl 4:9–12). Although these sentiments indicate the harmonious relationship of the sexes (Gen 2) before disobedience, other statements mirror female and male after disobedience (Gen 3). Qohelet demeans both creatures, but his more devastating judgment falls upon the female: "And I found more bitter than death the woman whose heart is snares and nets, and whose hands are fetters; he who pleases God escapes her, but the sinner is taken by her. . . . One man among a thousand I found, but a woman among all these I have not found" (Eccl 7:26,28). Subordination of female to male, a primeval sign of disobedient life (Gen 3:16), has become outright misogyny.

In its absorption with death Ecclesiastes echoes most poignantly vocabulary and themes from Genesis 2–3. "All are from the dust, and all turn to dust again" (Eccl 3:20b; *cf.* Gen 2:7, 3:19). Even though the sage includes animals in the verdict, he considers an alternative: "Who knows whether the spirit of the children of *haadam* goes upward and the spirit of the beast goes down to the earth?" (Eccl 3:21). The elements of spirit and dust signify, as in Genesis, the frailty of life. No individual (*adam*) "has power to retain the spirit, or authority over the day of death" (Eccl 8:8a). To conclude his testament, Qohelet reverses the imagery of creation. "The dust returns to the earth as it was, and the spirit returns to God who gave it" (Eccl 12:7; *cf.* Gen 2:7). Following the reversal comes the refrain "Vapor of vapors."

Summary. As a dominant motif in Ecclesiastes, *hevel* covers many subjects and offers many nuances of interpretation. It connotes emptiness, futility, irony, absurdity, and mystery. The persistence of the word distinguishes the book; at the same time, the meanings of the word relate it to other texts. By disassembling sapiential tradition, *hevel* corrects the idolatrous bias toward wisdom found in Proverbs. By reinterpreting the language of creation, it underscores the theology of Genesis 2–3 and expands the purview of wisdom. In myriad ways the voice of vapor speaks substantively within biblical faith.

But Vapor Is Not All

If *hevel* dominates the insights of Ecclesiastes, it does not exhaust them. Theological assertions abound.

The inscrutability of God. God is unknowable. Human beings "cannot find out what God has done from the beginning to the end" (3:11b). Never does the sage appeal to revelation, never does he use the covenantal name Yahweh, never does he speak to God, and never does God speak to him. In cultic activities he admonishes care, even detachment, for one does not establish a personal relationship with the Deity. "Guard your steps when you go to the house of God. . . . Be not rash with your mouth, nor let your heart be hasty to utter a word before God, for God is in heaven, and you upon earth; therefore let your words be few" (5:1–2). Another text witnesses eloquently to divine inscrutability. Playing on the double meaning of wind and spirit for the Hebrew word *ruah*, Qohelet limns divine mystery. "As you do not know the way of the wind and how bones grow in the womb," or, "As you do not know how the spirit comes to the bones in the womb of a woman with child, so you do not know the work of God who makes everything" (11:5). This use of the image wind diverges strikingly from wind as futility, the parallel of *hevel*. Here wind (or spirit) testifies to the mystery of divine creativity.

The activity of God. A theology of inscrutability does not prevent Qohelet from talking about God. Often the sage reports divine activity through the verbs *give*, *make*, and *do*. At places he claims that God gives a single gift to humankind. It may be negative, "unhappy business" (1:13), or positive, "food, drink, and pleasure" (3:13; *cf.* 3:10). At other places he declares that God gives different gifts to different groups. To the individual who pleases God, the Deity "gives wisdom and knowledge and joy; but to the sinner God gives the work of gathering and heaping, only to give to one who pleases God" (2:26). Again, God gives one everything for a good life— wealth, possessions, and honor—and yet does not give power to enjoy them (6:2). Though unfathom-

able (11:5), this Deity is hardly remote. Creation and preservation bespeak divine involvement with the world. God made everything "beautiful in its time. . . . I know that whatever God does endures forever; nothing can be added to it, nor anything taken from it. God has made it so, in order that people should fear before him" (3:11–14).

The fear of God. While elsewhere the concept of fear of God positively signals the religious life (e.g., Ps 34:9, Prov 1:7), in Ecclesiastes its particular meaning is moot. Some commentators suspect that editors have inserted this vocabulary to tame the heretical sage. Certainly the admonition in the epilogue to fear God carries an orthodox message (12:13). Other interpreters hold that Qohelet himself employs the term, but negatively to signify terror and dread before the divine. Still others assert that he uses it positively to displace traditional righteousness. Ecclesiastes 7:15–20 suggests this reading. In the midst of reflections on the irony of wisdom and its corollary righteousness, the sage affirms an alternative: "The one fearing God will come forth from all of them" (7:18b). Having exposed orthodoxy as *hevel*, Qohelet opens the way to true faith, which he designates as fear of God (Gese 1983). But the end of the matter is not yet (*cf.* 12:13).

Joy from God. If *hevel* subverts orthodoxy, joy (*simhah*) subverts *hevel*. Some scholars deny this thesis. Nonetheless, the book allows, even encourages, it. Seven texts proclaim divine joy as the way to transcend vaporous existence (Whybray 1982). In these passages Qohelet draws upon observation and confession rather than explanation and argumentation. The verbs "see" and "know" appear frequently in the first person. The vocabulary of the good and fit prevails, especially with the formula "There is nothing better than . . ." Though never analyzed, joy is emphatically God's gift. In some places the concept fear of God joins it. And throughout, *hevel* provides context and contrast.

The first reference to joy occurs amid the vapor of human strivings (1:12–2:26). So disillusioned is Qohelet by his effort to achieve success, pleasure, and security that he hates life. Then he shifts attention to find new vision. Apart from God everything is vexation and despair, but "from the hand of God" comes joy in toil (2:24–26). In a second passage (3:1–15)

Qohelet confronts the problem of time, how to live without knowing "what God has done from the beginning to the end." The answer returns: nothing is better than to embrace joy. That all "be happy and enjoy themselves as long as they live" constitutes God's gift. This joy relates to the fear of God. "God has made it so, in order that people should fear before him" (3:14c). The sage moves to a third concern, injustice (3:16–22). Two observations exacerbate the issue. Human beings do not know the appointed time for divine judgment, and judgment has no power beyond death. Rather than despair, Qohelet declares nothing is better than to enjoy work. Such is the lot of humankind. What comes after cannot be seen, but joy can be realized now.

Vanity in the pursuit of wealth brings Qohelet to a fourth recommendation (5:10–20). The love of money does not satisfy; the surfeit of the rich induces sleeplessness; and the possession of wealth may mean its loss. Further, riches cannot be carried into death, and the one who strives after them spends life in vexation, sickness, and resentment. If God gives wealth, that is a different matter. But in any case "to eat and drink and find enjoyment in all the toil" is good and fit. Thus has God arranged the lot of everyone. Those who accept find that "God keeps them occupied with joy in their hearts."

The fifth passage returns to the question of injustice (8:10–15). Two adjacent sections develop the thought. The first (8:10–13) observes the prosperity of the wicked. They receive decent burials, engage in cultic affairs, and get reprieve and praise. Then comes an opposing confession: "Yet I know that it will be well with those who fear God because they fear before him; but it will not be well with the wicked, neither will he prolong his days like a shadow, because he does not fear before God." In drawing this contrast between two groups, Qohelet does not employ the usual pairing of the righteous and the wicked, perhaps because the two terms together suggest orthodox wisdom. Instead, for the designation "the righteous," he substitutes "those who fear God" (*cf.* 7:15–20). Though no mention of joy appears here, the break with traditional language moves in that direction. The second section (8:14–15) completes the thought through a different approach. It too observes inequity but reverts to the pairing of the righteous and wicked,

thereby contrasting old wisdom with Qohelet's view. Structurally, the word *hevel* encircles the righteous who reap the deeds of the wicked and the wicked who reap the deeds of the righteous. Thus is human existence trapped on earth and traditional wisdom ensnared. From outside the circle, however, Qohelet counters: "But I recommend joy . . . through the days of life which God gives under the sun." Free of the circle, this recommendation enables one to overcome *hevel*.

The divine gift of joy sustains life even in the face of judgment and death. These issues provide the sixth context (9:1–10). Although some people respond to *hevel* and fate with evil lives or mad hearts, Qohelet shows a more excellent way. "Go, eat your bread with enjoyment, and drink your wine with a merry heart; for God has already approved what you do." The seventh setting for joy (11:7–12:7) is like the sixth. Since "all that comes is vapor," the brevity of life, even a long life, makes enjoyment imperative. "Rejoice, . . . let your heart cheer. . . . Know that for all these things God will bring you into justice" (11:9).

Overall, joy is a major theme in Ecclesiastes. The sage does not define it but does distinguish it from pleasure and laughter (*cf.* 2:1–2, 7:3–6). They are self-confirmatory pursuits that end in disappointment and vanity. Whenever Qohelet discusses them, he makes no reference to God. By contrast, to embrace joy is to receive a divine gift. It does not solve the incongruities of existence; it does not answer the problem of evil and suffering; and it does not conquer death. But joy does offer a transcendent perspective that turns life away from futility. If Qohelet undermines idolatry, especially the idolatry of wisdom, by insistence upon *hevel*, he also begins to subvert *hevel* by admonitions of joy. Though the subversion be incomplete, it is no less a witness to faith. Vapor is not all.

CONTEXTS

Various contexts produce different uses and interpretations of Ecclesiastes. Historical studies posit a postexilic date, ranging from the fifth to the second century B.C.E., most often settling upon the mid third. The book itself offers few clues, apart from late biblical Hebrew, but it does suggest a world of despotic and unpredictable monarchs (8:2–5, 10:16–17). Such political conditions prevailed after Alexander the Great (d. 323 B.C.E.), with the Ptolemies of Egypt and the Seleucids of Syria vying for control of Palestine. In this setting life might well be perceived as vapor, irony, and absurdity.

Correspondingly, sociological analyses locate Ecclesiastes in a period of insecurity when an old order fades (Crüsemann 1984). If in preexilic Judah a certain balance held between peasantry and monarchy, in postexilic times it no longer exists. Outside rulers levy taxes and duties. Pressure for greater production alters agricultural life to decrease the freedom of small farmers. At the same time, an upper class flourishes. Qohelet probably belongs to this group even though he devalues the profits of an acquisitive society. His stance on justice is mixed. He deplores the tears of the oppressed and the power of their oppressors (4:1–3); yet he admonishes obedience to the king whose word is supreme (8:2–5). In his reflection, opposite values clash without social, political, or economic resolution.

Sapiential circles in the ancient Near East broaden understanding of Ecclesiastes. Comparison to selected Akkadian proverbs, the Egyptian "Lamentations of Khakheperre-sonbe," the Babylonian "Dialogue of Pessimism," and other such literature discloses similarities in theme, vocabulary, and conclusion. Ecclesiastes is surrounded by a cloud of witnesses who grapple with absurdity, despair, and death. They show that his concerns exceed a single culture, history, and religious milieu.

Canonical perspectives offer additional insight. Besides referring to themes within the book, the three epilogues link it to wisdom literature in Israel. The first (12:9–10) probably alludes to Proverbs. The second (12:11–12) reinforces the allusion as it warns against unidentified collections beyond these "sayings of the wise." The third (12:13–14) expresses a point of view identical to Sirach but not found in the body of Ecclesiastes. It unites wisdom and *torah* by paralleling fear of God and observance of divine commandments. In the final form of the epilogue, then, redactors may have tried to impose a single theological focus on all wisdom (Sheppard 1977). A canonical view emerges thereby that alters, if not contradicts, the testimony of Qohelet himself.

Other canonical relationships are likewise instructive. The Greek Bible places Ecclesiastes between Proverbs and the Song of Solomon, an ordering that evokes multiple meanings. In following Proverbs, for instance, Ecclesiastes tempers assured optimism and corrects deficient theology. In being followed by the Song of Solomon, its somber tone is lightened and its joyous notes are expanded. Traditionally, all three books have been attributed to Solomon. The Hebrew Bible places Ecclesiastes among the *megillot*, the collection of the Five Scrolls, each read at an annual festival. Over time, the book became associated with Sukkot, the Feast of Tabernacles (or Booths), a harvest celebration (*cf.* Deut 16:13ff). But the import of Ecclesiastes in this liturgical setting is unclear. Some scholars hold that it injects a melancholy note into a festive occasion. Others maintain that it sounds joy for a happy feast. Again, the sage confounds; indeterminate meaning prevails.

EPILOGUE

Of the making of many Ecclesiasteses there is no end, and much scholarship is a weariness of the flesh. What might Qohelet say to all the toil that has produced such diverse interpretations of his work? "This also is vapor and a striving after wind." "There is ruin in a flood of words, but do you fear God" (5:7j). Readers who understand will know the liberating laughter of joy.

Bibliography

Bickerman, Elias. "Koheleth (Ecclesiastes) or the Philosophy of an Acquisitive Society." In *Four Strange Books of the Bible*. New York, 1967.

Crenshaw, James L. "The Chasing After Meaning: Ecclesiastes." In *Old Testament Wisdom*. Atlanta, 1981.

———. *Ecclesiastes*. Philadelphia, 1987.

Crüsemann, Frank. "The Unchangeable World: The 'Crisis of Wisdom' in Koheleth." In *God of the Lowly: Socio-Historical Interpretations of the Bible*, edited by Willy Schottroff and Wolfgang Stegemann. Maryknoll, N.Y., 1984.

Forman, Charles G. "Koheleth's Use of Genesis." *Journal of Semitic Studies* 5 (1960).

Fox, Michael V. "The Meaning of *Hebel* for Qohelet." *Journal of Biblical Literature* 105 (1986).

Gese, Hartmut. "The Crisis of Wisdom in Koheleth"

[1963]. In *Theodicy in the Old Testament,* edited by James L. Crenshaw. Philadelphia, 1983.

Ginsberg, H. L. "The Structure and Contents of the Book of Koheleth." In *Wisdom in Israel and in the Ancient Near East,* edited by M. Noth and D. Winton Thomas. Leiden, 1955.

Good, Edwin M. "Qoheleth: The Limits of Wisdom." In *Irony in the Old Testament.* Philadelphia, 1965, repr. 1981.

———. "The Unfilled Sea: Style and Meaning in Ecclesiastes 1:2–11." In *Israelite Wisdom,* edited by John G. Gammie. Missoula, 1978.

Gordis, Robert. *Koheleth, The Man and His World: A Study of Ecclesiastes.* New York, 1951, repr. 1968.

Kugel, James L. "Ecclesiastes." In *Harper's Bible Dictionary,* edited by Paul J. Achtemeier. San Francisco, 1985.

Loader, J. A. *Polar Structures in the Book of Qohelet.* New York, 1979.

Murphy, Roland E. "Ecclesiastes (Qohelet)." In *Wisdom Literature.* Grand Rapids, 1981.

Ogden, Graham S. "'Vanity' It Certainly Is Not." *The Bible Translator* 38 (1987).

Polk, Timothy. "The Wisdom of Irony: A Study of Hebel and Its Relation to Joy and the Fear of God in Ecclesiastes." *Studia Biblica et Theologica* 6 (1976).

Rad, Gerhard von. *Wisdom in Israel.* London, 1972.

Sheppard, Gerald T. "The Epilogue to Qoheleth as Theological Commentary." *Catholic Biblical Quarterly* 39 (1977).

Whybray, R. N. "Qoheleth, Preacher of Joy." *Journal for the Study of the Old Testament* 23 (1982).

Wright, Addison G. "The Riddle of the Sphinx: The Structure of the Book of Qoheleth." *Catholic Biblical Quarterly* 30 (1968).

———. "The Riddle of the Sphinx Revisited: Numerical Patterns in the Book of Qoheleth." *Catholic Biblical Quarterly* 42 (1980).

Zimmerli, W. "Das Buch Kohelet: Traktat oder Sentenzensammlung?" *Vetus Testamentum* 24 (1974).

PHYLLIS TRIBLE

Song of Solomon

TITLE

AS IS THE case with other biblical works, there is a superscription affixed to the Song of Solomon: The Song of Songs by (lit., "to") Solomon. The duplication of "song" is a Hebrew idiomatic expression for the superlative, that is, the best or greatest song. This view is echoed in the well-known statement of Rabbi 'Aqiva' ben Yosef (d. ca. 135 C.E.) that the world was not worth the day the Song of Songs was created (Mishnah, Yad. 3:5). In the Western tradition the book is also known as the Song of Songs (after its superscription) or as the Canticle (Canticle of Canticles), thanks to the Vulgate translation, canticum canticorum. In any case, the term "song" need not be pressed. Although it could have been set to music, entirely or in part, we have no evidence to confirm this. What is certain is that the eight chapters are poetry.

The superscription (1:1) associates the work with Solomon. Probably his authorship is intended, although the connecting preposition could be interpreted to indicate that he is the subject of the work. The reason for ascribing the work to Solomon is the occurrence of his name in 1:5, 3:7–11, and 8:11–12 and also the mention of a king in 1:4, 1:12, and 7:6 (EV, 7:5). Nevertheless, these arguments are weak; nowhere does the male speaker in the Song claim to be King Solomon. Solomonic authorship may also

have been suggested by Solomon's many wives (1 Kgs 11:3). Brevard Childs (1979, 574) has interpreted the claim for Solomon as a sign that the Song belongs within the context of wisdom literature, since he was the sage par excellence. The date of the work cannot be determined, although a majority of scholarly opinion inclines to assign it to the postexilic era. If this is a collection of poems from various periods, some may date from the preexilic period.

LITERARY CHARACTERISTICS

Many striking features combine to set this work apart from other biblical books. (1) There are several speakers: a woman, a man, the daughters of Jerusalem, and perhaps the poet (whether author or editor). (2) The movement within the work is created by dialogue, especially that of the man and the woman (who is given the most lines). (3) There are several literary genres.

The Speakers

The identity of the speakers is indicated by marginal references in many English translations (NAB, NEB). While there is not total agreement regarding the identity of the speakers, in over 90 percent of the cases the indications of the Hebrew text itself secure the identity of male or female, singular or plural. From this emerges a male, a female, and a

241

group of women (the daughters of Jerusalem, whose main function in the Song seems to be as a foil for the woman; *cf.* 2:7, 3:5, 5:9, 6:1). Some, however, have distinguished two male characters, a peasant shepherd (1:7) and a king (*cf.* 1:4, 12), and have proposed that the Song contains a drama. The conflict would be between Solomon (the king) and a peasant lover (the shepherd) for the hand of the woman. But this view has been more or less abandoned. The genre of drama seems to be absent from Hebrew writings; besides, the stage instructions provided for this interpretation are quite arbitrary. Moreover, the distinction between king and shepherd is tenuous. They are one character: the lover is described now as king, now as shepherd. This kind of make-believe is characteristic of the idealization process at work in love poetry especially. In Egyptian love poems, with which the Song can profitably be compared (Fox 1985, 98), the man is endowed with royal characteristics. The same phenomenon occurs in the Song, and so there is no reason to recognize two separate characters. But if the Song is not a drama, it is dramatic in the sense of dialogic exchange between the main characters.

There has been a question not only of the number of characters but also of their identity. The so-called cultic interpretation has identified the man and the woman with divine beings, the god and goddess who are celebrated in the sacred marriage songs of the ancient Near East (Ishtar and Tammuz in the Babylonian tradition). Some allusions in the Song may have a background in the mythological world of gods and goddesses (e.g., the role of Lebanon and leopards in 4:8; see Pope 1977, 474–478), but this is not enough to sustain the view that the Song celebrated the sacred marriage rite. Any description of love works on both the human and the divine level. What benefits human love is projected onto divine love and vice versa, hence the allusions that some commentators find in the Song. But at the most this may explain something of the prehistory of the Hebrew poetry. There can be hardly any doubt that as the text stands it deals with love between human beings (as Theophile J. Meek holds [1956, 95]).

The Use of Dialogue

Even if many of the poems in the Song were originally separate and distinct (e.g., 3:6–11), the glue that holds them together is dialogue between the man and the woman. Unlike the collection of Egyptian love poems (Fox 1985, 3–81), in which the characters discourse separately without directly revealing their love to each other, in the biblical poems the lovers address each other directly. At times it is not clear if the beloved is indeed physically present. Thus in the opening lines of 1:2–4, the woman exalts her lover and speaks to him and of him in such a manner as to suggest that he is present perhaps only in imagination. But the ensuing lines (1:5–8), which begin with an address to the daughters, contain a direct request to him for a rendezvous, a request that he personally answers.

This issue of presence is at the heart of the relationship between the lovers. The theme of presence and absence or finding and losing is celebrated in two remarkably parallel passages, 3:1–5 and 5:2–8. In the latter case it leads into an extended dialogue between the woman and the daughters about the "lost" lover (5:2–6:3), who suddenly appears in 6:4, describing the beauty of the woman.

The Diversity of Literary Forms

These forms derive from the nature of the love relationship between a man and a woman: (1) songs descriptive of the beloved's beauty, often designated by the Arabic term *waṣf* (4:1–7, 5:10–16, 7:2–6); (2) poems of yearning (1:2–4, 7:12–8:4 [EV 7:11–8:4]); (3) poems of admiration (1:9–2:3); (4) poems of reminiscence (2:8–17); and (5) poems of boasting (6:8–10, 8:8–10, 8:11–12).

It is not possible to determine the precise setting of these poems. It was popular at one time to designate them as marriage songs that would have accompanied the celebration of weddings. But there is no evidence that such an occasion gave rise to the poems, although they may have come to be used in this manner. It is true that there is a reference to Solomon's wedding day in 3:11, and the man calls the woman "sister" and "bride" (probably in anticipation) in 4:9–12, but this is not sufficient to establish a marriage setting. The general mood of these units fits the broader and less definable situations of mutual love (admiration, yearning, etc.).

CONTENT

Despite the lack of formal structure, an outline of the general contexts may be sketched. There is little agreement on the number of poems; hence this outline is designed merely to facilitate for the reader the key movements within the work.

1:2–4. In the introduction the woman expresses her yearning for her "royal" (v. 4) lover and associates the "maidens" (perhaps the daughters of Jerusalem) with her own feelings.

1:5–2:7. After explaining her sunburned appearance to the daughters (1:5–6), she asks her lover for a rendezvous, to which he responds in a teasing way (1:7–8). A loving conversation ensues, with mutual compliments being paid (1:9–2:7) before the woman concludes with an adjuration to the daughters about stirring up love.

2:8–17. In a reminiscence the woman recalls the lover's springtime visit and invitation, including their conversation. When he describes her inaccessibility (like a dove in a rocky cliff), she reminds him in a teasing ditty that young men (the "little foxes") are paying suit to young women (the "vineyards"; v. 15). She closes with the formula of mutual belonging (v. 16; *cf.* 6:3, 7:10) and invites him to herself (v. 17, which picks up in a literary inclusion the symbols of gazelle, stag, and mountain that began the poem in vv. 8–9).

3:1–5. The woman narrates the loss and successful recovery of her lover (contrast 5:2–7) and ends with an adjuration to the daughters (v. 5, a refrain of 2:7).

3:6–11. In this enigmatic poem Solomon's wedding procession is described by an unidentified speaker. In the context of the Song, this is another reference to the lover as king.

4:1–5:1. The man delivers a *wasf* describing the physical charms of the beloved (vv. 1–7), invites her to leave her mountain fastness (v. 8, the inaccessibility motif; *cf.* 2:14), and describes her bewitching effect upon him (vv. 9–11). She is a garden of exotic plants (vv. 12–15), to which he invites the winds to waft; and she replies by inviting him to herself ("his garden"; v. 16). With a jubilant cry he asserts his coming to the "garden" (5:1a–d). The scene concludes with an invitation to be in-

toxicated with love (perhaps directed to the lovers).

5:2–6:3. The woman takes up from chapter 3 the theme of the search for the absent lover. This time there is no success, and she enlists the aid of the daughters to tell him, should they find him, that she is sick with love (5:2–8). The daughters' request for a description of the lover affords her the opportunity to deliver a *wasf* about his physical charms (vv. 9–16). When they express a heightened interest in searching for such a person, she assures them that their hopes are in vain. He belongs to her; she is his garden (6:1–3).

6:4–10. The lover makes a sudden appearance, praising her beauty and uniqueness.

6:11–12. It is not clear who speaks these words (perhaps the woman); because the text is corrupt, the meaning of verse 12 escapes us.

7:1–11 [EV 6:13–7:10]. An invitation (by whom?) is issued to the woman to "turn" (JPS; to be gazed on admiringly? to dance?). Then someone (the man?) delivers a *wasf* (7:2–6). The speaker of verses 7–10a is certainly the lover, who expresses his passionate desire to be united with her. She interrupts his words in verse 10 with a reference to their kissing and concludes with the formula of mutual belonging (v. 11; *cf.* 6:3).

7:12[11]–8:4. This position can be construed as a continuation of the previous lines. The woman invites her lover to go out to the "vineyards" for the delights of love (vv. 12 [11]–14 [13]) and describes her desire (8:1–2). The conclusion (vv. 3–4) takes up the refrain of 2:6–7 (*cf.* 3:5).

8:5–14. These lines are best described as appendixes (Robert 1963) that appear to be snatches of poetry without any context. The meaning and identity of the questioner in verse 5a are not clear. According to the Masoretic vocalization of verse 5b, the man speaks and refers to some previous encounter with the woman. Verses 6–7 are spoken by the woman, who celebrates the power of love. The comparison of love to death and Sheol (the abode of the dead) is striking: In Old Testament thought, these are personified as the dynamic powers that pursue every living being until they finally win out. The supreme compliment to love is to compare its strength to that of such superpowers. Moreover, the woman goes on to comment on the fire of love and calls it "a most vehement flame" (so RSV and many other versions). But the Jerusalem Bible translation (and see the footnote in NIV) is closer to the Hebrew and is to be preferred: "a flame of Yahweh himself." This association of human love with God is remarkable.

Verses 8–10 seem to be a reminiscence by the woman of the overbearing and officious words of her brothers (vv. 8–9; *cf.* 1:6) about her as a child—to which she triumphantly responds that in the "eyes" of her lover, she is as one who brings "peace" (*shalom,* a play on Shelomoh, or Solomon). Verses 11–12 can be understood as spoken by the man or the woman. In either case, it is a boast that the woman ("my vineyard") is more valuable than Solomon's "vineyard" (the royal harem; *cf.* 6:8–10). Verses 13–14 are a reprise of earlier themes. The man desires to hear her voice (v. 13, as in 2:14), and she answers his request with words derived from 2:17.

HISTORY OF INTERPRETATION

The Traditional Meaning

It is a remarkable fact that the earliest attested interpretation is, for *both* the Jewish and Christian traditions, a symbolic meaning. The Song was understood to portray the covenantal relationship between the Lord and the people of God. Naturally, Christian tradition viewed the relationship from a Christian perspective, as between Christ and the church or Christ and the individual soul.

Jewish tradition is reflected in the Targum (the sixth-century Aramaic paraphrase), which interpreted the Song as an allegory of Israel's history from the Exodus to the messianic times. It is worth noting that this book came to be counted among the *megillot,* or scrolls, and is read in connection with the feast of Passover. Although questions arose about what might be called the canonicity of the book (whether it "defiled the hands," i.e., was "holy"), Rabbi 'Aqiva' strongly supported the Song: "All the writings are holy, but the Song of Songs is most holy" (Mishnah, *Yad.* 3:5).

Christian tradition was molded by the works of the great biblical commentator Origen (*d. ca.* 253), who developed particularly the concept of the personal relationship between God (Christ) and the

individual soul. This view became dominant in the medieval monastic interpretation, especially with Bernard of Clairvaux, who wrote eighty-six homilies on the Song. The theme was continued by mystical writers and poets, such as the Spanish Carmelite John of the Cross (1542–1591), whose *Cántico espiritual* is a kind of mosaic formed by phrases from the Song.

It is not difficult to understand the popularity of the exegetical trend that saw the relationship between God and the individual in personal terms. Other books of the Bible itself, in their portrayal of the covenant as a marriage relationship, can be brought to bear in trying to understand the Song. This is most vividly expressed in the life and message of the prophet Hosea, whose marriage to the unfaithful Gomer symbolized the undying love of the Lord for Israel (see Hos 1–3). The theme is taken up again in several of the prophetic books (Isa 1:21, Jer 3:1, Ezek 16:23–34). Most often the context is one of condemnation for Israel's infidelity. But Israel also appears as a loving spouse, restored by her God (Isa 62:4–5). The same theme is expressed by Paul in Ephesians 5:27–28 and in Revelation 21:9.

This is not the obvious meaning of the Song, as there is nothing in the text that explicitly refers to God and Israel. Nevertheless, this interpretation prevailed for centuries.

Early on, the traditional interpretation was supported by the allegorical exegesis that was much in vogue among Jews and Christians. Each detail in the text became subject to another, supposedly higher, meaning. With hindsight one may argue that this was a well-nigh fatal mistake because it opened the text to extremely artificial interpretation. One may apply a safe rule of thumb here: unless a work is written as an allegory, it should not be interpreted as one. The vagaries in the history of the interpretation of the Song might have been avoided. Rather, if one is going to hold to the traditional meaning, analogy—not allegory—is the key. There is an analogy between human love and divine love, and the dominant moods of the Song (yearning, fidelity, admiration) can be seen to work on a human-divine plane.

The Literal Historical Meaning

Despite its long and venerable history, the traditional understanding of the Song has been more or less replaced in modern times by the literal interpretation that derives from historicocritical methodology. It must be admitted that the literal interpretation is the rather obvious sense of the text. The opening line ("Let him kiss me with the kisses of his mouth"; Au. trans.) clearly suggests that one is dealing with human sexual love. The description of the flow of the dialogue, given above, underlines the appropriateness of the literal interpretation. Comparison with the Egyptian love poems provides further evidence that the Hebrew work fits into the genre of ancient Near Eastern love poetry. There are some differences, of course, because there is no direct dialogue in the Egyptian poems. In those the man and woman appear more to reflect their own inner emotion of love, whereas the biblical characters are more directed toward each other. But the world of make-believe, the fantasy world of love, is similar in both literatures. Exotic flowers, extravagant praise, lovesickness, descriptions of the other's beauty, and an extraordinary attention to the sensual (touching, tasting, smelling, seeing) are common to both. Merely to tick off the richness of fruits, flowers, and animals that figure in the Song is to envision another world: vineyard, henna, cedars and cypresses, lilies and thorns, apples and raisin cakes, figs and pomegranates, myrrh and aloes, nard and saffron, palms, nut garden, and so on. The animals cover a wide variety: horse, stag, gazelle, hind, fox, dove, goat, lion, and leopard—all in eight chapters!

Most modern readers interpret comparisons as representative of color, size, or shape, that is, some sensible aspect of the object. But the descriptions in the Song are unsettling. How does one understand the comparison of the woman's hair to "a flock of goats streaming down the mountains of Gilead" (4:1), or of her neck (cf. the nose in 7:5) to David's tower (4:4)? The ancients seem to go beyond merely representational comparisons; their symbols can reproduce the subjective pleasure afforded by various sensual stimuli. But they can also evoke new and dynamic dimensions. The eye, for example, is not merely the organ of vision but is imbued with power. Even wine has eyes, because it "sparkles" (Prov 23:31; RSV). Hence the eyes of the beloved bewitch the lover (4:9, 6:5). But more than that, the eyes are "doves" (1:15, 4:1, 5:12). Do the doves represent some physical quality? There is evidence from ancient Near Eastern iconography that doves were seen as messengers of love. The entire comparison is somewhat different from the prosaic shape, color, and size categories of our world, and the reader of the Song has to be alert to these startlingly new and strange dimensions of the imagery.

In view of the dispiriting history of sex and sexual attitudes in the West, the Song's affirmation of the joy, beauty, and fidelity of love between the sexes is a welcome testimony. It reinforces the noble human values that are implicit in the love relationship. This differs from the customary biblical perspective on love and marriage as the divinely instituted means of procreating the human race (Gen 1:27–28). Although the "romantic" aspect is hardly sounded in the Bible (but cf. Prov 5:15–19; Eccl 9:8–9), the ebullience of the lovers in the Song is unmistakable. It has been suggested (Childs 1979, 573–575) that the Hebrew sages may have been responsible for collecting and handing down this poetry as a witness to their social values. It is worthy to be "the voice of the bridegroom and the voice of the bride" (Jer 16:9, 25:10).

Nevertheless, the traditional interpretation (without the allegorical excesses) is not to be dismissed out of hand. As we have seen, it derives support from the marriage symbolism of the covenant, the meaning of 8:6, and the extraordinary agreement between church and synagogue. Every biblical book has come to mean more than its original author(s) intended. The open-endedness of human love challenges the modern reader of this magnificent poetry.

Bibliography

Childs, Brevard S. *Introduction to the Old Testament as Scripture*. Philadelphia, 1979. A general work that recognizes the wisdom orientation of the Song.

Fox, Michael V. *The Song of Songs and the Ancient Egyptian Love Songs*. Madison, Wis., 1985. A translation and analysis of Egyptian poems and of the Song, with an appreciation of the language, symbols, and emotions that express love.

Gordis, Robert. *The Song of Songs*. New York, 1954. A succinct, standard commentary that emphasizes the literal historical meaning.

Kramer, Samuel N. *The Sacred Marriage Rite*. Bloomington, Ind., 1969.

Meek, Theophile J. "The Song of Songs." In *The Interpreter's Bible,* vol. 5. Nashville, Tenn., 1956. Pp. 91–148. A standard commentary that is oriented to the cultic origins of the Song in ancient sacred marriage rites. The application to human love is seen as a secondary and later application.

Murphy, Roland E. "Towards a Commentary on the Song of Songs." *Catholic Biblical Quarterly* 39 (1977): 482–496. A summary of current scholarship. The article portrays the flow of action within the Song.

Pope, Marvin H. *Song of Songs.* Garden City, N.Y., 1977. A detailed commentary on the text and grammar, which brings to bear on the Song various aspects of ancient Near Eastern culture. It also provides a thorough treatment of the history of interpretation.

Robert, André. *Le Cantique des cantiques.* Paris, 1963. A valuable commentary along the lines of the traditional interpretation. It includes a lengthy excursus on representative love poetry from the ancient world.

ROLAND E. MURPHY, O. CARM.

Isaiah

THE BOOK OF the prophet Isaiah is one of the most interesting and complex writings contained in the Old Testament. Its intricate literary structure has made it a subject of controversy at more than one period in Christian and Jewish history, and it illustrates some of the most significant features of Old Testament prophecy. It contains a total of sixty-six chapters, making it the longest single book of the entire Bible, and it is the first of the major books of what the Hebrew scripture canon describes as the Latter Prophets.

The prophet Isaiah lived during the eighth century B.C.E. and was active in his ministry for almost forty years. Although, as was customary in ancient times, the words of the prophet were originally spoken orally to a public audience, there are strong indications that Isaiah himself began the process of recording several of his prophecies in writing (cf. Isa 30:8 with 29:11f., and see below under "Prophecies of Isaiah in Their Setting"). He was certainly not, however, the author who wrote down all sixty-six chapters of the book that now bears his name, and there are important reasons why this must be recognized. Prophecy contained two essential components. It consisted of a message given by a prophet concerning the intended action and attitude of God. It also contained some reason, or explanation, to show why this action was necessary or why this attitude had arisen. If, for instance, the prophet pronounced a warning of a threatening action by God, then this threat would be made intelligible by showing what features in the people's conduct had aroused the divine anger. Conversely, if the action was reassuring and hopeful of a blessed future, then the prophecy would refer to those aspects of the divine nature, or those divinely given promises, that provided the basis for such assurance. Sometimes in the formulation of a prophet's messages one aspect would predominate over the other, so that much would be said about why punishment was necessary and little about the form the punishment would take. At other times the prophet could present deeply disturbing and vivid pictures of threatened ruin and disaster but would say little as to the reason for them, on the understanding that these reasons were already well known.

This two-sided nature of recorded prophecy is important for an understanding of its meaning and lasting relevance. A prophecy was originally addressed to a specific situation, frequently one of a markedly critical, and often highly political, nature. To know what this situation was serves to clarify the reasons that lay behind the prophecy as well as the degree of reality ascribed to the threat or assurance it contained. It is very important, therefore, that we should know the life and circumstances of the prophet, since the national and international issues of the time are deeply reflected in the prophecies that he gave. With none is this more imperative than in the case of the prophet Isaiah. Unfortunately, the individual prophetic books contain relatively little of this detailed historical and political information, although often much of it can be quickly and confidently inferred. The historical books of 1 and 2 Kings fill out much of this information for us, and the description of Joshua, Judges, 1 and 2 Samuel, and 1 and 2 Kings as the Former Prophets points to the link between prophecy and its historical background.

A further point is also of great assistance in understanding the distinctive form of the prophetic books. Just as there was a prior background of events that helps to illuminate the purpose of a prophecy, so also there was a subsequent history of further events that reflected back on how the prophecy was understood. A prophetic threat or promise looked to a response in two ways. If people heeded the warning, then clearly God could modify or even revoke his intended action (see Amos 7:3, 6). If no such response was forthcoming, then when disastrous events transpired these could be seen as marking the fulfillment of the prophecy. Prophecy, therefore, whether it was threatening or hopeful, looked for some fulfillment (the Hebrew uses a verb meaning "to set up, establish") in events after the prophecy had been given. This fact serves to explain why there is so much material in the prophetic books of the Old Testament referring to a period after the time when the original prophet had spoken.

The prophet Isaiah was active over a long period of time, from at least 736 B.C.E. until 701 B.C.E. The political events in the sister kingdoms of Judah and Ephraim during this period are therefore the primary basis for understanding his message, and the events of these years are closely reflected in chapters 1–39 of the book. The major overshadowing background was the powerful intrusion of Assyria in the entire region of the Levant, as far as the border of Egypt. When Isaiah began his prophetic work Assyria was just beginning to influence affairs very strongly in both Judah and Ephraim. By the time of his last prophecies in 701, Judah was a vassal kingdom under Assyrian imperial control, and Ephraim in the north had been broken up and became largely absorbed into a new alignment of provinces under Assyrian jurisdiction.

These considerations serve to explain some of the most striking features of the book. A first group of

prophecies, central to chapters 1–12, is basically concerned with the events surrounding the arrival of Assyrian power into Judah and Ephraim. These events extended as far as the time of the accession of Hezekiah to the throne of Judah in 725 and the collapse of the northern kingdom after rebelling against Assyria in 723–722. During the years 705–701 Hezekiah of Judah also rebelled against Assyria, and the events of these years form the basis for a nucleus of prophecies in chapters 28–32. Since other nations besides Judah and Ephraim were deeply affected by these happenings, prophecies relating to Israel's neighbors are also found, in chapters 13–23. Already, therefore, we are provided with a basis for understanding a significant central nucleus of the Book of Isaiah.

Chapters 36–39 present a slightly expanded account of events linked with the rebellion of Hezekiah against Assyria and the subsequent siege of Jerusalem (see 2 Kgs 18:13–20:19). The narratives were certainly incorporated into the Book of Isaiah after having first been set out in 2 Kings. After Isaiah 39 there is no further explicit mention of the prophet Isaiah, and it becomes clear on detailed examination that the contents of chapters 40–66 belong to a period dating more than a century after the prophet's time. Persons and events are alluded to that had not been known in Isaiah's day. Yet other events from this later time are also referred to in chapters 13–14, and an even later age provides the background for the rather obscure chapters 24–27. How are we to explain the presence of this later material in a book concerned initially with prophecies from Isaiah in the eighth century? Two main theories have been canvassed by scholars, and each has enjoyed a period of popularity. A third, more recent explanation is more likely to offer a true understanding of the complexities of the book. The first of these theories, closely linked with the work of Bernhard Duhm in a commentary dating from 1892, argued that a substantial body of later prophecies, not originally connected with Isaiah, came to be added to the book for reasons that can no longer be clearly determined.

These later prophecies are to be found in two major groups, chapters 40–55 and 56–66, and scholars have referred to them as Deutero- (or Second) Isaiah and Trito- (or Third) Isaiah respectively. Yet there are some connections between the separate parts, even though evidence of a later historical background is not to be denied. Hence a second major attempt at explanation, put forward by Sigmund Mowinckel in 1926, has enjoyed intermittent support from scholars. It argued that the prophet Isaiah had formed a small group of disciples (see Isa 8:16), which continued to exist and subsequently formed a powerful religious circle in Jerusalem. This "prophetic school" gave rise to further influential prophetic figures, among whom we may place the great spiritual giant of Isaiah 40–55 and the author, or more probably series of authors, of chapters 56–66. The book is therefore to be seen as the product of the school of the prophet Isaiah and to have been in the process of composition over a period of more than two centuries. Each of these theories has its own insights and merits, but neither truly manages to clarify the purpose of such a complex literary work as this book.

More recent studies of the literary developments of prophecy in the Old Testament (Clements 1980, Fishbane 1985) have shown that various forms of supplementation, exposition, and reinterpretation became a natural part of prophecy once it had been fixed in writing. The subsequent history of institutions (such as the Davidic kingship) and peoples (Babylon) referred to in prophecies gave rise to intricate literary structures. Later editors would also reassemble prophetic collections to elicit a clearer divine plan that they saw to be implicit within them. In consequence it became natural to build up a prophetic book not around the theme of "authorship," as in a modern book subject to modern conceptions of authorial intention, but around the theme of "message." Once God had spoken concerning his people and their central religious institutions and attitudes, further divine words relating to these realities belonged quite properly to the book, or more precisely scroll, in which that message had first been given. We should therefore recognize that the Book of Isaiah is built up around the message of the prophet Isaiah, and this includes divine revelations given after the prophet's own lifetime had ended, but which were concerned with features about which the prophet had spoken very powerfully. Since Isaiah had spoken about the oneness of the divine purpose for Israel, about the role of the Davidic kingship, and about the advent of

Assyrian (Mesopotamian) imperial intervention in Judah and Ephraim, further information was needed to show how these prophecies had been fulfilled.

A further feature is also of great importance for a proper grasp of the purpose, character, and unity of the Book of Isaiah. Assyrian imperial control over Judah finally collapsed about a century after it had begun. However, it was very rapidly replaced by another Mesopotamian power, that of Babylon, within two or three decades after the Assyrians had removed their tight control. This rule was to prove even more disastrous for Judah than Assyrian rule had been, since whereas both the Jerusalem Temple and the Davidic kingship had survived the Assyrian depredations, they did not do so in the face of Babylon. It was of the utmost interest and importance therefore for the compilers of this magisterial prophetic book to show the connections between Assyrian and Babylonian power. The link between these two great powers of antiquity is carefully brought out in Isaiah 39 in such a way as to mark the transition from the first (Assyrian) phase of the book to the subsequent (Babylonian) phase.

A further feature also becomes evident from a close examination of the Book of Isaiah. As I have already mentioned, the prophet himself addressed what he had to say to specific situations, thereby acting as a religious interpreter of these events. He foretold how they would issue forth into future events in which the hand and intention of God would be evident. In the case of Isaiah these future events were predominantly of a threatening and punitive nature. So behind the intervention of Assyria in the internal affairs of Judah and Israel (Ephraim) the hand of God was seen to be at work. Yet the prophet was not a fatalist foretelling a fixed and unalterable destiny that was determined for his people. On the contrary, the future lay open to the plans and purposes of God, which could never be fully known to humankind. They could be discerned only partially and through the skillful search for the truth that lay behind the mystery that characterized the being of God. Even more important, God was recognized as a personal being, so that the dealings of all humankind with him were of a personal, spiritual, and moral nature. There was room for repentance and for a right, and spiritually serious, response to his declared intentions once he had revealed them. The prophet was a person who was most anxious to provoke a response of penitence and obedience toward God.

As later generations of prophetic scribes reflected upon the prophet's words, they naturally wished to reinforce this appeal for a positive response of obedience toward God and to show what form such obedience must display. They were also concerned to relate this awareness of the relevance of the prophet's words to the needs and demands of their own day by retaining and interpreting the imagery and phrases that the prophet had used. In no book is this activity more marked than in the case of the prophet Isaiah. We find that, in addition to the need to provide a measure of guidance to show how Isaiah's prophecies had been fulfilled in events and had then led to further major events, there was also a need to elaborate and apply the demand for repentance that his message had contained. If those who had first heard Isaiah preach had failed to respond positively, then it was still to be hoped that later generations who read his words would respond more worthily. This feature has been responsible for the fact that much of the later material that has been preserved in the book possesses a more general and even timeless character. It points to the need to turn away from idolatry and to obey the divine law in a manner that would have been applicable to almost any period of Israelite-Jewish history in biblical times.

In addition to this concern to define more clearly how men and women should respond to Isaiah's prophecies, a further feature is to be noticed in the later parts of the book. Not only is there no clear and distinctive information about the precise political and international background in those parts of the book that were added after the end of the Babylonian era, but these sections (especially in 56–66 and 24–27) make extensive use of elaborate word-pictures to convey their message. The element of mystery and the belief in a hidden revelation of a secret purpose of God disclosed through his prophets have become dominant characteristics. Such passages have become known as "apocalyptic" (revelatory) literature, and indeed the later parts of the Book of Isaiah contain the most important evidence from the Old Testament for the rooting of apocalyptic in the ground of prophecy. This is most clearly to be seen in chapters 56–66 (Hanson 1975) and 24–27 (Plöger 1968). Thus the Book of Isaiah is undoubtedly the most central and informative witness to changes in the understanding and interpretation of prophecy during the period between the Babylonian exile and the rise of the Christian community.

THE LIFE AND TIMES OF ISAIAH

The major feature of the historical background to the Book of Isaiah was the rise of the neo-Assyrian empire and the reimposition of Assyrian imperial control in the Levantine states of the eastern Mediterranean Sea. When Tiglath-pileser III came to the Assyrian throne in 745 B.C.E., he quickly set about reasserting his influence in the West as far as the kingdoms of Egypt and Phoenicia. The two sister kingdoms of Israel (Ephraim) and Judah were inevitably caught up in this development and suffered greatly on account of it. Judah, now a vassal kingdom, paid heavy annual tribute to its Mesopotamian overlord, and after a period of vassaldom Israel (Ephraim) fared even worse. Following a disastrous rebellion the kingdom was broken up and administered as an internal province of the Assyrian empire with no native kingship of its own. The former borders, which less than half a century before had stretched from Lebanon to the Red Sea (2 Kgs 14:25), were now redrawn and much of the population compulsorily removed to other regions of the empire. The northern kingdom of Israel ceased to be a kingdom or a single unified political entity at all. For a prophet of the God who was known as "the Holy One of Israel" these events could only be looked upon as disastrous. Yet this was the position of Isaiah, whose prophecies from the period provide a kind of spiritual commentary on these affairs, and whose explanations and interpretations offered to later generations a guide as to why such misfortunes had befallen Israel and Judah.

In view of the powerful political events that shook these two sister kingdoms, it is to be expected that Isaiah's words contain a strongly political element and relate directly to these events. More especially the major upheavals of the period clearly offered the most direct reasons for the preservation of prophecies from Isaiah and hence helped to draw together clusters of prophetic sayings, even though later editors have tended to break up these original clusters in the interests of a more thematic approach.

The four most prominent events concerning Israel and Judah during this period were as follows. First, between the years of 736–733 a conflict arose between Judah and Israel in which the latter kingdom (Ephraim) was in alliance with the Aramaean (Syrian) kingdom of Damascus. This upheaval, which marked the sharpest open breach between the two closely related kingdoms of Israel and Judah, has become known as the Syro-Ephraimite war. It ended with direct military intervention by Assyria to conquer both Samaria and Damascus and undoubtedly greatly strengthened the hold of this Mesopotamian power. Judah's king, Jehoahaz (Ahaz), acted treacherously in seeking to retain his throne. His death and the accession of his son and successor Hezekiah took place in 725. The opportunity for some rapprochement between Judah and Israel now presented itself, but it passed in confusion and bitterness. After a series of internal assassinations and coups the northern kingdom rebelled against Assyrian control again, and Samaria was besieged and taken in 723. From this point on, no native ruler was left on the throne of this province, and its collapse was further hastened. Taken together, the death of Jehoahaz and the fall of the northern kingdom of Ephraim mark the second of the major political phases of Isaiah's career in which the fate of Ephraim achieved prominence. A third, if relatively minor, political event took place in 711, when a coalition of minor states in the west, led by the Philistines of Ashdod, rebelled against Assyria. The extent to which Hezekiah of Judah was drawn into this conflict is not clear, but it undoubtedly offered a tempting opportunity for Judah also to break free from its irksome vassaldom. Isaiah strongly and visibly campaigned against such involvement on Judah's part (see Isa 20). In any event the rebellion came to nothing.

The most striking of all the political events of Isaiah's prophetic career began in 705, when the Assyrian ruler Sargon died. Taking advantage of the period of instability in the Mesopotamian homeland, Hezekiah joined a number of other neighboring states, backed by strong support from Egypt, in withdrawing allegiance to Assyria. The situation was slow to be resolved as the new Assyrian ruler Sen-

nacherib asserted his control in his homeland before moving to reestablish Assyrian rule over the rebellious western provinces. In 701 Judah was attacked, and in a major battle fought at Lachish the city was besieged and captured. The precise sequence of events after this attack is disputed, although much detail is provided from the Assyrian royal chronicles. After the defeat of the Egyptian forces, which sought to check Sennacherib at Eltekeh, an initial start was made on a siege of Jerusalem. Before the city suffered undue deprivation, Hezekiah surrendered and paid a heavy penalty for his temerity in withdrawing his allegiance to Assyria (2 Kgs 18:13–16). Yet surprisingly he retained his throne as an Egyptian vassal and Judah thereafter passed more than half a century before Assyrian rule over it finally crumbled and hastened on toward total collapse. The events surrounding the confrontation between Hezekiah and Sennacherib in 701 and the role that Isaiah's prophesying played in them are much disputed and need to be considered in specific detail. We have at least one prophecy from Isaiah made shortly after these events (Isa. 22:1–14), the last from him that is certainly datable. With this climactic threat to Jerusalem and its unexpected sequel the long ministry of Isaiah appears to have come to a close.

THE PROPHECIES OF ISAIAH
IN THEIR SETTING

The account that Isaiah gives of his call to be a prophet, set out in chapter 6, is dated to "the year that king Uzziah died" (Isa 6:1), most probably coming after that death had taken place. This was the year 736 B.C.E., following the chronology used by Joachim Begrich (1963). (The precise dates for the reigns of the kings with whom Isaiah was associated have been disputed.) A primary reason for Isaiah's remark must lie in the fact that because of Uzziah's illness (see 2 Kgs 15:5) his son Jotham served as coregent with him and after the latter's death his grandson Jehoahaz (Ahaz) also served briefly in this fashion. Uzziah's death therefore marked the time when Ahaz obtained full freedom to act as independent ruler.

At his experience of call, Isaiah received a vision of God in the Temple, seeing him sitting in splendor upon his heavenly throne. The report of the call opens an account, preserved in a first-person narrative form, that covers the events of the ensuing three years as well (the conclusion is probably at Isa 8:18). This "Isaiah Memoir" deals with the period of the Syro-Ephraimite war of 736–733 and appears to have been written down by the prophet toward the end of that period. This accounts for the ambivalent sense that the memoir displays of the prophet's message, which was initially hopeful and reassuring, but which became threatening after having been rejected by the king of Judah and those in authority in Jerusalem (Isa 7:13, 8:17). It also explains the heavy irony and anticipation of rejection that are reintroduced into the report of the prophet's call and commissioning (6:9–10). God had sent him to present his divine message to Israel and Judah, but if they refused this it would rebound to their own hurt.

Both in the call narrative and in the episodes that immediately follow there are indications of Isaiah's social and religious eminence, which enabled him to achieve ready access to no less a figure than the king himself. This points to Isaiah's upbringing either in a wealthy landowning family in the city of Jerusalem or more probably among the ranks of the temple priesthood. At all events his call brought him both cleansing to become the spokesman of God (6:5–7) and a knowledge that his proclamation of the divine message would have to continue until extensive ruin and devastation had been inflicted upon the land (6:11–12). The manner by which this would come about is not spelled out, but there are strong indications that it would result from military defeat and catastrophe.

After receiving his call, the prophet recalls in his memoir the events, interviews, and prophecies that he delivered personally to Ahaz, king of Judah, during the years 736–733, when the alliance of Syria and Israel (Ephraim) sought to attack Judah and lay siege to Jerusalem. This alliance intended to remove Ahaz from his throne and to replace him with a ruler who would support the policy of resolute military resistance against Assyria. Ahaz had evidently chosen to adopt a more flexible, even collaborationist, policy toward Assyria, which eventually led to his sending a massive payment of tribute gift to the Assyrian king (2 Kgs 16:7–9) in order to buy Assyrian support against his northern neighbors. Before this tribute gift was sent,

which even required the plundering of the Jerusalem Temple in order to provide its full extent, Isaiah sought a series of interviews with the king and gave his prophetic messages to him. The prophet's intention was clearly to dissuade the king from treacherous conduct that would embitter relations between Israel and Judah and compel the king himself to submit to Assyrian demands, however punitive they should prove to be. In order to encourage the king in remaining steadfast in this way Isaiah gave to the king assurances of God's support and protection, if only the king showed sufficient courage and steadfastness to trust in God. It is evident, however, that the king lacked such courage and was not prepared to trust the words that the prophet brought to him.

To strengthen and affirm his prophetic message, Isaiah gave the king "signs" that take the form of "sign-names" given to the children of the prophet. The sign-names, of which there are three (*cf.* the three sign-names given to Hosea's children in Hos 1:4, 6, 9), each contain a cryptic message from God providing an indication of the assurance that the prophet brought to the king, but which the king himself refused to heed. There is no doubt concerning the meaning of the names, since the prophet Isaiah himself explicitly interprets what they signify.

The first of these children bears the mysterious sign-name Shear-jashub ("A remnant returns") and is already old enough to be carried by the prophet to meet the king (Isa 7:3–9). The message of the name is interpreted (all translations by the author except as noted):

> It shall not stand,
>   and it shall never happen.
> For the head of Syria is Damascus,
>   and the head of Damascus is Rezin. . . .
> And the head of Ephraim is Samaria,
>   and the head of Samaria is the son of Remaliah.
> If you will not believe,
>   you will certainly not be kept firm.
>
> (Isa 7:7–9)

The prophet employs delightfully intriguing circumlocutions to convey his message and give it an air of solemnity, but its meaning is plain: those who are plotting against Ahaz to remove him from his throne are mere men, and since such a plan is contrary to God's it will not succeed.

Ahaz, however, remained unimpressed by this message and was in no way willing to set aside his plan to seek, and pay for, the aid of Assyria. After an interval, therefore, Isaiah arranged again to meet the king and to offer to him a further sign (7:10–17). Ahaz refused even to agree to any such sign, so that Isaiah declared:

> Listen then, you ruler of David's line! Is it not enough for you to weary men, that you weary my God also? Therefore the LORD himself will give you a sign. Behold the young woman who is pregnant will bear a son, and she will call his name Immanuel [God is with us]. (7:13–14)

The prophet then goes on to interpret the significance of the name, which implies God's protection, in terms of what it will mean for the king, regarding the threat that was still facing him: "Before the child knows how to refuse what is bad and choose what is good, the land before whose two kings you are in dread will be deserted" (7:16).

The prophet has added to the message of the sign-name of Shear-jashub an assurance of the time within which the deliverance sought by the king would have come: before the child knows how to refuse what is bad and choose what is good, that is, before it can be taught how to behave by being told what is right and wrong. There is an element of intentional vagueness, but Isaiah, who must undoubtedly have been referring to his own pregnant wife, implied that deliverance would have come before the child was more than a couple of years of age.

Still the king refused to listen to Isaiah, so yet a third interview was sought with yet a third sign-name, given to a child who had not even been conceived at the time the name was divulged (8:1–4). The name here is the lengthy one of Maher-shalal-hashbaz ("Spoil speeds, booty hastens"), referring to a military defeat for those who were currently threatening Jerusalem and its king. The message of the name is further spelled out: "Before the child knows how to call 'Mommy' or 'Daddy,' the wealth of Damascus and the spoil of Samaria will be carried away before the king of Assyria" (8:4).

However, all these elaborate messages and in-triguing sign-names, the latter solemnly inscribed upon a tablet of either wood or clay (8:1), were in vain. The king refused to listen to Isaiah and sent his faithless and treacherous gift to the king of Assyria (2 Kgs 16:5–12). Ahaz achieved his aim when both Damascus and Samaria were overthrown by the armies of Assyria. Ahaz had, however, shown himself devoid of any genuine faith in the God of Israel and indifferent to the fact that both Israel and Judah were part of one people in the eyes of God (and his prophet Isaiah). Nor did the intervention of Assyria stop at the border between Israel and Judah, for this aggressive imperial power imposed its will upon Judah as upon any other petty nation, exactly as Isaiah had foretold that it would (8:5–8).

Isaiah had set out, through the sign-names given to his children, to bring a message of hope and assurance to his ruler Ahaz in the time of conflict that had arisen. This message had been totally rejected by the king, however, so now the very assurance and protection that he had spurned would be turned against him to be his downfall. The sense that the king of Judah had betrayed his people, and that in seeking to maintain his position as king he had actually betrayed it, is brought out very strikingly and poetically by the prophet in 8:11–15. The very God of Israel, who should have been regarded as the "rock" of security and stability of the kingdom of Judah, would instead become "a stone of offense" and "a rock to stumble over" for both Judah and Israel ("both houses of Israel" in the prophet's words; 8:14).

How the ruin and disaster would come of which the prophet had been forewarned at the time of his call had now become plain to him, and he spelled it out to his people:

> He [God] will raise a signal-flag for a distant nation
> and whistle for it from the ends of the earth;
> then look, it will come swiftly and speedily!
> None is tired; none stumbles,
> none dozes or sleeps;
> not a waistcloth is untied,
> not a sandal-thong is broken;
> their arrows are sharp,
> and all their bows ready for use;
> their horses' hooves are like flint,
> and their chariot wheels like the wind.
> They roar like a lion,

growling like young lions.
    They growl and seize their prey,
        carrying it away so that none can rescue it.
                          (5:26–29)

In such terms Isaiah forewarns of the coming of the armies of Assyria, a force that was to become well known, and greatly feared, throughout Judah and Israel in the decades that followed. It is not surprising, therefore, that the memory of Isaiah's words forewarning of the arrival of this power that was destined to change the entire political face of the Near East during the next century became the subject of continued reflection and concern.

What prophecies Isaiah proclaimed during the remaining years of the relatively brief reign of Ahaz cannot certainly be determined, but he can hardly have laid all responsibility for the disastrous events that befell the northern kingdom at the door of Judah's king alone. Both in Ephraim and Damascus there were guilty leaders and political advisers whom Isaiah did not shun to condemn as having contributed to their own downfall (17:1–3 against Damascus and vv. 4–6 against Ephraim). Probably therefore we should also date the sharp criticism of the drunken rulers of Ephraim in 28:1–4 to this period. At any event, after much further internal conflict and dissension Ephraim rebelled yet again against Assyria, resulting in an even more ruinous siege and plundering of Samaria in 722. Before this took place, however, Ahaz had died, and this event brought to the throne of Judah in 725 a new ruler, Hezekiah, who appears to have been much more respectful of the religious inheritance of his kingdom than Ahaz had been and who may even have displayed some genuine concern to achieve some rapprochement with the alienated citizens of Ephraim. The death of Ahaz is reflected in the Book of Isaiah by a prophecy addressed to Philistia in 14:28–32, showing again how widely this prophet was alert to the international political scene. It also provided the opportunity for him to reassert his deep conviction that Zion (Jerusalem) had a vital part to play in God's plans for his people, and for all nations (v. 32).

The accession of Hezekiah provided Isaiah with the occasion for presenting to the nation the most momentous, and certainly the best known, of all his prophecies. Isaiah 9:2–7 follows the form and venerable language of ancient coronation oracles. When a new ruler came to the throne it was a part of the accompanying celebrations that a favorable oracle should be proclaimed to him recalling the divine promises upon which the royal dynasty was founded and looking forward to prosperity and greatness:

The people who walked in darkness
    have seen a great light;
those who were living in a land of intense gloom,
    upon them has light shone.
Thou [God] hast enlarged the nation,
    thou hast increased its happiness.
people rejoice before thee
    as at harvesttime,
    or when men divide the spoil of battle.
For the yoke of his burden
    and the staff upon his shoulder,
    the rod of his taskmaster,
    thou hast broken as on the day of Midian.
For every boot of the soldier marching into the
    din of battle,
and every tunic spattered with blood,
will be burned as fuel for the fire.
For to us a child is born,
    to us a son is given;
and the right to govern will be placed upon him,
    and his name will be called
"Marvelous Counselor, Divine Warrior,
    Everlasting Father, Prince of Peace";
Of the growth of his kingdom
    and of peace
there will be no end,
upon the throne of David, and over his kingdom,
    to establish it, and to uphold it
with justice and righteousness
    from this time forth and for evermore.
The zeal of the LORD of hosts will do this.

The reference to the "birth" of a royal child (v. 6) refers not to the birth of a royal heir but to the "new birth" of the king at his coronation, who is thereby elevated to become the "son" of God (cf. Ps 2:7, a royal coronation psalm that bears close comparison with the prophecy from Isaiah). In such terms Isaiah reminded the new ruler of his exalted office, of the divine promises that undergirded it, and of the possibilities of greatness that these conferred. In many respects Hezekiah's reign did mark some real improvement in the situation of Judah, certainly when its fortunes are compared with those of the almost unmitigated catastrophes that befell the sister kingdom of Ephraim. Nevertheless the later years of this king's reign were marked by a sharp and prolonged conflict between him and the prophet Isaiah that must engage much of our further attention. Therefore this royal coronation prophecy is of the utmost importance for an understanding of both the nature of prophecy and the particularly distinctive features of the Book of Isaiah. The prophet was not always a gloomy and threatening figure who castigated his people and condemned its rulers, although this often proved to be necessary. He also held out hope and glorious possibilities for his people's future. In many respects it was the greatness of this vision of a triumphant and prosperous future, in which peace and an end to warfare would form the most central of all blessings, that gave rise to the prophet's impatience with the present. It was also to prove the most lasting and enduring of the themes and images of prophecy, which has given it meaning and vitality centuries after the prophet had originally proclaimed it. This awareness of God's special commitment to the kingship and dynasty of the house of David was to make the Book of Isaiah the centerpiece of the messianic hope to be found in the Old Testament and to lead to a long sequence of further prophecies concerning the future greatness of the dynasty of David.

Isaiah appears clearly to have hoped that the arrival of Ahaz upon the throne of Judah might lead to better relations between Judah and Ephraim, since the conflict between them was one he bitterly regretted (see Isa 9:21). Yet this was not to be, and the prophet proclaimed a long and painful plea to the people of Ephraim, who had suffered so greatly in the decades since the great ruler Jeroboam II had died in 746. For all their sufferings, however, they were no nearer a return to their traditional loyalty to God and his law (9:8–21). So in fact the final collapse of the northern kingdom passed with little relief of its sufferings, and it came to be progressively absorbed in the many depredations and political realignments forced upon it by the Assyrians (see 7:8).

Isaiah certainly did not regard the king of Judah as an isolated and independent figure, and a series of sharply worded condemnations by him of the leaders and ruling classes in Jerusalem provide a powerful insight into the social and moral awareness of the prophet (5:8–20, 10:1–4).

At some stage in his prophetic ministry Isaiah appears to have delivered a memorable and deeply reflective prophecy affirming that ultimately God would overthrow Assyria for all its arrogance and pride, just as he had used it as a stick with which to punish his people Israel and Judah (10:5–11, 13–15). The prophecy has been widely acclaimed by scholars for the depth of its insight into the world-encompassing range of a vision of a divine providence that extended to all nations. It lifts the idea of God from that of a partisan national guardian to that of a mind and will that are genuinely universal in both power and range. It displays skillful use of metaphorical imagery to convey its message and appears also to show a familiarity with the arrogant and boastful tone of royal victory inscriptions such as imperial powers set up in conquered cities. Yet, for all this, its content creates difficulty for the scholar, since it is not clear that there was any turning point in his ministry when Isaiah could have believed or declared that the downfall of Assyria was imminent. In fact, what we know of his preaching firmly excludes this. At most we may consider that this reflective pronouncement of the ultimate downfall of Assyria, and the end of its control over Judah, was intended to show that such a collapse would ultimately lie in the hands of God. Far from intending to incite the kingdom of Judah to rebel against Assyria, this prophecy was intended to discourage such rash and premature ventures in the knowledge that all these issues lay in the mysterious power of God.

There were evidently two further opportunities for Judah to join in more widely planned attempts by the Levantine kingdoms of the eastern Mediterranean, strongly backed by Egypt, to withdraw allegiance to Assyria and to withhold the payment of tribute money. The first of these took place in the years 714–711, led by the Philistine kingdom of Ashdod, and is referred to in Isaiah 20. This short account of Isaiah's actions at the time of the rebellion states that he went about Jerusalem "naked and barefoot" for three years as a warning sign to his people. By adopting the garb of a prisoner of war Isaiah sought to impress upon all who saw him the futility and disaster that lay behind such ill-considered political acts, which could only bring further suffering upon those who had already suffered much. It enabled him to raise a theme that was to be repeated strongly and frequently throughout all his remaining years as a prophet: Egypt's help is vain and worthless (see Isa 30:1–5). It is possible that the prophecy against Egypt in 18:1–6 belongs to the time of this Ashdodite rebellion. The picture of a hostile army marching toward Jerusalem (10:27b–32) may also derive from this time, although no very certain and precise historical background to this has become clear. The strongly worded anti-Egypt prophecy of 19:1–15 is most probably not from the prophet but derives from a later time and has been added to present a more complete picture of God's intentions and plans for Egypt.

The later years of Isaiah's activity are taken up almost exclusively with the events that occurred between the years 705 and 701. In 705 the great Assyrian ruler Sargon died, to be succeeded by Sennacherib. It was this ruler who was to take part in one of the most significant campaigns in Judah by any Mesopotamian power, a campaign that was subsequently widely reflected upon in the biblical record and in the impressive memorials in carved wall-reliefs and the pretentious royal chronicles that the Assyrian ruler had prepared.

Sennacherib's accession to the throne was marked by a period of unrest and political turmoil in the provinces close to the Assyrian capital city of Nineveh. News of this unrest must have accompanied the reports of the ruler's death (which some have thought may even have been celebrated in the satirical dirge set in Isaiah 14:4–21 and later applied to a Babylonian ruler) and reached Judah and the neighboring kingdoms. A further attempt at breaking free from the heavy impositions of Assyrian control was thereupon made. Hezekiah was heavily involved, and it may even have been that Jerusalem became a center for the rebellious diplomacy. Egypt offered strong support for the rebel kingdoms. It is undoubtedly the promises of this Egyptian support, and those of the treaty negotiations in which they were embodied, that are so roundly and emphatically condemned by Isaiah in a whole series of prophecies (Isa 28:7–13, 14–18; 29:1–4, 13–14, 15–16; 30:1–5, 6–7; 31:1–3). Isaiah

branded the entire plan as futile—a "covenant with death" that was in no way the plan and purpose of God. It was a policy conceived in faithlessness and treachery that would have catastrophic consequences for the kingdoms embroiled in it. Once again the prophet Isaiah insisted that Egypt's help was worthless and that those who trusted in it had abandoned their faith in God as the God of Israel.

The outcome of the rebellion is told in 2 Kings 18:13–16, although the threatened siege of Jerusalem is ascribed to the fourteenth year of Hezekiah rather than the twenty-fourth (which it undoubtedly was). A much longer and fuller account is attributed to Sennacherib himself in a royal chronicle, heavily self-congratulatory in tone, prepared for the ruler. In spite of some obscurities over matters of detail there can be little doubt that the biblical and Assyrian records present us with complementary perspectives upon the same event. Far greater uncertainty attaches to the very much longer, and evidently composite, narrative in 2 Kings 18:17–19:37. (See Clements 1980.) The narrative account here, although it gives only a brief sketch of the major military moves, points to Sennacherib's having been frustrated in his intention of inflicting a costly siege and heavy penalties upon Jerusalem and her king. This has led many scholars to claim that it must be referring to some other attempt on Sennacherib's part to take Jerusalem, either shortly after the first blockade of the city (it seems likely that no full siege was made), when Hezekiah had surrendered, or possibly as much as a dozen years later. Neither assumption is either likely or necessary, and it is better to recognize that the more amplified account, which is also repeated in Isaiah 36:1–37:38, represents a later, more theologically reflective, account of the circumstances of Hezekiah's surrender in 701, whereby any costly bloodshed in Jerusalem was avoided. It could well have been the case that a popular memory survived that Sennacherib had acted under duress, and with unwanted haste, in allowing Hezekiah such relatively lenient terms of surrender.

A series of prophecies set in the Book of Isaiah refer to the overthrow of nations that threaten Jerusalem (see Isa 8:9–10), or even in one case specifically to God's plan to "break" the Assyrian in the land of

Judah-Israel (see Isa 14:25). These sayings, however, do not fit readily into the consistent pattern of Isaiah's preaching and are better understood as belonging to the phase of subsequent development of the prophet's message.

The last prophecies from Isaiah that we can date with confidence are two that belong to the immediate aftermath of the events of 701. The first of these has now been set by the book's later editors at the beginning to form a kind of preface to the entire collection in Isaiah 1:4–9. It portrays Judah as a sinful nation, torn and ravaged by suffering, with Jerusalem —the "daughter of Zion"—left as an isolated and beleaguered city. Amid a host of ravaged and plundered towns and minor cities (Sennacherib's Chronicle lists no less than forty-six) Jerusalem stood apart "like a hut in a field of melons" (Isa 1:8; NIV). Undoubtedly this picture of the plundered and ruined territory of Judah, and of Jerusalem's merciful and pitiable isolation, had come to be viewed as a symbolic picture of the condition of Israel and Judah throughout the following two centuries that succeeded Hezekiah's reign. It is for this reason that the note of hope contained in the concluding reference (v. 9) to "some survivors" was probably added later.

The other prophecy from the aftermath of the events of 701, which is also the last certainly datable prophecy from Isaiah, is an unexpected condemnation of the citizens of Jerusalem for their revelry and celebrations after the city had been spared from the sword by Hezekiah's surrender (22:1–14). It is wholly understandable that the ordinary men and women of the city experienced a great sense of relief, which is all the more fully brought home by the scenes of barbarism and cruelty inflicted by Assyria upon the defenders of Lachish after that city had fallen. These atrocities are recorded for all posterity to see in the wall-reliefs that decorated Sennacherib's palace in Nineveh. Yet, understandable as we may admit Jerusalem's celebrations upon its escape to have been, we may also endorse the deeper insight and wisdom of Isaiah's condemnation. So strong in fact were his feelings that such rejoicings were misplaced that he pronounces a virtual death sentence upon the people. Perhaps more deeply he felt that they had passed such a sentence upon themselves:

This is what the LORD God has revealed to me:
"This sin will not be forgiven you
until you die,"
says the LORD God.

(Isa 22:14)

Isaiah's attitude may appear unreasonable, yet it was a truly prophetic one. Rather than mourn the ruin and devastation that Hezekiah's policy of rebellion against Assyria had brought upon the kingdom, the people were congratulating themselves and their ruler upon their skillful diplomacy. They mistook survival for victory and closed their minds to the fate of hundreds, and possibly thousands, of their fellow countrymen who had died at the hands of the Assyrian masters of the territory. Hezekiah had ignored the condemnation of Isaiah when he had confirmed his plans, and now that they had come to their fateful conclusion he was rejoicing in the little that he had saved from the ruin.

KEY THEMES OF ISAIAH'S PROPHECIES

It is evident from this examination of the specific prophecies of Isaiah addressed to the developing political situation in Israel (Ephraim) and Judah during the years in which Assyrian domination in the region was established that his thinking was deeply political in its implications. Yet the sphere of politics was in no way separate from that of religion, and we can see underlying all that he had to say a consistent basis of religious and spiritual themes.

First among these fundamental convictions was the knowledge that God was in a special relationship to Israel that demanded of this people a consistent loyalty of allegiance and a responsible degree of moral integrity and concern. The favored title for God is "the Holy One of Israel" (Isa 1:4, 5:19, etc.), and this meant for the prophet not simply that God was holy and apart but that all of Israel was truly one people. In consequence he deeply opposed the division of this people into two kingdoms, which he himself was willing to define as no more than "two houses of Israel" (8:14). So he vigorously opposed the actions of Ahaz, which had embittered the relationships between these two kingdoms. In returning to God, the hope for what remained of the northern kingdom of Ephraim was that these people would also return to become one people again (9:8–21). When seen in religious perspective the sister kingdoms of Israel and Judah were one people and together constituted the "vineyard" of the Lord God (see Isa 5:7).

Implicit in this understanding of Israel as essentially one people bound by a common loyalty to one God, Yahweh, who had constituted them as his people, was a condemnation of the years of division after Solomon's death. In becoming separated into two houses with no focal point of unity in either the worship of the Temple in Jerusalem or the kingship of the Davidic dynasty, Israel had demonstrated its rebellion against God:

> Listen, you heavens, and pay attention, earth;
> for the LORD has spoken:
> "I have reared children and brought them up,
> but they have rebelled against me.
> Oxen know their owner,
> and asses their master's stall,
> but Israel does not know,
> my people do not understand."
> You sinful nation,
> a people burdened with sin,
> children of wrongdoers,
> sons who act wickedly!
> They have forsaken the LORD,
> they have despised the Holy One of Israel,
> they are completely estranged.
>
> (1:2–4)

This theme of Israel's alienation from God becomes a central one for Isaiah's understanding of what was taking place in the sister kingdoms of Israel and Judah in his days. In such a central affirmation Isaiah found the key to the interpretation of the confused political aims, widely rampant social injustice, and purely outward and formal religious observance of the communities he knew. They had forsaken their true identity as the people of the Lord their God and had, in consequence, forfeited their right to his protection and blessing. No longer could Yahweh speak of them as "my people" (1:3) but only as "this people" (6:9, 8:6).

Upon this basis Isaiah develops the theme of the "hardening" of Israel's heart, with its consequent spiritual blindness and deafness that made it impossible for the people to see and understand the true nature of their condition (6:9–10). They neither grasped the reasons for the misfortunes that befell them, nor were they able to make intelligent decisions to rectify their mistakes. Isaiah saw that the effect of his prophecies was in reality a negative one, driving the people deeper in their rebellion against God and making it more difficult for them to change their ways. The theme becomes of great importance for the whole written tradition of Isaiah's prophecies (see Isa 29:18, 35:5) and for the entire biblical understanding of the Word of God (cf. Mark 4:12). Various explanations have been put forward to assist in understanding the meaning of God's "hardening" the hearts of his people through the word of prophecy. In part there is an undoubted element of irony present, which sought to penetrate the people's complacency and awaken a fresh openness to hear God's word. There is present also an element of psychological realism, a recognition that "I will not" will eventually become "I cannot." Other scholars have discerned within the saying an element of historical and personal experience that would indicate that the saying had been written in Isaiah's "Memoir" of his call and early prophecies after some interval of time had elapsed. During this period the prophet would have sensed a deep frustration with the popular rejection of his prophecies (see 7:13, 8:16–18). All of these explanations contribute to the understanding of the theme, which in its comprehensiveness has a deep and enduring theological importance.

The central significance for Isaiah of the true nature of Israel as a single people bound by inescapable bonds to Yahweh, its God, sheds its own light on the major political event of the period in which he prophesied. This was an era that witnessed the progressive collapse and downfall of the northern kingdom of Israel (Ephraim), culminating in the fall of Samaria to the Assyrians in 722. The decline, however, began more than a decade before this, and its long-term consequences extended over a further period of more than half a century (cf. the editorial note in 7:8).

If the nature of Israel provides a basic theme for the prophet, this theme is fully matched by his understanding of God. The distinctive and favored title for Yahweh God is "the Holy One of Israel" (1:4). Even more prominent in the early prophecies is the simple title "the LORD of hosts" (Yahweh Sebaoth) (1:24, 6:3, etc.). This must certainly have been an ancient title, widely used in the Jerusalem Temple worship, which associated God with the military traditions of early Israel as the one who led Israel's armies ("hosts") into battle. It later came to be linked with the "hosts of heaven" (40:26), thus giving the title a broad cosmic significance. The sense of the majesty and power of God, who is truly Israel's "king" (see 6:5), pervades all of Isaiah's preaching. In comparison with him human beings are as nothing, and their advice and plans cannot be sustained against him (*cf.* 2:17, 7:8–9, etc.). This awareness of the unassailable power and superior wisdom of Yahweh the God of Israel sets him apart from all other gods who form the objects of human worship. Whether Isaiah can properly be described as a monotheist, that is, as denying the existence of any gods other than Yahweh, has been much discussed by scholars. Certainly he expresses many of the implicit essentials of such a faith (see especially Isa 10:5–15), yet it is not clear that he wholly repudiates the existence of other deities. The issue is not really an important one for him, since he knows that all such gods must be incomparably weaker and lesser than Israel's God.

The essential characteristics of how the divine nature is known and operative in the life of the world are to be seen in the prophet's emphases upon the holiness, righteousness, and justice of God. These are in all respects attributes of deity that were widely accepted and believed long before the time of Isaiah. Nevertheless this prophet lends to them a new seriousness and a new inner consistency and coherence. In 5:8–9 he draws attention to an issue that undoubtedly went deep in the social and moral transitions of his day:

Woe to those who join house to house,
 who add field to field,
until there is no more room,
 and you are left to live alone in the midst of the land.
The LORD of hosts has sworn in my hearing:
"Surely many houses shall be desolate,
 large and beautiful homes, with no occupant."

Here we certainly find drawn into the prophet's invective the awareness that the contemporary legal and social practice that enabled the powerful and wealthy citizens of Jerusalem to extend their estates at the expense of the rural population constituted a great injustice. Yahweh, Israel's God, was the guardian of justice, not the patron protector of the city of Jerusalem's rulers and administrators. So we find further that the notion of divine justice led Isaiah into a powerful condemnation of the ruling classes in Jerusalem (5:8–25, 10:1–2). In a memorable phrase the prophet insists that righteousness is at the very heart of holiness (5:16). He particularly singles out the maladministration of justice as calling down the divine wrath (1:17, 23; 5:23; etc.).

It is wholly in line with this condemnation that Isaiah could repudiate the value of the formal cultic worship offered by the community (1:10–17). For all its outward earnestness and rectitude such worship merely served to mask the corruption and injustice that everywhere prevailed in the society. It could not therefore claim to justify its intention of uniting the people with their God. Their very social and moral disorder demonstrated that they were living in open defiance of him.

For all this emphasis upon the moral attributes of God, it is noteworthy that Isaiah shows himself in all respects to be deeply and closely attached to the traditions and religious language of the Jerusalem Temple. For him God is in a very real sense the "God of Zion." He is "the LORD of hosts, who dwells on Mount Zion" (8:18; *cf.* 14:32). It is wholly in keeping with this close attachment to the traditions of the Jerusalem Temple that Isaiah should have received his call to prophesy in the Temple itself (6:1–13). In the visionary description of God that came to him on that occasion, he brings into the open much of the imagery and symbolism that belonged to the Temple cultus, showing it to have been much richer than might have been anticipated. God is portrayed as "the King," seated upon an exalted throne and surrounded by his heavenly courtiers, who offer him both praise and service. For a tradition of worship that sharply repudiated the use of images, it is striking that this repudiation did not preclude the retention of the belief in theriomorphic divine servants such as the seraphim (6:1–2). However, it is not the pictorial content but rather the sense of awe and majesty that dominates the prophet's awareness of God. It is God's will that prevails, not the will of humankind, a contrast that the prophet makes on more than one occasion (10:7–13, 28:14, 29:14). The extent to which the prophet draws upon the traditions of Jerusalem's worship, together with the evident facility of access that he enjoyed to many of the most powerful and influential figures in the kingdom, including the king himself, suggests that Isaiah came from the educated and wealthy section of the populace. Quite possibly this may point to some section of the Temple administration, although some explicit indication of this would normally be expected if it were the case.

The centrality of Jerusalem in the prophet's thinking and prophesying carries with it an almost unquestioned assumption that "the city" represents the natural and necessary form required for social life. His condemnation of Jerusalem and its rulers leads him not to abandon the idea that ultimately it must represent "the city of God" but rather to look to a time when it will truly fulfill its divinely ordained role (1:21–26). In drawing together both a sharp criticism of the abuse of justice and power in the city with a vision of a cleansed and purified city of the future, the prophet has himself created the vision that the fullness of human endeavor can be truly realized only in a city of God. It is wholly in keeping with this picture that the threat posed by military siege to the order and prosperity of Jerusalem should have been seen by Isaiah as the self-evident mark of the inescapable divine anger (3:1–8). When the city succumbed to confusion and violence, then the whole divine ordering of human life was at an end.

In his emphasis upon social justice Isaiah displays many points of similarity to the prophecies of Amos, so much so that it has been argued that he was familiar with a collection of these prophecies (see R. Fey, *Amos und Jesaja* [Neukirchen-Vluyn, 1963]). This could well be the case, but if so it should not be allowed to hide the marked differences between the two great prophetic figures. Amos finds his religious values most fully expressed in a rural, tribally ordered society. Isaiah, however, sees the complexities of urban life as themselves a mark of the complex way in which God has structured the human scene. That both men found abuses in their respective social worlds should not be allowed to suggest that either was looking for a wholly different type of social order.

Only in the longer term, as their prophecies were reflected upon and developed, did the idea of a wholly new social order emerge.

For Isaiah the supreme official of the realm was the king, whose position he clearly regarded as God-given and divinely necessary. Isaiah's endorsement of divine support for, and election of, the Davidic royal house (7:9, 13, etc.) should not, however, be taken to imply an unrestrained and open-ended divine commitment to the person of the king. Even though the prophet vehemently attacked Ahaz for his betrayal of the royal office, this condemnation does not seem to have carried with it any wholesale rejection of the idea of monarchy, even though Isaiah clearly regarded God himself as Israel's true "king" (6:5).

The most important of Isaiah's utterances concerning the divine origin of the institution of kingship and its divinely intended role in Israel's prosperity is to be seen in the oracle for a royal accession in 9:2–7. This should most probably be regarded as having been delivered by Isaiah on the eve of the accession of Hezekiah to the throne in Jerusalem in 725. (See A. Alt, "Jesaja 8, 23–9, 6: Befreiungsnacht und Krönungstag," in *Kleine Schriften*, vol. 2, Munich, 1959, pp. 206–225.) What is striking here is the very high place accorded to the role and status of the king:

Of the spread of his government and of peace
   there will be no end,
upon the throne of David, and over his kingdom,
   to establish it, and to uphold it
with justice and with righteousness
   from now and forever.
The zeal of the LORD of hosts will perform this.
(9:7)

It is most probable that the prophet's words here simply reflect the traditional and established royal tradition of the Jerusalem court and Temple circle. If so, it is possible that the prophet was reminding his hearers of the promise that God had made, and to which they were to respond in faith, if it were truly to be realized. Nevertheless, even if we recognize a degree of conditional promise in this famous prophecy, it accords a very high place to the office of the king and to the Davidic dynasty. It is the presence of this prophecy in the book, and of the many later prophetic developments relating to the further history of the Davidic dynasty (see especially 11:1–5, 32:1–2, 33:17, 55:3–5), which have made the book of Isaiah the central source of messianic prophecy in the Old Testament.

It in no way implies any necessary conflict, or inconsistency on the prophet's part, that he should have coupled this very high evaluation of the divine foundation for the office of the king with sharp criticisms of both Ahaz and Hezekiah. In some degree the coronation oracle represents the "ideal" state of affairs, which can only be achieved when the reigning holder of the divine office fulfills fully his responsibilities toward God. The prophet envisages all human society as based upon a divinely given order in which religion, morality, and prosperity are all part of one continuous whole. The true goal of this order is "peace"—a comprehensive term for a prosperous, just, and peaceful community. In spite, therefore, of the prophet's use of the title "the LORD of hosts" he is not a militarist but one very strongly committed to the notion that all power, both divine and human, must lead to an ordered and peaceable society. That the prophet could portray this as the return to an original earlier state of affairs undoubtedly indicates a certain idealizing of the past (1:24–26). Nevertheless, in such a portrayal he has revealed his own insight that peace and prosperity are not a "natural" condition that can arise from within the world but rather are to be seen as a gift of God, given from outside by the power of the divine spirit (see especially 11:2).

One theme begins to acquire a new character and eminence in Isaiah among the prophets that we have not found so emphasized among his predecessors. This is the theme of "faith" and of "trust" in God. It first comes to great prominence in the prophet's address to Ahaz at the time when Jerusalem, and more especially its royal house, was under threat in the Syro-Ephraimite war (736–733). The prophet faced a king who was unwilling to accept a message of assurance through the mediation of prophecy and who instead preferred to trust the rhetorical skills and generous payments of diplomatic appeals. Ahaz preferred to trust the brutal ruler of Assyria rather than put his faith in God (7:9–12). This theme of "lack of faith" thereafter becomes a central one for Isaiah's understanding of what it is that has gone wrong so as

to bring Israel into rebellion against the plans and purposes of God. God has been utterly faithful to his people, making incontrovertibly plain his intentions for them. Such a divine purpose, however, had to be grasped and acted upon if it were not to remain a mere empty word. The prophet himself therefore had to take care to ensure that he maintained the clarity and firmness of his own insight into God's plans and was not misled by the doubts and fears of the people (8:11–15).

It is as an aspect of this broad condemnation of the chief authorities in Jerusalem, especially the king himself, that we encounter the most strongly characteristic feature of Isaiah's prophecies. This is his total condemnation of the political alliances that Judah made, first with Assyria under Ahaz and then with Egypt in attempts to break free from Assyrian control.

The condemnation of treaty negotiations with Egypt, in which ambassadors from the Ethiopian territory of Upper Egypt came by sea to Judah, is expressed in Isaiah 18:1–6. Either the period of 714–711 or the more extensive cycle of anti-Assyrian negotiations in 705–701 provides the setting for this, giving rise to the characteristic range of rich poetic imagery and devastating threat that colors the brilliance of Isaiah as a prophet:

For thus the LORD has said to me:
"I will look out calmly from my dwelling
    as on a hot summer's day,
    as when the dew rises in the heat of harvest."
For before the harvest, and when the blossom has gone,
    and the flowers are ripening into grapes,
he will cut off the shoots with pruning knives,
    and cut off the freshly spreading branches.
All of them will be left
    to the birds of prey of the mountains
    and to the beasts that roam the earth.
The birds of prey will pass the summer upon them,
    and all the beasts of the earth will winter upon them.
                        (18:4–6)

By this satirical picture of God quietly sunning himself on a warm summer's day, just before the harvest ripens, the prophet affirms that God will not support the aims of such a treaty. He then introduces a picture of the devastation of the vines by vandals before the grapes are plucked, leaving what is left for birds and wild animals to enjoy. The treaty negotiations will prove utterly ruinous.

This sharp opposition to reliance upon the promises of Egyptian military support for the withdrawal of allegiance to Assyria in the period particularly of 705–701 (28:14–18; 29:15–16; 30:1–5, 6–7, etc.) characterizes Isaiah's attitude. That he opposed this treaty with Egypt very strongly cannot be doubted, although it is less clear what ideas motivated such a stance. The prophet contrasts the "trusting" in Egypt's promises of military support with a deeper "trusting" in God (see 30:15–17). This could be construed as a form of utopianism, believing that God would intervene in a very direct, almost mythological fashion to protect his people. Yet this cannot be what Isaiah intended or expected. Clearly he did mistrust Egypt as a political power and rightly recognized that the Egyptians were more concerned to use their northern neighbors to form a buffer between themselves and the Assyrians than they were to encourage the independence and self-determination of the several small nations of the Fertile Crescent. Isaiah also deeply mistrusted reliance on military strength and prowess, regarding it as an affront to God and to human dignity that must eventually give way to a genuine basis for peace (see 9:5). Yet he was not a pacifist in the modern sense. It is possible that he would have found reasons to oppose any alliance with a foreign power, sensing that all such implied some degree of recognition of foreign gods, but this is certainly not a clear or necessary inference to draw. It is better to recognize a strong note of political realism to which the prophet added an informed awareness that resistance to the political will and demands of Assyria had already shown itself to be futile and self-defeating, worsening the situation rather than improving it. For him faith in God meant a deep willingness to discern a larger Providence at work (see 10:5–6) in which the justice, righteousness, and honored name of God would ultimately be vindicated in human affairs. His opposition to the contemporary political scene in Judah therefore was a genuinely perceptive and constructive viewpoint.

As a prophet Isaiah evidently made frequent poetic use of sharp contrasts, especially setting the exalted holiness and majesty of God over against the frailty and ignorance of human beings. This sense of divine majesty and apartness is vividly presented in the account of his call-vision (6:1–3) and continues to color and shape his condemnations of human behavior. He sharply opposes all human pride and pretentiousness. It is supreme folly to display too great a self-esteem: "Woe to those who are wise in their own eyes,/and clever in their own opinion" (5:21).

The final judgment of God will take the form of the ultimate abasement of all that is proud and distorted with pretentious self-esteem (2:9–11, 5:15–16). The whole section of Isaiah 2:6–22 is a portrayal of divine judgment against the false values of human pride and human possessions, but it has been much disputed how closely the passage conforms to the prophet's actual words. In any event, so impressive and effective has been this theme in Isaiah that it appears to have attracted a substantial degree of subsequent elaboration.

This prophetic celebration of the ultimate triumph of God over human pomp and ceremony finds its most vigorous and lasting expression in the satire in 14:4–20 on the death of the great world-ruler. The words are now applied to the king of Babylon (14:4), but it has been plausibly suggested (see, e.g., Barth 1977) that the passage was composed by Isaiah himself at the time of the death of the Assyrian ruler Sargon II in 705. Certainty over such issues cannot be achieved, but its sharp contrasts fit well into a characteristic theme of Isaiah's prophesying.

Such an attitude of mind could easily have led to a measure of disparagement of human existence and civilization, but this was clearly not true of Isaiah. Of all the great prophets of the Old Testament he is the one who has most to say about human institutions, human ambitions, and human values. He was clearly a member of a well-educated Jerusalem society, literate (see 30:8), and deeply informed about matters of government even when the decision-makers tried to keep their plans secret (29:15). He valued the city and its life and has provided us with one of the most interesting and informed pictures of the social and moral tensions that characterized a large city, with strong international links, in the ancient world. He is also remarkably free of conventional religious polemic, although the editors of his prophecies have naturally related his prophecies to the perennial and more conventional needs of Jewish religious life.

It is in relation to his condemnation of the many counselors and would-be guides whom he found in Jerusalem, often centrally placed in administration and governmental affairs, that he affirms his claim that true "wisdom" lies in a deep and humble trust in God (besides 5:21 see also 19:11–15, 28:23–26, 29:14). The prophet's contrast of the conventional with divinely given wisdom has suggested to several scholars, particularly William Whedbee, that Isaiah had some special interest in those who taught and purveyed wisdom.

When the book as a whole is viewed as a fundamental conception of human society and its relationship to God, it is evident that Isaiah possessed a deep moral sense. For one who was undoubtedly very close to the Temple and its activities, he spurns any idea of sin as a purely formal, taboo-like affront to God. Rather it lies in an indifference to the greed, injustice, and corruption that all too readily flourish in a large city with a small and privileged elite at its center. Central to this social pyramid of political and economic administration is the office of the king. In supporting this office and portraying it as essential to the welfare of God's people, Isaiah nevertheless found strong reason for severe criticism of both rulers—Ahaz and Hezekiah—in whose reigns the major part of his prophesying was undertaken. In observing the consequences of individual bad actions and attitudes on the part of those who held responsible office in society, Isaiah expresses a strong awareness of the manner in which wrongdoing becomes a destructive force in the entire web of human affairs. Although his understanding of God is essentially determined by his experience of the symbolism and traditions of the Temple in Jerusalem, he nevertheless perceives that God must be the guardian and providential ruler of all nations. Although therefore he does not express an explicitly monotheistic doctrine of God, he nevertheless implies a familiarity with all the essentials of such a belief. The Lord God of Israel displays a control over all nations and determines the ultimate purposes and achievements of each of them, however much, in their ignorance, they adhere to the worship of other deities. Among the prophets we must undoubtedly regard Isaiah as one who achieved a truly impressive theological grasp of the nature of faith and its formative role in the fabric of human society.

THE FURTHER DEVELOPMENT OF ISAIAH'S PROPHECIES

It is very clear from what we have noted of the prophecies of Isaiah that, like the messages of other prophets, what he had to proclaim in his prophetic announcements was addressed to a specific situation and was deeply affected by the circumstances in which it was given. It warned, admonished, and threatened the people of Judah and Israel of the dangers that faced them and pointed to the inner wrongs and injustices in their religious and social life that had incurred the divine wrath. Yet it never failed to point back to the majesty, greatness, and holiness of God, which established a foundation of hope for the future. To a significant degree, therefore, the prophet himself looked to future events to establish the truth of his prophetic words and to fulfill them. For this reason the interest in what the prophet had said and the explanations he had presented for the momentous upheavals that had affected the political and religious life of Judah and Israel during his days retained their significance long after the prophet first delivered them. The prophet was foretelling the future not in a rigid, fatalistic fashion, but by insisting that a controlling divine Providence governed the affairs of all nations. We might even go so far as to say that the degree of interest in the words of a great prophet like Isaiah actually increased and intensified long after the time when he first delivered them.

This general recognition of the relationship of prophecy to historical events serves to explain the reasons for its retention and preservation in written form. There is little reason to doubt that the great majority of Isaiah's prophecies, if not all of them, were first publicly proclaimed orally to a distinctive circle of hearers. It is most probable therefore that those who constituted this first audience of the prophet's words can be identified to some degree by the contents of what he said. The castigation of the wealthy ruling classes of Jerusalem, which several times appears in Isaiah's threats, leads us to recognize that he had adequate opportunity for addressing such people directly at the time of their deliberations, or even at their festivities (see, e.g., 28:7–18).

Isaiah, however, did write down certain prophetic pronouncements after he had given them, apparently out of a sense of frustration at the refusal of the responsible authorities to heed his words and out of a desire to preserve for posterity a testimony to the faithfulness of God (see especially the "Memoir" of 6:1–8:18, 30:8). There is also little reason for us to doubt that the written records made by Isaiah of certain of his prophecies form a central nucleus of the preserved book that now bears his name. These written compositions, however, can have formed little more than a small part of the book that we have, which was put together as a collection, given shape and editorial introductions, and then supplemented and added to over a very extended period of time. Almost paradoxically, the very relevance and high level of importance of what the prophet had to declare necessitated the continuing growth and elaboration of his book.

It has been suggested that the prophet himself may have initiated the process of supplementing and adding further comments and interpretations to words that he had given earlier. More widely canvassed (e.g., by Sigmund Mowinckel) has been the view that Isaiah in particular formed a small circle of disciples around him who continued to act as the tradents of his message and who added to it further sayings and prophecies of their own. Such a view has pointed to Isaiah 8:16 ("Bind up the testimony, seal the teaching among my disciples"; RSV) as proof of the existence of such a company of disciples. In fact, however, the reference here can be more narrowly translated as "those I have instructed" and is a reference to the two named witnesses of Isaiah 8:2. It is not clear, therefore, that there ever existed any large organized body of disciples of the prophet Isaiah who formed a separately identifiable religious community. In reality, since Mowinckel identified this community of Isaiah's disciples with the cult-prophets of the Temple, it is more plausible to assume that the task of preserving and editing the recorded prophecies of Isaiah took place in close association with the main body of Temple officials and servants in Jerusalem. In fact we do not know a great deal about the nature and identity of those who were the tradents of the prophecies of Isaiah. In some sense they undoubtedly were disciples of the prophet, but such can only be a loose designation. They appear to have been closely linked to the

Temple and to have displayed a positive interest in preserving and interpreting the word of God given to Israel through prophecy by more than one individual. At all events the importance of their work, and the reasons that led them to undertake it, are largely to be inferred from the contents of the Book of Isaiah itself.

Two general points may be deduced with confidence from the preserved form of the Book of Isaiah. First, the political domination of Judah and Ephraim (Israel) by Assyria for more than a century after the time of the Syro-Ephraimite war (736–733) provided the groundwork for understanding Isaiah's prophecies. Accordingly the editors have expressly added comments to identify Assyria's incursions as fulfilling Isaiah's threats in 7:7, 7:20, and 8:4. The disastrous long-term consequences for Ephraim at the hands of Assyria are also spelled out with an explicit time reference in 7:8b. A second general inference must be that, whereas Isaiah himself addressed his messages to a people who were passionately resistant to his words and warnings, leaving him isolated and frustrated (see 8:17), those who found themselves entrusted with the task of editing and interpreting his prophecies to a later generation encountered a different attitude. They were living through the painful and evil consequences of the choices and decisions that their predecessors had made. No longer was there any doubt possible for them about the evil consequences of trusting in Assyria or those of making alliances with Egypt in the hope of breaking free of Assyrian control. All such possibilities now lay in the past; the need now was to understand why Judah and Israel had fallen on such disastrous times and what hope lay in the future. The past could not be changed, but the future still lay open and the question was whether Isaiah's prophecies held out any clear hope and guidance for an eventual restoration of Israel and Judah to their former glory. In this regard we can see how certain of Isaiah's prophecies came to take on a very special interest and importance in the years after Jerusalem's escape from the forces of Sennacherib in 701.

In the context of the preservation of Isaiah's prophecies in the years immediately following the siege and surrender of Jerusalem in 701, it is understandable that the mood of Judah was very different from what it had been during Hezekiah's days. The people were humbled and distressed by what had taken place. Although only very limited information is preserved for us, it is clear from the broad survey that is set out in 2 Kings 17:7–41, which must have been composed sometime later, that the situation in what was left of the northern kingdom of Ephraim was ruinous. The same conclusion is confirmed by the note that an editor has placed in Isaiah 7:8b: "Within sixty-five years Ephraim will be broken to pieces so that it will no longer be a people" (RSV). In Judah, however, after Hezekiah's surrender to Sennacherib in 701 we hear of no further act of rebellion. When eventually Sennacherib was killed in a palace intrigue (Isa 37:38, although no extrabiblical evidence exists to confirm this fact) there were plenty of devout hearts and minds in Jerusalem who discerned in such an act the retributive hand of divine justice. His successor, Esarhaddon, however, allowed no easing of the burden placed upon Judah, and Manasseh, the ruler who succeeded Hezekiah, drew forth from the Old Testament historian the sharpest and most severe rebuke for his disregard of Judah's religious interests (2 Kgs 21:1–16). It seems very likely, if only as a point of speculation, that much of this reprehensible behavior during the fifty-five years of his reign was a consequence of his readiness to accede to Assyrian demands. It would fit the picture that we have, from both Assyrian and Old Testament sources, of a ruler who secured his position by abusing his own people in order to comply with the avaricious demands of his foreign masters. If this is the case, it serves to clarify for us much of the thinking and concerns that controlled the work of Isaiah's editors. At any rate we find their work most strongly motivated by the elements of hope and of light coming at the end of a time of darkness.

Two prophecies above all others have gripped the editors' attention and have led to a fascinating sequence of interpretative additions and elaborations that demonstrate how prophecy continued to retain its significance long after the prophet's own days. These are the royal coronation oracle in 9:2–7, which celebrates the greatness of the Davidic dynasty, and the assurance given in 10:5–19 of an eventual divine judgment upon Assyria's arrogant boasting in its victories. The foremost consequences of the continued reflection upon the Davidic coronation oracle are

to be seen in the extensive development of royal messianic ideas and themes in the book (see below, "Isaiah's Prophecies in the Age of Babylonian Rule"). Most immediately relevant for consideration is the use of the metaphor of the breaking of the "rod" and "staff" of servitude from 9:4. This metaphor clearly offered a vivid image of the political subservience to Assyria that both Judah and Ephraim had experienced, so that its ending could be construed as implied by the prophecy. It is not surprising therefore that in seeking to draw out the full meaning of Isaiah's prophecies the editors should have spelled out this implication quite plainly:

> The LORD of hosts has sworn:
> "As I have planned,
>   so will it be,
> and as I have purposed,
>   so shall it come about;
> that I will break the Assyrian in my land,
>   and upon my mountains trample him under foot;
> then his yoke shall depart from them,
>   and his burden from their shoulder."
>
> (14:24–25)

The prophet's picture of God's hand stretched out in judgment (9:12, 17, etc.) is then coupled with this word picture in 14:26–27. An even more elaborate and detailed interpretive comment on the removal of the "rod" and "yoke" of Assyria is set out in 10:24–27. In a similar fashion the assurance of 10:5–15 that Assyria is no more than a rod in the hand of God that must itself ultimately suffer punishment for its arrogant and excessive claims is further developed to show that the nightmare of Assyrian rule over Judah will end. Most directly, Isaiah's image of Assyrian depredations of its subject peoples as that of a man plundering a bird's nest is taken up and used in 31:5 as a portrayal of God's special protection of Jerusalem. Furthermore, the portrayal of Assyria as a great forest of trees that must be cut down and burned (10:17–19, 33–34) appears to have been developed as a result of the prophet's image of "briers and thorns" taking over the "vineyard" of God in 5:6 (*cf.* 7:23–25, 10:17). Possibly this had been combined with the image of Assyria as a wooden "rod" from 10:5, just as the image of "light" from 9:2 has been extended to incorporate the idea of a fire that will burn down the forest (10:17).

Much of this appears to be a kind of subtle word game, developing and reinterpreting the prophet's vivid images in order to draw forth new meanings from them (see Fishbane 1985, 458ff.). There was, however, a far more serious and significant side to this interpretative development. By using the metaphors and words of the prophet and applying them to the historical situation as it unfolded itself in the years after the prophet's time, the possibility was explored of uncovering the divine "plan" for Israel at the hands of Assyria. In fact, the very word "plan" (Heb. 'ēṣāh; RSV, "purpose") had been used by Isaiah to describe God's intention, and this is further elaborated later as the prophecies have been reflected upon (14:24).

What is of most importance to the interpreter of the book is the fact that, in the majority of instances, this secondary elaboration of Isaiah's words and word imagery points to an ultimate defeat and overthrow of Assyrian power and an ending of its imperial rule over Judah and Israel. Earlier commentators upon the book have been inclined either to deny the connection of such passages with the prophet Isaiah at all or to look for some period in his prophetic ministry when he could have entertained such expectations of the overthrow of Assyria. By noting their secondary nature while yet acknowledging their essential connection with the words and prophecies of Isaiah, we have a much clearer and more convincing explanation of their origin and purpose. Isaiah had warned an obtuse and unresponsive people of the dangers that faced them through their misguided attempts to woo Assyria to their cause and then to wriggle free from its grip. Neither of these maneuvers had been successful, and a period of great destruction and suffering had overtaken them as a result. Most of the land of Israel now lay devastated and under foreign rule (see 1:7–8).

To a people groaning under the weight of Assyrian oppression in the half-century and more that followed the surrender of Hezekiah in 701 some word of hope and assurance was now in order. Had God proclaimed through his prophet a full and final end upon the land (see 6:11–12)? By drawing together Isaiah's prophecies into a connected and interpreted whole, those who edited them into a book sought to show that there was hope and light at the end of the dark tunnel beginning at the very time when Isaiah commenced his prophetic ministry.

In some cases, as in the rather broad pictures of ruined and devastated farmland developed around the "briers and thorns" image in 7:23–25, only a very general picture is made. Much more significant are the several passages where a very dramatic and complete overthrow of Assyrian rule is presented. Besides 10:16–19, 10:33–34, and 14:24–27 we find similar portrayals in 8:9–10, 17:12–14, and 29:5–8. In all three of the latter instances it is no longer simply Assyria that is explicitly named as the enemy who is to be overthrown, but a larger anonymous "multitude of nations." This point has occasioned much discussion and undoubtedly deserves careful attention since it is not readily to be assumed that all such assurances have a similar origin and refer to the same circumstances. Nevertheless it would seem to be most likely that in developing the Isaianic imagery concerning an eventual overthrow of Assyria and the ending of its rule over Judah the traditional language and phraseology of certain psalms celebrating Jerusalem's greatness have been employed (cf. Pss 46, 48, 76). This would certainly bear out my contention that the work of collecting and editing the prophecies of Isaiah took place in close association with the circle of Temple scribes and servants in Jerusalem. It is possible that Isaiah had himself been from among their number.

These messages of hope and assurance that Assyria's days of world dominion were also numbered in no way circumvented, or discounted, the message of judgment that Isaiah had given. On the contrary, they served to confirm it and to elucidate its meaning more fully by showing that it lay wholly within the demands of a holy and righteous God. What had changed by the time these words were added to Isaiah's prophecies was that the survivors of Judah were to be found suffering and smarting under the judgment that had befallen them.

The Old Testament historian writing in 2 Kings 21:1–16 paints a very different picture of Manasseh and his reign from that accorded his predecessor Hezekiah. This may in itself help to explain to us why, when seen in retrospect, the events that colored the last years of Hezekiah's rule appeared rather different in the years that followed Hezekiah's death. The next generation saw them from a different standpoint. The most important consequence of this for the interpreter of Isaiah and his prophecies concerns the two strongly contrasting Old Testament accounts of the circumstances of Hezekiah's surrender to Sennacherib in 701. The brief factual account of 2 Kings 18:13–16, which is not repeated in the Book of Isaiah, simply reports the Judean king's surrender and the amount of the heavy indemnity he was compelled to pay. The much fuller account of 2 Kings 18:17–19:37 contains detailed reports of certain prophecies of Isaiah purportedly given at the time when Jerusalem was under siege. It presents the fact that no actual bloodshed and fighting took place in Jerusalem as a great victory for Jerusalem and the Lord God. Various speculative suggestions have been made that a second siege of Jerusalem must have been involved in order to account for this very assured and triumphalist attitude on the part of the jubilant reporter of the events. However, since the actual events recounted are essentially the same in both cases, it is more probable that we are faced here with earlier and later accounts of the same historical happening. Hezekiah had surrendered to Sennacherib in order to avoid a prolonged siege and a costly battle in Jerusalem. Thereby, as if by a miracle, Jerusalem was spared the fate of so many other cities of Judah and Israel, and Hezekiah himself retained his throne as a vassal of Assyria.

The connection with actual prophecies from Isaiah is to be discerned in the manner in which the two Isaianic prophecies concerning the divine foundation of the Davidic royal dynasty (Isa 9:2–7) and the eventual certainty of divine punishment for Assyria (10:5–15) have influenced the reporting. So indeed it had appeared to be confirmed by the course of events that God had defended and saved Jerusalem "for [his] own sake and for the sake of [his] servant David" (2 Kgs 19:34). It may well have been the case that this revised and more hopeful interpretation of the major event of Hezekiah's reign, which had provided a central focus for some of the most important of Isaiah's prophecies, began to emerge during the reign of Manasseh. So dark and oppressive were the years of this king's long reign that it is highly probable that those whose task it was to preserve and interpret prophecy should have seized firmly upon every sign and signification of hope. Certainly his

successor Amon reigned for only two years before he was assassinated, to be followed by Josiah, who came to the throne as a boy of eight years of age and reigned for thirty-one years (639–609; 2 Kgs 22:1). Josiah's reign was of great importance for the entire subsequent history of Judah and Israel and has left a profound impression upon much of the literature of the Old Testament. Not least, it has affected the preservation and editing of the collection of Isaiah's prophecies.

In order to appreciate how and why this king's reign was so significant, and why a concern with it has increasingly attracted the attention of scholars endeavoring to uncover the literary growth of the Old Testament, some basic historical reflections are necessary. In the tenth century, under David and Solomon, Israel had become a powerful nation controlling virtually the entire land from the Egyptian border to the mountains of Syria. Thereafter this kingdom had become divided into two separate sister kingdoms (Judah and Ephraim), with only very limited collaboration between them. When Assyria intervened directly in their affairs at the time when Isaiah began to prophesy, the weakness of both kingdoms became painfully evident. The northern kingdom of Ephraim collapsed altogether and was gradually dismembered and depopulated. Only Judah retained any semblance of its former unity, and this in a much-reduced area. When the leaders of Judah sought to comprehend what had befallen them and why, they found in Isaiah's prophecies certain important aids toward an understanding of their situation. Four major points stand out: (1) Israel was indeed one people, so that division and disunity were a sign of rebellion against God; (2) the Davidic kingship was the divinely appointed government for the administrative expression of this unity; (3) Jerusalem, with its beautiful Temple and royal palace, was the religious capital of this people; and (4) the punishment brought about by the Assyrians was a sign of the righteous anger of God.

These four essential factors led to the emergence of a strong movement for reform in Judah, which looked to the time when Assyrian control would be ended in order to implement the demand for a whole new political and religious order for Israel. It was during the days when Josiah was growing to maturity that the opportunity for this reform came about, and it must be regarded as certain that this situation provided the background to the great reform reported in 2 Kings 22:3–23:25. Although it may at first appear that such events, coming almost a century after Isaiah's last prophecies, could have had little to do with the prophet, the opposite is in fact true. In a number of major ways Isaiah's prophecies provided a theological basis for the reform, and clearly those who were strongly supportive of the move for reform were eager to associate their aims with Isaiah's prophecies. If the people of the days of Ahaz and Hezekiah had been unwilling to heed the words of the prophet Isaiah, then those of Josiah's time were more willing to do so.

In a major work dealing with this question Hermann Barth (1977) has endeavored to show the importance of the editorial work on Isaiah's prophecies during Josiah's reign. The viewpoint adopted here is not wholly in agreement with his presentation, especially since he rejects the Isaianic origin of the prophecy of Isaiah 9:2–7. Nevertheless it certainly appears to be highly probable that it was during Josiah's reign, when the period of Assyrian domination of Judah ended, that Isaiah's prophecies took on added significance. Since he was the prophet who had foretold the manner and consequences of the military and political intervention of Assyria in the affairs of Israel (both Judah and Ephraim), his words could also serve to explain the ending of this. Much of the character of this retrospective interpretation of Isaiah's prophecies is distinctly hopeful and reassuring in its nature, contrasting with the heavily threatening character of the prophet's attitude to Ahaz and Hezekiah. Nevertheless there were genuine and important links with the actual words of the prophet that now served to illuminate the prospects of a new age. It ought seriously to be reckoned with, as I have already noted, that much of the groundwork for this concentration upon the hopeful features of Isaiah's words was laid during the dark years of Manasseh's evil reign.

It is highly feasible, as Barth suggests, that the original conclusion to this edited collection of Isaiah's prophecies is to be found preserved now as Isaiah 32:1–8, which marks a fitting close to a period of political upheaval and turmoil:

Behold, a king will rule in righteousness,
  and princes will administer just laws.
Every one of them will be like a shelter from the wind,
  a refuge from the storm wind,
and like streams of water in a dry place.
  They will be like the shade of a great rock in a sun-scorched land.
Then the eyes of those who see will not be closed,
  and the ears of those who listen will hear plainly.
The panic stricken mind will understand clearly,
  and the stammering tongues will speak readily and clearly.
The foolish person will no longer be called honorable,
  nor the scoundrel be described as noble.
Surely the fool speaks foolishness,
  and his mind plans evil things:
to do what is godless,
  and to speak perverse things about the LORD,
so that he leaves the longing of the hungry person unsatisfied, and deprives the thirsty person of drink.
The evil person plays evil tricks;
  he plots crafty schemes
to ruin the poor with lying words,
  even when the plea of the destitute is right.
But the man who is honorable plans honorable things,
  and remains steadfast in honorable deeds.

There is a strength and dignity about these words that have rightly left their mark on Christian and Jewish spirituality. At the same time the reader will notice immediately the direct connection with Isaiah's own words. The central importance of the Davidic kingship, which is rooted in Isaiah's prophecy of 9:2–7, begins the section and must clearly have looked to Josiah as a noble successor to the ignoble Manasseh and the ill-fated, and probably much hated, Amon. Even more strikingly the prophetic unit affirms that the time of Israel's blindness and deafness, unforgettably entwined in the account of Isaiah's call (9:6–10), will now come to an end. Israel will be able to see and hear clearly again. In line with this the new age of justice, peace, and prosperity will contrast with the avaricious injustice that Isaiah so firmly condemned (see 5:8–23). It would be difficult to find a more helpful and clear instance of the way in which the work of editing, structuring, and supplementing the prophecies of Israel's great inspired figures took place. Such a work sought to make clear on the basis of prophecy the plans and purposes that God had toward God's people. Prophecy served as the living word of God, which required, if it were truly to be heeded, to be applied and explained, not rigidly preserved in a fixed and unchangeable form. To insist therefore that a prophetic book like that of Isaiah must contain only the prophet's own words is to impose upon it a purely human basis of interpretation that conflicts with the very nature of prophecy as the living word of God, to be heeded and acted upon by God's people.

Barth presents in his study (1977, 203ff.) a reconstructed picture of what the prophecies of Isaiah, as they were edited during Josiah's reign, might have contained. Valuable as this is, we may be content here to note certain salient points. Isaiah had insisted that Israel should be one people, a feature that strongly motivated the movement for reform during this king's reign. He also pointed to the divinely given role of the Davidic kingship and the Temple in Jerusalem as central symbols for faith to respond to and showed how the suffering brought about by Assyria had been a necessary punishment that Israel had brought upon herself. All of these features gained a new impetus and a new measure of support during the reign of Josiah, culminating in the appearance of a powerful and influential circle of reforming leaders and officials. Much of the results of their further work, especially insofar as it has left a literary legacy in the Old Testament, is to be seen in the Book of Deuteronomy and the great history of Israel from its beginnings, which covers the books of Joshua through 2 Kings. Known in the Hebrew Bible as the Former Prophets, this long document comprising six books has come to be described by modern scholars as the Deuteronomistic History.

ISAIAH'S PROPHECIES IN THE AGE OF BABYLONIAN RULE

Isaiah 36–39 contains a series of narratives, the first dealing with the events of 701 B.C.E., the second with a serious illness and recovery of the king Hezekiah, and the third with the arrival in Jerusalem of emissaries from Babylon; in this last narrative Isaiah's prophetic ministry figures prominently. In the background to all three stories the divinely grounded importance to Israel of the Davidic dynasty and the Temple in Jerusalem also receives significant attention. These are themes regarded as strongly present in Isaiah's prophesying. Since these stories are closely parallel to 2 Kings 18:13–20:19, being in fact only

slightly varied in the two versions, it has been widely believed that the narratives were first located in the Book of 2 Kings and secondarily incorporated into the Book of Isaiah. It is possible that the reverse literary chronology may be the case, but the point is probably not overly important. The stories must have been of independent composition and are certainly representative of a type of narrative that enjoyed a widespread popularity. Their great importance for the understanding of the Book of Isaiah is that the last of them, which concerns the visit to Jerusalem of emissaries from Babylon (2 Kgs 20:12–19; Isa 39), shows clearly how the events of Hezekiah's reign, and their relationship to Isaiah's prophecies, came to be linked to the age of Babylonian rule over Judah (604–538). The main purpose of the narrative is to prepare the reader to recognize that the protection afforded to Jerusalem in Hezekiah's day, "for God's sake and the sake of the dynasty of David" (Isa 37:35), would not be maintained against the Babylonian armies, as is made clear in Isaiah 39:5–7:

> Behold, the time is coming when all that is in your palace, and that which your ancestors have preserved until now, will be carried to Babylon; nothing shall be left, says the LORD. And some of your own sons who are born to you shall be taken away; and they shall become eunuchs in the palace of the king of Babylon.

Thus the prophet Isaiah is reported to have addressed Hezekiah after he had welcomed the emissaries from Babylon into his palace. The background and circumstances of the story need not detain us unduly, since its greatest interest for us lies in the way in which it serves to unravel some of the most important literary features concerning the composition and unity of the Book of Isaiah.

The medieval Jewish scholar Ibn Ezra (1092–1167) came to recognize how completely chapters 40–66 of the Book of Isaiah reflect the period after 550, when a significant section of the Jerusalem population had been carried into exile in Babylon and when the Temple lay in ruins. Furthermore, there was no longer a ruler of the Davidic dynasty on the throne in Judah; the surviving heirs of the royal house were themselves in Babylonian exile. Later the Jewish philosopher Baruch Spinoza (1632–1677) also noted this Babylonian background to chapters 40–66 of the

Book of Isaiah and since the work of the German scholar J. C. Doederlein in 1788 such a recognition has progressively prevailed in Christian scholarship. In a widely adopted view Bernhard Duhm suggested that chapters 40–55 were the work of an anonymous prophet living in the Babylonian exile before 538, who has generally been known as "Deutero- (or Second) Isaiah." Such a view has many points to commend it but has most often been too little concerned to explain the connections between chapters 40ff. and the material contained in the earlier chapters 1–39.

Only recently has greater attention been devoted to this question and to the overall unity that has been imparted to the book. It is evident, for instance, that the Babylonian background of the sixth century is reflected not only in chapters 40–55 but also in chapters 13–14 and in fact in a number of other parts of the book (notably in chap. 35). Chapters 56–66 are from an even later age than 40–55, probably dating from the early fifth century, and the contents of 24–27 are later still.

The evidence is quite unmistakable, therefore, that the processes of composition and editing that led to the formation of our extant Book of Isaiah were prolonged and complex. To assume, as has often mistakenly been done, that the concern of this process of compilation was simply to preserve the words (or the supposed words) of Isaiah has imposed false criteria of interpretation. God's word through the prophet Isaiah was a "living" word to be applied, interpreted, and further understood in relation to the ongoing history of God's people. Most central here were the questions concerning the people of Israel as a single nation (whom God had called "my people"), the Davidic kingship whom God had appointed to rule over them, and the Temple in Jerusalem, where God had demonstrated that his presence would be with them. The further history of these great institutions was required to be understood and interpreted in the light of the prophet Isaiah's words.

It is valuable for us to note briefly the chief outline of events marking the arrival of Babylonian forces in Judah. After a short period of self-determination of its internal affairs once Assyrian rule had collapsed, Judah passed briefly under the control of Egypt. Josiah was killed in battle at Megiddo in 609

in a vain attempt to thwart an Egyptian move to strengthen the Assyrian armies fighting against Babylon (2 Chr 35:20–27). By 604, Judah, under the Davidic king Jehoiakim, fell under Babylonian control. Shortly afterward Judah joined a rebellion that resulted in the Babylonian forces under Nebuchadnezzar besieging and sacking Jerusalem in 598. By this time Jehoiakim was dead and his son Jehoiachin was on the throne in the city. He and many of the leading citizens of Judah were deported to Babylon to live as exiles there. The king's uncle Zedekiah was placed on the throne but less than ten years later attempted a further rebellion against Babylon. This led to a prolonged siege of Jerusalem and the fall of the city in 587. Subsequently, in a deliberate punitive measure, the Temple and royal palace were destroyed and the Davidic dynasty deposed. Undoubtedly, the tragic consequences of these events for the royal house of David and the Jerusalem Temple encouraged a continued interest in the interpretation of the prophecies of Isaiah. At its simplest this interest led to an "updating" of prophecies in regard to the new oppressor from Mesopotamia, such as we find in the prophecy against Tyre (Isa 23:13): "Behold the land of the Chaldeans! It is this people; it was not Assyria. God gave it over to the wild beasts." In this relatively simple instance, a prophecy concerning the destruction of Tyre has been seen to be applicable to the later threat to that city from Babylon (Chaldea).

Very much more significant is the way in which Isaiah's condemnation of the behavior of the citizens of Jerusalem after the deliverance of 701 has been related to the destruction of that city in 587. Already we can see from the narrative episode of chapter 39 that the events of the year 598, when Jerusalem first fell to Babylon after a siege (cf. 2 Kgs 24:10–17), have been closely linked to Isaiah's prophesying. The events of 587, when far greater physical destruction was inflicted on the city, are to be seen in Isaiah 13:4–8 and 22:5–8a, 8b–11. The command in 13:4–8 is quite clearly indicated as "concerning Babylon," and the description of the destruction of a city can best be regarded as applicable to Jerusalem.

This being the case, we are probably meant to recognize that the descriptions of devastation and darkness at a number of points in chapters 2–8 of the book are intended to relate to the devastation that followed the Babylonian destruction of Jerusalem in 587:

> Then one will pass through the land distressed
>   and hungry;
>   and in his hunger he will become enraged and will
>   curse both his king and his God!
> Then whether he looks upward, or down to
>   the earth,
>   he will see only distress and darkness,
>   overpowering gloom and dense blackness.
>
> (8:21–22)

It is very probable also that the assertion incorporated into the account of Isaiah's commissioning—that even after the widespread devastation and ruin brought upon the land by the Assyrians there will be a time of further ruin—also applies to the Babylonian menace (6:13). The concluding word of hope, "The holy seed is its stump," was undoubtedly added later still in the age of Ezra and Nehemiah. The portrayal of ruin and disaster overtaking Judah and Jerusalem that is set out in 3:1–4:1, with a clear indication of the death of many in battle, must also have taken on a new range of meaning once the threat from Babylon materialized. There are very clear indications therefore that Isaiah's warnings of divine judgment to be inflicted upon Jerusalem came to be revived and supplemented more than a century after Isaiah had delivered them at the time when the Babylonian armies attacked the city. We find a very similar situation concerning the later application of threatening prophecies of doom upon Jerusalem by Isaiah's contemporary Micah. His words about the destruction of the Temple and its sacred site acquired a new depth of meaning and interest when the Temple was destroyed in 587 (Mic 3:9–12, *cf.* Jer 26:18f.).

The question of the extent to which it is possible to find evidences of the catastrophes of 587 in Isaiah 1–39 may be regarded as of secondary interest beside the larger issue of the reasons that led the compilers of the book to supplement it with the remarkable prophecies of chapters 40–55. These sixteen chapters, long recognized by scholars as originating after 550 and as addressed to those Judean citizens who were in exile in Babylon, are now an important and intrinsic part of the book. It is wholly unsatisfactory to leave aside the question of why they have been joined to the earlier collection of Isaiah's prophecies when we have already found ample indication that the events that brought about this exile to Babylon were of immense interest to the continued preservation and interpretation of Isaiah's prophecies.

A number of scholars have been content to describe the prophetic author of chapters 40–55 as a "disciple" of Isaiah. Yet this fails to do more than offer a loose designation without showing wherein his connection with the great prophet Isaiah was truly to be found. At another level of scholarly investigation it could be claimed that the insight of a later editor (or editors) was responsible for combining the later chapters with the earlier ones. There are, however, sufficient indications to suggest that from the outset the prophecies of 40–55 were recognized as possessing a connection with Isaiah and were positively intended to do so.

There remains a measure of uncertainty over the extent to which chapters 40–55 are a coherent unity in themselves. Belief that they are such has been widely assumed by scholars, with the result that insufficient attention has been paid to the possibility of later insertions into the material. Undoubtedly the long diatribe against the making of idols in 44:9–20 shows many signs of having been added later. For the rest, the message and historical context of these chapters are made remarkably clear. Israel, which is sometimes addressed as "Jacob" and sometimes as "Zion," is in exile in Babylon. These people have evidently been there for some long period of time, have come to the brink of total despair, and have largely lost all expectation of a return to their homeland. The message of the prophet is therefore strongly hortatory in tone and full of positive affirmation and encouragement.

The opening words of the new prophecies address themselves to this situation and set the tone for most of what follows:

> Comfort, comfort my people,
>   says your God.
> Speak lovingly to Jerusalem, and tell her
> that her time of military servitude is over,
>   that her wrongdoing is pardoned,
> that she has suffered at God's hand
>   in double measure for all her sins.
>
> (40:1–2)

271

The portrayal in 40:3–5 of a great highway back from Babylon, the land of exile, to Jerusalem thereafter remains a central and recurrent theme of the chapters (40:9–11, 27–31; 41:17–20; etc.). The effect of this God-given highway will be to make possible the triumphant return of the exiles to Jerusalem (51:11, 52:7–10). The further goal of this great return to the homeland will be the rebuilding of Jerusalem in splendor (54:11–17).

Nor does the prophet leave any uncertainty as to either the time when this great deliverance will come or the agency through whom it will be achieved. He explicitly refers to Cyrus as the head of the Medo-Persian empire who will conquer Babylon and set free the exiles from Jerusalem:

> "who [God] says of Cyrus, 'He is my shepherd,
>   and he shall fulfil all my purpose';
> saying of Jerusalem, 'She shall be built,'
> and of the temple, 'Your foundation shall be laid.'"
> (44:28; RSV)

Further references to Cyrus and his achievements are to be found in 41:1–8 and 41:25, and his early conquests, which made him a major threat to Babylonian rule, are clearly presupposed at a number of points. These references, with their recognition that certain important events threatening the rule of Babylon had already taken place, show clearly that we are dealing here with prophecies given subsequent to 550. Cyrus' rise to power is already presupposed and the bold assertion that particular events have already taken place demonstrates the certainty that others of a like nature will quickly follow them.

On two major themes expressed by the prophet Isaiah there are clearly formulated further developments in chapters 40–55. The first of these concerns Israel's election by the Lord to be a people in a unique relationship to him. I have noted how Isaiah declared that God had now spurned God's people, because they had first spurned and rejected God. Now the prophet of the exile counters this with a firm and bold declaration that Israel is, and remains, a people chosen and elected by God. The very opening words, "comfort my people" (40:1), counter the implicit rejection in God's commission to Isaiah, "Go, and say

to this people" (6:9). So there are repeated assurances that, in spite of all appearances to the contrary, Israel is indeed chosen of God:

> But you, Israel, are my servant,
>   Jacob, whom I have chosen,
>   the descendants of Abraham, my friend;
> you whom I took from the ends of the earth,
>   and called from its farthest boundaries,
> saying to you, "You are my servant,
>   I have chosen you and not cast you off";
> fear not, for I am with you,
>   be not dismayed, for I am your God;
> I will strengthen you, I will support you,
>   I will sustain you with my victorious right hand.
> (41:8–10)

Further assurances of Israel's divine election are to be found in Isaiah 43:6f., 44:1f. and elsewhere. It is then wholly in line with this affirmation that, just as the rejection of Israel was countered by a renewed assurance of her election, so there should be further resumption of Isaianic themes. The most clearly demonstrable of these is the conscious echoing of the theme of Israel's blindness and deafness, which figures so centrally in Isaiah's commission (6:9–10). This theme continues to be employed in the exilic prophecies as a description of Israel's condition (42:7, 16, 18f.; 43:8; 44:18).

The extent to which the contents of chapters 40–55 were consciously influenced at the time of their origin by a familiarity with the collection of Isaiah's prophecies must remain open. Many important connections appear, but they lack the demonstrable firmness evident in other parts of the book—parts composed as a part of the ongoing development of the Isaianic collection of prophecies. Beyond any serious doubt, however, this prophetic message concerning the future return from exile and the rebuilding of Jerusalem formed a fitting and appropriate sequel to the collection of prophecies in which the fates of Israel and Jerusalem were seen to be so closely interlocked.

The continuing action of God toward Israel that had been announced in advance and interpreted through the voice of prophecy is referred to by the prophet in a contrast of "former things" with "new things":

Remember not the former things,
  nor consider the things of old.
Behold, I am about to perform a new thing;
  now it emerges; can you not perceive it?
I will make a way in the desert
  and rivers in the desolate land.

(43:18; and *cf.* 48:3–8)

As the prophecies are now set within the Book of Isaiah it is apparent that we should understand by these "former things" the events covered by the earlier prophecies of Isaiah. Whether the prophet originally intended this or was referring to earlier prophecies of his own cannot certainly be determined. In any case, this continuity between God's actions in the past toward Israel and the new actions, which will bring back from exile in Babylon those who had been taken from Jerusalem, is used to demonstrate that Yahweh, the Lord God of Israel, is the true and only God. The gods whom other peoples worship have no effective power over events and so are not true deities, as is indicated in 45:20–23:

"Assemble yourselves and come,
  gather together to hear,
  you who are left among the nations!
Those who carry about wooden idols
  have no true knowledge;
they keep on praying to a god
  that cannot save.
Speak out and present your case;
  let them talk it through together!
Who told this long ago?
  Who declared in the distant past?
Was it not I, the LORD?
  There is no other god apart from me,
a righteous God and Savior;
  there is none at all besides me.

"Turn to me for your salvation,
  all the ends of the earth!
I am God, and there is no other.
I have taken oath on my own name,
  a word has gone forth from my mouth
with complete assurance and it will not fail:
'To me every knee shall bow,
  every tongue shall swear.'"

This forthright teaching that the Lord God of Israel alone has the power to control human affairs, and that this is demonstrated by the fact that God alone announces events in advance through prophets, has made chapters 40–55 of Isaiah the most explicit teaching of monotheism in the entire Old Testament. Out of the earlier awareness that the Lord God was incomparably superior to all other deities who claimed to possess power has emerged the sense that these other deities have no power at all. They effectively do not exist. The use of images to simulate their existence is then regarded as a further aspect of the complete falsity of their claims. It is likely that this rejection of deities whose existence was portrayed through images attracted to itself a later diatribe in 44:9–20. It would appear likely that other short polemical rejections of idolatry in the Book of Isaiah were also introduced at a late stage.

It is certainly of great importance that full weight should be accorded to the manner in which this exalted and refined teaching about the nature of God has been derived from prophecy. What was implicit in the teaching of Isaiah of Jerusalem concerning the divine control over all human affairs, and especially over the imperial pretensions of Assyria, has been developed into a more comprehensive doctrine of Yahweh, the God of Israel, as the one and only God.

The precise historical situation to which the prophecies of chapters 40–55 are addressed is clear, and their overall message is readily summarized:

"Listen to me, you who are obstinate in heart,
  who are far from deliverance:
I am bringing near my deliverance, it is not far off,
  and my salvation will not be delayed;
I will put salvation in Zion,
  for Israel my glory."

(46:12–13)

Yet for all the directness of the message, and the transparent certainty regarding the situation to which it is addressed, many of the prophet's words have proved tantalizingly elusive. The style is very close to that of psalmody, indicating an author whose mind and language were steeped in the traditional forms of praise and hymnic psalmody (see especially Begrich 1938). Among the results are a marked repetitiveness in certain themes and also a complex fusion of images that have often proved difficult to interpret with complete clarity. Several major themes recur that have left a profound mark upon the overall structure of the Book of Isaiah. Besides the theme of the great highway that will make possible the return of the exiles from Babylon to their homeland, there is stress upon the future beauty and splendor of the new Jerusalem that will be rebuilt (see especially 54:11–17). This vision incorporates the assertion that a whole new age will begin for Jerusalem in which it will truly live up to its name as a city of peace and great prosperity. We find here a fresh shift of emphasis away from the concern for the restoration of Israel to the status of full national existence. Jerusalem, rather than the land of Israel, will have pride of place in the age of salvation shortly to appear. Furthermore, although the rebuilding of the Temple is openly asserted to be a major aspect of this new era for Jerusalem (44:28), it is the city as a whole, rather than the Temple in particular, that holds the center of attention. Thus the title "Zion," which refers specifically to the mount on which the Temple was built, comes to be applied to all Jerusalem and, by a kind of natural extension, to all Israel. A new interest, of a distinctly nonpriestly character, is made to attach to Jerusalem.

A similar and somewhat enigmatic extension is given to the tradition of the divine covenant with the dynasty of David, which is so important a part of the inheritance of the preaching of Isaiah. The later prophet declares the future role that this Davidic covenant will play in the restored Israel:

> Incline your ear, and come to me;
>   listen, so that you may live;
> I will then make with you an eternal covenant,
>   my dependable loving commitment to David.
> I made him a ruler over peoples,
>   a leader and commander over many peoples.
> Behold, you shall summon nations that you do
>   not know,
>   and nations that did not know you shall run to you,
> because of the LORD your God, and of the
>   Holy One of Israel,
>   for he has given glory to you.
>
> (55:3–5)

The meaning here is strongly dependent upon understanding of the identity of the "you" who are the addressed. Assuming, as several scholars do, that this word is intended to apply to all Israel, there is then a deliberate widening and extension of the tradition of the divine covenant with the dynasty of David to make it more extensively applicable to the nation. The covenantal elements of love, permanence, and leadership are retained; these, however, are no longer invested solely in the family of David, but rather in the nation as a whole.

The most enigmatic feature of Isaiah 40–55 has concerned the presence of four passages that since the work of Bernhard Duhm (1892) have frequently been regarded separately from the remainder of the prophecies and have been entitled the "Servant Songs" (42:1–4, 49:1–6, 50:4–11, 52:13–53:12). By separating the four units in this fashion from their context it became possible to interpret them quite independently of the rest of Isaiah 40–55 and to look for a specific individual who could be identified as the Servant. Yet this is clearly a dangerous proceeding, which is not properly justified by any marked discrepancy between the songs themselves and their context. Since it is unquestionably and repeatedly made clear in the contextual chapters that "the Servant" is a title for Israel, it should be assumed a priori that this meaning is the most likely understanding of the title in these four passages (41:8–9, 42:19, etc.; see Mettinger 1983). At most we might suggest that the prophet has narrowed his understanding of Israel as God's servant to the point where he identifies the servant wholly with the Israel in Babylonian exile. In the last of these four passages (52:13–53:12) there is a remarkable disquisition upon the significance of Israel's suffering justly for her sins and yet also suffering far beyond the measure that any just reckoning of her deserts could merit. Overall it is better to recognize that the so-called songs are highly compressed images of the role of Israel through its experience of judgment and exile, such as these chapters develop more widely. They belong to their context and are neither temporally nor in their literary form significantly distinct from that context.

Undoubtedly it is the rich theological content of chapters 40–55, the strange anonymity occasioned by their incorporation into the Book of Isaiah, and their memorable lyrical quality that together have made them the subject of a great deal of individual attention. Their place within the Book of Isaiah is clearly important and demands adequate recognition. Whether, as was at one time widely believed, they once existed as an entirely independent collection and were added only at a much later stage to the present Book of Isaiah is far from certain. They betray some significant connections with the remainder of the book, sufficient to suggest that the tradition of Isaiah's prophecies formed an important constituent of the author's background.

FROM PROPHECY TO APOCALYPTIC

So far I have examined the growth and structure of the Book of Isaiah and have noted that it consists of two major parts. The first of these, now preserved within chapters 1–39, contains the original prophecies of Isaiah and the series of editorial notes and additions to them concerning the period of Assyrian imperial domination over Judah that ended in the reign of Josiah. The second part, with its central focus in prophecies concerning the overthrow of Babylon and the return of the Judean exiles from there, is to be found within chapters 40–55. The question of when, and how early, the prophecies of chapters 40–66 were joined in a written collection to the earlier part of the book remains a disputed issue. As a number of indications in chapters 1–39 show, the tradents of Isaiah's prophecies came to affirm that God had determined that Babylon should replace Assyria as the punitive "rod" with which Judah must be punished. However, a number of factors suggest that chapters 40–66 may not originally have been part of the same literary connection as the emergent collection in chapters 1–39 but came to be joined to this in the postexilic age. This joining inevitably led to the incorporation of further references to Babylon, and to many of the central themes of chapters 40–66, into the earlier (Assyrian) part of the book. At all events, the contents of chapters 56–62 are closely related to the themes of chapters 40–55 and appear to have been combined with these in the early postexilic age.

It is further evident that the prophetic pronouncement of the fall of Babylon, still viewed as a future event, has become a major theme for the earlier part of the book:

Behold, I am about to rouse up the Medes against them,
  who pay no attention to silver
  and take no delight in gold.
Their bows will slaughter the young men;
  they will have no mercy on infant children;
  nor will they take pity on the young.
Then will Babylon, the most splendid of kingdoms,
  the glory and pride of the Chaldeans,
become like Sodom and Gomorrah
  which God overthrew.
It will never again be inhabited
  or lived in throughout all generations;
No Arab will pitch his tent there,
  nor will shepherds make their flocks lie down there.
Instead wild beasts will settle there,
  and porcupines will inhabit its homes;
there desert owls will dwell,
  and wild goats will play.
Jackals will howl in its towers,
  and wolves in its elegant buildings.
Its end is close at hand
  and it will not last much longer.

(13:17–22)

A further declaration of the fall of Babylon and its perpetual ruin is to be found in Isaiah 14:22–23. Furthermore, the brilliant satire on the downfall of a great world ruler, which some scholars have suggested may have been composed by Isaiah for the death of Sargon II in 705, has now been applied to "the king of Babylon" (14:4–21). As it is now preserved it serves as a song of exaltation over the ending of an oppressive world power. The presence of such material in the collection of Isaiah's prophecies in chapters 1–39 indicates that the theme of Israel's salvation wrought through the overthrow of Babylonian power appears as a major theme in both parts of the Book of Isaiah.

As Babylon's overthrow marks the negative side of the message of the book, so the theme of Israel's restoration and the return of all those dispersed exiles among the nations marks the positive side of the hope that the final form of the book expresses. These prophecies derive from an extended period of the postexilic age. Undoubtedly the prophecies of chapters 40–55 envisaged the return from exile in Babylon and the rebuilding of Jerusalem as imminent events that would ensue upon the fall of Babylon to the Medo-Persian ruler Cyrus in 538. It is evident, however, that the scale of the returns and the achievements of those who sought to reestablish themselves in

Jerusalem fell far short of the hopes that had been aroused. In consequence, the themes of Israel's return from exile and of the rebuilding of Jerusalem continue to reappear at a later time (60:1–22, 61:1–7, 62:1–12). It is noteworthy that among these prophecies, the concern for the rebuilding of Jerusalem comes to occupy a central place. Correspondingly, the expectation of Israel's restoration as a nation to a fully independent place among the nations of the world falls further into the background.

> Upon your walls, O Jerusalem,
>   I have set guards;
> Continually, both day and night
>   they shall never be silent.
> You who are the heralds of the LORD
>   do not be quiet.
> Nor give to anyone rest
>   until he establishes Jerusalem
>   and makes it an object of praise in the land.
>   (62:6–7)

In keeping with the great importance accorded by Isaiah to the Davidic kingship, it is not surprising to find that the restoration of the surviving heirs of the much-chastened and reduced Davidic dynasty to this office should have been proclaimed:

> Then a shoot shall spring up
>   from the stump of Jesse,
> and a branch shall grow out of his roots.
> The spirit of the LORD shall come upon him,
>   the spirit of wisdom and discernment,
>   of wise counsel and of power;
> the spirit of understanding and of reverence for
>   the LORD.
> He will take pleasure in reverence for the LORD.
> He shall not judge by appearances,
>   or issue rebukes merely on what he hears.
> He will judge the cases of the poor fairly,
>   and administer justice impartially
>   for the afflicted of the land.
> He will strike the earth with the rod of his mouth,
>   and kill wicked persons with the breath of his lips.
> Righteousness will be the belt around his waist,
>   and faithfulness the belt upon his thighs.
>   (11:1–5)

It is worth noting that this portrayal of the return to office of the heirs of David's dynasty was further elaborated at a later stage by an affirmation that this would mark a return to the paradisiacal condition of the world as God intended it to be from the beginning (11:6–9).

The declaration of a still-future return of all the scattered remnants of Israel remains one of the unfulfilled promises present in the final stages of the book's compilation. It reappears at a number of points within the collection, notably at 11:12–16, where the still unfulfilled aspect of this hope is further emphasized by the addition of 11:11. Noteworthy, too, is the suggestion in 11:10 that it will be the royal heir of David's line who will be the "signal flag" (RSV "ensign") that God will raise as a sign for all the dispersed exiles to return to their home. See also Isaiah 27:12f. and 35:8–10 for the continued recurrence of this theme of the "Great Return," which originated with the prophecies of chapters 40ff.

A number of major literary problems remain unresolved in respect of the later stages of the formation of the Book of Isaiah in the postexilic period. Regrettably, the earlier critical view that the book is to be regarded as composed of three major literary sections (chaps. 1–39, 40–55, 56–66) paid too little attention to their interrelationships. Undoubtedly three such self-contained and independent literary sections never existed as such. Of the three, only chapters 40–55 have retained scholarly confidence as having once comprised a separate literary whole, and even this must be regarded as highly questionable. For long scholars have recognized that chapters 24–27 in the earlier major part of the collection, together with chapters 34–35, display a distinctively different character from much of the remainder of the book. The former unit has been identified as the "Apocalypse of Isaiah" and has been allocated as a separate composition to the late fifth century B.C.E. (Wildberger 1984) or to an even later period. Similarly the chapters 34–35, which have sometimes been described as the "Little Apocalypse of Isaiah," must belong to the postexilic age. Since there are no overwhelmingly clear indications of the date of these sections, it is understandable that opinions have varied between locating them as far back as the preexilic age and dating them to the late Hellenistic era.

We may here set aside the inconclusive debate regarding the date of these difficult chapters and concentrate attention on some more fundamental literary considerations. First of all, it is highly improbable that the contents either of chapters 24–27 or of 34–35 ever existed, or were intended to exist, as separate and self-contained prophetic units. The contents indicate that these passages were composed in order to present a later interpretation and development of themes already present in the Book of Isaiah. As such they reveal to us the way in which the earlier prophecies, which had by the postexilic age been formed into a substantial book, had come to be reinterpreted and reapplied to new historical situations. Moreover, they display all the characteristics of what has been described as "apocalyptic" or, perhaps more narrowly, "proto-apocalyptic." This term refers not to a new kind of literature, nor yet to an entirely new and distinctive type of religious thought, but rather to a way in which the earlier prophecies were interpreted and applied to the continuing history of God's people in the trials of their existence after the exile. Such texts are less overtly historical in the sense that few direct references to known events are made. Instead they are replete with images and themes drawn from the earlier parts of the Book of Isaiah. Apocalyptic represents a form of "prophecy among the scribes" that reveals how the word of God was adapted and reinterpreted to a new series of situations. The precise chronology of its emergence has not been satisfactorily established, although it is evident that the book of the prophecies of Isaiah formed a primary source for its development (see, e.g., Vermeylen 1977). Odil Hannes Steck (1985) has further argued that Isaiah 35 should be regarded as a composition specifically intended to assist in the combining of the main part of "First Isaiah" with "Second Isaiah." Such observations, from a literary point of view and in connection with the concern to understand the later stages of the formation of the Book of Isaiah, indicate that a number of obscurities still remain in tracing this development.

What we should note, however, is that the latest additions to the book were intended as a guide and supplement to the earlier material, rather than as wholly separate compositions. We can readily see this, for example, in the way in which the "New Song of the Vineyard" of 27:2–6 is intended as a complement and development of the original Isaianic "Song of the Vineyard" in 5:1–7.

Several major themes mark the latest literary additions to the book. Already I have drawn attention to the divine promise of the "Great Return" that would mark the ending of Israel's dispersion among the nations. Alongside this—and rather surprisingly so, in view of the earlier hostility shown by Isaiah to Hezekiah's treaties with Egypt—is the promise that eventually Egypt itself will be converted to a true trust in Yahweh, the God of Israel: "At that time Israel will be the third with Egypt and Assyria, a blessing in the center of the earth, whom the LORD of hosts will have blessed, saying, 'Blessed be Egypt my people, and Assyria the work of my hands, and Israel my inheritance'" (19:24).

The entire section of Isaiah 19:18–24, which serves as a supplement to the threatening prophecy against Egypt in 19:1–15, reveals how in the late postexilic era, when a very large Jewish community had come to be established in Egypt on a more or less permanent basis, earlier prophecies came to be seen, and added to, from a wholly new perspective.

The gradual transition in the understanding of earlier prophecy that is to be found in the Book of Isaiah shows a shift to a more world-embracing and cataclysmic view of God's plan for the nations of the world. Two themes tend to dominate this view and lend to the final edited form of the Book of Isaiah a very distinctive character. The first of these concerns a great threat posed to the existence of Israel by all the nations of the earth. The images of doom and disaster presented here show a worldwide cataclysm through which the purified remnant of God's people will attain their salvation (13:9–16, 24:1–20, 29:5–10, 34:1–4.). In such a passage as 30:29–33 it is further evident that even the name "Assyria" has come to be employed as a cover name for the otherwise unidentified opponents of Israel.

The second theme of this final editorial stratum in the book is, quite appropriately, one of Israel's final vindication and blessedness in the land that God had long before promised to the nation's ancestors and in the city in which Isaiah had prophesied with such dramatic effect:

On this mountain the LORD of hosts will make for all peoples a sumptuous feast. It will be a feast of good wine, rich food, and the very best wines, well kept and refined.

277

Then he will destroy on this mountain the covering that is spread over all peoples, that is the veil that covers all nations. He will overthrow death completely, and the LORD God will wipe away tears from all faces. Then the ignominy suffered by his people he will take away from all the earth; for it is the LORD who has spoken. (25:6–8)

We may compare further such passages as Isaiah 10:24–27, 12:1–6, 24:17–23, 27:12–13, 30:19–26, and 33:17–22. They add up to a picture of strong hope in the power of God to fulfill his word and a deep awareness that the continuing history of Israel reflects the trials and tensions of human rebellion against the divine will. Eventually the will of God, declared long ago through the prophets and fulfilled through a long history, will be brought to a final fulfillment in the triumph of God's people from Jerusalem. Such is the concluding message of the Book of Isaiah. It has passed through a long literary history and has marked the transition from the simple word of prophecy addressed to a single historical situation to the revelatory unfolding of God's plan for the final destiny of his people Israel. It shows the deep changes that came to prophecy once it had assumed a written form. The earlier words could be reflected upon and seen to be fraught with new meanings. Prophecy could be compared with prophecy until a larger understanding of the divine purpose could be discerned within it. It gave rise to a new type of scribe, versed in the meaning and interpretation of the prophetic writings that were not accessible to the illiterate or the undiscerning. To this extent the book contains a most challenging comment about its own inner mysteries and meaning, penned no doubt by a teacher and a scribe who had become enthusiastic over the understanding that he had acquired of its hidden truths:

Then the vision of all this will have become to you like the words of a book that is sealed. When men give it to one who can read and say, "Read this," he will reply and say, "I cannot, for it is sealed." Then when they give the scroll to one who cannot read and say, "Read this," he will say, "I cannot read." (29:11–12)

Bibliography

Commentaries

Barth, Hermann. *Die Jesaja-Worte in der Josiazeit.* Neukirchen-Vluyn, 1977.

Clements, Ronald E. *Isaiah 1–39.* Grand Rapids, 1980.

Duhm, Bernhard. *Das Buch Jesaja.* Göttingen, 1892 5th ed., 1968.

Elliger, Karl. *Jesaja 2. Isa. 40.1–45.7.* Neukirchen-Vluyn, 1970.

Fohrer, Georg. *Das Buch Jesaja.* 3 vols. Zurich, 1964–1967.

Gray, George Buchanan. *A Critical and Exegetical Commentary on the Book of Isaiah 1–27.* The International Critical Commentary. Edinburgh, 1912.

Herbert, A. S. *The Book of the Prophet Isaiah, 1–39.* Cambridge, 1973.

Kaiser, Otto. *Isaiah 1–12.* Rev. ed. Translated by J. Bowden. London, 1983.

———. *Isaiah 13–39.* Translated by R. A. Wilson. London, 1974.

Knight, George A. F. *Deutero-Isaiah: A Theological Commentary on Isaiah 40–55.* New York, 1965.

———. *The New Israel: A Commentary on the Book of Isaiah 56–66.* Grand Rapids, 1984.

McKenzie, John L. *Second Isaiah.* Anchor Bible, vol. 20. Garden City, N.Y., 1968.

Mowinckel, Sigmund. *Jesaja-disiplene.* Oslo, 1926.

North, Christopher Richard. *The Second Isaiah.* Oxford, 1964.

Skinner, John. *The Book of the Prophet Isaiah.* Cambridge, 1905, 1917.

Torrey, Charles Cutler. *The Second Isaiah: A New Interpretation.* New York, 1928.

Westermann, Claus. *Isaiah 40–66: A Commentary.* Translated by David M. G. Stalker. Philadelphia, 1969.

Whedbee, J. William. *Isaiah and Wisdom.* Nashville, Tenn., 1971.

Wildberger, Hans. *Jesaja 1–39.* 3 vols. Neukirchen-Vluyn, 1965–1979.

Whybray, Roger Norman. *Isaiah 40–66.* Grand Rapids, 1981.

Isaiah's Life and Times

Blank, Sheldon H. *Prophetic Faith in Isaiah.* New York, 1958.

Blenkinsopp, Joseph. *A History of Prophecy in Israel.* Philadelphia, 1983.

Bright, John. *Covenant and Promise: The Prophetic Understanding of the Future in Pre-exilic Israel.* Philadelphia, 1976.

Childs, Brevard S. *Isaiah and the Assyrian Crisis.* London, 1967.

Clements, Ronald E. *Isaiah and the Deliverance of Jerusalem.* Journal for the Study of the Old Testament Supplements, vol. 13. Sheffield, England, 1980.

Cogan, Morton. *Imperialism and Religion: Assyria, Judah, and Israel in the Eighth and Seventh Centuries B.C.E.* Missoula, 1974.

Dietrich, Walter. *Jesaja und die Politik.* Munich, 1976.

Donner, Herbert. *Israel unter den Völkern.* Vetus Testamentum Supplements, vol. 11. Leiden, 1964.

Erlandsson, Seth. *The Burden of Babylon: A Study of Isaiah 13.2–14.23.* Translated by George J. Houser. Lund, Sweden, 1970.

Hoffmann, Hans Werner. *Die Intention der Verkündigung Jesajas.* Beihefte der Zeitschrift für die alttestamentliche Wissenschaft, vol. 136. New York, 1974.

Huber, Friedrich. *Jahwe, Juda, und die anderen Völker beim Propheten Jesaja.* Beihefte der Zeitschrift für die alttestamentliche Wissenschaft, vol. 137. New York, 1976.

Irwin, William Henry. *Isaiah 28–33: Translation with Philological Notes.* Rome, 1977.

Kilian, Rudolf. *Jesaja 1–39.* Erträge der Forschung, vol. 200. Darmstadt, 1983.

———. *Die Verheissung Immanuels: Jes. 7.14.* Stuttgart Bibel Studien 35. Stuttgart, 1968.

Koch, Klaus. *The Prophets.* Vol. 1, *The Assyrian Period.* Translated by Margaret Kohl. Philadelphia, 1982.

Isaiah 40–66

Begrich, Joachim. *Studien zu Deuterojesaja.* Stuttgart, 1938, reprinted Munich, 1963.

Boer, Pieter Arie Hendrik de. *Second Isaiah's Message.* Leiden, 1956.

Clements, Ronald E. "Deutero-Isaianic Development of First Isaiah's Themes." *Journal for the Study of the Old Testament* 31 (1985): 95–113.

Lindblom, Johannes. *The Servant Songs in Deutero-Isaiah.* Lund, Sweden, 1951.

Mettinger, Tryggve N. D. *A Farewell to the Servant Songs.* Lund, Sweden, 1983.

North, Christopher Richard. *The Suffering Servant in Deutero-Isaiah.* London, 1948.

Schoors, Antoon. *I Am God Your Saviour: A Form-Critical Study of the Main Genres in Isaiah 40–55.* Vetus Testamentum Supplements, vol. 24. Leiden, 1973.

Stuhlmueller, Carroll. *Creative Redemption in Deutero-Isaiah.* Rome, 1970.

Whybray, R. Norman. *The Second Isaiah.* Sheffield, England, 1983.

The Editing of the Book of Isaiah

Barth, Hermann. *Die Jesaja-Worte in der Josiazeit.* Neukirchen-Vluyn, 1977.

Clements, Ronald E. "The Unity of the Book of Isaiah." *Interpretation* 36 (1982): 117–129.

Fishbane, Michael. *Biblical Interpretation in Ancient Israel.* New York, 1985.

Hanson, Paul D. *The Dawn of Apocalyptic.* Philadelphia, 1975.

Johnson, Dan G. *From Chaos to Restoration.* Journal for the Study of the Old Testament Supplements, series 61. Sheffield, England, 1988.

Mays, James L., and Paul J. Achtemeier, eds. *Interpreting the Prophets.* Philadelphia, 1987.

Plöger, Otto. *Theocracy and Eschatology.* Translated by S. Rudman. Richmond, Va., 1968.

Seitz, Christopher R., ed. *Reading and Preaching the Book of Isaiah.* Philadelphia, 1988.

Steck, Odil Hannes. *Bereitete Heimkehr.* Stuttgart, 1985.

Vermeylen, Jacques. *Du prophète Isaïe à l'apocalyptique.* 2 vols. Paris, 1977.

Wildberger, Hans. *Königsherrschaft Gottes: Jesaja 1–39.* 2 vols. Neukirchen-Vluyn, 1984.

RONALD E. CLEMENTS

Jeremiah

THE BOOK OF Jeremiah has always played a crucial role in the study of ancient Israelite literature and religion. For the historian, the book has provided a vivid firsthand account of events in Jerusalem during the ten years that preceded the Babylonian sack of the city in 587 B.C.E. For students of Israelite prophecy, Jeremiah has supplied an explicit description of prophetic activity and unparalleled insight into the nature of the prophetic experience itself. For the theologian, the prophet's words have furnished a cogent explanation for the traumatic events surrounding the beginning of the exile and have helped later Jewish and Christian communities to understand their own experiences of suffering and loss. For students of literature, Jeremiah has been a fascinating collection of moving poetry and gripping narratives.

At the same time, Jeremiah has never yielded its treasures easily. The book bristles with difficulties that have frustrated scholars and puzzled the casual reader. Although the text is fairly clear about the general dates of the prophet's activity, many of his individual oracles are undatable and cannot easily be correlated with specific historical events. The narratives of Jeremiah's prophetic activity that are dated are not arranged in chronological order. Rather, narratives from different historical periods are interwoven according to no discernible pattern. Some passages seem to be duplicates or at least to represent different perspectives on the same event (6:12–15 and 8:10–12; 10:12–16 and 51:15–19; 16:14–15 and 23:7–8; 23:5–6 and 33:15–16; 23:19–20 and 30:23–24; 30:10–11 and 46:27–28; 7:1–15 and 26:1–24; 25:1–29 and 36:1–32). Literary analysts have been frustrated by their inability to uncover a clear organizational pattern within the book as a whole and have been puzzled by Jeremiah's unusual mixture of divine oracles, theological commentaries, and extensive biographical narratives about the prophet's activities. To make matters even more complex, the Greek translation of the book in the Septuagint is roughly seven-eighths the length of the Hebrew text followed by most English translations. Furthermore, chapters 46–51 of the Hebrew text appear after 25:13 in the Greek version, and the contents of those chapters are arranged in a rather different order. All of this suggests a complex compositional history.

At first glance, then, the problems associated with reading Jeremiah appear to be literary ones that might be solved through more careful attention to the book's rhetoric and overall literary structure. However, the reader who focuses only on the literary aspects of the text overlooks an important interpretive clue provided by the book itself. Throughout the entire text, but particularly after chapter 20, the Book of Jeremiah is obsessed with current historical events and with their proper theological interpretation. Twenty-eight passages in the book are assigned specific dates. Over fifty of the prophet's contemporaries are mentioned by name, often with detailed references to their family histories and to their occupations. There are numerous references to the Babylonian invasion of Judah, to the siege of Jerusalem, and to the reactions of various individuals to these events.

Clearly, then, an informed reading of Jeremiah must take place against the background of the historical and theological concerns that seem to have dominated the consciousness of the writers and editors of the book. Attention to Jeremiah's historical and religious background will not provide a detailed solution to all of the book's literary problems, but an awareness of the authors' original concerns will provide a helpful perspective that can clarify many of the book's obscurities.

THE PROPHET AND HIS TIMES

According to the book's own superscription, Jeremiah prophesied from the thirteenth year of King Josiah (*ca.* 627/626) until the fall of Jerusalem to the Babylonians (587/586). The prophet was thus active during forty of the most tumultuous years in Israelite history. During this period the nation's political, economic, social, and religious systems were altered in major ways that left a permanent imprint on the people's understanding of their own identity. Equally important, the fall of Jerusalem and the subsequent Babylonian exile changed forever the shape of Israelite religion and had a profound impact on the shape of much of the biblical text. To understand why this is so, it is necessary to understand Israel's political and religious situation during the years that led up to the exile.

The Prophet's Political Context

For much of the century preceding Jeremiah's call to prophesy, political life in Israel was dominated by the Assyrian Empire, which had subjugated most of Palestine and Syria and forced local rulers to pay tribute. To be sure, occasional turmoil in Assyria sometimes encouraged the empire's distant vassals to revolt, but these breaches of treaty were later severely punished, and the cohesion of the empire was maintained. The power of the Assyrians was demonstrated sharply to Israel in 722/721, when the rebellion of the northern kingdom of Israel (Ephraim) was met with an Assyrian invasion, the destruction of the capital city, Samaria, and the deportation of much of the population (2 Kgs 17). After the fall of Samaria, only the southern kingdom of Judah, itself an Assyrian vassal, remained under Israelite control. King Hezekiah of Judah briefly rebelled against Assyria, instituted a religious reform, and attempted to lay claim to former Ephraimite territory in the north, but the Assyrians retaliated by invading Judah and threatening Jerusalem (701). In the end Hezekiah was forced to capitulate and pay heavy tribute to Sennacherib, the Assyrian monarch (2 Kgs 18–20).

However, after the death of the Assyrian king Ashurbanipal (627), the empire's power began to wane. Internal political instability encouraged a rebirth of nationalism on the periphery of the empire, particularly in Babylon, Egypt, and Palestine. As a result, the Judean king Josiah was able to rule with relatively little interference from Assyria, and he even attempted to regain Assyrian territory that had historically been part of the northern kingdom of Ephraim. At the same time, he instituted, or at least supported, a religious reform that restored the worship of Israel's national God, Yahweh, to the land (2 Kgs 22–23; 2 Chr 34–35). The precise chronology of these events is unclear, but it is likely that he began his reforms relatively early in his reign. However, Judah's independence was short-lived. While Josiah was attempting to enlarge his own kingdom, Egypt and Babylon were struggling for control of the old Assyrian empire. When Josiah became involved in this struggle, in 609, he was killed, and Judah entered a period of political instability from which it never fully recovered.

Josiah's successor, his son Jehoahaz, reigned only three months before he was deposed by Pharaoh Neco II of Egypt, who placed another son of Josiah, Jehoiakim, on the Judean throne. Judah thus became an Egyptian vassal and was forced to pay heavy tribute (2 Kgs 23:31–35), a situation that triggered much opposition in the land and led to the formation of political groups opposing Jehoiakim's pro-Egyptian stance. In the meantime, the power of Babylon continued to grow, and in 605 the Babylonians defeated the Egyptian army at Carchemish. By 603 the Babylonian king Nebuchadrezzar II was clearly a threat to Palestine, and Jehoiakim became a Babylonian vassal. This shift in Judah's allegiance caused further internal dissension as pro-Babylonian, pro-Egyptian, and nationalist factions quarreled over the wisdom of the king's foreign policy.

In 601 Jehoiakim, believing that Babylonian power was declining, again made an alliance with Egypt, a move that soon cost him dearly. Late in 598 the Babylonians invaded Judah and laid siege to Jerusalem. King Jehoiachin, who had replaced his father, Jehoiakim, on the throne, was forced to surrender the city to the Babylonians in 597. He was deported to Babylon, along with a number of palace and Temple officials and craftsmen, including the prophet Ezekiel (2 Kgs 24:14–16; Ezek 1:1–3). The Temple and royal treasuries were drained to pay tribute to the Babylonians, and some of the Temple vessels were either destroyed (2 Kgs 24:13) or taken to Babylon (Jer 27).

For some Judeans, the year 597 marked the beginning of the exile. However, for Jeremiah and those left in Jerusalem, little seemed to have changed. The Babylonians placed Zedekiah, Jehoiachin's uncle, on the throne but continued to use the title "king" to refer to the exiled Jehoiachin, a move that provoked some of the exiles to doubt the legitimacy of Zedekiah. However, in spite of this confusion Zedekiah managed to restore some political stability to the land and remained a faithful Babylonian vassal, even though some of his advisers advocated pro-Egyptian and nationalist policies. Eventually, though, the pro-Egyptian faction prevailed, and Zedekiah conspired with other Babylonian vassals to rebel (Jer 27–28). The attempted revolt was not successful, and Judah was forced to reaffirm its loyalty to Nebuchadrezzar (Jer 29:3–14, 51:59).

Even though Zedekiah was forced to return to the Babylonian fold, some factions in Jerusalem continued to press for revolt. Zedekiah seems to have had doubts about the wisdom of such a move (Jer 21:1–7; 37:3–10, 17; 38:14–23), but he eventually yielded to internal pressure and rebelled, probably with the expectation of receiving aid from Egypt. Nebuchadrezzar's reaction to Judah's revolt was both quick and decisive. In 588 he invaded, destroying a number of cities and laying siege to Jerusalem. After a protracted siege, the city finally fell in the summer of 587 or 586. In the confusion, Zedekiah and some of the royal court attempted to escape but were soon captured by the Babylonians. The king's sons were killed, he himself was blinded and taken captive to Babylon, Jerusalem was destroyed, and the Temple was burned.

Most of the inhabitants of the city were deported to Babylon, although some, including Jeremiah, went to Egypt, at least temporarily. Other refugees may have remained in Judah. Nebuchadrezzar attempted to restore political stability by appointing a Judean noble, Gedaliah, to be governor over the "poor of the land" who still remained in Judah. However, Gedaliah was soon murdered, and the land again became politically unstable. This unrest may have led to an additional deportation in 582 and to the incorporation of Judah into the Babylonian province of Samaria, but the precise course of events during this period is unclear.

The Prophet's Religious Context

Just as Jeremiah lived in an age of great political and social instability, so he also witnessed a major crisis in Israel's traditional faith. This crisis began with the deportation of 597 and reached its peak with the fall of Jerusalem in 587, but its roots lay much earlier in Israel's history. By Jeremiah's time Israel's religion was dominated by two general perspectives on the nature of God's relationship to the nation in general and to the city of Jerusalem in particular. The first of these perspectives was closely associated with Jerusalem and had developed in conjunction with the royal court and the Temple. According to this royal Jerusalemite theology, God had elected David and his descendants to be the eternal rulers of the whole nation of Israel and at the same time had chosen Jerusalem as the place where God would dwell forever (2 Sam 7).

The divine election of the dynasty and the city was symbolized by God's eternal presence in the Temple, where the Deity was enthroned above the cherubim in the Holy of Holies. Because God had promised to dwell in Jerusalem in perpetuity, both the city and the Temple were considered to be inviolable and therefore safe from foreign attack. The eternality of God's election of Israel and the invulnerability of Jerusalem were celebrated in Israel's worship (Pss 2, 46, 78, 110, 132) and were supported in varying degrees by some of Israel's prophets. Isaiah, for example, prophesied that God would punish the people for their sins but would not totally destroy Jerusalem. After the judgment, a remnant would remain, and a Davidic king would still occupy the throne in order to demonstrate God's fidelity to the promises of election (Isa 7:10–25, 8:1–10, 28:1–22, 29:1–24, 30:15–28, 33:1–24). Isaiah's words were proved to be true both during the Syro-Ephraimite War (*ca.* 734–733), when Ephraim and Syria unsuccessfully sought to overthrow the Davidic ruler in Jerusalem, and during the Assyrian invasion of 701, when Jerusalem was miraculously delivered from imminent destruction. It is therefore not surprising that prophets continued to proclaim Jerusalem's inviolability in Jeremiah's own time, even during the final days of the Babylonian siege (Jer 23:9–40, 27–29).

The second general perspective on God's relationship to Israel is represented by the Book of Deuteronomy and by the Deuteronomistic History of Joshua, Judges, Samuel, and Kings. In contrast to the royal theology of Jerusalem, Deuteronomistic theology held that God's election of the Davidic monarchy, the people of Israel, and the city of Jerusalem was not necessarily eternal but was contingent on Israel's obedience to the divine law, particularly the law preserved in the Book of Deuteronomy. As long as Israel and its kings obeyed the law and listened to the prophets who interpreted and elaborated it, the Davidic king would remain on the throne, the people could continue to live in the land that God had given them, and God's name would continue to dwell in the Temple in Jerusalem. But if the people or the king disobeyed the law and refused to listen to God's servants, the prophets, then God would forsake Jerusalem, the Davidic dynasty would end, and the people would be punished by death and exile.

Just as the royal Jerusalemite theologians could point to events in Israelite history that supported their theological views, so also the Deuteronomistic theologians claimed historical support for their view of God's relationship to Israel. When the Assyrians destroyed the northern kingdom of Ephraim and brought an end to this part of the Israelite nation, the Deuteronomistic theologians interpreted the event as divine punishment for Ephraim's long history of disobedience (2 Kgs 17:7–41). Furthermore, they warned that if the southern kingdom of Judah did not

learn from the sad history of Ephraim and turn once again to following the law, then God would also reject Judah and would abandon Jerusalem to its enemies.

The precise sources of Deuteronomistic theology are uncertain, but its origins may lie in northern sanctuaries such as Shiloh, where the Ark of the Covenant resided before David moved it to Jerusalem. In any case, Deuteronomism seems to have become influential in Judah not long after the fall of the northern kingdom. By the time of Hezekiah the theology seems to have influenced foreign policy in Jerusalem and to have triggered the king's religious reforms, which receive unqualified praise from the Deuteronomistic writers of the Books of Kings (2 Kgs 18–20). At least according to the account in Kings, the theology was ignored by Hezekiah's successors until the reign of Josiah, who also instituted a religious reform based on Deuteronomistic principles. A part of this reform was a "book of the law," possibly an early version of Deuteronomy, which was found in the Temple (2 Kgs 22–23). The prophet Jeremiah, who began to prophesy during Josiah's reign, was heavily influenced by Deuteronomistic theology and continued to advocate it throughout his career, even though Deuteronomistic influence in Jerusalem waned after Josiah's untimely death. Deuteronomistic influence can also be found in the prophecies of Jeremiah's contemporary, Ezekiel, who advocated a radically transformed version of the royal Jerusalemite theology.

The political ferment of Jeremiah's time raised several serious theological questions that his contemporaries had to answer on the basis of the theological options open to them. These questions were stimulated by the first deportation of exiles from Jerusalem in 597 and reached a critical point when the Temple was destroyed in 587. Modern readers of the Bible, who have the advantage of historical and theological perspective, tend to underestimate the difficulty of these questions, but people living at the time did not know what the future had in store for Israel. For them the questions were both difficult and important, for the answers that the people supplied had very real political and religious consequences.

The first and most general question concerned the proper theological interpretation of political events. Was the growing threat of a Babylonian invasion a warning that Judah should return to the proper worship of God, or was the Babylonian presence simply a normal part of political life in the ancient Near East? If the Babylonians were a divine warning, then what was the proper response? Was repentance required in order to remove the threat, as the Deuteronomistic theology claimed, or was it necessary only to trust in God's fidelity to the promises of election made long ago to the city and to the people, as Isaiah and others had argued? Were religious responses alone an adequate way of dealing with the threat, or should political action of some sort be taken as well? These questions continued to be debated in Jerusalem until the moment of the city's fall, and afterward they became important topics for discussion as the exiles attempted to understand what had happened to them. The ways in which specific people and groups answered the questions, along with the practical implications of those answers, were of enormous interest to Jeremiah and his supporters and constitute the subject matter of many of the book's narratives.

When Jerusalem fell to the Babylonians in 587, a second, very specific, question was raised concerning God's special relationship to the city and to the Davidic line. Were the destruction and exile simply God's temporary punishment for the people's accumulated sins, a punishment to be followed by a restoration of the nation and the monarchy? Or did the exile signal the end of Israel's special status as God's people? Had God left Jerusalem, never to return, and thus brought an end to the people and the Davidic dynasty? This question, in turn, led to another. If the exile did not mean a complete end to Israel, then who would constitute the new Israel that would be allowed to return to the land? Would the entire nation be brought back, or would a particular community in Palestine, Egypt, or Babylon be singled out as the true successor to preexilic Israel? This question had been argued hotly after the first deportation (Ezek 11:14–21), but it arose anew when the people found themselves scattered throughout much of the Mediterranean world.

Yet another question raised by the events leading up to the exile concerned the difficulties that the people experienced in discerning the true word of God. Even those inhabitants of Jerusalem who were genuinely attempting to discover what God wanted them to do during the crisis were frustrated by the presence of numerous prophets, each of whom claimed to be proclaiming the word of God. When these prophetic messages conflicted with each other, then the people had to determine which was true and which was false. This problem of recognizing genuine prophets was of great concern to Jeremiah and his supporters, for throughout his career he was opposed by prophets giving oracles that conflicted with his own.

Finally, the exile itself forced the survivors to create a new way of living as the people of God. Removed from their land and without the support of the Temple, they not only had to render to themselves a satisfying theological account of their recent past, but they also had to determine how they could live faithfully in exile in such a way as to make possible a return to the land. One of the primary resources that they employed in this task was the collection of Jeremiah's oracles, which they read and reinterpreted in the light of their new situation.

The Prophet's Biography

Because of the importance of the political and religious events in which Jeremiah was directly involved, his biography has intrigued readers of the book since antiquity. Interest in the details of the prophet's life began during his own lifetime and can be found within the book itself. Besides the editor's biographical superscription (1:1–3), which would normally appear at the beginning of any prophetic book, the Book of Jeremiah also preserves several unusual "complaints" or "laments," which give an intimate picture of the prophet's private reactions to his task (11:18–23, 12:1–6, 15:10–21, 17:14–18, 18:18–23, 20:7–18). In addition, the book contains a number of narratives about Jeremiah's activities during the years immediately before Jerusalem's fall (chaps. 27–29, 32:1–15, 35–36, 37:1–43:7). To be sure, these sources do not provide as much information as the modern historian would like, and, as an examination of the book's literary structure shows, it is likely that their inclusion resulted from factors other than a simple curiosity about the details of the prophet's life. Nevertheless, the book does provide enough information to permit the reader to reconstruct Jeremiah's life in some detail.

Jeremiah was born in Anathoth, a small Benjamite town about four miles northeast of Jerusalem (1:1). He came from a priestly family that owned property in the village (32:7–9), and it is likely that his ancestors traced their lineage to Abiathar, a descendant of the priestly house at the old northern sanctuary at Shiloh, whom David had installed as high priest in Jerusalem. Abiathar was exiled to Anathoth by Solomon (1 Kgs 2:26–27), and the priest's descendants probably remained there, on the periphery of the Jerusalem priesthood, until the destruction of the Temple.

It is impossible to determine whether or not Jeremiah's father, Hilkiah, is to be identified with the high priest of the same name who played a leading role in Josiah's religious reforms (2 Kgs 22:3–20). However, there can be no doubt that Jeremiah was strongly influenced by the Deuteronomistic theology on which the reforms were based. This influence presumably came directly from his family as well as from the writings that were already a part of the Deuteronomistic corpus: Hosea and early forms of Deuteronomy and the Deuteronomistic History. Jeremiah adopted not only the characteristic theology of the Deuteronomistic tradition, but he was also fond of using Deuteronomistic language and literary images. Particularly notable is his use of marital images to speak of the covenantal relationship between God and Israel (2:2–3, 20–25, 32–37; 3:1–5, 19–25; 4:1–3), a usage that was pioneered by Hosea.

Jeremiah began to prophesy in the thirteenth year of Josiah (627/626). If the chronology of 2 Chronicles 34:2–7 is correct, then the king had already begun his political and religious reforms by the time the young prophet gave his first oracles. Given the fact that Jeremiah's theology has striking affinities with the theology of the reform, it is strange that he does not mention it anywhere in his book. Nevertheless, it is possible that some of his early oracles were given as part of the reform. Josiah reasserted Judean control over parts of Ephraim, an area with which Jeremiah's priestly family had traditionally had strong ties. If some of the prophet's judgment and promise oracles dealing with Ephraim come from this period (2:4–25, 3:6–25, 4:1–2, 31:1–22), then it may be that he participated in an early phase of the reform by delivering prophetic warnings and promises to the north in an attempt to reintegrate the people into the Davidic empire. However, if he did so, his participation in the reform must have been short-lived, for the bulk of his words deal with Judah and Jerusalem rather than Ephraim.

It is not clear how far Jeremiah's prophetic activity extended into Josiah's reign. Almost all of the dated material in the book is ascribed to the period between Jehoiakim's first year and the fall of Jerusalem (26:1; cf. 3:6), a fact that may indicate that there was a sizable gap in Jeremiah's prophetic work during the last years of Josiah. Possibly the prophet became disenchanted with the sincerity or the thoroughness of the reform and refused to participate in it further. Or, the predominance of late material in the book may simply indicate that the prophet and his followers were more concerned with the traumatic events leading up to the fall of the city than they were in his earlier oracles, with the result that in the final form of the book Jeremiah's early words have been obscured or absorbed into later narratives about the fall.

Throughout his prophetic life Jeremiah's message was remarkably consistent. Accepting the Deuteronomistic notion that God's covenant with Israel was contingent on the people's obedience, Jeremiah called them to repent so that they might avert the judgment that God would otherwise send (3:12–25). The prophet originally spoke of this judgment in rather vague terms, although he sometimes specified it as a drought (14:1–6) or an attack by an unnamed enemy (4:5–31). But as the Babylonian threat began to loom larger on the horizon, he began to predict that the Babylonians were the instruments that God had chosen to punish Jerusalem. At this late stage of events, even the people's repentance would no longer be able to avert the judgment, so during the last days of the siege Jeremiah advised the inhabitants of Jerusalem to accept God's punishment and surrender peaceably to Nebuchadrezzar's army (27:1–22). After a long exile, it would indeed be possible for some of the exiles to return to the land, but only if they admitted their sins and sincerely repented (31:15–40, 32:9–44, 33:1–26).

Given the harshness of Jeremiah's message, it is not surprising that he faced strong opposition from several quarters throughout his prophetic career. His own complaints indicate that some of his harshest critics were to be found among his own family at Anathoth. They tried to prevent him from delivering his prophetic messages and at one point even tried to kill him (11:18–23, 12:1–6). The reason for their opposition is unclear, although if they were indeed involved in Josiah's religious reforms they might have been upset by Jeremiah's refusal to support the reforms fully. In this case they would have also been stung sharply by his criticisms of contemporary religious life in Jerusalem, a religious life that the reformers had helped to shape. For the priests from Anathoth, Jeremiah's negative comparison between the fate of Jerusalem and the fate of their old shrine at Shiloh would have been particularly irritating (7:1–15).

A second source of opposition was "the prophets," whom Jeremiah accused of misleading the people by prophesying that God would protect Jerusalem in spite of their violation of the covenant (5:31, 6:13, 14:13–16, 23:9–32, 27:1–29:32). These prophets were clearly supporters of the Jerusalemite theology, which held that God would remain faithful to the city and not allow it to be destroyed. From Jeremiah's perspective, these prophets were simply wrong, and their oracles were preventing the people from hearing God's true word. Jeremiah accused the prophets of lying and inventing their own oracles rather than receiving them from God. These accusations of false prophecy continued with increasing harshness until the fall of Jerusalem, when, of course, it became clear that Jeremiah's accusations had been correct.

Finally, Jeremiah was opposed by a number of Jerusalem officials who did not accept his prophetic authority (20:1–6, 26:1–24, 36:1–32, 37:1–43:7). Some of this opposition was motivated by religious concerns, but much of it was related to the prophet's political stance as an opponent of the royal theology. Particularly during the last days of the siege, his advocacy of surrender to the Babylonians was considered treasonous by many government officials, and they strongly advised that the prophet be executed. Zedekiah, however, refused to punish Jeremiah in this way but did permit the officials to imprison him. Even in prison the prophet refused to change his message and was unwilling to cooperate with the king by interceding with God on the city's behalf (37:1–43:7).

However, just as Jeremiah had opponents in Jerusalem, so he also had friends. Opposition from his family is not mentioned in the narratives of the last days of the siege, and it may be that his family finally realized that he was indeed a true prophet. In addition, Jeremiah received support from several members of the royal establishment, particularly the family of Shaphan, a scribe who had earlier been involved in Josiah's reform (2 Kgs 22:3–14). During the tense days before the city's fall, these supporters protected Jeremiah from those who sought to kill him and served as buffers between the prophet and the king (36:1–43:7).

When Jerusalem finally fell, Jeremiah was treated kindly by the Babylonians, presumably because they interpreted his message to be supportive of their cause (39:11–40:6). Rather than being deported to Babylon, Jeremiah was allowed to join the newly appointed governor, Gedaliah, at Mizpah. After Gedaliah's murder, Jeremiah was taken to Egypt, along with a number of other Judean survivors, an action that was condemned in a divine oracle (42:7–44:30). At this point the story of Jeremiah comes to an end, and there is no additional biblical information on his later life. Postbiblical sources have a great deal to say on this subject, but this information is contradictory and unreliable.

THE LITERARY SHAPE OF THE BOOK

While the overall message of Jeremiah is relatively clear, the literary structure of the book is often obscure. A number of different literary forms are represented: poetic oracles addressed to the people, private dialogues between God and the prophet, prophetic complaints and prayers addressed privately to God, speeches from the people addressed to the prophet or to God, third-person narratives about the prophet's activities, prose sermons addressed to the people, and prose interpretations of poetic oracles. This material does not seem to be arranged according to any discernible pattern. Occasionally oracles are organized on the basis of their contents, as in the case of the oracles against foreign nations (25:1–38, 46:1–51:64), the oracles inspired by the potter (18:1–19:15), or the promise oracles (30:1–33:26), but this does not seem to be the book's overall organizational principle. Beginning with chapter 21 a number of the narratives are assigned specific dates; yet the narratives themselves are not arranged in strict chronological order. Incidents and oracles from various times in the reigns of Jehoahaz, Jehoiakim, Jehoiachin, and Zedekiah are intertwined in a way that seems to blur rather than clarify any sort of chronological scheme. This apparently haphazard style of organization leads to confusion when the book is read as a whole and hinders a clear understanding of the prophet's message.

Since antiquity there have been numerous attempts to solve Jeremiah's literary puzzles, but to date no completely successful solution has been advanced. However, an understanding of the book's structure can certainly be enhanced by a brief examination of its literary components and their probable history. Once the form, setting, and function of the book's constituent parts are understood, the reasons for its overall shape will become clearer.

The Prophet and the Book

In ancient Israel prophecy was originally an oral phenomenon. Prophets received their oracles directly from God and then delivered them to the appropriate recipients. During or sometime after a prophet's career, the oracles were collected and eventually written down, either by the prophet or by the prophet's supporters and disciples. The prophetic process worked in this way until the exile, when, for the first time, prophetic oracles and even entire books were created initially in writing. Jeremiah's contemporary, Ezekiel, was probably the first to bypass the oral stage and circulate prophecy primarily in written form. Jeremiah also made use of writing as part of his prophetic work, and the book itself indicates that his oracles underwent a complex process of development before reaching their final shape.

The lack of obvious literary structure in parts of the book suggests that a number of the prophet's oral oracles have been collected and arranged in various ways sometime after they were originally delivered. At the same time, the book records that on several occasions Jeremiah dictated oracles to be written down and circulated to a particular audience and that he even revised the written material at a later date. In the fourth year of Jehoiakim, God commanded the prophet to write on a scroll all of the words that had been given to him up to that time. Jeremiah accordingly dictated to Baruch the scribe a scroll full of oracles, and Baruch then read the scroll to the people, to the princes of Judah, and finally to Jehoiakim himself. The king was unmoved by the contents, however, and burned the scroll section by section as it was read. God then commanded Jeremiah to dictate a second scroll containing all of the same material as the first. The prophet did so and added to it "many similar words" (36:1–32; *cf.* 45:1–5). At a later date Jeremiah himself is said to have written a collection of prophecies concerning Babylon (51:59–64), and he is also known to have written oracles to the Israelites who were exiled to Babylon in 597 (29:1–32).

All of these stories about prophetic writing suggest that oral transmission and written transmission of the prophet's words occurred simultaneously during his own lifetime, a fact that greatly hinders any effort to understand the book's compositional history. Furthermore, the fact that the book contains a large number of narratives about the prophet's activities shows that writers other than the prophet were involved in its creation and that the process of shaping the presentation of his words and deeds continued well after the end of his prophetic career. This latter point is reinforced by the observation that the Greek text of Jeremiah differs in major ways from the Hebrew text, probably an indication that the book continued to develop in different ways in the various communities that preserved it. The precise details of this development are unclear, but it is possible to isolate within the book four different types of literary material, each of which presumably had its own distinct history before becoming part of the present book. These four types—poetic oracles, prose oracles and supplementary material, biographical narratives, and prose sermons—have often been delineated and analyzed on the basis of their distinctive linguistic features, but their differing individual interests have not always been recognized.

Poetic oracles. In biblical Hebrew the distinction between poetry and prose is not absolute. However, in general, poetry is composed of relatively short lines arranged in pairs. These pairs are normally internally "parallel," with the result that the second line of each pair echoes or elaborates the first. In the Book of

Jeremiah, poetic oracles (sometimes called source A) are found primarily in chapters 1–25, 30–31, and 46–51. They are usually thought to have been created by the prophet himself, although occasionally introductory comments have been added by others during the process of the book's compilation. The oracles were probably created at various times throughout the prophet's working life, beginning in the Josianic period, although it is now rarely possible to date them precisely. The relationship of the poetic units to the scroll mentioned in chapter 36 is unclear, but most scholars assume that at least some of the oracles now contained in the book were first written down during Jehoiakim's reign.

Jeremiah's poetic oracles are characterized both by literary variety and by a lack of specificity. Metaphors, similes, wordplays, and literary images abound, a fact that gives the book an evocative quality that resists strict historical interpretation. There are frequent shifts of voice, and the identity of the speaker is often unclear. Sometimes God addresses the prophet with a private oracle or words to be delivered to the people. At other times the people seem to speak to God through the prophet, or the prophet speaks on his own behalf to God. The people are quoted, invited to reply to real questions, or asked rhetorical questions. Announcements are made, exhortations are delivered, and commands are given. Speakers change suddenly, often without warning. This sort of literary variety can confuse the unwary reader, but it also gives the book a sense of urgency and vitality that reflects the oracles' original oral setting.

In the present form of the book, the prophet's poetic oracles have been collected in three major groups on the basis of content. The first collection, chapters 1–24, consists primarily of announcements of judgment against Ephraim, Judah, and Jerusalem. Throughout the collection, the emphasis is on the people as a whole. Individuals, such as the king, the priests, or the prophets, are mentioned only in the context of the people in general. The sins that the people have committed are described rather generally, but it is clear that they are being condemned for violating their covenant with God and for failing to observe the divine law, particularly the law as it is outlined in the Book of Deuteronomy. Similarly, the judgment that their disobedience brings is described

only in vague terms, usually as a natural disaster or a military defeat.

In keeping with Deuteronomistic theology, however, the prophet seems to have felt that sincere repentance could avert the threatened judgment. Therefore the announcements of disaster are sometimes accompanied by exhortations to the people to repent. These exhortations are most frequent in the early part of the collection (chaps. 1–6) and then become extremely rare. Their disappearance allows the announcements of judgment to dominate the material and thus to create an increasing sense of tragedy and impending doom.

Within the first collection of poetry, oracles have sometimes been arranged further according to content. Thus, for example, oracles based on family and sexual images have been collected in chapters 2–3, while chapters 14–15 contain oracles relating to drought. In addition, oracles are sometimes organized to form a dialogue between God and the people (chap. 6). This dialogue, which is facilitated by the prophet, points to a crucial theological concept in Jeremiah's thinking: the importance of the prophet in divine-human communication. From the very beginning of the book (1:4–10), Jeremiah is presented as a prophet like Moses, a figure who, according to Deuteronomistic theology, is the only legitimate means of communication between God and the people (Deut 18:9–22). Mosaic prophets hear the word of God more clearly than do other prophets (Num 12:6–8) and therefore are able to pass on that word to the people without distortion. Deuteronomic law therefore requires Israel to listen to Mosaic prophets, whose word inevitably comes true. Such prophets, however, do not only deliver divine words to Israel. They also provide a means by which the people can approach God. When the people have a request or a question to place before God, they are to go to the Mosaic prophet, who will intercede on their behalf. This understanding of the prophetic office has influenced the arrangement of some of Jeremiah's judgment oracles and plays an even greater role in some of the book's prose texts.

The second collection of poetic texts in the book (chaps. 30–31) consists of oracles of promise. Many of these oracles seem originally to have been addressed to the northern kingdom of Ephraim and are likely to have been delivered initially during Josiah's reform. However, in the final version of the book they have been augmented by promise oracles addressed to the southern kingdom of Judah, so that the whole collection now indicates that all of Israel will return to the land after the exile.

The final collection of poetic oracles (25:30–38, 46:1–51:58) consists of oracles against foreign nations. These oracles announce judgment on Israel's enemies and couple their punishment with Israel's triumphant return to the land. Oracles against foreign nations thus function as promises for Israel and allow a word of hope to predominate in the last part of the book.

Prose oracles. In addition to a large body of poetic oracles, the Book of Jeremiah also contains a few brief oracles in prose. These are always added to existing poetic oracles and serve both as a supplement and as a guide to the reader (1:1–3; 2:4; 3:24–25; 4:9–12, 27; 5:18–19; 9:12–16, 23–26; 10:11; 11:21–23; 12:14–17; 18:18). It is likely that these prose supplements entered the book after the poetic oracles were already in written form, but little can be said about their origin. They do not share a common theme and so are unlikely to have been part of an independent collection before they were added to the book. Many scholars attribute them to later editors, but Jeremianic authorship is certainly not out of the question, given the fact that the prophet used writing in his work. Deuteronomistic language and theology are common in the prose oracles, but this fact in itself says little, for numbers of people connected with the book, including the prophet himself, were influenced by Deuteronomism. The prose oracles were thus probably added to a written collection of poetic oracles, either by the prophet himself or by his disciples, in order to clarify parts of the original poetry. The additions may well have been made over a period of time, a possibility that would account for their diverse contents and functions.

Biographical narratives. The Book of Jeremiah is unique among the prophetic books because it contains a large number of prose narratives about the prophet's life and professional activities. These narratives (sometimes called source B), which appear in the last half of the book (20:1–6, 26:1–29:32, 36:1–43:7, 45:1–5, 51:59–64), have a distinctive vocabulary and literary style that betray only a small amount of Deuteronomistic influence. Many scholars attribute the narratives to the scribe Baruch, who is known to have produced written documents for Jeremiah on several occasions (32:12–16, 36:4–32, 45:1–5). Baruch's work is usually thought to focus on the prophet's sufferings during the reign of Zedekiah (37:15–16, 21; 38:7) and thus to elaborate the motif of prophetic suffering already present in Jeremiah's own poetic laments.

This traditional understanding of the narratives is skewed for two reasons. First, although the narratives reflect an intimate knowledge of the royal court during Jeremiah's time and preserve many accurate details concerning life in Jerusalem between the two deportations, the book contains no evidence to indicate that Baruch was actually the author of these accounts. Second, the narratives are concerned with Jeremiah's life only incidentally and are thus not really biographical at all. Rather they focus on the reactions of a large number of royal officials, particularly the king himself, to Jeremiah's message. The narrator seems to assume that the characters already know the contents of Jeremiah's oracles, and for this reason his words are usually summarized rather than being given in full. After the summary the narrator describes, often in minute detail, the degree to which specific individuals obey or refuse to obey oracles that the prophet brings. Jeremiah thus appears in the narratives primarily as a symbol, as a concrete embodiment of the divine word.

The overall effect of focusing the narratives in this way is to shift the emphasis of the book from the people as a whole to certain state officials, who may be seen as representatives of the people. While the poetic oracles are normally addressed to the people, who must bear the responsibility for their own responses, the narratives place the responsibility for Jerusalem's fate squarely on the king and his court. According to the narratives, several kings had the opportunity to obey the prophet and thus to avoid the city's tragic fate, but they did not heed his warning.

In addition to being concerned with individual reactions to Jeremiah, the narratives are also extraordinarily interested in the appropriate mode of life for Israel after the disasters of 597 and 587. Lying behind this interest are the questions of the identity of the true Israel and the conditions under which a restoration of the community might be possible. The narratives indicate that already in the time of Jehoiakim, Jeremiah was advising submission to the Babylonians as the only way for Israel to survive. This message remained consistent throughout the remainder of the prophet's life. According to the narratives, Jeremiah therefore interpreted the exile of 597 as God's just punishment on the nation and believed that the exile would be a long one. At the same time, the people who remained in Jerusalem continued to be under the threat of judgment and were in no way superior to those already in Babylon (*cf.* Ezek 11:14–21). Since by this time the prophet believed that repentance was either impossible or ineffective, he advised the Jerusalemites to accept God's judgment peacefully by submitting to the rule of the Babylonian king. If they did so, they might continue to live in the land, although not necessarily in Jerusalem itself. If Jeremiah's advice had been followed, the true Israel might have suffered slavery in the land or in Babylon, but both communities might have restored the nation after a suitable period of repentance. However, the narratives also make clear that Zedekiah did not obey the prophet's words. The result was death or exile in Babylon for most of the inhabitants of the city, including the king and the royal court. Jeremiah himself and a few of "the poor of the land," who had believed the prophet's words, were allowed to remain in Judah as a continuation of the Israelite community. The narratives imply that this Palestinian community might have rebuilt the nation, but its members made the fatal error of ignoring God's command to remain in the land. Instead they went to Egypt, a move that Jeremiah immediately condemned. As a result the Egyptian community was completely rejected. In the end, then, the only hope for restoration lay with the community in Babylon. Israelites living in Palestine or Egypt would be excluded from the reconstituted community.

The decidedly political focus of the narratives suggests that they originated in a group concerned with identifying and preserving the true Israel during the exilic period and with reconstructing the Israelite state once it was possible for the exiles to return. By assigning praise or blame to the officials who were active just before the exile, the group was at the same time able to make value judgments about the exilic descendants of those officials. Only those who were in exile in Babylon and who believed the words of Jeremiah would be part of the reconstruction.

Prose sermons. In addition to the so-called biographical narratives, the Book of Jeremiah also contains a large number of prose sermons (sometimes called source C). These sermons are characterized by the fact that they have been heavily influenced by Deuteronomistic language and theology. Because they are so similar to the sermons in the Deuteronomistic History (for example, Deut 1–11; 2 Kgs 17), most scholars assume that they are additions made by Deuteronomistic editors working long after Jeremiah's death. However, it is important to realize that in Jeremiah's own time Deuteronomistic influence was pervasive and that even the prophet himself was touched by it. The sermons might therefore simply be examples of a different prophetic genre (sermon instead of oracle), or they may be the creation of Jeremiah's immediate disciples. Alternatively, the sermons might have been created during the exile as a way of disseminating Jeremiah's basic message.

No matter what the origin of the sermons, their contents and function are relatively clear. In contrast to the biographical narratives, where the narrator's interest is in the reactions of Jeremiah's audience, the prose sermons focus on a word of the prophet or a word directly from God. If the activities of the prophet or the people are described, as in the case of the prophet's symbolic acts (13:1–14, 17:1–18:12, 25:1–29, 32:1–44), they are simply the setting for the divine message. The sermon typically reminds the people of their obligations under the covenant with God and exhorts them to repent of their sins, which are described in stereotypical Deuteronomistic terms. A judgment, usually in the form of exile away from the land, is threatened if repentance does not occur.

The prose sermons have been scattered throughout the book in order to restate Jeremiah's poetic oracles in orthodox Deuteronomistic terms (3:6–12, 15–18; 7:1–8:3; 11:1–17; 13:1–14; 14:11–16; 16:1–21; 17:19–27; 18:1–12; 19:1–15; 21:1–10; 24:1–10; 25:1–29; 32:1–44; 33:1–34:22; 43:8–44:30). Thus, for example, in 3:6–12 Jeremiah's preceding condemnation of the northern kingdom (3:1–5) and his following call for the Ephraimites to repent (3:12–14) are explained by the Deuteronomistic note that Ephraim had been destroyed because the people "played the harlot" by worshiping other gods (*cf.* 2 Kgs 17). Still, the sins of Judah have been much worse, and this fact prompts God to allow the northern kingdom's return. Similarly, all of the ambiguities of Jeremiah's poetic oracles in chapters 1–6 have been resolved by the prose sermon in 7:1–8:3. Everything that precedes is now subsumed under the typical Deuteronomistic schema of obedience and reward, disobedience and punishment.

Throughout the book the sermons stress the conditionality of the covenant and hold that Israel's prospects for remaining in the land depend totally on the people's obedience rather than on the actions of the king or the royal court. It is not surprising, then, that the sermons also explain the exiles of 597 and 587 as God's just punishment of Israel because of its long history of persistent rebellion. God had sent a number of prophets to warn the people to repent, but they ignored the prophets and continued to rebel. For the prose sermons, Jeremiah's own personal experiences of rejection and persecution are simply the most recent examples of the people's stubbornness. However, God's forbearance has limits, and eventually the people must suffer for their sins. The only hope of restoration lies in Babylon, among the exiles who recognize the theological meaning of their recent history and admit their guilt.

The Growth of the Book

The relatively loose way in which the various components of Jeremiah have been put together suggests that the book grew into its present shape over a long period of time and that it was not the product of a single systematic editor. This growth took place as Jeremiah, his disciples, and later generations of Israelites attempted to make sense of the exile and to understand its implications for Israel's future. Nevertheless, the finished book does possess an overall coherence, with each of the major components contributing something to the overall effect.

At the heart of the book are the poetic oracles, which have been arranged in such a way as to give the reader an increasing sense of Jeremiah's despair concerning Israel's fate. This arrangement presumably reflects the actual course of the development of the prophet's oracles, as well as the later interests of his disciples. After chapter 6 the sense of despair is enhanced through the incorporation of the prose oracles and sermons, which give the book a consistent theological focus. These additions are in harmony with Jeremiah's poetic oracles, and the former may in fact have grown out of the latter. The prose supplies systematic theological statements that the original poetry lacked.

The abstract Deuteronomistic theological concepts that dominate the first half of the book are given specific content in the "biographical narratives" that begin in chapter 20. Rather than simply speaking of the people rejecting God's messengers, the prophets, the book supplies examples of the rejection of a particular prophet. At the same time, the narratives, which often contain specific dates and names, help to give the reader the impression that all of the earlier oracles and sermons, whatever their real origin, actually apply to the events that occurred during the last years of Jerusalem's life. The mixing of narratives from the reigns of Jehoiakim and Zedekiah further gives the impression that both of these periods were treated by the prophet in the same way. There was no historical development in his message from the beginning of his professional life to the end. He gave the same oracles to Jehoiakim as he did to Zedekiah, and both kings ignored him. In both cases the result was the same. People from Jerusalem were taken into exile in Babylon (597 and 587). Yet among the Babylonian exiles, after 597 and 587, there was still hope for repentance and for a return to the land. Thus in the last half of the book the original political interests of the narratives and the original theological interests of the sermons are combined to provide a comprehensive theological explanation for the exile and an indication of the nature of the restored Israelite community. The historical events that are recounted demonstrate conclusively the validity of the Deuteronomistic theology and attest to the authenticity of Jeremiah, the prophet who articulated that theology in a time of great crisis.

THE MESSAGE OF JEREMIAH

Although Jeremiah contains a relatively coherent message, the book is not arranged in such a way as to present that message logically and systematically. Traces of the individual interests of the book's various components still remain in the finished product, and little has been done to eliminate contradictions or smooth out the literary rough spots. Instead, Jeremiah's final message is conveyed impressionistically as the reader moves through the book. Through the repetition of the theologically oriented prose sermons and the editorial interaction of the book's other components, the theological and political message is gradually impressed on the reader until the point finally becomes overwhelming. The best way, then, to understand Jeremiah's message is to follow the course of the present text, paying particular attention to the subtle shifts of emphasis that occur as the book moves through its major sections.

Poetic Oracles (Chapters 1–6)

The book's first major collection of poetic oracles is introduced by an account of Jeremiah's call (1:4–10), which supplies the reader with important information that is necessary for understanding the remainder of the material. The call story has two noteworthy features. First, it indicates that Jeremiah was actually called while he was still in his mother's womb. The event being described in chapter 1, which is dated to the thirteenth year of Josiah, is therefore strictly speaking not a call at all but a reminder of a call that has already been given. The implication of this curious situation is that Jeremiah is not now able to reject the call to be a prophet. He was made a prophet when he was conceived, and no amount of complaining on his part can alter his condition (1:7–8). This point will be made repeatedly later in the book, when Jeremiah's complaints are met only by God's renewed command to deliver the divine word (12:5–17, 15:10–21, 20:7–18). The second noteworthy feature of the account is that Jeremiah is clearly portrayed as a prophet like Moses. In 1:7–9 portions of Deuteronomy 18:15–22 are quoted verbatim in order to indicate to the reader something that the people in Jeremiah's own time did not realize until the fall of Jerusalem (52:1–34): Jeremiah's prophetic word will inevitably come true, and the people who hear him must pay attention to that word or risk divine punishment. This motif of the Mosaic prophet plays an important role in the later stories of Jeremiah's conflicts with other prophets, the princes, and the kings, for it allows the reader to locate the true word of God in the narratives. Any confusion that may have been felt by Jeremiah's original audience has been removed for the reader.

Jeremiah's privileged status as a Mosaic prophet is immediately reinforced by two initial visions (1:11–19), which indicate both his authority and the content of his message. The first vision, an almond rod, is taken to be an assurance that God will indeed perform the word that the prophet speaks. In the second vision, a boiling pot facing away from the north is interpreted to mean that God is about to send judgment against Jerusalem in the form of an attack by an enemy from the north.

The oracles now collected in chapters 2–6 were probably originally directed at the northern kingdom of Ephraim as part of Josiah's efforts to reunify the old Davidic empire, and traces of these northern concerns still remain in the text. However, in the present form of the book references to Judah have also been inserted in order to indicate that the same message applies to both the north and the south. The divine word is timeless and can therefore be reused with different audiences on different occasions. The oracles themselves present Jeremiah's basic message by using literary images that were developed by Hosea and the later Deuteronomistic theologians. Israel, both north and south, has violated its covenant with God by "playing the harlot" with other gods. God has repeatedly sent prophets to warn the people of the consequences of their actions (6:17), but they have refused to hear. Such behavior will eventually lead to their destruction unless they sincerely repent. The nature of the threatened judgment is graphically but vaguely described. An unnamed enemy will rage like a lion in the land (4:5–10); an invincible army will attack, striking terror in the hearts of all Israelites (4:13–22, 5:15–18). God will personally lead the charge (6:2–8) until the land is gleaned like a vineyard and only a remnant remains (6:9–12). So serious will be the devastation that for one terrifying moment the prophet actually sees the whole earth revert to its primordial state of chaos:

> I looked on the earth, and lo, it was waste and void;
>   and to the heavens, and they had no light.

I looked on the mountains, and lo, they were quaking,
  and all the hills moved to and fro.
I looked, and lo, there was no man,
  and all the birds of the air had fled.
I looked, and lo, the fruitful land was a desert,
  and all its cities were laid in ruins
  before the Lord, before his fierce anger.

                                          (4:23–26; RSV)

However, in spite of the gravity of the people's sins, the oracles indicate that the judgment is still only a future threat and that God's real desire is not punishment but repentance. Calls for Israel to return to the covenant and the true worship of God are given throughout the oracles (3:12–25, 4:1–4). Yet these calls are unheeded. Even when the voices of the people are occasionally heard acknowledging their sin (3:24–25), their repentance does not seem to be sincere. In the end the people appear to accept their fate and give up all hope of avoiding the judgment (6:24–26). The collection thus ends on an ominous note, which will be strongly reinforced by the oracles and sermons that immediately follow.

Interpreted Poetic Oracles (Chapters 7–24)

The second collection of Jeremiah's poetic oracles differs from the first in that the second also contains a number of prose sermons that develop the Deuteronomistic motifs found in the poetic oracles. The prophet's basic message does not really change, but it is brought into conformity with orthodox Deuteronomistic language and theology. As part of this process the ambiguities of the poetic oracles are resolved and the message acquires a more predictable and consistent form. Because of the periodic repetition of these sermons, the reader gets the clear impression that the prophet's message has stabilized.

The second collection opens with a typical Deuteronomistic sermon (7:1–8:3), which both summarizes all of the preceding oracles and anticipates those that are to come. Regardless of the original addresses and functions of the poetic oracles, the sermon suggests that everything that the prophet has said relates to the fate of Jerusalem and the Temple. The sermon is delivered in the Temple court and unambiguously condemns the traditional royal theology of Jerusalem. The people are warned not to put their trust in the claim that God dwells eternally in the Temple and thus protects the city from destruction. Rather, God's protection of the city is dependent on the people's faithful performance of their covenantal obligations. If Israel reforms its behavior, then God will allow the people to continue to dwell in the land. If they do not, then God will desert the Temple and allow the city to be destroyed.

Although the sermon appears to hold out the hope that Israel will listen to Jeremiah and repent, thus averting the threatened judgment, this hope is tempered almost immediately. God continues the sermon by forbidding the prophet to intercede on the people's behalf (7:16). This prohibition is a restriction of the traditional role of the Mosaic prophet, who was responsible both for delivering God's words to the people and for mediating the people's words to God. Because of the seriousness of the people's sins, their right to approach God through the prophet is now removed. While this prohibition does not necessarily mean that the destruction of the people is inevitable, it does mean that they must be responsible for their own salvation (7:16–34).

The pessimistic tone of this major prose sermon colors the oracles and sermons that follow it. In chapters 8–10 another collection of poetic oracles continues Jeremiah's condemnation of Judah and Jerusalem. He criticizes the Jerusalemite prophets for misleading the people with false assurances of salvation and holds out the possibility that repentance will still be effective in preventing the judgment. However, because of the setting in which the oracles have been placed, they take on an aura of hopelessness. The punishment of the people seems increasingly inevitable. In a major departure from normal biblical practice, even God is portrayed as grieving over the destruction that must certainly come (8:18–22, 9:1–3).

The dark tone of the oracle collection is reinforced again by a prose sermon that underlines the precariousness of Israel's position (11:1–17). God commands the prophet to remind the people of the conclusion of the Book of Deuteronomy (Deut 27–30), which mandates curses for all those who break the covenant. In fact the people in Judah and Jerusalem have already broken the covenant many times in the past, and the present generation is simply maintaining that tradition. Therefore the judgment has already been pronounced. God will bring evil on the people, and they cannot escape it. Their protests will be of no avail. God will not listen to them. Again the prophet is warned not to intercede on their behalf. Nothing can be done to save them. The judgment has now become inevitable. There will be no further opportunity for repentance.

Just at this point, when the fate of Jerusalem seems to be sealed, the first of Jeremiah's complaints has been inserted into the text (11:18–12:17). These remarkable poems give the reader an unparalleled view of the anguish that the prophet experienced during the performance of his task. Originally they probably reflected his genuine surprise and pain at the opposition that he met from his own family and from the society in general. They also expressed what many prophets knew. To be God's prophet was to experience a sort of divine tyranny. God's spirit possessed the prophet so completely that the person virtually lost the ability to act independently. It is not surprising then that individuals tried to avoid the prophetic office whenever possible, and Jeremiah's complaints undoubtedly reflect his own dismay at the absolute control that God was exercising over him.

However, in the context in which the complaints have now been set, they raise a number of new issues that seem to have been of great concern to the compilers of the book. First, the complaints raise the possibility that Jeremiah will simply revolt and refuse to deliver the divine message that he has been given. If this were to happen, then all hope really would be lost for Israel. Even though the inevitability of the judgment has already been announced, it might still be possible that divine mercy could prevail over divine justice. This had happened before in Israel's past, and theoretically it might happen again in the present if the prophet's announcement of certain judgment were to shock the people into repenting. However, if the prophet refused to deliver the divine word, then even this slim hope would be lost.

Second, the complaints indicate that Jeremiah was under a great deal of social and psychological pressure because of opposition from his enemies. If the prophet were to crumble under this pressure and cease to carry out his prophetic functions, it would indicate

that human opposition could successfully thwart God's will for Israel and could thus provide a direct challenge to God's power in the world. Finally, for the reader Jeremiah functions not only as a historical individual with a particular task to perform but also as a representative of people everywhere who seek to obey God's will for themselves and for the society in general. The prophet's reactions to outside pressure are therefore important because of the lessons that they hold for later faithful individuals struggling under similar circumstances. All of these issues raised by the complaints dominate the latter portion of the second oracle collection (chaps. 11–20) and help to shift the focus of the whole book from the divine message itself to the human embodiment of that message. They thus facilitate the transition to the second half of the book, which concentrates on individual reactions to the prophet.

The major issues connected with the complaints are treated in 11:18–12:17. The prophet begins the first complaint by expressing his shock at the revelation that his own family is seeking to destroy him:

> The Lord made it known to me and I knew;
>   then you showed me their evil deeds.
> But I was like a gentle lamb led to the slaughter.
> I did not know it was against me
>   they devised schemes, saying,
> "Let us destroy the tree with its fruit,
>   let us cut him off from the land of the living,
>   that his name be remembered no more."
>   (11:18–19; RSV)

He then asks for divine vengeance and protection. God responds favorably to this request, promising punishment for Jeremiah's enemies (11:18–23). The prophet, however, continues to press the matter and turns the complaint against God, demanding to know why the Deity permits innocent people to suffer. In this case the divine response is less reassuring. Rather than responding directly to the question, God chides the prophet for asking it and promises that opposition from the prophet's family will increase rather than diminish (12:1–6).

Jeremiah tries again, and complains about the personal burdens he has borne because of his prophetic office. God reassures the prophet that he will be protected and that his enemies will be punished, but there will be no release from his prophetic tasks (12:7–17). The first series of complaints thus makes it clear that Jeremiah will be compelled to continue to function as God's prophet. The divine word will continue to be proclaimed, and no human opposition will be able to stop it. At the same time, God will provide divine protection for the prophet and will preserve his life so that he can continue to carry out his mission.

Having considered for the first time the personal problems of the prophet, the book returns to the dreadful message that he must proclaim. Jeremiah is told to bury a waistcloth by the Euphrates River. When the waistcloth is ruined through decomposition, the prophet is told that this is a symbol of what will happen to Israel during exile in Babylon (13:1–11). The symbolic act with the waistcloth then becomes an opportunity for giving another series of judgment oracles against Judah and Jerusalem (13:12–27).

The desperateness of Israel's situation is illustrated graphically by a series of oracles in 14:1–15:4. These oracles, which may have originally circulated independently, have now been arranged to illustrate the degree to which Israel has already been cut off from God. At the beginning of the collection, a poem describing the severe effects of a drought is followed by a lament by the people (14:1–9). In the lament, which resembles those in the Psalter, the people confess their sins and ask for God's forgiveness. Although this sort of repentance is precisely what Jeremiah had hoped would occur, the lament is met by a judgment oracle rather than an oracle of forgiveness (14:10). Jeremiah then attempts to intercede on behalf of the people by arguing that they have been misled by the prophets, but he is forbidden to do so and is told to deliver another judgment oracle (14:11–18). The people again confess their sins (14:19–22), but this confession is no more effective than was the first. Jeremiah is assured that even Moses and Samuel would not be able to convince God to listen to the people's prayers. The only response that God will now give is a fresh word of judgment:

Then the Lord said to me, "Though Moses and Samuel stood before me, yet my heart would not turn toward this people. Send them out of my sight, and let them go! And when they ask you, 'Where shall we go?' you shall say to them, 'Thus says the Lord:

Those who are for pestilence, to pestilence,
    and those who are for the sword, to the sword;
those who are for famine, to famine,
    and those who are for captivity, to captivity.'

I will appoint over them four kinds of destroyers, says the Lord: the sword to slay, the dogs to tear, and the birds of the air and the beasts of the earth to devour and destroy." (15:1–3; RSV)

The remainder of the second oracle collection continues the editorial pattern that has already been set up in the first part of the unit. Poetic oracles announcing unconditional judgment on Judah and Jerusalem are supplemented by prose sermons that explain the judgment in strict Deuteronomistic terms (16:1–21, 17:19–27, 18:1–12, 19:1–15, 21:1–10). Interspersed among these sermons are additional confessions (15:10–21, 17:14–18, 18:18–23, 20:7–18), which reiterate God's protection of the prophet and the necessity for him to persist in his prophetic task. This sort of repetition reinforces the themes of the first part of the collection and leaves the reader with a growing sense of inevitable doom.

The sermons, oracles, and confessions reach their climax in chapters 23–24, which take up three topics that will play a major role in the last half of the book. In 23:1–8, Israel's kings ("shepherds") are condemned for leading the people astray and allowing them to be destroyed. This point will be illustrated later in detail in the narratives chronicling Jehoiakim's and Zedekiah's reactions to Jeremiah. In 23:9–40, Jeremiah condemns the prophets who articulate the Jerusalemite theology, charging them with inventing the oracles that they deliver. This conflict with the prophets will be described later in the narratives of Jeremiah's activities in Jerusalem (chaps. 27–29). Finally 24:1–10 describes Jeremiah's vision of two baskets of figs that are placed before God's altar in Jerusalem. One basket is full of good figs, and they are accepted. One is full of bad figs, and they are rejected. The two baskets are then identified respectively with the exiles in Babylon and the exiles in Egypt and in Palestine. Only the former can be considered to be part of the true Israel, a motif that is

The striking feature of these climactic chapters of the second oracle collection is that they repeatedly speak of hope for Israel's future. Although there is no indication that the judgment can be avoided, the texts indicate that God's rejection will not be total or permanent. God will provide Israel with new, faithful kings who will reestablish the Davidic line (23:5–8) and preside over a restored nation. God will also call new prophets who will deliver true divine oracles (23:33–40). Finally God will rebuild the nation from the exiles who are in Babylon and who remain the true Israel (24:4–7). In the midst of the darkness there is a ray of hope for the future, and that hope too will be amplified in the second half of the book.

Narratives of Conflict (Chapters 25–45)

The section that follows the first two oracle collections is composed primarily of biographical narratives interspersed with prose sermons (25:1–29, 32:16–44, 33:1–34:22, 43:8–44:30) and a few poetic oracles (25:30–38, 30:4–31:37). Although the oracle collections in their present form have left the reader with a clear sense of the inevitability of Israel's judgment, the theological reasons for that judgment, and the singlemindedness of the prophet in carrying out his task, the material has still lacked specificity. The reader gets an impression of the development of the prophet's message, but nothing can be pinned down to a specific historical context unless the reader already knows a great deal about the political and religious events of Jeremiah's time. This situation changes, however, when the reader reaches the narratives of conflict, for they supply very specific contexts within which to place the preceding material. They are thus in a sense a retrospective framework to aid the reader in understanding the entire book.

Of course the historical framework supplied by the narratives is far from objective and is intent on encouraging the reader to understand the book in a particular way. In the narratives everyone in the royal court who comes in contact with Jeremiah is placed in one of two groups: those who obey the prophet's word and those who reject it. For the latter there can be no hope and no future. People in this group, particularly the two major kings of the period, Jehoiakim and Zedekiah, are assigned all of the blame for the destruction of Jerusalem and the exile of the people. All of those who reject Jeremiah are condemned to death, and by implication their descendants can play no role in any reconstruction that may occur after the exile. Rather the only hope for Israel's future lies with the descendants of those who accepted Jeremiah as a true prophet and who tried to prevent the coming disaster. Only members of this group who are in exile in Babylon (rather than in Egypt or Palestine) will be allowed to return to the land.

While the theology of the narratives represents a development of certain themes in the earlier narratives and sermons, it also represents a narrowing and refocusing of Jeremiah's original message. Where the prophet preached that all of the inhabitants of Judah and Jerusalem were responsible for their own fates, the narratives place the responsibility for Israel's future solely on the government. Furthermore, the few words of hope in Jeremiah's message were not originally aimed only at the exiles in Babylon but were directed to any faithful people who would confess their sins and repent. Only with the vision of the figs (chap. 24) is the Babylonian community elevated to the status of the true Israel. This narrowing undoubtedly represents an attempt by Jeremiah's exilic followers to understand more clearly the implications of his message for their own time.

The narratives of conflict begin with a prose sermon that makes explicit what the reader has already been able to glean from the second oracle collection: the destruction of Jerusalem is inevitable (25:1–29). The sermon is dated to the fourth year of Jehoiakim (*ca.* 605, the date of the Babylonian victory at the Battle of Carchemish). Thus relatively early in the king's reign the fate of the city was already sealed. All of Jeremiah's oracles since the beginning of his prophetic work have been ignored, just as the Israelites ignored the earlier prophets that God sent to warn them. Therefore God announces an irrevocable judgment against Judah and Jerusalem: the people will be exiled to Babylon for seventy years, and only after that time will a return to the land be possible. The sermon thus anticipates the deportation of 587 and indicates that the earlier deportation of 597 is to be considered only the first installment of the complete judgment, which is yet to come.

The reasons for the pessimism of the prose

sermon are dramatized in the biographical narrative that immediately follows (chap. 26). At the beginning of Jehoiakim's reign Jeremiah is said to have stood in the Temple court and delivered an oracle exhorting the people to repent and warning them not to ignore the prophetic word as they had in the past. This warning echoes those found in chapters 1–7 and implies that these earlier oracles represent the specifics of the message that the prophet gave in Jehoiakim's time. Jeremiah's Temple oracle provokes two different reactions from his hearers. The priests and the prophets claim that Jeremiah should be killed because he has spoken against the city and the Temple. Jeremiah defends himself on the grounds that he has been commanded by God to prophesy. This explanation temporarily satisfies the princes, until certain elders point out that in the past kings have treated prophets in two different ways. Sometimes the kings have listened to the prophets and thereby saved the nation, just as Hezekiah listened to the prophet Micah and instituted a religious reform. However, at other times the kings have killed prophets like Jeremiah, as Jehoiakim has already done in the case of the prophet Uriah. The issue remains unresolved, and Jeremiah's friends rescue him from the trial, but Jehoiakim's attitude toward prophets like Jeremiah is already clear. The king rejects them, just as he will eventually reject Jeremiah.

From the story of Jehoiakim's reaction to Jeremiah, the narrative moves forward in time to Zedekiah, who ruled after Jehoiakim's folly had already made the judgment inevitable and brought about the deportation of 597. Because nothing can be done to prevent the completion of the judgment sometime after 597, Jeremiah turns his attention to the question of who will survive the exile in order to rebuild the nation. In chapters 27–29 the prophet engages in a series of confrontations designed to illustrate how Israel must live in the future. At the beginning of Zedekiah's reign Jeremiah is told to wear a yoke and appear before the king, who was at that time contemplating an alliance against the Babylonians. Because, from the standpoint of the narrative, God has already determined to destroy Jerusalem, Jeremiah uses the yoke to dramatize an oracle advising submission to the king of Babylon. If the people bow to the inevitable judgment, God will allow them to survive and will give them the opportunity to return to the land (27:1–22).

The king, however, is receiving exactly the opposite advice from the Jerusalemite prophets, who believe that God will remain faithful to the city and will not allow it to be destroyed. The king's dilemma is graphically illustrated in chapter 28, which describes a confrontation between Jeremiah and the prophet Hananiah. Following the Jerusalemite royal theology, Hananiah predicts that the exiles who were deported in 597 will soon return and that God's anger has come to an end. Jerusalem has been punished for its sins, as Jeremiah himself had prophesied, but God's election of the city still stands. The divine presence remains in Jerusalem, and the city will not be destroyed in a future judgment. To dramatize his point, Hananiah breaks Jeremiah's yoke and contradicts his earlier oracle.

The conflict being portrayed in the narrative is not only between two prophets who have dramatically different oracles but also between two legitimate theological positions. The Jerusalemite position holds that God's election of the city and the people is eternal, while the Deuteronomistic position holds that election is contingent on the people's obedience. In this case the reader already knows which position will turn out to be correct. Jeremiah is, after all, a Mosaic prophet, and his word will inevitably come to pass. However, for people living in Jeremiah's time the issue was not that simple. Even Jeremiah himself, when challenged by Hananiah, backs down and expresses his hope that Jerusalem can still be saved. Only after God commands Jeremiah to replace his wooden yoke with an unbreakable iron yoke does he realize the truth of his own message and accuse Hananiah of false prophecy. This accusation is proved to be true when Hananiah dies unexpectedly, the traditional punishment for false prophets (Deut 18:20).

Having made the point that the people left in the land after 597 are doomed to destruction if they do not submit to the authority of Nebuchadrezzar, the conflict narratives turn to the question of the fate of the exiles who are already in Babylon. In chapter 29 Jeremiah writes a letter to the exiles counseling them to prepare for a long exile. Prophetic advice to the contrary is to be ignored. At the same time, Jeremiah explicitly promises the exiles that after seventy years they may return and rebuild the land (29:10–14).

Jeremiah's epistolary promise oracle is strengthened by the addition of a collection of promise oracles in chapters 30–32. Some of these oracles seem to have originally been addressed to the northern kingdom and may have originated during the Josianic period, when Jeremiah was concerned with the repentance of Ephraim (30:10–11, 18–22; 31:2–22). At a later time the prophet seems to have modified them to include Judah as well and seems to have envisioned a restoration of both north and south in a re-creation of the old Davidic empire (31:23–34). However, Jeremiah's broad vision of salvation for the whole nation has been narrowed considerably by the setting in which the oracles have been placed. In chapter 29 promises of restoration are given only to the exiles already in Babylon, and by implication the promises in chapters 30–31 apply only to them as well. This interpretation of the material is even clearer in chapter 32, where Jeremiah buys a field in Anathoth to dramatize the point that normal life in Judah will return after the exile. However, the promise given here is only for those in Babylon; exiles in other parts of the world do not seem to be included. Even for the Babylonian exiles, the return to the land will not occur automatically. They must first acknowledge the sins that brought them into exile in the first place and then must repent (31:18–30). Only when this is done will God bring them back to the land and make a new covenant with them, an eternal, unbreakable covenant engraved on the human heart:

> Behold, the days are coming, says the Lord, when I will make a new covenant with the house of Israel and the house of Judah, not like the covenant which I made with their ancestors when I took them by the hand to bring them out of the land of Egypt, my covenant which they broke, though I was their husband, says the Lord. But this is the covenant which I will make with the house of Israel after those days, says the Lord: I will put my law within them, and I will write it upon their hearts; and I will be their God, and they shall be my people. And no longer shall each man teach his neighbor and each his brother, saying, "Know the Lord," for they shall all know me, from the least of them to the greatest, says the Lord; for I will forgive their iniquity, and I will remember their sin no more. (31:31–34; RSV)

The remainder of the conflict narratives (chaps. 33–45) simply reiterate the patterns that have already been established and continue to underline the inevitability of Jerusalem's destruction. Although much interesting historical information is contained in these chapters, their major function in the present book is to reinforce the narrative message through the sheer repetition of examples. Stories from the reigns of Jehoiakim and Zedekiah are mixed together, but the basic point is always the same. Because of Jehoiakim's rejection of Jeremiah's oracles, Jerusalem is doomed to be destroyed. Zedekiah had the opportunity to save some of the people in the city by submitting peacefully to Babylonian control, thus accepting the punishment that God had decreed, but the king forfeited this opportunity through his indecision.

The story of Jehoiakim's rejection of the prophetic word is told in chapter 36, which describes the writing of a scroll containing all of the words that Jeremiah has spoken up to that time, the fourth year of the king's reign. The scroll is then read to all of the people assembled in the Temple, and as usual it polarizes the audience. Some of the royal officials are apparently impressed by the prophet's message and have the scroll read before the princes and the king. Jehoiakim's reaction is decidedly negative. He burns the sections of the scroll as they are read and thus rejects the message that it contains. It is no accident, then, that Jerusalem's judgment becomes inevitable in Jehoiakim's fourth year (chap. 25).

Zedekiah's role in the disaster of 587 is recounted in greater detail (37:1–39:10). The king's initial unwillingness to follow Jeremiah's political advice (chaps. 27–28) continued during his entire reign. At various times he flirted with the idea of submitting to the Babylonians, but in the end he was always unwilling to do so, perhaps because he feared reprisals within the royal court. On several occasions he protected Jeremiah from those who sought to kill him and frequently implored the prophet to intervene with God on the city's behalf. But as the book's readers have already learned, Jeremiah is no longer allowed to intercede. The prophet can only repeat the oracles of judgment. Nothing can be done to prevent the city's destruction.

However, even after the Babylonians captured the city and deported most of the remaining inhabitants to Babylon, the few people who were still left in Judah were given yet another opportunity to avoid destruction, to become part of the true Israel, and to participate in the reconstruction of the land. In a historical coda to the narrative of the city's fall (chaps. 40–45), the narrator has included a detailed and somewhat confusing account of the Judean remnant. These people, along with Jeremiah himself, were allowed by the Babylonians to settle in Judah outside of Jerusalem and to begin a new government under the leadership of Gedaliah. The text clearly implies that if these people had remained in the land, then they could have begun the restoration immediately. However, after Gedaliah's murder they decided to go to Egypt, a move that Jeremiah warned them not to make. Because these survivors left the land, they were condemned to be destroyed. In the end the only hope for Israel's restoration is to be found among the exiles in Babylon. The conflict narratives thus end where they began (chap. 24), with the assertion that the true Israel is to be found only within the Babylonian exilic community.

Oracles Against the Nations (Chapters 46–51)

For the modern reader, the next section of the book, a collection of poetic oracles against foreign nations, seems to be an anticlimax after the dramatic account of Jerusalem's last days and the vindication of the truth of Jeremiah's prophecies. In fact, however, these oracles serve an important function at the end of the book by reintroducing a motif that has been muted since chapter 32: the promise of restoration. Jeremiah may well have delivered oracles against foreign nations at various times earlier in his career, and he may have viewed them as a way of interceding on Israel's behalf. By destroying Israel's enemies, the people could be protected. However, in the oracles' new setting at the end of the book they serve as an oblique promise. The foreign nations, particularly Babylon, supply the force necessary to keep the Israelites enslaved in a strange land and to prevent their return to their homeland. The destruction of these foreign powers is thus the first step in Israel's restoration, and the process of destruction begins as soon as the oracles are given.

Historical Conclusion (Chapter 52)

The entire book ends with another chapter that appears to be anticlimactic. The book's editors have inserted a version of 2 Kings 24:18–25:30, a historical chronicle of Jerusalem's destruction. The unit simply repeats information that has already been given more graphically earlier in the book and appears to add nothing to the overall argument. Nevertheless, chapter 52 serves two important functions in its present location. First, it demonstrates one final time the truth of Jeremiah's prophetic word. All of his oracles against the city have come to pass, and the people have been justly punished for their sins. The prophet's Deuteronomistic theology has thus been vindicated and may therefore be accepted as the basis of a restored nation. Second, the passage supports the hope that Jeremiah's promises to the exiles will also be fulfilled. Since Jeremiah has been shown to be a true Mosaic prophet whose words inevitably come true, the reader of the book can also rely on the soundness of the oblique promises in the preceding chapters.

In its final form, then, the Book of Jeremiah stands as a testimony to the power of God's word and to the folly of human attempts to ignore that word. The actions of individuals and the people as a whole during the last years of Jerusalem's life have been arranged and interpreted as an object lesson for future generations. Preexilic Israel refused to obey the covenant with God and thereby brought upon itself the curses attached to covenant-breaking. Future Israelites are challenged to learn from this negative example and to avoid making the same mistakes. If they repent and avoid the sins of their ancestors, then a new nation can be restored in the land, and Jeremiah's promises will at last be realized.

Bibliography

Commentaries

Bright, John. *Jeremiah.* Garden City, N.Y., 1965.

Carroll, Robert P. *Jeremiah.* Philadelphia, 1986.

Holladay, William L. *Jeremiah One: A Commentary on the Book of the Prophet Jeremiah Chapters 1–25.* Philadelphia, 1986.

McKane, William. *A Critical and Exegetical Commentary on Jeremiah.* Vol. 1, *Introduction and Commentary on Jeremiah I–XXV.* Edinburgh, 1986.

Thompson, J. A. *The Book of Jeremiah.* Grand Rapids, 1980.

Studies

Ackroyd, Peter R. *Exile and Restoration.* London, 1968.

Blenkinsopp, Joseph. *A History of Prophecy in Israel.* Philadelphia, 1984.

Bogaert, P.-M., ed. *Le livre de Jérémie.* Louvain, 1981.

Carroll, Robert P. *From Chaos to Covenant: Prophecy in the Book of Jeremiah.* New York, 1981.

Holladay, William L. *The Architecture of Jeremiah 1–20.* Lewisburg, Pa., 1976.

Klein, Ralph W. *Israel in Exile: A Theological Interpretation.* Philadelphia, 1979.

Malamat, Abraham. "The Last Years of the Kingdom of Judah." In *The World History of the Jewish People,* edited by Abraham Malamat, vol. 4. Jerusalem, 1979.

Mays, James Luther, and Paul J. Achtemeier, eds. *Interpreting the Prophets.* Philadelphia, 1987.

McKane, William. "Relations Between Poetry and Prose in the Book of Jeremiah, with Special Reference to Jeremiah 3:6–11 and 12:14–17." *Supplements to Vetus Testamentum* 28 (1980): 220–237.

Mowinckel, Sigmund. *Prophecy and Tradition.* Oslo, 1946.

Nicholson, Ernest W. *Preaching to the Exiles: A Study of the Prose Tradition in the Book of Jeremiah.* New York, 1970.

Perdue, Leo G., and Brian W. Kovacs, eds. *A Prophet to the Nations: Essays in Jeremiah Studies.* Winona Lake, Ind., 1984.

Rowley, H. H. "The Prophet Jeremiah and the Book of Deuteronomy." In *Studies in Old Testament Prophecy Presented to Professor Theodore H. Robinson,* edited by H. H. Rowley. Edinburgh, 1950.

Seitz, Christopher R. *Theology in Conflict: Reactions to the Exile in the Book of Jeremiah.* Berlin, 1989.

Wilson, Robert R. *Prophecy and Society in Ancient Israel.* Philadelphia, 1980.

ROBERT R. WILSON

Lamentations

LAMENT BELONGS TO human existence, for suffering is intrinsic to human life, and lament expresses this suffering. When a child is born, its first utterance is a cry. The cry of pain remains throughout one's life the immediate, inarticulate expression of pain. Jesus' cry on the cross ("and he cried aloud . . .") is understandable to every person in all times. More than that, the yet unspoken cry of pain is common to all creatures who can give tongue to their suffering; it is part of the essence of all creatures.

FUNCTION AND SIGNIFICANCE

When pain finds expression in words, it becomes lament, which may be a mere cry or may be expanded into a sentence. The cry of lament also is part of being human; it is found among all human beings on earth. It appears in the narratives of the Bible: the lament of Cain, of Samson, of Rebecca, and many others. This cry of lament is wholly connected with the situation in which it is evoked and can be transmitted only as part of the particular situation that is being related.

The lament, however, may also be expanded to a larger literary structure, to a song of lament or a psalm of lament, and thereby it receives an independent existence, removed from a life situation. A distinction must be made between lament as a reaction to the death of a human being (dirge) and lament as a reaction to personal suffering (complaint). These concepts are fundamentally different, even in their original usage. The Hebrew word qinah can only mean a dirge, never a complaint about suffering. Although both forms give expression to human suffering, a complaint is raised by those who are immediately affected by suffering, while a dirge is raised by the survivors who are affected by the loss of the deceased. Further differences are implicit in this distinction. In the lament, what is at stake is the change of the situation that is lamented; therefore, in it an appeal is made to Yahweh; this is not the case in the dirge. The dirge is a secular, the lament a cultic, affair. Petition belongs to the lament, but not to the dirge.

Dirge and Lament in the Old Testament

Actual dirges are rarely found in the Old Testament; usually, it is only stated that they were performed, as in the case of Abraham's dirge over Sarah (Gen 23:2). David's dirge over Saul and Jonathan is substantially preserved in 2 Samuel 1:17–27, and over Abner in 3:33–34. In a larger sense the dirge can also announce to the people the coming of the day of judgment, as in Amos 5:2 ("Fallen, no more to rise, is the virgin Israel"; RSV) and Jeremiah 9:16–21.

Laments constitute a considerable part of the Old Testament, especially of the psalms of lament, both communal and individual. Moreover, they form a major element of the Book of Job (individual lament) and the Fourth Book of Ezra (communal lament). The proclamation of Deutero-Isaiah and other salvation oracles that reflect the lament of the people after the fall of the nation contain many lament motifs. The same holds for other prophetic books—sometimes even whole psalms of lament such as Isaiah 63 and 64.

The Combination of Dirge and Lament in Lamentations

Only in the Book of Lamentations are dirges and laments combined. This is a result of the unique situation that prevailed after the catastrophe of 587 B.C.E., when the survivors experienced the conquest of Jerusalem as the death of the city. The experience of the demise of a city has a parallel in the Sumerian dirge over Ur, as well as in prophetic proclamations of judgment in the Old Testament that are clothed in the literary form of a dirge, such as Amos 5:2 and Jeremiah 9:16–21.

The Literary Form of the Dirge and the Lament

In its original form the dirge is always brief. It is connected closely with funeral rites and is transmitted orally. The death wail, consisting of a word or short sentence, recurs again and again, and, in contrast to the lament, is self-contained. The lament may take a variety of forms and has no fixed structure. The most frequent motif is the announcement of death (as in Amos 5:2). This can be connected with the summons to lament, or it can stand alone. The proclamation of death may contain information about how death came upon the one who is being lamented (2 Sam 3:33–34). The anguish of death finds concrete expression in the motif of contrasting what was with what is now. The description of pain is the subjective unfolding of the cry of desolation ("Woe"). In particular instances further motifs can be added (Jahnow 1923).

The lament received its form in the worship of ancient Israel, in which it was transmitted orally; then it was fixed in small collections as communal and individual psalms of lament, out of which—together with other genres of psalms—the Psalter developed. In contrast to the dirges, these psalms are prayers. Here the lament constitutes an element of prayer, to which belong, besides the complaint, the address to God, the expression of trust, the confession of guilt, the petition to God, and the vow of praise (Gunkel-Begrich 1933; Westermann 1977).

Unlike dirges, the Psalms are not mere portrayals of misery but, rather, are divided into "God-laments" (or accusations against God: "You have done . . ."), "I-" or "we-laments" (subject in the first person), and "enemy laments" or complaints against enemies ("The enemies have . . ."). The dirge is directed toward death, the lament toward life. Because the lament belongs to human existence, it has a correspondingly existential structure. Just as, in Genesis 2, being a self, being with others (community), and being in the presence of God, the Creator, all belong to human existence, so human existence is affected by suffering in these three aspects, as is evident already in the very first lament, that of Cain in Genesis 4. That the laments in the Psalms are articulated according to these three aspects is shown, for example, by Psalms 13 and 22 (see the tables in Westermann 1977, 132 and 139). The peculiarity of Lamentations 1, 2, and 4 lies in the fact that here dirges and laments form a union in which the community lament constitutes the basic framework mixed with elements of the dirge.

ORIGIN AND HISTORICAL SETTING

The Book of Lamentations is designated in the Hebrew Bible as Qinoth (pl. of qinah, "lament") or, following the initial cry of lament, as 'ekah ("Oh, how!"). In the Septuagint it is designated as Threnai, in the Vulgate Lamentations; some manuscripts add "of Jeremiah" or place "Laments of Jeremiah" at the conclusion. In modern translations the title has been adopted from the Septuagint or the Vulgate. According to an early Jewish tradition (2 Chron 35:25), Lamentations was affixed to the Book of Jeremiah in the canon of the Old Testament. In the Hebrew canon, the book is found among the five festal scrolls (megilloth). In our time scholars no longer believe that Jeremiah was the author.

The Text

The text consists of five songs of lament. Three of these songs, which constitute the kernel of the book, 1, 2, and 4, show great similarities inasmuch as the lament of the people is connected with motifs of the dirge. Song 5 is a community psalm of lament that is structured like the community laments of the Psalter. Song 3 comprises several parts: verses 42–51 form an abbreviated community lament, whereas the other parts deal not with the suffering of the people but with the suffering and deliverance of an individual (with some expansions). Each song is a self-contained entity, as shown also by the alphabetical formulation; for each in itself extends from *aleph* to *taw*, from A to Z. Each one, therefore, is to be understood and interpreted individually.

Date and Circumstances of Origin

Lamentations is among the few parts of the Old Testament whose time of origin we can know with a high degree of certainty. The origin of the laments can be traced back to the conquest of Jerusalem and the subsequent deportation of its people in the year 587 B.C.E. In the language of these songs, the suffering of the city and its inhabitants is portrayed with poignant immediacy. Indeed, no other event in the history of Israel has been transmitted to us as vividly and concretely as the fall of Jerusalem and its consequences for the survivors.

Situation in Life

There is a particular reason why the fall of Jerusalem evoked such an immediate chorus of response from those affected by the tragedy. In ancient Israel there was a tradition, reaching back into an early period, that in cases of misfortune experienced by the whole people a rite of lamentation (Şom, lit. "fast") was held in which the misfortune was lamented before God, and God was implored for help. Such a rite of lamentation was again observed after the fall of Jerusalem and the destruction of the Temple; it is mentioned in 1:7a: "Jerusalem remembers in the day of her affliction . . ." Now, however, the rite is changed in that those who have experienced the city's fall seemed to regard that event as having finality, and therefore it was a lamentation for the death of Jerusalem. In the period immediately after the catastrophe these rites were probably the only possible form of worship; sacrificial worship had ceased. Rites of

fasting and mourning are also mentioned in Zechariah 7:5–7 and 8:19. Later, then, these lamentations, together with other liturgical texts, became the festal scroll for the worship service of the ninth of Av, when the Jewish community commemorates to this day the destruction of the Temple. Here we have the rare case where the occasion for the lamentations and the inception of a traditional practice can be clearly identified.

Literary Form

The five songs contain twenty-two strophes each. In number 5, each strophe consists of one line; in 4, each has two lines, giving a total of forty-four lines; in 1, 2, and 3, each strophe contains three lines, or sixty-six lines altogether. Only in number 5 does the number of strophes correspond to the number of letters in the alphabet. In 4, each strophe begins with a letter of the alphabet; the same is true for 1 and 2, where each strophe has three lines. In 3, all three lines of each strophe begin this way. Lamentations 1, 2, 3, and 4 are considered "alphabetic," Lamentation 5 "alphabetizing." Alphabetic psalms are also found in the Psalter, especially in Psalm 119. The purpose of this form may be to express a totality (from A to Z) or to provide a mnemonic device; both are possible. In any case, this "artificial" form is of late origin and presupposes that the psalms are more to be read than heard. The lateness of the form is evident from the fact that in Hebrew poetry, form is always determined by content. In the case of the alphabetic psalms or songs, however, the alphabetic beginning and sequence have nothing to do with the content of the songs of lament. Therefore, it is improbable that these laments originated in this alphabetic form; rather, they must have assumed their form only in the course of transmission. Such a transformation according to the alphabet was quite possible in a time when ancient songs were collected and preserved.

As far as the rhythm is concerned, here too form and content cannot be separated. The ancient Hebrews did not yet have a poetic "meter" that was independent from content. Rather, their poetry displays a rhythm, corresponding to the particular poetic content, which can change within a song or psalm. An especially marked rhythm is that of the *qinah*, or funereal lament, a descending 3/2 rhythm (the numbers in this case designate not syllables but accents). It occurs especially often in Lamentations 1, 2, 4, and 5, but here too other rhythms are added.

In addition, there is also the sentence rhythm, the so-called *parallelismus membrorum*, a movement of two sentences in a relationship of correspondence, which constitutes the real uniqueness and beauty of Hebrew poetry. In these songs the significance of the form of speech is found in their nature and purpose, namely lament. Several passages give an invitation to share in lamentation (1:12–18, 2:18–19), and in these cases the form of the lament as a whole has the basic task of summoning the people to participate in the suffering that is here lamented.

GENRE AND STRUCTURE

Songs 1, 2, and 4 display more or less clearly the structure of a community psalm of lament, with which motifs of the dirge have been combined. Song 5 is a lament of the community, differentiated from those of the Psalter only by the length of the "we-lament" in verses 2–18, which makes this similar to portrayals of affliction and the apprehensive question at the end. On the other hand, 3 deviates markedly from the other songs. It is not a lamentation over the fall of Jerusalem but a composition of several parts, of which only verses 42–51 constitute part of a communal lament. All else belongs to the lament of an individual, to which expansions and an abbreviated psalm of praise of an individual have been added (vv. 52–58). Song 3 must therefore be treated separately from the others.

Lamentation 1 begins (as do 2 and 4) with the cry of lament, "Oh, how . . ." This is followed by a "we-lament" that is modulated into a portrayal of affliction (vv. 1–6), a confession of guilt in verses 8a and 9a, a petition for God's favor in verses 9c and 11, an "enemy lament" in verses 7c and 10, a "God-lament" in verses 12–15 (concluding with the sentence in verse 18a: "Yahweh is in the right"), a summons to be involved (v. 18b), a petition for God's favor in verses 20a and 21a, and a petition against enemies in verses 21c–22.

In Lamentation 2, the "God-lament" follows the cry of lament (vv. 1–8b); then comes the "we-lament" with its portrayal of misery (vv. 11ab, 13), the guilt of the prophets (v. 14), enemies and neighbors (vv. 15–17), a summons to lament (vv. 18–19), and a "we-lament" (vv. 21ab, 22bc).

In Lamentation 4 the "we-lament" follows the cry of lament (vv. 1–10), which includes the guilt of the people (v. 6) and the guilt of the prophets and priests; then comes the "God-lament" in verses 11–13, a "we-lament" in verses 14–16, the imprisonment of the king (vv. 17–20), the punishment of Edom, and the blotting out of Israel's sin (vv. 21–22).

Lamentation 5 begins (and also ends; v. 21) with a petition for Yahweh's favor; there follows in verses 2–18 a long "we-lament," similar to the portrayal of misery, though recounted in the second person. In it are found the sins of the ancestors (v. 9), a general confession of sin (v. 16), restrained praise of God (instead of confession of trust), a God-lament (v. 20), a petition for God's intervention (v. 21), and at the end the apprehensive question "Or have you utterly rejected us?"

Lamentation 3:42–51 (a fragment) consists of a "God-lament" (vv. 42–45) in which is found a confession of guilt (v. 42), an "enemy lament" (v. 46), a "we-lament" (v. 47), a description of pain (vv. 48, 49, 51). The plea for God's favor is only suggested, in verse 50.

By and large the five texts have the same structure, even though their sequence, because of the alphabetical arrangement, is not symmetrical. All five feature the following elements:

1. The cry of lament (only in 1, 2, 4)
2. The lament in three parts, in which the "we-lament" (objective) is sometimes connected with descriptions of pain (subjective)
3. Confession of guilt or attribution of guilt
4. Petition for God's favor with address to God (petition for God's intervention only in No. 5)
5. Petition against enemies

Several additional themes appear only once or twice. Apart from the cry of lament at the beginning, these are the themes of the community lament in the following order, but with some important differences:

1. The cry of lament at the beginning has

the effect of making it appear that a song with this kind of introduction is a dirge, hence the designation *qinoth*.

2. The "we-lament" and the "God-lament" are transformed to a description of pain by changing the first person of the "we-lament" and the second person of the "God-lament" to the third person. In both structures there are exceptions, however, that permit the basic form to be preserved.

3. The dirge introduced with the cry of "woe" is a secular (profane) form that has no address to God. In Lamentations 1 and 2, however, the address to God, together with the petition for God's favor, have been added secondarily, with the result that the song of lament becomes a prayer: "O Yahweh, behold my affliction!" (1:9c, 11c, 20a; 2:18, 19, 20a). In Lamentation 4 an address to God is lacking. In Lamentation 5 the petition for God's favor is especially emphasized (vv. 1, 21), whereas in 3:42–51 it is only suggested, in verse 50.

4. In Lamentations 1 and 2 a change can be seen. At the beginning the style of the dirge prevails; in the later course of the song we find the style of the lament of suffering. This gradual transition brings about a movement within the text. The songs do not linger over the death of Jerusalem, but they boldly beseech God again to show favor toward the remnant of his people. It is a movement faintly similar to the movement discernible in the psalms of lament, from lament to confidence.

5. Befitting the peculiar character of the songs of lament, two themes of the community lament are entirely or almost entirely lacking. One of these is a remembrance of God's previous saving action (e.g., Ps 80) or a confession of trust. Lacking also is the petition for God's intervention on behalf of his people, or even a plea for restoration. The latter appears only in Lamentation 5, a community lament. Those who speak in the songs of lament are so overcome by the severe blow they have suffered that they are able neither to look back to God's saving deeds in the past nor to hope for a change that brings restoration. The absence of these two themes accords completely with the situation in which these songs arose.

6. Except for the cry of lament at the beginning,

the clearest characteristic of the dirge is the contrast between "then" and "now." This theme, however, is not equally distributed in Lamentations 1–5. Rather it is concentrated only in two passages: in the "we-lament" of 1:1–6 and in the "we-lament" of 4:10, 14–16. From this it is evident that the "we-laments," being the laments of the survivors, agree at this point with the laments of those left behind, that is, with the dirge. This makes the combination of dirge and lament in these lamentations more understandable.

MOTIFS

The "We-Lament"

Like the laments of the people found in the Book of Psalms, the Lamentations include several characteristic features, especially complaint in distress, confession of trust in God, and petition for help. In these poems the people's lament expresses various aspects of suffering. (On the threefold organization of laments see Claus Westermann, *Ausgewählte Psalmen* [Göttingen, 1984], Excursus on Psalm 13.)

The fall of the nation. Throughout, the Lamentations are defined by the collapse of the kingdom of Judah, which occurred with the fall of Jerusalem, an event on which they look back:

> Jerusalem remembers the days of her
> affliction and bitterness
>
> . . . .
>
> how her people fell into the hand of the foe
> and no one helped her.
>
> (1:7)

> She has fallen terribly,
> and no one comforted her.
> (1:9b)

This event evokes lament, mourning:

> My eyes are dissolved in tears
> for the fall of the daughter of my people.
> (2:11)

> Horror and pitfall have come upon us;
> devastation and destruction,
> my eyes flow with rivers of tears
> because of the destruction of the daughter of
> my people.
>
> (3:47–48)

Above all, the conquest of the city of Jerusalem is in view:

> The kings of the earth will not have believed it,
>> nor any of the inhabitants of the earth,
> that besiegers would come in,
>> enemies into the gate of Jerusalem.
>>> (4:12)

> He caused wall and rampart to lament,
>> together they crumbled,
> Her gates have sunk into the dust,
>> he has ruined and broken her bars.
>>> (2:8c, 9a)

Survivors are deeply afflicted by the imprisonment of the king, which signifies the fall of the house of David (4:17–20):

> Our eyes failed,
>> looking—in vain—for help!
>
> . . . .
>
> Our end drew near, our days were numbered. . . .
> The breath of our life, the anointed of Yahweh,
>> was captured in their pits,
> in whose shadow we supposed that we would
>> live among the nations.

The human toll. Terrible and incalculable in extent is the loss of human lives, those who died during and after the battle for the city, and those taken away into exile in a foreign land:

> How lonely sits the City
> that once was so populous!
> Like a widow she became,
>> she that was great among the nations!
>>> (1:1)

> We mourn the roads to Zion . . .
> all its gates are desolate.
>>> (1:4)

Death has spared no one; it has taken a terrible harvest:

> On the day of Yahweh's wrath
>> none escaped and survived.
>>> (2:22b)

> Those whom I nurtured and reared
>> my enemy has destroyed.
>>> (2:22c)

Even greater in dislocating impact is the loss through deportation into exile:

> Judah has gone into exile because of affliction
>> and hard servitude;
> she dwells now among the nations
>> but finds no resting place.
>>> (1:3)

> My maidens and young men
>> have gone into captivity.
>>> (1:18c)

> Her kings and her princes are among the nations,
>> instruction (*torah*) is no more.
>>> (2:9b)

Misery after the catastrophe. In addition to bereavement a state of misery prevailed that afflicted the entire people—great and small, high- and low-born, young and old. Above all, it was the children, the women, and the aged upon whom affliction and misery came. They are mentioned recurrently and with particular anguish. However, along with them mention is made of the entire nation, every member of the body politic: children (1:16; 2:11, 12; 1:5; 2:21; 4:4) and their mothers (2:12, 20; 4:3, 5, 10; 5:11); maidens and young men (1:15, 18, 46; 2:10, 21, 22; 5:11, 13, 14); old people (2:21; 5:12, 14); nobles and heroes (1:6, 15; 4:1, 2, 7, 8); princes (2:2, 9; 5:12); the king (2:6, 9; 4:17–20); priests, prophets, and elders (1:19; 2:6, 9, 10, 20; 4:14–16).

Especially the loss of leadership is emphasized:

> Her king and princes are among the nations,
>> instruction is no more;
> and her prophets receive no more
>> revelation from Yahweh.
>>> (2:9bc)

Furthermore, the upper social level was affected by suffering and disgrace:

Her princes have become like harts that
　find no pasture;
They went away powerless before their hunters
　　　　　　　　　　　　　　　　(1:6)

Hunger. Elemental afflictions like hunger, thirst, and bodily pain impress themselves on the people's memory with lasting force. The laments of the hungry and the thirsty and those who saw their neighbors die of hunger speak with the language of real experience:

All her people groan;
　they seek after bread.
They trade their treasures for food
　to quiet their hunger.
　　　　　　　　　　　　(1:11)

Happier were the victims of the sword
　than the victims of hunger
who pined away
　stricken by lack of food.
　　　　　　(4:9; cf. 2:19; 4:5; 5:10)

It was possible to procure food only with great effort and danger:

We acquire our bread at the peril of our lives,
threatened by the sword from the wilderness.
　　　　　　　　　　　　(5:9; cf. 5:6)

We must pay for the water we drink,
and the wood we get must be bought.
　　　　　　　　　　　(5:4)

The hunger was so terrible that mothers nourished themselves on their own children:

Should women eat their offspring,
　the children of their tender care?
　　　　　　　(2:20; cf. 4:10)

Slavery and disgrace of the vanquished. In those days foreign rule was nothing new for Israel; but here something else is meant, namely, that a people is ruled in its own land by an occupying force whose presence is felt everywhere in daily life, which treats the surviving population arbitrarily and can dispose over all areas of life.

She that was a princess among the nations
　has become a vassal.
　　　　　　　　　　　　(1:1)

Slaves rule over us;
　there is none to deliver us from their hand.
　　　　　　　　　　　　(5:8)

Young men are compelled to grind at the mill,
　and boys stagger under loads of wood.
　　　　　　　　　　　　(5:13)

Suffering and the disgrace of suffering always belong together in the Old Testament. Thus Lamentation 5 is introduced:

Remember, Yahweh, what has befallen us;
　behold, and see our disgrace!

Again and again the lamentations express how unbearable is the burden of disgrace for its victims, the triumphant attitude of the adversary, the taunts of neighbors and former friends (1:8, 11, 17; 2:15).

Loss of inheritance, houses, and buildings. For a people whose identity was closely tied to a land, the loss of family inheritance and property was painful.

Our inheritance has been turned over to enemies,
　our homes to aliens.
　　　　　　　　　　　　(5:2)

For this our heart has become sick,
　for these things our eyes have grown dim,
for Mount Zion which lies desolate;
　jackals prowl over it.
　　　　　　　　　　　　(5:18)

The roads to Zion mourn. . . .
　all her gates are desolate.
　　　　　　　　　　　　(1:4)

Loss of treasures, joy, and festivals. Moreover, the catastrophe had robbed the people of the joys of life, especially those associated with the pilgrimage festivals held in Zion, when they had passed through the streets singing and dancing. All this was now no more.

From the daughter of Zion has departed
   all her splendor.
(1:6)

The roads to Zion mourn
   because none come to the appointed feasts.
(1:4a)

The old men have quit the city gate,
   the young men their music.
(5:14)

The joy of our hearts has ceased;
   our dancing has been changed to mourning.
(5:15)

Is this the city of which people said:
   "The perfection of beauty, the joy of all the earth"?
(2:15c)

The loss of treasures is indicated in the contrast between then and now:

How the gold has grown dim. . . .
The precious stones lie scattered at the
   head of every street;
The precious sons of Zion,
   worth their weight in gold,
how they are reckoned as earthen pots. . . .
(4:1–2; *cf.* 4:5, 7–8).

In all these instances the lament gives expression to the fact that, for those who speak thus, beauty, elegance, and graciousness belong to a wholesome life. The catastrophe has deprived them of the gift of divine blessing.

Loneliness, desolation, disconsolation. Streets and open squares, once filled with a joyous multitude, are now desolate. The city ifself seems in mourning:

How lonely sits the city once full of people!
. . . .
None of her friends is there to comfort her.
(1:1–2; *cf.* 1:7, 9, 16, 17, 21; 2:13)

Portrayal of Suffering. The people experienced not just physical adversity but also inward suffering and heartache:

She weeps bitterly in the night,
   tears stream over her cheeks.
(1:2)

Her maidens have been oppressed,
   she herself suffers bitterly.
(1:4)

Hear how I groan!
(1:21)
(*cf.* 1:22c; 2:11)

In all the above passages the pain and the weeping of a particular individual is portrayed: Zion is personified as a woman who is afflicted with severe pain. Long before this, Israel or Judah or Jerusalem had thus been personified, as in Amos 5:2. The intention of this device is to intensify the portrayal of suffering. A collective entity cannot weep, so it is a woman who weeps here. However, this personification can be laid aside now and then, as in 1:4: "Her maidens are oppressed, she herself suffers bitterly." In another passage it is said of this suffering:

What can I say for you,
To whom can I compare you, daughter of Jerusalem?
What can I liken you to that I may comfort you,
O virgin daughter of Zion?
For deep as the sea is your ruin,
   Who can restore you?
(2:13)

Or she may be exhorted to lament:

Let your tears stream down like a brook,
Day and night give yourself no rest. . . .
(2:18–19)

The same sentiment is expressed in Lamentation 5(and in 3:42ff.) without personification:

The joy of our hearts is at an end,
   our dancing is turned to mourning!
(5:15)

Therefore our heart has become sick.
(5:17)

Or the sorrow and suffering of the inhabitants of Jerusalem are described:

> The elders of the daughter of Zion sit
> silently on the ground,
> They have strewn dust on their heads
> and put on sackcloth.
> The maidens of Jerusalem have deeply
> bowed their heads.
>
> (2:10)

The many sentences dealing with the motif "portrayal of suffering" present the subjective side of the "we-laments," whose objective expression consists in lamenting the miserable conditions prevailing after the catastrophe, all they had to endure and what they lost. Lamenting means both weeping and putting into words what one is weeping about. Together they enable us to perceive the hidden cause of the lament, its releasing function, which eases the heaviness of suffering.

The "God-Lament" (Reproach of God)

A great number of sentences in Lamentations have Yahweh as the subject, with the structure "Yahweh has done . . ." This is the complaint directed to God, the accusation against God, which is also an aspect of the psalms of lament and the Book of Job. When one considers the great number of "God-laments" in Lamentations 1, 2, 4, 5, and 3:42–51, the designation of Lamentations as variants of the dirge (Jahnow 1923) must be ruled out. For the dirge is a secular genre; it does not speak of God. Rather, the "God-lament" is an aspect of the lament that is at the same time prayer. To be sure, the many "God-laments" in Lamentations are not, for the most part, direct address (such is the case only in the community lament in 5, in 3:42–51, and in a few other passages). The direct address has been converted into a description of affliction in the third person. But that does not alter the fact that God is reproached; God is reproved for what he has done to his people and his city.

Yahweh has brought suffering upon Israel. In these songs the anguish of lamentation is intensified by the realization that God—not accident or fate—has brought suffering upon Israel:

> . . . is there any sorrow like my sorrow
> which was brought upon me,
> which Yahweh afflicted
> on the day of his fierce anger?
>
> (1:12bc)

> Yahweh has trodden as in a winepress
> the virgin daughter of Zion.
>
> (1:15)

> . . . that you have done it,
> that you have brought the day which
> you have announced.
>
> (1:21c)

> Yahweh has cast down from heaven to earth
> the splendor of Israel;
> Yahweh has not remembered his footstool
> in the day of his anger.
>
> (2:1)

> and Yahweh has multiplied in the daughter of Zion
> mourning and lamentation.
>
> (2:5c)

Sometimes this suffering is portrayed as bodily affliction or sickness suffered by the personified Zion:

> Yahweh has left me stunned,
> faint all the day long.
>
> (1:13c)

And in some passages suffering is regarded as punishment for sin:

> Heavy is the yoke of my sins,
> fastened by Yahweh's hand.
> (1:14; *cf.* 4:16a; 3:42)

Yahweh has destroyed Zion in anger. Zion was regarded as the dwelling place of God and the seat of the Davidic monarchy. Therefore its destruction has the dimension of tragedy:

Yahweh has destroyed without mercy
all the habitations of Jacob.
(2:2; also v. 3)

Yahweh gave full vent to his wrath,
he poured out his hot anger;
And Yaweh kindled a fire in Zion,
which consumed its foundations.
(4:11)

In the day of your anger you have slain them,
slaughtering without mercy.
(2:21c)

God has destroyed the city and its buildings:

In the tent of the daughter of Zion
he has poured out his fury like fire.
(2:4)

Yahweh has destroyed all its palaces,
laid to ruin its strongholds . . .
Yahweh has broken down his booth like that of a garden,
Laid in ruins the place of his appointed feasts.
Yahweh has brought to an end in Zion
appointed feast and Sabbath.
(2:5–6)

Yahweh has scorned his altar,
disowned his sanctuary,
Yahweh has delivered into the hand of the enemy
the walls of her palaces.
(2:7; also vv. 8–9, 17)

God has rejected kingship and priesthood:

In his fierce indignation Yahweh has spurned
king and priest.
(2:6c)

Yahweh has brought down to the ground in dishonor
the kingdom and its rulers.
(2:2c)

Yahweh has become an enemy. God has treated Zion like an enemy. A terrible thought for the vanquished: God is not on their side but on the side of their opponents.

Yahweh has become like an enemy,
has devastated Israel.
(2:5)

Yahweh gave me into the hands
of those whom I cannot withstand.
(1:14c; also vv. 15, 17; 2:3)

Yahweh is compared to a hunter and a warrior:

Yahweh spread a net for my feet;
he turned me back.
(1:13b)

Yahweh has bent his bow like an enemy,
with the arrow in his right hand.
(2:4a)

In both of the community laments the "God-lament" has the form of direct address:

Why will you forget us forever,
why forsake us for all time?
(5:20)

You have wrapped yourself with anger and pursued us,
slaying without pity;
You have wrapped yourself like a cloud
so that no prayer can get through.
(3:43–44)

In a few places in the actual songs of lament, however, direct address appears together with the third person:

In the day of your anger you have slain them,
slaughtering without mercy.
(2:21c)

"Enemy-Laments"
(Accusation of Enemies and Neighbors)

It is striking that the "enemy-laments" (structure: "The enemies have . . .") are not much developed and, in relation to the other two aspects of lament, occupy only a small place. This restraint in the "enemy-laments" is displayed particularly in two ways: (1) the lament is raised only in individual sentences, never in longer pericopes, and (2) expressions of passionate hatred for enemies or of embitterment for what they have done are hardly present. Anger against enemies arises only because they have desecrated the Temple and robbed its treasures:

> The enemy has stretched out his hands
> over all her precious things;
> yea, she has seen the nations
> invade her sanctuary.
>
> (1:10)

> Should priest and prophet be slain
> in the temple of Yahweh?
>
> (2:20c)

Of the conquest of Jerusalem by enemies it is only reported objectively that an overwhelming power prevailed:

> My children are desolate,
> for the enemy has prevailed.
>
> (1:16c)

> They were set upon my neck;
> he caused my strength to fail.
>
> (1:14b)

However, bitterness does arise over the triumphal attitude, the scorn and derision of the enemy:

> Her oppressors are uppermost,
> her enemies prosper,
> because Yahweh has . . .
>
> (1:5)

> The foe gloated over her,
> mocking at her downfall.
>
> (1:7c)

> All my enemies have heard of my trouble,
> they are glad that you have done it.
>
> (1:21b)

Closely related to "enemy-laments" are laments raised over former friends who have not given help and have become enemies, and who after the fall of Jerusalem have boasted and mocked:

> All her neighbors have been unfaithful to her,
> they have become enemies. . . .
> none comforted her.
>
> (1:2, 7, 9)

> Yahweh has commanded against Jacob
> that his neighbors should be his foes.
>
> (1:17b; also 1:19, 2:15)

Thus shame was added to suffering:

> Remember, O Yahweh, what has befallen us,
> behold, and see our disgrace!
>
> (5:1)

> You have made us offscouring and refuse
> among the peoples.
>
> (3:45; also 1:8, 17)

The reason why "enemy-laments" are not nearly as prominent as "we-laments" and "God-laments" is shown in sentences like "Yahweh has made the enemy rejoice over you" (2:17c).

It was the judgment of God upon Israel that led her enemies to execute divine punishment. The insult of enemies is necessarily subdued when they are the instruments of God, as the prophets of judgment had been saying for a long time. However, when the catastrophe is perceived as God's judgment upon his people, lament cannot be raised without an accompanying confession of guilt.

Confession of Guilt

Confession is the only element, except for the lament, that occurs in all five songs, albeit in different forms. Like the description of distress, the confession is formulated in the third person:

> . . . because Yahweh has made her suffer
> for the multitude of her transgressions.
> Jerusalem sinned grievously. . . .
>
> (1:5, 8)

> Her uncleanness was in her skirts,
> she took no thought of her future.
>
> (1:9; also vv. 4, 6)

Strikingly, however, in some passages the confession of guilt has retained its proper form:

> Heavy is the yoke of my sins,
> by his hand they were fastened together.
>
> (1:14a)

> Righteous is Yahweh,
> for I have rebelled against his word.
> (1:18; *cf.* vv. 20, 22)

> Woe to us, for we have sinned!
> (5:16; *cf.* 3:42)

One can hardly judge this cluster of passages in any other way than to say that here an actual confession of guilt is preserved, based on the recognition that Israel has sinned against its God. The accusations raised in vain by the prophets of judgment against their people before the fall of the nation are now perceived to be justified by those who make this confession of guilt. The prophets were thus rehabilitated in retrospect. Accordingly, to the prophets of salvation of the preexilic time is now attributed guilt for the divine punishment in a special degree:

> This happened on account of the sins
> of her prophets. . . .
> (4:13a)

> [Your prophets] have not exposed your iniquity. . . .
> (2:141b)

In one passage the confession of guilt seems to be rejected or refused:

> Our ancestors sinned, and are no more,
> and we bear their punishment.
> (5:7)

The fact that this sentence occurs in the same lament as the spontaneous confession of guilt, "Woe to us, for we have sinned!" (5:16), shows how the admission of sin was not self-evident in the period after the destruction of Jerusalem. There were also those who rejected the view that children should suffer for the sins of their parents (Ezek 18:1ff), and these testimonies were likewise given a place.

Petition for God's Favor

The confession of trust has its place in the individual psalms of lament; in the community la-ments, however, the expression of trust is found only rarely. Instead, there is a remembrance of God's previous saving deeds. It is a peculiarity of Lamentations that both the above elements are lacking. But the distress and misery of the people do embolden them to beseech God's favor again. It is this motif that marks the lamentations as prayers and distinguishes them from the dirge.

> Remember, O Yahweh, what has befallen us,
> behold, and see our disgrace!
> (5:1)

> Look, O Yahweh, and see!
> With whom hast thou dealt thus?
> (2:20)

> O Yahweh, behold my affliction,
> for the enemy has triumphed!
> (1:9; *cf.* vv. 11, 20)

In all these passages the petition for God's favor seeks to motivate God to look favorably upon the supplicant. Viewed separately, they all contain themes of lament: "we-lament" in 5:1, "enemy-lament" in 1:9, description of pain in 1:20. Therein is shown the inextricable connection between lament and petition: the lament is made not only for its own sake but also as an appeal for a way out of distress.

This aim is also the focal point of the expansive invitation to lament in 2:18–19:

> Cry aloud to the Lord, O daughter of Zion!
> . . . .
> Pour out your heart like water
> before the presence of the Lord!
> Lift up your hands to him
> for the lives of your children!

The urgency in this series of imperatives is intended as encouragement to turn to the helper who can change the distress. But this passage too stops short with a plea for divine favor. The second element of the petition, namely, for Yahweh's intervention on behalf of his people and for restoration, is lacking in Lamentations 1, 2, and 4, as is the confession of trust. The reason for this lack is the same in both cases.

Those who speak here are still so overwhelmed by the blow that has struck them that a plea for Yahweh's intervention does not pass their lips. Of course, one could argue that such a plea is implied in the petition for Yahweh's favor, but this only underscores the fact that in no case is the petition fully enunciated—not even in Lamentation 5, a community lament that is placed within the framework of both elements of the petition. It begins with a plea for Yahweh's favor (5:1) and ends with a plea for intervention (5:21):

> Restore us to thyself, O Yahweh, that
> we may be restored.
> Renew our days as of old!

But precisely this community lament ends with the anxious, doubting question, which accords with the songs of lament:

> Or hast thou utterly rejected us?
> Art thou exceedingly angry with us?
> (5:22)

Here also should be mentioned two other statements that—instead of a confession of trust—stand between lament and petition. The first is 1:18: "Righteous is Yahweh,/for I have rebelled against him." In the structure of Lamentation 1 this sentence stands in the place belonging to the confession of trust. Here, however, the sentence does not serve as a confession; rather, it must be explained in connection with the particular emphasis of the confession of guilt in Lamentation 1 (vv. 14, 18, 20, 22). The verse is a reflection that furthers the thought: we ourselves are at fault, not God! God is righteous, and we have rebelled against him (cf. Ps 51:6).

Also standing in the place of a confession of trust is 5:19: "But thou, O Yahweh, dost reign for ever/Thy throne endures to all generations." Manifestly the sentence is a quotation from a psalm of praise. Those who pronounce this recall the words of praise to God, but not in a jubilant tone, for the meaning has become ambivalent. The God who is forever en-throned in the heights of the cosmos is incomprehensibly distant. Hence the note of restraint in the poet's praise of God.

Petition Against Enemies

In many individual and community psalms of lament the plea for Yahweh's favor and for his intervention appears as a third element of a petition directed against enemies. Such is also the case in Lamentations 1 and 4:

> . . . let them be as I am,
> Let all their evildoing come before thee;
> and deal with them as thou hast dealt with me.
> (1:21d–22a)

> Rejoice and be glad, O daughter of Edom
> . . . .
> to you also the cup shall pass
> . . . .
> The punishment of your iniquity, O daughter of Zion,
> is accomplished.
> He will keep you in exile no longer,
> but your iniquity, O daughter of Edom, he will punish.
> (4:21, 22)

What is striking is not so much the lack of a petition against the enemies in Lamentations 2 and 5 as its presence in 1 and 4. Some scholars interpret this to mean that what was said concerning the laments about the enemies is true here also: namely, that the discourse against the enemies is suppressed because Yahweh executed his judgment upon Israel through her enemies and thus they, to a certain degree, carried out his mandate. However, the situation here is different than in the laments over enemies. For the texts of both petitions against the enemies agree in saying that the enemies have covered themselves with guilt and Yahweh must therefore punish them as he punished Israel: "Do to them, as you have done to me!" Thus what is involved is God's righteous governance in history. The nations must undergo catastrophe just as it befell Israel. Verse 4:22a ("the punishment of your iniquity, O daughter of Zion, is accomplished") must be interpreted along the same lines. To be sure, this statement is not meant as a proclamation of forgiveness extended to Israel (as in Isa 40:1); it merely affirms that the iniquity of the people has been blotted out through Israel's suffering (as in Isa 40:2).

THEOLOGICAL SIGNIFICANCE

The theological significance of the Lamentations has usually been seen in the answer given to a theological question. Thus Norman Gottwald (1954) sees the key to their theological significance in an answer to the tension between the Deuteronomic teaching of retribution and the experienced reality of the fall of the nation. For Bertil Albrektson (1963), the tension lies in the contrast between the doctrine of the inviolability of Zion and the shattering of this belief by the city's destruction. Such and similar questions may resound in the Lamentations, but these songs were not created to answer such questions. They arose as the reactions of those who experienced the catastrophe, as actual laments in which actual suffering finds expression.

In recent years some scholars have maintained that the key to the theological understanding of the Lamentations is found in the third song. This is the view of Otto Kaiser (1981), who ascribes to this song a paradigmatic meaning. Brevard Childs expresses the same view even more emphatically: "The function of chapter 3 is to translate Israel's historically conditioned plight into the language of faith, . . . to incorporate the history of the nation in its . . . despair within a liturgical context" (Childs 1979, 594). But apart from the question of how Lamentation 3 is related literarily to chapters 1, 2, 4, and 5, one can ask what is meant by a transfer into a liturgical context, if 1, 2, 4, and 5 as well as 3 are liturgical texts. They too contain the address to God and the plea for divine favor. Likewise, it is questionable whether one can describe Lamentation 3 as "language of faith" because it is the lament of an individual, while 1, 2, 4, 5 are not because they are laments of the people. In my view, the answer to the question of the theological significance of Lamentations must come from these poems themselves. Lamentations 1, 2, 4, and 5 are unambiguous laments over the fall of Jerusalem; chap-

ter 3, on the other hand, contains no unambiguous sentence indicating that the fall of Jerusalem is involved.

The theological significance of the Lamentations arises from the uniqueness and distinctiveness of these canonical writings of the Old Testament: the combination of lament and dirge. Their significance in the discourse about God is shown in their peculiar movement from lament over death (dirge) to prayer. They express the question of the survivors: Is this the end? (5:22). At the same time, however, they show that those who come together to remember the fall of Jerusalem (1:7) despite this question, hold to the One who in his wrath had brought about the catastrophe and implore him to turn once again to the remnant. Their confession of sin makes it possible to give meaning to the catastrophe: the wrath of God had a basis, so God is still at work. Those who were decisively struck by misfortune (as stated in the lament over death) hold firmly to the lament over suffering. The lament was preserved and handed down as an element of the service of worship. The "passion" of the people of God will speak further to the remnant; it has received a positive, constructive significance.

Furthermore, the Lamentations have a historical-theological significance. The repeated mention of the prophets (1:21; 2:14, 17) is not properly a motif of the community lament; it belongs to the motifs in Lamentations 1–5 that can be explained only within the historical context of the Book of Lamentations. In the course of the remembrance of the "days of her distress and bitterness" (1:7) it was only natural to remember also the prophets and their work. Those who remembered the catastrophe asked about the causes and historical antecedents. The Lamentations are thereby endowed with historical-theological significance. The prophets of judgment were rehabilitated; the prophets of salvation were seen as those who led Israel astray and were condemned on that basis. Here it is perceived that the work of the prophets of judgment made possible a continuity beyond the abyss of the fall of the nation: "Yahweh has fulfilled his word, as he ordained long ago" (2:17; cf. 1:21). Deutero-Isaiah will elaborate this start toward bridging the abyss.

The account of the imprisonment of the king (4:17–20) unfolds the lament over the end of the monarchy (2:2, 6, 9), and is probably part of a poem dealing with the end of the kingdom. It belongs to the multifaceted theological reworking of this event that begins just after 587. The end of the monarchy, seen in the perspective of the historical account in 2 Kings 25:1–7, with which Lamentations 4:17–20 corresponds closely, was lamented and recounted in song in a very different manner. In Psalm 89 the end of the monarchy is contrasted with the promise given by the prophet Nathan; in Lamentations 4:17–20, however, a member of the royal court speaks (probably an eyewitness, as shown by the language of verse 20, which corresponds to the words customarily used in praise of a king; cf. the royal psalms). This language connects the lament over the end of the kingdom with the later expectation of a messianic king. Here too the fall of the nation is linked with the preceding history of Israel and seems to point toward the future.

LAMENTATION 3

Lamentation 3 does not belong to the genre of the laments, as do Lamentations 1, 2, and 4. It was inserted into the collection of Lamentations because, like them, it is an alphabetical acrostic song. Also, in verses 42–51 the fragment of a communal lament is present.

Lamentation 3 is composed of various parts, brought together by the alphabetical sequence and some loose associations; for example, the lament of an individual follows the song of praise of an individual (compare Ps 22). It is not an organic composition; in style and sentiment it is comparable to the parts of psalms interspersed in the Chronicler's Work or even with the alphabetical acrostic Psalm 119.

The composition (3:1–66) contains three (or four) elements: 1–25 and also 52–66 are parts of an individual psalm of lament; 26–41 consist of expansions in the form of reflection and paraenesis; 42–51 constitute part of a community psalm of lament; 52–58 are part of a hymn of praise. The composition is singularly introduced as a personal confession: "I am a man who has experienced affliction . . ."; in this respect the opening is similar to Job 30 (Lam 3:14 ≅

Job 30:9). The long "God-lament" and "I-lament" in verses 1–16 are joined with a description of pain (vv. 17–19) and a confession of trust (vv. 20–25). Verses 26–41 expand this confession of trust into a paraenesis, and this is followed by a fragmentary community lament. Verses 52–61 are part of a hymn of praise, in which the specifically liturgical parts at the beginning and end are missing. The conclusion (vv. 59–66) could be the conclusion of a psalm of lament; it contains the lament about enemies and the petition against the enemies.

The understanding of Lamentation 3 depends on a prior decision: whether to regard Lamentations 1–5 as a book with five chapters or a collection of individual songs (as in the case of the small collections within the Psalter). A decisive point to consider is the fact that not a single sentence in Lamentation 3:1–60 refers unambiguously to the catastrophe of 587. If one wants to reinterpret the suffering of the individual portrayed in Lamentation 3 as the suffering of Jerusalem after the destruction of 587, then the entire book must be understood allegorically. How shall we, for instance, understand the sentence in 3:27 ("It is good for a man that he bear the yoke of his youth") when it is applied to Israel? Moreover, the paraenesis in 3:26–41 is similar to a *midrash*, in contrast to the psalms of lament. In these verses, the sufferers are denied lamentation; instead of lamenting, they are exhorted to consider their sins and return to Yahweh. The author of this expansion intends to move away from lament toward a wisdom piety (vv. 39–40).

If Lamentation 3 is an independent composition combining various parts, then these parts are to be explained and interpreted within the context of their own literary form: the context of the individual lament and its variations, the hymn of praise of the individual, and the community lament. Only then is it possible to inquire about the meaning of the composition as a whole—a question that belongs to the history of redaction.

Bibliography

Commentaries

Hillers, Delbert R. *Lamentations*. The Anchor Bible, vol. 7A. Garden City, N.Y., 1972.

Kaiser, Otto. Commentary in *Das Hohe Lied; Klagelieder; Das Buch Esther,* translated and annotated by Helmer Ringgren and Otto Kaiser. *Das Alte Testament Deutsch,* vol. 16/2. Göttingen, 1981.

Kraus, H. J. *Klagelieder. Altes Testament,* vol. 20. Neukirchen (Moers), 1956.

Meek, Theophile J. Introduction and Exegesis in *The Interpreter's Bible,* edited by George Arthur Buttrick et al., vol. 6. Nashville, Tenn., 1956. Pp. 3–38.

General Studies

Albrektson, Bertil. *Studies in the Text and Theology of the Book of Lamentations, with a Critical Edition of the Peshitta Text.* Lund, Sweden, 1963.

Childs, Brevard S. *Introduction to the Old Testament as Scripture.* Philadelphia, 1979. Pp. 590–597.

Gottwald, Norman K. *Studies in the Book of Lamentations.* Chicago, 1954.

Gunkel, Hermann, and Joachim Begrich. *Einleitung in die Psalmen.* 1933; 2d ed. Göttingen, 1966.

Jahnow, Hedwig. *Das hebräische Leichenlied im Rahmen der Völkerdichtung.* Giessen, 1923.

Westermann, Claus. *Praise and Lament in the Psalms.* Translated by Keith R. Crim and Richard N. Soulen. Edinburgh, 1981.

CLAUS WESTERMANN
Translated by Bernhard W. Anderson

Ezekiel

THE BOOK OF Ezekiel stands among the Old Testament prophets, after Isaiah and Jeremiah, and before the Book of the Twelve, the so-called Minor Prophets. The "prophetic" books, while containing large sections of sayings of one kind and another, are intimately tied into the periods to which they refer. Ezekiel's prophecy, for example, is rooted in the catastrophe of the fall of Jerusalem in 587 B.C.E. While the historical background to much of the material remains uncertain, we may nevertheless assume that the words both of the prophets and of the successors who contributed to the books as we have them were closely linked with the actualities of political and social life. We may often suspect, though much less proof is available, that more could be discovered about the history of the people if we were able to know exactly when particular sayings were uttered, or when particular elaborations of those sayings—in the form of comments, expositions, or "sermons"—came into being. The problems thus perceived are particularly relevant to the full understanding of the Book of Ezekiel.

CONTENTS

A simple division of the book may be made: (1) chapters 1–24, prophecies of judgment from the years leading up to the fall of Jerusalem in 587 B.C.E.; (2) chapters 25–32, oracles against foreign nations; (3) chapters 33–48, oracles of restoration. But such a division does not do justice to the complexity of the book, and a more detailed survey points to other levels.

Chapters 1–24 form a large unit containing within itself several types of material and several separable groupings.

1. In 1:1–3:27, various types of material are built together around the broader understanding of the commissioning of Ezekiel: a complex vision of a flying throne, experienced in Babylonia and set in the thirtieth year (1:1), identified as the fifth year of Jehoiachin (1:2, i.e., 593 B.C.E.); in 1:1–28a, a call to the prophet that involves his receiving a scroll of woe (1:28b–3:3); a commissioning of the prophet to his people (3:4–11); a translation of the prophet (from Jerusalem?; cf. chaps. 8–10) to the exiles in Babylonia (3:12–15); the prophet as watchman (3:16–27).

2. Next follows a series of symbolic actions proclaiming the siege of Jerusalem, total disaster, and exile (4:1–5:17), closely linked to a series of oracles of imminent judgment (6:1–7:27) that are centered on the theme of "the end" (7:1–4).

3. In 8:10–11:25, the prophet's translation to the doomed Temple and city of Jerusalem is described,

echoing the departure of God as a counterpart to the appearance in Babylonia in chapter 1.

4. There follow sermons and allegories on the coming disaster (12:1–19:14), initiated in a symbolic action representing siege and exile (12:1–7, 8–20). The section incorporates an elaborate sermonic allegory on Israel's history (chap. 16) and a complex statement on responsibility (chap. 18). The section ends in a lament over Israel and her rulers (19:1–14).

5. Oracles and symbols of judgment are presented in 20:1–24:27, reaching a climax in the announcement of the fall of Jerusalem (chap. 24) and incorporating an elaborate allegory on Israel and Judah (chap. 23).

The foreign-nation oracles of chapters 25–32 are curiously unbalanced. Judah's neighbors—Ammon, Moab, Edom, Philistia—are briefly dismissed (25). Tyre is treated at length in 26–28: judgment (26), dirge in prose and poetry (27), poetic allegory (28). Egypt is handled in a series of dated oracles in chapters 29–32: they are linked to the tenth (29:1), eleventh (31:1), and twelfth (32:1, and also 32:17) years, with a reference also to the twenty-seventh year (29:17). The absence of any judgment material on Babylon is noteworthy.

The restoration material in 33–48 is broken into two quite distinct parts by 38–39, where Gog, king of Magog, again in a complex section, is interpreted as showing the overthrow of all nations and their acknowledgment of the restoration of Israel. Its climax is to be seen in the picture of the nations as witnesses of the reality of the God of Israel (39:21–29).

Chapters 33–37 are directly linked back to 3:16–27, the watchman theme; in the exposition of this there is a link to the responsibility theme both there and in chapter 18. Chapters 34–36 are concerned with the condemnation of earlier rulers and the establishment of true rule, together with particular judgments on Edom. The whole section culminates in symbols of restoration: resurrection of the people, joining of the divided nation, establishment of renewed Davidic rule (37).

Chapters 40–48, dated (40:1) to the twenty-fifth year of exile, the fourteenth year after the fall of Jerusalem (i.e., 573–572), are deliberately linked (43:1–5) with the vision of the flying throne: the whole section concerns the complete renewal of the land and the rebuilding and reordering of the Temple; it represents an ideal for the future state of land and Temple. The relationship of this section to the remainder of the book is clear, yet its origin remains perplexing and its differences from what precedes mark it off as separate.

THE LIFE AND TIMES OF EZEKIEL

The book itself provides a number of dates that may give clues to the activity of the prophet, but the dates are not easy to interpret. They may, in any case, refer only to particular sections of material, and the book may have been schematically ordered to some degree, which suggests an annalistic approach to the message of the prophet.

Earlier prophetic books sometimes "date" oracles either by giving an actual date or, more often, by alluding to a particular event. The dates in Ezekiel point forward to the schematic ordering of Haggai and of Zechariah 1–8, where the various oracles or groups of oracles are given precise historical contexts in this way, though the full significance of the dates escapes us. Later, too, the Book of Daniel offers such a sequence. In these cases, there is the possibility that the compilers are using dates to give precise applicability and authenticity to particular elements in the prophetic message.

In Ezekiel, the initial date (1:1, 2) provides what looks like a double dating system: fifth day, fourth month, thirtieth year (1:1), apparently to be understood as the same as the fifth day of the month (which?) of the fifth year of Jehoiachin's exile (1:2). It is not impossible that the two dates were originally quite separate: if they refer to the same year, then "thirtieth" remains unexplained. Is it the prophet's age? or the period since Josiah's reform? or—perhaps the most probable answer—a later scribal attempt to explain why Jeremiah spoke of seventy years of exile (Jer 25:11f.) where Ezekiel speaks of forty years of punishment for Judah (Ezek 4:6)? Such a supposition receives some support from the evidently symbolic use of numbers in Ezekiel 4:4–6. But whereas the forty-year figure of 4:6 makes use of a well-established number for the punishment of Judah (*cf.* the reference to forty years in the wilderness, cited in Exod 16:35, frequently in the wilderness material, in the Psalms, in various prophecies, and in the New Testament; and *cf.* significantly Ezek 29:11, 13 as a theme of judgment on Egypt), the symbolism of the other figure of 390 years, which is said to refer to the "punishment of Israel," is by no means clear.

The Greek translation offers an alternative of 190, made up of 40 plus 150, and this has been linked to the figures for the days of the flood in Genesis 6–8. It is probably a later interpretation, designed to associate the disaster of the sixth century with the major calamity of ancient legend. Attempts have been made at relating the 390 or the 190 back to the division of the kingdom in the reign of Rehoboam (1 Kgs 12, perhaps *cf.* Isa 7:17), or to the disaster at the fall of Samaria in 722; still less sure are the suggested associations of these figures with later disasters. The nearest such would appear to fall close to the period of Alexander the Great (332 falls very neatly 390 years after 722); what we know of biblical chronological systems in the later Old Testament period (*cf.* Dan 9) does not support the idea that such exactitude was available. While we may suppose there to be some endeavor to show the significance of the figures, none of the possible explanations does more than hint at the way in which later interpreters have sought to correlate Ezekiel's actions and prophecies with the experiences of their own day. The obscurity of much of the detail in the book would seem to lend itself very readily to such speculation; it is one of the ways in which prophecy is understood to remain meaningful.

The dates in Ezekiel cover a period from the fifth year of Jehoiachin (1:1f., 593), through the sixth, seventh, and ninth years (8:1, 20:1, 24:1), to the twelfth (33:21), at which point the news of Jerusalem's fall is described as reaching the prophet. The oracles against Tyre are linked to the eleventh year (26:1); those against Egypt extend over the tenth to twelfth (29:1; 30:20; 31:1; 32:1, 17), with one (29:17) that moves right on to the twenty-seventh (571) and probably represents an updating of earlier material. The opening of chapter 40 sets the vision of the future of land and Temple in the twenty-fifth year.

If the range of dates appears to provide a reasonable limitation to the period of Ezekiel's activity, their relationship to the material with which they stand is not necessarily readily determinable. Nor does it follow that they can all be treated at the same level. The presence in 4:5f. of what appear to be symbolic dates allows the possibility that some others may be of this kind: in particular, the date that marks the start of the vision of the new land and Temple in chapters 40–48 could indicate the endeavor by another and perhaps later writer to dovetail that visionary sequence into the period of Ezekiel and thus give it authority for those to whom it was directed.

If the dates in some measure provide a frame for Ezekiel's activity, it must be acknowledged that our information about him remains limited to the references to his name, his priestly status (1:3), his wife, who died at about the time of Jerusalem's siege in 587 (24:18), his presence at Tel-abib (1:1, 3:15), near the Great Canal. We might have expected some play to have been made with the prophet's name (Ezekiel, "God strengthens," *ḥazaq*), but no explicit statement is made. The use of the related verb is marked in 3:8f. and 3:14, both as suggesting the prophet's position ("I have made your face hard . . . "; "like adamant harder than flint I have made your forehead"; RSV) and as expressive of divine control or empowering ("the hand of the LORD being strong upon me"). But this latter idiom is found elsewhere (Isa 8:11), and the verb finds only limited use in the book as a whole.

If the prophet's intimate concern with the fate of Jerusalem has suggested to some the possibility that he was in reality still in Jerusalem at the time of the siege and disaster (note chapter 12), the view that the book itself presents—that he was taken into captivity in 598—appears more probable. The fate of Jerusalem and its significance occupied a central place within a message that is concerned both with the absoluteness of divine judgment and with the true nature of hope, which is shown to belong within the divine prerogative.

If we know little about the prophet himself, we are much more fully informed from other sources about the events in which he was involved. The fact that the dates are linked to the reign of Jehoiachin (king of Judah in 597, then taken into captivity in Babylonia) does more than provide a chronological frame, however elusive its information may be. It implies a view that sees the first capture of Jerusalem in that year as effectively marking the end of the kingdom of Judah, and, insofar as hope attaches to the Davidic line, sees in the captive king a figure of at least some significance. The book does not mention the release of Jehoiachin from prison in 562 (*cf.* 2 Kgs 25:27–30 and the parallel text in Jer 52:31–34), an event that has been variously interpreted as pointing to a hope for the future, perhaps to be linked with speculations concerning Zerubbabel as descendant of the captive and released king at the time of upheavals in the early years of Darius I (*cf.* Hag 2:21–23); or alternatively as marking the end of any such hope, in that there is no subsequent echo of it, and the final phrase of the account indicates his death.

So far as Ezekiel is concerned, 17:12 alludes to the taking captive of Jehoiachin (though he is not named), but no indication appears of any hope attaching to him. Had such been intended, it could readily have been included in the hopeful oracle of 17:22–24. While there are other expressions of Davidic hope (34:23f., 37:22f., and, more explicitly, 37:24f.), at no point is such hope attached to the specific figure of Jehoiachin. The absence of any such precise reference could imply that, for Ezekiel, no particular hope for the future was associated with Jehoiachin; and the paucity of reference to the Davidic theme points in the same direction. This could carry with it the probability that the dating by Jehoiachin is part of an attempt to fit Ezekiel into a certain kind of thinking of the postexilic period in which both Davidic promise and descent from the captive king were seen to be significant. But if this is so, it remains the case that the Book of Ezekiel is at no point explicit on this issue; later glossing of the text could have been expected to make it clear but does not do so.

Many passages in the judgment sections in chapters 1–24 draw out the inevitability of doom for Jerusalem and Judah. This is true of the symbolic actions of 4–5; of the "end" theme in 7; of the portrayal of divinely enacted disaster for city and Temple in 8–11; and repeatedly in the chapters that follow, in particular in 21, where the theme is of the divine sword of judgment and of the directing of the king of Babylon by divination to Jerusalem; and again

in 24 in the climax of the fall of the city (the news reaching Ezekiel "on that day," 24:26; *cf.* 33:21f., which offers the alternative of the twelfth year, 586 or 585). Much in these chapters is directed to the deported community in Babylonia, by implication countering any hopes of the speedy downfall of Babylon and of the sparing of Jerusalem from final disaster (*cf.* Jer 29). The rather gruesome cauldron symbol of Ezekiel 11—the cauldron as a protective picture in 11:3 giving place to that of the dead in the city as the contents of the cauldron that is Jerusalem (11:7), and typified in the sudden death of Pelatiah in 11:13—stresses that no hope remains in Judah. The short narrative and prophecy are set in the context of the final departure of God from Temple and city (11:22–25).

Our knowledge of Judah during the years that follow remains scanty. A brief period of possible revival under Gedaliah (2 Kgs 25:22–26; Jer 40–41) ends with his assassination and the escape to Egypt of some of the community (Jer 43–44). The Book of Ezekiel gives no further clue, except in allusions to his being consulted (see, e.g., Ezek 14:1) and as the book sees hope in terms of the bringing to life of a dead people and the joining into one of the separated elements of Judah and Israel under one Davidic ruler (37). For other clues we have to go to the inferences that can be drawn from the stories of restoration (Ezra 1–6) and from the prophecies of Haggai and Zechariah, which suggest some degree of continuous life; and to the archaeological evidence, which, while witnessing to much destruction, probably also shows some continuity of occupation and life in Judah. This we should expect. But we may observe that the Book of Ezekiel contributes to the major emphasis on the future as belonging to the deportees in Babylonia, both by its stress on destruction and by its setting. (See, on this theme, 2 Chron 36, which is more emphatic than 2 Kgs 25.)

EZEKIEL AND THE PROPHETIC TRADITION

The Book of Ezekiel is like other prophetic books in that considerable space is devoted to oracular sayings and poems that deal with the wide spectrum of condemnation of various evils (notably apostasy in his case), with the reality of the divine promises of life and well-being (though these are less prominent), and with the failures and judgments of other nations, thus exhibiting the universal quality of divine rule. In these respects, the Ezekiel material is close to other prophetic collections, in particular to Jeremiah, whose prophetic activity substantially overlaps Ezekiel's own in time, and to Hosea. The affinities with Jeremiah invite a comparison with Hosea in view of the close links between these two prophets in language, style, and content; and it is not easy to be sure how far Ezekiel is dependent on Hosea directly and how far through the mediation of Hosea's thought and style in Jeremiah. In chapters 16 and 23, there are particularly close links with Hosea, very much connected with the use of marriage imagery to represent the relationship between God and his people; and though such ideas are markedly present in Jeremiah (e.g., Jer 2), the detail of the elaboration in Ezekiel suggests that the Ezekiel passages represent an exegesis of the corresponding themes in Hosea.

Ezekiel thus represents a particular element in the development of prophetic material, and one that would appear to explain in part the elaboration of ideas and pictures that is so noteworthy in the longer expositions, particularly in those often described as "allegory." Whereas earlier prophetic material often uses pictures drawn from the natural and human worlds to express religious ideas, the Ezekiel passages develop the detail of such themes extensively. The application of the term "sermon," however much it is necessary to avoid an oversimple view of what is involved, has often seemed most appropriate to these expositions, though they show not simply the exegetical expansion of earlier prophecy but also a fuller elaboration of the pictorial details. Such elaboration may indicate an attempt at more precise application to the particular situation addressed by the prophet or by his successors.

But while the links between Ezekiel and Jeremiah and Hosea are important, they should not obscure another aspect of the presentation of Ezekiel that shows a close relationship with prophecy as it appears in the narrative books, and in particular with the prophets Elijah and Elisha, whose traditions form a substantial section of the Books of Kings (1 Kgs 17–2 Kgs 9). If the prophets known to us in the prophetic books are rarely to be found mentioned in the narrative works (the so-called Former Prophets, consisting of Joshua, Judges, 1–2 Samuel, and 1–2 Kings), the apparent separation between the "pre-writing" and the "writing" prophets is evidently an artificial one. Such clues as we find point to a much closer similarity between the one group and the other; and in the case of Ezekiel numerous features provide such links. The "hand of the LORD" as empowering and controlling the prophet (e.g., in 3:14) and as carrying him from place to place (e.g., in 8:3) appears in a not dissimilar way for Elijah (1 Kgs 18:46) and Elisha (2 Kgs 3:15). The concept of the "spirit of God" (as in Ezek 2:2), one that is rare in or absent from some of the prophetic books, appears in a number of stories concerning earlier prophetic figures (1 Kgs 22:23; 2 Kgs 2:9, 15f.). The use of symbolic acts, found in numerous prophetic books, is a particular mark of stories told about prophets in Samuel and Kings and becomes very evident in Ezekiel, as also in Jeremiah. The indications of paranormal behavior and experience (e.g., Ezek 4:4–8, 8:3), while they may be found in other prophetic books (e.g., Mic 1:8; *cf.* Isa 20), are common in Ezekiel, who for this reason in particular appears to be a strange and remote figure, at first sight much stranger than some of the other major prophets.

It would clearly be incorrect to draw sharp lines of affinity and distinction, yet there is evidently a certain tendency to think of Ezekiel as belonging to a different type of prophecy than other major figures. In part this is due to the tendency to overlook or underestimate the strangeness of their behavior, as in the case of Isaiah (see Isa 20, already noted; Isa 8:11, with the concept of the "strong hand" of God taking hold of the prophet; and 2 Kgs 20:1–11, in contrast to Isa 38:21, where the motif of the prophet as healer is merely appended to a narrative from which that element has been largely eliminated). The strangeness of Ezekiel, suggested by stories and imagery, is certainly evident in much that the book contains. But it is not unique: the style of presentation has parallels in the stories gathered around such a figure as Elisha.

The strangeness of Ezekiel in the prophetic group is further emphasized by the close relationship between Ezekiel and priestly-legal material, in particular that of the so-called Holiness Code (Lev 17–26). This has even led to the supposition that Ezekiel was himself the author of that legal corpus. But while such an assumption is inappropriate, it is evident either that Ezekiel himself as priest was closely influenced by the style and language of those chapters, or that those responsible for the collection and arrangement of his prophetic sayings saw him as potentially so linked. The figure and the words of Jeremiah have been mediated in somewhat similar fashion through association with Deuteronomistic thought and style. In both cases, it is clear that the separation between prophetic, priestly, and legal material, however convenient for discussion, is less than adequate to full understanding. (Compare the use of similar words in Jer 18:18, Ezek 7:26.) At any rate, the interpretation of Ezekiel, evident in so much elaboration in the prophetic oracles, has tended to make of him an interpreter of laws and of priestly directives and hence a fitting recipient for the elaborate cultic and other material to be found in chapters 40–48.

STRUCTURES

At first sight it may appear that the prophetic books, including Ezekiel, show little sign of orderly arrangement. Closer examination, however, reveals a kind of organization. Thus, chapters 4–5 contain a series of symbolic actions and exposition, and 26–28 have several distinct elements, yet all are intimately related to the judgment of Tyre. Study of the text shows that even where connections are not immediately obvious there may be verbal and thought links between different passages now standing close to one another.

Much attention has been directed by scholars to such matters of structure. Books need to be considered whole if we are to decide what their ultimate purpose may be; sections within a book may reveal particular stages of the book's formation. There is room for difference of opinion on various aspects of this kind of study, but it has brought illumination to

the understanding of ways in which the material as it now stands may show the hand of the prophet himself, of his immediate disciples (or successors, since we have little evidence of "disciples" in a more precise sense), and of later readers and expounders endeavoring to make clear to their own contemporaries the significance of particular passages or of sections or the whole of the book. This applies to the original Hebrew and to its ancient and modern translations. These translations bring their own particular contributions to the understanding of the book as we know it, since translation, particularly of ancient and religious literature, must contribute something of the translators' own understandings of what the text means to their contemporaries. Among commentators on Ezekiel, a marked difference may be seen between those who attribute the material more or less as its stands to the prophet himself and those who see in this book, as in others, many indications of the continuing process by which the words and deeds of a prophet are made intelligible and applicable to later generations.

Subdividing the book is itself a partly subjective process. Still, some sections are marked off reasonably clearly, and it is appropriate now to say a little more about some of these: for fuller discussion, the various commentaries need to be consulted.

Chapters 1–3 form a single unit, clearly grouped around the "call" experience of the prophet: opinions differ about its unity, but its general coherence is clear enough. Yet the chapters are made up of very distinct elements. The vision of the flying throne in 1:4–28a is continued in 1:28b–2:7 and 2:8–3:3 with two sections (perhaps really one) that move into quite different imagery, in particular that of the scroll of woe that tastes like honey. Whereas the vision reappears in some measure in chapters 8 and 10, the theme of the scroll is unique. After an exposition of the prophet's mission in 3:4–11, the vision theme returns and is concluded in 3:12–15. This is followed by the exposition of the watchman theme in 3:16–21, and by a final exposition of the prophet's task with a return to the vision theme in 3:22–27. While the interlinkages between the various sections are explicit, the differences of level and style strongly suggest that the final unit has been skillfully built up, explicating the nature of the prophet's commission, the responsibility resting upon him, the doom that he has to pronounce, but also pointing forward in the book both to the carrying through of doom and beyond that to the return of the glory of God to Jerusalem in 43:2–5. Such skillful interweaving suggests a purposeful exposition of several distinct elements in which the themes of relentless judgment, the people's and the prophet's responsibility, and the real nature of the hope for the future are tellingly combined.

We may note that a not-unrelated structure appears in chapters 8–11, linked by the use of the vision theme but elaborating the nature of the failure of Israel's leadership in the irreligious acts described in 8:7–18. The total judgment in chapter 9, where the possibility of sparing only those who truly lament the abominations of the people suggests a modicum of hope, but no more, and the departure of the glory of God in chapter 10, preface the symbolizing of judgment in the death of Pelatiah (11:1–13). Yet here again, before the final departure of God to Babylon (11:22–25), the hope of restoration is made more explicit in the prospect of reassembly of the scattered, and total renewal and purification (11:14–21). Again, we have not a single unit of material, but a subtle weaving together of different elements looking ahead to prospects and realities of recovery.

Chapters 4–7 present a different example. These chapters are built up around a group of symbolic actions, which depict or symbolize what Ezekiel understands to be the divine will; the relationship between action and event may be understood as the expression of the reality of divine action, already inherent in the symbol performed. Thus 4:1–3 depicts a portrayal of siege: the symbol and its interpretation are closely interwoven. In 4:9–17 a more elaborate rationing of food is presented as a sign of the coming siege with its scarcity of food; this theme has been extended with a theme of uncleanness, which links it to the conditions of deportation. In 5:1–4 the virtually total destruction of the people of Jerusalem is depicted in terms of the dividing and destruction of the prophet's hair: it appears to be elaborated first with a remnant theme (5:3), but even this remnant is reduced by fire (v. 4); the following verses elaborate this theme in a passage that also comments on siege

conditions (5:5–12), and this in its turn is followed by a more general exposition of disaster (5:13–17).

Within this whole section, and also in part commented on within it, is a symbolic action portraying the length of punishment for Israel and Judah (4:4–6, with a sequel in vv. 7–8, perhaps a comment on 4:1–3), which shows the prophet bound for a period of days symbolic of the length of the disaster. There is a relationship here between symbols and prophecies of siege and exile, with the possibility that the concept of their duration has been extended to comment on subsequent ideas of exile as a condition from which release belongs not to the end of Babylonian rule but to some more remote future (cf. Daniel 9 for one exposition of this theme, found also in other later writings).

Chapters 6–7 may, with a separate inception in 6:1f., be a distinct unit, perhaps centered on the proclamation of the end in 7:1–3, elaborated in 7:5–9 and 10–13 (possibly linked to the prophecy of "end" in Amos 8:1–3). A series of oracles on doom and disaster takes up the theme of scattering, of idolatry, of wrath and the sword, of the city and its rulers, partly linked to what precedes and also, in a number of details, linking with fuller material subsequently in the book.

The collections in chapters 12–19 and 20–24 are in some respects much looser, but within them we may find the development of the same or similar themes. In two sections—16 and 23—there is more elaborate presentation of the people's past, in the first in terms of the unfaithful wife (cf. Hosea and Jeremiah), in the second in the story of two sisters who symbolize Israel and Judah (cf. Jer 3:6–14). In both cases, there are indications that the long homiletic expositions have been elaborated to bring out more details of the interpretation. In some respects the material is close to earlier prophecy; but the greater detail of interpretation distinguishes Ezekiel, though we may note parallels with Jeremiah, where exposition is also often to be observed (e.g., Jer 7–8). The overall picture is of total judgment on kings and people; false prophecy (13), idolatry (14), the failure of kings and princes (17, 19), the inevitability of judgment (21) on city and people (22), lead on to the actual doom and the drawing together of the death of the prophet's wife and the loss of the city (24). Chapters 20–24 begin with a review of Israel's history and an interpretation that expresses both the absoluteness of failure, religious and moral, and the assurance of reentry to the land because God is God: "And you shall know that I am Yahweh, when I bring you into the land . . . " (20:42). The section ends with the death of Ezekiel's wife and the acceptance of doom, the prophet himself a sign, and "they will know that I am the LORD" (24:27).

The foreign-nation oracle section in chapters 25–32 is notable for its poetry and for exposition, to be found in the two main sections (26–28) on Tyre, in which a long poem on the city as a merchant ship is interleaved with explanatory comment, and the glory of Tyre, embodied in its king, is depicted in language that utilizes the Eden theme (*cf.* Gen 2–3) and shows variant forms of that story; 29–32, on Egypt, also employs poetry and prose, both to bring out the nature of judgment on Egypt at the hand of Babylon and also (in 29:17–20) to set forth the despoiling of Egypt as recompense for the labor of the siege of Tyre. The judgment of the nations is, in these chapters, closely related to the gathering of Israel and the acknowledgment that "I am Yahweh their God" (e.g., 28:24, 26; 29:16, 21, and so frequently). This explicit purpose of judgment and restoration is echoed in the final verses of the overthrow of Gog in 38–39 (see 39:25–29), so that although that elaborate section appears to draw together the theme of the nations in a climax of assault and judgment, it also serves to draw together the themes of judgment and restoration and provides a point of attachment for the final chapters of the book.

The two restoration sections, 33–37 and 40–48, differ sharply from one another. The former echoes many of the themes of the first half of the book—watchman, responsibility, judgment on rulers and on the mountains; it also picks up themes of hope, especially in its final sections, which show the restoration of the community to life and to ideal rule.

THEMES OF EZEKIEL'S PROPHECY

Responsibility

The theme of responsibility has been one of the major areas of discussion in regard to the contribution of Ezekiel and the Book of Ezekiel to the development of Old Testament thought. The question most often raised has been that of the relation between individual and corporate responsibility, since Israel had a strong sense of corporateness. This can be seen in narratives that stressed ways in which the whole community or a particular family group bore responsibility for the failure of individual members. Thus the story of the sin of Achan (Josh 7), in which his whole family and possessions had to be destroyed, appeared to suggest both a certain contagiousness of sin and a unity of the family in responsibility; the story of Jonathan's infringement of an oath laid upon the whole people by Saul (1 Sam 14) showed how disastrous could be the consequences for the whole people of one man's failure. Yet in each case it is clear that, while the result of an individual's failure could be felt as far-reaching, the removal of the culprit was central to the action taken to remedy the situation. Psalms such as 15 and 24, laying stress on declarations of innocence, may be understood to mean that each member of the community recognized such responsibility; and indeed the whole legal system rested on the assumption that it was the guilty who should be identified and punished. Where a criminal was undiscoverable, action had to be taken by the community (Deut 21:1–9) to purge the guilt in the absence of the individual responsible. In such thinking the recognition of responsibility was combined with the awareness that the consequences of failure, of whatever kind, can be felt by the community.

One consequence of the stress on corporate responsibility was to see in certain Old Testament passages, and most clearly in Ezekiel 18, a development from that concept to one of individual responsibility. While, clearly, different understandings of human behavior may be found in various parts of the Old Testament, such an emphasis, resulting from a failure to appreciate the particular concerns of Ezekiel, led to an artificial dividing of periods.

It is helpful, in attempting to understand the thought of Ezekiel, to avoid isolating any single passage. Whether it is possible to indicate some material as belonging to the prophet and other material as belonging to disciples or successors, interpreters of his message for new situations, we may nevertheless link together the different elements in the book and appreciate its whole impact. Particular note may be taken of the "watchman" passages in chapters 3 and 33. There we may see Ezekiel's own appreciation of his task, or perhaps in some measure his successors' understanding of how he saw it, and recognize the stress that is laid on responsibility. In these passages, we see what is laid on the prophet: the duty of warning the wicked of the consequences of his wickedness. The wicked is himself held responsible; but failure to give due warning of the consequences of wicked actions brings responsibility also on the prophet. An intimate relationship is expressed between the prophet's response to the divine injunctions laid upon him and his own sense of responsibility for those to whom he is sent. It is out of his own consciousness of divine demand that he comes to take upon himself the consequences of his carrying out or failing to carry out this demand.

Scholars have described this sense of responsibility in terms of "pastoral" concern. While it may be unsatisfactory to use terms belonging to another context, pastoral concern does describe an aspect of prophecy that is to be found elsewhere—an intimate relationship between the prophet and the community that he addresses. This intimacy shows itself in the agonized expressions of inner anguish of Micah (Mic 1:8f.) and in the "confessions" of Jeremiah (e.g., Jer 20:7–18). My concern lies not in attempting to discuss the full significance of such passages or their possible or probable source, but in considering how they illustrate the reality of prophetic personalities that are never detached from, or narrowly antagonistic to, those whom they address (as in Jesus' weeping over Jerusalem, e.g., in Luke 19:41). It is easy to form the impression that the prophets were simply passing judgment on their contemporaries—which they were —and not to appreciate the strong sense of involvement that they had (see also the description of Moses in Exodus 32:32 and Amos' appeals for clemency in Amos 7:2, 5).

The full nature of the thought in Ezekiel 18 is likely to be concealed by the use of legal formulas for its presentation ("if a man . . ."), and also by the whole presentation in the form of a hypothetical example of a family succession that offers a vivid actualization but in fact uses an instructive technique such as we may find in Old Testament wisdom (cf. Job 4:7–11, Ps 37:25). The pictures conceal an urgent concern.

Disaster and Hope

The dominant impression of the Book of Ezekiel is inevitably that of judgment: the first part of the book is concentrated there, and so too are the foreign-nation oracles. Hopes for the future do appear in some passages, and, though these do not reverse the general impression, they do underline that hope emerges beyond the immediacy of judgment and that the future is impossible without the present. In the later chapters, where promise is evident, it is itself qualified with words of warning; and while the vision of the future land and Temple offers assurance, it does so within material that frequently stresses the preservation of holiness, with its implication that the possibility of disaster is not really so far away. From whatever date individual passages may come, the whole is dominated by the experience and the interpretation of the destruction of city and Temple in the sixth century B.C.E. and the consequent loss of monarchy and of other aspects of political and religious organization. The messages of hope stand out against this background, seen both as it immediately affected the community and as it was reflected on as having continuing significance for the community in later and other experiences. At no point is this relationship between hope and disaster minimized, so that words of promise are never superficial alleviations of disaster.

Basic to the book is the use of phrases underlining the reality and nature of God. In one form or another, expressions such as "because of my name" and "you shall know that I am Yahweh" act almost like punctuation marks in the text. (Compare the similar use in Leviticus 17–26.) Promise and hope, so it is frequently emphasized, rest in the reality of God. The motif of the name, that is, the nature or person, of God is fully developed (cf. Ezek 20:44). Ezekiel in this relates closely both to the emphases of Deuteronomy and the Deuteronomistic writings, and to the Holiness Code (cf. e.g., Deut 12:5ff.,

Lev 18:5). Relationships may also be traced with Jeremiah (*cf.* Jer 7:10, 14) and the Book of Isaiah (Isa 43:7, and elsewhere in 40ff.). It is because God is God, and for no other reason, that he acts to restore.

The Temple and Land of the Future (Chapters 40–48)

The content of these chapters covers the vision and the fulfillment of the vision of a new Temple, city, and land. It is described first in terms of a vision of the new city, its detail set out by the device of a heavenly being—"a man, whose appearance was like bronze, with a line of flax and a measuring reed in his hand" (40:3). The description of the actions of this man (for the theme, *cf.* Zech 1:16 and 2:1–5) enables the detail of a restored Temple to be set out—courtyards, gates, inner court, rooms for the priests. Its detail is measured—the sizes of the courts and the gateways, and the inner shrine, the thickness of the walls. In addition, precise description is given of carvings, doorposts, and doors. This is to be seen not as a mere building design but as a vision of what the Temple ought to be; it is closely related to what had preceded in the monarchical period but is not simply bound by it (40–42).

With 43:1–5, the glory, which had been seen in the vision of chapter 1 and echoed at the end of chapters 10 and 11 as departed from the Jerusalem Temple and appearing in Babylonia "by the river Chebar," is identified as returning through the east gate and filling the Temple. The full purification and restoration of the Temple is ordered in response to the divine intention to dwell in the midst of Israel forever (43:6–9). The detail of the building, seen in a vision, is now to be laid out for the people by the prophet. So it is set out still further by the prophet as the agent of God's ordaining of altar, sacrifices, purity of worship, and true priesthood (43–44).

With the completion of the shrine is set forth the allocation of the land, first that which is for God and next that for the priesthood to live in, their support coming not from possession of the land but from the offerings and first fruits (44:27–45:5). An allocation for the city follows (45:6) and that for the prince

(45:7ff.). It is followed by a detailed exhortation to right conduct by princes and people, and precise indications of the offerings to be made, the observance of the Sabbath, and, within these provisions, note of the special responsibility of the prince (45:8–46:24).

The picture, then, is of a marvelous river flowing out from the Temple, a river that becomes deeper as it moves toward the south; eventually it flows into the stagnant waters of the Dead Sea, bringing life to it, while leaving the marshes for salt. The banks of the river are lined with trees that provide both food and leaves for healing (47:1–12). The whole land is to be reallocated (*cf.* Josh 13–19), the detailed boundaries for the tribes set out in due order, but now based on an idealized view of the land (Ezek 47:13–23, 48:1–7). Further indications are given of the allocation of priestly lands, of the city area, and of the lands of the prince (48:8–22); and this is followed by the allocations to the remaining tribes (48:23–29). The gates and the measurements of the city lead on to its being renamed "The LORD is there" (*Yahweh shammah,* 48:35), as an expression of its true nature.

Opinions about this section of the book vary widely. The natural first approach is to see it as a later supplement to the prophet's own message (40:1, "twenty-fifth year"); whether it is attributable to Ezekiel himself or to a "disciple" is a further point to be resolved. One line of argument here has been to claim that certain elements in the Temple description show precise knowledge of the preexilic building, and that the description must therefore lie within the living memory of that earlier building and must in any case precede the rebuilding associated with the restoration of the community under the first Persian rulers (*cf.* Ezra 1–6). The lack of any reference to or use of the material of these chapters is held to argue for their offering an idealized picture that could not be utilized in the real situation of the years of restoration.

There is clearly strength in this view, though the arguments are by no means conclusive. We may observe that the author of the Books of Chronicles was able to utilize the description found in Kings of the preexilic Temple; it is not unnatural to suppose that a strong tradition about that building or knowledge of architectural style persisted into the later period. But it is more difficult to account for the lack of any precise reference back to these chapters, even though it may be claimed that the outlook of the prophets Haggai and Zechariah places them in the line of Ezekiel. More difficult is the presence in chapters 40–48 of material dealing with the position of the prince. It is evident that this material offers an implicit critique of the status of the earlier kings, in that although the part played by the rulers in support of Temple worship is plainly recognized and becomes an important part in the portrayal of the future Temple's organization, there is little support for their role in the earlier part of the book. Here we find harsh criticism of the kings (e.g., in 17; compare also the passages dealing with the "shepherds" in 34), combined with some indications of a hope of restoration of the Davidic line (in 17:22–24; and in the explicit promises of 34:20–24; 37:22, 24f.). But Davidic promise is absent from the final chapters of the book; the "prince" of those chapters is never Davidic, and though attempts have been made at reconciling these two hopes for the future, it is difficult to believe that chapters 40–48 saw anything but a non-Davidic future, with the prince carefully restricted religiously even if enjoying something of the status of the former Davidic rulers.

It is to be noted, too, that 40–48 are not all of a piece; elaborations, for example in 45–46, suggest a longer process of formation for the material, even if its origins go back to the time of Ezekiel himself or at least to that of his immediate successors. As it now stands, the section needs to be considered in relation to later possible situations.

There is little to provide indications of date, but there are clues to the context of thought found here. Arguments about the dating of the material in the Priestly sections of the Pentateuch remain. There have been numerous attempts to prove an earlier date for these than has normally been accepted; and certainly considerable evidence suggests that, whatever the final date, much incorporated here is of earlier origin. Insofar as the material of those Priestly sections—particularly the tabernacle descriptions in Exodus 25–30 and 35–40, and the large collections of laws in Leviticus and Numbers—draws together older traditions and laws, we may legitimately ask for what purpose this was done. Part of the answer may be that the collecting of older material and its prominent setting in the wilderness context, associated with Moses as national and cultic founder and thereby given authority, was a critique of the contemporary situation. This could involve critique of the preexilic cult in the Temple in the later years of the Judean kingdom, and hence the Priestly material could stand side by side with the Deuteronomistic critique; or, from a somewhat later standpoint, it could involve a critique of that earlier period, with a pointer to the necessity for an adequate refoundation of cult and people after the disruption of the Babylonian period; or it could belong later still as critique of the postexilic Temple and religious setup.

In that later period, we find the author of the Books of Chronicles offering in 2 Chronicles 1–9 very nearly a repeat of the description of the first Temple building under Solomon in 1 Kings, after having already, by the account of David's reign, shown David as the true founder or refounder of Temple worship, thus effectively making of monarchy the upholder of the religious tradition. In each of these, there may be an attempt at arguing for the continuity of the postexilic worship and belief with that of the preexilic Temple, as well as a critique, expressed in terms of what the later Temple and its religious life ought to be. Whether or not the tabernacle traditions go back to an early period, their presentation at such impressively duplicated length in Exodus 25–30 and 35–40 implies both what is and what ought to be.

The significance of the presentation in Ezekiel 40–48 becomes clearer when we consider later material of a comparable kind. The so-called Temple Scroll from the Dead Sea area contains material that points to later speculation about the nature of the Temple, and expresses, in the form of injunctions given in the past to Moses, both a critique of existing cult practices and hope for a future and properly constituted building and contents. This scroll, for which there is evidence of several copies, and which can probably be traced back to the later second century B.C.E., is still very much under discussion. It may be questioned whether "Temple Scroll" is the most appropriate title;

Yigael Yadin, in his more popular account of the scroll, its findings and its contents, gives as a subtitle "The Hidden Law of the Dead Sea Sect," and others have argued for its being a "Law Scroll" rather than the narrow "Temple Scroll." It provides, in first-person form, a divine speech designed to be set after Exodus 34, including a revelation of the Temple building as its main theme, but including other and wider sections of legal material. This provides links with *Enoch* (90), with *Jubilees* (1:29, 32:23, possibly dependent on *Enoch*, and connected with the story of Jacob at Bethel in Genesis 28), and also with Revelation 21. In the details of the furnishings, there are many links with Exodus 25–27 and 36–38.

A full discussion of the topic does not belong here, but it is now possible to place Ezekiel 40–48 in a broader context and to see the significance of those chapters in relation to this wider literature. Whatever the precise relationship between the various allusions to or descriptions of an ideal Temple, divinely ordained or divinely built, it is clear that these chapters are one example of a particular genre. The significance of such a genre lies in its twofold quality as critique of existing institutions and exposition of ideal replacements. As such, the material belongs in the context of postexilic and postbiblical thought concerning the nature of the Temple and land. It expresses the need to understand the concept of continuity from the first Temple to the later one and offers hope for a better future in the prospect of a replacement, whether divinely provided (explicitly in Rev 21) or humanly built. With regard to any one example of the genre of Temple literature, it is possible to argue as to whether we are to think of a proposed actual building or to have a heavenly or eschatological concept: the lines between the two approaches are difficult to define. The whole genre would seem to belong in that area of thought which looks critically at the contemporary situation and believes in a better reality.

Such a mindset is related to ancient beliefs in the divine provision of a building as temple—expressed in the concept of a primeval Eden, the garden of God that is the deity's own dwelling or pleasance (Gen 2; *cf.* Ezek 28). It is expressed in the statements about the provision of a pattern or plan for temple-building

in Exodus 25. (Such a plan is shown as provided for Gudea of Lagash in *Ancient Near East in Pictures*, pl. 430f., 749, and notes to pl. 749 on p. 338). The attitudes expressed here are like that of Moses in regard to the tabernacle, or of David in regard to the prospect of a rebuilt Temple after the exile (1 Chron 28:11). In the Ezekiel chapters, such a picture of rebuilding is incorporated within the concept of a newly occupied and allocated land, and the connections between land and Temple are close. We may compare the ideas of Zechariah 14, as well as those which are associated with the occupation and allocation of Canaan by Israel (*cf.* Josh 13–19, Deut 12, the tabernacle in Exodus, and that same tabernacle in Num 1–2 at the center of the precisely arranged tribes on the march).

Wherever, on the grounds of the detailed consideration of the text, we place chapters 40–48 in relation to the remainder of the book, these points remain valid, and offer an aspect of critique and hope in the Judean community of the years of Babylonian, Persian, or later foreign rule.

EZEKIEL IN PERSPECTIVE

The Book of Ezekiel is not easy reading. The flow of some of the poetic passages does make them stand out—for example chapter 19, the main parts of 27 and 28, and the strongly rhythmic opening of 37. In most instances, however, the forcefulness of the oracles is undermined by expositions that are repetitive and often loaded with technical legal language. In addition, the commonly held supposition that prophets are better and more interesting than priests has tended to undervalue Ezekiel, whose priestly status overshadows the book and has made him suspect in some circles of interpretation. In part this is the result of the weight of interpretative and homiletic material in the book. In part it is the lack of elements that strike a sympathetic response in the reader, except for the brief use of the theme of his wife's death, the loss of "the delight of your eyes" (24:16); but even her death, accompanied by the command not to mourn, has sometimes made him seem insensitive. Yet under the cover of such language and of the harshness of much that is attributed to him, there appears the figure of one who, living through the sixth-century disaster to Jerusalem and Judah, stands out as an interpreter of doom and as a proclaimer of a hope that centers on the reality and holiness of God.

We need to think ourselves both into the world of his experience and into the strangeness of the language. We need also to recognize the significance of the indications of later interpretation, found both in the book and beyond it. If, as has been suggested, much is here that shows the relevance of the prophetic tradition about Ezekiel to the circumstances of later experience, the importance of Ezekiel as interpreter of disaster and hope can be seen to speak to many generations. Insofar as the Babylonian exile became a symbol of disaster and restoration, Ezekiel must occupy a preeminent place as its interpreter.

Among other aspects of later appreciation must rank two that are of primary importance. One is the way in which the imagery of restoration, and in particular of resurrection, in chapter 37 appears in later thought and especially in art: of this, the supreme example is given by the paintings in the Dura Europos synagogue on the Euphrates in Syria (third century C.E.). The other is the significance of the "flying throne" vision of chapter 1 in the development of *merkavah* (chariot) mysticism. That opening chapter is treated with caution in some later Jewish writings: the holiness of its content, which led to its use in mystical writings, also marked its danger if read without care. It is possible that in part the very growth of mystical interpretation suggested the desirability of its restriction in use. The influence of Ezekiel may also be seen substantially in later apocalyptic writings, not simply as a result of the interpretation in new contexts of biblical prophecies but also because the many obscure elements in oracles and allegories led easily to their use as one component in the development of the much more elaborate visions and allegories of later writings.

It is important that Ezekiel be appreciated both for the range of ideas to be found in the book and for the place that the book occupied in the developing self-understanding of the Jewish community as well as that of the Christian community that grew out of it. Not least, interpretation of the events of the sixth century B.C.E., with their radical effect upon the history of subsequent years, is impossible without taking full account of this endeavor to understand the nature and meaning of disaster. The experience of disaster, of whatever kind, had to be so understood as to be seen to belong in the overall picture of the nature of divine rule and the consequences of divine demand. The fact that these problems are perennial makes the Book of Ezekiel, however strange it may appear to us, a significant part of contemporary understanding of religious experience and an important aspect of literary expression.

Bibliography

Commentaries

Carley, Keith W. *The Book of the Prophet Ezekiel.* New York, 1974.
Cody, Aelred. *Ezekiel, with an Excursus on Old Testament Priesthood.* Wilmington, Del., 1984.
Cooke, George A. *A Critical and Exegetical Commentary on the Book of Ezekiel.* Edinburgh, 1936.
Eichrodt, Walther. *Ezekiel.* Translated by Cosslett Quin. Philadelphia, 1970.
Greenberg, Moshe. *Ezekiel 1–20.* Anchor Bible, vol. 22. New York, 1983.
Wevers, John W. *Ezekiel.* New Century Bible Commentary. Grand Rapids, 1982.
Zimmerli, Walther. *Ezekiel: A Commentary.* Vol. 1. Translated by Ronald E. Clements, edited by Frank Moore Cross and Klaus Baltzer. Vol. 2. Translated by James P. Martin, edited by Paul D. Har and Leonard Jay Greenspoon. Philadelphia, 1979–1983.

Special and General Studies

Boadt, Lawrence. *Ezekiel's Oracles Against Egypt: A Literary and Philological Study of Ezekiel 29–32.* Biblica et Orientalia, 37. Rome, 1980.
Carley, Keith W. *Ezekiel Among the Prophets.* Naperville, Ill., 1975.
Joyce, Paul. *Divine Initiative and Human Response in Ezekiel.* Journal for the Study of the Old Testament Supplements, 50. Sheffield, England, 1989.
Lust, J., ed. *Ezekiel and His Book: Textual and Literary Criticism and Their Interrelation.* Leuven, 1986.
Zimmerli, Walther. *Ezechiel: Gestalt und Botschaft.* Biblische Studien, 62. Neukirchen-Vluyn, 1972.

The Temple Scrolls

Maier, Johann. *The Temple Scroll: An Introduction, Translation, and Commentary.* Translated by Richard T.

White. Sheffield, England, 1985. The translation takes account of more recent works than the original German of 1978.

Schürer, Emil. *The History of the Jewish People in the Age of Jesus Christ (175 B.C.–A.D. 135)*. Translated by T. A. Burkill et al.; revised and edited by Géza Vermès and Fergus Miller. Vol. 3. Edinburgh, 1986. Pp. 406–420.

Yadin, Yigael, ed. *The Temple Scroll*. 3 vols in 4. Jerusalem, 1983.

———. *The Temple Scroll: The Hidden Law of the Dead Sea Sect*. New York, 1985.

Dura Europos

Du Mesnil du Buisson, Robert. *Les peintures de la synagogue de Doura-Europos*. Rome, 1939.

Goodenough, Erwin Ramswell. *Jewish Symbolism in the Greco-Roman Period*. Vol. 1. New York, 1953. Pp. 246–248.

Riesenfeld, Harald. *The Resurrection in Ezekiel 37 and in the Dura-Europos Paintings*. Uppsala, 1948.

Sukenik, Eleazar Lipa. *The Ancient Synagogue of Beth Alpha*. London, 1932.

Merkavah Mysticism

Scholem, Gershom. *Jewish Gnosticism, Merkavah Mysticism, and Talmudic Tradition*. 2d ed. New York, 1965.

———. "Merkabah Mysticism (Ma'aseh merkavah)." In *Encyclopaedia Judaica*, vol. 11. Jerusalem, 1971.

Essays on Related Subjects

Bickerman, Elias Joseph. *The God of the Maccabees*. Translated by Horst B. Moehring. Leiden, 1979.

Collins, John J., ed. *Apocalypse: The Morphology of a Genre*. Missoula, 1979.

Hanson, Paul D. *The Dawn of Apocalyptic*. Philadelphia, 1975.

Hellholm, David, ed. *Apocalypticism in the Mediterranean World and the Near East. Proceedings of the International Colloquium on Apocalypticism, Uppsala, 12–17 August 1979*. Tübingen, 1983.

Koch, Klaus. *The Rediscovery of Apocalyptic*. Naperville, Ill., 1972.

Moore, Carey A. *Daniel, Esther, and Jeremiah: The Additions*. Anchor Bible, vol. 44. Garden City, N.Y., 1977.

Plöger, Otto. *Theocracy and Eschatology*. Translated by S. Rudman. Richmond, Va., 1968.

Pritchard, James B., ed. *Ancient Near Eastern Texts Relating to the Old Testament*. 3d ed. Princeton, 1969.

Tcherikover, Avigdor. *Hellenistic Civilization and the Jews*. 1930. Translated by S. Applebaum. Philadelphia, 1959.

Vermès, Géza. *The Dead Sea Scrolls in English*. 2d ed. Harmondsworth, 1975.

PETER R. ACKROYD

Daniel and Additions to Daniel

THE STORY OF DANIEL

THE BOOK OF Daniel opens with a collection of six stories (chaps. 1–6) told in the third person about the Jewish wise man and visionary Daniel and his three young Jewish friends Hananiah, Mishael, and Azariah (better known by their Babylonian names, Shadrach, Meshach, and Abednego; see Dan 1:7). It concludes with a collection of three dream visions concerning the culmination of human history (chaps. 7–8, 10–12) and a great prose prayer accompanied by an angelic response (chap. 9), all recounted by Daniel himself.

The Hero

The Book of Daniel tells us that its hero was brought to Babylon by order of King Nebuchadrezzar sometime after the first Babylonian capture of Jerusalem in 597 B.C.E., along with other noble "youths without blemish, handsome and skilful in all wisdom, endowed with knowledge, understanding learning, and competent to serve in the king's palace" (Dan 1:4; RSV). We are also told that "Daniel had understanding in all visions and dreams" (1:17), a competence that soon led to his establishment as "ruler over the whole province of Babylon, and chief prefect over all the wise men of Babylon" (2:48), as "the third ruler in the kingdom" (5:29), and even as one of the

three presidents of the kingdom of Darius the Mede (6:2). His piety and steadfast loyalty to the God of Israel got him both into and out of trouble with his foreign masters; his status as "greatly beloved" by God (9:23) opened the way for dream visions and angelic interpretations of history that laid bare both its scope and its meaning (chaps. 7–12). His career as a Babylonian civil servant and Jewish seer spanned sixty or seventy years (taking the figure given in 1:21 together with the outside dates of 606 [Dan 1:1] and 535 [Dan 10:1]).

Ancient Israel knew more about Daniel, however, than the author(s) of the Book of Daniel revealed. The hero of the Book of Daniel is probably the same Daniel who in Ezekiel 14:14 and 14:20 is listed along with two ancient non-Israelite worthies—Noah and Job—as preeminent in righteousness. (The inclusion of the name of Daniel in a list of gentile heroes suggests that he too may have originated outside of the Old Testament tradition.) In Ezekiel 28:3 his name is raised once again in connection with a foreign figure, the king of Tyre, whose great wisdom could be described in no better way than by comparison with Daniel's: "You are indeed wiser than Daniel;/no secret is hidden from you."

Although these earlier allusions to an ancient figure stress Daniel's righteousness and wisdom, neither points to his skill as a judge. Since the very name Daniel means "'El [God] is my judge" or 'El is a judge," the lack of association with the function of judgment might seem unusual. However, this competence is in fact identified with another ancient Daniel figure known outside the Old Testament in the Canaanite texts from Ugarit (Ras Shamra in modern Syria), which date from the fourteenth century B.C.E. In *The Tale of Aqht* we hear of a king named Dnil who is almost Solomon-like in his fame as a wise judge: "He judges the cause of the widow,/And tries the case of the orphan" (2 Aqht 5:7–8).

These bits of evidence, coupled with the enlarged Daniel tradition preserved in apocryphal texts and the Greek Bible (see "The Larger Tradition: Additions to the Book of Daniel," below), suggest that stories about a righteous, wise, and powerful hero of the past named Daniel were current in the environment in which the canonical Book of Daniel was written and that the author(s) of the biblical book selectively determined which of the memories of Daniel should be preserved. Undoubtedly theological interests—about which more will be said below—guided the author(s) in that selection.

The Hero's Deeds

The first half of Daniel can be described as the outer history, or public career, of the hero and his friends. Recently characterized as "court tales of contest" and of "conflict" (Humphreys 1973), these are "saints' tales," hagiographies, which glorify the scrupulous steadfastness, piety, and wisdom of Daniel and his friends. In a general way they can be compared to the wisdom literature of the Old Testament, for they put into narrative form the etiquette and professional ethics that wisdom teachers such as the writer of Proverbs 1–9 sought to inculcate in young men of the prominent families of Jerusalem. These six stories may also be compared to the other tales told by the sages about righteous men and women who, through trust in God and unswerving allegiance to God's sovereignty, were able to survive in the face of overwhelming opposition and to glorify God by their piety. In the process, they experienced upward social mobility because of their extraordinary virtues. The only other canonical example is the Book of Esther, but the apocryphal stories of Judith and Tobit, the tale of the three young courtiers of 1 Esdras 3–4, and the beloved international tale of Ahiqar (see Pritchard

1969, 427–430) fully demonstrate the genre. Clearly, Daniel 1–6 and the extracanonical lore of the Daniel cycle belong to this tradition.

The Daniel of the second chapter of the book is rather obviously presented as a new Joseph; he and his friends, like Joseph of old, are ideal courtiers who possess the skills of administration, dream interpretation, and all-purpose wisdom that make them suitable for high rank in the court of the foreign king. The Daniel cycle, like the other narratives before it, deals with the problem of theodicy. The stories exhibit an international and intercultural perspective, and display human beings making decisions in mature and responsible ways. All of these themes are at home in the sapiental tradition of Israel.

Chapter 1 of Daniel is set in the school of wisdom of the royal court of Babylon. Here young captives from Judah are being taught "the letters and language of the Chaldeans" (1:4). In this environment, Daniel and his three friends elect not to eat the rich food and wine that the king has assigned them as a daily portion, but rather to eat nothing but vegetables and to drink nothing but water. In spite of the misgivings of the steward who brings them their food, and who, together with his supervisor, the chief of the king's eunuchs, fears that these lads who are supposed to be fattened up and trained will not fare well on such a diet, the test is carried out. After ten days, the Jewish youths are "better in appearance and fatter in flesh than all the youths who ate the king's rich food" (1:15). Indeed, the king, who may never have known about the vegetable contest, ultimately finds them "ten times better than all the magicians and enchanters that were in all his kingdom" (1:20). The primary issue of this first story is not the observation of dietary law, for no evidence exists that the writer of the story intended to link the disciplined behavior of the Jewish youths to the fully articulated dietary tradition of later Judaism. Rather, the major issue is the importance of Jewish identity; readers are encouraged to insist on maintaining that identity, even in the most threatening circumstances of a foreign court, in the confidence that God vindicates such loyalty.

The second narrative, contained in Daniel 2, is the famous account of Nebuchadrezzar's dream. In this "court tale of contest," Daniel outdoes not only "the magicians, the enchanters, the sorcerers, and the

Chaldeans" (2:2) who staffed the king's advisory council, but even the most successful of Jewish courtiers, namely Joseph, who served in Pharaoh's court. Nebuchadrezzar does not know the meaning of his dream; in fact, he has forgotten the dream itself. When Daniel is found and brought before him, the young man attributes his knowledge of the dream not to his own sagacity but to "the God in heaven who reveals mysteries" (2:28). (The Aramaic word *razin*, "mysteries," refers to those matters that can be known only by divine revelation and that particularly have to do with the end of history.) The interpretation of the king's dream of a colossal statue with body parts descending in value from the golden head to the iron-and-clay feet has to do with five kingdoms. Daniel makes clear that this sequence of kingdoms, beginning with Nebuchadrezzar's, who is represented by the golden head, culminates when the fourth and weakest kingdom is destroyed by yet a fifth kingdom, presented as a "stone [that] was cut out by no human hand" (2:34), which smashes the entire statue and becomes "a great mountain and fills the whole earth" (2:35). Nebuchadrezzar expresses great gratitude to Daniel and praises Daniel's God as "God of gods and Lord of kings and a revealer of mysteries" (2:47). The devout contemporary readers of old and readers ever since have been left to make what they could of the four kingdoms, though it is common among scholars today to regard them as the Babylonian, Median, Persian, and Hellenistic kingdoms that succeeded each other in Middle Eastern history. The fifth kingdom, the stone cut out by no human hand, is the coming kingdom of God, which at the day of judgment displaces all the others and assumes dominion in an eternal heavenly empire on earth.

The "court tale of conflict" of chapter 3 pits Daniel's three friends, Shadrach, Meshach, and Abednego, against King Nebuchadrezzar's proclamation that every person in his empire should fall down and worship a golden image of himself that he had set up on the plain of Dura in the province of Babylon. When the Jewish lads are accused by certain malicious enemies of refusing to do this, they are hauled before the king and threatened with being cast into a fiery furnace. The king challenges them: "Who is the god that will deliver you out of my hands?" (3:15). The three youths, of course, trust that precisely the God of

Israel will prove to be such a god, but they tell the king that even if their God proves unable to do it (or so 3:17 seems to say), they will not serve the golden image. The three lads walk out of the fire without so much as the smell of smoke on them, and again Nebuchadrezzar promotes them and praises the God who could effect such a great deliverance.

The fourth chapter of Daniel is the story of Nebuchadrezzar's madness. This affliction results from his pride and his failure to recognize "that the Most High rules the kingdom of men, and gives it to whom he will, and sets over it the lowliest of men" (4:17). Though he is warned of this danger in a dream, Nebuchadrezzar still says, "Is not this great Babylon, which I have built by my mighty power as a residence and for the glory of my majesty?" (4:30). The moment he utters these words, a heavenly voice announces the onset of his madness. Forthwith he was "driven from among men, and ate grass like an ox, and his body was wet with the dew of heaven, until his hair grew as long as eagles' feathers, and his nails were like birds' claws" (4:33). Only after he acknowledges the rule and the power of the Most High God, does Nebuchadrezzar's strength return to him. Daniel's role in the story is to interpret the dream and to indicate how Nebuchadrezzar might achieve restoration and tranquillity.

The fifth chapter contains the dramatic story of Belshazzar's feast. This king is not remembered as such in Babylonian records but was perhaps regent in Babylon during the end of the reign of Nabonidus, the last and slightly mad monarch of that empire. Belshazzar throws a feast for a thousand of his lords, together with assorted wives and concubines. He has the wine served in the gold and silver vessels that Nebuchadrezzar had stolen from the Temple in Jerusalem. In the midst of the feast, a ghostly hand appears and writes the words *mene, mene, tekel,* and *parsin* on the wall. No one can understand the mysterious text until Daniel is brought into the hall. He is promised a great reward and a high place in the kingdom if he can interpret the message, and he readily does so. He understands the four mysterious words neither as weights nor as coins (as they have often subsequently been understood) but rather as verbs. Their meaning: God had *numbered* the days of Belshazzar's kingdom, had *weighed* him in the balance and found him wanting, and had *divided* his kingdom between the

Medes and the Persians. "That very night," says the text, "Belshazzar the Chaldean king was slain" (5:30).

The first half of the Book of Daniel closes with the famous account of Daniel in the lions' den. Once again Daniel refuses to compromise his faith in the God of Israel. He deliberately violates an edict that King Darius "the Mede" (a personage not actually attested in history, though perhaps to be identified with the Persian king Darius I, 522–486) had been persuaded by certain jealous satraps and counselors to issue. This proclamation forbade "petition to any god or man" except Darius; naturally, it led to Daniel's arrest and condemnation to death by lions. The king—like Pilate in a later generation—was much distressed at this outcome. For his part, Daniel—like Pilate's victim, according to the memory of the early Christians—rose again from the pit of death with no hurt upon him, leading Darius, like Nebuchadrezzar before him, to praise the God of Daniel: "He delivers and rescues,/he works signs and wonders/in heaven and on earth,/he who has saved Daniel/from the power of the lions" (6:27).

These first six stories of the book, set in the context of the Jewish Mesopotamian Diaspora, show a pious, powerful, and faithful Daniel who could be taken by generations of Jews and Christians as the very model of appropriate behavior. It is no surprise that this half of Daniel, rather than the apocalyptic section, has been most frequently honored in painting and in song. Great renditions of these stories in art began in the third century C.E. in the catacombs of Rome and continued through Rubens' masterpiece of Daniel in the lions' den, Rembrandt's unforgettable study of Belshazzar watching the hand as it wrote upon the wall, down to the impressionistic painting of Daniel in the lions' den by the twentieth-century black American painter Henry Ossawa Tanner. It gave rise to musical interpretations ranging from Negro spirituals and the "talkin' blues" operetta of Buryl Red and Grace Hawthorne *It's Cool in the Furnace* (1973) to, at the other extreme, Sir William Walton's 1931 oratorio *Belshazzar's Feast*. And yet in terms of intrinsic theological significance and impact on the history of Jewish and Christian thought, the mature apocalyptic vision of the second half of the book has been more important.

The Hero's Dreams and Visions

The second half of the Book of Daniel can be described as the inner history of the public man. In these chapters (7–12) Daniel recounts his dreams and visions of the end of human history and the culmination of God's righteous purposes. Chapter 7 is a complete vision in itself and in many ways is the center of the entire book. The vision begins with four beasts that rise up out of the sea, each representing a world empire (7:3–17). Using as guides the specific identifications made in comparable historical allegories in the book (see Dan 2:37–38, 8:20–25), most modern commentators understand that the lion with eagles' wings stands for Babylon, the bear with three ribs in its mouth for Media, the leopard with the wings of a bird and four heads for Persia, and the dreadful beast with no name but with iron teeth and ten horns for the Hellenistic empire of Alexander the Great and his successors. Amid the ten horns an eleventh springs up, with the eyes of a man and "a mouth which uttered enormities" (Lacocque 1978, 135). This little horn frequently is taken in modern scholarly literature to represent Antiochus IV Epiphanes, the tyrant of Antioch in Syria. His reign, 175–163 B.C.E., was marked by the inauguration of the first pogrom against the Jews in recorded history and the desecration of the Temple in Jerusalem on 15 Kislev 167. None of that is mentioned here specifically; we only watch as the "little horn" is brought before the Ancient of Days in judgment. In the aftermath of this act of judgment by the heavenly king, who is seated on a fiery throne and surrounded by ten thousand times ten thousand angels, the world empire is taken away from all the others and given to "one like a son of man," who comes "with clouds of heaven" (7:13). To the puzzled Daniel, an angelic interpreter explains that the beasts are world empires and that the one like a son of man is "the saints of the Most High," who shall "receive the kingdom and possess the kingdom for ever, for ever and ever" (7:18).

In the history of Christian interpretation of Daniel, this chapter has been at the very center of the discussion. In every generation interpreters have been convinced that they knew which historical figure was represented by the little horn whose appearance in history ushers in the day of judgment. Very early, perhaps even in the times of the canonizers of Daniel, the fourth beast of chapter 7 had come to be regarded not as the Hellenistic empire of Alexander (which had faded from the Jewish scene by 63 B.C.E. with the arrival of the Roman general Pompey in Palestine) but as Rome itself. That identification is quite obvious in the transformation of Daniel 7 in Revelation 13. If the fourth beast is Rome and the Roman empire can be said to have endured even beyond the sack of Rome and the deposition of the last of the Western emperors in the fifth century C.E., then it could be argued that the seer had in mind a king arising out of some yet-unknown member of the political progeny of the Roman empire. So it came about that diverse commentators linked the little horn in whose days the final judgment should take place with Charles I, king of England, beheaded in 1649; with his opponent, Oliver Cromwell; with Adolf Hitler; and even with some yet-unknown figure who will arise out of one of the nations of the European Common Market.

A more likely assessment of the allegorical significance of the four beasts and the little horn assumes that the writer was trying to make sense of events under way at the time of writing—perhaps during the latter years of the reign of Antiochus IV Epiphanes, or even specifically in 164. The assumption also explains why Daniel's prophecy of the near approach of the last day goes so wide of the mark. The writer and his audience stand, in fact, at the junction of the known and the unknown. The "prophecy" of the appearance of the four beasts rather nicely parallels the already well-known rise and fall of imperial powers in the Near East from the neo-Babylonian empire down to the second century B.C.E. But prophecy of the imminent end of history (7:26) and the displacement of the succession of human kingdoms by the everlasting rule of the saints of the Most High (7:18) does not match the known facts. It could not do so, because the events of history after 164 had not yet become facts.

Chapter 8 is another apocalyptic vision in which the seer beholds a ram with two horns charging west, north, and south. This beast is displaced by a rampaging one-horned he-goat. His great horn is replaced in time with smaller horns; during the growing period of one of these lesser horns the sanctuary is overthrown, and "the transgression that makes desolate" (8:13) is

perpetrated upon Israel. The angelic interpreter makes clear that the rampaging he-goat out of which the final horn grows is the king of Greece, that is to say, Alexander the Great. This chapter shows continuing interest in the calendar and in the foreordained periods of time in which tribulation, divine intervention, and the restoration of the kingdom to the hands of the saints shall take place. To the burning question of all apocalyptic literature, "For how long . . . ?" comes the answer, "For two thousand and three hundred evenings and mornings; then the sanctuary shall be restored to its rightful state" (8:13–14).

Chapter 9 is largely given over to a lengthy prayer of confession offered by Daniel, expressed in priestly language reminiscent of Nehemiah 9:6–37. Because of the concluding words, "O Lord, hear; O Lord, forgive; O Lord, give heed and act" (Dan 9:19), this prayer has sometimes been called the Old Testament *Kyrie eleison*. The prayer sits rather oddly in its context because the surrounding material deals with Daniel's concern over the meaning of the seventy years of the desolations of Jerusalem, which the prophet Jeremiah had spoken of in Jeremiah 25:11, 12 and 29:10. At the end of the prayer, the angel Gabriel appears and assures Daniel that he has come to bring him wisdom and understanding. He then multiplies the seventy years by seven, creating seventy weeks of years (490 years), and then divides that figure into three periods: seven weeks of years (presumably of Babylonian exile); then sixty-two "weeks" of a rebuilt and yet troubled Jerusalem; then one final "week" of trouble. During the last half of this last "week," "the [one who makes desolate shall come] upon the wing of abominations" (9:27). In the history of Christian interpretation of this chapter, many efforts have been made to link this timetable with known history, often with a view to proving that the present is counting down toward the final period of the time of desolation.

Chapters 10–12 conclude the Book of Daniel with a lengthy apocalypse. After an ecstatic experience of revelation in chapter 10, the prophet is shown a detailed and historically quite accurate, though entirely nameless, picture of Jewish history from the time of the Persian conquest down to the rule of Antiochus IV Epiphanes. The accurate rendition of events ceases at 11:39, and from 11:40 on the prophecies of the ultimate end of Antiochus and the double resurrection of the dead in the context of the last judgment (12:1–2) depart widely from any known history. It is safe to assume, then, that the writer was living exactly at the point reached in 11:39, and was turning in 11:40 toward the future in order to anticipate the end of Antiochus and the full manifestation of divine sovereignty in the world.

The Daniel of these last six chapters is not the beloved figure of the first six chapters, but his words have had an awesome impact on Western religious thought. These chapters constitute the first fully developed apocalypse in the Old Testament tradition and in Jewish lore. This new literary and theological genre of apocalyptic writing had descended from the earlier eschatological visions of the classical prophets. Daniel 7–12 has elaborated and projected onto a vast screen the older prophetic notion of a Day of Yahweh in which Yahweh settles up accounts with the divine enemies and restores the saints to their rightful place. Furthermore, the old themes of divine warfare, destruction of evil, and vindication of good have been touched with the mythic dimensions of new creation. The human community that emerges from the struggle is fundamentally altered because resurrection has taken place (12:2–3); the king of the dominion that is everlasting is reminiscent of a new Adam (7:13–14).

In Christian art and music, this portion of the book has received less direct interpretation than chapters 1–6, partly because it is assimilated to its New Testament counterpart, the Book of Revelation. Michelangelo's great *Last Judgment* in the Sistine Chapel in Rome, for example, shows a heavenly judge seated on a throne. His disposition of good and wicked persons is reminiscent of both Daniel 7:9–10 and Revelation 20:11–15. However, it is also in the Sistine Chapel that Daniel is depicted as a clean-shaven, pensive youth sitting and looking into a great book wherein he undoubtedly is perceiving the meaning of the seventy years of desolation of the prophet Jeremiah.

THE LARGER TRADITION: ADDITIONS TO DANIEL

The Daniel cycle was considerably more extensive than that part of the tradition which is still preserved in the Masoretic text. Since ancient times Jews and Christians have been aware of the additional narratives about Daniel and his friends preserved in the Greek Old Testament. Now, in our own time, hitherto unknown texts related to Daniel have appeared among the scroll fragments from the Dead Sea. Evidently the figure of Daniel inspired the imaginations of Jewish storytellers and writers of the second century B.C.E. and later, no matter what their language and sectarian views might have been.

Daniel in the Greek Bible

Alone of all the books of the Old Testament, Daniel was received by the Western church in the Greek translation traditionally attributed to Theodotion, a Greek-speaking Jew of the second century C.E. Actually the work is as early as the first century B.C.E. Perhaps Hellenistic Jews and early Christians were already baffled by the bizarre visions of Daniel and appreciated this more literal Greek translation (here known as Theod-Dan). The Septuagint text of Daniel (LXX-Dan), perhaps finished at Alexandria around 100 B.C.E., has come down to us in only two early manuscripts. In both Greek versions, however, the Daniel cycle is enlarged with three additions: the story of Susanna, Bel and the Dragon, and the Prayer of Azariah and the Song of the Three Young Men.

About the latter little more need be said than that it is inserted between Daniel 3:23 and 3:24, and that it provides the reader of the Greek Daniel with the text of what the young men said while they "walked about in the midst of the flames." Azariah's prayer is a psalm of communal lament (reminiscent of Psalm 44). It is not the cry of an individual from the crematorium, but rather the cry of a desolate people who have no "prince, or prophet, or leader, . . . no place to make an offering before [God], or to find mercy" (v. 15). The exultant Song of the Three Young Men, built around the thirty-two-fold refrain "Bless the Lord," exhorts all of creation to affirm God the Creator and Preserver. It expands the worshipful and joyous theme of Psalm 148; it is fitting, therefore, that the two parts of the Song, *Benedictus es Domine* (vv. 29–34) and *Benedicite, omnia opera Domine* (vv. 35–68), should stand alongside the great *Te Deum Laudamus* as canticles for morning prayer in the Christian liturgical tradition.

Susanna. Among the many traditions that gathered around the figure of Daniel, the wise Jewish sage of Babylonian exile, none boasts more charm and literary excellence than the story of Susanna and the Elders. This narrative appears as a thirteenth chapter of the Book of Daniel in the Septuagint text and the Latin Vulgate, but in Theodotion's translation, the received Greek text, it serves as a preface to the entire book. Perhaps it was placed there for no other reason than that Daniel is presented as a young lad.

Briefly told, the story first introduces Susanna, the very beautiful daughter of one Hilkiah and the wife of a rich member of the Babylonian Diaspora named Joakim. Because a spacious garden adjoined the latter's house, the community used to gather there, and the two elders appointed as judges would hold court in the same garden. Every afternoon Susanna walked in the garden; such constant exposure to her beauty soon awakened lust in the elders' hearts.

One hot Mesopotamian day Susanna makes up her mind to bathe in the privacy of her garden. But she is not alone. The two esteemed elders suddenly emerge from the shadows of the trees and demand that she lie with them. They even threaten to frame her, if she refuses them, by reporting that a young man was with her. Like Joseph with Potiphar's wife, Susanna finds herself in a dire predicament. However, she does not tarry long; because she is a virtuous woman who prefers the image of corruption to its reality, she calls for the servants.

The next day the elders follow through with their threat before the full assembly, adding perjury to lecherousness by reporting that they had found Susanna embracing a young man in the garden. Needless to say, the people believe them and Susanna is led away to be executed. However, the Lord hears her prayer and arouses "the holy spirit of a young lad named Daniel" (v. 45), who cries with a loud voice, "I am innocent of the blood of this woman."

While the stunned people struggle to make sense of this message, Daniel charges them with inadequate judicial procedures, especially the failure to cross-examine the accusers. Daniel himself then undertakes that examination. His method is simplicity itself. He separates the two elders and asks each one, "Under what tree did you see them being intimate with each other?" (v. 54). One locates the deed under a mastic tree, and the other says it happened under an evergreen oak. Their lies exposed, the two elders are condemned to death, as demanded by the law against bearing false witness (Deut 19:16–21). Susanna lives on to become the paradigm of innocent virtue falsely accused; for his part, "from that day onward Daniel had a great reputation among the people" (v. 64).

The story fits very nicely into the cycle of stories celebrating the wisdom of Daniel. It may have failed to achieve the status of scripture simply because the canonizing community did not have it available in a Hebrew or Aramaic text. It has all the ingredients necessary for an effective human-interest story: a beautiful and virtuous heroine, dirty old villains, a brave and wise hero, and a happy ending. The values of integrity and trust in God that Susanna exemplifies, together with the Solomon-like judiciousness exhibited by Daniel, are in no way to be made light of. In fact, the story conforms nicely to the overarching faith of the Book of Daniel, which holds that God faithfully backs faithfulness and that wickedness will ultimately be brought to its knees.

Bel and the Dragon. The earliest apocryphon on the account of Daniel in the lions' den is the story of Bel and the Dragon (*ca.* third century B.C.E.), which appears in Theodotion's translation as an addition to chapter 12, and in the Septuagint text and the Vulgate follows Susanna as chapter 14. This two-part narrative begins with a conflict between Daniel and the priests of the Babylonian god Bel, who claim that their idol is a living god because he eats the twelve bushels of flour, forty sheep, and six measures of wine offered to him every day. At great personal risk, Daniel challenges this claim. The food is left in the temple overnight, but unbeknownst to the priests of Bel, Daniel strews ashes on the temple floor. In the morning the footprints of the priests, their wives, and their children are found; they admit to taking the food away every night through a secret door. The impostors are then slain by the enraged King Cyrus.

After destroying the idol and its temple, Daniel destroys a great dragon that the Babylonians had also been worshiping. He does so by feeding it cakes made of pitch, fat, and hair, which cause it to bloat and burst. This is too much for the enraged populace, however, and they demand that the king execute the

Jewish courtier. Daniel is thrown into a den with seven lions that are accustomed to receiving a daily ration of two human bodies and two sheep. Sometime during the six days in which Daniel is in the den, an angel of the Lord brings the prophet Habakkuk by the hair of his head from Judaea to Babylon (the reverse of a trip another prophet made; see Ezek 8:3) and has him feed Daniel a meal of pottage and bread. When the king comes to the den on the seventh day to mourn Daniel, he finds him sitting there quite contentedly. Immediately Cyrus cries out, "Thou art great, O Lord God of Daniel, and there is no other besides thee" (v. 41).

Obviously an expansion of the theme of Daniel 6 enriched with folkloristic motifs, the story of Bel and the Dragon was as beloved as the former through the ages of typological and iconographic interpretation. Daniel's act in poisoning the dragon is taken by some medieval interpreters as a type of Constantine's rejection of paganism. The lions' den is of course understood to be hell, and the seven lions are the seven deadly sins. Some even go so far as to interpret Habakkuk's food as signifying the Eucharist and his entry into the den without rolling away the stone (understanding that detail from Daniel 6) as a type of the impregnation of Mary by the Holy Spirit without breaking her hymen. This kind of typology, based upon the mere surface features of the text rather than the theological claims it is making, strikes us as absurd. But this evidence at least illustrates the richness with which the religious imagination could apprehend the situation of a saint coping with life-threatening torture and oppression.

Daniel in the Dead Sea Scrolls

Although they lack the deuterocanonical status enjoyed by the additions to Daniel in the Greek Bible, the four Aramaic pseudo-Daniel fragments found in Cave 4 at Qumran further demonstrate that the cycle of stories about the Jewish wonder-worker Daniel was larger and richer than our canonical text suggests. Of particular interest is the so-called Prayer of Nabonidus, found in 1955, which reads as follows:

> The words of the prayer uttered by Nabunai king of Babylon, [the great] king, [when he was afflicted] with an evil ulcer in Teiman by decree of the [Most High God].

> I was afflicted [with an evil ulcer] for seven years . . . and an exorcist pardoned my sins. He was a Jew from among the [children of the exile of Judah, and he said], "Recount this in writing to [glorify and exalt] the Name of the [Most High God." And I wrote this]:
>
> "I was afflicted with an [evil] ulcer in Teiman [by decree of the Most High God]. For seven years [I] prayed to the gods of silver and gold [bronze and iron], wood and stone and clay, because [I believed] that they were gods."
>
> (Vermès 1975, 229)

The Prayer of Nabonidus has important affinities with Daniel 4. Without entering into the debate about which represents the older version of the tradition, we can simply acknowledge the similarities and differences. A Babylonian king is incapacitated, not to the point of madness, but painfully and for a long term of seven years. Prayers to the idols avail not. (The list of idols made of various materials is nearly identical to the list cited by Daniel against King Belshazzar in Daniel 5:23.) And no wonder, for the suffering, as in the case of Nebuchadrezzar in Daniel 4, is by the decree of the Most High. It takes a Jew from among the exiles in Babylon to cure the king and to command the king to make a written glorification and exaltation of the name of the Most High.

The Prayer of Nabonidus lacks much of the refinement and finesse of the biblical version of the same tradition, perhaps because it is only a fragment. The only justification we are given, for instance, for God's decision to punish the king, is the rather general charge of "sins." The disease is an inflammation or boils, not the full-blown "monomania" (Hartman and Di Lella 1978) or "lycanthropy" (Montgomery 1927) of the canonical king. The Jew is a mere exorcist. The king is cured by him, not by God, through the pardon of his sins. (Others have understood the text to mean that God removed the illness following the king's confession of sin, and that the seer simply gave the meaning of the event, putting it in a letter to the king; see Mertens 1971, 35–36; also Hartman and Di Lella 1978, 178–179.) However, the same essential moral is driven home: the God of Israel, the Most High God, is sovereign in Babylon, too, and it is a wise Babylonian king who will acknowledge that reality.

The most significant variation of this fragmentary Dead Sea narrative from the cognate narrative in Daniel is the fact that the chief character is a different king altogether. Nabunai/Nabonidus (556–539 B.C.E.), the fourth king to succeed Nebuchadrezzar (605–562), has long been known from several sources (especially the "Nabonidus Chronicle"; see the text in Pritchard 1969, 305–307; see also the "Verse Account of Nabonidus," *ibid.*, 312–315) as a kind of derelict or even mad king. When the neo-Babylonian empire was collapsing around his head, he stayed out of the way at the oasis of Tema in Arabia, leaving the regency to his son Bel-shar-usur (the Belshazzar of chap. 5), and refused to function in his role at the New Year's festival in Babylon. Worst of all, it was his fate to be the last king Babylon ever had; he had the doubtful distinction of presiding over the demise of the empire. In short, the story of a royal affliction or even madness fits the historical Nabonidus as well as or better than it does the historical Nebuchadrezzar.

The significance of this blending of identities of two Babylonian monarchs in the Jewish tradition about a mad king healed by the Jewish God is simply this: the time, place, and characters of the story are neither verifiable nor significant data. Though we have no reason to think that the writer of Daniel 4 was consciously writing fiction when he repeated the folk story about the madness of a pagan king, we have very good reason to think that the writer's real point in preserving the story was to teach an important lesson about divine sovereignty. The actual king in question is not really important at all; in the context of the canon, looking forward to the vindication of those of low degree by the sovereign of all the world, he is really a type. This Nebuchadrezzar/Nabonidus stands for every human of power and prestige, those who run the real risk of hubris. Because, according to the story, he learned the lesson and came to a happy ending, he can be presented in a more positive light than the historical Nebuchadrezzar.

ONE BOOK OR TWO?

Few books of the Old Testament have fueled more fires of critical controversy than has the Book of Daniel. Much of the difficulty arises from the radically different character of the two halves of the book. Could the sapiental legends of chapters 1–6 possibly have come from the same hand as did the apocalyptic visions of chapters 7–12? If not, did the two folios emanate from the same historical period? And why was the book written in two languages, yet not with the neat and logical allotment of six chapters to each one?

Language

Daniel shares with the Book of Ezra the distinction of being the only book of the Old Testament of which a substantial portion is written in Aramaic. That language (a northwest Semitic language like Hebrew, though not of the same Canaanite family to which Hebrew belongs) had become the lingua franca of the Assyrian empire perhaps as early as 1000 B.C.E. and achieved its widest use throughout the eastern Mediterranean, Mesopotamia, and Egypt late in the Persian period (538–330). The Aramaic portion of Daniel begins at chapter 2:4a after the sentence that opens with the words "Then the Chaldeans spoke to the king [in] Aramaic." The text then continues in Aramaic through chapter 7. The Aramaic portion of the book thus contains both the tales of the first half of Daniel and some of the apocalyptic visions of the second half.

Efforts to assign the Hebrew and Aramaic portions of Daniel to different authors have proved unsatisfactory, largely because the most logical redactional separation—the tales of chapters 1–6 from the apocalyptic texts of chapters 7–12—won't work with the language distinction. Daniel 1 contains a court tale like the others of chapters 1–6 but is written in a language different from the others, even as the Hebrew chapters 8–12 contain apocalypses very similar to the Aramaic chapter 7. One widely used way of accounting for the bilingual character of the book is to suggest that it was originally written entirely in Aramaic and that some portions were then translated into Hebrew to make it more acceptable to the zealous nationalists of the later Jewish community. While this suggestion is strengthened by the fact that the Hebrew of the book is rife with Aramaisms, it suffers somewhat from the fact that the shifts from Hebrew to Aramaic and back again take place at exactly the same points in the fragments of Daniel from Qumran. Since these fragments must date to a time within a century or a century and a half of the composition of the book and rather well ahead of the period after 70 C.E. in which the final decisions were being made about what writings belonged in the canon, the translation would have to have taken place within only decades of the composition of the book.

Redaction History

Even though no definitive answer has yet been given to the question of why Daniel is written in two languages, the mere fact that it is suggests that the book underwent a process of growth. This suggestion receives considerable additional support from the fact that chapters 1–6 differ in form and spirit so radically from the apocalyptic chapters 7–12. Many commentators have discerned the presence of at least two and often more hands in the growth of the Book of Daniel into its present form. John Gammie (1976), for example, believes that the book underwent three stages of growth. Hartman and Di Lella (1978, 12–14), mostly following Ginsberg (1948, 1954), describe the redaction history of the book as follows: (1) Daniel 1–6 comes together as a cycle of hagiographic stories about the ancient worthy and sage; (2) Daniel 7, with certain exceptions, is appended to the earlier collection as its first apocalypse; (3) Daniel 8, with certain exceptions, is appended as a second apocalypse; (4) Daniel 10:1–12:4 plus 8:18–19 is appended as a third apocalypse; and finally (5) Daniel 9, plus all those verses which use the "little horn" as a symbol of Antiochus IV Epiphanes (7:8, 11a, 20b–22, 24b–25), plus all those verses which deal with angels and with the specification of the time remaining before the end (8:13–14, 16, 26a, 27b; 11:1; 12:5–10, 13), are added to form the final stratum. According to this view, the prayer of Daniel 9:4–19 and the two glosses intended to update the chronological scheme of the time of the end (12:11, 12) were added even after the book had undergone all the previously mentioned stages of development. These redactional strata are discerned by means of correlations within the book between comparable images, chronological notices, and linguistic tags, and also correlations between the book and events of Judean history known from secular sources. Certain clues found within the book indicate that various writers either knew or did not yet know of those secular events.

While such refined efforts at discerning the

stages of growth of Daniel may be less than definitive, it seems safe to assume that the stories about Daniel in chapters 1–6 reflect a Diaspora outlook that is familiar with both the Persian and the Hellenistic environments in which Jews lived during the fifth through third centuries B.C.E. The apocalypses of Daniel 7–12, on the other hand, can be dated rather more precisely to the first third of the second century B.C.E. That being the case, we can assume that the circles that composed the apocalypses in the name of Daniel, the wise judge and prescient seer, had in hand an already extant cycle of Daniel stories to which, for reasons of their own, they appended their apocalyptic visions. Whether it was their intention or not, the effect of combining the two very different types of literature was to give a picture of the kind of "interim ethics" practiced by those observant and Torah-true Jews who looked to the imminent culmination of the divine purpose in history. The result is helpful and surprising. The heroes are anything but quietistic figures who, having lost their grip on any significant role in history, now simply try to keep their noses clean until the great day of judgment arrives. On the contrary, as the stories of chapters 1–6 present them, they are vigorous in defending the cause of their people and observing the commandments of the covenant against idolatry and syncretism.

Date

The question of the date of Daniel has been much debated, particularly in Christian biblical scholarship. Conservative commentators generally have taken as reliable the ostensible setting of the book in the Babylonian exile during the later Babylonian and early Persian monarchies; less conservative commentators, on the other hand, have looked to a date in the second century B.C.E. The latter half of the book, at least, provides enough internal clues to enable us to date it quite successfully if these clues are correlated with the historical information preserved in 1 and 2 Maccabees and in Josephus.

The lengthy apocalypse of Daniel 10–12 provides the best clues. As already noted, the critical tradition now suggests that the writer of the book lived in the period represented by the gap between Daniel 11:39 and 11:40. Up to 11:39, the great review of the political maelstrom of Near Eastern politics portrays historical events quite accurately, from the rise of the Persian empire down to a time somewhat after the desecration of the Temple in 167 B.C.E. That desecration and the accompanying persecution of observant Jews by Antiochus IV Epiphanes are described in 1 Maccabees 1:54–61:

> They erected a desolating sacrilege upon the altar of burnt offering. They also built altars in the surrounding cities of Judah, and burned incense at the doors of the houses and in the streets. The books of the law which they found they tore to pieces and burned with fire. Where the Book of the Covenant was found in the possession of anyone, or if anyone adhered to the law, the decree of the king condemned him to death. . . . According to the decree, they put to death the women who had their children circumcised, and their families and those who circumcised them; and they hung the infants from their mothers' necks.

All of this horror is alluded to very simply in Daniel 11:31, culminating with the prophecy that "they shall set up the abomination that makes desolate" (see also 2 Macc 6:3–6, Dan 8:11–13, 9:26–27, 12:7, 11). It is widely believed that Antiochus installed a Syrian garrison in the Temple area, and that the garrison took over the Temple for its own purposes. Quite naturally the soldiers sacrificed swine on the altar, because the pig was the sacrificial animal in the Canaanite cult to which they adhered.

All such allusions can be substantiated by the text up through verse 39. Beyond that point the events predicted in the apocalyptic vision no longer correspond to the actual sequence of history. For example, the prediction that "the king of the north [Antiochus] shall pitch his palatial tents between the sea and the glorious holy mountain; yet he shall come to his end, with none to help him" (11:45) does not correspond with known events in Antiochus' latter years. Ancient sources such as Polybius (Histories 31.9) report that the king died in Persia while on a campaign there; 1 Maccabees 6:1–16 and 2 Maccabees 9 agree. There is certainly no reason to believe that he died anywhere west of Jerusalem, or that following his death the angel Michael introduced a period of tribulation and the resurrection of the dead, "some to everlasting life, and some to . . . everlasting contempt" (Dan 12:1–3).

All of this suggests, then, that the last portion of

the Book of Daniel was brought into final form late in the reign of Antiochus IV Epiphanes, after he had brought about the desecration of the Temple but before the Maccabean rebels under Judas expelled the Syrian garrison and reconsecrated the Temple on Kislev 164 B.C.E.—the day now celebrated in Jewish tradition as Hanukkah (see 1 Macc 4:36–59; 2 Macc 10:1–9). Had the writer of Daniel known of that great success, surely he would have mentioned it. With the possible exception of minor updating glosses and possibly the prayer of chapter 9, then, the Book of Daniel came into its complete form sometime between 167 and 164. It must have been quickly accepted as authoritative scripture, for, as noted, it exists in its present form in fragments from Qumran that date back to the first century B.C.E. Furthermore, in a list of great scriptural heroes, including Abraham, David, and Elijah, 1 Maccabees 2:59–60 mentions Daniel as having been delivered from the mouth of the lions, and his friends from the flames. Since 1 Maccabees is thought to have been written around 100 B.C.E., this provides us with a *terminus ad quem* for the reception of the Daniel cycle as scripture.

AUTHOR AND AUDIENCE

Everything about the Book of Daniel suggests that its addressees were observant Jews who sought to maintain the covenant tradition of Israel in the face of overwhelming outside pressure to conform to imperial religion. Daniel and his friends would have been their ideal figures and role models. They were wise men, versed in dream interpretation and conversant with angels. But even more than that, they were utterly loyal to their only sovereign, Yahweh, God of Israel. In the stories of chapters 1–6, they insist on maintaining their sharp individual identity by refusing to eat the king's food and to bow to the imperial cultic symbols, and by attaining a purity and excellence of life that lifted them in quality above all the other wise men and courtiers of their age. In the second part of the book, the heroes are less clearly spotlighted and are known by such rather cryptic titles as "the saints of the Most High" to whom the eternal kingdom is given (Dan 7:18, 22, 27); "the people of the saints" (8:24); and "the people who know their God," who can "stand firm and take action" (11:32). Above all, they are "those who are wise" and "those who turn many to righteousness." At the resurrection day promised in 12:3, they will "shine like the brightness of the firmament . . . like the stars forever and ever."

According to the ancient sources that deal with this same period, the most likely authors and readers of Daniel were the "company of the Hasideans, mighty warriors of Israel, every one who offered himself willingly for the law" (1 Macc 2:42). That these mighty warriors were also observant persons is suggested by the fact that their allies in the struggle against the Antiochene regime and the hellenizing Jews, "the many who were seeking righteousness and justice," at first refused to fight on the Sabbath and consequently suffered defeat and massacre (1 Macc 2:29–38). In 1 Maccabees 7:13–18, the Hasideans reappear, ready to make peace with the foreign powers as soon as the legitimate Zadokite priesthood has been restored.

> The Hasideans were the first among the sons of Israel to seek peace from them, for they said, "a priest of the line of Aaron [Alcimus, who was in fact an ungodly man, though high priest] has come with the army, and he will not harm us." And he spoke peaceable words to them, and swore this oath to them, "We will not seek to injure you, or your friends." So they trusted him; but he seized sixty of them and killed them in one day, in accordance with the word which was written,
>
> "The flesh of thy saints [hasidim] and their blood
> They poured out round about Jerusalem,
> And there was none to bury them."
>
> [Psalm 79:2–3]

Perhaps we should view the Hasideans of Maccabees simply as representatives of a larger wing of the Judaism of their day, namely, the *hasidim*—the pious or observant ones—to which side of the Jewish community the actual authors of Daniel also belonged. This position (strongly advocated by John J. Collins in his 1984 book and 1985 article) would permit us to recognize a strong kinship between the two groups without asserting an actual identity between the "mighty warriors" of Maccabees and "those who are wise" of Daniel. They would all have stood together in the larger party of the *hasidim*, and as such would have been among the spiritual ancestors of those sects of later Judaism that we know as the Pharisees and the Essenes. Like the *hasidim* before them—and unlike the ultranationalistic Zealots of

their own time—the early Pharisees were willing to work with the ruling power as long as the demands of the Torah upon their own lives and fellowship were not violated. Like Daniel 12:1–3, the Pharisees anticipated the resurrection of the dead. We can reasonably assume, then, that the Book of Daniel was written for and by persons who sought with all their might to remain true to Yahweh and to the practices of the covenant people. In the face of overpowering Hellenistic pressures toward accommodation, syncretism, the elimination of Jewishness, and the incorporation of Judaea into a harmonious Syro-Palestinian Hellenistic empire, we can be sure they paid dearly for their faith. Everything about the Book of Daniel, as well as 1 Maccabees 1–4 and all of 2 Maccabees, points to this fact. But by taking a strong stand against such tyranny, even to the point of announcing in apocalyptic terms that its demise would constitute the very turning of the ages and the introduction of the kingdom of heaven on earth (Dan 7:9–18), these *hasidim* set a standard for refusal to cooperate with corrupt worldly power that has characterized Jews and observant Christians alike throughout the subsequent centuries. The powerful encouragement to say no to the powers that be in order to say yes to the kingdom of God has been the abiding legacy of the Book of Daniel.

THEOLOGICAL PURPOSE

Throughout much of the history of the interpretation of the Bible in the Jewish and Christian traditions, biblical apocalyptic literature in general and the Book of Daniel in particular have been approached from one or the other of two extreme positions. On the one hand, some have discovered in the apocalyptic announcement of an imminent time of tribulation (often set at three and a half "times") followed by the culmination of history a literal road map of the future. Such interpretations have typically identified the eleventh horn on the fourth beast of Daniel 7:8 with a historical personage of their own time and have announced that the end was at hand. By combining Daniel with other apocalyptic texts, some interpreters, such as the premillennial dispensationalists (represented in the United States by the once-ubiquitous Scofield Reference Bible and more recently by the widely read author Hal Lindsey), have created a vast scenario of end times involving persecution by the forces of Antichrist, the beast whose number is 666, the rapture of the saints in the midst of the premillennial tribulation, the first judgment and thousand-year rule of the saints, and the final judgment and destruction of the world. They have found it possible to draw a time line, to place a dot on that chart, and then to say, "We are here."

At the other extreme are those who have tried either to ignore this material or to treat it as at best a highly mythic and probably very naive attempt to write history in advance. This has been the fate of the Book of Daniel in the mainstream of Judaism for many years, and in various modern Christian traditions as well. Stationing itself between these two radical treatments of Daniel and biblical apocalyptic is the interpretive stance, ever more popular since the dawn of the nuclear age, that biblical eschatological literature is invaluable to religious thinking because its bright vision draws readers into the future. And that is good because, as the sage observed long ago, "Where there is no vision, the people perish" (Prov 29:18; KJV).

The encompassing purpose of Daniel is to offer vision and to inculcate hope, not simply for individual escape from death and damnation but for the people of God as a whole. Before addressing that large theological purpose, however, several less central theological issues raised by this fascinating book should be noted. The unswerving affirmation of the sovereignty of God over all human sovereignties emerges as a theme in Daniel 1 and continues to be proclaimed vigorously throughout the book. The question of interim ethics, or how to live until the Day of the Lord dawns, is addressed throughout Daniel 1–6, always with an eye to the culmination of history envisioned in Daniel 7–12. The doctrine of revelation, with the corollary issues of the significance of dreams and the interpretation of mysteries, surfaces as a major issue by chapter 2. So does the difficult theological problem of determinism as well as the question of whether what the future holds is already written in the divine book of destiny. The affirmation of God's power to complete the divine work of redemption, and the possibility that this work is absolutely universal in its scope, emerge in the discus-

sion in Daniel 2. Chapter 6 raises and answers the question of whether God is trapped in the immutability of divine law just as Darius is by the law of the Medes and the Persians. Daniel 7 provides an opportunity to think about the impact of myth on biblical literature, for surely the great beasts that appear out of the sea have their roots in the mythic theme of the profound opposition of evil forces to the creative power of God.

The latter part of the book treats the difficult question of the relation of the end of history to history itself. Is history a meaningless series of events that gain what meaning they have merely by pointing toward the relative approach of the end of history, or does God's intervention to culminate history have implications for what goes on in history itself? Angels and their relationship to human beings become topics of importance beginning with chapter 8, and the great prayer of Daniel 9 raises the issue of retributional thought: Must everything that happens to the people of God be interpreted as either punishment or reward? Of course, the appearance in Daniel 12:1–3 of the notion of the resurrection of the dead, some to eternal life and some to eternal death, introduces into the biblical tradition for the first time (except for a cryptic reference in the apocalyptic section of Isaiah [Isa 26:19]) a motif that will assume major proportions in the New Testament. Interwoven with these theological issues are problems that Daniel as a whole presents: What happens when the end does not come on schedule? Can an incarnate Word of God accurately map the future in advance? Is apocalyptic theology a "failure-of-nerve theology" written by oppressed groups who have no other hope left than divine intervention, or does it—as has been suggested— seriously address a perennial theme, "How long, O Lord, must the righteous suffer?"

Overarching these significant theological issues is the problem of theodicy, of God's way of dealing with evil in the world. Daniel projects a clear solution to this problem: God will not be mocked. God will achieve the divine purpose of the redemption of the world in God's own time. God will win, and everything will be all right. Because this is the case, the Daniel who survives in exile and outshines the other wise men is not a passive figure who simply sits quietly until the last divine intervention, but issues forth into the fray. That is why we can speak of the first chapters of Daniel as interim ethics, that is, ethical instruction illustrative of how the saints should live in the time before the culmination. The saint does not simply hang on, observe all the strictures of the sect, and survive. The saint's courage inspires others to believe and gives hope to those who are losing their hope. The saint helps bring about a world in which God is honored, idolatry is ended, the needs of the needy are met, and the oppressed are liberated. Like those of his contemporaries Esther and Tobit, Daniel's deeds ultimately lead to the vindication of the believers, tied closely to the vindication of the God of Israel.

Christian readers will also recognize a similarity to the picture of the ministry of Jesus in the New Testament. The little apocalypses of the Gospels (Matt 24–25, Mark 13, Luke 17:20–37) are to the account of Jesus' ministry (per se) what the last chapters of Daniel are to the deeds of Daniel. The new age is surely coming, and God will surely be the victor. The vision of the coming kingdom is a stimulus, just as the pearl of great price was a stimulus to the man who went out and sold everything to buy the field in which it was found (Matt 13:45–46). Jesus' ministry of healing and of liberating persons from the bondage of sin and despair was shot through with a strong sense of the immediacy of the coming kingdom, which would vindicate God's way of combating evil in the world. His message, too, was a call not to quietism but to action, an invitation to people to offer in their own lives a foretaste of the character of the coming kingdom.

Taken as a whole, then, under the rubric "foretaste," the Book of Daniel is an invitation to its readers to proceed with hope and energy into the future. It offers a vision that is intended to pull its readers into that future like a magnet, rather than to leave them terrified in the face of the end. It is clear that although God alone can cut out of the mountain that stone that fills the whole earth (Dan 2:34–35, 44–45), those who have the vision of God's coming victory can imitate in their individual and communal lives the coming kingdom. They can give previews of what the world will be like when justice prevails, idolatry is quashed, and wolves dwell with lambs. Placed within the context of the whole sweep of eschatological vision in the Bible, the Book of Daniel points ultimately toward a reconciled and peaceful community in the future, one in which even foreign kings like Nebuchadrezzar and Darius acknowledge the sovereignty of God and praise God's saving power.

This confidence in God's ultimate victory in the struggle with evil may be the single most profound source of hope available to our modern culture. Science and fiction alike give only ambiguous readings of the future, encouraging us when they point to the evolution of the human species toward ever greater perfection, but more often discouraging us as they point to totalitarian "big brothers" whose strength is underwritten by technology and nuclear fear. The most radical forms of Marxism and Islam offer alternative eschatologies to our age, but both require the destruction of significant parts of the human community in order that the purposes of emancipation be achieved. In comparison, biblical apocalyptic literature sometimes attains a vision that is universal in scope and that is rich with hope for all things. On the great day that is coming, "the creation itself will be set free from its bondage to decay and obtain the glorious liberty of the children of God" (Rom 8:21; RSV). On that great day, "the one like a son of man" will be given "dominion and glory and kingdom . . . his dominion is an everlasting dominion, / which shall not pass away, / and his kingdom one / that shall not be destroyed" (Dan 7:13–14).

Bibliography

Commentaries

Baldwin, Joyce G. *Daniel: An Introduction and Commentary.* Leicester, 1979.

Calvin, John. *Commentaries on the Book of the Prophet Daniel.* Translated by Thomas Myers. Grand Rapids, 1948.

Collins, John J. *Daniel, with an Introduction to Apocalyptic Literature.* Forms of the Old Testament Literature, vol. 20. Grand Rapids, 1984.

Delcor, Mathias. *Le Livre de Daniel.* Paris, 1971.

Hartman, Louis F., and Alexander A. Di Lella. *The Book of Daniel.* Anchor Bible, vol. 23. Garden City, N.Y., 1978.

Heaton, Eric William. *The Book of Daniel: Introduction and Commentary.* London, 1956.

Koch, Klaus. *Das Buch Daniel.* Erträge der Forschung, vol. 144. Darmstadt, 1980.

Lacocque, André. *The Book of Daniel.* Translated by David Pellauer. Atlanta, 1978.

Montgomery, James A. *A Critical and Exegetical Commentary on the Book of Daniel.* The International Critical Commentary, vol. 22. New York, 1927.

Plöger, Otto. *Das Buch Daniel.* Kommentar zum Alten Testament, vol. 18. Gütersloh, 1965.

Towner, W. Sibley. *Daniel.* Atlanta, 1984.

Other Works on Daniel

Casey, Maurice. *Son of Man: The Interpretation and Influence of Daniel 7.* London, 1979.

Collins, John J. *The Apocalyptic Vision of the Book of Daniel.* Missoula, 1977.

———. "Apocalyptic Eschatology as the Transcendence of Death." *Catholic Biblical Quarterly* 36 (1974): 21–43. Reprinted in *Visionaries and Their Apocalypses,* edited by Paul D. Hanson. Philadelphia, 1983.

———. "Daniel and His Social World." *Interpretation* 39, 2 (1985): 131–143. This entire issue is devoted to the Book of Daniel, with other major essays by Gammie, Koch, and Towner.

Gammie, John. "The Classification, Stages of Growth, and Changing Intentions of the Book of Daniel." *Journal of Biblical Literature* 95 (1976): 191–204.

Ginsberg, Harold Louis. *Studies in Daniel.* New York, 1948.

———. "The Composition of the Book of Daniel." *Vetus Testamentum* 4 (1954): 246–275.

Humphreys, W. Lee. "A Life-style for the Diaspora: A Study of the Tales of Esther and Daniel." *Journal of Biblical Literature* 92 (1973): 211–223.

Lacocque, André. *Daniel et son temps.* Geneva, 1983.

Mertens, Alfred. *Das Buch Daniel im Lichte der Texte vom Toten Meer.* Würzburg, 1971.

Rowley, Harold Henry. *Darius the Mede and the Four World Empires in the Book of Daniel.* 1935. Reprint. Cardiff, 1964.

Essays on Related Subjects

Bickerman, Elias J. *The God of the Maccabees: Studies on the Meaning and Origin of the Maccabean Revolt.* Translated by Horst R. Muchring. Leiden, 1979.

Collins, John J., ed. *Apocalypse: The Morphology of a Genre* [*Semeia* 14]. Missoula, 1979.

Hanson, Paul D. *The Dawn of Apocalyptic.* Philadelphia, 1975.

Hellholm, David, ed. *Apocalypticism in the Mediterranean World and the Near East: The Historic and Sociological Roots of Jewish Apocalyptic Eschatology.* Proceedings of the International Colloquium on Apocalypticism, Uppsala, 12–17 August 1979. Uppsala, 1983.

Koch, Klaus. *The Rediscovery of Apocalyptic.* Translated by Margaret Kohl. Naperville, Ill., 1972.

Moore, Carey A. *Daniel, Esther, and Jeremiah: The Additions.* Anchor Bible, vol. 44. Garden City, N.Y., 1977.

Plöger, Otto. *Theocracy and Eschatology.* Translated by S. Rudman. Richmond, Va., 1968.

Pritchard, James B., ed. *Ancient Near Eastern Texts Relating to the Old Testament.* 3d ed. Princeton, 1969.

Tcherikover, Avigdor. *Hellenistic Civilization and the Jews.* Translated by S. Applebaum. Philadelphia, 1959.

Vermès, Géza. *The Dead Sea Scrolls in English.* 2d ed. Harmondsworth, England, 1975.

W. SIBLEY TOWNER

hosea

THE PROPHET HOSEA, the only native Israelite among the great "writing" prophets of the
eighth century B.C.E. (Amos, First Isaiah, Micah),
has often been characterized as the "prophet of love"
over against Amos, the "prophet of doom." As with
most stereotypes, there is both truth and falsehood
lodged within this conception of the prophet, whose
name in Hebrew means "[God] has saved." As he
foresees the turbulent end of the northern kingdom
(Israel), Hosea's message is as violent as any delivered
by Amos, and his use of familial imagery is by no
means always positive or evocative of tender feelings.
Indeed, because of the overall tone of the book, many
scholars have come to doubt that such hopeful passages as 14:1–9 (Masoretic text 14:2–10) and so on
could have originated with the author of the bulk of
the work.

The book comes from a time period falling
approximately between the death of Jeroboam II in
746 and the fall of Israel (the northern kingdom, also
referred to as "Ephraim" by Hosea, in order to
distinguish it from the southern kingdom of Judah) to
Assyria in 722/721. The prophet's oracles were probably collected and preserved by disciples who fled to
safety in Judah when the Assyrians destroyed the
capital city, Samaria, and deported the upper-class
Israelite population. As with the lives of most of the
great prophets, we do not know what became of
Hosea at that time. His work may have undergone one

or more reorganizations and supplementations in the
hands of Judean editors both in the early seventh
century and during the Babylonian captivity, when
the message of Hosea was particularly relevant for
those seeking to understand the meaning of Judah's
sufferings (Andersen and Freedman 1980). In its
final form, the book may be divided into two unequal
complexes, the first comprising chapters 1–3 (Hosea's
family mirrors God's relationship with Israel), and the
second comprising chapters 4–14 (prophetic utterances). One noted scholar (Wolff 1974) further subdi-
vides the second part into 4:1–11:11 and 11:12–14:9
(Masoretic Text 12:1–14:10).

SOCIOPOLITICAL CONTEXT

As with any prophetic book, it is impossible to
grasp the major concepts of Hosea without some
understanding of the social and political realities to
which his prophecies were directed. Even though
there is considerable debate about the proper chronological order of the oracles found in the work, the
broad outlines of the period from which the book
comes are clear, and these give some insight into the
time frame and meaning of the individual passages.

The politics and social practices of the northern
kingdom of Israel were always conditioned by the
peculiar geographical position of that nation. Israel
was a land of rich, productive valleys and upwarped

hill country. Along with Judah, its less geographically favored sibling to the south, it lay nestled like a choice nut in the politically volatile nutcracker formed by the great river valley civilizations to the south (Egypt) and east (Assyria and Babylon). Pressures exerted by the great imperialistic powers inevitably crushed those small states occupying the Palestinian land bridge that had the misfortune to lie directly in the path of Egyptian and Mesopotamian ambitions, and the two often appear together as a word pair in Hosea's doom-filled prophecies (7:11, 9:6, 11:5, 11:11, 12:1 [MT, 12:2]). Periods of ascendancy in the political fortunes of Judah and Israel always came during times when the great empires of the river valleys were weakened at home or overextended abroad, thus allowing "breathing space" to the petty kingdoms of the Levantine.

The survival of Judah for almost two centuries following the fall of Israel owed more to its geographical inaccessibility and undesirability when compared with the privileged position of the northern kingdom than to any moral or theological superiority on Judah's part. Geographically, Israel occupied a territory where the great north-south and east-west trade routes crossed. Although this location gave the kingdom access to greater trade possibilities and foreign interchange, it also made the land a primary target for Egyptian or Mesopotamian kings who wished to march their armies through it to meet their great rival in the quickest, most efficient way available. (The only other possibilities for crossing the land bridge lay far to the north in the Palmyrene Corridor or in the south through the waterless Negev.) Like Belgium in the era of modern world wars, Israel simply happened to be in the way of the power struggles and expansionist policies of two great adversaries. Hosea, of course, envisions Israel's coming destruction as the result of the country's apostasy from Yahweh, the delivering God of Moses and the ancestors. However, the geographical and political realities undergirding the situation of the eighth-century kingdoms of Israel and Judah make one wonder whether any degree of faithfulness, however strong, could have averted the catastrophes that lay ahead.

In the tenth century, the recently divided kingdoms of Judah and Israel had been devastated by an Egyptian invasion led by the pharaoh Sheshonk I. By the mid ninth century, Egypt lay dormant and the Assyrian menace from the northeast had forced the kings of Israel into an alliance with Aram-Damascus and other local kingdoms against the Assyrian Shalmaneser III. They were briefly successful, apparently defeating the "Great King" at the battle of Qarqar on the Orontes River in 853. However, this allied victory was short-lived, for in 841 the Israelite usurper-king Jehu was forced to pay heavy fines to keep his kingdom (he is shown kissing Shalmaneser's feet in submission on that king's "Black Obelisk"). For about a century afterward, Assyria was occupied with reorganization and problems in its own territory, allowing Judah and Israel a period of recovery that issued in the prosperous reigns of Uzziah of Judah and Jeroboam II of Israel. It was during this time of false security and blind optimism that Amos of Judah took his message of coming disaster to the northern kingdom and was met with a predictably negative response. Chapters 1–3 of Hosea may reflect the fortunes of the nation at the very end of Jeroboam II's reign.

Following Jeroboam's forty-one-year reign, his son, Zechariah, was assassinated within a year of his father's death in 746, thus bringing Jehu's dynasty, begun in violence in the Jezreel Valley, to a fittingly violent end. More palace coups followed, with King Menahem (ca. 745–ca. 738) emerging as the victor. Like Jehu before him, this king's policy for keeping his throne included pacification of the Assyrians by payment of huge amounts of tribute, for which he had to levy cruel taxes on Israelite landholders. This naturally alienated him from his local power base, and with Menahem's death the series of assassinations resumed as pro-Assyrian factions struggled with Israelite nationalists. His son Pekahiah was assassinated after two years by Pekah, who was in turn assassinated by Hoshea, Israel's last king. In part, the anarchy in Israel was prompted by the all-too-evident resumption of Assyrian aggression with the accession of Tiglath-pileser III in 745.

The rule of the new king, an able administrator and warrior, spelled the beginning of the end for Israel and the neighboring petty states. Subduing his Babylonian enemies to the south, Tiglath-pileser defeated the kingdom of Urartu in the north and waged war as far away as the Caspian Sea. This accomplished, he turned his attention to the west and implemented previous policies with new zeal. Rather than simply punishing rebellions with massive displays of military might, this king annexed as Assyrian provinces any vassal states who refused tribute. Wholesale deportations of the ruling social classes of conquered states now held as provinces eroded local resistance by those peasants left on the land. Given that submission to Assyria was the only sure way for a ruler to retain some remnants of autonomy for himself and his country, Menahem's payment of tribute to Tiglath-pileser suddenly becomes understandable in the light of the unpleasant alternatives. It is clear from subsequent events, however, that the heavy tax burdens imposed by Menahem fueled the assassination of his son Pekahiah by anti-Assyrian factions.

Pekah, the usurper, made common cause against Assyria with Rezin, the king of Damascus, and certain Philistine allies along the coast. They tried to press Judah into joining their doomed alliance, and, finding first Jotham of Judah and then his son Ahaz unwilling to join their coalition, invaded Judah from the north (2 Kgs 15:37). In desperation, young King Ahaz sent to Tiglath-pileser for help (against the advice of the prophet Isaiah) and voluntarily made Judah an Assyrian vassal (2 Kgs 16:7ff., Isa 7:1–17). This episode is known as the Syro-Ephraimite War; Hosea's oracles in 5:1ff., 5:8–6:6, 7:8–12, 8:7–10, 9:11–14, 11:1–7, and 12:1 (MT 12:2) probably come from the period immediately preceding the war and during the war itself.

With the Syro-Ephraimite coalition of Pekah and Rezin at the gates of Jerusalem intending to depose Ahaz, Tiglath-pileser was swift to respond. Attacking the coalition from the north, Judah was spared as Israel and its anti-Assyrian allies were driven into fighting the Great King long before planned and with a hostile Judah at their back. First destroying Philistia in 734 (and thereby rendering potential aid to the coalition from Egypt impossible), Tiglath-pileser then devastated Israel, annexing Israelite holdings in the Galilee and Transjordan and deporting their ruling populations. At this point, Pekah was assassinated by Hoshea, who then wisely surrendered to Assyria. In 732 the Assyrians conquered Damascus, executing Rezin and proceeding with annexation and deportation of the Syrian kingdom.

When Shalmaneser V succeeded his father,

Tiglath-pileser, in 727, Hoshea tried to take advantage of the unrest that inevitably attended the death of a powerful king. Making overtures to Egypt for support, Hoshea refused tribute to Shalmaneser. Israel's fate was thus sealed: Shalmaneser attacked in 724 and took Hoshea prisoner. The capital of Samaria held out for two years as the Assyrians occupied the territory remaining to Israel after the earlier annexations of 733, but finally fell in 722/721 to Shalmaneser's successor, Sargon II. As thousands more were deported to Mesopotamia and Media, some fled to the relative safety to be found in Judah, carrying the sacred traditions of the now-defunct northern kingdom. Israel had come to an end, but the literary and theological heritage of its people endured.

The Book of Hosea accurately reflects the social and political turmoil that attended the last days of Israel. The heavy burdens of vassalage to Assyria were various and demoralizing, since the price of survival was greater than the simple payment of tribute. The draining away of resources from the vassal country worsened its economic situation automatically, since surpluses could not be amassed for normal trade, nor could profits be plowed back into the land. Large, wealthy landholders routinely passed their tax burdens to the crown along to the peasant tenants who worked their land. General indebtedness rose, small landholdings—the "heritage" of the poor—were swallowed up by greedy land speculators, and the ranks of the poor swelled. Similarly, the constant struggle to unite against Assyria, the Syro-Ephraimite war against Judah, and the court rivalries between pro- and anti-Assyrian factions also exacerbated the economic situation, since money siphoned away for militaristic reasons could not be used to improve the lot of the common folk.

Part of the price tag of vassalage usually included the adoption of the religious practices of the conquering suzerain. Although there is no direct evidence that Assyria interfered in Israel's cult before the fall of Samaria (Cogan 1974), from the time of Jehu's submission to Shalmaneser III, Israel's exclusive worship of Yahweh had been threatened by the demands of political expediency. Actually, outside influences on its religious practices had always been a problem for the northern kingdom, at least in part because of its geographical position. Not only did Israel have greater contact with outsiders than did Judah, on account of its position on the international trade routes, but from the beginnings of statehood, its territories contained a fairly large, unassimilated population of Canaanite city-states. These people naturally tended to retain their own religious traditions of Baal worship. Marriage alliances with the Phoenician city of Tyre in the ninth century brought official toleration of Baal worship to Israel in the person of Queen Jezebel, since foreign princesses were permitted to retain their religions of origin as a matter of course in imperial marriages. Jehu's purging of Tyrian Baal worship as he founded his own ruling house did not deal with the popular fusion of Yahweh with local *ba'alim* and left unaddressed the problems of two coexisting populations with differing and purportedly inimical religious traditions. Further, the various alliances with Aram-Damascus against Assyria brought Israel into close contact with Syrian religious practices, at least some of which may have included human sacrifice, though only as a last resort during times of public or national emergencies.

In a modern age that values ecumenical dialogue (or at least religious tolerance), it is often difficult to understand the bitter hatred of the "conservative" Israelite Yahwists for the fertility religions that surrounded them. It is important to remember that the rivalry between Yahwism and Baalism was based on far more than Israelite sensibilities about the inappropriateness of sexuality as a legitimate form of worship. One modern reconstruction of this conflict focuses on the social and political differences between Israel and surrounding neighbors (Gottwald 1985). Israel had covenanted with Yahweh, the redeemer god of the slaves in Egypt, to worship that god exclusively. Such fidelity was to be manifested not simply in the purity of Israel's cult (much of which was, in fact, adapted from Canaanite neighbors) but in a new social order that overturned the ruling ideologies of the surrounding city-states. There, the local king stood as a representative of the god Baal (whose name means simply "owner" or "master"), and by his celebration of the sexual act with a priestess representing a goddess who was Baal's consort, fertility for the land was assured. Like Baal, the king owned the land and all the people on it; power was concentrated in the hands of the few members of a military aristocracy

who exploited all those beneath them. Cults that worshiped the royal dead effectively took grain surpluses out of the bellies of the poor and put them into the control of the priesthood that served the royal houses. This practice reduced possibilities for trade and growth and kept the lower-class population trapped in the struggle for simple daily survival. The manipulative sexuality that sought to stimulate divine fertility provided a convenient focal point for all the abuses of a religion that served and cemented an unjust social organization. To adopt parts of this worship for Yahweh's cult or to publicly profess the religion of the overlord was equivalent to a rejection of Yahweh's call for justice and equality among Israelite and Judean men. (Unfortunately, the patriarchal biases of the ancient world had a negative impact on Yahwism's ability to proclaim equality for women and certain others considered "outsiders.")

Thus, for the great prophets, both foreign alliances and foreign worship, however expedient politically, were sinful lapses from true fidelity to Israel's god. From Hosea's perspective—one he shares with all the eighth-century prophets—reliance on Egyptian, Assyrian, or Aramaean allies instead of a reassertion of dependence on God through covenantal relationships and the social justice they entailed only witnessed to Israel's fundamental moral and theological bankruptcy. This, more than any particular sexual perversity, represents the core of the nation's "harlotry," though the prophets certainly took the strongest exception to the presence of cultic sexual practices that had infiltrated the worship of Yahweh.

THEOLOGICAL HERITAGE

Quite naturally, the Book of Hosea reflects the particular perspective of its native Israelite author, and this difference is felt in both diction and content. While frequent mention of Judah is made (perhaps the additions of a zealous Judean editor of later times), Hosea is primarily interested in the theological history and future of his own land, as the prophet's continued use of the northern term "Ephraim" suggests. Hosea's emphasis on Israel's past history is more than a mere rehearsal: Israel's present and future realities can be intuited from an understanding of the nation's past relationship to God, for the notion of "corporate identity" infuses all the prophetic writings of the Hebrew Bible. The entire people living at any time was felt to bear the characteristics, and hence the potentialities and liabilities, of its forebears. Thus the Jacob traditions mentioned in 12:2ff., 12:12f. [MT 12:3ff., 12:13f.]) indicate the contentious nature of the Israelite people in the eighth century; the deliverance experienced in the Exodus of the Late Bronze Age (11:1–4) foreshadows Yahweh's present anguish and future compassion (11:8–11); and so on. Hosea's use of national traditions makes it clear that, from the outset, faithlessness had marked Israel's response to Yahweh's redemptive labors on the people's behalf. The defection to Baal at Baal-Peor recorded in Numbers 25 is recalled in 9:10; the bloody beginnings of Jehu's dynasty find their way into a symbolic name for one of Hosea's children in 1:4. In 9:15 and 13:10ff., the beginnings of kingship at Gilgal, where Saul was chosen as the United Kingdom's first monarch, marks another wrong turning point in the people's history.

Hosea's particular attention to the beginning and end of ruling dynasties (8:4, 13:10–11) is naturally related to the violence that marked the political fortunes of the royal houses in the eighth century, when assassination became the rule rather than the exception. However, more ancient northern traditions are reflected here as well. First, Israel and Judah each had their own covenant traditions, and prophets tended to articulate their messages from the perspective of the covenant that had been most important in their national history. In Judah the covenant with David and his house was viewed as "unconditional": God swore to preserve David and his descendants on the throne as reward for their past fidelity, and while such rulers might be chastised for wrongdoing, the covenant was viewed as inviolable and unbreakable (2 Sam 7). In the North, the Mosaic or "conditional" covenant model prevailed: the people swore to fulfill certain obligations in gratitude for Yahweh's delivering acts in the Exodus. If the people did not uphold their side of the agreement, the Mosaic covenant could be broken and God would no longer be Israel's protective deity (Exod 19–20). When Hosea names his second son "Not-my-people," he is giving symbolic form to his belief that Israel's apostasy had resulted in God's rejection of the now-broken Mosaic covenant.

Because of the importance of the differing views of the two covenant traditions, it is no surprise that both Judah and Israel viewed the legitimacy of political power in ways compatible with their individual covenants. From the division of the united kingdom upon the death of Solomon in the tenth century, rulership in Israel tended to find its legitimation through prophetic circles. Since there was no stable ruling house (comparable to the one in Judah) that was authorized by the Davidic covenant, charismatic leadership confirmed by prophetic approval became the method whereby Israelite rulers gained and held power. Likewise, prophetic challenge to a royal house could bring it down (cf. 1 Kgs 19). It is easy to see, then, why Amos' prophetic challenge to Jeroboam II resulted in his expulsion from the land (Amos 7:10–15). Hosea's oracles and the symbolic actions revolving around his family life no doubt earned him the same public dislike and humiliation that attended the careers of the other great prophets of Israel. His positive view of the true prophet's vocation (12:10, 13 [Masoretic text 12:11, 14]) and scathing attacks on the rulers of Israel show that he stands firmly in the heritage of the northern prophetic traditions.

Given the strong theological affinities found between Hosea's thinking and that expressed in the Book of Deuteronomy, it is not unlikely that both were influenced by the traditions kept alive among the circles of the Levites, Israel's teaching priesthood, and that the survival of both works is owed at least in part to Levites who fled to Judah after 722/721. Certainly, those who edited the Book of Hosea shared many theological attitudes with those who produced Deuteronomy and the Deuteronomistic History in Joshua-Kings. Such contact points included a belief in the unity of Israel and Judah (hence the prophetic message to one could be applied to the other, as in 5:10, 12–14, etc.), the future reuniting of Israel and Judah under the House of David (3:5), and a fervent hope that the events of 722/721 were not God's last word on Israel's future (14:4–8 [MT 14:5–9]; Clements 1975). The effects of this theological outlook may be felt throughout the book, where originally negative prophecies are toned down and "updated" in the process of editing; though some scholars believe that at least a few of the hopeful passages, such as 11:8–9, may contain the authentic wording of the prophet. Such a reversal from doom to hope is not unique in the prophetic writings: Isaiah, Jeremiah, and Ezekiel all shift to the articulation of more hopeful messages concerning long-term survival as they see their predictions of doom fulfilled.

LITERARY FEATURES

Prophetic works usually contain three types of materials: (1) autobiographical passages in prose or poetry, including "call passages" (where a prophet is commissioned as such by God), reports of visions, and explanations of symbolic actions; (2) narrative passages in the third person, usually assumed to be from the hand of disciples, which relate significant events in the prophet's career and the nation's history; and (3) prophetic utterances, generally in poetic form, which may include prophecies of doom, oracles of salvation, "woe" oracles, threats, reproaches, and covenant lawsuits. Many speakers may be heard in the poetic oracles: sometimes the voice speaking is conceived of as that of God (2:1–5 [MT 2:3–17], 7:11–16, 11:1–9, etc.); sometimes it is that of the prophet, either speaking as himself (7:8–10, 9:7–9, etc.) or satirizing the people's responses to the prophetic message (6:1–3). In Hosea, chapters 1–3 contain third-person (1:1–9) and first-person (3:1–5) prose accounts that explain the meaning for Israel of the symbolic actions taking place in Hosea's family. A poetic lawsuit between Yahweh and Israel in chapter 2 is sandwiched between the two accounts of Hosea's domestic troubles, giving the lawsuit context and meaning. Prophetic utterances form the rest of the work in chapters 4–14, with the book ending on a decidedly didactic note in 14:9 (MT 14:10), where forms borrowed from the wisdom tradition exhort the audience to take the prophet's message seriously.

The reader without knowledge of Hebrew will probably wonder at the great range of modern translations given for a single passage in Hosea. This is due to the poor condition of the original text, which is second in difficulty only to the Book of Job. Some speculate that the corrupt state of the text is a result of the adverse effects of political and social turmoil during the period in which it was written and smuggled to safety in Judah.

Hosea's Family Mirrors God's Relationship with Israel (Chapters 1–3)

One of the most interesting features of the prophetic ministry is the performance of "symbolic actions." When commanded by God (as in 1:2, 4, 6, 9; 3:1), prophets would carry out unusual or unexpected acts that became "visual aids" illustrating their messages. In all likelihood, such behavior was influenced by both the concepts underlying "sympathetic magic" and the belief that words, like actions, had magical power to create the very thing to which they referred. It is not clear whether the prophets themselves believed that they were merely "illustrating" the present and future circumstances of the people, or if they thought they were actively forging the fates of doom or restoration to which they pointed symbolically through their actions. It is clear from the political and priestly authorities' reactions to prophetic symbolic actions that the latter, more "magical," view held sway in the minds of those in power, who felt threatened by the prophet's ministry. Hence, we see typical responses of repression, attempted censorship, and physical coercion used to attempt to restrain such prophetic behaviors, lest they create the doom-filled outcome by their peculiar acts. Symbolic actions are often dramatic and outrageous by the standards of their communities; often they may seem simply inexplicable or silly (e.g., in Jer 32 that prophet purchases a plot of land in Anathoth when Judah is about to fall to the Babylonians). By the very drama that surrounds them, symbolic actions are designed to get the attention of a hostile or panic-stricken audience. They baffle and excite the imagination. Perhaps the best-known and most intriguing of all symbolic actions performed by the Hebrew prophets is Hosea's marriage to a woman named Gomer.

Symbolic actions that are rooted in the normal (and not so normal) events of family life are not unique to Hosea, though it is there that they make their first appearance among the "Writing Prophets." Like Hosea, Isaiah also gave his children symbolic names that heralded events in the nation's future (Isa 7:14, 8:4). Jeremiah is commanded not to take a wife in order to dramatize the coming rupture in Judah's daily life (Jer 16:2), and Ezekiel is told not to mourn the death of his wife, the "delight of his eyes," as a sign of the grief to come (Ezek 24:15–24). However, no other prophet was commanded to make quite so long-term and distressing a commitment as was Hosea when told to wed a "woman of harlotry." Such scandalous behavior on the part of a Hebrew prophet seems so inconceivable to some that a few scholars have attempted to give the events recounted in Hosea 1–3 an entirely allegorical meaning. However, since we see the family as an acceptable arena for symbolic actions in the other prophets, there is little reason to allegorize Hosea's reports.

Hosea's marriage was, no doubt, as interesting a topic for gossip in eighth-century Israel as it is for scholarly reconstructions in the present. Unfortunately, the text is by no means clear as to what actually transpired: does chapter 3 recapitulate the same events as chapter 1, now viewed from a later perspective, or does it refer to a subsequent reconciliation with Gomer, Hosea's encounter with yet another woman, or something else altogether? Not only is it difficult to sort out the identity of the woman (women?) in chapters 1–3, but the actual status of Gomer is unclear, since the text does not call her a prostitute per se. It has been suggested that "wife/woman of harlotries" in 1:2 might mean someone who shares the general ethos of her surroundings, that is, a member of a "harlotrous" people (see Isa 6:5 for a similar situation), rather than referring to Gomer's alleged profession or adulterous behavior (Gordis 1971).

To further complicate matters, we cannot say whether Gomer, if she was a prostitute, was merely a secular prostitute or was attached in some way to cultic activities, which would have scored considerably higher on the scale of sinfulness in prophetic thinking. One scholar has suggested that Gomer was not a prostitute, but rather took part in the supposedly common practice of dedicating her virginity to Baal by servicing a stranger within the precincts of the temple, in return for the blessings of fertility from the god (Wolff 1974). However, sources used to reconstruct a "sex cult" in eighth-century Israel are late and speculative at best. Even in Mesopotamia, where better documentation for the existence of a cult of sacred sexuality exists, the relationship between "secular" and "sacred" practices is unclear (Lerner 1986).

It is Hosea's particular literary and theological achievement that he is able to use the very form of the practices he hates (sacred sexuality) as a vehicle for his message about Yahweh. While vehemently denying the appropriateness of conceiving of Yahweh in ways influenced by Baal worship (2:12–13, 16 [MT 2:14–15, 18]), Hosea then images Yahweh in a marital relationship with Israel, and attributes to Israel's God all the bounties and acts usually associated with Baal, the fertility deity (2:8, 21–22; 14:5–8 [MT 2:10, 23–24; 14:6–9]). One wonders whether the "mixed messages" sent by this technique were confusing to those hearing his oracles. It may be that the fusion of Yahweh with Baal was so complete that such an approach was the only one that could have made the psychic connection between the people's espoused theology and Hosea's insights about God.

The marriage metaphor used to describe God's relationship to Israel, though laden with dangerous overtones of the fertility religions, provides an excellent illustration of the prophet's conception of Yahweh's suffering over Israel's faithlessness. Marriage in the patriarchal societies of the ancient world served varied social purposes and was the foundational unit of society. By the acquisition of wives and the production of sons, young men were acknowledged as adults and gained social standing. In this respect, wife and children were living extensions of the husband's ego boundaries, enhancing his social position and personal power. Since women and children were absolute dependents (though later legal traditions restrict somewhat the father's right to dispose of wife and children in wholly arbitrary ways), the thought that they might turn against the one who supported and owned them was probably a dreadful one to men, who profited from this social system (cf. Esth 1:13–22). Women's sexuality was closely guarded because through it male inheritance passed from father to son; women who had more than one partner struck at the very heart of patriarchal society's transmission of power, standing, and the means of production. For this reason an adulterous wife did more than betray the man who owned and supported her; the living symbol of disorder, she lessened him in his own eyes and the eyes of society. Hence the husband's confusion, hurt, and anger in such a situation would have been extreme and would have been experienced as humiliating and shameful.

Hosea's experience of these emotions brings him to a point where he sees them as a human mirror of God's response to the people's apostasy. What Hosea does not see is that a covenant built on a master-slave relationship like that embodied in patriarchal marriage or the conditional covenant (which was developed from models of vassal treaties between a great king and those just defeated by him) can never satisfy the deep emotional needs of the one in the position of the slave. Hosea's use of the parental metaphor to describe Yahweh's love for Israel actually predominates outside of chapters 1–3 and represents a more hopeful model in his theology than does the husband-wife relationship. Male children—and Israel is always conceived of as male—outgrow their position of dependence in ways not allowed to women in the ancient world, becoming mature, responsible, and productive companions for their parents. Thus the parent-child relationship better embodies the kind of developmental growth that God envisions for Israel.

It has been argued that the meaning of Hosea's marriage is to be found not in the passages that look to a hopeful restoration of the marital relationship (i.e., 2:14–3:5 [MT 2:16–3:5]) but in the symbolic names given to Hosea's children (1:4–8). In ancient society the name held a power that harks back to the magical power contained in all words. The name explained the essence of a person or thing, conferring the power of that knowledge on all those who knew it. It was definitely *not* the custom to give children negative names, since this would certainly shape their destinies. The names given Hosea's children would have been vivid, daily reminders of the unpleasant fate in store for the nation. In this reconstruction, the positive interpretations later given these names, the hope for marital restoration, and the insights about the enduring nature of love are seen as additions by disciples or Judean editors after the prophecies of doom had come to pass (Clements 1975).

Prophetic Utterances (Chapters 4–14)

At first glance, one is struck by the loose, "collection"-like character of the second complex comprising the Book of Hosea. Abrupt shifts in speaker and topic occur throughout, openings and closings of units are not clearly marked, and prose and poetic styles intermingle in a way that has been

suggested as characteristic of eighth-century prophecy. Not all of these features need be attributed to the hands of later well-meaning editors. As we come to understand preexilic prophecy better, some commentators are beginning to find a greater unity in style and content in Hosea than was previously thought.

Viewed in terms of literary form, the second complex is composed mainly of divine speeches (4:4–9; 5:1–3; 5:8–7:16; 8:1–12; 9:10–13, 15–16; 10:9–15; 11:1–9, 11; 12:10–11 [MT 12:11f.]; 13:4–14; 14:4–8 ([MT 14:5–9]), with a smaller number of prophetic speeches where God is spoken of in the third person. This varied structure accounts for the shifts in speaker, often occurring within a single unit (*cf.* 4:10–15, 8:11–13, 11:12–12:14 ([MT 12:1–15]). The language of legal disputes is prominent in 2:2 (MT 2:4); 4:1, 4; 12:2 (MT 12:3), and laments, complaints, exhortations, threats, and diatribes also make an appearance. The presence of wisdom forms in 8:7 and the affinity of parts of Hosea with wisdom thinking on the natural order has led some to suggest that Hosea was trained as a sage. However, this may be too great a conclusion to draw from the evidence, since wisdom forms occurred among the folk as well as among the educational elite in ancient Israel. Generally, the Book of Hosea is difficult for form criticism, that branch of biblical literary criticism which attempts to pinpoint original "generic" form, social context, and use. Little precise historical information is present in the second complex, and this effectively limits the critic's ability to assign a given oracle to a particular time and place.

Hosea's style is particularly notable for its use of varied similes and extended metaphors, drawn mostly from the natural world and the life of the family. Both Yahweh and Israel are imaged in innovative and striking ways. Yahweh is pictured as a devouring lion (5:14, 13:7–8), a she-bear robbed of her cubs (13:8), a leopard (13:7), a moth and dry rot (5:12), an evergreen tree (14:8 [MT 14:9]), and dew (14:5 [MT 6]), as well as by the more typical images of parent (11:1ff.), husband (2:2ff. [MT 2:4ff.]), fowler (7:12), owner of stock animals (10:11, 11:4), and doctor (7:1, 11:3, 14:4 [MT 14:5]). Israel/Ephraim appears as a child (11:1ff.), an adulterous wife (2:2ff. [MT 2:4ff.]), an invalid (5:13; 7:1, 9; 14:4 [MT 14:5]), an unborn child and mother in labor (13:13). Similes from the natural world are also used to characterize Israel, including various birds (7:11f., 9:11), cattle (4:16, 10:11), grapes and a grapevine (9:10, 10:1, 14:7 [MT 14:8]), figs and lilies (9:10, 14:5 [MT 14:6]), chaff, smoke, dew, and mist (13:3), the olive tree and the forests of Lebanon (14:6f. [MT 14:7f.]). More colorfully, the people are like a smoldering oven and a half-baked cake (7:4–8), with leaders who are like snares and nets (5:1). The sheer variety of imagery used in this one small book is an index of the poetic creativity of its author; it must have had a powerful impact on hearers who were left unable to imagine God absent from even the most mundane spheres of action (Wolff 1974).

The second complex in the book is difficult to characterize in terms of structure of poetic units, in part because opening and closing formulas are usually omitted. Hosea prefers the use of synonomous parallelism (where the second half-line restates the thought of the first) in the creation of his poetic lines, with bicola (two half-lines to a verse) and tricola (three lines to a verse) predominating as his favorite forms. A typical example of his use of synonomous bicola is found in 6:6: "For I desire steadfast love and not sacrifice,/the knowledge of God, rather than burnt offerings."

Hosea's use of tricola may be observed in 9:4, 9:6, and often at the beginning and end of oracles, as in 8:9, 13 and 9:3, 6 (Wolff 1974; Lundbom 1979). Hosea's poetry plays with typical Hebrew word order, and this characteristic contributes to a feeling of "distance" in the prophet's message, almost as though the grammar of the oracles reflects the movement of God away from the people. One scholar has suggested that such "delaying" tactics may also have served the purpose of holding the attention of an angry or indifferent audience for the duration of the oracle (Lundbom 1979). The routine use of poetic parallelisms creates an air of expectation in the hearers, who are naturally primed to wait for the second half of the verse to complete the poetic thought. By postponing this fulfillment, Hosea puts his audience on edge and gains more time to hammer home his point.

Hosea's creative use of language, tradition, and theology lends a power to his message that transcends the events of the eighth century. His masterful depiction of the pathos of a betrayed God and a faithless people is given special force by the parallel events taking place in his own family. As the celebrated Jewish theologian Abraham Heschel puts it in his penetrating study *The Prophets* (1962), Hosea—perhaps because of his own experiences—has intuited the "dramatic tension" existing between God's burning anger and intense compassion for the people. Such passages as 13:4–8 and 11:1–9 resound with a divine fury at betrayal, which is, nevertheless, held in check by an unquenchable love:

When Israel was a child, I loved him,
    and out of Egypt I called my son.
The more I called them,
    the more they went from me;
they kept sacrificing to the Baals,
    and burning incense to idols.
Yet it was I who taught Ephraim to walk,
    I took them up in my arms;
    but they did not know that I healed them.
I led them with cords of compassion,
    with bands of love,
and I became to them as one who eases the
    yoke on their jaws,
    and I bent down to them and fed them.
They shall return to the land of Egypt,
    and Assyria shall be their king,
    because they have refused to return to me.
The sword shall rage against their cities,
    consume the bars of their gates,
    and devour them in their fortresses.
My people are bent on turning away from me;
    so they are appointed to the yoke,
    and none shall remove it.
How can I give you up, O Ephraim!
    How can I hand you over, O Israel!
How can I make you like Admah!
    How can I treat you like Zeboiim!
My heart recoils within me,
    my compassion grows warm and tender.
I will not execute my fierce anger,
    I will not again destroy Ephraim;
for I am God, and not man,
    the Holy One in your midst,
    and I will not come to destroy.

(11:1–9)

Hosea's marriage taught him more than the meaning of betrayal and humiliation. If a human parent could feel a sustaining love for the living fruit—legitimate or not—of his unhappy union, how much more abiding must be the love of a divine parent for wayward Ephraim! Though he could not avert the terrible fate that overtook the northern kingdom, Hosea left a literary and theological legacy whose influence is still felt. By delving into the deepest darkness of human emotions, Hosea came into contact with the heart of his god. It is this luminous moment of understanding between creator and creature, captured so powerfully in Hosea's writing, that has continued to move and enlighten readers of the book over the centuries.

Bibliography

Andersen, Francis I., and David Noel Freedman. *Hosea: A New Translation with Introduction and Commentary.* Anchor Bible, vol. 24. Garden City, N.Y., 1980. A special look at the literary texture of Hosea that finds more integrity to the work than was previously held to be the case.

Clements, Ronald E. "Understanding the Book of Hosea." *Review and Expositor* 72 (1975): 405–423. Argues for a Judean editing of the text of Hosea, and looks at the complex in chapters 1–3 from this perspective.

Cogan, Morton. *Imperialism and Religion: Assyria, Judah, and Israel in the Eighth and Seventh Centuries* B.C.E. Missoula, 1974. This revised doctoral dissertation catalogs the effects of Assyrian imperialism on the states of the Palestinian land-bridge, concluding that Assyria did not interfere in internal religious affairs until Israel's annexation as an Assyrian province.

Emmerson, Grace I. *Hosea: An Israelite Prophet in Judean Perspective.* Journal for the Study of the Old Testament Supplements, vol. 28. Sheffield, England, 1984. Looks at the various levels of editing of Hosea and comes to conclusions strikingly different from those of Andersen and Freedman.

Gordis, Robert. "Hosea's Marriage and Message." In *Poets, Prophets, and Sages: Essays in Biblical Interpretation,* edited by Robert Gordis. Bloomington, Ind., 1971.

Pp. 230–254. Reviews the various options for understanding the actions described in Hosea 1–3 and concludes that we have two accounts, each from a different time period, of the same incident.

Gottwald, Norman K. *The Hebrew Bible: A Socio-Literary Introduction.* Philadelphia, 1985. Emphasizes social scientific and literary approaches in its reconstruction of Israelite and Judean tradition and history.

Heschel, Abraham Joshua. *The Prophets.* 2 vols. New York, 1962. Provides excellent, extremely readable discussions of the phenomenon of prophecy in ancient Israel and Judah. A landmark in theological scholarship. Especially notable is Heschel's treatment of divine pathos in Hosea.

Lerner, Gerda. "The Origin of Prostitution in Ancient Mesopotamia." *Signs* 11 (1986): 236–254. Reviews the cuneiform evidence from Mesopotamia on prostitution, with special attention to the way the sexual control of women cemented the power and class relations in ancient society.

Lundbom, Jack R. "Poetic Structure and Prophetic Rhetoric in Hosea." *Vetus Testamentum* 29 (1979): 300–308. Looks at Hosea's use of broken bicola to convey a message of divine distance.

Schmitt, John J. "The Gender of Ancient Israel." *Journal for the Study of the Old Testament* 26 (1983): 115–125. Surveys the use of masculine and feminine imagery to designate Israel and concludes that the harlot metaphor in the prophetic writings originates in city language (cities are feminine in Hebrew), while the gender of Israel remains overwhelmingly masculine in the Hebrew Bible.

Wolff, Hans Walter. *Hosea: A Commentary on the Book of the Prophet Hosea.* Translated by Gary Stansell. Philadelphia, 1974. This standard commentary on Hosea makes use of frequent emendations of difficult texts and takes a form-critical approach in the explication of the units. For a very different treatment of the text of Hosea, see Andersen and Freedman, above.

CAROLE R. FONTAINE

Joel

THE SINGLE MOST important feature that sets Joel apart from the other books of the prophets is its peculiar preoccupation with an insect, the desert locust. As this insect commands the attention of the author of Joel for the first two-thirds of the book, any attempt to understand the work must first determine the significance of the locust: Why should it dominate the thought of a biblical prophet? What sort of crisis did it create? Is the locust really a locust, or only a symbol for something larger than itself? Joel's interpreters have wrestled with these basic questions over the years, and any reader who hopes to understand this unusual prophetic book and why it was preserved in the biblical canon must address them as well.

The Book of Joel actually has two parts. The lengthier initial section is dominated by the locust (1:2–2:27). The shorter final section, however, does not mention the locust (2:28–3:21; 3:1–4:21 in the Masoretic text). Instead, it describes a future outpouring of God's spirit and the apocalypse, a great and final war in which Israel will be victorious and all its enemies defeated. Most interpreters since the 1950s have seen a close connection between the two parts of Joel, viewing the locust threat as the sign of a greater crisis, the last war described at the conclusion of the book. Some scholars, however, see the two parts of Joel as quite distinct, the initial section describing a

locust plague and the final section being added by an editor who anticipated the apocalypse.

The merits of these two views of the unity of the Book of Joel will be evaluated later. Both views, however, recognize the crucial place of the locust in Joel. This insect produced the human and ecological crisis that brought the Book of Joel into existence and thus provides the obvious place to begin an investigation into the meaning of Joel.

A LITURGY FOR THE LAND (1:2–2:27)

The event around which the entire first part of Joel revolves is an ecological crisis of national proportions caused by the swarming of the desert locust. Lengthy descriptions of the locust (1:4–12, 16–20; 2:1–11) indicate a massive invasion of the Land of Israel: locusts are spread out like the light of dawn on the mountains; they crowd into the cities, covering the walls and houses and coming through the windows like thieves.

This infestation causes no mere inconvenience but the complete loss of the produce of an entire growing season. Fields of grain, vineyards, orchards, and pastureland have all been stripped bare by the voracious appetites of the invading swarms. To use Joel's own metaphor, the countryside has been turned from a garden of Eden into a desert wasteland (2:3).

The specters of widespread malnutrition and starvation and, ultimately, a considerable loss of life loom large.

The magnitude of the plague and of the agricultural devastation described in Joel appears to be an accurate portrayal of the damage that can be inflicted by the insect in question, *Schistocerca gregaria,* the desert locust (Krebs 1978; Whiting 1915). The desert locust regularly inhabits and breeds in the immense desert stretching from Saharan Africa through the Arabian Peninsula and into western India, an area including the Sinai Peninsula and Judean desert. Given the right combination of circumstances, still not completely understood by scientists but involving climate as well as biological and behavioral changes in the insect itself, the desert locust multiplies rapidly, crowds into dense, gregarious swarms, and migrates in large bands into neighboring fertile areas in search of food.

The seriousness of such an outbreak to food supplies and human populations can be illustrated by statistics from an invasion of Somaliland in 1957. A swarm of desert locusts there was estimated to include 16 billion locusts and to weigh 50,000 tons. Since locusts eat their own weight in green food each day, the threat to vegetation from the swarming locust is enormous. Though controlled in the modern era by insecticides sprayed on breeding areas, the desert locust remains a serious threat. For thirty-seven of the fifty-six years between 1908 and 1964 it was in a state of plague and is now monitored constantly by the United Nations Food and Agriculture Organization's Emergency Center for Locust Operations.

The first two chapters of Joel contain one of the oldest detailed descriptions of the desert locust in a state of plague in the Middle East, although the account is not journalistic or scientific. It is a highly personalized response—poetic in form and religious in substance—to an extraordinary human tragedy.

The ancient Hebrew poetry found in Joel is composed of verses of two or three parallelistic lines; it relies heavily on metaphor and simile to communicate the experience of an event that seemed unreal in its magnitude. The insect hordes are described as a massive nation occupying the land, as brush fires crackling through the stubble, as lions with fearful teeth, as thieves who steal in through windows, and as thunderclouds darkening the sky. But most of all, they are compared to an invading army (1:6, 2:4–9).

Joel selects literary forms closely related to Israel's religious life for his response to the locust crisis because the crisis is perceived as one of religious dimensions. Some of these forms derive from the prophetic tradition; others, from religious services and liturgies and from public worship developed by official Temple personnel.

The Book of Joel opens, following its title (1:1), with an appeal traditionally used by prophets to gain the attention of their audience and alert it to the delivery of a solemn proclamation (2:2–4). Like other prophets who employed this conventional form (e.g., Isa 1:2, Mic 1:2, Jer 2:4, Amos 8:4), Joel understood himself as a messenger delivering a divine decree.

This opening summons is followed by a series of speeches in which Joel urges different sectors of the population—consumers (drinkers of wine, 1:5–10), farmers (1:11–12), and priests (1:13–18)—to respond to the extreme agricultural crisis by declaring their distress and appealing to God for help. Joel begins each speech with a verse containing a series of imperative verbs; the second line of each verse begins with *helilu* (wail), a term frequently used in the Bible in descriptions of ceremonies of lamentation (e.g., Jer 4:8, Amos 8:3). Indeed, the first two elements of the lament genre, a prayer employed in Temple liturgy to appeal to God for assistance in a crisis, are recognizable in these speeches: a cry to God, followed by a description of distress, in this case the catastrophic losses of food to the locusts. Concluding this series of speeches is the prophet's own prayer of lament (1:19–20).

The description of the locust infestation in these prayers of lament is concluded in a vivid poem (2:1–11), in which the appearance of the locust in the Land of Israel is closely related to the arrival of the Day of Yahweh. The concept of the Day of Yahweh has a rich and varied history in biblical literature, and Joel's exact intention in using it in this poem, as well as in 1:15, has been actively debated.

Originally a designation for Yahweh's victory in holy war, and later connected with the celebration of

Yahweh's kingship in Zion, the Day of Yahweh was given a radically new interpretation by the classical prophets. According to them it would be a day of darkness and not light, a day on which Yahweh would be victorious, not over Israel's enemies, but over Israel itself as a judgment for the corruption in its society (e.g., Amos 5:18–20). Early apocalyptic writers would reverse the image yet again, describing the Day of Yahweh as an essentially positive event, the day of the great apocalypse, on which Yahweh would defeat the wicked permanently and vindicate the people of God (e.g., Zech 14:1–9).

Of these different meanings, the one given by the classical prophets best explains Joel's use of the concept in this poem (*cf.* Bourke 1959). Joel perceives the invasion of the locusts as an army brought by God against his own people and the devastation of the land as God's day of judgment on Israel. Even the darkening of the sun caused by the black clouds of locusts whirling into the land must have called to mind for Joel the prophetic notion and conventional language of darkness accompanying God's judgment day (2:2, 10; *cf.* Amos 5:18–20, Zeph 1:14–16).

Joel's interpretation of the appearance of the locusts as the arrival of Yahweh's day of judgment is clear in his consequent call for repentance on the part of his society (2:12–17). He insists that the priests gather the entire community for a public ceremony in order to grieve for its sins and appeal to God for pity and assistance. In the tradition of the classical prophets, however, Joel emphasizes that true religious life and worship do not consist in the public rituals of the Temple service but are essentially an inner orientation and commitment (2:12–13). Using a conventional expression about God's compassion (*cf.* Exod 34:6), Joel suggests that sincere repentance will result in divine help (2:13).

Joel's delivery of a divine oracle of salvation concludes the initial section of the book (2:18–27). The message promises an end to the locust plague, a complete revival of the land, and the well-being of the society. The oracle assures the people that God has heard their appeals and that a response is imminent. Using language that carefully echoes the earlier description of the disaster, Joel reverses image after image. The invading locust will be driven out into lands as desolate as those it leaves behind (2:20; *cf.* 2:3). The land that had mourned is told to rejoice (2:21; *cf.* 1:10). The animals who once longed for pasture will graze in it again (2:22; *cf.* 1:19–20). Trees and vines once stripped even of bark will again yield produce (2:22; *cf.* 1:12). All that the locust devoured will be restored (2:25; *cf.* 1:4). A people summoned to wail (*helilu*) will again praise (*hillaltem*) its God (e.g., 2:26; *cf.* 1:5).

Joel's religious response to the ecological crisis pervades this initial section of the book. Believing the locust to be God's own destroying army (2:11, 25), he urges his contemporaries to raise laments to God, calls them to national self-examination and repentance, and finally delivers in an oracle actual divine words promising assistance. This response to a natural disaster as a religious event is predicated on two basic conceptions of the biblical prophets, conceptions they shared for the most part with other ancient Near Eastern cultures.

First, they perceived reality as an integrated whole, with no sense of the clear divisions between the realms of nature, human experience, and divine activity, a sense that is pronounced in modern societies dominated by a scientific worldview. For them, everything was part of a single reality, ultimately controlled by divine forces and wills. A disruption within any one of the realms was apprehended as a disruption within all realms of experience. A natural disaster such as a locust plague could be explained not by discovering its natural causes alone (i.e., the biology or habitat of the locust), but only by discerning human and divine influences that might also be involved.

Second, Joel's response was based on the notion that exemplary behavior was invariably rewarded by God with good fortune, and immoral behavior with misfortune. This key element in Israel's understanding of its covenant with God (e.g., Deut 27–28) was vigorously proclaimed by Israel's prophets, who viewed Israel's political reversals as the inevitable divine response to corruption in its society (e.g., Amos 3:9–11). Thus Joel regarded ecological misfortune as a divine response to social corruption and foresaw renewal in nature as the inevitable divine response to communal self-examination and renewal.

Joel's conception of reality as an integrated whole also explains his sense of the close bond between human society and its natural environment. He recognized to how great an extent the fate of human life is linked to the fate of the earth, and he expressed this by his repeated use of the same terms and images to describe the responses of humanity and nature to the locust infestation. As the priests mourn so does the land (1:9–10). As the vines wither and dry up so do the farmers and so does the joy of the people (1:11–12). As Joel cries out to God so do the animals in the barren pastures (1:19–20). The land and its people are inextricably linked in the tragedy. Thus the ceremony to which Joel calls the people is not just an affair between the people and God. It is a liturgy for the land, a land that has been decimated and upon whose renewal society depends for its survival.

Because of the liturgical characteristics of Joel's compositions—his summons to a public ceremony of lament at the Temple in Jerusalem and his use of literary forms designed for community worship—Joel has often been viewed as a Temple official, a "cult prophet." His book has even been analyzed as a unified liturgy that with its prayers and oracles provides the order for the very ceremony to which he summoned the people (Kapelrud 1948). There can be no doubt that Joel was familiar with Temple worship and that he considered it crucial to the appeal for divine assistance in a crisis, but it is difficult to say whether he was acting on behalf of the Temple hierarchy and writing for its worship. More likely, Joel, as was typical of Israel's classical prophets, had no official position with the Temple (Wolff 1977). Rather, in customary prophetic fashion, he called all segments of his society, farmers as well as priests, to recognize God's displeasure, amend their ways, and appeal to God for help. In this prophetic role, he delivered the divine promise of help.

Regularly debated without a completely satisfactory solution is the question of exactly when in Israel's history the land was hit with the invasion of locusts that inspired Joel's response. The title of Joel does not identify his career with the reign of any Israelite king, as do the titles of most prophetic books. Nor are there any historical allusions, at least in the initial section, that would provide clues to the date of the plague.

Joel's language and basic religious ideas—disaster as punishment for societal sins, the need for national renewal—are much like those of Israel's preexilic prophets, and some, such as Wilhelm Rudolph, have placed the composition of Joel during Israel's monarchy, not later than the seventh century B.C.E. The editors of the Hebrew Bible must have had these considerations in mind in placing the Book of Joel between those of the eighth-century prophets Hosea and Amos.

But most scholars, noting that Joel makes no reference to a king and that some terminology is close to that found in later biblical literature, place Joel after Israel's monarchy, during the postexilic period of the sixth, fifth, or fourth centuries (Ahlström 1971; Wolff 1977). A definite solution to the date of Joel is in the final analysis not crucial for understanding the initial section of the book. A plague of desert locusts of the dimensions Joel describes would have been catastrophic for Israelite society at any time in its history.

It is the catastrophic, life-threatening character of the plague that explains Joel's complete preoccupation with the desert locust in the initial section of the book. The ecological crisis caused by the invading armies of locusts was no less desperate than the international crises caused by the invading armies of the Assyrians and Babylonians, about which better-known prophets such as Isaiah and Jeremiah composed responses. When Joel came forward to address his people his aim was nothing less than to save the life of a society.

ARMS FOR AN APOCALYPSE (2:28–3:21)

Considering the dominance of the locust in the initial section of the book, it seems somewhat surprising that the second section does not mention the locust at all. That section focuses instead on the apocalypse, a great final war in which God will defeat all corrupt powers on earth and inaugurate a new age of security and well-being for the upright. The major literary composition in this section is a hymn celebrating the victory of the divine warrior (3:1–21), a hymn that can best be understood by examining the traditional sources on which its author drew.

As old as Israel itself is the idea that Israel's God was a warrior, fighting on Israel's behalf against nations hostile to it. Hymns celebrating divine victories over Israel's enemies are among the oldest poems in the Bible, composed before the Israelite monarchy as early as the twelfth and eleventh centuries B.C.E. (e.g., Exod 15:1–18, Judg 5). Many hymns from the monarchy, established at the end of the eleventh century, contained this tradition and praised the military exploits of God on behalf of the Davidic king reigning in Jerusalem (e.g., Pss 2, 24, 29, 68, 89, 97).

These hymns in turn are based on an even older tradition, the ancient Near Eastern conflict myth found in both Canaanite (the Baal cycle) and Mesopotamian (Enuma Elish) texts. In this myth the storm god is threatened by his enemy, the sea, and goes out to battle shaking the cosmos with his thunderous power. After defeating the sea, the storm god returns to his holy mountain to be enthroned king of the cosmos by the gods whom he has saved. Fertility and plenty are bestowed on all creation.

These mythic and hymnic traditions were taken up by Israelite poets after the fall of the kingdom of Israel in 587 to express their hopes that God, in the role of divine warrior, would restore their national, economic, and religious status among the nations. In these late divine warrior hymns, poets often express apocalyptic thoughts, imagining that God's next military campaign will defeat Israel's enemies for good and thereby bring an end to ordinary human history. God's appearance would be so cataclysmic that reality would be restructured. These poets anticipated the end of the present age of Israel's suffering and the creation of a new order of complete peace and abundance (e.g., Isa 66:14b–16, 22–23; Zech 14:1–21; Ezek 38–39). It is among such poets that the author of Joel 3 is to be found.

Joel 3, an apocalyptic adaptation of the old mythic and hymnic traditions of the divine warrior, incorporates the major elements of the ancient Near Eastern conflict myth: the sovereignty of the divine warrior is threatened by Israel's enemies, who have exiled God's people, sacked his Temple, and taken his land (3:1–8); the divine warrior goes into combat and defeats the enemy nations (3:9–14); the cosmos is shaken by God's appearance (3:15–16); the victorious warrior is enthroned on his holy mountain (3:17); fertility and well-being are bestowed on creation (3:18); and the salvation of God's people is affirmed (3:19–21).

A remarkable image in this hymn is the poet's order to the nations to manufacture arms for the apocalypse from agricultural implements (3:10)—an exact reversal of the command in another well-known biblical poem (Isa 2:2–4, Mic 4:1–3) to beat swords into plowshares and spears into pruning knives, to give up the study of the tactics of war. For this poet the new age would be brought into being not by negotiation among nations but by a decisive conflict between divine and human armies.

The hymn gives every indication that the war in question does not occur within ordinary history; rather it is a cosmic conflict that will introduce a substantively new period of human experience. The divine warrior fights alone without Israel's armies. He defeats all the nations. The nations actually singled out—Tyre, Sidon, Philistia, Egypt, Edom—are Israel's traditional enemies and are meant to symbolize all hostile powers. And the battle is fought in the valley of Jehoshaphat, not an actual place but a symbolic one meaning "Yahweh has judged," thus describing the significance of the war. The images of fertility and abundance are so excessive that they suggest a re-creation of the natural order.

By adapting old, revered traditions about Israel's divine warrior for this hymn, its poet gave these words legitimacy in the mind of his audience and at the same time reminded it of divine assistance Israel had received in many crises in the past. In using these traditions to picture the future cosmic victory of the divine warrior, the poet proposed a solution to a predicament that looked hopeless in light of current political and historical circumstances. He shared the national pain of his fellow Jews, subjugated and demoralized since the fall of the Israelite kingdom, but was convinced that justice would be done to nations guilty of war crimes and atrocities and that Israel would experience a new peace and prosperity.

This divine warrior hymn is preceded by a much shorter composition (2:28–32; chap. 3 in the Hebrew text), which anticipates the same events described in more detail in Joel 3: the salvation of God's people in a cosmic event (2:30–32). The unique element here is the description of the ideal human community that will populate the new age (2:28–29), an egalitarian society in which all possess the spiritual powers and insights once granted only to exceptional prophetic figures. Traditional social, sexual, economic, and religious hierarchies and divisions are overcome, so that no one is excluded from full participation in the life of the community.

THE BOOK SEEN AS A WHOLE

The central question for understanding the Book of Joel as a whole is how these two sections of Joel are related to one another. What does this picture of the apocalypse and the new age at the conclusion of Joel have to do with the locust infestation with which the book begins? Two basic responses to this question have come from Joel's interpreters.

Many scholars, especially since the early 1950s, have seen the book as the unified composition of a single author (e.g., Wolff 1977). According to this position, the two sections are linked by similarities in language and by intentional parallels. The crisis caused by the locust prefigures for the prophet Joel an even greater crisis, the final conflict between God and the nations. The locust armies symbolize the national armies. As God drives out the locust, so will he defeat the nations. As the Land of Israel is restored to fertility following the locust plague, so will it be after the apocalypse. Thus references to the Day of Yahweh throughout Joel (1:15; 2:1–2, 10–11, 30–31; 3:14–15) are essentially apocalyptic and refer to God's imminent final victory.

Other interpreters, such as Bernhard Duhm, have emphasized the distinct differences between the two sections of Joel and have portrayed the book as a collection of compositions by two authors, which have been combined to reorient old prophecy to new crises. This approach sees the two sections as reflecting distinctly different settings and concerns. The first section is totally absorbed with the agricultural crisis

caused by the locust, whereas the second, which does not even mention the locust, focuses on the political crisis of exile caused by the fall of Jerusalem (conversely not mentioned in the first section). Although God's assistance is viewed in the first section in terms of the restoration of crops and food supplies within the normal sphere of human history, divine aid is represented in the second section as the reconstitution of Israel as a nation in Judah by a cosmic event that will usher in a new age.

This latter approach to the Book of Joel deserves to be taken more seriously than it has been in the last several decades. The social situations and worldviews reflected in the two sections of Joel are so distinct that they suggest separate historical settings and religious minds at work. Similarities in language are explainable as a common use of formulaic poetic expression or even direct quotation from older prophetic literature. And parallels may be described as the secondary result of the editorial addition of new apocalyptic poetry.

Collections of prophetic speeches in other prophetic books have received just this sort of editing to provide them with apocalyptic conclusions. Isaiah 56–66 and Zechariah 9–14, studied by Paul Hanson, are two of the best examples. These apocalyptic additions were intended to carry forward the original prophet's thought with the claim that previously expressed hopes for salvation would be realized when God acted in cosmic fashion to destroy evil and re-create the world as a secure home for God's people. The genre of the divine warrior hymn, like that in Joel 3, was particularly popular with these apocalyptic poets and editors.

Understood in this way the Book of Joel provides us with a glimpse into two crises that threatened the integrity of the nation of Israel and its faith in God. The first of these was an ecological crisis of massive proportions, the swarming of the desert locust and consequent catastrophic losses of crops and food. The second was a political crisis, the end of the kingdom of Israel and consequent killing, subjugation, and deportation of its citizens.

Both crises produced figures who came forward with responses designed to save the life and faith of the threatened community. One was the prophet to whom we owe the name of the book. He urged his people to respond to the ecological crisis with a period of national self-examination and recommitment to the ideals of community within its covenant with God. He offered, as relief from despair, the anticipation of relief from the infestation and the hope of a new, abundant harvest. The other figure was an anonymous apocalyptic poet who added new compositions affirming that Israel would not be annihilated by recent political tragedies but would ultimately be protected by a greater power who would deal out justice to the guilty and provide security and well-being for God's people.

Bibliography

Ahlström, Gösta W. *Joel and the Temple Cult of Jerusalem.* Leiden, 1971. A study of selected topics from Joel, especially the book's reflection of Jerusalem Temple practices.

Bourke, J. "Le jour de Yahvé dans Joël." *Revue biblique* 66 (1959): 5–31, 191–212. A defense of both prophetic (1:15; 2:1, 11) and apocalyptic (2:31, 3:14) uses of the Day of Yahweh in Joel.

Duhm, Bernhard. "Anmerkungen zu den zwölf Propheten." *Zeitschrift für die alttestamentliche Wissenschaft* 31 (1911). The classic statement on the dual authorship of Joel.

Hanson, Paul D. *The Dawn of Apocalyptic.* Philadelphia, 1975. An analysis of the apocalyptic additions to Isaiah (chaps. 56–66) and Zechariah (chaps. 9–14).

Kapelrud, Arvid S. *Joel Studies.* Uppsala, 1948. A presentation of Joel as unified liturgy composed by the "Temple prophet" Joel for Israelite worship.

Krebs, Charles J. *Ecology: The Experimental Analysis of Distribution and Abundance.* 2d ed. New York, 1978. Chapter 16 contains a brief introduction to the behavior of the desert locust.

Plöger, Otto. *Theocracy and Eschatology.* Translated by S. Rudman. Richmond, Va., 1968. Pp. 96–105 contain an examination of the apocalyptic features in Joel, especially in 2:28–3:31.

Rudolph, Wilhelm. *Joel, Amos, Obadja, Jona.* Gütersloh, 1971. A detailed commentary treating Joel as a unity.

Weiser, Artur. *Das Buch der zwölf Kleinen Propheten.* Vol. 1. *Das Alte Testament Deutsch,* vol. 24. Göttingen, 1956. A proposal that Joel was written by one author in two distinct stages.

Whiting, John D. "Jerusalem's Locust Plague." *National Geographic* 28 (1915): 511–551. A vivid description of Jerusalem's last great locust plague.

Wolff, Hans Walter. *Joel and Amos.* Translated by Waldemar Janzen, S. Dean McBride, Jr., and Charles A. Muenchow. Philadelphia, 1977. The most complete and thorough commentary in English.

THEODORE HIEBERT

Amos

AMOS IS THE third book of the twelve minor prophets and is named after the first prophet whose pronouncements were collected and preserved as an independent literary work. His oracles date from around the middle of the eighth century B.C.E. The book has attracted special interest, both for its intrinsic literary qualities and as a key to the development of prophecy in ancient Israel—and hence to our understanding of the prophetic literature in the Hebrew Bible. Its appeal lies particularly in its short, pungent sayings, its vivid imagery, and its telling criticism of social, religious, and economic wrongdoing. Although some of the language and references are strange to modern readers, there is much that transcends history and culture to strike the imagination (all translations are by the present author):

> A lion roars; who will not fear?
> God speaks; who will not prophesy?
> (3:8)

Or again:

> Let justice roll along like rushing water,
> and righteousness like a perennial stream.
> (5:24)

The book opens with a superscription (1:1) and motto (1:2) and then continues with a series of eight oracles against various nations, concluding with Israel (1:3–2:16). The chapters that follow present groups of shorter sayings, each beginning with the general call to attention: "Hear this word" (3:1, 4:1, 5:1). Within chapters 5–6 other sayings are gathered in two or three groupings beginning with the cry "Woe to . . ." (5:7 [disputed], 5:18, 6:1). There is a sudden shift to prose narrative in chapter 7. Three vision reports in the first person (7:1–9) are followed by two narrative fragments in the third person (7:10–17). A fourth vision report (8:1–3) is followed by yet another collection of poetic sayings (8:4–14); and a fifth vision report (9:1–4), by a final group of sayings (9:7–10). These in turn are followed by the concluding divine promises of 9:11–15. Also distinctive are the passages of hymnic praise that punctuate the text at several points (4:13, 5:8–9, 9:5–6).

The sayings of Amos range in length from two poetic lines (e.g., 3:8, 6:12) to the series of oracles against various nations, bound together with refrains, in 1:3–2:16 (though the oracles against Tyre, Edom, and Judah were probably not part of the original series). The most common form of oracle in the book is the announcement of disaster preceded by a justification; for example, "I detest the arrogance of Jacob, I hate its palaces; so I will hand over the city in its entirety" (6:8).

Many of the individual sayings undoubtedly derive from Amos himself, but their collection and arrangement is the work of epigones. Although the arrangement of the sayings seems random or even arbitrary at times, various editorial motivations have been found for setting particular sayings side by side. Thus 1:3–2:15 is followed by 3:1–2 because both consider Israel's relationship to its God, Yahweh, in the context of Yahweh's relationship to other nations. And 3:3–6 follows 3:1–2 because both attempt to convince the audience that their own God may bring suffering upon them. Verses 9–11, 12, and 13–15 in chapter 3 share a focus on buildings and their furnishings (as well, perhaps, as having the inhabitants of Samaria as their target—though Samaria is not explicitly mentioned in vv. 13–15).

THE CONDITION OF ISRAEL AND AMOS' MESSAGE

Amos prophesied in a time of renewed prosperity for Israel. After repeated depredations by the Aramaeans, the Israelite king, Jeroboam II, finally recovered Israelite territory from these northeastern neighbors and secured the borders. This renewed control of trade routes north and south led to a period of peaceful growth. The king's efforts, encouraged by a prophet (2 Kgs 14:25), were also seen by a later writer as Yahweh's doing (2 Kgs 14:25, 27). It is understandable that many Israelites, believing themselves to be Yahweh's special people, felt reassured of Yahweh's presence and blessing. They were confident that whenever Yahweh intervened in human affairs it would be on their behalf, as it was when he brought them out of Egypt.

Unfortunately prosperity turned confidence into complacency. Creditors used or consumed pledges (Amos 2:8) or sold debtors into servitude to get immediate payment (2:6); sellers in the market used false scales to get more silver for less grain (8:5); and corrupt judges denied legal redress to those who had been wronged (5:10, 12b). As these references indicate, the injustices were not limited to one group or class, but were practiced at all levels of society. The breakdown in traditional values was particularly striking among the wealthiest in the society, who cultivated and enjoyed considerable luxury. While some were losing their land and homes and family, others had both winter and summer houses (3:15), lived in

homes of ashlar masonry (5:11), or enjoyed furnishings decorated with fine ivory work (3:15, 6:4; excavations have produced numerous examples of Samarian ivories). In 6:1–6 there is a graphic description of the sybaritic banquets enjoyed by the elite of the society, with choice meats, wine (cf. 4:1b), unguents, and music.

Amos castigates those who enjoy a life of carefree luxury and remain at the same time oblivious to the violence and oppression on which it is based. Indeed, having lost sight of the right direction for the society (3:9–10), the elite are said to "hoard violence and oppression for themselves" (3:10–11). The core of Amos' message, then, is that because of these misdeeds, God will destroy this society. The finality and thoroughness of this coming disaster, as well as its inescapability, are a persistent theme.

The finality of the catastrophe is perhaps most vividly expressed in the dirge of 5:2, which portrays Israel as a dead young woman, her body abandoned on her land. Similarly, 5:16–17 and 8:10 refer to universal mourning throughout the country; and 8:3 conjures up the picture of corpses everywhere, over which the palace singers wail. Armies will be decimated (5:3) and households left empty (6:9–10). The thoroughness of the coming scourge is conveyed in vivid images. What will be left is likened to a single log snatched from a conflagration (4:11) or a pair of shinbones or scrap of ear that a shepherd might retrieve in trying to rescue a sheep from the mouth of a lion (3:12).

Amos mercilessly destroys any hope for escape. The strong and the swift will find that their strength and speed fail them; the skill of archers and horsemen will avail them nothing; and the boldest warrior will run away naked (2:14–16). Their hopes will be like those of one who escapes from a lion only to run into a bear; who gets home safely and leans against the wall only to be bitten by a snake (5:19). In the fifth vision Yahweh announces that not one of them will flee or escape, even though in their desperation they break into the underworld or go up into the heavens, hide on the tops of mountains or on the floor of the sea. Yahweh will find them and seize them everywhere, commanding the sword to kill them even in exile (9:1–4).

The enormity of this announcement cannot be

AMOS

underestimated. It is as if the One God announced he were going to destroy Judaism; or Jesus Christ, the church; or Allah, Islam. How can Yahweh destroy his own people? Israel had enjoyed Yahweh's special intervention (2:9–11), and had been especially recognized by Yahweh (3:2a), uniquely delivered by Yahweh from slavery in Egypt (9:7b). It is characteristic of Amos that he relativizes this special relationship between Israel and Yahweh. Certainly the Exodus of Israel from Egypt was Yahweh's doing—but so was the exodus of the Philistines from Caphtor and of the Aramaeans from Kir (9:7b). Israel, says Amos, is in fact no more special to Yahweh than the remotest of peoples (9:7a). Exactly as Yahweh calls the nations to account for their crimes and announces their punishment, so he calls the Israelites to account and announces their punishment (1:3–2:16). Far from being exempt from such general judgment, Israel is the more accountable because of the special favors it has received (3:2b, 2:9–11). The other nations, even Egypt, are summoned to witness Israel's misdeeds (3:9) and testify against it (3:13).

For Israel this is a complete overturning of its values, a reversal of its theology. Yahweh's "eye," hitherto fixed benevolently on Israel, is now fixed malevolently on it (9:4b). The Day of Yahweh, eagerly awaited as the time when Yahweh would intervene among the nations on Israel's behalf to give it victory over its enemies, would be a day not of light but of darkness, not of victory but of defeat, as Yahweh fights not for but against Israel (5:18, 20). The motif of Yahweh turning light to darkness recurs in two of the hymnic passages (4:13a, 5:8a), and the same reversal opens the announcement of disaster in 8:9–10.

The visions reported by Amos do not disclose any explanation for the impending catastrophe. But the prophet has no doubt about the reasons: the common people are being trampled (2:7a, 4:1a, 8:4); they are taxed relentlessly (5:11a), cheated of fair measure and fair payment (8:5b), and then sold into servitude to pay off even small debts (2:6b, 8:6). Their access to the courts for redress is blocked (2:7a, 5:12b), so that "justice" has a bitter taste (5:7, 6:12b). It is particularly offensive to Yahweh that those who thus mistreat their fellow Israelites continue all the while to practice traditional worship. Hence

the ironic call to worship in 4:4–5; the contrast between taking Yahweh seriously and taking cultic worship seriously in 5:4–5; and the hyperbolic rejection of traditional worship in 5:21–23.

Amos singles out for condemnation those who see themselves as the elite, who live comfortably and confidently in Samaria (6:1, 4–6a; 3:15; these include specifically the great ladies of the town [4:1]), and those who glory in their military achievements (6:13). It is particularly against these that God's wrath is directed. Samaria will be stripped of its strength, and its splendid palaces plundered (3:9–11). The great and fancy houses will be demolished (3:15). The fine ladies will be dragged off through the broken city walls into exile (4:2–3). Those who enjoy their comforts at the head of the nation will be at the head of those being deported (6:7). And those who gloat over their military successes will find themselves beaten from one end of the country to the other (6:14).

THE RESPONSE OF ISRAEL AND AMOS' RHETORIC

Even from this prosaic, summary account of the prophet's message, the power of Amos' rhetoric is evident. He fashions his words in response, first, to the complacency and indifference of his listeners, and, second, to their hostility. To attract their attention and engage them in his discourse, he frequently begins by saying something with which they will readily agree—thus raising their expectations and winning their sympathy. Only then does he expose their guilt and the consequent punishment. In the series of oracles in 1:3–2:16 (unified by general form and particular refrains), for example, Amos works to win his listeners' enthusiastic endorsement of Yahweh's judgment against various neighboring nations. The reiteration of the same refrain at the beginning of the final oracle presses his audience to go on to assent to the rightness of Yahweh's judgment against the last nation: Israel itself. Another oracle opens in 3:2 with a strong assertion of Yahweh's special relationship with Israel alone—only to conclude that that relationship entails special accountability. And the beginning of 3:12 suggests the idea of redemption: "As a shepherd rescues . . . " The unsuspecting listener's attention has been caught, but it is then directed to

369

contemplate the mere scraps that will be rescued.

Amos frequently uses a rhetorical question or a series of rhetorical questions to engage the listeners and push them into giving the same answer to the final critical question as they gave to the earlier commonsense ones. Thus 3:3–6 constitutes a series of six questions, based on familiar relationships, that elicits the answer "No, of course not!" and leads the audience to give the same answer to the seventh question: "Is there a calamity in a town without Yahweh being responsible?" Presupposing the accepted theological relationship, 9:7b has Yahweh ask: "Did I not bring Israel out of Egypt?" The answer is: "Of course!" But the text immediately goes on to suggest by its use of parallel questions that Yahweh brought other peoples from their previous homelands in just the same way—thus denying the uniqueness of the Exodus and Yahweh's special relationship to Israel.

The aforementioned rhetorical devices are used to bring the reluctant audience to hear the unbearable message. Amos employs other rhetorical forms to defend himself and his heirs from the attacks of an opposition aroused by the radical and provocative nature of that message. Thus he tells those who would silence him that they cannot blame him for his message but must address themselves to Yahweh, whose speech is the irresistible force behind the prophecy. His most succinct apologia is found in 3:8: "Is there anyone who will not fear when a lion roars?" The answer is obviously no. Then follows immediately: "Is there anyone who will not prophesy when Yahweh speaks?" The strict parallelism of the two questions presses the same answer on those unwilling to admit it. A striking metaphor and the parallel construction compel acceptance of Amos' claim that when Yahweh has spoken one cannot help prophesying.

The vision reports of 7:1–8, 8:1–2, and 9:1–4 also serve to justify the prophet's role and, more specifically, his message. Twice, on seeing a vision of destruction, Amos pleads with Yahweh to spare Israel and recognize its helplessness, and twice he causes Yahweh to change his mind (7:1–3, 4–6). But by the third and fourth visions, Yahweh takes the initiative and addresses Amos, stating with finality that he will no longer pass by Israel (7:7–8, 8:1–2), which is now

beyond intercession. And in the fifth vision there is no dialogue: Yahweh simply announces that he will utterly destroy Israel—it will not be able to escape anywhere in the universe. Yahweh's will toward Israel has changed from good to bad (9:1–4). In these vision reports, Amos' authenticity as a prophet is demonstrated by his having twice successfully interceded with God (cf. Jer 27:18) to avert the impending disaster. But the validity of his announcement of Yahweh's punishment of Israel is also vindicated, as it is shown to have been God's intention from the beginning, and to have been impressed upon the prophet with increasing severity. How can Amos be expected to compromise when Yahweh has finally revealed himself to be uncompromising?

Also serving an apologetic function in the book are the two unique fragments of third-person prose narrative in 7:10–17. Although presumably written by Amos' followers, these narratives draw on observations or accounts of his experiences. In the first, the priest of Bethel, Amaziah, reports the words of Amos to the king: "Jeroboam will die by the sword and Israel will go into exile" (7:11; cf. 7:9 and 7:16b, 5:27, 6:7). He infers from these that Amos has conspired against the king and concludes that such statements cannot be tolerated (7:10). The narrative does not record the king's reply, and what follows neither builds nor depends on this first narrative fragment. It seems, then, simply a device to show how seriously Amos was taken by the authorities and how dangerous his message was taken to be.

In the second narrative fragment Amaziah addresses Amos directly, telling him to go and prophesy in Judah and forbidding him to continue to prophesy in Bethel because of its status as a royal sanctuary: the issue here is not the content of Amos' prophesying but its legitimacy in such a shrine. Amos responds by asserting his legitimacy, which derives from direct divine arrest. Not a professional prophet, at first he had been a breeder of livestock and a cultivator of fig trees until Yahweh took him and told him to prophesy. His defense here is much the same as in 3:8, namely, that Yahweh is responsible for his present activity.

Amos proceeds to announce God's punishment of Amaziah. He indicates that the punishment is for the king's attempt to prevent Amos from prophesying (*cf.* 2:12b). Then he details the consequences of Amaziah's order for his wife, children, land, and self. The speech culminates in a reiteration of the basic theme: Israel will have to go into exile (7:17).

Here too the outcome is left open. How did Amaziah react to this oracle concerning his person? Did he arrest Amos for insubordination? Or did Amos go, as he was told? The narrative does not address those issues because it is not interested in such historical questions. It seeks, rather, to influence the reader through what it has made explicit: the conflict between the priest and the prophet and between the authorities they each represent. Each claims jurisdiction over the other. The priest, accountable to the kings, represents the state religion. His authority is temporal and local ("You shall not continue to prophesy *in Bethel*" [7:13a]). Amos, by contrast, represents only Yahweh and is accountable only to Yahweh. His authority has the stamp of divine command, which cannot be gainsaid; therefore he must prophesy against Amaziah when Amaziah has ordered him not to prophesy. As the first narrative fragment exhibits the general, official impact of the word of the prophet on the land and its leader, the second focuses on a personal confrontation and exhibits the irresistibility of the prophetic word and the personal vulnerability of any who would attempt to resist or reject it. This narrative thus seeks to convince its readers that Amos' authority far exceeds that of any religious official.

MAJOR ISSUES OF INTERPRETATION

The preceding discussion attempts to lay out the main features of the Book of Amos, as they are now generally understood. However, several issues of interpretation remain to be settled to general satisfaction. One is the relationship between the announcement of disaster and the justification for it. It is usually assumed that the vision reports are the starting point of Amos' mission—that once he was convinced of the finality of God's sentence on Israel, he set about looking for reasons that would explain such terrible punishment. This assumes that the message of the prophet came from outside his previous experience, that the literary references to the source of his mission are historically and psychologically descriptive, and

that the reasons given for the announced disaster are Amos' rationalizations of it.

But it is also possible that Amos, perceiving both the breakdown of traditional values and the injustices in Israel, came to be convinced of the finality of Yahweh's judgment. Amos' perception of prevailing conditions would then be the starting point of his mission, and the visions of disaster would be the outcome of Amos' previous reflections, rather than the stimulus of such reflections. This accords not only with the interpretation of the vision reports as apologetic but also with a view of the prophet as one who interprets the world in which he or she lives and moves from diagnosis to prognosis.

It is also customary among scholars to understand Amos' pronouncements literally, that is, as straightforward predictions of impending disaster. If that is so, however, why does he hone his language for such rhetorical effectiveness? Why should one who has heard God's final judgment take such trouble to communicate with the condemned? Is he really trying to reach those who may constitute a wise minority whom God might spare from the general disaster? Verses such as 9:8–10 suggest such a discrimination between the nation as a whole and those individuals who do not fit the general pattern. However, these verses are often attributed to a later hand, one arguing precisely for a discrimination between the guilty and the innocent, and for the exemption of the latter from the general fate. Alternatively, one might cite what seem to be direct appeals for change from elsewhere in the text: "Let justice roll along like rushing water" (5:24); "Seek me [Yahweh] that you may live" (5:4); "Seek good and not bad, that you may live . . . hate wrong and love right" (5:14–15). However, 5:24 in its context, following 5:21–23, serves to show why the people's worship is unacceptable, and 5:4, 14–15 have similarly been interpreted as merely exposing how far the Israelites' behavior is from anything that could save them (and in any case Amos' authorship of these verses has been contested). The fact remains: Amos' rhetoric raises the question of whether his aim goes beyond merely announcing bad news.

Again, it is common to see in the Book of Amos a reflection of a two-class society in which the rich and powerful oppress the poor and powerless. There is certainly some evidence of the two extremes, both in

Amos and in the remains uncovered by excavation. But such passages as 2:6, 8; 5:11; and 8:5–6 have been shown to imply that the oppressed extend from the most vulnerable members of the society to middle-ranking landowners, and the oppressors from the most privileged ranks to those struggling to maintain a small patrimony. The view one holds of the complexity of the society and of the sensitivity of Amos' criticism has a definite bearing on the interpretation of his intentions. For Amos, it is not simply a matter of separating the good from the bad (*cf.* 9:8–10), but of recognizing the depravity of a whole society and the consequences of such behavior.

There has been considerable disagreement over the originality of the message of Amos. An earlier generation of biblical scholars saw Amos as a great, creative visionary; others have considered him a tradition-bound conservative. Some have seen in the book a new vision of the nature of God and of God's relationship to the world. Others claim Amos based his message on the covenant between Yahweh and Israel and on publicly stated laws—he was merely pronouncing the appropriate judgment on the people for transgressing those laws. In fact, it seems that little in Amos' thought was radically new. On the other hand, nowhere does he cite or make explicit reference to the law, or invoke the covenant.

He seems rather to have taken traditional values and norms for granted (including expectations concerning the relations between nations) and to have wrestled with certain theological traditions in order to show how seriously God takes violations of those values and norms. Shocked by the breakdown of traditional mores and norms, Amos foresaw only disaster for Israelite society. He took traditional theological assumptions one by one and either emptied them of special significance (9:7) or reversed their significance (3:2, 5:18–20). Thus, in common with similar writings, Amos contains elements of both traditional values and new perceptions. The tension between traditional values and contemporary conditions drove him to find new ways of looking at tradition.

Perhaps the most vexing question is the extent to which the book, as we now have it, is a compilation of Amos' own pronouncements. Some scholars claim that almost the entire book is a record of his utter-

ances; others see it as the product of two or three centuries of living with Amos' sayings, during which time they were extended, interpreted, applied to new circumstances, and amended. The implications of such alternative views for the interpretation of the book are significant. Evaluation of the final verses is particularly revealing in this respect.

For example, Amos himself could have been the author of those sayings if (1) the reference to God's raising of the "fallen booth of David" (9:11) refers to contemporary Judah's recovery of its empire under David and if (2) the promises of the last verses (9:13–15) address those who were not among the condemned "sinners of my people" (9:10a), and who, therefore, were expected to survive the predicted cataclysm. But if Amos is indeed the author of these verses, then it was he who modified the threat of inevitable annihilation by promising that the entire nation would not be destroyed (9:8b–10) and that Yahweh would restore Israel to peace and prosperity (9:13–15). But an unconditional divine promise that the people would never again be uprooted from their land is scarcely compatible with an announcement of the people's deportation from the land and the utter uselessness of their reliance on previous divine promises.

On the other hand, if "the fallen booth of David" with its breached walls and ruins (9:11) refers to Jerusalem, the city of David, after the Babylonian conquest in 587, and if the "uprooted people" and "abandoned towns" of 9:15 and 9:14 refer also to conditions following the Babylonian invasion, and if the promises of those verses are based on familiarity with those conditions, then clearly those promises could not derive from the eighth-century prophet Amos. But, if this is the case, then Amos' authorship must be restricted to those sayings that cleave more consistently to the theme of deserved disaster. In the society of his day those pronouncements would have had unmitigated force. Moreover when his prophecies were fulfilled in the destruction of the northern kingdom of Israel, they would have gained in authority and acquired wider and lasting influence. For they would have significance not only for those who in the last decades of that kingdom shared Amos' views but also for all who subsequently remembered the end of Israel. His words would be preserved and recited as a warning to future generations, who, like their ancestors, might be led to ignore the traditional norms of justice and honesty.

Thus, although it may be presumed with reasonable confidence that the activities of the *man* Amos took place in the middle of the eighth century B.C.E. during the reign of Jeroboam II, fixing the date and setting of the *book* of Amos depends on one's understanding of the passages that contain these final promises. Since the nineteenth century most scholars have judged that the last verses presuppose the fall of the Davidic dynasty in 587 B.C.E.; and that the expression of hope for God's restoration of the devastated land and uprooted people presupposes at least the imminence of the return of the exiles to Judah in the last third of the sixth century. This view leads to the conclusion that the book grew out of the utterances of Amos in the mid eighth century, but was not completed until the postexilic period. Composition over such a long period—in this case, from the mid eighth to the late sixth century—accords well with the composition of most other books in the Hebrew Bible. These were not written at one time by one person, but rather were the products of oral traditions written down over long periods of time by many people.

In the case of Amos, it is widely agreed that within the time period of 750 and 500 B.C.E. other contributions were made to the book. There is disagreement on how extensive those contributions were, but it seems clear that many of Amos' sayings occasioned reflection and debate in light of later circumstances. As a result of this, comments or interpretations were added at times to a saying; or a saying may occasionally have been recast to suit a later situation. One good example of such adaptation is the insertion of the references to Judah (2:4–5) and Zion (1:2, 6:1) during the transmission of the Amos tradition in Judah.

Even initially, the text of the "words of Amos" (1:1) was not fixed, but was flexible and adaptable to new situations. Thus the process of understanding the sayings and applying them to contemporary situations, an occupation of all subsequent ages, was already underway as the sayings were being compiled and transmitted. At that stage explanatory and applicatory comment was incorporated into the text.

Most would agree, however, that it is not the final, postexilic edition of the work that determines its governing perspective; rather, it is the earliest edition, presumably by Amos' immediate followers, that preserves the stamp of the prophet himself and has persisted in its essentials, only marginally affected by later additions and modifications. It is less appropriate, therefore, to read the book as a postexilic work that frequently preserves earlier material than as an eighth-century deposit of the work of the prophet Amos, to which occasional phrases or passages have been added in subsequent centuries.

Whatever its precise historical origins and formation, the Book of Amos, a collection of brief utterances and reports of telling rhetorical effect, persists as a powerful poem: a penetrating indictment of a society that disregards traditional values of justice, honesty, and integrity in social relations and religious practices and a gripping vision of the inescapability of the doom to which such a society is subject. In the final analysis it also bestows a divine promise of new beginnings and abundant enjoyment of the goods of the earth.

Bibliography

Auld, A. G. *Amos*. Old Testament Guides. Sheffield, England, 1986.

Barton, John. *Amos's Oracles Against the Nations: A Study of Amos 1:3–2:5*. New York, 1980. A valuable monograph on the conventions and assumptions with which Amos worked.

Fendler, M. "Zur Sozialkritik des Amos." *Evangelische Theologie* 33 (1973). A study of the social realities implied by the text and of Amos' evaluation of them.

Hayes, J. H. *Amos, The Eighth Century Prophet: His Times and Preaching*. Nashville, Tenn., 1988.

Koch, Klaus. *The Prophets*. Vol. 1, *The Assyrian Age*. Translated by Margaret Kohl. Philadelphia, 1983. A slightly idiosyncratic but stimulating assessment of Amos.

Koch, Klaus, *et al. Amos: Untersucht mit den Methoden einer strukturalen Formgeschichte*. Kevelaer, 1976.

McKeating, Henry. *The Books of Amos, Hosea, and Micah*. Cambridge, 1971. A short, simple, but judicious commentary for the beginner.

Mays, James L. *Amos: A Commentary*. Philadelphia, 1969.

Melugin, R. F. "The Formation of Amos: An Analysis of Exegetical Method." *Society of Biblical Literature Seminar Papers* 1 (1978). A brief review of the work of Koch

(1976) and Wolff (1977) and a fresh study of the composition of the book.

Rudolph, Wilhelm. *Joel, Amos, Obadja, Jona.* Gütersloh, 1971.

Soggin, J. A. *The Prophet Amos: A Translation and Commentary.* London, 1987.

Wolff, Hans Walter. *Joel and Amos.* Translated by Waldemar Janzen, S. Dean McBride, Jr., and Charles A. Muenchow. Philadelphia, 1977. The most detailed, comprehensive, and masterly commentary available in English, with extensive bibliography.

Woude, A. S. van der. "Three Classical Prophets: Amos, Hosea, and Micah." In *Israel's Prophetic Tradition: Essays in Honour of Peter R. Ackroyd,* edited by Richard Coggins, Anthony Phillips, and Michael Knibb. New York, 1982. A brief survey of the important literature and issues of the 1960s and 1970s, with bibliography.

SIMON B. PARKER

Obadiah and Nahum

Obadiah

OBADIAH, THE SHORTEST book of the Hebrew Bible, has a large theme—God's justice and his faithfulness to his covenant with Israel. The book has sometimes been criticized as a nationalistic and vengeful judgment on the nation of Edom for its violence against Judah at the time of the fall of Jerusalem to the Babylonians in 587 B.C.E., and certainly that is the reason for the judgment pronounced in the book. When Judah succumbed to the troops of Nebuchadrezzar, ending her existence as a national state, Edom failed to come to her aid. On the contrary, Edom gloated over Judah's misfortune (v. 12), joined in the looting of Judah's goods (v. 13), and even cut off the escape of some of her refugees, turning them over to the Babylonian conquerors (v. 14). For that violation of its brotherly covenant with Judah, Edom is to be punished by God, who takes both his covenant with Judah and the covenants between human beings seriously. That is the principal message of this fourth book of the twelve minor prophets.

Of the prophet who delivers this message to Edom from the Lord, we know nothing. Obadiah, which means "servant or worshiper of Yahweh," is a familiar name in the Old Testament (*cf.* 1 Kgs 18:3, 7, 16; 1 Chron 27:19; 2 Chron 34:12), but none of the other references are to be identified with this prophet. Verses 1–4 of the book are paralleled, in a different setting, in Jeremiah 49:14–16; verse 5 is paralleled in Jeremiah 49:9; verse 8 echoes Jeremiah 49:7. Scholars have therefore theorized either that an older oracle was used by both Obadiah and Jeremiah or, more probably, that Jeremiah 49:7–22 is a postexilic composition, dependent in part on Obadiah. There are also some similarities with the book in Joel 3:19 (*cf.* v. 10); 3:3 (*cf.* v. 11); 1:15; 3:4, 7, 14 (*cf.* v. 15), and 2:32; 3:17 (*cf.* v. 17), but Joel is undoubtedly the later work. The parallels and similarities show how prophets used earlier traditions and adapted them to their own situation. They believed that the word of God remained in effect and was therefore pertinent to their own time and place.

Serious arguments have been raised, however, concerning the unity of the Book of Obadiah. Many scholars hold that the original work consisted of verses 2–14, 15b, which were uttered shortly after 587 B.C.E. as a particular judgment on the perfidy of Edom. To this, they hold, verses 15a, 16–18, or 16–21 were later added, perhaps in the time of Nabatean raids (500–450 B.C.E.) against Edom that forced her from her territory. This addition therefore sets the original oracle of verses 2–14, 15b in the context of God's universal judgment against the nations at the time of the Day of the Lord. To support this contention, such scholars point out that in those verses Edom is punished through the instrumentality of foreign nations, whereas in the rest of the text all nations are judged through the instrumentality of Israel.

On literary and rhetorical grounds, however, it is impossible to separate the book into two distinct oracles, and verse 15 as it stands reflects the proper order. Edom is the central object of judgment throughout the book, and the Day of the Lord figures in both sections (vv. 8a, 15–18). The theme of the reversal of fortunes permeates the book from beginning to end. And rhetorically, the decisive Hebrew word *ki* (for) at the beginning of verses 15 and 16 must be connected with what has gone before, since in general such *ki* phrases in Hebrew are used to give the theological rationale to what has been previously stated. We are, therefore, justified in reading the book as a unit, as it has been handed down to us in the canon.

With the exception of verse 20, which can only be read by emendation (as the RSV reads it), the text is in fairly good shape. Its style is passionate and poetic, interlaced with exclamations (e.g., v. 5) and repetitious verbal clauses in the Hebrew (e.g., v. 2) that punctuate the basic thought.

To understand the message of the book, we must know something of the history of Jacob and Esau, the forebears of the nations of Israel and Edom. The two were brothers (Gen 25:19–26), but from the first their relationship was marked by deceit and hatred (Gen 25:29–34; 27; 32–33), an enmity that continued between the peoples descended from them. Control of the territory of Edom, to the southeast of the Dead Sea, with its trade route running to Ezion-geber on the Gulf of Aqaba, was maintained during the time of David and Solomon. Thereafter, kings of Israel and Judah were characterized by whether or not they could hold on to Edom (*cf.* 2 Kgs 14:22, 16:6), and wars were frequent (*cf.* 2 Chron 21:8–10). Nevertheless, Edom's people were considered Israel's brothers, and the law of Deuteronomy 23:7 forbids the Israelite to abhor an Edomite. But in violation of that brotherly relationship, Edom turned against Judah in the latter's hour of greatest need, celebrated Judah's downfall, and joined in its ruin. Such disregard of a covenant was an unforgivable breach of righteousness, and Obadiah therefore announces that God will punish Edom for its sin.

God takes human covenants, founded in natural relationships, seriously, and he is the guardian of those human bonds—of parents with children, of husbands with wives, of siblings with siblings—just as he is the guardian of the bonds between kings or judges or princes and their people, and of prophets and priests with their followers. The sanctity of human and societal relationships is a *sine qua non* throughout the Hebrew Bible.

Beyond that, Israel is the chosen people of the Lord, his designated instrument for bringing his blessing to all the earth (Gen 12:3), the object of his special love and promise for the fulfillment of his purpose (Exod 19:4–6, Deut 7:6–8). To harm Israel, therefore, when God does not intend harm, is to attack God's purposes (e.g., Gen 12:3, Jer 2:3). In such an event God's defense of Israel, the apple of his eye, is as instinctive as a wink (Deut 32:10, Zech 2:8). Thus does God faithfully keep his covenant with his chosen people.

The book begins with the prophet's ecstatic vision, by which he is made privy to the plan: unspecified nations will rise up in battle against Edom (v. 1). Such battle, however, is not the work of the nations, but that of the Lord. God himself is rising up against Edom to make it small and cause for mockery among all peoples (v. 2).

As so often happens to nations in the prophecy of the Hebrew Bible, Edom's pride has led it astray. It thought itself invincible, fortifying itself amidst the sandstone cliffs and crevices, some of them 5,000 feet high, to the southeast of the tip of the Dead Sea. But nothing is too high for the Lord to bring down (e.g., Amos 9:2–3; Isa 2:12–17, 14:12–15), even from the heights of heaven (vv. 2–4). At the hand of the Lord, Edom will experience a stunning reversal of fortunes. Having plundered Judah's goods (v. 11), so too will it be thoroughly plundered, with nothing whatsoever left of its resources (vv. 5–6). It violated its covenant with the Israelites; therefore its allies and friends will violate their covenant with Edom and drive it from its land (v. 7). Edom was renowned for its wise men and wisdom tradition, but God will destroy its counselors along with its warriors, after which it will be renowned only for its shameful treachery against Jacob, that is, Judah (vv. 8–10; Teman in v. 9 is a district of Edom). As Edom has done to its brother Judah, so will be done to Edom (v. 15). Edom's sins will return upon its own head. God's judgment will take the form, as often in the Bible, of returning the evildoer's own wrong upon him (*cf.* 1 Kgs 8:31–32; Rom 1:24, 26, 28).

This judgment upon Edom, however, will not stand in isolation; rather it will be an integral part of God's judgment on all nations at the time of the Day of the Lord. Over against the day of Edom's participation in the ruin of Judah (vv. 11–13) is the decisive Day of Yahweh (vv. 8, 11, 15), which is to come soon. And when it comes, all the enemies of God's people will be destroyed. Edom has drunk and reveled on Mount Zion at the time of the fall of Jerusalem, but she and all nations will be forced to drink the cup of God's wrath (*cf.* Jer 25:15–29) until they stagger and completely disappear (v. 16). Israel has already experienced God's judgment in the form of the Babylonian destruction. Now her fortunes will be totally reversed, and on God's day she will be the object of his favor.

This view of the Day of the Lord is not the usual one found in the prophetic literature. Typically the prophets picture the Day of Yahweh as a time of judgment for Israel as well. The concept of the Day of the Lord had its roots in Israel's tribal league (1220–1000 B.C.E.), when it was believed that God the divine warrior fought for Israel against her enemies. From these roots, popular piety therefore projected a future, decisive day, on which God would defeat every enemy and exalt his chosen people. Most of the prophets dispute the popular view, however, and hold that the Day of the Lord is, for sinful Israel as for all other nations, a day of battle, wrath, darkness, and destruction. On that day only a faithful remnant will be left in Israel and all human pride and sin will be destroyed, leaving God alone exalted (*cf.* Amos 5:18–20; Isa 2:6–22; Ezek 7:5–27; Joel 1:1–15, 2:1–11; Mal 4:5). Obadiah reverses the traditional prophecies. There will indeed be left only a remnant of Israel (v. 17), but that remnant will be the instrument of God's judgment on Edom (v. 18), which will have no remnant whatsoever. Israel's remnant, furthermore, will regain not only the former territory of Judah (v. 17), but the whole of the ideal kingdom from Halah in the north to the Negev in the south, from the western coast of Palestine and Syria to the eastern limits of Gilead and Edom beyond the Jordan (vv. 19–20). On that day, God will set up his kingdom over all the earth, in which the saved of Judah shall share (v. 21; for "saviors" read, with many versions, "saved").

Edom's history is rather obscure. We do know, however, that Edom was driven from its land during the first half of the fifth century B.C.E., probably by Nabatean raiders from the desert. Forced to move into the Negev, south of the territory of Judah, it established there the kingdom of Idumea, with its capital at Hebron (1 Macc 4:29, 5:3, 65; Mark 3:8). At the time of the Maccabees under John Hyrcanus (135–104 B.C.E.), this area was, according to Josephus, forcibly incorporated into the Jewish commonwealth. Edom became, however, the prophetic prototype for all of those who oppose God, and its downfall was understood by the prophets as an indispensable precondition for the messianic age (*cf.* Isa 34:5–6, 63:1–6). Thus, in the Book of Revelation, God's enemies are gone and the kingdoms of the world have become the kingdom of the Lord and of his Christ (11:15).

Nahum

NAHUM, THE SEVENTH of the twelve minor prophets in the Hebrew Bible, is a celebration of the fall of Nineveh, the capital of the Assyrian empire, in 612 B.C.E. As such, the book has often been ignored in worshiping communities as unworthy of being included in their canon, and it has been criticized by scholars as the nationalistic and vengeful product of a false prophet. To be sure, scholars praise the literary value of the book because it contains some of the finest war poetry ever written, but its religious value is considered to be far less than that of other prophetic writings.

Such views are questionable, however, and part of the downgrading of the book is due to scholars' proclivity to omit the opening oracle in 1:2–11. That passage is built upon an older acrostic oracle, with insertions made by Nahum in verses 2b and 3a and an extension in verses 9–11. Actually, the whole of the book constitutes a carefully ordered unity, of which 1:2–11 forms the key to the prophet's message and from which it cannot be excluded.

The Assyrian empire dominated the ancient Near East from 745 until its total capitulation to the Babylonians in 609. One of the most ruthless conquerors in history, the Assyrians practiced a policy of deporting whole populations from conquered areas and replacing them with peoples from other areas, a policy that led to the deportation and disappearance from history of the ten northern tribes of Israel about 722 B.C.E.

Assyria's capital was Nineveh, an immense settlement, with sprawling suburbs, on the eastern bank of the Tigris River. Enclosed by a wall eight miles in circumference, the city constituted the largest fortified space in the Near East at the time. Almost impregnable, it was surrounded by fortified hills on three sides and the Tigris River on the other, and was guarded beyond its wall by an elaborate system of moats, canals, and outer bulwarks. The city reached its height as the administrative, cultural, and economic center of the empire under the rule of Sennacherib (704–681), who built the "Palace with No Rival," and Ashurbanipal (668–627), whose library of 22,000 clay tablets now forms one of our principal sources of knowledge of ancient Mesopotamia.

Nineveh was besieged without success by the Medes in 614. However, in 612 the Medes were joined in their war against the Assyrians by Scythian tribes from the Caucasus and, above all, by Nabopolassar of Babylonia (626–605). They laid siege to the city for two and a-half months; then they finally breached the wall and took the city. A number of the Ninevites fled to Haran, under the leadership of Asur-uballit, but they were decisively defeated by the Babylonians in 609. There is some evidence, part legend and part history, that Nineveh's fall was engineered by redirecting its canals, moat, and rivers so that the city was flooded (*cf.* Nahum 1:8; 2:6, 8).

Nahum was apparently written shortly before the fall of Nineveh, to celebrate the city's imminent collapse and to place that defeat in a theological context. We know nothing about the author beyond his book. His name means "comforting" or "comforter," and certainly Assyria's fall was comforting to Judah. Nahum came from Elkosh, whose location is unknown. His book is the only prophetic corpus with two titles and the only one to be called a "book" (v. 1), although its message was undoubtedly first delivered orally. Following the initial oracle of 1:2–11 are four judgment oracles on Nineveh, each a word of the Lord climaxing in Hebrew with *hineh* ("Behold!"; 1:12–15, 2:1–13, 3:1–7, 3:8–13). The final oracle (3:14–19) complements 1:2–11 and closes (in the Hebrew) with the same word as that which concludes 1:11 and the whole book.

The initial oracle forms the theological context within which the rest of the book is to be understood. It opens in a drumbeat announcement that is somewhat obscured in the English translation: "An avenger is Yahweh . . . an avenger is Yahweh . . . an avenger is Yahweh . . . and a keeper of anger against his foes (1:2; Au. trans.), for the Lord is a "jealous God." That is, he is working out his purposes through his chosen people, Israel. He is zealous for that purpose, and he will not be deterred from it. Assyria was once used as an instrument of God's purpose to punish Israel for her sin (*cf.* Isa 10:5–19), but Assyria in her proud might overstepped her bounds, and now God will destroy her.

God is very slow to come to such anger, however (v. 3)—as Israel experienced in her long subjugation to Assyria. Indeed, this passage emphasizes the goodness of God, who is always a stronghold in the day of trouble and a refuge for those who trust him (v. 7). But above all, God is the mighty Lord over all nature and nations (vv. 3–5). If any people or power should defy his lordship, he "will by no means clear the guilty" (v. 3) but will make a full end of his adversaries (vv. 8–9). There is no protection for Assyria against God's destroying wrath (vv. 6, 9); having plotted evil against the Lord, she will be consumed by the fire of his anger (vv. 10–11).

The passage calls posterity to self-examination and repentance before the lordship of God. He is good, patient, forbearing toward the sins of humankind, very slow to anger, and of great might. However, in pursuit of his sovereign purpose, God will by no means pass over those who oppose him.

Nahum's four judgment oracles on Nineveh apply the theological message of the first oracle to his own time. All these oracles depict the siege and fall of Nineveh, but they are not to be understood as a sequential account of that battle. Rather they illumine first one scene and then another in some of the most vivid war poetry ever written. Some scholars even think that Nahum must have been an eyewitness to the battle, but the oracles are more likely the product of the creative word given the prophet, since prophets depended on the Word and not on external events for their message.

The initial announcement of Nineveh's defeat is presented in 1:12–15 (English version). God will "cut off" Assyria's armies (v. 12), her offspring, her gods (v. 14), and "Belial" (v. 15; MT 2:1). The latter title is a compound of two Hebrew words meaning "nothingness" or "worthlessness." For Nahum, it means evil incarnate, which he equates with Assyria. Later it becomes a term for Satan (*cf.* 2 Cor 6:15). The announcement of Assyria's "cutting off" (the term dominates the poem) means good news for Judah. She now will be freed from her Assyrian slave master (v. 13), and Nahum borrows the picture of the herald of good news from Isaiah 52:7 to announce that *shalom,* or abundant life and peace, will come to Judah and that she will be able to live again by her former customs (v. 15). Though expressed in the present tense, the announcement concerns Judah's future.

In 2:1–13 (MT 2:2–14), the actual siege and fall of Nineveh are foreseen by the prophet in an ecstatic vision of vivid pictures. A "shatterer" rises up against Assyria in the form of the scarlet-clad troops of Babylonia (vv. 1, 3), but they are acting at the instigation of the Lord (v. 2). The Babylonian onslaught begins in the suburbs outside of Nineveh's walls, with war chariots wheeling and cavalry dashing about (vv. 3–4). The Assyrians try vainly to defend their city (v. 5). The wall is breached, the city is flooded (v. 6), and the Ninevites are led off into captivity—portrayed in verse 7 as a woman led into exile while her maidservants wail and bemoan her fate. No Ninevite tries to stay and fight. All attempt to escape (v. 8). The city is plundered by the conquerors and bereft of its treasures and power (vv. 9–10). Verses 11–12 then form a prophetic taunt song, in which Assyria is portrayed as a lion who has himself now become a prey. But the determining word is in verse 13: "Behold! I am against you, says the Lord of hosts" (RSV). It is God who rises up against Assyria to defeat her, and none can stand before him.

The woe oracle of 3:1–7 portrays Nineveh's doom. As such, verses 1–4 detail Assyria's crimes

against a foreign city, which form the accusation against her; verses 5–7a announce God's judgment; and verse 7b is a dirge uttered over the fallen city of Nineveh.

Assyria's slaughter of a city's populace is vividly portrayed. Her cavalry and war chariots wreak such destruction that her soldiers stumble over heaps of corpses in the streets of the captured city (vv. 2–3). Verse 4 pictures her as a harlot who, by treacherous alliances and international deals, has lured other nations to their death.

Once again, however, God's word determines all: "Behold! I am against you, says the LORD of hosts" (v. 5). He will expose the ugliness and corruption of the harlot Assyria before all and sentence her to death (vv. 5–6). The funeral dirge sounds in verse 7b, but no one mourns her demise, and there is none to comfort her.

A taunt song (3:8–13) uses another vivid metaphor to portray Nineveh, this time as drunk, weak, and dazed (v. 11). In verses 8–10, the city is compared with Thebes, the capital of Ethiopia and Egypt that was captured by the Assyrian ruler Ashurbanipal in 663 B.C.E. Thebes, a great city for over 1400 years, had also relied on a system of fortified moats and rivers for protection, but it fell to Assyria, which slaughtered its children, enslaved its nobles, and took its leading citizens into exile. So too would Nineveh be taken, despite its reliance on forts and moats and warriors (vv. 11–13), for there is no defense against God, who will make Nineveh drink the cup of his wrath (v. 11; *cf.* Jer. 25:15–29).

The final oracle (3:14–19) portrays Nineveh's futile last defense and ultimate defeat. Verses 14–17 are a taunt song, in which the prophet sarcastically urges Nineveh to prepare for siege by storing extra water, by repairing her wall with bricks, and by multiplying her goods and defenders. All will be in vain. Nineveh's defenders will be like fleeting grasshoppers, who eat and run to disappear before the heat of the day. God will sweep through in the form of the fire and sword of Babylonia, and Nineveh will be no more.

Verses 18–19 are a final funeral dirge, uttered over the fallen city and empire. Assyria's military commanders and nobles are dead, her people are scattered like sheep without a shepherd. Her wound is fatal; there is no healing. But there is also no mourning for dead Assyria. Instead, the peoples of the world, all victims of Assyria's unrelenting evil, clap their hands in joy and triumph over the death of their persecutor (*cf.* Rev 18:20, 19:6–7).

The message of Nahum is clear: God is not to be mocked. Though slow to anger and of great might, God will by no means clear the guilty but will do away with human evil in order to establish the rule of peace and good.

Bibliography

Obadiah

Childs, Brevard S. *An Introduction to the Old Testament as Scripture.* Philadelphia, 1979. Pp. 411–416.

Muilenburg, James. "Obadiah, Book of." In *The Interpreter's Dictionary of the Bible*, vol. 3. Nashville, Tenn, 1962. Pp. 578–579.

Rudolph, Wilhelm. *Joel, Amos, Obadja, Jona.* Gütersloh, 1971.

Thompson, John A. "The Book of Obadiah: Introduction and Exegesis." In *The Interpreter's Bible*, vol. 6. Nashville, Tenn., 1956. Pp. 857–867.

Wolff, Hans Walter. *Dodekapropheton 3.* Neukirchen-Vluyn, 1969–1982.

Nahum

Achtemeier, Elizabeth. *Nahum, Malachi.* Atlanta, 1986.

Calvin, Jean. *Commentaries on the Twelve Minor Prophets.* Vol. 3. Translated by John Owen. Edinburgh, 1846–1849. Reprint 1950.

Davidson, Andrew B. *The Books of Nahum, Habakkuk, and Zephaniah.* Cambridge, 1920.

Gadd, Cyril J. *The Fall of Nineveh.* London, 1921–1923.

Keil, Karl Friedrich. *The Twelve Minor Prophets.* Vol. 2. Translated by James Martin. Edinburgh, 1868. Reprint, Grand Rapids, 1954.

Kleinert, Paul. "The Book of Nahum." In *A Commentary on the Holy Scriptures*, edited by John P. Lange. Translated and edited by Philip Schaff. New York, 1874.

Speiser, E. A. "Nineveh." In *The Interpreter's Dictionary of the Bible*, vol. 3. Nashville, Tenn., 1962.

Taylor, Charles L., Jr., and James T. Cleland. "The Book of Nahum: Introduction, Exegesis, and Exposition." In *The Interpreter's Bible*, vol. 6. Nashville, 1956.

ELIZABETH ACHTEMEIER

Jonah

THE BOOK OF Jonah tells of a recalcitrant Israelite prophet who unwillingly assists in the deliverance of an enemy city. Although it consists of only forty-eight verses, the work enjoys enormous popularity among Jews and Christians. Elie Wiesel reflects upon Jonah's broad appeal:

> At the mention of his name one's mind begins to wander in search of adventure and enchantment; we think of the whale, hear the roaring tempest, roam the streets of noisy cities with their seductive nightlife and their corrupting daylife; we watch the sky and expect it to burst open at any moment and send down fire and brimstone upon all those who forget that the earth too is the Lord's. (p. 130)

Jonah appears in the second section of Hebrew Scripture (Prophets), numbering fifth in the Book of the Twelve Minor Prophets (*Dodekapropheton*). Unlike other prophetic collections, it is not a compendium of sayings attributed to Jonah (who is never actually called a *navi'* [prophet] in the work). This is a story about a prophet, rather than a book of prophecy. The author maintains anonymity throughout, writing from a third-person perspective and nowhere claiming to be Jonah himself. We know only that he, or she, possessed remarkable literary skills and was thoroughly versed in Israel's prophetic and cultic traditions.

GENRE

What type of literary work is Jonah? Few contemporary scholars argue that it relates historical facts, for events and details in the story strain credulity. However, no single attempt to classify Jonah has commanded universal assent; and the work has been variously identified as folklore, prophetic legend, *midrash*, allegory, satire, and parable. Among these categories, parable is perhaps the most satisfying, for the work tells a simple, powerful story that calls for both identification and decision on the part of the reader. Of course, a lengthy parable like Jonah can have more than one point, or teaching.

STORY

The author claims to tell of an incident in the life of Jonah ("dove"), son of Amittai. Although 2 Kings 14:25 mentions a prophet by that name who brought God's optimistic word of national expansion to Jeroboam II, ruler of the northern kingdom of Israel from 786–746 B.C.E., there is no mention in Kings of events recorded in the Jonah scroll.

Scene 1. The story begins without introduction, stating only that the word of Yahweh commanded Jonah to go to Nineveh and decry its wickedness. Jonah offers no verbal response to God's order, but his actions proclaim his unwillingness to go to a city that was, for Israelites, a byword for cruelty and godlessness. Rather than traveling east, Jonah heads west, booking passage on a ship bound for Tarshish.

The divine mandate is not so easily escaped, however. Yahweh hurls a great wind that stirs up the sea; and the sailors, fearing shipwreck, entreat their gods for help while Jonah sleeps below deck. Finally, they wake him up and cast lots, which implicate him. Jonah confesses that his God is "Yahweh, the God of heaven, who made the sea and the dry land" (1:19; RSV). The terrified sailors struggle to ride out the tempest, but ultimately they must follow Jonah's instruction to throw him overboard. Immediately, the storm subsides; and the sailors become God-fearing Yahwists, offering sacrifice and vows.

Scene 2. Yahweh "appoints" a great fish (there is no reference to a whale), which swallows Jonah and retains him for "three days and three nights" (1:17 [MT 2:1]). At the end of that time, Jonah prays (the ostensible content of his prayer, a psalm filled with water and underworld imagery, follows in 2:2–9 [MT 2:3–10]). Thereafter, the fish obeys Yahweh's command and vomits the man onto dry land.

Many scholars think that the psalm is a later addition to the text, inserted by an editor who missed the content of the prophet's prayer and/or wished to render Jonah more "pious." One can certainly argue that it does not fit the situation well, for while we might expect from Jonah a lament, or a prayer of repentance, we find instead a thanksgiving psalm. In its present context, the psalm probably adds one of many satirical notes to the story. The audience would have recognized that Israel's poets frequently used water and underworld imagery metaphorically to describe distress (see, for example, Pss 18:16, 71:20, 130). In Jonah's case, however, "his troubles are not 'like' waves rushing over his head. [They] *are* waves rushing over his head" (Miles 1975, 174).

Scene 3. Again, Yahweh orders Jonah to Nineveh. Walking one day's distance into the city, hyperbolically described as three days' journey in breadth, the prophet proclaims his only oracle—an unconditional pronouncement that in forty days Nineveh will be destroyed.

The reaction of Nineveh's citizenry is both immediate and astonishing. At the king's command, humans and livestock fast, don sackcloth, and beseech God's mercy. In response, Yahweh "repents," that is, changes the divine plan to destroy the city.

Scene 4. Jonah reacts to his success, unparalleled in the history of any Israelite prophet, with anger. For the first time, he voices a reason for his unwillingness to obey Yahweh and go to Nineveh: "I knew that thou art a gracious God and merciful, slow to anger, and abounding in steadfast love, and repentest of evil" (4:2). Jonah's words, which echo the theophany at Sinai (Exod 34:6), are, in effect, an accusation that Yahweh has justified Jonah's worst fear, discrediting him by refusing to carry out his unconditional prophecy of Nineveh's destruction. Like his prophetic predecessor, Elijah, Jonah asks that Yahweh take his life (4:3; see also 1 Kgs 19:4). Unlike Elijah, however, Jonah's disgruntlement is motivated by the deliverance of those to whom he prophesied rather than by oppression and threat of violence. To Yahweh's question, "Do you do well to be angry?" (4:4), the prophet offers no response. Instead, he goes out of Nineveh and constructs a shelter, beneath which he sits to observe what will become of the city.

Scene 5. Yahweh "appoints" a plant (4:6; the same verb appears in 1:17 [MT 2:1], 4:7, 4:8), which provides shade for the prophet until a worm attacks it and it withers. Plagued by a brutal sun and a searing east wind, Jonah again asks to die. Yahweh counters with a question once more: "Do you do well to be angry for the plant?" (4:9).

Jonah's retort, "I do well to be angry, angry enough to die" (4:9), is his last recorded remark in the book. The final words belong to Yahweh. Gently, it seems, God remonstrates this prophet, who cares more for infallible prophecy and mechanical justice than for mercy in the face of wholehearted repentance. If Jonah pitied the plant (himself?), which he had no part in creating, should not God feel pity for a repentant city with many thousands of human and animal inhabitants? With this question posed by Yahweh to Jonah, and to the reader, the story ends.

TEACHINGS

Central to the Book of Jonah are the concepts of divine freedom and mercy in the face of human repentance. The story is, in fact, illustrative of the perspective found in a text like Jeremiah 18:7–8, wherein Yahweh says: "If at any time I declare concerning a nation or a kingdom, that I will pluck up and break down and destroy it, and if that nation, concerning which I have spoken, turns from its evil, I will repent of the evil that I intended to do to it." God exercises freedom to pronounce judgment against, and be moved by compassion toward, Nineveh. Jonah knows that "deliverance belongs to Yahweh" (2:9 [MT 2:10]); he also knows of the divine propensity for showing unmerited mercy (4:2). Yet he balks at the notion that Nineveh, capital of Assyria and Israel's bitter foe, should be the recipient of such mercy, despite the very genuine repentance of its inhabitants.

Jonah's story refutes any notion that Israel alone deserves divine mercy, whereas the other nations of the world merit only divine justice. In this regard, the reference to Jonah ben Amittai in 2 Kings 14:24–27 needs further consideration, for there we read that Yahweh acted mercifully toward Israel, despite its persistent sinfulness. If Yahweh acts in such fashion toward Israel, should not Israelites rejoice when divine mercy also is extended to others, particularly when their repentance exceeds Israel's own? The author of Jonah may well have selected this little-known prophet as the subject of his or her tale because his word of weal to a sinful nation demonstrates the divine freedom to exercise grace, despite human culpability.

Divine freedom impinges upon another issue addressed by the Jonah scroll as well: the problem of distinguishing between true and false prophets. No less than we, ancient Israelites struggled to recognize the bearer of God's authentic word. They sought criteria by which to resolve uncertain cases. So, for example, we read in Deuteronomy 18:20–22:

But the prophet who presumes to speak a word in my name which I have not commanded him to speak, or who speaks in the name of other gods, that same prophet shall die. And if you say in your heart, "How may we know the word which Yahweh has not spoken?"—when a prophet speaks in the name of Yahweh, if the word does not come to pass or come true, that is a word which Yahweh has not spoken; the prophet has spoken it presumptuously, you need not be afraid of him.

According to this criterion, Jonah would be judged a false prophet, deserving of death, for his unconditional prophecy of destruction in forty days failed to materialize. The author of our story suggests, however, that so mechanical a view of prophecy overlooks Yahweh's desire always to be merciful, even after the prophetic word has been proclaimed. God's freedom cannot be constrained by human pronouncements.

The Book of Jonah is also filled with affirmations that divine sovereignty and care extend to all of creation. "Yahweh, the God of heaven, who made the sea and the dry land" (1:9), controls the world and everything in it—storms and sea creatures, worms and wind—regardless of Jonah's attempt to escape Yahweh's commission by fleeing to Tarshish! Furthermore, the sovereign creator does not restrict concern for humans to Israelites alone. On the contrary, God wills to save all people, even those whom Israel regards with fear and loathing.

DATE

Although decisive evidence for dating the Book of Jonah is lacking, most biblical scholars regard it as a postexilic composition (fifth–third centuries B.C.E.). First, the author demonstrates familiarity with Israel's prophetic traditions, including prophecies in Jeremiah and Ezekiel. Second, the teachings of the book address theological issues of particular concern in the aftermath of exile (e.g., whether Yahweh's salvific plans for the future were inclusive, or exclusive, of people and lands outside the Land of Israel). In fact, some scholars have argued that the work is an allegory, wherein Israel (represented by disobedient Jonah) is swallowed by Babylon (the fish) and finally freed to witness to the gentiles. Such a view flounders at fundamental points within the book; however, allegorical interpretation flourished among the early Christians, who saw Jonah's three-day-and-night captivity within the fish as a portent of the death and resurrection of Jesus (e.g., Matt 12:39–41). Among Jews, the story of Jonah is read on Yom Kippur, the Day of Atonement.

Bibliography

Burrows, Millar. "The Literary Category of the Book of Jonah." In *Translating and Understanding the Old Testament*, edited by Harry Thomas Frank and William L. Reed. Nashville, Tenn., 1970. An informed discussion of scholarly views concerning the genre of the book of Jonah.

Landes, George M. "The Kerygma of the Book of Jonah: The Contextual Interpretation of the Jonah Psalm." *Interpretation* 21 (1967): 3–31. An attempt to explain how Jonah's psalm fits into its canonical context.

———. "Jonah, Book of." In *The Interpreter's Dictionary of the Bible*, supplementary vol. Nashville, Tenn., 1976. Pp. 488–491.

Miles, John A., Jr. "Laughing at the Bible: Jonah as Parody." *The Jewish Quarterly Review* 65 (1975):168–181. The author explores instances, as well as the function, of parody in Jonah.

Trible, Phyllis L. "Studies in the Book of Jonah." Ph.D. diss., Columbia University, 1963. An exhaustive study of Jonah by an author of remarkable literary sensitivity and skill.

Wiesel, Elie. *Five Biblical Portraits.* Notre Dame, 1981. A well-known author guides the reader through the stories of Saul, Jonah, Jeremiah, Elijah, and Joshua.

KATHERYN PFISTERER DARR

Micah

INTRODUCTION

THE NAME "MICAH" means "Who is like . . .?" It is the shortened form of Micaiah ("Who is like Yahweh?"). In the literary style of the ancient Near East, such a rhetorical question asked about a deity was an assertion of the god's incomparability. Micah's name is a confessional claim that Yahweh, the God of Israel, is the true and highest deity, the God to whom no other can so much as be compared!

The Book of Micah is a prophetic testimony to that confession. It begins with a call on all the peoples of the earth to hear the following prophecy as evidence that Yahweh is sovereign over history (1:2). The book concludes with a hymn of praise asking, "Who is a God like you, pardoning the iniquity of his people?" (7:18). God of the world and shepherd of his flock—that is the God for whom Micah speaks. Yahweh is a God who uses the judgment and salvation of Israel to reveal his universal reign. He is a God who requires justice of people and forgives their sins.

In the course of critical study of the prophecy, the name Micah has come to refer to two separate but related entities. One is Micah of Moresheth, who was active as a prophet in Judah during the latter part of the eighth century. The other is the book that bears his name. Like the great Book of Isaiah, the Book of Micah contains material composed not only during the Assyrian period in the eighth century, but also during the Babylonian and Persian periods of Israel's history. The sayings of Micah of Moresheth are found in the first three chapters of the book. The other prophecy incorporated in the book is a response to the tradition of Micah in later times of crisis. (There are, of course, other views of the relation between prophet and book, which can be considered through the use of the works cited in the bibliography.) Because of the distinction between the historical prophet and the book as a literary entity, it is useful to treat them separately.

MICAH OF MORESHETH

The Time of Micah

The scribes who composed the full title of Micah's book dated his activity in the reign of Jotham, Ahaz, and Hezekiah, kings of Judah (1:1). It was during those years, they said, that the word of the Lord came to Micah, making of him an intermediary through whom Israel's God spoke. The reigns of these three kings covered approximately the second half of the eighth century B.C.E., so these regnal dates allow for quite a long period of activity. Jotham's reign may have begun in 742 (his dates are uncertain); Hezekiah died in 687.

Those were the years of the Assyrian crisis. Not

long before King Jotham's accession to the throne, Tiglath-pileser III guided Assyria's swift rise to dominance in the Near East. This Mesopotamian monarch was determined to control the Mediterranean seacoast for economic and strategic reasons. From the time of Tiglath-pileser to well into the next century, Assyrian armies assaulted the small states in the western area. The northern kingdom of Israel and Syria became subject vassals in 738. Twice they sought to throw off the Assyrian yoke. Once, in 734, acting in concert, the northern kingdom and Syria tried to force King Ahaz of Judah to join them in a common revolt. Ahaz appealed to Assyria for help, becoming a vassal himself, and Israel was reduced to a province of the empire. Another attempt at independence was made in 724, but by 722/721 the capital city, Samaria, was captured and razed, and the population was deported.

In 704 Hezekiah of Judah was drawn into a general uprising. The Assyrian ruler Sennacherib methodically crushed the rebel states. By 701 his armies were in Judah. One city after another succumbed to gruesome revenge until Jerusalem alone was left surrounded. In the account in his annals (Pritchard 1966, 287–288), Sennacherib reports that "himself [Hezekiah] I made a prisoner in Jerusalem, his royal residence, like a bird in a cage." He implies that the city escaped destruction because Hezekiah paid a huge ransom, resumed paying tribute, and became an obedient vassal again.

It was in this period that the first generation of classical prophets appeared. Amos of Tekoa was active in Bethel and Samaria, followed in the northern kingdom by the great Hosea, whose prophecy forecast and interpreted the demise of the northern kingdom. In Jerusalem, Isaiah, son of Amoz, spoke the word of the Lord from the time of Uzziah's death recurrently in the reigns of Jotham, Ahaz, and Hezekiah. It may well be that the scribes who dated Micah's book by the reigns of these three kings were identifying a period and its conditions rather than referring to a precise chronology. The first generation of prophets in all their individuality shared two broad convictions: the character of their societies had become unacceptable to their God, Yahweh, and Yahweh created the international crisis to enact his judgment.

The sayings preserved in the Book of Micah do not contain any references to known persons or events

that would make it possible to determine more nearly the time of Micah's prophetic activity with convincing certainty. In 1:6–7 there is a prediction of Samaria's destruction, which as a word of Micah's would indicate that he was already active before Samaria fell in 722. In 1:8–16 there is a lament over disaster that has befallen (or will strike) several towns in Judah, reaching to the very gate of Jerusalem. Some scholars think the lament reflects Sennacherib's Judean campaign of 701, which ended in a siege of Jerusalem. But others see the lament as a prophecy of yet unidentified disaster that will befall the region.

There is one fascinating bit of evidence about Micah's career found outside the Book of Micah. According to the twenty-sixth chapter of Jeremiah, the prophet Jeremiah was put on trial during the reign of Jehoiakim for predicting the destruction of Jerusalem and its Temple. During the trial, certain "elders of the land" gave testimony in Jeremiah's behalf by reminding the court that "Micah of Moresheth prophesied in the days of Hezekiah king of Judah, and said to all the people of Judah: 'Thus says Yahweh of hosts, Zion shall be plowed as a field; Jerusalem shall become a heap of ruins, and the mountain of the house a wooded height'" (Jer 26:18; RSV). A century after his time, knowledge of Micah's activity was alive as oral tradition among these elders, who were able to quote one of his sayings (Mic 3:12). They dated this saying to the days of Hezekiah and remembered him as a prophet whose message was a threat to Jerusalem.

The Book of Micah is so short that it does not require a career that spanned four decades. Indeed, the book includes sayings that are not consistent with the time and its conditions. It seems likely that Micah was active only during the reign of Hezekiah, toward the close of the eighth century; the saying about Samaria's fall can be accounted for as the work of those who produced the book.

The Man

The prophet Micah is named only twice in the Hebrew Bible—in the title of his book and in the account of Jeremiah's trial. Both times he is called Micah the Moreshtite ("of Moresheth"). The name Micah seems to have been a common one in Judah; the designation as the Moreshtite must have been given him when he was in Jerusalem, in order to identify him in particular. Like Amos of Tekoa, Micah of Moresheth was a man from one of the towns that ring the capital at a distance of a day's walk.

Micah refers to his hometown in his lament over the disaster Sennacherib's invasion of Judah brought upon its towns and villages (1:14). Moresheth-gath has been identified with an ancient ruin, Tell el-Judeideh, which lies some twenty-five miles southwest of Jerusalem. From its location at the edge of the Shephelah it overlooks the coastal plain.

The town had obvious strategic importance in planning the defense of the country and its capital. (One important north-south route ran through it.) That is why King Rehoboam selected it as one of the sites to be fortified as part of a defense system to guard the western approaches to Jerusalem. In Micah's time, with the Assyrians active in the region, the militarization of such strategic towns would have been intensified, and local life would have been disrupted by the presence of military and administrative officials. It was probably an experience of this invasion of his hometown by the arrogant officials from Jerusalem that gave Micah his vehement attitude toward such figures (see chapters 2 and 3). The book reveals nothing about his personal life. We do not know what his vocation was or what happened to him before or after his prophetic activity. He is not even identified as a "prophet" in the title of his book or in the account in Jeremiah, although the latter does use the verb "prophesied" of his speaking. His sayings are quite like those of Amos and Isaiah in formal style, and he clearly functioned as an intermediary between the divine and human realm, announcing the opinions and plan of the deity to his audience. If we do not call him prophet or seer, we should lack a social role with which to identify his activity.

Micah does speak of himself and his mission once (3:8). He contrasts himself with prophets, seers, and diviners who promise prosperity, safety, and health (*shalom*) to those who pay their fees and support their professions. Micah, instead, challenges Israel for its rebellious sins against Yahweh and warns that Yahweh will intervene in human affairs to punish Israel for those sins (1:3–5). He announces that the calamities befalling the nation were caused by its transgressions. Micah, reporting that he has been endowed with strength and courage to give voice to the verdict of Yahweh's justice, specifically addresses those officials who are responsible for administering justice in the society (3:1, 9). Micah, it appears, was commissioned by the spirit of Yahweh to represent Yahweh and declare his justice to precisely those who should have meted out justice but did not.

The vehemence with which he speaks to and about the powerful of society is matched by his passionate empathy for the oppressed, whom he repeatedly calls "my people" (2:4, 8, 9; 3:3, 5). This expression of kinship and intimacy is frequently used as a lament over the suffering of those with whom one is identified. It is thus no accident that one of the most powerful sayings in the collection is a skillfully composed lament over the towns endangered by the punishment Yahweh sent because of the sin of the country's powerful (1:8–16).

It is certainly no surprise that Micah's prophetic message was met by disdain and threats from those it exposed. Once Micah quotes the scornful rebuke of his audience (2:6–7), and there are hints of their rejection of his announcements of doom (3:11). But he carried out his calling "to declare to Israel his sin," and left the rest to God.

The Message

Micah's sayings are collected in the first three chapters of the book. As they are now arranged, the sequence is introduced by the announcement of Yahweh's appearance to deal with Israel's transgressions (1:3–5a) and concluded by the prediction that the holy city of Jerusalem would be reduced to ruins in the midst of woods and fields (3:12). This arrangement displays the basis and the climax of Micah's message. His sayings were announcements of what Yahweh was about to do—a judgment that would culminate in the destruction of the center of that sinfulness, the capital city.

Micah's central concern, the criterion by which he measured society, can be summed up in a term he repeatedly used: justice (3:1, 8, 9). Indeed, all the sayings in chapter 2 and 3 turn on that concern. Justice for Micah was the tradition of values and customary precedents that should govern society's conduct in economic and social matters. It inhered in the old ways of life that had been established in Israel as a people ruled by Yahweh. Micah always spoke of the nation as Israel and Jacob, never Judah. His notions of equity and right were those found in the Covenant Code (Exod 20:21–23:33), which viewed the nation as a community of mutual responsibility and rights under God. For that reason justice for him was not reducible to the decisions of a government and the laws it promulgated and enforced. He showed what a deeply moral and religious notion it was for him by the other words he used to talk about justice, such as "good" and "uprightness," and by the language he employed to speak of injustice, such as "evil," "perverting the straight way," and "iniquity."

The injustice Micah condemns is economic in character. Micah lived in a time when an alliance between the royal government and an urban business class was reshaping the social fabric of the nation. An old agrarian society of landowners who participated in local self-government was being replaced by a new social order. A burgeoning monarchy, needing assets for its officials, allied itself with the urban business class, which had begun to accumulate land, not as patrimony and for livelihood, but as capital. The interests and personnel of the two groups largely overlapped; and with the military crisis, the need to intrude on the governance of localities beyond Jerusalem was intensified.

The devastating effect of this development is the injustice Micah sees among those who covet fields and houses and seize the rightful inheritance of citizens (2:1–2), and who are themselves like an invading army driving women and children out of their homes (2:8–9). He accuses them of acting like cannibals in their avarice (3:2–3). They raise resources to support and develop the capital city through executions and wrongdoing (3:9).

Micah speaks in these indictments to one particular group—the powerful who run the government and local courts. Micah calls them to account by labeling them "chiefs and leaders," the old names of those who had been responsible for justice in earlier Israelite society (3:1, 9). They exercise their greed against others "because it is in the power of their hand" (2:1; RSV). These officials and the emerging rich have turned the prophets and priests into sycophants who gravitate to the wielders of power and the holders of wealth. For these latter Micah has only scorn and contempt (3:5–7, 11) because they give

their blessing to the situation with pronouncements of *shalom* (peace, welfare) and condone the evil that is done.

Micah expects the judgment to fit the crimes. Land seized would be torn from the new owners (2:4–5). Those who preyed on the helpless would themselves cry out in helplessness (3:4). The words of prophets and priests would become worthless (3:6–7). And Jerusalem, the holy city, which the powerful claim as divine refuge against the dangers of history and the threats of Micah (2:6, 3:11), would be reduced to rubble in a field.

Jerusalem, of course, did not vanish into the oblivion of rural obscurity. Sennacherib's armies devastated the country, and the general suffering and disruption must have been severe. The elders at Jeremiah's trial explained the unfulfillment of Micah's prophecy by attributing Jerusalem's escape to the repentance of King Hezekiah. But, even as Jeremiah's trial proceeded, Assyria had been replaced by another empire whose armies were preparing the doom of the city. When Nebuchadrezzar of Babylon in 587 breached Zion's defenses, razed the city, and destroyed its Temple, it seemed to those who remembered Micah's prophecy that his sayings were of immediate relevance. It was that connection which led other unknown prophets to add further sayings to the Book of Micah in order to fill out the disclosure of God's plan for Zion and its population.

THE BOOK OF MICAH

The creation of the Book of Micah proceeded in phases over a long time. The exact course of the book's growth is difficult to discern. Accounts of just how it occurred will always remain hypothetical, but there seems to be evidence for the following tentative sketch. The Deuteronomistic scribes who composed the title (1:1) saw Jerusalem's fall in 587 as a sequel to Samaria's in 722. Both were, they believed, part of Yahweh's judgment on his people for apostasy and idolatry. They bore witness to this insight by adding 1:5b–7 and other small comments to chapters 1–3.

Chapters 4–5 are a response to the prophecy of judgment on Israel and especially to the announcement of Jerusalem's destruction. The recurring topics in these chapters are Zion, the remnant of Israel, and

THE PROPHETIC VISION OF MICAH

the nations. All the sayings arranged in these chapters deal in one way or another with the question: What will become of Jerusalem and Israel in the midst of the nations after the catastrophe of Yahweh's judgment? The sayings seem to be the work of prophets who were speaking to that question during and after the exile.

Chapters 6–7 are arranged in two parts. The first (6:1–7:7) takes up Micah's theme of justice and relates it to the harsh years after the exile. The second part (7:8–20) is composed of a blend of psalmic and prophetic material, which suggests a liturgical use of chapters 6–7, if not the whole book.

The book was probably completed after the Temple had been rebuilt by 515 B.C.E. Sayings like 4:1–5 assume the Temple's existence. The whole process of the book's creation was a response to Micah's prophecy. It deals with the questions set by his proclamation for later times and applies his theme of justice to the conditions of the new beginning of Yahweh's people after the period of judgment was over.

The original sayings of the prophet Micah and the Book of Micah are different in genre and have different functions. Micah's sayings were spoken to particular persons on specific historical occasions, to an audience that had to decide how to respond to what he said to them. Later readers have a book in which many sayings are collected and arranged as part of a larger whole. The book bears witness not just to Yahweh's word to the powerful in Hezekiah's time but to a prophetic design of what God has been doing in the whole history of judgment that brought about the fall of Samaria and Jerusalem, the exile of their populations, and the new beginning centered in Zion. The book itself remains prophecy because of its origin and especially because there are parts of its scenario of Yahweh's grand design for history that have not come to pass. The book locates the early readers of the postexilic period fairly well along in the course of Yahweh's strategy to deal with the world of nations in general and with his chosen people and sanctuary in particular. Like the other prophetic books, Micah tries to make theological sense of what the people have already experienced and gives hope for what lies ahead. It perceives past and future in light of a revelation of Yahweh's will and purpose.

The first three chapters deal with the era of judgment, Yahweh's punishment of Samaria and Jerusalem. The sayings that compose these chapters are arranged in a sequence that is almost like a narrative. They begin with a description of how Yahweh's wrath was aroused by the sins of the two kingdoms of Israel and Judah and their capital cities (1:3–5). Then the destruction is portrayed as a disaster (1:6–7) that moves to the very gate of Jerusalem. A lament depicts the woe that moves across Judah's villages to lap at the walls of Zion (1:8–16). Chapter 2 indicts those whose covetous greed brought on the punishment (2:1–5) and records the prophet's debate with those who rejected his message (2:6–7). Chapter 3 lays the responsibility for the punishment on the leaders of the nation and concludes with the announcement of the destruction of Jerusalem (3:9–12). Since Zion is the city of God, the dwelling place of the Most High, its obliteration meant that Yahweh no longer had any place in Israel, any special connection with this people. Yahweh, the judge of idolatry and injustice, is free in divine sovereignty from dependence on any people or place previously chosen.

Chapters 4–5 deal with the era of salvation, when Yahweh will use the conditions created by his judgment to manifest his universal sovereignty. The consummation of Yahweh's rule is announced at the very beginning in an eschatological proclamation (4:1–5) that stands in sharp contrast to the announcement of Zion's destruction. In the latter days, Mount Zion, God's dwelling place, will be accepted as the center of the world, and all nations will be subject to the will of the divine king who reigns there. War will end; peace will prevail. The rest of the sayings in this section describe how this will come about and what effect it will have on the people of God.

In 4:9–5:4, three sayings beginning with "now" introduce situations of distress for the population of Jerusalem-Judah and then go on to announce how the coming kingdom of God will relieve that distress. Now the leaderless people cry out in distress and leave their city for Babylon, but the hand of Yahweh will rescue them from captivity (4:9–10). Now they are surrounded and threatened by many nations, but

Yahweh will give them the victory over all their foes (4:11–13). Now they are besieged and their ruler is humiliated, but a new ruler shall arise from Bethlehem who will be the true shepherd for Israel (5:1–4). Yahweh's actions will overcome the loss of their country, the threat of the nations, the collapse of the monarchy.

The other sayings tell how Yahweh will gather the people who have been driven from their land and how he will make this remnant of Israel into a secure nation, strong enough to prevail against the threats of history (4:6–8, 5:5–9). The final saying (5:10–15) declares that Yahweh will purge the restored nation of everything and anything on which it could rely instead of trusting Yahweh—weapons, fortifications, images, mediums, even cities will be cut off. Yahweh and his rule, Zion and the kingdom of God, will be and must be all in all.

At the very beginning (1:2) and at the end (5:15) of these two sections on the punishment and restoration of Zion there are verses that offer the entire scenario of Yahweh's historical and eschatological action as a witness to the nations concerning the universal rule of Yahweh.

The section that is made up of chapters 6 and 7 issues, like the first, an invitation to consider it as the word of Yahweh (6:1a; see 1:2). Unlike chapters 1–5, which are arranged according to the eras of judgment and salvation, these chapters speak of one time, a time of weariness, failure, and discouragement. It is a time when the faithful must wait for Yahweh. It is a time when trust in the forgiveness of God and hope in his promises will provide comfort.

In 6:1–7:6 the theme of justice that was so prominent in chapters 1–3 is resumed, but in a quite different way. It is not just the leaders who lack justice, but the entire society in which life must be lived. At 7:7 there is an adversative statement ("but as for me . . .") that corresponds to 3:8. In the earlier passage, the prophet declares that he, in contrast to false prophets, is filled with justice. Here he declares that, in contrast to a corrupt society, he will trust in the Lord and wait for him to act. Then in 7:8–20 we hear the prayer and promises and praise that are the expressions of that trust and waiting.

Chapters 6–7 form a concluding section that opens with an argument in which Yahweh takes his people to task because they have grown weary of him and have lost the motivation that remembering the salvation history would create (6:1–5). The question is raised: What is the proper response to that history? The answer given is that it is not sacrifice, but doing justice, loving mercy, and walking humbly with the God one worships (6:6–8). But what is required is not what is done. A word from Yahweh describes the lack of justice in "the city" and announces the appropriate punishment (6:9–16) as if in response. The prophet describes in a lament what life in this unjust society is like (7:1–6) and then declares that the only thing left for the faithful to do is to rely on Yahweh and wait for him to act (7:7).

The rest of chapter 7 brings those who read and hear the book into participation. The corporate community speaks—first as an individual (vv. 8–10) and then as a congregation (vv. 18–20)—and is addressed (vv. 11–13). Verses 14–17 are difficult to assess because of their uncertain text, but they seem to be a prayer by the community (see the translation of JPS). The book thus, at its conclusion, offers the community words with which to express and live out trust and hope: a psalm of confidence in Yahweh's salvation for a sinful people (vv. 8–11), a promise of restoration (vv. 11–13), and a prayer to Yahweh to be again shepherd of Israel as he was of old (vv. 14–17). Last comes a hymn of praise (vv. 18–20), which may well be the most marvelous description in the Bible of the God who forgives sin (vv. 18–20).

Bibliography

Hillers, Delbert R. *Micah.* Philadelphia, 1983.
Koch, Klaus. *The Prophets.* Vol. 1, *The Assyrian Period.* Translated by Margaret Kohl. Philadelphia, 1982.
Mays, James L. *Micah: A Commentary.* Philadelphia, 1976.
Pritchard, James B. *Ancient Near Eastern Texts Relating to the Old Testament.* 2d ed. Princeton, 1966.
Wolff, Hans Walter. *Micah the Prophet.* Translated by Ralph D. Gehrke. Philadelphia, 1981.
———. *Dodekapropheton 4: Micha.* Neukirchen-Vluyn, 1982.

JAMES LUTHER MAYS

habakkuk

HABAKKUK OCCUPIES EIGHTH place among the twelve minor prophets, coming between Nahum and Zephaniah. The twelve are designated minor prophets because of their relatively short length compared with the much longer books of the major prophets, Isaiah, Jeremiah, and Ezekiel. Habakkuk, with only three chapters, is one of the shorter of the minor prophets. But despite its brevity, the profundity of its theological insight gives it a value that transcends its "minor" status.

THE SUPERSCRIPTIONS

Most prophetic books begin with short headings or superscriptions that often give significant background information about the prophet's family or home, the period of his prophetic activity, and the focus of his message. Sometimes additional superscriptions are found within a book, providing useful historical information about the particular oracle that follows it. Habakkuk contains two superscriptions, but neither provides much help in understanding the background of the book. The opening superscription (1:1) identifies the content of the book, or at least the content of the first two chapters, as an oracle (*massa'*) of Habakkuk the prophet (*navi'*). The final chapter has its own superscription, which identifies it as a prayer (*tefillah*) by the same prophet. This meager information, which amounts to little more than the prophet's name, is all that is known about the prophet apart from what may be surmised indirectly from the contents of his prophecy. The prophet is mentioned in the apocryphal or deuterocanonical work Bel and the Dragon (vv. 33–39), and identified in the Old Greek version of it (v. 1) as a Levite with a father named Jesus; but this is late Midrashic expansion with no historical support.

Unfortunately, the name Habakkuk provides no clue to the personality of the prophet or to the interpretation of the book. It belongs to a rather common Israelite type in which plant names are used as personal names; Tamar, Elon, Keziah, and Hadassah are other examples. Habakkuk appears to derive from Akkadian *habbaququ*, a garden plant. The Greek form, Ambakoum, can be explained by simple dissimilation; it does not suggest a different derivation.

Nor does the designation of Habakkuk as a prophet (*navi'*) and of his word as an oracle (*massa'*) add much to our knowledge of the background of the book. Some scholars have taken these terms as clear indications that Habakkuk was a professional prophet employed in the Temple, but it is doubtful whether either *navi'* or *massa'* will bear the weight assigned to it by this theory. The content of the book shows that the prophet was familiar with Israel's liturgical forms, and there is no reason to doubt that the Temple was the locus of at least some of his prophetic activity. But the evidence does not allow one to say more. Isaiah and Jeremiah are generally not considered cult prophets, but both on occasion act as prophets in the Temple, and both are referred to as *nevi'im* (e.g., Isa 38:1, 39:3, Jer 1:5, 20:2). Moreover, although Jeremiah objects to the prophetic use of the term *massa'* (Jer 23:33–39), it is used as a designation for some of Isaiah's oracles (note especially Isa 17:1, 19:1, 22:1, 30:6). Nor is there any clear evidence of how Isaiah and Habakkuk supported themselves; the sources of income, even for the relatively well-known figure Jeremiah, are simply unknown.

Even if Habakkuk was a professional prophet employed by the Temple, that provides no basis for denigrating his message. There is little justification for the sharp dichotomy drawn by many scholars between the professional cult prophets ("false" prophets) and the nonprofessional, independent, classical prophets ("true" prophets). This sharp distinction, based on a problematic reading of Amos 7:14 and a few other highly polemical passages, fails to take into account how little we know of the sources of income of any of the prophets—"true" or "false." The classical prophets as a group may have been just as professional as the "false" prophets as a group. To judge from the account of the encounter between Jeremiah and Hananiah (Jer 28:1–17), the contemporaries of the prophets had no such easy yardstick for deciding who was a true prophet.

MESSAGE AND STRUCTURE

If the attempt to learn something about the man Habakkuk yields disappointing results, this failure is partially offset by the relative ease by which the message of Habakkuk may be discerned.

Following the superscription in 1:1, Habakkuk utters a lament to God over the oppression that the just experience at the hands of the wicked (1:2–4). Yahweh responds to that lament with a surprising oracle in which he promises to use the Babylonians as his tool for punishing the wicked (1:5–11). Habakkuk then objects that the Babylonians are themselves unrighteous oppressors. How, the prophet asks, can a righteous God watch idly while such a nation destroys people more righteous than they (1:12–17)? Having questioned God's justice, the prophet takes his stand

to await another oracle in response to this challenge (2:1). Yahweh's response comes in 2:2–20. God tells Habakkuk to write the vision down and to wait for its fulfillment, which will certainly come (2:2–3): the one who trusts in God's faithfulness will live, while the unrighteous will not (2:4). The end of the Babylonian oppressors is then graphically portrayed in a series of so-called "woe oracles" (2:5–19). (These passages might be better designated *hôy* oracles, since the particle *hôy* is a simple exclamation whose function is to get the attention of the hearer, like the colloquial English "Hey!"; any overtones it may acquire derive from the context, not from the inherent meaning of the word.) The series ends with a call to all the earth to keep silence before Yahweh, who is in his holy temple (2:20)—thus setting the stage for the poem that follows in chapter 3.

Chapter 3 has its own superscription (3:1), its literary genre differs radically from the literary genres encountered in the first two chapters, it is not found in the Qumran commentary on Habakkuk, and it ends with a musical directive in 3:19d. These observations have led numerous scholars to assign an independent literary history to this chapter, and many would not attribute the piece to the prophet responsible for chapters 1–2. Nevertheless, in the present form of the book, chapter 3 contributes to the argument developed in the two preceding chapters. Following the new superscription, the prophet speaks of the report he had heard of Yahweh's awesome deeds (3:2), thus introducing the old theophanic hymn to the divine warrior that he cites in 3:3–15. The hymn praises Yahweh for executing awful judgment on his famous enemies of the past. Habakkuk's second reference to hearing in 3:16 picks up the motif of 3:2, and together the two references bracket the hymn. The hearing of the hymn profoundly affects the prophet and convinces him that the God whose judgments on his former enemies were celebrated in the hymn will soon appear to crush his current enemies, the Babylonians (3:16). In the light of this certainty, Habakkuk owns the demand God made in 2:3 and vows to wait for Yahweh no matter how hopeless the present may seem (3:17). This resolution of the prophet's earlier questioning ends in a hymn of praise to the God of his salvation, and a short musical rubric concludes the book (3:18–19).

PROBLEMS OF INTERPRETATION

Despite the coherence of the preceding outline, there remain several disputed points of interpretation that must be discussed: (1) the identity of the wicked oppressor in the various sections of the book, (2) the meaning of the famous passage in 2:4, and (3) the unity of the book.

The Wicked Oppressor

The substantivized adjective *rasha‘* (wicked [man]) occurs three times in the Book of Habakkuk. The word first occurs in the prophet's original lament, where Habakkuk complains that justice is perverted because the wicked man surrounds the righteous (1:4). Following Yahweh's response, in which God announces that he is about to raise up the Chaldeans as his agents of judgment, Habakkuk again uses the word in his second lament, complaining to God, "Why do you look on the treacherous? Why do you keep silent when the wicked man swallows one more righteous than he?" (1:13; Au. trans.). The third occurrence is in the hymn in chapter 3, in which Yahweh is praised as the one who, to save his people and his anointed, crushed the leader from the house of the wicked (*mibbit rasha‘*; 3:13). This third occurrence clearly refers to some enemy of the past whom God destroyed, but the first two occurrences of *rasha‘* (1:4, 1:13) refer to present enemies. Do both references, however, refer to the same wicked oppressor? Who is this oppressor?

A variety of interpretations have been proposed. Most of the commentators who equate the wicked oppressors of 1:4 and 1:13 identify this oppressor as the Neo-Babylonian empire or its king, Nebuchadrezzar. The Chaldeans, the Aramaic tribe that controlled Babylon during this period and from which the Neo-Babylonian rulers sprang, are mentioned in 1:6 as God's agents of judgment, and since Habakkuk's description of the oppressor in 1:12–17 seems to refer to the same agents, this identification seems obvious. Those who equate the oppressors of 1:4 and 1:13, yet wish to avoid the identification of this oppressor with the Babylonians, find themselves compelled to rearrange verses, emend away the reference to the Chaldeans, read each individual unit in isolation from its literary context, or otherwise do violence to the present text of Habakkuk.

If one takes the present literary contexts of 1:4 and 1:13 seriously, however, it is difficult to equate the *rasha‘* in these two verses. The wicked oppressor in 1:13 appears to be the Babylonian power for the reasons stated above, but since God announced he was raising up the Babylonians to take care of the wicked oppressor mentioned in 1:4, the *rasha‘* in that verse can hardly be the same as the Babylonians. If the two oppressors are different, the range of possibilities for identifying the first oppressor is much wider. Scholars have identified the wicked in 1:4 with the Assyrian power, with the Egyptians under Necho, or with native Judean oppressors.

It is hard to choose between these alternatives, but the vocabulary used to characterize oppression in 1:2–4 seems to point to internal problems in Judean society. The language is strikingly similar to Jeremiah's laments over his persecution by the Judean officials (Jer 12:1–4, 15:15–18, 18:19–23, 20:7–12) and lacks any of the clear references to foreign oppression that one finds sprinkled through Habakkuk's second lament; note especially the expression "slaying nations" (Hab 1:17). The parallels between Habakkuk 1:2–4 and the Jeremianic material suggest a date for Habakkuk's first lament sometime during the troubled days after Jehoiakim's appointment to the throne in 609 B.C.E., while Yahweh's "surprising" response to Habakkuk, that God was raising up the Babylonians as his agents (1:5–6), requires a date no later than 605 B.C.E. Once the news reached Israel that the Babylonians had crushed the Egyptian army at Carchemish and Hamath (605 B.C.E.), such an announcement as Yahweh's would not long remain surprising.

Habakkuk's second lament, in which he complains of the injustice of the Babylonian oppression, implies some experience of Babylonian rule and thus must be dated sometime later than the first lament. Here one must distinguish between the presumed oral setting of the original independent units and their present literary juxtaposition. Obviously the book as a whole dates from the period after Babylon had imposed its yoke on Judah, and the bitterness of Habakkuk's lament suggests the period after the Babylonians first sacked Jerusalem in 597 B.C.E. If

Habakkuk shared Jeremiah's estimate of Jehoiakim (Jer 22:13–19) as the parallels between the laments of the two prophets suggest, Habakkuk probably did not lament the death of this wicked king in 598 B.C.E.; Jehoiakim had been the chief representative of the native Judean *rasha'* against whom the prophet had announced the sending of the Babylonians. But it would have been difficult for the prophet to have experienced the plundering of the Temple and the deportations after the fall of the city in 597 without feeling that the Babylonians, like the Assyrians of Isaiah's day (Isa 10:7–15), had overstepped their legitimate role. What then was God going to do about this new oppressor, this even more overbearing *rasha'*? How could a just God possibly allow such injustice to continue?

This is the real issue in the Book of Habakkuk and the perspective from which the book as a whole was composed. Habakkuk's first lament and Yahweh's first response, while they probably had an independent existence and function at an earlier period in the prophet's ministry, function in their present literary context merely to set the stage for the problem. The presence of this earlier material juxtaposed with Habakkuk's second lament from the later period serves to undercut any theological attempt to justify the Babylonian conquest in terms of a simple pattern of sin and punishment. The oppression in Judean society cried out for correction, but the Babylonians had not brought justice to the oppressed righteous. God's will to save the oppressed was still in question.

Yahweh's Answer

The second major crux in the book concerns the interpretation of Habakkuk 2:4 and its connection with the oracles against the oppressor in 2:5–20. Habakkuk 2:4 is cited three times in the New Testament, twice by Paul to give scriptural authority to his doctrine of justification by faith (Rom 1:17, Gal 3:11) and once by the author of the Hebrews letter to encourage an oppressed and discouraged Christian community to persist in their faith (Heb 10:38). Paul's use of the text made a particularly profound impression on the later Christian tradition, and the heavy theological weight that the tradition consequently assigned to the passage has made it difficult for

Christian exegetes to give a fresh reading to Habakkuk 2:4. Added to this difficulty is the uncertainty about the precise meaning of the second word in the verse, *'uppelah*. The notes of the Revised Standard Version render it as "is puffed up," but its text presupposes a different reading, though still verbal. And many commentators would emend the verb form to a noun or substantivized adjective designating the unrighteous person so that the word would stand in antithetical parallelism to the noun *tsaddiq* (the righteous man) in the second half of the verse. Moreover, the beginning of verse 5 is very difficult and widely assumed to be corrupt. Thus the logical connection between verses 4 and 5 is less than crystal clear.

An adequate resolution of all these difficulties would require an extensive philological commentary well beyond the scope of this article; the best that one can offer here is an indication of the direction that such a treatment would take. Following the general lines laid out in Gerald Janzen's seminal studies, I would translate 2:2–4 as follows:

> Yahweh answered me and said:
> "Write the vision and make it plain on the tablets
>   so that the one who reads it may run.
> For the vision is a witness to the appointed
>   time.
> It testifies to the end and does not lie.
> If it seems slow, wait for it.
> For it will surely come; it will not delay.
> The *faint-hearted* [?] soul will not walk in it,
> But the righteous person will live by its
>   faithfulness."

The vision that Habakkuk is to receive has an eschatological dimension to it: it is a reliable witness that points to a set time in the future. Although it may seem slow in coming, that vision will come to pass at the end of the appointed time. The righteous person, trusting in the reliability of that vision, will find life, but his unbelieving counterpart will refuse to walk in the light of that vision. The antithetical parallelism between "will not walk in" (*lo' yisserah b-* [emended from *yaserah*], lit., "will not go straight in") and "will live by" (*b- . . . yihyeh*) creates an ambiguity that the prophet exploits. The vision creates the possibility of life by giving hope to the oppressed, but that life must be lived according to the vision—one must go straight in it.

If this reading correctly conveys the sense of the passage, the question that remains to be answered concerns the vision itself. Where in Habakkuk is the actual vision recorded? Three main answers are possible. Scholars have sought the content of the vision in 2:4 itself, in the *hôy* oracles that follow (2:5–20), or in the theophanic material in the following chapter (3:3–16). Despite the weight of scholarship that identifies the vision with 2:4, this verse makes a very lame vision. The verse continues the instructions on how to respond to the vision, but no vision whose coming could be anticipated in the future is communicated. Rather, this verse tells one how to behave in the present in the light of a future development that has not yet been communicated.

The following oracles against the foreign oppressor (2:5–20) have a better claim to being the vision: they express a future judgment, and their message is one that would give hope for survival to Judeans suffering under Babylonian oppression. On the other hand, *hôy* oracles placed in the mouths of foreign nations (2:5b–6) seem a strange vehicle for communicating so important a vision. Moreover, the introduction to this section in 2:5 with the expression *ve'af ki* (and moreover) suggests an elaboration or undergirding of the preceding instructions rather than an introduction to the climactic vision. This section (2:5–20) actually functions to retard the final resolution of the work while anticipating that resolution. It retards the resolution by standing between the announcement of the vision and the vision itself, and it anticipates the vision's portrayal of God's coming in judgment when it attributes the threatened destruction of Babylon to God's action (2:13–14, 16) and when it calls the whole earth to keep silence before Yahweh, who is present in his Temple (2:20).

One does not reach the resolving vision itself until one encounters the old theophanic hymn in 3:3–15. This hymn, which draws much of its powerful imagery from the old myth of the storm god's battle against the chaotic sea, graphically envisions the coming of God to destroy his enemies and to save his people and his anointed; but the hymn is bracketed by verses that direct the reader back to the instructions in 2:3–4. The prophet's appeal to God to bring his former deeds back to life (*ḥayyehu* 3:2) picks up on God's promise that the righteous would live (*yiḥyeh*)

by the reliability of the vision (2:4). The expression "in the midst of the years" (3:2) recalls God's promise that the vision witnessed to "the appointed time," testified to "the end" (2:3). And Habakkuk's statement that he had heard the report about Yahweh (3:2) reminds one that the vision is characterized as a witness (*'ed*), as one who testifies (*yapeaḥ*; 2:3). Following the hymn, Habakkuk again reaffirms that he has heard, and he vows to "wait quietly for the day when disaster would overtake the people who plunder us" (3:16; Au. trans.). The reference to the appointed day and Habakkuk's vow to wait patiently clearly refer back to the instructions in 2:3–4. Moreover, the concluding vow to exult in Yahweh as one's salvation and strength even when the visible sources of life are failing (3:17–19) embodies the admonition to wait for the realization of the vision even when it seems slow in coming; it recalls the promise that the vision would not prove false, that by it the righteous would find life (2:3–4). Finally, the coming of Yahweh in the opening line of the hymn (*yavo'*; 3:3) points back to the certainty of the vision's coming (*bo' yavo'*; 2:3).

The hymn's powerful vision of Yahweh's certain coming in judgment brings a resolution to Habakkuk's earlier struggle with God's justice. Although not yet apparent, its promised appearance allows the faithful to do more than merely endure the present; the faithful, exulting in God and living by the vision of his coming, can begin instead to endow the present with the contours of that vision of the future.

The Unity of the Book

The preceding discussion has demonstrated the coherence of the three chapters of Habakkuk. In my view, at any rate, there is no reason to excise any of the material as secondary. The omission of chapter 3 from the Qumran commentary does not demonstrate that the chapter was lacking from the biblical manuscript the Qumran scribe was commenting on. The Qumran commentaries are not famous for their completeness: the scribe may simply have grown tired of writing commentary; or he may have felt his treatment of chapters 1–2 was sufficient for his purposes. Chapter 3 is found in the Septuagint and in the Hebrew scroll of the minor prophets found at Murabba'at. Moreover, the prophetic use of a reworked ancient hymn is not out of character for a prophetic figure, since the prophets as a class adapted a wide range of both secular and religious genres for their own unique purposes.

The issue is more complex with 2:5–20. It clearly intervenes between the announcement of the vision (2:2–4) and the vision itself (3:3–15), but rather than deleting the material as a secondary insertion, I have explained this placement of 2:5–20 as serving a retarding and anticipatory function. More, however, needs to be said. Eckart Otto (1977) has pointed out that a significant portion of the *hôy* oracles in 2:5–20 could be read as directed at social oppression within Judean society. The elements that direct this material toward a foreign oppressor could be easily removed, suggesting that the core of these oracles was originally directed against the native Judean oppressor mentioned in Habakkuk's first lament, but it does not require that one consider them a secondary insertion in the literary composition of the book. Just as the first lament reflects a setting earlier in the prophet's ministry than the time of the composition of the book as a whole and yet finds its present literary formulation from that later period, so the reformulation of similarly early *hôy* oracles could be attributed to Habakkuk himself and dated to the time of his final composition of his book.

His reformulation of them to address the wrong-doing of the foreign oppressor, however, has not emptied these oracles of their applicability to Judean injustice. The designation of these oracles as a "parable" (*mashal*) and "mocking riddles" (*melitsah ḥidot;* 2:6) suggests that they be read on more than one level, as Otto already noted. If Judeans could be guilty of oppression, if, as 1:4 indicates, a Judean could be a wicked person (*rashaʿ*), then these *hôy* oracles could serve, on one level, as a warning not to participate in the oppression threatening Judean society. The righ-

teous person (*tsaddiq*) was to live in the light of the vision of God's coming judgment, but what it means to be a righteous person is given concrete shape when set over against the description of wicked behavior contained in the opening formulations of the *hôy* oracles. Thus the *tsaddiqim*, defined by their rejection of injustice and oppression, patiently await God's coming judgment, but even in the present they may already anticipate in their own just behavior God's eschatological vision for the future.

Bibliography

Achtemeier, Elizabeth. *Nahum, Malachi.* Atlanta, 1986.

Anderson, Bernhard. *Creation Versus Chaos.* New York, 1967.

Brownlee, William H. *The Midrash Pesher of Habakkuk.* Missoula, 1979.

Hiebert, Theodore. *God of My Victory: The Ancient Hymn in Habakkuk 3.* Atlanta, 1986.

Humbert, Paul. *Problèmes du livre d'Habacuc.* Neuchâtel, 1944.

Janzen, J. Gerald. "Habakkuk 2:2–4 in the Light of Recent Philological Advances." *Harvard Theological Review* 73 (1980): 53–78.

———. "Eschatological Symbol and Existence in Habakkuk." *Catholic Biblical Quarterly* 44 (1982): 394–414.

Keller, Carl A. "Die Eigenart der Prophetie Habakuks." *Zeitschrift für die alttestamentliche Wissenschaft* 85 (1973): 156–167.

Otto, Eckart. "Die Stellung der Wehe-Worte in der Verkündigung des Propheten Habakuk." *Zeitschrift für die alttestamentliche Wissenschaft* 89 (1977): 73–107.

Rudolph, Wilhelm. *Micha, Nahum, Habakuk, Zephanja.* Gütersloh, 1975.

Smith, Ralph L. *Micah, Malachi.* Waco, Tex., 1984.

Woude, Adam S. Van der. *Habakuk, Zefanja.* Nijkerk, 1978.

J. J. M. ROBERTS

Zephaniah

INTRODUCTION

THE BOOK OF Zephaniah contains, in expanded form, the collected oracles of the prophet who spearheaded the revival of the prophetic movement in the late seventh century B.C.E., after nearly a century of silence. Zephaniah was the first prophet to speak out against certain conditions and practices found in Judah and Jerusalem since Isaiah and Micah had done so in the waning years of the eighth century B.C.E.

Historical Background

Although Assyrian might had ended the existence of the northern kingdom of Israel in 722–721 B.C.E., Judah was able to retain its independence with the help of the balance of power Egypt represented at the time. King Hezekiah (715–687) exploited this situation to Judah's advantage. Eventual Assyrian ascendancy over Egypt, however, ended this power balance and forced the southern kingdom into the Assyrian orbit. The subsequent subservience of Kings Manasseh (687–642) and Amon (642–640) to Assyria reflected in their accommodationist policies had a devastating effect on the religious and social fabric of the kingdom of Judah. Prophetic protest was long stifled under these conditions until a palace coup placed Josiah (640–609) on the throne and set the stage for reform. The new king and his supporters took advantage of the rapid decline of Assyrian power at the close of the seventh century B.C.E. and initiated reforms that would restore the Yahwistic faith as the exclusive law of the land. Not since the reign of Hezekiah almost a century earlier had prophets raised their voices in protest against governmental policy and religious practices that deviated from Israel and Judah's covenantal beliefs. Indeed, it was not only the trauma of the demise of the northern kingdom of Israel but also the vindication of the earlier mid-eighth-century warning cries of Amos and Hosea in the north that had then prompted the southern reforms of King Hezekiah.

Furthermore, at that time the Cushite twenty-fifth Egyptian Dynasty (716–663) provided a much-needed political counterbalance to Assyrian power, allowing Hezekiah some breathing space for internal change. Isaiah, whose ministry stressed reliance on faith in God rather than in foreign political pacts, had harsh words for the royal alliance with the Egyptian Cushite Dynasty. Isaiah 18 is a powerful expression of his belief that Hezekiah's pro-Egyptian policy was doomed. Judah's independence was ultimately preserved by the Babylonian revolt at the end of the seventh century, which drew Assyrian attention away from Judah and Egypt toward the east. In rather brief time Assyrian hegemony ended in the west, giving King Josiah in turn breathing space to restructure

Judah with a revived, purified Yahwistic faith. The prophet Zephaniah spearheaded this movement with a warning message describing in dramatic imagery the coming Day of Yahweh. It was his voice, taking up the work of Isaiah and Micah, which subsequently fed into the ministries of Jeremiah, Nahum, and Habakkuk.

ZEPHANIAH, THE PROPHET

The Book of Zephaniah is our only source of information about the prophet, and that is limited almost exclusively to the superscription that heads the material collected under the prophet's name. The opening verses of biblical books of prophecy generally provide the title, authorship, location, and date of composition. This information is usually added by the hand of an editor or redactor of a later period. Biblical scholarship identifies the redactor(s) with a disciple of the prophet or those who cherished the prophet's message and sought to keep it before the community of believers. Consequently, what now appears to be only a terse statement was originally seen as sufficient to identify the author and validate what followed as vital to the life of the faithful, all in the compass of few words.

In the case of Zephaniah's identity, three clues are given. First, he is marked and authenticated as a prophet; next his family tree is given for four generations; finally, the date of his ministry is set during the reign of Josiah: "The word of the Lord which came to Zephaniah the son of Cushi, son of Gedaliah, son of Amariah, son of Hezekiah, in the days of Josiah the son of Amon, king of Judah" (1:1; RSV). Two aspects of Zephaniah's genealogy stand out: his African ancestry and his possible royal background. In Hebrew, Cushi stands for African, as related in Numbers 12 in the controversy over Moses' Cushite (Ethiopian in RSV) wife; moreover, 2 Kings 19:9 identifies the Cushite ruler of the Twenty-fifth Dynasty, "Tirhakah, king of Cush," as an ally of Hezekiah against the Assyrians. The term Cush is the Egyptian designation for the region of her darker-skinned neighbors to the south along the cataract region of the Nile River. The Hebrews also use Cush to identify Africa and her people. The Greek classical sources and the Greek Bible use Ethiopia ("land of burnt faces") as its equivalent, whereas the people of that region called their land Nubia. The widespread use of Ethiopia in modern English versions of the Bible stems from the impact of the Greek Bible in the West.

Prophetic genealogies seldom go beyond the first or second generation, but this one reaches into the fourth, doubtless in order to link Zephaniah with the name Hezekiah. Though the identity of this Hezekiah with King Hezekiah is not certain, the combining of African and royal heritage points this way. The Cushite presence is identified with the monarchy from David's Cushite guard (2 Sam 18:21) down to Africans at the court of Jehoiakim and Zedekiah as told by Zephaniah's later contemporary Jeremiah (Jer 36:14, "Jehudi the son of Nathaniah, son of Shelemiah, son of Cushi"; and 38:7, Ebed-melech the Cushite "who was in the king's house"). Other evidence intrinsic to the message of Zephaniah, for example, his special concern for Jerusalem and its royal traditions (Zeph 1:7–13) shows his knowledge of and personal feelings for this segment of society.

The name Zephaniah derives from two elements: the divine name "Yah(weh)" and the place-name "Zaphon," the great mountain in the north, where, like Olympus in Greek mythology, the gods dwell. Yoked thus, the name literally means "Yahweh is Zaphon," which, as an attack on the claims to power of the Canaanite gods, yields the extended meaning: "(It is) Yahweh (who) protects." The name occurs elsewhere (2 Kgs 25:18; 1 Chr 6:36; Zech 6:10) and always in a royal or priestly context, before and after the time of the prophet. The name, like the genealogy in which it appears, points to a deeply religious tradition and one with royal, or at least Jerusalem priestly, connections as well.

The prophet's ministry is best placed during the reign of the king Josiah (640–609 B.C.E.), who, after the decline of Assyria, reasserted Judah's political and religious independence. Given the close correspondence between key elements in Josiah's reforms and the crimes condemned in Zephaniah's preaching, it may be inferred that the prophet's ministry came during the early part of Josiah's reign or even before the cleansing of the Temple of Assyrian accretions. The idolatrous and syncretistic practices he condemns are similar to those condemned by the reform movement, suggesting that Zephaniah preceded that effort and may even have influenced the direction it took.

The Deuteronomic reform, reflecting the style and content of the core of Deuteronomy, began in earnest in 621 B.C.E. Its program called for the purification of religion through centralizing cultic worship at the Jerusalem Temple. It was also an expression of national self-assertion against Assyrian rule. During this period of religious and political ferment, Zephaniah called for return to the rule of Yahweh, lest the nation fall under the heavy hand of divine judgment. The prophets Nahum, Habakkuk, and Jeremiah also joined the fray, with Jeremiah's long ministry spanning the beginning as well as the demise of the Deuteronomic reform movement soon after Josiah's death in 609 B.C.E. While we hear no more of Zephaniah during or after this time, his words are nevertheless remembered and preserved. Like many collections of the sayings of the preexilic prophets, the Book of Zephaniah began to take on its present canonical shape during the Babylonian exile. Despite the paucity of information about him, Zephaniah's place in the succession of prophets marks him as initiator of this final outpouring of prophetic fervor before the fall of Judah and the destruction of the Temple in 587 B.C.E.

THE BOOK OF ZEPHANIAH

Form and Composition

The Book of Zephaniah is similar in structure to other prophetic books. The collected sayings and deeds of the prophets themselves form a larger anthology or corpus known as the Latter Prophets, consisting of Isaiah, Jeremiah, Ezekiel, and the twelve minor prophets. The Book of Zephaniah stands in the ninth position among the Twelve, following Nahum and Habakkuk and preceding Haggai, Zachariah, and Malachi. The canonical order of these works reflects another underlying reality, namely, the strong sense of continuity and identification among the prophets and their followers. The prophets had both their personal identity and a shared identity with the prophetic movement and tradition.

Although they are distinctive individuals, Zephaniah and those others who have held the prophetic office used a common, shared repertoire of theological expressions and images, as well as certain literary

forms and conventions that have come to be associated with the prophetic office and tradition. Jeremiah noted, for example, "The law (torah) shall not perish from the priest, nor counsel ('etsah) from the wise, nor the word (davar) from the prophet" (Jer 18:18; RSV). The prophetic "word" was either a word of woe, predicting disaster for the community's disloyalty to God, or a word of weal or peace, promising blessing and vindication out of God's love for God's people. Like the ancient covenantal ceremonial blessing or curse for either obedience to the covenant or disobedience, the prophet too proclaims the coming of either destruction or peace (shalom), in return for either loyalty or apostasy. The Book of Zephaniah thus can be divided into three parts: (1) threats of woe against Judah (1:2–2:3); (2) threats against foreign nations (2:4–3:8); and (3) promises of peace and good fortune (3:9–20). This threefold division of oracles can be further divided into smaller units that may reflect the different occasions on which the prophet addressed the community.

Within the established literary canons of woe oracles and peace oracles, Zephaniah stands by itself on account of certain distinctive characteristics that reflect the prophet's particular background and theological position. One of the hallmarks of its prophetic message is the elaboration of the concept of the Day of the Lord (yom Yahweh) to a fuller extent than was done before in Amos (5:18–20, 8:9–14) or later in Isaiah (13:6–16). Another distinguishing feature is the universalizing of both threat and peace. The words of weal as well as the expected oracles of woe apply also to the foreign nations. Even though the Book of Amos opens with oracles against foreign nations (chaps. 1–2), these serve only as prologue to the prophetic threat against Israel. Zephaniah's oracles against the nations, however, are integral to his proclamation of universal doom on the Day of the Lord. Similarly, his words of future restoration include the nations within the scheme of universal renewal.

Literary Style

Only the superscription (1:1) and two explanatory verses on retribution (2:10–11) are in prose. The remainder of these prophetic utterances are in poetic form. Poetry is a more emotionally expressive vehicle, and gives the prophet a fuller range to convey the emotions and the divine pathos by which he is overwhelmed and compelled to cry out. The verse form also works to make a deep emotional impression on the audience. It lends itself to repetition and is grasped more quickly and retained in the mind and heart longer. The oracles are rehearsed and transmitted orally. The oral transmission and poetic form are complementary and are congenial vehicles for the prophet, the hearers, and those followers who preserve and transmit the prophetic word.

Assonance and repetition are key poetic devices in Zephaniah's repertoire. The opening unit on the threat of universal destruction (1:2–6), for example, repeats the key word "sweep" (Hebrew root '-s-f) four times, twice in the opening verse for emphasis, asof asef, "I will utterly sweep away." The expressions "from the face of the earth" and "human"/"humankind" again occur twice with paranomasia on similar-sounding Hebrew words for "earth" and "human" (adamah and adam, respectively). In like fashion, the expression "Day of the Lord" (Hebrew, yom Yahweh) is repeatedly mentioned in the second unit on the Day of the Lord (1:7–2:3). The third prophetic unit, containing oracles against foreign nations (2:4–15), dramatically opens with assonance and a punning wordplay, "Gaza shall be deserted . . . and Ekron shall be uprooted" (Hebrew, 'azzah, 'azuvah . . . ve'ekron te'aqer).

Powerful metaphors, dramatic imagery, and clever turns of phrase mark this work in the Hebrew original. Subsequent translations into other languages, such as Greek, Latin, and English, have retained the rhetorical power of the original. This is particularly true of that most influential portion of Zephaniah's speech on the Day of the Lord (1:7–2:3), which portrays God searching Jerusalem with a lantern to expose those who drink their lives away, in the belief that God does not care and will not intervene (1:12). Proverbs 20:27 carries the same image and message: "The spirit of man is the lamp of the Lord, searching all his innermost parts." What follows is among the best poetry in the Bible. Zephaniah 1:15 is in the form of a battle hymn that depicts the effects of God's marching to battle: "A day of wrath is that day." Western liturgy and music for the burial of the dead have been strongly influenced by this passage

through the medieval Latin hymn *Dies irae*. The divine anger is expressed in a veritable cascade of nouns modifying the ominous repetition of the word "day" (*yom*):

> A day of wrath is that day,
> a day of distress and anguish,
> a day of ruin and devastation,
> a day of darkness and gloom,
> a day of clouds and thick darkness,
> a day of trumpet blast and battle cry.
>
> (1:15, 16a; RSV)

Threat of Universal Destruction (1:2–6)

The superscription in 1:1 serves as the book's title and authenticates that Zephaniah, offspring of Cushi, received "the word of the Lord" that is herewith given. Then follows a message of judgment over all creation, opening with a dramatic flourish of God sweeping the earth clean of all habitation. One thinks today, as the prophet's audience doubtless did then, of the Genesis account of creation and universal judgment by flood. The process of creation is reversed not by a deluge that returns everything to watery chaos, but by sweeping. The Hebrew words that open the collected oracles of Zephaniah, asof asef, "I will utterly sweep away," have an obvious connection with the word from the same Hebrew root meaning "gather" (asaf), and its derivative, "ingathering"/"harvest" (asif), also an early name of the important religious feast of Ingathering listed in the ancient calendars (Exod 23:16, 34:22). Of the three ancient Israelite pilgrimage festivals, Unleavened Bread (linked with Passover), Weeks (also called First Fruits and Pentecost), and Ingathering (also called Booths/Tabernacles), the last (asif) was the most important and best attended. It was popularly called "the feast of Yahweh" (Lev 23:39) or simply "the feast" (Ezek 45:25; 1 Kgs 8:2, 65). All of these associations with the opening words of Zephaniah suggest that the prophet and his audience made a similar connection and perceived the message that their joyous occasion was going to be changed into a tragic one because of their apostasy. The prophet condemns his people for adopting the idolatrous, foreign cults of the Canaanites (Baal), the Ammonites (Milcom), and the hated Assyrian overlords ("host of heavens" or astral worship). Perhaps his woe oracle was delivered at the

Ingathering festival, which originally marked the end of the agricultural year and was thus a particularly festive occasion. It would have caught the crowds unawares and made them take special notice. In this opening oracle Zephaniah threatens the destruction of all humankind and ends with a specific threat against Jerusalem and its inhabitants.

The Day of the Lord (1:7–2:3)

The prophet invokes the whirlwind- or tornado-like appearance of God by bidding the audience to be quiet (in sound, Hebrew *has*, "be silent," is not unlike English "hush"), and then he solemnly announces, "The day of the Lord [*yom Yahweh*] is at hand" (1:7). This invocation is liturgical in tone, like the familiar "The Lord is in his holy temple; let all the earth keep silence before him" (Hab 2:20; RSV). This unit consists of two parts: 1:7–13 and 1:14–18, with 2:1–3 as a word of hope to the humble and righteous. First person address or God's direct speech predominates in verses 7–13, whereas the heavy consequences of God's wrath are spelled out by repetition of the word "day" and accompanying descriptive nouns in verses 14–18.

In the first part the officials of the land are threatened with punishment for adopting foreign dress and religious practices. God searches the place with lamps to ferret out those who think the just God ignores their wicked deeds and that the righteous God is not incensed at their sloth and indifference. George Adam Smith is eloquent in his comment on verse 12: "'To settle upon one's lees' became a proverb for sloth, indifference and the muddy mind. . . . All this starts questions for ourselves. Here is evidently the same public temper, which at all periods provokes alike the despair of the reformer and the indignation of the prophet: the criminal apathy of the well-to-do classes sunk in ease and religious indifference. . . . The great causes of God and Humanity are not defeated by the hot assaults of the Devil, but by the slow, crushing, glacier-like mass of thousands and thousands of indifferent nobodies. God's causes are never destroyed by being blown up, but by being sat upon" (1898, 52–54).

The solemn introduction to the second and central section on the Day of the Lord shifts the focus away from sinful Jerusalem to the hastening, destructive presence of God: "The great day of the Lord is near, near and hastening fast" (1:14). Then follows the rumbling, irresistible onslaught of God as divine warrior. The poetic portrayal of the Day of the Lord as the final judgment day now encompasses all humanity. Whereas the rainbow-signed covenant between God and Noah signified that God would never again destroy the earth by flood (Gen 9:11–13), Zephaniah warns: "In the fire of his jealous wrath, all the earth shall be consumed" (1:18).

The concluding section of this battle hymn, which spills over into chapter 2, is very difficult because of obscure Hebrew words that have double meanings. The section could focus on the gathering of the people as chaff, as kindling for the coming conflagration. The very first words, translated "Come together and hold assembly" (RSV), are verbs derived from the Hebrew noun for "straw" (*kash*) and thus can mean "gather/collect together (straw)." But the section can be understood differently because this word can also mean "enter hard labor," implying the people's refusal to acknowledge their delicate (pregnant) state. Those same people who themselves care about nothing and think God does not care are warned to gather themselves together, to acknowledge their sin, and prepare for the coming (birth) pangs of divine judgment. Zephaniah offers suggestions for surviving that day: "Seek righteousness, seek humility; perhaps you may be hidden on the day of the wrath of the Lord" (2:3). Those so addressed are called "the humble of the land," an expression used not for the wealthy exploiters and irreligious folk, but for those (few) who do (obey) God's law. The prophet makes no promise; his "perhaps" offers only the possibility of survival.

Oracles Against Foreign Nations (2:4–15)

Previously the act of cursing neighboring states was part of the vindication and blessing of God's people, but Zephaniah's and Amos' reinterpretation of the Day of the Lord as negative rather than favorable judgment for God's people opened new ways of viewing oracles against the nations. These oracles of woe express something more complex than the reverse side of God's vindication of Israel through the defeat of the foreign nations. This form was put to various rhetorical and liturgical, as well as theological, uses. Amos used it to arouse his audience, and then included them among the enemies of God. The geographical ordering of the nations in Amos 1–2 moves from the distant to the near neighbor. Zephaniah moves from the near neighbor to the distant: those in the west are condemned first (2:4–7; Gaza and Ashkelon, the Philistines and Canaanites), then those in the east (2:8–11; Moabites and Ammonites), to the south (2:12; Cush/Ethiopia) and to the north (2:13–15; Assyria). Furthermore, these woe oracles are followed by condemnation of God's people (Jerusalem in 3:1–5). Zephaniah 2:13–15, with its portrayal of the destruction of Nineveh, the Assyrian capital, anticipates the Book of Nahum. Only brief mention is made of Cush, perhaps because its day of dominance had passed, and it is to be listed among the converts to Yahweh (3:10). However, the same woe cry of cursing can also be the funeral cry of mourning, of lament, since the nations who descend from Noah are conceived as a family and closely linked to Israel (Gen 10).

Oracles Against "the Oppressing City" (3:1–5)

Though not named, Jerusalem is "the oppressing city," whose leaders (judges, prophets, priests) are corrupt, pervert justice, and violate the law they are called to uphold. Almost a century earlier Isaiah (1:21–23) had leveled similar charges against Jerusalem. Continuing in the tradition of Isaiah, Zephaniah can also proclaim that God is in the midst of the city, dispensing justice even though its officials have failed in their responsibilities. Morning was the time when the court was in session and justice was dispensed; hence the beautiful depiction of God as the faithful judge: "Morning by morning he gives judgement, without fail at daybreak" (3:5; NEB).

Summation of God's Threat Against Jerusalem and the Nations (3:6–8)

The prophet tries to convert wayward Jerusalem, which shares the sentence of universal judgment with the nations, by using imagery and language borrowed from the law courts. He also employs the didactic style and exhortation used in the classroom, along with one of the key terms for instruction in Israel's wisdom tradition, *musar* (correction): "I said, 'Surely she will

fear me, she will accept correction'" (3:7; RSV). When it is clear that prophetic rebuke and warning have failed to change the people, God stands before the assembled nations as "witness" and "judge" who decides to "pour out upon them my indignation, all the heat of my anger" (3:8). God's wrath is aroused by the injustice of his own people as well as by that of the nations.

Conversion of All Peoples (3:9–10)

The symmetry of these last units, like that of the entire book, is the movement from the universal to the particular, from divine wrath against the nations to divine wrath against God's people. Here too, the process of conversion moves from the nations and the Diaspora (Israel scattered among the nations) to that of Jerusalem itself. The tradition of Genesis prior to the call of Abraham is recalled in the ideal of the family of nations speaking a universal language, a situation that was shattered with the dispersion of peoples and the confusion of speech owing to the destructive results of the Tower of Babel (Gen 11).

Nineteenth- and early-twentieth-century scholars have maintained that this and the following units are not Zephaniah's but are later additions primarily because the tone changes from condemnation to conversion and from destruction to restoration. This view is less persuasive now that the prophets are no longer placed in the straitjacket of uttering but one kind of oracle. The words of woe and threats of calamity were real, were spoken in the hope of conversion and change on the part of those marked for God's wrath. It was not so much that the threat of doom would be rescinded, but that out of the devastation a purged remnant of survivors would emerge and life begin again. That new situation would not be just a return to a former state, but would be a wholly new era when all enmities would cease. Zephaniah's message contains these seeds even though his ancient editors have arranged and expanded the materials of the book that bears his name.

The Deuteronomic flavor in 3:9–10—with its concern for "pure speech" and calling on "the name of the Lord" and the call for unity in serving God "with one accord"—may reflect Zephaniah's influence upon the Deuteronomic reform movement of which he was a contemporary or it may be a sign of a later editorial interpretation. Admittedly, the reference to Cush here (3:10), as in Isaiah 18:1, appears to be a convention; but the impact of the Cushite Twenty-fifth Egyptian Dynasty on the political and religious life of Israel and Jerusalem was significant and made itself felt within the prophetic literature down to and beyond Zephaniah's time. Zephaniah's own ancestry and the Cushite official's role in saving Jeremiah (Jer 38:7–13, 39:15–18) are contemporary with the reform movement and doubtlessly helped shape its ideals of unity and universalism. The idea that the conversion of the nations begins with Cush may have begun with Zephaniah 3:10, if not Isaiah 18:1–2 and 7. In any event, it took hold in the tradition (Ps 68:31), and is expressed again in the New Testament story of Philip's baptism of the Cushite (Nubian) official (Acts 8:26–40) that precedes the conversion of the Roman centurion Cornelius (Acts 10).

A Purified Remnant Takes Refuge in God (3:11–13)

In 3:12 the remnant in Jerusalem is seen as the "afflicted and poor" (NEB) ("humble and lowly"; RSV), that is, those who are dependent upon God rather than upon their own resources. The rebellious wealthy and arrogant, those who rejected God and God's justice, are expressly excluded. The survivors will know the peace that God alone can give, and they will experience it in solemn worship as portrayed in the pastoral imagery of the concluding verse 13: "For they shall pasture and lie down, and none shall make them afraid" (RSV).

Jerusalem Summoned to Rejoice (3:14–20)

Jerusalem is addressed as "daughter of Zion"; moreover the call (feminine imperative in Hebrew) to "sing/cry out" is similar to the summons to rejoice found in the Yahweh enthronement psalms (e.g., Pss 47, 98). These psalms proclaim God as king; so also Zephaniah 3:15 declares, "The King of Israel, the Lord, is in your midst; you shall fear evil no more" (RSV). The Day of the Lord is no longer a time of fear: the divine warrior has been victorious and has purged God's enemies from Jerusalem's ranks. This festival is an ingathering of the dispersed from the land; their changed condition will be an example to

the peoples of the earth. In this coming Day of the Lord, "I will make you renowned and praised among all the peoples of the earth" (3:20).

Zephaniah's consistent message—of God's will to intervene and silence those who think God is indifferent—reached into the exilic community of the next generation and was cherished in that age as it had been in his own. The dramatic, moving portrayal of the Day of the Lord as destruction was also coupled with a promise that God would intervene to save. The relationship between the preexilic original and the postexilic redactional use of Zephaniah is succinctly expressed by Brevard Childs: "The post-exilic redaction, when viewed from its effect on the canonical text, was not an attempt to make older material relevant by tying it to the exile, rather the reverse. It gave the exile its true meaning in the light of the divine promise" (1979, 461).

THE MESSAGE OF ZEPHANIAH

This preexilic prophet stresses the inevitability and universality of the day of judgment. Condemning the injustices and the apostasy of the leaders of God's people, Zephaniah does not call for reform and a return to God; he stresses, instead, the hope for the survival of the humble and obedient poor of the land (3:12). Like his later contemporary, Jeremiah, Zephaniah could only muster a "perhaps" (Hebrew 'ulai; 2:3) as a message of hope for those who might find shelter on that dreadful day. Anticipating the concept of a new heart (Jer 31:33, Ezek 11:19), Zephaniah prophesies the emergence of people of "pure speech" who will worship God "with one accord." Doubtless because of his own ancestry and the tradition of African elements within the royal household of Jerusalem, Cush is represented in the forefront of nations who will honor God (3:10; cf. Amos 9:7; Isa 18:7; Pss 68:31, 87:4). Caught up in the reality of the Day of the Lord, Zephaniah could only proclaim the wrath of the just God; however, he perceived it as a universal phenomenon and saw beyond it a coming universal worship. His message of the divine end, which included the vision of a new beginning for God's people and all humankind, was an important step in emerging prophetic eschatology in which the end marks the threshold of a new age. Zephaniah's prophetic career thus helped lay the groundwork for the postexilic prophets of return and restoration.

Bibliography

Bennett, Robert A. "Africa and the Biblical Period." *Harvard Theological Review* 64 (1971): 483–500.

Childs, Brevard S. *Introduction to the Old Testament as Scripture.* Philadelphia, 1979.

Christensen, Duane L. "Zephaniah 2:4–15: A Theological Basis for Josiah's Program of Political Expansion." *Catholic Biblical Quarterly* 46 (1984): 669–682.

De Roche, Michael. "Zephaniah 1:2–3: The 'Sweeping' of Creation." *Vetus testamentum* 30 (1980): 104–109.

Kapelrud, Arvid S. *The Message of the Prophet Zephaniah.* Oslo, 1975.

Smith, George Adam. *The Book of the Twelve Prophets.* Vol. 2. New York, 1898.

Watts, John D. W. *The Books of Joel, Obadiah, Jonah, Nahum, Habakkuk, and Zephaniah.* New York, 1975.

Wilson, John R. *Prophecy and Society in Ancient Israel.* Philadelphia, 1980.

ROBERT A. BENNETT

haggai, Zechariah, and Malachi

HAGGAI AND THE first eight chapters of Zechariah are explicitly set in Israel's postexilic era, in the years following the Persian defeat of Babylon in 539 B.C.E. Each addresses in its own way the issues of restoration and renewal that affected the community in Judah during this period. The second half of Zechariah (chaps. 9–14) is later, perhaps from the fifth century, but it is impossible to date with precision. Malachi reflects a setting near the middle of the fifth century, since it deals with issues also addressed in the Book of Nehemiah, from the same period.

When Babylon defeated Judah in 587, it took Judah's religious, political, and economic leaders into exile and destroyed the principal institutions centered in Jerusalem, Judah's capital city. The city itself was demolished along with the Temple, the symbolic and material center of Jewish life. Not long after Cyrus the Persian overthrew Babylon in 539, the Jews and other prisoners in Babylon were permitted to return to their native lands and cities. The accounts in Ezra and Nehemiah portray an immediate and massive return from exile, but there is also evidence in those very books that the return was slow and gradual; perhaps the greatest number of Jews came from Babylon to Judah between 526 and 520, during the reigns of the Persian kings Cambyses II and Darius I.

Upon their return to Judah, the returnees faced severe difficulties. Haggai, Zechariah, and Malachi testify to economic hardships plaguing the community, which remained firmly within the orbit of Persian sovereignty, and they reflect disputes within the community concerning its political and cultic leadership, the role and form of the cult itself, and perhaps even the question of who was eligible for membership in the community. The texts address these and other issues, however, from a theological perspective whose primary feature is Yahweh's promised intention to create a new order in which Jerusalem and its people enjoy unlimited blessing and glory by virtue of Yahweh's presence among them. This would of course require a decisive rearrangement of the present order, as Zechariah 9–14 makes abundantly clear.

haggai

Haggai's concern centers on the Temple, and he urges the people to join in its reconstruction. Since the Temple is Yahweh's dwelling place, from which he exercises royal dominion, the people can expect blessing and prosperity to follow their obedient response. The reconstructed Temple and the revitalized cult surrounding it signal a reversal of the community's fortunes and of current international arrangements. Temple reconstruction is thus an act of faith in circumstances that make it seem unreasonable. The Book of Haggai consists of three different types of material. First, there is a series of disputation speeches (1:2–11, 2:10–14, 2:15–19). Second, there are two oracles of promise addressed to the community and its leaders (2:6–9, including perhaps 1:15b–2:5 and 2:20–23), which articulate Yahweh's promises for the future. And third, surrounding these major portions of the book, is an editorial framework, which supplies circumstantial details such as dates and casts the entire book in the form of a narrative (1:1, 3, parts of 12–15a, 15b–2:2, 2:10, 20).

EDITORIAL FRAMEWORK

The framework establishes a chronological sequence for the prophetic speeches and places them in the context of events and circumstances in the Jewish community. Furthermore, it specifies to whom these words were spoken and emphasizes that Haggai's words were really Yahweh's. The language of the framework, which resembles that of the Deuteronomists (Mason 1977b), suggests that it is truly editorial, the work of redactors who collected and transmitted Haggai's speeches and thereby interpreted them.

This interpretation was accomplished first of all by supplying specific dates along the way (1:1, 15; 2:1, 10, 18, 20). Thus, the editors located the speeches in relation to (1) initial resistance to the building of the Temple, (2) a positive response to Haggai's first speech, (3) fears and disappointments as the work began, and (4) the glorious prospects of the community, now and even more so in the future. The specific dates all fall in the second year of the reign of the Persian king Darius, probably 520, the year in which Darius consolidated his rule—although not everyone agrees with this dating (see Bickerman 1981). Thus, Haggai's speeches are set against the backdrop of an international situation increasingly unfavorable to Jewish hopes and apparently (in the view of Haggai's audience) inimical to the reconstruction of the Temple (1:2).

Those to whom Haggai speaks are clearly identified: Zerubbabel the governor, Joshua the high priest, and the rest of the people. The official designations of Zerubbabel and Joshua are probably intended to emphasize their roles as the preeminent civil and cultic leaders, respectively, of the Jewish community. Some scholars have sought to find in the various

references to the people—"this people" (1:2), "the remnant of the people" (1:12; RSV), "the people of the land" (2:4), "this people and this nation" (2:14)—a religious and social distinction between two or more groups (Steck 1971). Some of these terms may have such implications in other biblical texts, but they do not seem to here. The "remnant" in 1:12, for example, refers merely to the remainder of the people (as in Nehemiah 7:72) in addition to their leaders, Zerubbabel and Joshua. It is not possible on the basis of either the editorial framework or the rest of Haggai to draw distinctions in his audience, for example, between Jews and Samaritans or between returned exiles and those who had remained in the land. Nor can one say anything certain about Haggai's own biography. The precise language of the framework seems designed to make clear that Haggai addressed everyone—"all the people of the land," including the civil and cultic leaders.

DISPUTATION SPEECHES

Each of these speeches revolves around a question that Yahweh commands Haggai to pose to the audience (1:4; 2:12, 13, 16a [RSV], 19). The question in chapter 1 is preceded by a quotation (1:2), and in the first and third disputation speeches Haggai expands on the question by making a series of observations (1:5–7, 9; 2:15–16). The questions are rhetorical; they are meant to elicit the assent of Haggai's audience. In the second disputation (2:10–14) the questions are straightforward and easily answered. On the basis of the agreement thus established between him and his audience, Haggai goes on to draw a radical conclusion (2:14), the implications of which were not obvious in the question. In the first and third disputations, he follows the rhetorical questions by asking the audience to reflect on their circumstances (1:5, 7; 2:15, 18). Expecting no disagreement, Haggai then moves from shared premises to an unexpected conclusion in order to persuade his audience to do what they were initially unprepared to do, namely, to reconstruct the Temple (Whedbee 1978).

The text does not tell us why the people believed it was not yet time to rebuild the Temple. They may have believed that its destruction by Babylon represented Yahweh's curse, which had not yet been lifted.

In addition they likely believed that the Jerusalem Temple was the site of Yahweh's dwelling, from which Yahweh exercised dominion as divine king, establishing and maintaining universal order. Since the people recognized, as Haggai pointed out, that Yahweh's dominion and the order it should reflect were nowhere in evidence, they may have believed that the time had not yet come to build the Temple. Temple-building would have to wait until Yahweh overcame the controlling alien forces and again ruled as divine king, as promised, for example, in Ezekiel 34:24–29 (cf. Hag 1:5–11, Zech 8:9–13).

Haggai, while agreeing with the community's dire assessment of the present situation, turns its logic around. The present distress is not a signal that alien forces have dominion; rather, Yahweh (1:9–11, 2:17) was and remains in sovereign control—it was precisely Yahweh who brought the distress. The situation requires not passive despair, but action—the reconstruction of the Temple as the site of Yahweh's royal dwelling, the place from which Yahweh will establish peace and welfare (*shalom*; 2:9).

The editorial framework makes obvious the link between Temple reconstruction and a decisive turn in the community's welfare by associating the dedication of the Temple's foundation (apparently the meaning of 2:18; cf. 2 Chr 24:27) with the end of futility and the beginning of blessing. This notice comes in the midst of Haggai's third disputation (2:15–19), in which he asks the people to contrast their present circumstances with those prevailing before Temple construction began. The conclusion is drawn: the Temple is the place from which peace will be established (2:9) and blessing begins today (2:19).

The second disputation (2:10–14), which seems out of place, likely responds to an implied question on the part of the priests and the people: why have cultic offerings not brought about their intended communion with Yahweh? The legal opinion (*torah*) sought by Haggai from the priests is designed to make the point that in the present circumstances the cult is ineffective because the Temple (or the altar? cf. Ezra 3:1–5) has not been reconsecrated following its desecration by the Babylonians. In these circumstances, rather than mediating Yahweh's presence the cult site conveyed impurity and rendered the people unclean. Haggai here associates the destroyed and desecrated Temple with spiritual as well as material futility: both "the work of their hands and that which is offered there are unclean" (2:14; Au. trans.).

ORACLES OF PROMISE

Material well-being is promised in the two future-oriented oracles. The first oracle (2:6–9) is introduced by the editorial framework of 1:12–15a and 1:15b–2:2, with 2:3 providing the immediate background. These verses presuppose that construction on the Temple has begun—that Haggai's rhetoric in the disputation speeches has had its intended effect (1:12–15a) and that there is great disappointment over the condition of the Temple in comparison with its former glory (2:3). Haggai answers this disappointment by employing language otherwise used to encourage those about to encounter a military foe (Deut 31:1–8) but used also in postexilic texts in relation to the task of constructing the Temple (1 Chr 28:20–21): Take heart and do not fear because Yahweh's presence is with you (2:4–5; Conrad 1985, 71–73). This encouragement is supported by the oracle in 2:6–9, which promises that Yahweh will upset the current order of things in the heavens and on the earth and will adorn the Temple with the wealth of the nations, wealth that is really Yahweh's after all.

Here Haggai decisively sets aside the conclusion the community has drawn from its present circumstances: that sovereignty is in hands other than Yahweh's. Yahweh's sovereignty, although not now in evidence, is nonetheless real; the promised manifestation of this reality provides motivation and encouragement for building the Temple as the site of Yahweh's royal rule, the place from which peace (well-being and harmony) will be established (2:9). The people should not be discouraged (2:4) or fear (1:13) because Yahweh is with them and promises to demonstrate that sovereignty that is symbolized by the Temple.

The second oracle, addressed exclusively to Zerubbabel, the governor of Judah, in 2:20–23, is unique among Haggai's speeches. The editorial framework emphasizes that Haggai delivered this oracle on the same day as his previous twofold disputation (2:10–14, 15–19). But whereas those speeches had settled matters internal to Judah—specifically, the effectiveness of the cult and the productivity of the land—this oracle addresses international affairs. Yahweh promises to effect a revolution by means of a cosmic upheaval (2:21; *cf.* 2:6), in which those currently exercising international power will go down to defeat (2:22; *cf.* Exod 15:1, Ezek 38:21). Following this, Zerubbabel himself will be invested with royal authority as Yahweh's servant, Yahweh's chosen, wearing Yahweh's signet ring (2:23; *cf.* Jer 22:24–27).

This concluding passage thus repeats one of the themes of 2:6–9 but also adds a significant political dimension. This oracle reveals the international order achieved by Darius of Persia in the sixth century to be temporary, pending an intervention by Yahweh to bring the world into a new alignment under Yahweh's sovereignty and with Zerubbabel as its executor. This promise concerning Zerubbabel went unfulfilled, and was no doubt challenged by some of Haggai's peers and their Persian sponsors.

The Book of Haggai is a compact witness to a coherent theological view of the relationship among Yahweh's universal sovereignty, the Temple as the site from which that rule is to be exercised, and the welfare of the restored Jewish community. On this theological basis Haggai urges the community to gauge the appropriateness of its action not on the past nor on its present circumstances, but on the future that Yahweh promises to bring about. Their rebuilding and reconsecrating the Temple are but the conditions that make possible the fulfillment of those promises.

Zechariah
Chapters 1–8

Like Haggai, Zechariah is provided with a chronological framework (1:1, 7; 7:1). These dates (at the same time as and two years later than Haggai) are set within a larger framework that consists at least of 1:1–6 and chapters 7 and 8, which portray Zechariah as a prophet preaching repentance and hope. The language of these chapters again resembles that of the Deuteronomists and, especially in 8:10–13, that of Haggai. Set within this framework is a series of visions that form the major portion of sixth-century Zechariah (1:7–6:15). (The Hebrew and English versions are divided differently in Zechariah 1 and 2; thus 1:18 in English is 2:1 in Hebrew. This discussion follows the English versions.)

There are eight distinct visions in Zechariah, all of which are said to have occurred in the same night (1:7). Furthermore, there is a kind of dramatic symmetry among them (Gese 1973, 36), which can be illustrated by outlining the structure of the visions:
1. Horses and riders patrolling the earth (1:7–17)
2. Removal of international threats to the community (1:18–21)
3. Yahweh's presence in Jerusalem (chap. 2)
4. Purification of the priesthood (chap. 3)
5. Yahweh's guiding presence (chap. 4)
6. Removal of the curse from the community (5:1–4)
7. Removal of internal threats to the community (5:5–11)
8. Horses and chariots patrolling the earth (6:9–15)

In other words, this structure focuses attention on the central visions, the fourth and fifth, which symbolize the cultic renewal of the community and Yahweh's immediate presence to it and its leaders. It places them—as with Haggai—in the wider context of Yahweh's sovereignty over the whole earth.

The visions, carefully structured though they are, include additional material, in particular oracles of the prophet's expectation of the fulfillment—and thus vindication—of his prophecies (2:9, 11; 4:9; 6:15; Petersen 1984a, 120–122). It is, however, easier to identify these additions than to understand their relation to the visions; thus, we will treat the texts according to their present sequence.

The introduction (1:1–6). This introduction to the work as a whole portrays Zechariah as a prophet of repentance and combines oracular material (vv. 1–3) with rhetorical questions (v. 5), as in Haggai 1:1–11. Zechariah reminds the people that Yahweh's wrath had fallen upon their ancestors (v. 2), and he urges them to repent, to "return to Yahweh," rather than ignoring the prophets as their ancestors had done (vv. 3–4). The somewhat confusing questions in verse 5 seem to imply that both the ancestors and the prophets, neither of whom are any longer alive, are irrelevant. But more likely these questions probably summarize the view of the people, who believe themselves free of past judgments. This is made clearer in verse 6a, in which Zechariah asks them to agree that the words and statutes of former prophets eventually "overtook" the ancestors. The language is drawn from Deuteronomy 28:15 and 2:45, where the people of

Israel are warned that Yahweh's curse will "overtake" them if they do not heed Yahweh's commandments and statutes.

Thus, the community is called to identify with its ancestors, on whom Yahweh's anger was inflicted. Although difficult to interpret, verse 6b is probably the response of Zechariah's audience: they accepted his word and repented, acknowledging that Yahweh had "purposed" to deal with them appropriately. (Yahweh's purposes are also noted in 8:14–15; and there are other verbal links between 1:1–6 and chapters 7 and 8, as well, suggesting that the introductory and concluding material comes from the same hand.) Thus the introduction to the book depicts the situation (in the year 520) as still subject to Yahweh's anger. But the community's repentance (1:6b) prepares the way for a turn: from Yahweh's anger to the community's renewal, which is the subject matter of the visions.

The Visions (1:7–6:15). Zechariah's stance shifts from that of a preacher of repentance to that of an observer of activity and conversations within the divine realm, perhaps even within Yahweh's council. In most cases the import of what he observes is not clear to him; he must rely on an angelic intermediary, who also replays and even proclaims messages from Yahweh (1:12–17). At the same time, Zechariah is not entirely removed from the earthly scene; he also observes people and events in Jerusalem. In effect, the visionary experience is located midway between the divine and human realms, and it embraces both the community's past and its future (Petersen 1984b).

The first three visions concern Jerusalem and its fate. In the first (1:7–17), Zechariah sees four horses and riders, which, as explained by the angel, are Yahweh's agents sent to patrol the earth. Their report that the earth is at rest is met with dismay. The response is one of dismay, because an earth at rest means that Jerusalem remains under foreign dominion, and that Yahweh has not yet reversed the decree that issued in Jerusalem's destruction (1:12). Yahweh responds to the angel's expression of dismay with words of encouragement. The angel's message to Zechariah in 1:14–17, delivered in Yahweh's name, is that Yahweh is now prepared to disturb the earth's peace, since the nations took advantage of the divine anger to further their own ends. While Yahweh's anger was only slight against Jerusalem, it is now great against the nations (1:15). Thus, Yahweh has returned to Jerusalem, will have the Temple rebuilt, and will once more comfort Zion and rebuild Jerusalem (1:16–17). This change of heart is here prompted by Yahweh's anger against the nations, whereas in 1:1–6 it was dependent upon the people's repentance.

The second and third visions expand upon the first. The second (1:18–21) portrays four horns representing the nations that humiliated Jerusalem and Judah (Israel may be an addition to 1:19) and four smiths or metalworkers who will humiliate the nations. In the third vision (chap. 2) Zechariah sees a man measuring Jerusalem (*cf.* Ezek 40). The angel's response (2:3–5) seems to imply that such measurements are unnecessary for two reasons: (1) Jerusalem's population and wealth will exceed any walls, and (2) Jerusalem will not require walls for defense because Yahweh will be her defender (whereas usually an unwalled village is a symbol of defenselessness [Ezek 38:11]). The Hebrew word for "young man" in 2:4 can also mean soldier, and he is understood here to be making unneeded defensive preparations. This vision is expanded by two commands to flee Babylon and come to Zion, directed to those still in exile, and by the prophet's promise that he will be vindicated as Yahweh's messenger when this reversal of international fortunes comes to pass and Yahweh is present in Jerusalem (2:9–11). This material probably was not originally part of the vision sequence. The language of 2:12 is remarkably similar to that of 1:17 but makes the additional and unique claim that Judah, "the holy land," is Yahweh's portion; with the change of one Hebrew letter 2:12 speaks of Yahweh inheriting rather than comforting (1:17).

The first three visions conclude appropriately with an appeal for universal silence in the face of Yahweh's impending decisive action (see Zeph 1:7, Hab 2:20).

The fourth and fifth visions are both the most important and the most difficult to interpret in the book. In chapter 3, which is less a vision than a revelation, the angel has a counterpart in Satan, who accuses Joshua (*cf.* Ps 109:6). It is probably the angel, rather than Yahweh, who speaks in 3:2, defending Joshua and describing him as one rescued from disaster—"a brand plucked from the fire" (RSV; *cf.*

Isa 7:4, Amos 4:11). The remainder of the scene, through 3:5, symbolizes the purification of the high priest by means of a change of clothes. The issue here cannot be Joshua's investiture because he is already the high priest. Rather, it is the same as in Haggai 2:10–14: the cult cannot mediate the presence of Yahweh because, according to Zechariah, its leadership is impure. Only after Joshua's iniquity has been removed (3:4) is he crowned with the turban, which here seems to be the sign of the high priest's regal status (3:5).

In the second half of the fourth vision (3:6–10) Joshua is granted authority in the Temple and access to Yahweh's council, on condition of continued faithfulness (3:7). While 3:8–10 is very difficult, and may be an addition to the vision proper, it appears that Joshua and his friends are being described as portents of what will come to pass (cf. Isa 8:18, 20:3), namely, that Yahweh will bring "my servant the Branch," a term referring to the royal designee (Jer 23:5–6), who is here unnamed. This promise is related to the stone that Yahweh places before Joshua, a stone with seven eyes (RSV "facets") and inscribed by Yahweh (3:9). The stone and its inscription symbolize the removal of the iniquity of "this land in a single day," or all at one time, and the land's prosperity that is to follow (3:10; cf. Mic 4:4). The inscription could be related to the turban (Exod 28:36–38; Petersen 1984a, 211) or to the foundation stone of the Temple (cf. 4:10b; Halpern 1978). It is more likely the latter, since here it is the land's guilt that is removed in one day, not Joshua's (3:4, 3:8), and since the turban is already on Joshua's head while the stone is before him (Rudolph 1976, 100). The point here is that the land is to enjoy prosperity. The number seven (3:9) may reflect the sevenfold punishment that the land has endured and the sabbath rest that it has enjoyed during the exile (Lev 26, esp. vv. 40–44). The inscribed stone is connected with the Temple, the site of Yahweh's dwelling, symbolizing both peace and the freedom from past iniquity that makes peace possible.

The fifth vision uses the imagery of a menorah to elaborate on the presence of Yahweh in the midst of the community and on the renewal of its leadership (4:1–6a, 10b–13). The inserted passage, 4:6b–10a, identifies half of this leadership, and thus the Branch

of 3:8, with Zerubbabel, who is nowhere else mentioned in Zechariah. The seven "eyes of Yahweh" mentioned in 4:10b refer back to the lamps of 4:2; however, an editor has connected them in 4:6b–10a with the "seven eyes" of 3:9, providing him the opportunity to introduce Zerubbabel and his role of Temple builder into the fifth vision and to bring the Book of Zechariah more closely into line with Haggai. By implication, then, the two anointed in 4:10 are Joshua and Zerubbabel, the cultic and civil leaders of the community, who govern it in dependence on Yahweh, who governs the earth.

The sixth and seventh visions (chap. 5) address the question of the purity of the community from still another angle. In 5:1–4, Zechariah sees a flying scroll that symbolizes a curse on all who swear falsely or steal; it will destroy their houses. The community is thus protected against internal treachery, which must have been a threat. In 5:5–11, the community's guilt is seen departing in a covered ephah, or basket, borne by two winged women who carry it to Shinar (Babylon). There, ironically, a temple (house) is built for it and it is set on a pedestal as if to be worshiped. This is both a sarcastic comment on Babylon, which will venerate what is evil in Judah, and a claim that Judah's own iniquity is far removed (cf. 1:1–6, 3:8).

Finally, the eighth vision repeats the basic imagery of the first. Here, however, it is announced that the horses and chariots have brought Yahweh's spirit to rest in the north country, the place of exile (6:8; cf. 1:12). Significantly, it is not Persia but Yahweh who is Lord of all the earth (6:5).

Following this final vision is a complicated text in which Zechariah orders a crown ("crowns" in Hebrew) to be made of gold taken from three returned exiles (6:11) and placed on Joshua's head. Then, an oracle follows concerning the Branch, who is twice designated as Temple builder (6:12, 13; cf. 4:6b–9) and who will rule in harmony with a priest at his side (6:13; cf. 4:13). Apparently, the Branch is not yet present, so the crown(s) will be kept in the Temple as a reminder (6:14). Concluding the whole vision cycle is a promise in 6:15 that those who are far off (in exile) will come to build the Temple. This will be the final vindication of the prophet (cf. also 2:9–11, 4:10). Whoever contributed this concluding verse is probably also responsible for the similar texts that emphasize Temple construction and Zerubbabel's role in it. In the visionary material itself, as in 6:11, Joshua the high priest is the central figure. That emphasis may have led to the alteration of 6:9–14, so that Joshua, already wearing a turban, is given a royal crown.

Concluding sermons (chaps. 7, 8). The concluding material is the counterpart of chapter 1 and carries its themes further in light of the visions. These sermons are occasioned by a question to the priests concerning ritual fasting to lament the destruction of the Temple (7:1–3; *cf.* Hag 2:10–14), to which Zechariah responds with a series of rhetorical questions (7:4–7). The answer to the ritual question is delayed until 8:18–19, and the intervening material gives the reasons that lament (7:3) will be turned into joy.

First, a summary of the preaching of the former prophets explains why Judah was sent into exile (7:8–14). Chapter 8 then turns to the present and announces Yahweh's intentions for Jerusalem (*cf.* 8:2 with 1:14): the return of both Yahweh and the exiles (8:3, 8). With 8:9, a second sermon seems to begin; it bears striking resemblance to the message of Haggai in its association of the community's welfare with the building of the Temple. This sermon concludes with a contrast between the fate of the ancestors and the expected fate of the community, followed by a prophetic exhortation to justice and peace (8:14–17). Finally, the question posed in 7:1–3 is answered: the times set aside for fasting will be times for rejoicing.

These chapters are concluded with the expectation that the nations will join the Jewish community in worship of Yahweh (8:20–23; *cf.* Isa 2:2–4). They will not be forced to come (contra Isa 49:22–23), but will be drawn to Jerusalem because they recognize that God is with the Jews (8:23). The first part of the Book of Zechariah is devoted to showing, in its diverse ways, that this is so.

Chapters 9–14

Few portions of the Bible are as difficult to interpret as these chapters. There are no clear historical references to illumine them and their language is often cryptic. They reflect serious divisions within the community and diverse expectations concerning the future. There are affinities between chapters 1–8 and 9–14 (Mason 1976), but the differences are even more obvious (Hanson 1975). There is possibly even a division between chapters 9–11 and 12–14; each of these units is introduced by the word "oracle" (or "burden"; 9:1, 12:1). Despite many attempts, however, it is difficult to see a consistent structure governing this material, which is of two general kinds. First, there are prophecies of Yahweh's decisive and final triumph over all rebellious powers, including both foreign nations (9:1–17, 10:3–11:1–3, 12:1–13:1) and the city of Jerusalem (14:1–21; *cf.* 13:7–9). Second, there are prophecies of judgment against the community's leaders, the "shepherds" (11:4–17), and against the prophets (13:2–6)!

Judgment against the shepherds. Much of chapters 10–13 concerns the shepherds, but the term is used ambiguously. Chapters 9 and 10 (and 11:1–3) are concerned primarily with Yahweh's triumph on behalf of Judah (Yahweh's flock) over the kings (the shepherds) of the nations (their goats) (10:3). The term "shepherds" here occasioned the addition of 10:1–2, which describes Judah as being without a shepherd (or leader). Thus, a portrayal of Yahweh's anger at and triumph over the foreign shepherds and nations (10:3–11:3) becomes, with the addition of 10:1–2 as its preface, a portrayal of the leaderless Jewish community. This use of the shepherd motif is then extended to depict Judah's own internal problems in 11:4–16: the prophet is described as a shepherd, as are the rapacious leaders whom Yahweh has given to the community as a judgment on its faithlessness. Finally, Yahweh's judgment condemning the unreliable shepherd who deserts his flock is summarized in 11:17, which may originally have been independent of the story preceding it (Willi-Plein 1974, 112). From the body of the story (11:4–16) it would seem that the bad shepherd is the prophet himself (11:9), who follows Yahweh's instructions to bring division and oppression to the community (11:10, 15–16).

Chapter 13 takes the shepherd imagery still further: Yahweh commands that his own shepherd be slain, again as a judgment on the community (sheep), two-thirds of whom will perish. The remaining third will be faithful to Yahweh. The justification for this action is provided in 13:2–6: the people have turned to idols and the prophets have been inspired by an unclean spirit. Since the people are unfaithful, Yahweh provides them with false leadership in order to lead them to ruin (11:4, 15–16; 13:7–9).

Future expectation. But ruin is not Yahweh's ultimate aim for Judah; thus, the shepherd imagery is interrupted in 12:1–13:1 with a portrayal of Yahweh's and the community's defense against the nations and the purification of the community. This action prompts repentance and remorse for the one "whom they have pierced" (12:10)—probably Yahweh's shepherd, who was "pierced" at Yahweh's command (13:7). The fate of this shepherd introduces a purging of the community that leads, ultimately, to its salvation (13:9). Many of these themes reappear in the New Testament.

The ultimate salvation of the community is vividly depicted in chapters 9 and 14, which frame the book. In 9:1–8, Yahweh's triumphal march against the nations is portrayed; in 9:9–10 this triumph climaxes with the entry of the king into Jerusalem and, significantly, the destruction of all armaments. Chapter 14 offers a very different picture: Yahweh summons the nations against Jerusalem, inflicting a defeat that leaves half of the city in exile. Then, at the decisive moment, Yahweh turns to fight for Jerusalem, inflicting a plague on all those who have fought against her—including Judah (14:14)! The result will be a transformation of the cosmic and earthly landscape (14:4–11), as well the imposition of Yahweh's universal kingship and the elevation and sanctification of Jerusalem as Yahweh's royal residence (14:9, 16–21). Not only will all the nations then venerate Yahweh as king, but they will come to Jerusalem annually to do it, even if unwillingly (14:17–18; *cf.* 8:20–23).

While it is clear that the diverse material in Zechariah 9–14 reflects serious conflicts within the Jewish community, and perhaps rivalries between Judah and Jerusalem (12:7, 14:14), it is impossible to say anything certain about the concrete circumstances of these conflicts. What can be said with certainty is that their ultimate resolution is to accompany Yahweh's triumph.

Malachi

The name Malachi means "my messenger" (*cf.* 3:1). Some have thought that this book is really an anonymous addition to Zechariah 9–14. It is introduced, for example, with the term "oracle" (or "burden"), as are Zechariah 9:1 and 12:1. Others contend that although nothing at all can be known about the author, the book is clearly an independent literary unit distinct from Zechariah (Baldwin 1972, 212). It is convenient and makes sense to speak of its author as "Malachi."

The Book of Malachi was written later than Zechariah 1–8, since it reflects public dismay over the absence of Yahweh's blessings as Zechariah had promised them. It also presupposes the completed Temple and speaks of Judah's "governor," suggesting a date in the fifth century. Similarly, it deals with the same problems of intermarriage (2:10–16) and economic neglect of the Temple (3:6–12) that concerned Nehemiah (Neh 13:10–13, 23–29).

As did Haggai, Malachi pursues a particular rhetorical strategy with his audience, the priests and the people. Typically, he begins with an observation or statement, then quotes the audience's response, and follows with his message. This message itself, again like Haggai's, often revolves around a rhetorical question (*cf.* 1:2–5). The book is divided into six such rhetorical units: 1:2–5, 1:6–2:9, 2:10–16, 2:17–3:5, 3:6–12, 3:13–4:3 (English versions). These are disputations; each of them intends to counter a prevailing view and to move the people to agreement and to action. The first, third, and fifth are addressed to all the people, whereas the others focus on the priests. In addition, 4:4–6 adds the authority of the law and the prophets to Malachi's message, concluding it with both a promise and a threat.

In his introductory speech, Malachi addresses the people's fundamental suspicion that Yahweh's love is ineffective and that Yahweh is powerless. Malachi counters this suspicion by contrasting Jacob with Esau (Gen 25:21–26). But rather than stressing Yahweh's love for Israel he emphasizes Yahweh's hate for Edom (*cf.* Rom 9:13); that is, although the effectiveness of God's love may not yet be evident in Israel, the lasting destruction caused by Yahweh's hate for Edom is certainly apparent to all (1:3–4). The people should conclude, therefore, that Yahweh's love, too, will have its effects: Yahweh's greatness will extend to Israel as well (1:5; *cf.* RSV).

The problem, then, as Malachi will diagnose it,

does not reside with Yahweh. Rather, the people by their unfaithfulness have prevented Yahweh from acting on their behalf. In the second speech the disposition of the community is reflected in that of the priests, who pollute the altar by bringing offerings so unacceptable that not even the governor would accept them (1:8). As a consequence, the community cannot expect to enjoy God's favor (1:9). In striking fashion, Malachi contrasts the impurity of Israel's offerings with the purity of those brought among the nations from east to west that revere Yahweh's name (1:11, 14). But this is neither a comment on the higher unity of all religions nor a projection into the future. Malachi indicts Israel by comparing its failings with the reverence shown for Yahweh elsewhere, among those not regulated by Israel's sacrificial laws (Rudolph 1976, 265). The present attitude and behavior of the priests violate the content of their original calling, here expressed as the covenant with Levi (2:4; cf. 3:3, Jer 33:21, Neh 13:29). Since the priests, as Yahweh's messengers, were charged with instructing the community (2:6–8; cf. Deut 33:8–11), they bear the responsibility for the community's guilt.

Attention shifts to the community in the third speech (2:10–16). The argument of this text is somewhat difficult to follow, but its principal point is, once again, that Yahweh does not accept the people's offerings because they have been unfaithful (2:13–14). At issue in this case is divorce, that is, Jewish men divorcing their wives to marry foreign women, perhaps for economic advantage (Locher 1981).

The fourth speech makes explicit the viewpoint of the people and their priests. As in 1:2 they had contested the effectiveness of God's love, and in 1:12 had said that Yahweh's table was polluted, so in 2:17 they contend that "the God of justice" is absent and the one who does evil is good in Yahweh's sight. All of this is finally summed up in 3:14: "There is no purpose in serving God." In opposition to this view the prophet stresses that Malachi, "my messenger," is preparing God's way. The Lord whom the people seek will then be present. This announcement is expanded in 3:1b–4, which speaks of a messenger of Yahweh's covenant who will purify the priests so that they will bring acceptable offerings, implying perhaps that the present priesthood will be replaced (cf. 3:18). The

continuation of 3:1a in 3:5 stresses the impending judgment on all moral inequity, for, unlike the priests (2:17, 3:14–15), Yahweh discerns good from evil. For that reason, God's presence is potentially ominous.

Following a disputation about the Temple treasury (3:6–12; cf. Neh 13:10–13), Malachi returns in the final speech to the complaint of the people and priests (3:14–15). In what follows, the complaint of 3:14 is answered obliquely. The disputation is broken off with the report that those who feared Yahweh deliberated together, resulting in Yahweh's promise to designate them his special possession to be spared in the coming conflagration (3:16–17). At that time proper discernment—between evildoers and the righteous—will be restored (3:18), and through Yahweh's acts the evildoers will perish, whereas those who fear Yahweh will enjoy prosperity and even vengeance (4:1–3).

Two conclusions have been appended to the Book of Malachi. The first summarizes the book by invoking the authority of Moses and the law (4:4). The second conclusion (4:5–6) seems to identify the messenger of 3:1 with Elijah, the prophet who will return prior to the day of the Lord to reform the community. That promised reform is accompanied by a threat, which heightens the importance of Malachi's own message.

Malachi's message is quite simple and straightforward. The present difficult situation calls for greater faithfulness and more rigorous moral discernment, not less. God's absence implies neither weakness nor rejection of Israel: "If you return to me, I will return to you" (3:7). As do Haggai and Zechariah, Malachi testifies to the graciousness of this offer and to the decisive choices that it entails.

Bibliography

Achtemeier, Elizabeth. *Nahum, Malachi*. Atlanta, 1986. This homiletical commentary is most appropriate for preachers. Its conclusions are often at odds with other commentaries, and it should be used in conjunction with them.

Ackroyd, Peter R. *Exile and Restoration*. London, 1968. Indispensable for understanding the context of exilic and early postexilic literature, this work provides a detailed and reliable treatment of the texts. The discussion is quite technical but eminently worthwhile.

Baldwin, Joyce. *Haggai, Zechariah, Malachi.* Downers Grove, Ill., 1972. Baldwin adopts a conservative stance toward the texts, but in responsible conversation with other scholars. This commentary is useful for beginners and scholars alike.

Bickerman, Elias J. "En marge de l'écriture." *Revue biblique* 88 (1981): 19–41.

Childs, Brevard S. *Introduction to the Old Testament as Scripture.* Philadelphia, 1979. Written in opposition to the standard critical approaches, this work proposes a canonical reading of the texts. It provides a comprehensive bibliography and survey of research.

Conrad, Edgar W. *Fear Not, Warrior.* Chico, Calif., 1985.

Gese, Martmut. "Anfang und Ende der Apocalyptik." *Zeitschrift für Theologie und Kirche* 70 (1973): 20–49.

Halpern, Baruch. "The Ritual Background of Zechariah's Temple Song." *Catholic Biblical Quarterly* 40 (1978): 167–190.

Hanson, Paul. *The Dawn of Apocalyptic.* Philadelphia, 1975. In an argument about the origins of apocalyptic eschatology, Hanson gives a detailed and highly technical treatment of Zechariah 9–14. He offers a controversial account of its social location and relation to other postexilic literature.

Locher, Clemens. "Altes und Neues zu Maleachi 2, 10–16." In *Mélanges Dominique Barthélemy*, edited by Pierre Casetti, Othmar Keel, and Adrian Schenker. Göttingen, 1981.

Mason, Rex A. "The Relation of Zechariah 9–14 to Proto-Zechariah." *Zeitschrift für die alttestamentliche Wissenschaft* 88 (1976): 227–239.

———. *The Books of Haggai, Zechariah, and Malachi.* New York, 1977a. This book, intended particularly for students, is a short commentary on the text of the New English Bible. Mason frequently (and correctly) departs from that translation and rearrangement of the text.

———. "The Purpose of the 'Editorial Framework' of the Book of Haggai." *Vetus testamentum* 27 (1977b): 413–421.

Mitchell, Hinckley G. *A Critical and Exegetical Commentary on Haggai and Zechariah*, and John M. P. Smith, *A Critical and Exegetical Commentary on the Book of Malachi*, published together in the *International Critical Commentary*. New York, 1912. These have long been the standard English commentaries on the Hebrew text. While severely dated in many respects, they are still valuable.

Niditch, Susan. *The Symbolic Vision in Biblical Tradition.* Chico, Calif., 1980. Niditch offers a reliable and comprehensive treatment of the vision genre in the Hebrew Bible. The greatest part of her work is devoted to Zechariah 1–8. Much of her work is concerned with text criticism and requires a knowledge of biblical languages.

Petersen, David L. *Late Israelite Prophecy.* Missoula, 1977. The study helps to place Haggai, Zechariah, and Malachi in the context of postexilic prophecy as a whole, including the views of prophecy in the books of Chronicles, Ezra, and Nehemiah. The book assumes considerable prior knowledge.

———. *Haggai and Zechariah 1–8.* Philadelphia, 1984a. This superb commentary draws upon and advances previous academic discussion but is useful for general readers as well. The full range of questions—textual, historical, literary, and interpretive—is treated responsibly and creatively. It provides, in addition, clear summaries of works in French and German, such as those by Petitjean, Beuken, and Rudolph.

———. "Zechariah's Visions: A Theological Perspective." *Vetus Testamentum* 34 (1984b): 195–206.

Rudolph, Wilhelm. *Haggai, Sacharja 1–8, Sacharja 9–14, Maleachi.* Gütersloh, 1976.

Smith, Ralph L. *Word Biblical Commentary: Micah, Malachi.* Waco, Tex., 1984. Smith's commentary provides a useful overview of the texts and of previous interpretations of them, although the author's own conclusions are sometimes hard to detect. The commentary contains notes on the Hebrew text but can be used by those who do not know biblical languages.

Steck, Odil Hannes. "Zu Haggai 1:2–11." *Zeitschrift für die alttestamentliche Wissenschaft* 83 (1971): 35–79.

Whedbee, J. William. "A Question-Answer Schema in Haggai 1: The Form and Function of Haggai 1:9–11." In *Biblical and Near Eastern Studies*, edited by Gary A. Tuttle. Grand Rapids, 1978.

Willi-Plein, Ina. *Prophetie am Ende.* Cologne, 1974.

BEN C. OLLENBURGER

List of Contributors

ELIZABETH ACHTEMEIER Adjunct Professor of Bible and Homiletics at Union Theological Seminary in Virginia. Author of numerous books. Ordained minister of the Presbyterian Church of America.
Obadiah

PETER R. ACKROYD Samuel Davidson Professor of Old Testament Studies Emeritus at King's College, University of London. Author of *Doors of Perception, Second Book of Samuel, First Book of Samuel, Israel Under Babylon and Persia.*
Ezekiel

BERNHARD W. ANDERSON Professor of Old Testament Theology Emeritus of Princeton Theological Seminary and Adjunct Professor of Old Testament, Boston University School of Theology. He received his B.A. from the College of the Pacific, his M.A. and B.D. from the Pacific School of Religion, and his Ph.D. from Yale University. His numerous books include *Understanding the Old Testament, Creation vs. Chaos, Out of the Depths: The Psalms Speak for Us Today,* and *Creation in the Old Testament* (editor and contributor).
The Bible as Sacred Literature

ROBERT A. BENNETT Professor of Old Testament at the Episcopal Divinity School, Cambridge, Massachusetts. Author of books on the Old Testament and articles on Africa and the Bible. Past member of the National Council of Churches of Christ committee that produced the *Inclusive Language Lectionary.*
Zephaniah

BRUCE C. BIRCH Professor of Old Testament at Wesley Theological Seminary. An ordained minister in the United Methodist Church. Author of *What Does the Lord Require?* and *Singing the Lord's Song;* coauthor of *The Predicament of the Prosperous* and *Bible and Ethics in the Christian Life.*
1 and 2 Samuel

WALTER BRUEGGEMANN Professor of Old Testament at Columbia Theological Seminary. Author of

Genesis, Prophetic Imagination, and *Israel's Praise: Doxology Against Idolatry and Ideology.* He is on the editorial council of *Theology Today* and is an editor of *Overtures for Biblical Theology.*
Genesis

MARVIN L. CHANEY Nathaniel Gray Professor of Hebrew Exegesis and Old Testament at San Francisco Theological Seminary. Author of *Ancient Palestinian Peasant Movements and the Formation of Premonarchic Israel* and other books and articles.
Joshua

RONALD E. CLEMENTS Samuel Davidson Professor of Old Testament Studies at King's College, University of London. Ordained minister in the Baptist Church. Author of *Isaiah and the Deliverance of Jerusalem, Old Testament Theology: A Fresh Approach,* and numerous articles.
Isaiah

DAVID J. A. CLINES Professor of Biblical Studies, University of Sheffield. Author of *The Theme of the Pentateuch, The Story of the Story,* and *Ezra, Nehemiah, Esther, Job 1–20.* Editor of *Journal for the Study of the Old Testament* and *Dictionary of Classical Hebrew.*
Job

JOHN J. COLLINS Professor of Theology at the University of Notre Dame. Author of *Between Athens and Jerusalem: Jewish Identity in the Hellenistic Diaspora, The Apocalyptic Imagination,* and *Daniel, with an Introduction to Apocalyptic Literature.*
Wisdom of Solomon

JAMES L. CRENSHAW Professor of Old Testament at Duke Divinity School. Author of *Prophetic Conflict, Hymnic Affirmation of Divine Justice, Samson, Gerhard von Rad, A Whirlpool of Torment, Story and Faith,* and *Ecclesiastes.* Former editor of the Society of Biblical Literature Monograph Series.
Proverbs

KATHERYN PFISTERER DARR   Assistant Professor of Hebrew Bible at Boston University School of Theology. Author of numerous articles on the prophetic literature of ancient Israel and of educational materials for the United Methodist Publishing House.
Jonah; Ruth; Esther and Additions to Esther

CAROLE R. FONTAINE   Associate Professor of Old Testament at Andover Newton Theological School. Author of *Traditional Sayings in the Old Testament: A Contextual Study*, as well as numerous articles on wisdom literature, goddess worship, and feminist spirituality. Member of the editorial board of *Semeia*.
Hosea

DAVID NOEL FREEDMAN   Arthur F. Thurnau Professor of Biblical Studies at the University of Michigan. Ordained minister in the Presbyterian Church. Author of *Pottery, Poetry, and Prophecy*. Coauthor of *The Paleo-Hebrew Leviticus Scroll, Hosea, An Explorer's Life of Jesus*, and *Studies in Ancient Yahwistic Poetry*. Editor or coeditor of volumes in the *Biblical Archaeologist Reader, Computer Bible*, and *Anchor Bible* series.
1 and 2 Chronicles, Ezra, and Nehemiah

WALTER HARRELSON   Distinguished Professor of Hebrew Bible at the Divinity School of Vanderbilt University. Past president of the Society of Biblical Literature. Author of numerous books and essays on the Bible and the religions of the ancient Near East, including *The Ten Commandments and Human Rights*. Vice-chair of the Revised Standard Version Bible Committee.
Introduction to the Old Testament

THEODORE HIEBERT   Assistant Professor of Hebrew Bible/Old Testament at Harvard Divinity School. Author of *God of My Victory: The Ancient Hymn of Triumph in Habakkuk 3* and various essays.
Joel

PHILIP J. KING   Professor of Biblical Studies at Boston College. Past president of the Society of Biblical Literature, the American Schools of Oriental Research, and the Catholic Biblical Association of America. Author of *American Archaeology in the Mideast* and other books and articles concerning the intersection of archaeology and biblical interpretation.
Judges

BURKE O. LONG   Professor of Religion at Bowdoin College. Author of *The Problem of Etiological Narrative in the Old Testament, 1 Kings, with an Introduction to*

Historical Literature, and numerous articles. Member of the editorial boards of *Journal for the Study of the Old Testament* and *Journal of Biblical Literature*.
1 and 2 Kings

JAMES LUTHER MAYS   Cyrus McCormick Professor of Hebrew and Old Testament at Union Theological Seminary in Virginia. Author of the commentaries *Leviticus, Numbers; Ezekiel, Second Isaiah; Hosea; Amos;* and *Micah*. Editor of *Interpretation: A Bible Commentary for Teaching and Preaching, Harper's Bible Commentary*, and *Interpretation: A Journal of Bible and Theology*.
Micah

JACOB MILGROM   Professor of Hebrew and Bible, University of California at Berkeley. Author of *Studies in Levitical Terminology, Commentary on the Book of Numbers, Studies in Cultic Theology and Terminology*, and *Cult and Conscience*. Member of the editorial boards of *Biblical Archaeology Review* and *Bible Review*.
Leviticus

PATRICK D. MILLER, JR.   Professor of Old Testament Theology at Princeton Theological Seminary. Author of *Interpreting the Psalms* among other works.
Psalms

ROLAND E. MURPHY, O. CARM.   George Washington Ivey Professor Emeritus of Biblical Studies at Duke Divinity School. Author of *Psalms, Job; Wisdom Literature;* and *Wisdom Literature and Psalms*. Former editor in chief of the *Catholic Biblical Quarterly*. Member of editorial boards of *Concilium, Vetus Testamentum, Interpretation, Theological Studies, Old Testament Abstracts, Biblical Theology Bulletin*, and *Hermeneia*. Contributor to translation of the *New American Bible* and board member for revision of the *Revised Standard Version*.
Song of Solomon

BEN C. OLLENBURGER   Associate Professor of Old Testament at the Associated Mennonite Biblical Seminaries, Elkhart, Indiana. Author of *Zion, the City of the Great King* among other scholarly writings. Editor and contributor to *Understanding the Word*.
Haggai, Zechariah, and Malachi

SIMON B. PARKER   Associate Professor of Hebrew Bible at Boston University School of Theology. Author of *The Pre-biblical Narrative Tradition* and numerous articles on aspects of Ugaritic and Israelite literature, religion, and social life. Editorial board member of *Writings from the Ancient World*.
Amos

CONTRIBUTORS

J. J. M. ROBERTS   William Henry Green Professor of Old Testament Literature at Princeton Theological Seminary. He is the author of *The Earliest Semitic Pantheon*, coauthor of *The Hand of the Lord*, and coeditor of *Unity and Disunity*.
Habakkuk

KATHARINE DOOB SAKENFELD   Professor of Old Testament Literature and Director of Ph.D. studies at Princeton Theological Seminary. Ordained minister of the Presbyterian Church of America and representative to the Consultation on Church Union and the Commission on Faith and Order of the National Council on Churches. Author of *The Meaning of "Hesed" in the Hebrew Bible: Faithfulness in Action*.
Numbers

JAMES A. SANDERS   Professor of Biblical Studies at the School of Theology at Claremont and Professor of Ethics at Claremont Graduate School. President of Ancient Biblical Manuscript Center for Preservation and Research. Author of *The Psalms Scroll of Qumran Cave 11*, *Torah and Canon*, *Canon and Community: A Guide to Canonical Criticism*, and other books and articles.
Deuteronomy

NAHUM M. SARNA   Dora Golding Professor Emeritus of Biblical Studies at Brandeis University. Editor and translator for the *Tanakh*, the Bible translation of the Jewish Publication Society. General editor of the JPS Bible Commentary Project. Past president of the Association for Jewish Studies. Author of *Understanding Genesis*, *Exploring Exodus*, and numerous essays.
Exodus

W. SIBLEY TOWNER   Reverend Archibald McFadyen Professor of Biblical Interpretation at Union Theological Seminary in Virginia. Author of *Daniel* in the *Interpretation* Bible commentary series among other books and articles on Jewish apocalyptic.
Daniel

PHYLLIS TRIBLE   Baldwin Professor of Sacred Literature at Union Theological Seminary. Author of *God and the Rhetoric of Sexuality* and *Texts of Terror*.
Ecclesiastes

CLAUS WESTERMANN   Professor of Old Testament at the University of Heidelberg. Honorary member of the Society of Biblical Literature and the Society for Old Testament Study. Author of *Praise and Lament in the Psalms* and commentaries on Isaiah and Genesis. Editor of *Theologisches Handwörterbuch zum Alten Testament*, *Forschung am Alten Testament*, and *Prophetische Heilsworte*.
Lamentations

BRUCE E. WILLOUGHBY   Managing Editor for the Center for Japanese Studies at the University of Michigan. Author of numerous popular and scholarly articles on a variety of topics relating to the Bible and the Ancient Near East.
1 and 2 Chronicles, Ezra, and Nehemiah

ROBERT R. WILSON   Professor of Old Testament and Religious Studies at Yale Divinity School. Author of *Genealogy and History in the Biblical World*, *Prophecy and Society in Ancient Israel*, and *Sociological Approaches to the Old Testament*, and numerous articles. Editor of *Canon, Theology, and Old Testament Interpretation*.
Jeremiah

Index

A

Aaron
  challenge to Moses' leadership by, 75a, 77a–b, 78b,
    79b–81a
  death of, 80b
  descendant of, 163a
  Exodus role, 52a, 52b, 54a, 54b, 57a, 75b
  and golden calf, 57b–58a
  Korah's challenge to, 78b, 79b
  priesthood of, 58b, 66b, 72b, 73b, 75b, 78b–79b, 84b
  rod of, 80b
Aaronic Benediction, 84b–85b
Abdon of Ephraim, 115a
Abednego (Azariah), 335a, 338b, 343b–344a
Abel, 12a, 31b
Abiathar, 79a, 138b, 143b, 286a
Abigail, 129a
Abihu, 66b
Abimelech (king of Shechem), 13a, 118a–b
Abner, 135a, 135b, 165b
Abraham, 50a, 118a
  in Christian tradition, 1b, 6a, 41b–42a
  dirge over Sarah, 303b
  family of, 32a, 33a–36a, 38a
  as founder of Israel, 16a, 28a, 47b–48b, 160b
  God's promises to, 12a–b, 22a, 28b, 35a–36a, 38a,
    40b–41a, 41b–42a, 91a, 96b
  Jerusalem linked to, 34b
  testing of, 35a–b, 119a
Absalom, 134b, 138a–139a, 146b, 165b
Achan, 111a, 326b
Acts of the Apostles, 144b
Adam, 30b, 41b, 160b, 161b, 234b, 235a, 338a
Adar, 174a
Adonijah, 146a, 146b
Adultery, as metaphor for Israelites' idol worship, 325b,
    355a–356b
Afflictions
  associated with Ark's capture, 130a–b
  associated with Jerusalem's fall, 307a–311b
  in David's reign, 139b
  locust invasion in Joel, 359a–365b
  of Nabonidus, 340a–341a

  ten plagues in Exodus, 53a–b, 59b
  see also Job, Book of; Sickness and health; Suffering
Afterlife
  Job and, 187b
  see also Heaven; Hell; Judgment Day; Resurrection
Agag, 132b, 174b, 175b
Agur, 225a, 228a, 229b
Ahab (king of Israel, northern kingdom), 147a, 147b,
    151a, 168a
Ahasuerus (king of Persia), 173a–179b
  see also Xerxes I
Ahaziah (king of Israel, northern kingdom), 151b
Ahaz (king of Judah)
  Assyrian alliance, 261a–b, 351a, 385b, 386a
  death and successor, 251a
  Isaiah as prophet for, 251b, 252a, 253a–254a,
    255a, 257b
  Isaiah's criticism of, 260b–261b, 263a, 268a–b
Ahijah, 167a
Ahiqar, 334a
Ai, 111a, 114a
Ain Jalud. See Harod
Akkad, 51a
Akkadian literature, 238a
Albright, William Foxwell, 29a, 29b, 83b
Alcimus, 344a
Aleppo Codex, 159b
Alexander the Great (king of Macedon), 238a, 321a,
    336b, 337a, 337b
Alexandria, 338b
Amalek, 54a–b, 117a, 132b
Amaziah (king of Judah), 110a
Amaziah (priest of Bethel), 370b–371a
Ambakoum. See Habakkuk
Amenemhet (Egyptian prince), 225a
Amenhotep II (pharaoh), 50a
American Bible Society, 18a
Amestris, 177a
Ammonites, 109a, 115a, 118b–119a, 165b, 168a, 320a,
    400b, 402a
Amnon, 17a, 138b
Amon (king of Judah), 105b, 145b, 267b, 397a
Amos, 14a, 158b, 260a, 327a, 349a, 386a, 397b,
    401b–402a

Amos, Book of, 304a, 310b, 362a, 367a–373b
Amram, 69a
Anathoth, 286a, 287a, 299a, 354b
Angels, 53a
    in announcement narratives, 117b
    Daniel's visions of, 336b, 337b, 340a, 343a,
        343b, 345b
    humans' relationships with, 345b
    Zechariah's visions of, 409a–410a
    see also Cherubim
Animals
    as food, 67a–b, 192a–b
    impurities of, 67a–b
    Job on, 189a, 193a–b
    sacrificial, 68a, 192b–193a, 343a
Ankh, 228b
Antichrist, 345a
Antioch, 336b
Antiochus IV Epiphanes (Seleucid ruler), 177b, 336b,
        337a, 337b–338a, 342a, 343a–b, 344a
Anti-Semitism
    in Esther story, 117b, 175a–b, 178a–b
    first pogrom, 336b
Aphek, 147b
Apocalypse of Isaiah, 276b
Apocalyptic literature, nature of, 14b–15a, 338a
Apocrypha, 2a–b, 5b, 11a, 15a, 178a, 179b
Apostasy
    Deuteronomists on, 388b
    Ezekiel on, 323a
    Hosea on, 350a, 353a, 356a
    Zephaniah on, 399b, 400b, 403b
Aqaba, Gulf of, 376a
'Aqiva' ben Yosef (Rabbi), 241a, 244a
Arad, 77a
Aramaeans, 50b, 147b–148a, 167b, 251a, 350b, 352b,
        368a, 369a, 393a
Aramaic language, 341b
Aramaic literature, 223a
Ark of the Covenant, 59a, 75a, 150b, 284b
    Philistines' capture of, 13b, 128a–130b
    return to Jerusalem, 130a, 136a–b
Artaxerxes I (king of Persia), 156a, 157a, 158a, 162b,
        163a, 163b
Artaxerxes II (king of Persia), 158a, 159b
Asa (king of Judah), 149b, 167b–168a
Asaph, 214a, 217a
Ashdod, 119b, 199b, 251a, 255b, 256a
Asher, 96a, 116b
Asherah (Canaanite goddess), 115b, 168b
Ashkelon, 119b, 402a
Ashurbanipal (king of Assyria), 105a, 282b, 378a, 379b
Assassinations. *See* Murder
Assyria
    and Babylonia, 249b, 270a–b

decline in power, 105a, 105b
deportation policy, 378a
empire's power, 284a, 378a–b, 385b–386a
Hezekiah's rebellion against, 248b, 251b, 256a–b,
        257a–b, 267a
Isaiah's prophecy against, 255b, 256b–257a, 265a–b,
        266b, 273b, 277b
Jonah at Nineveh, 381a–383a
Judah's disengagement from, 397b, 398b
Judah's fall to, 386a, 387a, 397a, 400b
Judah's relationship with, 99b, 109b, 252a–b, 253a–b,
        261a–262b
jurisdiction over both kingdoms, 248a, 250b, 264b,
        266a–b, 267b
Nineveh's fall, 377b–380a, 402a
northern kingdom's fall to, 251a, 254a, 255a, 267b,
        282a–b, 349a, 350a–353b, 378a
Assyrian literature and mythology, 17b, 143a, 150a
Asur-uballit, 378a
Atonement, Day of. *See* Yom Kippur
Atrahasis, 30b
Av, ninth of, 305b
Awil-Marduk. *See* Evil-merodach
Azariah. *See* Abednego
Azariah (Solomon's officer), 143b

B

Baal (Canaanite deity), 135a
    destruction of altars to, 117a–b
    Elijah on, 147a–b
    Israelites' worship of, 113b, 115b, 168b, 353a, 400b
    sexual fertility rites for, 352a–b, 355a–b
Baasha (king of Israel, northern kingdom), 145b,
        149b, 167b
Babel. *See* Tower of Babel
Babylon
    and Assyria, 249b, 270a–b
    Habakkuk and, 392a–395a
    Isaiah's prophecies against, 275a–b
    last king, 341a
Babylonian captivity, 16b, 104a, 149b, 281a–300b, 349b,
        372b, 389a, 389b–390a, 399a
    as allegory in Jonah, 383b
    in Daniel, 333a–346b
    Davidic cultic responsibility in, 98a, 137a, 166b
    events leading to, 270b–272b
    in Ezekiel, 319a–331b
    Isaiah's prophecies and, 269a–275a
    in Jeremiah, 281a–300b
    Kings on, 90b, 91b
    in Lamentations, 307b–317a
    priestly writings during, 72a, 81b, 93b

return from, 14b, 50a, 155b, 160a, 161a–163a, 270b, 272b, 274a, 275a, 275b, 404a, 405a–b
Babylonian literature and mythology, 17b
    Ecclesiastes parallel, 238a
    Job parallel, 199a
    Kings parallel, 143a, 145b, 150a
    proverbs in, 223a
    Purim's derivation from, 176a
    Song of Solomon relationship, 242a
    Tower of Babel parallel, 31b
Balaam, 74b, 75b, 82b–84b, 90a
Balak, 75b, 82b, 84a, 84b
Bamidbar. See Numbers, Book of
Barak, 116a–117a, 119a
Bar Kokhba, 84a
Barrenness
    Hannah's, 129a, 208a–b, 209a
    as theme in Genesis, 33b, 34a–35a, 38a
    as theme in Ruth, 123a, 124b, 125a–b
    see also Conception
Barth, Hermann, 268a
Baruch, Book of, 15a
Baruch (scribe), 288b, 290b
Barzillai, 145a
Bathsheba, 134a, 134b, 137b–138a, 146b, 165b, 166b
Bava' Batra', 177b
Beast whose number is 666. *See* Number of the beast
Beersheba, 77a
Behemoth, 189a
Bel and the dragon, 338b, **339b–340a,** 391b
"Belial," 379a
Bel-shar-usur. *See* Belshazzar
Belshazzar (king of Babylon), 335b–336a, 340b, 341a
Benaiah, 143b
Benedicite, 338b
Benediction. *See* Blessing
Benedictus es Domine, 338b
Benjamin, 39b–40a, 96a, 116b, 119b, 120a, 135b, 139a, 165b
Ben Sira. *See* Sirach, Book of; Sirach, Jesus ben
Bernard of Clairvaux, Saint, 244b
Bethel, 36b, 37b, 79a, 106a, 111a, 120a, 150a, 151a, 169a, 330a, 370b, 371a, 386a
Bethlehem, 120a
Bethshemesh, 130a
Bezalel, 58b
Bible
    Catholic, 2b
    Christian, 1a, 1b, 2a, 5a–6b, 11b–12a
    as history, 2b–3b
    modern approach to, 6b–8a
    origin of word, 1a
    relationship between Old and New Testaments, 5a–6b, 11a
    sources and study methods, 4a–5a

    translations of, 2b, 17b–18a
    see also New Testament; Old Testament; specific books and versions
Biblia hebraica, 159b
Biblia hebraica Stuttgartensia, 159b
Bildad, 182b, 183a, 185a, 186b, 198b
Blasphemy, 69a–b
Blessing. *See* Aaronic Benediction
Boaz, 124a–125b
Book of the Covenant. *See* Covenant Code
Bowing, in Israel's tradition, 173b
Bronze Age, 113a, 114b, 117a, 120a, 353a
Burning bush, 52a, 108a
Burnt offering. *See* Sacrifices
Byblos, 1a

C

Cain, 12a, 31b, 33a, 303a, 304b
Caleb, 73b, 74a, 75a, 77a, 81b
Cambyses II (king of Persia), 405a
Canaanite literature and mythology, 115b, 198b, 334a, 363a, 398b
Canaan (Promised Land)
    Deuteronomy on, 92b
    Holiness Code and, 63b, 68b
    Israelites' land division, 81a–82b, 90a
    Israel's control of, 113a, 114a–b, 116a–117a, 118b, 144b, 330b, 352a
    Moses' leadership toward, 12b, 24a, 52a, 54a, 75a, 76b, 80b, 89a
    Paul's interpretation of, 6a
    political turmoil surrounding, 50a–b
    religious cults, 343a, 400b; *see also* Baal
    woe oracle against, 402a
Caphtor, 369a
Carchemish, 282b, 393b
Caspian Sea, 350b
Caucasus, 378a
Census
    David's, 139b
    Moses', 72a, 73a–b, 75b
    scholars' interpretation of, 77b–78b
Chaldea, 270b, 334b, 341b, 393a
Chanukah. *See* Hanukkah
Chariot imagery, 151b, 331a, 408b
    see also Merkavah (throne) mysticism
Chebar River, 328a
Cherubim, 57b, 59a, 130a, 235a
Chilion, 123a
Chosen People. *See* Israel, covenant with God; Yahweh, promises to Israel

Christian Bible, 1a, 1b, 2a, 5a–6b, 11b–12a
    see also New Testament; Septuagint; specific versions
Christianity (early period)
    rejection of Esther story, 179a
    Septuagint as Bible, 2a–2b
Christ. See Jesus Christ
Chronicles, Books of, 11b, 78b, 90b, 91b, 144b,
    155a–169b, 328b, 329b
Circumcision, 12b, 33b, 92b, 343a
Conception
    of Jeremiah, 293a
    of Jesus, 340a
    Yahweh's role in, 125a, 125b, 129a
    see also Barrenness
Confession of sin. See Sins, confession of
Cornelius (Roman centurion convert), 403a
Coronation oracle, 150b, 254b, 260b–261a, 265a
Covenant Code
    and Baal worship, 352a–b
    conditionality of, 14a, 60b, 142b, 286b, 292a–b,
        294b–295a, 361b
    contents of, 50a–61a, 55b–57a, 60a–b
    Hosea's personal view of, 356a
    Israel's and Judah's differing views of, 353a–354a
    Micah's adherence to, 388a
    renewal of, 58a–b
    and Yahweh's role with other nations, 368a, 369a–b,
        372a, 375a, 383a
    see also Sinai, Mount
Creation literature, 5b, 16a, 31a–b, 42a–b, 43a
Crete, 119a
Cush, 398a–b
Cushan-rishathaim (king of Upper Mesopotamia), 115b
Cushites. See Ethiopia
Cyrus II (king of Persia)
    in Daniel, 339b, 340a
    declaration ending Babylonian captivity, 50a, 91b,
        155a, 156b, 160a, 161b–162b, 405a
    in Isaiah's prophecies, 339b, 340a

D

Dagon (Philistine deity), 119b, 130a
Damascus, 253b, 254a, 350b, 351a
Dan (city), 79a, 144a, 151a
Danel (ancient Israelite hero), 197a
Daniel, Book of, 11b, 14b–15a, 16b, 91b, 320b,
    333a–346b
Daniel in lions' den, 336a, 339b–340a, 343b
Danites, 96a, 116b, 119a, 119b, 120a
Darius I (king of Persia), 162a, 162b, 177a, 336a, 405a,
    406a, 408a
Darius the Mede (in Book of Daniel), 333b, 336a,
    345b, 346b

David (king of Israel)
    Absalom's revolt against, 134b, 138a–139b, 165b
    and Bathsheba, 134a, 134b, 137b–138a, 146b,
        165b, 166b
    condemnation for sins, 214b
    death of, 13b, 139b, 144b, 145a
    dirge over Saul and Jonathan, 303b
    disasters during reign of, 139b
    genealogy of, 123a, 125a, 126a, 151a, 160b,
        161b, 267a
    as Philistine mercenary, 133a, 135a, 165b
    psalms of, 136a, 139b, 216a, 216b
    reign of, 13b, 16b, 84a, 128a, 133b, 134a,
        135a–137b, 141a–b, 145a, 147a, 149b, 156a, 160b,
        165a, 249a, 258a, 268b, 269a, 270a, 276a, 376a
    religious policies, 79a, 110a
    return of Ark to Jerusalem by, 130a, 136a–b
    reverence toward God, 141b, 149a
    rise of, 132a–133b, 134b
    and Saul, 133b, 135a–b, 137b, 165a–b, 166b, 303b
    Sheba's revolt against, 139a, 165b
    Temple founding by, 156a, 166a–b
Day of Atonement. See Yom Kippur
Day of Judgment. See Judgment Day
Day of the Lord. See Judgment Day
Day of Yahweh. See Judgment Day
Dead Sea, 116a, 376b
Dead Sea Scrolls, 89b, 177b, 329b–330a, 338b,
    340a–341a, 341b, 343b, 392b, 395b
Death
    dirges for, 303a–304b
    Qohelet's view of, 233a–234b, 235b
    significance of Pelatiah's, 322b, 325a
    see also Afterlife; Heaven; Hell; Judgment Day;
        Resurrection; Sheol
Debir, 115b
Deborah, 115a, 116a–117b
Decalogue. See Ten Commandments
Deuterocanonical writings. See Apocrypha
Deuteronomistic historian, 13a, 108a–b, 120b,
    128b–129b, 132a, 134a–b, 137a, 142b, 284a–b,
    286a
Deuteronomy, Book of, 2b, 11a, 23a, 23b, 24a, 38a, 67a,
    69a, 69b, 73a, 75b, 77a, **89a–101a,** 106b, 108b,
    109a, 110b, 142b, 146a, 199a, 218a, 229b, 284a,
    289a, 291b, 292b, 294b, 323a, 329b, 353b, 376a,
    388b, 399a, 402b
Devil. See Satan
Diaspora, 92b, 93a, 94b, 100a, 215b, 336a, 339a, 342b,
    351b, 402a
Dies irae, 400b
Dietary code, 67a–68a, 68b, 334b
Dirges, 303a–304b, 307a
Disasters. See Afflictions; Flood
Disciples, Isaiah's, 264a–b, 271b

Disease. *See* Afflictions; Sickness and health; specific conditions
Divine promise. *See* Messiah; Promise; Yahweh, promises to Israel
Divorce, 413a
Dnil (Canaanite hero), 334a
Documentary Hypothesis, 25b, 26a, 26b
Doves, 245a
Dragon, Bel and, 338b, 339b–340a, 391b
Dreams
    Daniel's, 334b–335a
    in Joseph story, 38b–40b
    Mordecai's, 178a
Drunkenness, 147b
Dura Europos synagogue, 331a
"Dust to dust" phrase, 235b
Dynamic equivalency translations, 18a
Dynastic oracle, 136b–137a

E

Easter, 3b
Ebal, Mount, 95a, 118a
Ecclesiastes, Book of, 11b, 14b, 15a, 199b, 200a, 223a, **231a–238b**
Ecclesiasticus. *See* Sirach, Book of
Eded-melech, 398b
Eden, 96b, 234b, 235a, 326a, 330a, 359b
Edom, 36b, 84a, 90a, 109a, 117a, 163b, 167a, 168a, 197a, 225a, 315b, 320a, 363b, 367b, 375a–377b, 412b
Eglon (king of Moab), 115b
Egypt
    Aramaic language in, 341b
    Assyrian power and, 282b, 397a
    Cushite dynasty, 403a
    Exodus from, 3a–b, 28a, 53a–54b, 73b, 74a, 76b, 100a, 142b, 163a, 369a, 370a
    in Isaiah, 250b, 251a–b, 255a, 256a, 261b–262a, 264b, 270a, 277b
    in Jeremiah, 285a, 287b, 291a, 296b, 297b, 322b
    Joel's hymn against, 363b
    Joseph in, 38b, 39a–b, 40a–b
    judgment on, 326a
    Moses' return to, 52a
    portable shrines in, 59a
    ten plagues in, 53a–54b
Egyptian literature and mythology, 17b
    Ecclesiastes and, 233a, 238a
    Job analogy in, 198b–199a
    love poems, 242a, 242b, 245a
    Proverbs' parallel in, 223a, 224a
    Wisdom as goddess in, 228a–b
Ehud, 115b–116a

Ekron, 119b, 400a
Eldad, 77a
Eleazar (Aaronite high priest), 73b, 75b, 81a
Eli, 129a–130b
Elihu, 182b, 183a, 186a, 186b, 198a–b
Elijah, 13b, 26a, 147a, 151a, 151b–152a, 168a, 323b, 413b
Elimelech, 123a, 124a
Eliphaz, 182b, 185a, 192b
Elisha, 13b, 26a, 147a, 148a, 151b–152a, 323b
Elkanah, 208b
Elkosh, 378a
Elnathan, 156a
Elohim. *See* Yahweh
Elon of Zebulun, 115a
Eltekeh, 251b
Enoch, Books of, 330a
En-rogel, 146b
Enuma Elish, 30b
Ephesians, Epistle to the, 244b
Ephod, 118a, 120a
Ephraim (northern kingdom). *See* Israel
Ephraim (son of Joseph), 78a, 96a, 116b, 118a, 119b
Esarhaddon (king of Assyria), 265a
Esau, 36a, 36b, 37a–b, 376a, 412b
Esdraelon. *See* Jezreel Valley
Esdras, Books of, 41b, 90b, 160a, 334a
Essenes, 344a
Esther, 346a
Esther, Book of, 11b, 14b, 90b, **173a–179b,** 334a
Ethan, 217a
Ethiopia, 397a, 398a–b, 402a, 403a, 403b
Eucharist, 3b, 340a
Eunuchs, 334b
Euphrates River, 296a, 331a
Eve, 30b, 191a
Evil. *See* Antichrist; Satan; Theodicy
Evil-merodach (king of Babylon), 90b, 156b, 161a
Exodus, Book of, 2b, 3a–b, 11a, 12b, 21a, 21b, 38a, 38b, **47a–61a,** 64b, 69a, 72a, 77a, 79b, 80a, 80b, 108a, 329a, 329b, 330a
Exodus from Egypt. *See* Egypt, Exodus from
Ezekiel, 158b, 284b, 354b
Ezekiel, Book of, 11b, 40b, 68a, 69b, 78b, 92b, 124a, 197a, **319a–331b,** 383b, 391a, 399a, 407a
Ezion-geber, 376a
Ezra, 11b, 93b, 271a
Ezra, Book of, 78b, 90b, **155a–169b,** 304a, 341b, 405a

F

Fables, Jotham's, on kingship, 13a–13b
Faith
    kingship relationship to, 136a–137a

Faith (*cont.*)
   testing of Abraham's, 35a–b
   as theme in Isaiah, 261a–b, 262a
Faithfulness, of Ruth to Naomi, 123b–126a
Fall, the. *See* Genesis, Book of
Fall of Jerusalem. *See* Jerusalem, fall of
False accusations, 207b, 209a, 339a–b, 410b
False prophets. *See* Prophets, false
Famine
   in Egypt, 39b
   in Judah, 123a
Feast of Booths (Sukkot), 96a, 164a, 238b, 400b,
   401a
Feast of Tabernacles. *See* Feast of Booths (Sukkot)
Feast of Unleavened Bread. *See* Passover
Feast of Yahweh. *See* Feast of Booths (Sukkot)
Feminist interpretations, 7a–7b, 190b, 191a, 193b
Fertility
   images of, 363b
   of the land, 364a
   rites, 352a–b, 355a–b
   as theme in Ruth, 123b–126b
   see also Barrenness; Conception
Festival of First Fruits. *See* Pentecost
Festivals, Israelite, 14b, 61a, 69a; *see also* specific names,
   e.g., Purim
Festival of Tabernacles. *See* Feast of Booths (Sukkot)
Festival of Weeks. *See* Pentecost
Fidelity. *See* Faithfulness
Five Books of Moses. *See* Torah
Five Scrolls. *See* Megillot
Flaming sword, 235a
Flood, 31b, 32b, 321a, 400b, 401b
Flying throne visions, 319b, 320a, 324b, 331a
   see also Chariot imagery
Forbidden fruit, 31a
Forced labor. *See* Slavery
Former Prophets. *See* Prophets

G

Gabriel (angel), 337b
Gad (tribe), 73b–74a, 76a, 82a, 96a
Galatians, Epistle to the, 42a
Galilee, 113b, 116b, 351a
Galilee, Sea of, 114a
Garden of Eden. *See* Eden
Gath, 119b
Gaza, 119b, 400a, 402a
Gedaliah, 283b, 287b, 300a, 322b, 398a
Gehazi, 148a
Gemara, 5a
Genesis, Book of, 11a, 12a, **21a–43a,** 47b, 49b, 59b,

   67a, 72a, 72b, 73a, 84a, 92b, 94a, 144b, 145a,
   160b, 234b–235a, 304b, 321a, 400b, 401b, 403b
Gerizim, Mount, 95a, 118a
Gershom, 51b
Gibeah, 119b, 120b
Gibeon, 110b–111a, 114a, 137b
Gideon, 13a, 16a, 117a–118a, 119a
Gilead, 73b–74a, 116b, 118b, 119a, 135a, 245a
Gilgal, 353a
Gilgamesh Epic, 30b
Gleaning, 68b, 124a
God. *See* Yahweh
Gog (king of Magog), 320a, 326a
Golden calf, 49a, 57b–58a
Goliath, 133a
Gomer, 244b, 354b–355a
Gomorrah. *See* Sodom and Gomorrah
Good News Bible (GNB), 18a
"Good News." *See* Gospel
Goshen, 50b
Gospel, 3a, 94a
Graven images. *See* Idolatry; Golden calf
Greece, 337b
Greek mythology, 398b
Greek translation of Bible. *See* Septuagint
Gunkel, Hermann, 26b–28a, 28b, 29b, 30a, 36b

H

Habakkuk, 340a, 398a
Habakkuk, Book of, **391a–396b**
Hadassah. *See* Esther
Haftarah, 93b
Hagar, 34b
Haggadah, 93a
Haggai, 162b, 163a, 169b
Haggai, Book of, 156b, 161a, 320b, **405a–408a**
Halah, 377a
Halakhah, 93a
   see also Law, Jewish, daily
Haman, 173a–179b
Hamath, 393a
Hananiah (false prophet against Jeremiah), 298b, 392a
Hananiah (friend of Daniel). *See* Shadrach
Hannah, 99a, 129a, 208a–b, 209a
Hanukkah, 343b
Haran, 378a
Harod, 117b
Harvest
   as theme in Ruth, 124a, 126a
   see also Feast of Booths (Sukkot); Fertility
Hasideans, 344a
Hasidim, 344a–b

Hazor, 111a, 114a
Health. *See* Sickness and health
Heaven, 187b
    see also Afterlife
Heber, 116b
Hebrew Bible. *See* Old Testament
Hebron, 81a, 377b
Hell, 340a
    see also Sheol
Heman, 217a
Herodotus, 141a
Heshbon, 77a
Hevel, 233a–238b
Hexateuch, 22b–23b, 93a–b
Hezekiah (king of Judah)
    as Davidic ideal, 167b, 169a
    death date, 385b
    Isaiah's criticism of, 261a, 263a, 268a–b
    rebellion against Assyria, 105a, 248b, 256a–b, 257b,
        266a–267a, 282b, 386a
    reforms of, 168a–b
    reign of, 223b, 251a, 254a–b, 260b, 267a–268a,
        269a–b, 385b, 386a
    religious standards, 141b, 149a, 284b, 388b, 397a–b
    Zephaniah's genealogy from, 398a, 398b
Hilkiah, 339a
Holiness
    Covenant Code on, 68a–69a
    H Code for, 63b–64b
Holy of Holies, 57b, 59a–b
Hope, as theme in Ezekiel, 327b–328a
Horeb, Mount. *See* Sinai, Mount
Hormah, 77a
Hosea (king). *See* Hoshea
Hosea (prophet)
    children's sign-names, 252b, 353a, 354b
    marriage to Gomer, 244b, 354b–356a, 357b
    and other prophets, 158b, 323a
    prophecies of, 93a, 98b, 386a, 397b
Hosea, Book of, 16b, 92b, 137a, 286a, **349a–358a,** 362b
Hoshea (king of Israel, northern kingdom), 151a,
    350b, 351b
Hoy oracles, 396a
Huldah, 94b, 169a
Huleh, Lake, 120a
Hyrcanus. *See* John Hyrcanus I (high priest)

I

Ibn Ezra, Abraham ben Meir, 269b
Ibzan of Judah, 115a
Idolatry, 325b, 411b
    Asa's campaign against, 167b

Baal worship, 352a–b, 355a–b, 357b
    Daniel's challenge to, 335a–b, 339b, 340b, 342b,
        343a, 346a
    Exodus' prohibitions against, 60b
    Golden calf worship, 49a, 57b–58a
    H Code on, 64a
    Jerusalem's fall and, 388b, 389b
    Judah's destruction and, 292a
    and northern kingdom's fall, 291b–292a
    prophets' warnings on, 128b–129a, 134a, 250a, 271b,
        273a–b
    Zephaniah on, 398b, 400b
Idumea. *See* Edom
Immanuel, Isaiah on significance of name, 253a
Imprecatory psalms, 213b–214a
Impurities, in daily Jewish law, 66b–68a
Incest, 17a, 64a
Ingathering. *See* Feast of Booths (Sukkot)
Insanity. *See* Madness
Intermarriage, 157b, 158a, 163b, 164a, 165a, 412b, 413a
Iron Age, 113a–b, 114b
Isaac, 12a, 12b, 16a, 28a, 34a, 35b, 36b, 37a, 40b,
    47b, 48a
Isaiah, 354b, 386a, 397b
    prophecies' verification, 283b–284b, 285a
Isaiah, Book of, 4b, 6a–6b, 14a, 40b, 93b, 99b, 137a,
    156b, 161a, 197a, 218b, **247a–278a,** 270a, 277a,
    328a, 345b, 354a, 364b, 391a, 399a
Ishbaal. *See* Ish-bosheth
Ish-bosheth, 135a, 135b, 165a, 165b
Ishmael, 34a, 34b
Ishtar (Mesopotamian goddess), 176a, 228b, 242a
Islam, 346b
Israel
    covenant with God, 55b, 57b–61a, 114b, 169b,
        283b–284a, 354a–356a, 368a, 369b, 376b,
        387a, 389a
    as nation among other nations, 35b–36a, 369a, 383a
    Old Testament's relationship to, 15b–16a
    twelve tribes of, 78a–b, 96a, 116b; *see also* specific
        names
    see also Covenant Code; Judah (southern kingdom);
        Yahweh; Zion
Israel (Ephraim: the northern kingdom)
    Assyrian control of, 282a–b, 284a, 349a, 397a–b
    conflicts with Judah, 13b, 135b, 251a, 255a, 257b
    Davidic line, separation from, 167a–167b, 258a–b
    dissolution of, 248a–b, 249b, 250b, 254a, 257b, 258b,
        264b, 265b, 267b
    fall, idolatry and, 291b–292a
    fall, Jeroboam's transgressions and, 151b
    fall, reasons for, 149a
    Hosea on, 352b–353a, 356b–358a
    Jeremiah's oracles on, 286a–b, 289a, 289b, 299a
    name, 1b

Israel *(cont.)*
  see also Samaria; Syro-Ephraimite war; names of
    specific kings
Israelite kingdom, 13b, 130b–139b, 260b, 261a, 270a;
  see also Israel; Succession Narrative
Israel stela. *See* Merneptah stela
Issachar, 116b

J

Jabbok River, 117b, 118b
Jabesh-Gilead, 120b, 131b
Jacob
  at Bethel, 36b, 37b, 330a
  death of, 39a
  enmity with Esau, 36a, 36b–37a, 376a, 412b
  as father of Israel, 12a, 12b, 16a, 28a, 28b, 40b, 47b
  narrative of, 38a–b
  sons of, 39b–40a, 48a
Jaddua, 159a, 159b
Jael, 116b–117a
Jehoahaz (king of Judah). *See* Ahaz
Jehoahaz (king of Judah) (son of Josiah), 282b, 288a
Jehoash (king of Israel), 147a
Jehoiachin (king of Judah), 90b, 103b, 104b, 149b,
  151a, 152b, 155b, 156b, 270b, 283a, 288a, 319b,
  320b, 321a, 322a
Jehoiakim (king of Judah, son of Jehoiachin), 270b,
  282b–283a, 286b, 288a, 292b, 296b, 299b, 386b
  blame for Jerusalem's destruction, 297a, 297b, 393b,
    394a, 398b
Jehoram (king of Israel), 147a, 148b, 151b
Jehoshaphat (king of Judah), 168a
Jehoshaphat (symbolic valley), 363b
Jehu (king of Israel), 147a, 147b, 350b, 351b–352a, 353a
Jehudi, 398b
Jephthah, 118b–119a
Jeremiah, 93a, 99b, 197a, 208a, 327a, 338a, 354b, 393b,
  398a, 398b, 403a
  Lamentations' authorship and, 304b
  other prophets and, 158b, 323a
  trial of, 386b, 388b, 392a
Jeremiah, Book of, 2a, 11b, 16b, 69b, 92b, 99a,
  137a, **281a–300b,** 304a, 319a, 328a, 375b, 383b,
  391a, 399a
Jericho, 75a, 76a, 114a, 116a
Jeroboam I (king of Israel, northern kingdom), 16b, 79a,
  92b, 106a, 120a, 141b, 145b, 149a, 150a,
  150b–151b, 167a, 255a
Jeroboam II (king of Israel, northern kingdom), 349a,
  350b, 353b, 370b, 373a, 381b
Jerome, Saint, 178a
Jerubbaal. *See* Gideon
Jerusalem
  Abraham linked to, 34b

Ark of Covenant brought to, 136a–b, 284b
David's capture of, 135b–136a
Ezra and Nehemiah in, 157a–159a
fall of (587), 283a–b, 297a–b, 299b, 305a–b, 331a,
  387b, 388b, 389a, 393b
importance to Israelites, 135b–136a, 260a, 283b–284a,
  285a
prophets on inviolability of, 283b–284a
siege of, 167b, 256a, 267a, 270b, 275b–276a, 278a
walls, rebuilding of, 163b
Zephaniah's oracles against, 402a–402b, 403a–b
see also Temple; Zion
Jerusalem Bible (JB), 17b
Jeshua. *See* Joshua (high priest)
Jesse, 276a
Jesus ben Sirach. *See* Sirach, Jesus ben
Jesus Christ, 3a, 3b, 5a, 5b, 6b, 41b–42a, 84a
  conception and birth of, 340a
  crucifixion and death of, 303a
  ministry of healing, 346a
  parables of, 194b
  resurrection portent, 383b
  suffering of, 193b–195b
  temptation of, 90a
Jethro, 51b, 52a, 55a
Jewish Bible. *See* Old Testament
Jewish law. *See* Covenant Code; Law, Jewish; Ten
  Commandments
Jezebel (queen of Israel), 147a, 352a
Jezreel Valley, 116b, 350b
Joab, 135b, 138a, 138b–139a, 145a
Joakim, 339a
Job, Book of, 6a, 11b, 15a, 16b, 40b, 100b, **181a–200b,**
  223a, 229a, 304a, 317a, 333b, 354a
Joel, Book of, **359a–365a**
John Hyrcanus I (high priest), 377b
John of the Cross, Saint, 244b
Jonah, Book of, **381a–383b**
Jonathan (son of Saul), 128a, 132a, 133a–b, 135a, 137b,
  303b, 326b
Jordan. *See* Transjordan
Jordan River, 74a, 82a, 89a, 90a, 103b, 108b, 111b,
  116a, 117a, 117b, 119a, 120a, 151b
Joseph (Israelite leader), 12a, 12b, 38a–40b, 48a, 50a,
  73a, 78a, 96a, 334b, 335a, 339a
Josephus, Flavius, 177b, 178b, 342b, 377b
Joshua (high priest), 406a–b, 410a–b
Joshua (Israelite leader), 41a, 55a, 73a, 74a, 75a, 81a,
  81b, 84a, 94b, 144b–145a, 146a, 151b, 162a,
  218a, 410a
Joshua, Book of, 11a, 11b, 12b, 13a, 13b, 22b, 23a, 23b,
  28b, 90a, 93b, **103a–112a,** 104b, 115a, 128b,
  142b, 144b, 248a, 284a, 323b
Josiah (king of Judah), 26a, 77b, 142a, 275a
  Assyrian relationship, 282b, 397b, 398b

as Davidic ideal, 167b
Joshua relationship, 108a–110a
kingship prophecy for, 104a
reforms of, 79a, 92b, 95b, 99b, 104a, 104b–107a,
    111a–b, 168b–169a, 267b–268a, 268b, 282b, 284b,
    286a–b, 287b, 397a–b
religious rectitude of, 141b, 146a, 149a
Jotham (Gideon's youngest son), 13a–b, 118a
Jotham (king of Judah), 251b, 351a, 385b, 386a
Joy, 236b–237b
Jubilees, Book of, 330a
Jubilee year, 69b, 82b, 96b
Judah (southern kingdom), 158a, 160b
    Assyrian relations, 98a, 248a–b, 249b, 251b,
        254a–255b, 267a
    Chronicles' focus on, 155b, 158a, 160b, 166b,
        167a
    conflict with northern kingdom, 13b, 135a–b, 255a
    Covenant tradition of, 353a–b
    exile's duration, 320b–321a, 325b
    fall to Babylon, 151b, 152a, 270a–b, 307b–308b,
        310b, 354b, 411a
    formation of, 90b
    geographical inaccessibility, 350a
    Haggai's oracles and, 407b–408a
    Isaiah's condemnation of, 257a–b, 267b
    Josiah's reforms, 104b–107a
    judgment on Edom and, 375a, 377a
    Lamentations on fall of, 307b–308b, 310b
    Nahum's oracles and, 378a, 379a
    northern kingdom's fall and, 351b, 354a
    oracles and judgments against, 284a–285b, 289a–b,
        293b, 294b–296b, 297b, 367b
    political situation, 141a, 282b, 397a–399a
    prophets in, 14b
    return from exile to, 405a–b
    shepherd imagery for, 411b–412a
    Temple's importance to, 137b
    ultimate salvation for, 412a
    see also Babylonian captivity; Jerusalem; Josiah;
        Syro-Ephraimite war; Temple
Judah (tribe), 96a, 116b
Judges, Book of, 11a, 11b, 13a, 23a, 107a, 109a,
    113a–120b, 142b, 248a, 284a, 323b
Judges (concept), 55a, 56a, 72a, 77b
    see also Law, Jewish
Judgment Day
    in Daniel, 338a
    in Joel, 360b–361a, 364a
    in Obadiah, 377a
    universal destruction linked to, 369a–b, 377a,
        400b–401b
    Zephaniah's warning of, 398a, 400a–401b, 403a–404a
Judith, 90b, 334a
Justice, as theme in Exodus, 60a–b

K

Kadesh, 75b, 77a
Keret, epic of, 198b
Ketuvim. *See* Writings
Khirbet Rabud. *See* Debir
King James Version (KJV), 17b, 18a
Kings, Books of, 11a, 13b, 16b, 23a, 38a, 134b, 139a,
    139b, **141a–152b,** 160b, 224b, 248a, 266b, 284a,
    300b, 323b
Kingship. *See* Coronation oracle; Israelite kingdom;
    Kings, Books of; Succession Narrative
Kir, 369a
Kiriath-jearim, 130a
Kiriathsepher. *See* Debir
Kish, 174a
Kislev, festival in, 343b
Korah, 78b, 79b, 214a, 217a
Koran, 2b
Kyrie eleison, 337b

L

Laban, 36a, 36b, 37b
Lachish, 114a, 251b, 257a
Laish. *See* Dan
Lamentations, Book of, 11b, 14b, **303a–317b**
Laments
    Abednego's prayer, 338b
    function and significance, 303a–304b
    psalms of, 213b–214a
    see also Afflictions; Suffering
Land rights. *See* Property rights
Law, Jewish
    Covenant Code, 56a–57a
    for daily living, 2b, 5a, 12b, 56a–b, 66b–70b, 75a–b,
        79b, 82a, 82b, 96b, 213a, 334b
    see also Halakhah; Ten Commandments; *Torah*
Leah, 36b, 37b
Lemuel (king of Massa), 223b, 225a
Leningrad Codex, 159b, 160a
Leprosy, 148a, 340b
Leviathan, 189a
Levirate marriage, 124b
Levites, 52b, 119b, 161b, 163b, 164b, 166a
    and Aaronite priesthood, 77b, 78b, 79a–b
    census of, 73a–b, 75a, 78a
    Habakkuk as, 391b
    land rights, 78a, 82b
    Moses and, 58a, 78b, 96a
    religious duties, 63a, 75a, 75b, 77a, 79a–b, 120a, 168a
    revenge against Benjaminites, 120b
Leviticus, Book of, 2b, 5b, 11a, **63a–70a,** 72a, 72b, 73a,
    77a, 84b, 92b, 327b, 329a

Life, meaning of, 15a, 194a, 233b–234a
Locusts, plague in Joel, 359a–365a
Loss. *See* Lamentations, Book of
Lot (nephew of Abraham), 34b
Lot (*pur*)
    choosing Saul as king, 131b
    Haman's, 174a, 176a
Love poetry, 242a–244a, 245a–b
Loyalty. *See* Faithfulness
Luke, Gospel According to, 5b, 41b, 129a
Luther, Martin, 179a
Lycanthropy, 340b
Lysimachus, 178b

M

Ma'at (Egyptian goddess), 228a–b
Maccabees, Books of, 11a, 90b, 144b, 176b, 343b, 344a, 344b
Maccabees, rule of, 12a, 377b
Madness
    of Nabonidus, 341a
    of Nebuchadrezzar, 335b, 340b
Magnificat, 5b, 129a
Magog, 320a
Maher-shalal-hashbaz, 253a
Mahlon, 123b, 124b, 125a
Malachi, Book of, 156b, 399a, **412a–413b**
Manasseh (king of Judah)
    Assyrian policy of, 99b, 105a, 109b, 397a
    sins linked to Jerusalem's fall, 104b, 145a, 149a, 151a, 168b, 169a–b, 266b–267b, 268b
Manasseh (tribe), 76a, 78a, 96a, 116b, 117a
Manna, 54b, 74b, 76b
Mara. *See* Naomi
Marcion, 5b
Marduk, 176a
Marriage
    Hosea to Gomer, 244b, 354b–356a, 357b
    ideal wife description, 229b
    imperial, 352a
    intermarriage prohibition, 157b, 158a, 163b, 164a, 165a, 412b, 413a
    levirate, 124b
    as metaphor for God's relationship with Israel, 244b, 323a, 354b–356a, 357b–358a
    in Song of Solomon, 242a–b, 244b
    "wife-sister" motif, 28b
Marxism, 346b
Mary (mother of Jesus), 41b, 129a
    virgin impregnation of, 340a

Mashiach. See Messiah
Masoretic text, 90b, 92a, 99a, 109b, 176a, 224a, 243b, 338a, 349a, 359a
Massa, 225a
Materialism. *See* Wealth
McCarter, Kyle, 134b
Medad, 77a
Medes. *See* Media
Media, 175a, 176a, 335a, 336b, 351b, 378a
Megiddo, 116b, 270a
Megilloth, 126a, 238b, 244a, 304b
Menahem (king of Israel, northern kingdom), 350b–351a
Menorah, 410a
Mephibosheth, 137b, 138b
Mercy, as theme in Exodus, 60a–b
Meribbaal. *See* Mephibosheth
Merikare (Egyptian prince), 225a
Merkavah (throne) mysticism, 151b, 319b, 320a, 324b, 331a, 408b
Merneptah (pharaoh), 50b, 113b
Merneptah stela, 113b
Merodach. *See* Marduk
Meshach, 335a, 343b–344a
Mesopotamia
    Aramaic language, 341b
    Diaspora in, 336a, 339a, 351b
    monarchs, 115b, 256a, 386a
    prophecies against, 270b, 350a
    sacred sexuality cult in, 355a
    see also Assyria; Babylon
Mesopotamian literature and mythology, 228b, 363a
Messiah
    Isaiah's prophecies of, 6a–6b, 253a, 254b
    in Psalms, 212a
    see also Jesus Christ
Micah, Book of, **385a–390b**
Micah (character in Danite migration), 120a
Micah (prophet), 14a, 158b, 271a, 372a
Micaiah (prophet at Ahab's court), 13b, 16b
Michael (angel), 343a
Michal, 133a, 135b
Michelangelo, 338a
Midian, 51b, 52a, 76a, 115b, 117a, 117b, 254b
Midrash, 317b, 381b, 391b
Milcom (Ammonite deity), 400b
Miller, Patrick D., Jr., 130a
Migreh, 233b–234a
Miracles, of Moses, 54a–b
Miriam, 51a, 75a, 75b, 77b, 78b, 79b, 80b
Mishael. *See* Meshach
Mishnah, 5a, 15b, 100b, 241a, 244a
Mizpah, 131b, 287b
Moab, Plains of, 109a
    Israelites' encampment on, 71a, 73a, 75a, 82b–84b, 93b, 95b

Moses' death, 94a–b, 98b
Moses' speech at, 89a–b, 91a
Moabites, 75b, 168a
    Balaam's oracles, 82b–84b
    Ehud's victory over, 115b–116a
    Ruth and, 123a–b
    woe oracles for, 402a
Molech (pagan deity), 69a
Monogamy, 229b
Mordecai, 173a–179b
Moresheth-gath, 387a
Moses, 60b, 94a, 105b, 109a, 150b, 156a, 160b, 329b,
    330b, 413b
    Aaron's and Miriam's relationships with, 77a–b, 78b,
      79b–81a
    birth of, 50b–51a
    and burning bush, 52a, 108a
    census of Israelites, 72a, 73a–b, 75b
    character of, 51b, 218a
    Covenant with God, 55b–57a, 58a–b, 144b, 146a
    death of, 80b, 89b, 93b, 94a–b, 96a, 96b, 98b, 107b
    Exodus from Egypt, 53b–55a
    Five Books of. See Torah; specific books
    and golden calf, 57b–58a
    and Jerusalem Temple site, 99b
    and Pharaoh, 52b–54a
    and Priesthood, 77a–b, 78b
    prophetic tradition of, 293a–b, 296a
    speech at Moab, 89a–b, 91a
    Torah authorship, 24a–25b, 72a–b
    tribulations in wilderness, 28a, 54b–55a, 73b, 76b,
      81b, 82b
    see also Ark of the Covenant
Mourning
    of Abraham for Sarah, 303b
    of David for Absalom, 139a
    see also Dirges
Murabba'at, 395b
Murashu archives, 162a
Murder, 12a, 119b, 165b
    conspiracies against kings, 145a–b, 350b, 351a
    of Gedaliah, 300a
    of Zechariah, 350b

N

Nabatea, 375b, 377b
Nablus, 118a
Nabonidus (king of Babylon), 335b, 340a–341a
Nabopolassar (king of Babylon), 378a
Nabunai. See Nabonidus
Nadab (son of Aaron), 66b
Nadab (son of Jeroboam), 145b

Nahash (king of Ammon), 131b
Nahum, 398a
Nahum, Book of, **377b–380a,** 391a, 399a, 402a
Names. See Sign-names
Naomi, 123a–125b
Naphtali, 96a, 116b
Nathan, 128b, 134b, 135a, 136b, 137a, 137b, 138a,
    143b, 146b, 317a
Nazirite, 63b, 75a, 119a
Nebo, Mount, 96a
Nebuchadrezzar (Nebuchadnezzar II, king of Babylon),
    72a, 177a, 270b
    control of Judah, 282b, 283a, 283b, 286b, 298b, 375a,
      388b, 393a
    and Daniel, 333a, 334b–335b, 346b
    madness of, 335b, 341a
Neco II (pharaoh), 104a, 282b, 393b
Negeb, 55a, 117a, 350a, 377a
Negev. See Negeb
Nehemiah, 271a
Nehemiah, Book of, 11b, 90b, **155a–169b,** 405a, 406b
Nevi'im, 11a
New English Bible (NEB), 17b
New International Version (NIV), 18a
New Jerusalem Bible, 17b–18a
New Jewish Version, 17b
New King James Version, 18a
New Moon festival, 69a
New Testament
    citations of Habakkuk in, 394a
    relationship with Old Testament, 1a, 1b, 2b, 5a–6b,
      11a–12b, 41b–42a, 100b, 178b–179a, 193b–194b
    resurrection of the dead theme, 345b
    translations of, 17b–18a
New Year's feast, 211a–b
Nile River, 49b, 50b, 51a, 398a
Nineveh
    fall of, 377b–380a, 402a
    Jonah and wickedness in, 381b–383a
    royal palace, 257a
Ninth of Av (commemoration of Temple's destruction),
    305b
Noah, 30b, 197a, 333b, 401b, 402a
Northern kingdom. See Israel (Ephraim)
Noth, Martin, 23a–b, 24a, 103b
Number of the beast (666), 345a
Numbers, Book of, 11a, 24a, 58a, 63a, 64b, 67a,
    71a–85b, 72b, 74a, 329a, 353a

O

Obadiah, Book of, **375a–377b**
Obed, 125a

Og (king of Bashan), 74a, 75b, 90a
Old epic tradition, 72b
Old Testament
    Christian Bible's arrangement of, 11b–12a
    in Christian tradition, 1a, 1b, 5a–6b, 41b–42a, 100b,
        142a, 178b–179a, 193b–194b, 394a–b
    Greek text of. *See* Septuagint
    historical writings in, 12b–14b
    interpretations of, 17a–b
    laments as recurring theme in, 303a–304a
    literary diversity in, 16a–17a
    promise as theme in, 6a, 12a–12b, 13a, 13b
    relationship with Israel, 15b–16a
    role of Genesis, 40b
    three-part division of, 2a, 11a–15b
    translations of, 17b–18a
    see also New Testament, relationship with Old
        Testament
Onomasticons, 224b
Ophrah, 118a
Oracles
    Ahab's, 147b
    Amos', 367a–373b
    Balaam's, 82b–84b
    coronation, 150b, 254b, 260b–261a, 265a
    dynastic, 136b–137a
    Ezekiel's, 158b, 319a–331b
    on foreign nations, 401b–402a
    Habakkuk's, 391a, 391b, 392a–396b
    Haggai's, 406a–408a
    Hosea's, 349a, 353b–354a, 356a–357a
    Isaiah's, 218b, 392a
    Jonah's, 382a
    Malachi's, 412b–413b
    Micah's, 387a–388b, 389b–390b
    Nahum's, 378b–380a
    Nathan's, 138a
    Zechariah's, 408a–412a
    Zephaniah's, 397a, 399a–404a
Orontes River, 350b
Orpah, 123b
Othniel, 114b

                          P

Palestine, 282a, 282b, 285a, 291a, 296b, 297b, 337a,
    377a
Palmyrene Corridor, 350a
Papponymy, 159a
Parables
    condemning David's actions, 138a
    Habakkuk's *hoy* oracles, 396a
    Jesus', 194b

of Jonah and great fish, 381b–383b
Passover
    commemoration of, 3b, 14b, 56a, 400b
    commemoration's reinstatement by Joshua, 106b,
        111a–b, 160a, 169a
    commemoration under Hezekiah, 168a
    prior to the Exodus, 53a
    Song of Solomon and, 244a
    tabernacle dedication and, 75a
Paul the Apostle, 1b, 6a, 41b, 42a, 244b
    justification by faith, 394a
Pekah (king of Israel, northern kingdom), 350b–351a
Pekahiah (king of Israel, northern kingdom), 350b–351a
Pelatiah, 322b, 325a
Peninnah, 208a–b
Penitential psalms, 213b, 214b
Pentateuch. *See* Torah
Pentecost, 400b
Penuel, 36b, 37b, 117b–118a
Perjury. *See* False accusations
Persia, 173a–178a, 335a, 336b, 343a, 345b, 410b
Pestilence. *See* Afflictions; Plagues
Pharaoh (Exodus), 12a, 28b, 39b, 49b, 52b–54b, 335a
Pharisees, 99a, 344a–b
Philistines
    Ark's capture by, 13b, 128a, 130a–b
    Ashdod's rebellion, 251a, 255b
    David as mercenary for, 133a, 135a, 165b
    David's containment of, 136a
    Pekah's alliance with, 351a
    Samson and, 119a–b
    as threat to Israel, 90b, 115a, 115b, 127a, 135a, 363b
    woe oracles for, 320a, 402a
Phoenicia, 50b, 250b
Pilgrimages to Zion, 220a
Plagues
    locust, 359a–365a
    ten in Egypt, 53a–b, 59b
Plain of Esdraelon. *See* Jezreel Valley
Plain of Megiddo. *See* Megiddo
Pogrom, first in recorded history, 336b
Polybius, 343a
Polygamy, 229b
Pompey (Roman general), 337a
Poverty
    exploitation by rich, 164a
    retribution doctrine and, 195a
Pregnancy. *See* Conception
Priests, 120a, 229a, 286a, 330b, 371a, 398b, 413a
    Aaronic, 58b, 78b
    duties of, 66b, 71b, 77a, 80a, 156a
    Ezekiel as, 330b
    high priests' genealogy, 159a–b
    Levite, Aaronic, and Zadokite relationship, 78b–79b
    in Malachi, 413a–b

Moses' lineage, 78b–79b
Old Epic tradition writings by, 72a–b
ordination of, 66a, 66b
P and H Codes, 63b–64b
relationship with kings, 143b, 371a
vestments of, 63a, 66a, 410a
Zadokite line, 78b–79b, 129b
see also Levites
Priests' Manual. *See* Leviticus, Book of
Promise
    as Old Testament theme, 6a, 12a–12b, 13a, 13b
    see also Yahweh, promises to Israel
Promised land. *See* Canaan (Promised Land)
Property rights, 78a, 82a–b, 90a, 124b–125a
Prophets
    as division of Old Testament, 2a, 2b, 6a, 11a–b, 12a–14b, 323a–b
    false, 287a, 298b, 383a, 390a, 392a
    function of, 131a
    literary components of writings of, 354a
    see also Dreams; Oracles; Visions; specific prophets
Prostitutes, 168a, 355a
Proverbs, Book of, 5b, 11b, 31a, 156b, 199b, 200a, **223a–229b,** 232a, 234a–b, 238b, 400a
Psalms, Book of, 11b, 14b, 15a, 40b, 156b, **203a–220b,** 229b
Psalter. *See* Psalms, Book of
Ptolemies (Egyptian dynasty), 238a
Pur. See Lot
Purification offering. *See* Sacrifices
Purim, 14b, 175a–176b, 177a, 177b–180a

Q

Qarqar, battle of, 350b
Qohelet, 225a, 231a–238b
Qumran. *See* Dead Sea Scrolls

R

Rabbi 'Aqiva'. *See* 'Aqiva' ben Yosef (Rabbi)
Rachel, 36b, 37b, 38a
Rahab, 110b
Ramses II (pharaoh), 50b
Rape, of Tamar, 17a, 165b
Rasha' (wicked man), 393a, 393b
Ras Shamra. *See* Ugarit
Rebecca, 303a
Rehoboam (king of Israel), 105b, 167a, 321a, 387a
Reparation offering. *See* Sacrifices

Repentance
    Jeremiah on, 291a, 294a
    as theme in Jonah, 382b–383a
Rephidim, 54b
Responsibility, as theme in Ezekiel, 326a–327a
Resurrection
    of the dead, 338a, 344b, 345b, 383b
    imagery of, 331a
    Jesus portent, 383b
Retribution
    Daniel's prayer and doctrine of, 345b
    Job and doctrine of, 184b–186a, 188a, 189a–b, 190a, 191b, 194b, 195a, 196a, 199b
Reuben, 52b, 73b, 76a, 77b, 82a, 96a, 116b
Revelation, Book of, 244b, 330a, 338a, 377b
Revised Standard Version (RSV), 17b, 18a, 394b
Rezin (king of Damascus), 351a
Roberts, J. J. M., 130a
Roman Empire, symbolism for, 337a
Romans, Epistle to the, 41b, 42a
Rost, Leonhard, 134b
Ruth, Book of, 11b, 90a, 90b, **123a–126b,** 156b

S

Sabbath, 410a
    as creation's culmination, 31a
    Hasideans' refusal to fight on, 344a
    P and H Codes concerning, 64a, 64b
    slaves' right to rest on, 60a
    Ten Commandments concerning, 59b
    Torah concerning, 12b
Sabbatical year, 69b
Sacrifices
    Abraham's test, 35a–b
    animals as, 192b–193a, 343a
    of Jephthah's daughter, 118b–119a
    Leviticus on, 64b–66a, 66b, 68a, 69a–b, 84b–85a
    Malachi on impurity of Israel's, 413a
    Manasseh's offering of human, 168b
Saints, Daniel on, 338a, 343b, 345a, 346a
Samaria
    fall to Assyria, 110a, 251a, 253a, 253b, 258b, 321a, 349a, 386b, 389a
    friction with Jerusalem's Jewish community, 162a, 163b
    woe oracles for, 368a, 369b, 386a–b
Samaritans. *See* Samaria
Samson, 115a, 119a, 303a
Samuel, 91a, 165a, 296a
Samuel, Books of, 11a, 11b, 13a, 13b, 23a, 38b, 78b, 90b, 99b, 109a, **127a–139b,** 141a, 142a, 146b, 160b, 165a–b, 209a, 248a, 284a, 323b
Sanballat, 159a, 163b
Sarah, 28b, 33a–35b, 36a, 38a, 96b, 303b

Sargon II (king of Assyria), 51a–b, 251a, 256a, 262b, 351b
Satan, 401a, 409b
  Beliel as term for, 379a
  and David's guilt, 165b
  Job's wife as echo to, 190b–191a
Saul (king of Israel)
  David's dirge over, 303b
  David's relationship with, 133b, 135a–b, 137b, 165a–b, 166b
  death of, 133b, 135a, 160b
  military exploits of, 128a, 131a, 132a–b, 133a–b, 175b
  reign of, 90b, 127b–129a, 130b–132b, 141a, 149b, 326b, 353a
Science, and Biblical interpretation, 6b
Scrolls, Judaic. See Megillot
Sea of Galilee. See Galilee, Sea of
Seder, 3b
Seleucid Empire, 238a
Sennacherib (king of Assyria)
  death of, 265a
  Hezekiah's surrender to, 267a
  Hezekiah's uprising against, 282b, 386a
  invasion of Judah by, 386b, 387a, 388b
  palace at Nineveh, 257a
  siege of Jerusalem by, 167b, 168b, 251a–b, 256a–b, 257a
Septuagint
  Apocrypha and, 2a–b
  Daniel in, 338b–340a
  on duration of Judah's exile, 321a
  as early Christians' official Bible, 2a–b, 47a
  Ecclesiastes in, 238b
  Esther in, 174a, 178a, 178b–179a
  Ethiopia in, 398a–399b
  Ezra in, 160a
  Habakkuk in, 395b
  Jeremiah in, 281b, 288b
  Kings in, 142a
  Lamentations in, 304b
  Moses' death in, 96b
  order of biblical books in, 11b, 89a, 90a, 90b
  Proverbs in, 223b
  Samuel in, 127a–b, 142a
Serpent, 31a, 235a
"Servant Songs," 274b
Seven deadly sins, 340a
Sexual relations
  daily Jewish law on, 67b, 68b–69
  fertility rites, 352a–b, 355a–b
  Genesis on, 235b
  Song of Solomon on, 245b
  symbolism for, 124b
Shadrach, 335a, 343b–344a
Shalmaneser III (king of Assyria), 350b, 351b

Shalmaneser V (king of Assyria), 351a–b
Shamgar, 115a
Shaphan, 287b
Shavu'ot, 126a
Shear-jashub, 252b–253a
Sheba, Queen of, 166b
Sheba (Benjaminite), 139a, 165b
Shechem, 13a, 36b, 95a, 103a, 118a
Shema, 89b, 95a, 99a, 101a
Shenazzar. See Sheshbazzar
Sheol (netherworld), 185b
  see also Hell
Shepherd imagery for Judah's relationship with Yahweh, 411b–412a
Sheshbazzar, 161a, 162a
Sheshonk I (pharaoh), 350a
Shibboleth, 119a
Shiloh, 120b, 284b, 286a, 287a
Shimei, 145a
Sickness and health
  God as healer metaphor, 92b
  in Psalms, 207b, 209a
  skin (scale) disease prohibitions, 67b, 79b, 80a
  see also Leprosy; Plagues
Sidon, 363b
Sign-names, 252b, 253b
Sihon (king of Amorites), 74a, 75b, 90a
Simchat Torah, 93b
Simeon, 52b, 116b
Sinai, Mount
  burning bush at, 52a
  covenant at, 21b, 28a, 49a, 95b, 98b, 150b
  Israelites' arrival and encampment at, 55a–b, 69b, 71a, 93a
  Moses' speech to Israelites at, 89b–90a, 91a, 92a, 100b
  tabernacle as extension of, 59a
  theophany at, 55a–55b, 59a
Sinai Covenant. See Covenant Code
Sinai region, 28a, 55a, 73b, 74b, 75b–76a, 76b–77a, 360a
Sins
  Christian vs. Jewish view of, 41b
  confession of, 210a, 296a–b, 306a, 340b, 401b
  forgiveness of, 382a–383a, 385a, 390a
  seven deadly, 340a
  suffering linked to, 185a–186b
  see also Retribution; Theodicy
Sirach, Book of, 5b, 223a, 229b, 238a
Sirach, Jesus ben (son of Sirach), 177b, 225a, 226b–227a
Sisera, 116b–117a
Sistine Chapel, 338a
666 (mystical number), 345a
Skehan, Patrick, 223b, 224a–b
Skin (scale) disease, 67b, 79b, 80a
  see also Leprosy

Slander. *See* False accusations
Slavery, 368a
  associated with fall of Jerusalem, 309a
  Covenant Code laws governing, 56a, 60a–b
  in Solomon's reign, 144a
  see also Exodus, Book of
Snake. *See* Serpent
Sodom and Gomorrah, 6a, 35a, 275b
Solomon (king of Israel), 79a, 105b, 217a
  association with Ecclesiastes, 231b, 238b
  infidelity of, 166b–167a
  kingship's transfer to, 166a
  association with Proverbs, 224b, 238b
  reign of, 50a, 143b–144a, 145a, 146a, 150b, 286a
  association with Song of Solomon, 238b, 241a–b
  in Succession Narrative, 13b, 134b, 138a–139a, 139b
  tabulation of royal officials, 140b–144a
  as *torah* keeper, 110a
  wedding of, 242b
  wisdom of, 231b, 339b
  see also Wisdom of Solomon
Song of Solomon, 6a, 11b, 14b, 156b, 238b, **241a–245b**
Song of Songs. *See* Song of Solomon
"Song of the Sea," 54b
Song of the Three Young Men, 338b
Southern kingdom. *See* Judah
Spinoza, Baruch, 269b
Succession Narrative, 134b, 138a–139a
Succoth (town), 54a, 117b
Suffering
  Jesus', 193b–195b
  Lamentations' portrayal of, 310a–311a
  problem of, 183b–184b
  see also Afflictions
Sukkot. *See* Feast of Booths
Sumerian literature and mythology, 223a, 304a
Susa, 165a, 174a, 174b, 176b, 177a
Susanna, 338b, 339a–b
Swearing falsely. *See* False accusations
Syria, 167a, 251a, 252a, 267b, 331a, 334a, 336b, 351a, 377a, 386a
Syro-Ephraimite war, 251a, 252a, 261a, 264b, 284a, 351a, 351b

T

Taanach, 116b
Tabernacle, 57a–b, 58b–59b, 63a, 66a, 75a, 329a, 329b, 330b
Tablets of stone, 57b, 58a, 58b, 59a
Tabor, Mount, 116b
Tale of Aqht, The, 334a
Talmud, 5a, 100b, 125b–126a, 177b, 178a

Tamar, 17a, 138b, 165b
Tammuz (Babylonian deity), 242a
Tanakh (Tanach), 2b, 11a, 17b, 47b
Targum, 178a, 244a
Tarshish, 382a, 383b
Te Deum Laudamus, 338b
Tehillim, 220a
Tekoa, 386a
Tel-abib, 321b
Tel Dan. *See* Dan
Tell Balatah. *See* Shechem
Tell Deir Alla. *See* Succoth (town)
Tell el-Ful. *See* Gibeah
Tell el-Judeideh, 387a
Tell el-Mutesellim. *See* Megiddo
Tema, 341a
Teman, 376b
Temple in Jerusalem (first; Solomon's), 58b, 134a, 252b, 258a, 270a
  building of, 50a, 150a–b
  building preparations, 166a, 166b
  desecration of, 313a, 398b
  destruction of, 72a, 249b, 270b, 271a, 283b, 305a–b, 327b, 388b
  destruction prediction, 386b
  Deuteronomistic theology on, 142b, 284a, 294a–b, 399a
  Isaiah on role of, 258a–260a, 263a, 267b
  Joel and, 262a
  kingship and, 136b–138b, 141b, 142b, 143a, 145b, 149a, 160b
  priesthood, 79a–b, 129b
  as sole worship site, 99b–100a
Temple in Jerusalem (second; restoration), 3a, 77a, 77b, 211b, 389a, 409b
  building of, 162a
  Cyrus' decree allowing, 155b, 156b, 160a, 161a–162a
  desecration of, 336b, 343a–b
  Ezekiel's vision of, 320a, 327b, 328a–330b
  as Josiah's royal assertion, 105a–b, 106a, 168b
  opposition to rebuilding, 162a–b
  as sole worship site, 106a, 167a
  as theme in Haggai, 405b–408a
Temple Scroll. *See* Dead Sea Scrolls
Ten Commandments, 55b, 57a, 59a, 59b, 95a
Tent of meeting, 58a–b
Terah, 32a
Teraphim (cultic objects), 120a
Tetragrammaton, 60b, 69b
Tetrateuch, 23a, 23b
Thebes (Egypt), 379b
Thebez, 118b
Theodicy
  in Daniel, 345b–346a
  see also Retribution

Theodotion, 338b, 339a, 339b

Theology. *See* Bible, sources and study approaches; Old Testament, interpretations of; *specific approaches*

Theophany, 55a–b, 59a

Throne mysticism. *See Merkavah* mysticism

Thummim, 118a

Thutmose III (pharaoh), 50a

Tiglath-pileser III (king of Assyria), 105a, 250b, 350b–351a, 386a

Tigris River, 378a

Timnah, 119b

Tirhakah (king of Ethiopia), 398a

Tobiah, 163b

Tobit, 334a, 346a

Tobit, Book of, 90b

Today's English Version (TEV), 18a

Tola of Issachar, 115a

Torah, 2a, 2b, 100a
  Christian interpretation of, 6a–b
  composition of, 24a–25b, 72a–b, 92b, 93a, 94b, 99a, 157a, 215b
  contents of, 11a–b, 15b
  dating of, 329a
  editing of, 91b
  function of, 93b, 216b
  historical scholarship on, 24b–30a
  historical validity of, 76a–77b
  obedience to, 229a, 344b
  overview of, 12a–12b
  sources in, 4a
  see also Ark of the Covenant; Deuteronomy; Exodus; Genesis; Leviticus; *Megillot;* Numbers

Torah (law), 2b, 109b, 110a, 144a, 144b, 238a
  psalms on, 213a–b

Torat Kohanim. *See* Leviticus, Book of

Tower of Babel, 31b, 402b

Transjordan, 50b, 74a, 74b, 76a, 76b, 77a, 82a, 83b, 84a, 95a, 95b, 103a, 107b, 109a, 113b, 118b, 351a

Translation, Biblical. *See* Bible, translations of

Troy, 50b

Trust, as theme in Isaiah, 261a–b, 262a

Tulul edh-Dhahab. *See* Penuel

Twelve Prophets, Book of. *See* Prophets

Tyre, 270b, 333b
  judgment oracles on, 320a, 321a, 324a, 326a, 363b, 367b

U

Ugarit (Ras Shamra), 17b, 334a

United Bible Society, 18a

Ur, 304a

Urartu, 350b

Uriah, 138a

Urim, 118a

Usury, 68b, 164a

Utopia, Joel on, 364a

Uzziah (king of Judah), 251b, 350b, 386a

V

Vashti (queen of Persia), 173b

Vegetarianism, 192a, 192b, 193a

Virgin Mary. *See* Mary (mother of Jesus)

Visions
  Amos', 367b, 368b–369a, 370a–b, 371b, 372a–b
  as component of prophetic work, 354a
  Daniel's, 333a, 336b–337b, 344b–346b
  of flying throne, 319b, 320a, 324b, 331a
  Habakkuk's, 392b, 394b–395a, 396a
  Jeremiah's, 293b–294a, 296b–297a
  in Kings, 144b
  of restoration of Temple, 327b, 328a–330b
  Zechariah's, 408a–411a

Von Rad, Gerhard, 22b–24a, 28a, 28b, 29a, 32a, 35b, 38a–b, 92a, 93a, 134b, 228b

Vulgate, 47a, 160a, 241a, 304b, 339a, 339b

W

Wealth
  inequity and abuse of, 164a, 259b, 351b, 352b, 368a–b, 369a, 371b–372a, 388a, 403a
  lamentation for loss of, 310a
  materialist reading of Job, 195a–196b
  Qohelet on possession and use of, 237a
  see also Poverty

Well-being offering. *See* Sacrifices

Westermann, Claus, 27a

Whale. *See* Great fish

Wiesel, Elie, 381a

Wilderness
  Moses in, 28a, 54b–55a, 73b, 76b, 81b, 82b
  see also Sinai region

Wisdom, woman personifying, 228a–b

Wisdom literature
  nature of, 5b, 199b–200b, 223a, 228a–229b, 238a
  psalms, 212b–213a
  see also Sirach, Book of; Wisdom of Solomon

Woe oracles, 401b–402a

Women, status of
  Deborah and Barak, 116a–117a
  ideal wife description, 229b
  in Job, 190b–192a

as possessions, 355b–356a
property rights, 82a–b, 124b–125a
Qohelet's views on, 235b
in Ruth, 125a
as wisdom personification, 228a–b
see also Feminist interpretations; Marriage; Prostitutes
Writings (Ketuvim), 2a, 2b, 6a, 11a, 11b, 14b–15a, 91a,
    91b, 159b; *see also* specific books

X

Xerxes I (king of Persia), 173a, 176b–177a, 178a–b

Y

Yahweh
    Asa's faith and, 167b–168a
    and biblical interpretation, 4a
    characteristics and nature of, 59b–61a, 147b, 148a,
        236a–237b, 259a–b, 356b, 378b, 386a, 386b,
        412b, 413a
    commands of, 22a, 22b, 33b, 368b, 371a, 381b–383b,
        395a, 406b, 411b–412a
    and conception, 125a, 125b, 129a
    as creator, 59b–60a
    and Esther story, 173b, 178a, 178b
    faith and trust in, 151b, 261a–b, 262a, 343b, 390a–b,
        395b
    fear of, 236b, 237a
    as healer, 92b
    and house of worship concept, 136a–b, 167a
    Israelite disobedience to, 115b, 117b
    and Job's afflictions, 182a–199a
    joy from, 236b–237b
    and kingship, 107a, 107b, 109a, 118a, 131a–b,
        136a–b, 141a, 144a, 147a, 148b, 150b
    Lamentations' petitions to, 306a–316a
    name, 52a, 60b, 160a, 197b, 225a, 258b–259a, 326a,
        327b, 398b
    as one and only God, 273a–b, 385a

power of, 130b
promises to Israel, 12a, 13a, 13b, 22b, 23a, 23b,
    107b–109a, 110a, 277b–278a, 405a, 406a,
    407b–408a, 413b
and Prophets, 132a
punishments by, 387a–b, 389b, 392a–b, 393b
shepherd imagery for Judah, 411b–412a
worship of, 113b, 167a, 282b, 352b, 371b, 413a
wrath of, 408b–409a, 411b
see also Covenant Code; Idolatry; Israel, covenant with
    God; Temple in Jerusalem; Ten Commandments
YHVH. *See* Tetragrammaton
Yom Kippur, 383b

Z

Zacchaeus, 42a
Zachariah. *See* Zechariah; Zechariah, Book of
Zadok, 78b, 79a–b, 129b, 138b
Zaphon, 398b
Zealots, 344a
Zebulun, 96a, 115a, 116b
Zechariah, 162b, 163a, 169b, 322a, 329a, 330b, 350b
Zechariah, Book of, 156b, 161a, 305b, 320b, 364b,
    399a, **408a–412a**
Zedekiah (king of Judah), 270b, 283a, 287a, 288a, 290b,
    291a, 292b, 297a–b, 299b, 398b
Zelophehad, 74b, 75b
Zephaniah, Book of, 391a, **397a–404b**
Zeresh, 174b
Zerqa River. *See* Jabbok River
Zerubbabel (governor of Jerusalem), 155b, 156a, 161a,
    162a, 162b, 169b, 322a, 406a–b, 407b–408b, 410b
Ziba, 137b, 138b
Zimri (king of Israel, northern kingdom), 145b
Zion, 211b, 217a, 217b, 219b–220a, 254a, 273b, 274a,
    309b, 310a, 373a, 388b, 389b; *see also* Jerusalem
Zion, Mount, 377a, 389b
Zionism, 41a
Zipporah, 51b, 52b, 55a
Zophar, 182b, 185a, 185b–186a, 198b